Jewels from the Treasury

Jewels from the Treasury

Vasubandhu's

Verses on the Treasury of Abhidharma

and Its Commentary,

Youthful Play

An Explanation of the Treasury of Abhidharma

by the Ninth Karmapa Wangchuk Dorje

Foreword by Khenchen Thrangu Rinpoche

Translated from the Tibetan with reference to the Sanskrit

by David Karma Choephel

KTD Publications

Woodstock New York

KTD Publications and the translator David Karma Choephel would like to acknowledge the generous support of the Tsadra Foundation in the publication of this book.

Published by:
KTD Publications
335 Meads Mountain Road
Woodstock, NY 12498, USA
www.KTDPublications.org

Cover painting of Vasubandhu and illustrations of Vasubandhu and the Ninth Karmapa Wangchuk Dorje by Karma Dradul.

Library of Congress Control Number: 2011944417
ISBN 978-1-934608-25-8
Printed in the United States on acid-free paper.

Contents

FOREWORD BY

Khenchen Thrangu Rinpoche

Among the abhidharma of the Foundation and Great Vehicles, the main text that students in monastic colleges study these days is *The Treasury of Abhidharma.* There are many commentaries on the *Treasury.* The great Chim Jamyang's commentary and the Eighth Karmapa Mikyö Dorje's commentary, *The Springtime Cow of Easy Accomplishment,* are very clear and good, but they are too long. When new students study them, they are unable to find a way into them. In order to help such students, the Ninth Karmapa Wangchuk Dorje composed a commentary that is very clear and concise. Students who read it are able to develop definite comprehension of the abhidharma in general, and within that, clearly understand the points taught in the *Treasury of Abhidharma.* That is why it is so beneficial that the Ninth Karmapa Wangchuk Dorje's commentary on the *Treasury* has been translated.

Among the three baskets of Buddhist teachings, it is important to understand the abhidharma teachings. There are three main trainings: the superior training in discipline taught by the vinaya, the superior training in samadhi taught by the sutras, and the superior training in full knowing taught by the abhidharma. Of these three trainings, the primary one for destroying the afflictions and attaining the ultimate result is the superior training in full knowing. Developing this training depends mainly on the *piṭaka* of abhidharma, and that in turn depends mainly on the treatises of abhidharma. Of all these treatises, the easiest and clearest is the *Treasury of Abhidharma,* so if you study the *Treasury,* it will bring great benefit.

Khenchen Thrangu Rinpoche
Sarnath, India
February 17, 2008

Translator's Introduction

English-speaking students of Buddhism are very fortunate these days: there are more and more books on Buddhism, and in-depth study of Buddhist philosophy and practice is becoming possible in an English medium. Important texts from all Buddhist schools and traditions, in particular the Indian and Tibetan, are becoming available in excellent, clear English translations that are understandable and beneficial for general readers and specialists alike. Since many students of Buddhism are primarily interested in meditation, many of the texts initially translated focused on meditation. But in order to receive the full benefits of meditation practice, it is necessary to have a thorough understanding of the views of Buddhist philosophy. As Master Vasubandhu says in the *Treasury of Abhidharma*:

> With conduct, listening, contemplation,
> Completely train in meditation.

In other words, in order to achieve results in our meditation practice, we must first maintain the conduct of good discipline and then develop the *prajñā* or "full knowing" born of listening and contemplation through study of the Buddha's words and the treatises that explain them. Without study we are like blind people trying to climb a cliff, it is said, but with the proper understanding that comes from thorough study and contemplation, our meditation will improve and we will be able to enjoy its fruits.

Of all the subjects to study, masters in all Buddhist traditions consider the abhidharma to be one of the most important. Abhidharma is like an encyclopedia of Buddhism: it pulls together the teachings the Buddha gave in many different sutras and discourses and presents them in a systematic way. Studying it gives an understanding of what things are and why they are called by the names they are given. It provides a solid foundation for further study because other treatises often refer to concepts and phenomena that are covered most thoroughly in the abhidharma. But most important, it gives answers to such pressing questions as, what are the natures of our bodies and minds? How are we born? How do our minds work? How does karma work? What causes suffering? How do we free ourselves from suffering?

Although the Buddha himself said that his teachings could be divided into the three baskets of sutras, vinaya, and abhidharma, it would be difficult to pinpoint a specific set of his discourses that could be called *abhidharma*. Rather, Shariputra, Kātyāniputra, and other arhats collected and systematized the teachings the Buddha had given on many disparate occasions in many sutras and the vinaya, compiling what are called the *seven treatises of abhidharma*. As the different schools of Buddhism developed, each school also developed its own tradition of interpreting and explaining the abhidharma, and so there came to be several distinct presentations of the abhidharma.

The basis for the study of abhidharma in the northern Buddhist traditions that spread to Tibet, China, Korea, and Japan was provided by Master Vasubandhu's *Verses on the Treasury of Abhidharma* (often called the root verses) and his accompanying *Explanation of the Treasury of Abhidharma* (usually called the autocommentary). Written in the fourth century, these brilliant works eclipsed earlier treatises on the abhidharma to such an extent that Tibetan translators did not even consider most of the treatises it was based upon necessary to translate. Within the Tibetan tradition, Vasubandhu's *Treasury* is considered one of the five great works of Buddhist philosophy. The root is especially prized for the way in which it condenses an immense topic into clear, concise, and memorable verses. Several of the verses are so often quoted in works on other topics that they are among the most commonly quoted lines in Tibetan Buddhism. When studying abhidharma, students memorize the root—in some monastic colleges, gathering every morning to recite the verses aloud from beginning to end. The meter of the verses makes them easy to recite and remember, so that as students recite them over and over, passages that at first seem impenetrable become clearer and clearer. Eventually they become reminders that flow easily over the tongue, bringing to mind the meaning described in the commentaries.

For a student new to the abhidharma, however, Vasubandhu's work on its own is difficult. The root verses are like a key that opens the gate to a vast field of knowledge, but they are too terse to understand without explanation. On the other hand, the autocommentary is imposing for beginners. Not only is it lengthy—one English translation was published in four volumes—it covers many doctrinal disputes between different Buddhist schools in such detail that beginners might find it difficult to discern what is important. Other points are given only cursory explanation, as if it is assumed that the reader already knows the point or that a master will explain it.

For these reasons among others, many Indian and later Tibetan masters wrote commentaries on either the root verses, the autocommentary, or both. Among these, the Ninth Karmapa Wangchuk Dorje's explanation of the root verses entitled *Youthful Play* is especially useful for those who are new to the abhidharma. About a third the length of the autocommentary, its explanations of the root verses are succinct and clear; its synopses of the disputes between different schools outline the main points without providing so much detail that a new student might get confused; and it fleshes out several topics covered only briefly in the autocommentary. *Youthful Play* gives a thorough overview of the abhidharma for those who wish to study it but cannot do so exhaustively and provides a basis for those who wish to delve further into abhidharma studies.

When most students of Buddhism first learn about the abhidharma, at first it seems as if it is a set of scriptures—one of the three baskets or *piṭaka* of the Buddhist canon. However, this is only one aspect of what the word *abhidharma* refers to. In Vasubandhu's presentation, there are three types of abhidharma: ultimate abhidharma, path abhidharma, and scriptural abhidharma. Ultimate or genuine abhidharma is the stainless, undefiled full knowing that correctly discerns what is and what is not, as well as the five undefiled aggregates which accompany it. The name abhidharma is also given to the defiled full knowing and treatises through which one can achieve stainless wisdom. The defiled full knowing of individuals on the path is path abhidharma, and treatises such as the seven treatises of abhidharma and this *Treasury* are scriptural abhidharma.

The reason it is important to study the abhidharma is that only this undefiled full knowing can liberate us from the suffering of samsara. Ordinary sentient beings lack this full knowing and are unable to properly distinguish what is from what is not. This confusion leads to greed for the things one wants and aversion toward things one finds unpleasant. This in turn leads to the actions which on a longer timeframe bind us to the cycle of rebirth, but in the short term as well lead to the difficulties of our lives. One only has to look at how many of our everyday problems—whether major or petty, real or imagined—result from misunderstandings or misplaced hopes and fears to see how important it is to develop the wisdom that sees what is as it is. As Vasubandhu says near the beginning of the *Treasury:*

> Without full discernment of dharmas, there is not
> Any method to totally quell the afflictions.
> Because of afflictions, the world wanders the seas of existence.

Although the necessity for studying the treatise is to realize the undefiled full knowing that correctly discerns dharmas, the actual topic is all defiled and undefiled dharmas—in effect, all dharmas, as there are no dharmas which are neither defiled nor undefiled. As Wangchuk Dorje notes in his commentary, the reason to divide dharmas into these two categories is to indicate which dharmas we need to give up and which dharmas we need to adopt in order to bring ourselves to liberation and happiness. Defiled dharmas are those dharmas in relation to which our defilements or afflictions can occur and are primarily the dharmas included in the two truths of suffering and origin. Undefiled dharmas include the truths of cessation and path—those dharmas, which when we understand them correctly, either are liberation or bring us to liberation.

Following a brief overview that identifies defiled and undefiled dharmas, the *Treasury* then presents eight areas or chapters.[1] The first area, "Teachings on the Elements," gives an overview of the classification of all phenomena into the aggregates (*skandha*), sense bases (*āyatana*), and elements (*dhātu*). It then further classifies dharmas by what realm they are present in; whether they are virtuous, nonvirtuous, or neutral; how they are produced; and so forth. The second area, "Teachings on the Faculties," presents an overview of the sensory and other faculties, mental factors, nonconcurrent formations, and causes, results, and conditions. Taken together, these two areas provide a general categorization of all phenomena and demonstrate how phenomena relate to one another as perceiver and perceived, cause and result, and so forth.

The next area, "Teachings on the World," gives a presentation of sentient beings and the world that contains them. Although many Western texts call this "Buddhist cosmology," Tibetan commentaries say that this is a presentation of the truth of suffering: by understanding what possible rebirths there are, how one is reborn, and the places one can be reborn, one can see how none of these transcend impermanence and suffering. The first half of the area describes the different types of wanderers, or sentient beings, and explains how they take birth, what sustains them during their lives, and how they die. This includes a thorough explanation of the between or *bardo* state and the twelve links of interdependence. The second half of the area presents the arrangement of the outer world with Mount Meru surrounded by rings of mountains, oceans, and continents, including detailed descriptions of the god realms above and the hell realms below.

This area is one of the most fascinating for Tibetans and non-Tibetans alike, not least because the description of the outer world does not match our modern understanding of the physical universe. Many modern Tibetan khenpos and scholars explain that this is because our common perceptions of the world arise out of our shared karma. Since beings today have different karma than those of Vasubandhu's time, the world naturally appears quite differently to us today. Another possible explanation is that the Buddha and later scholars including Vasubandhu needed to teach in ways that the people of their time could understand, and therefore they described the world according to the prevalent beliefs of their times. However we reconcile ourselves to this, at the very least this area is rich with descriptions of the mountains, seas, and places that provide much of the imagery of Buddhist literature.

The fourth and fifth areas then present the causes for the world as we know it to arise: karma and the afflictions, which are the two parts of the truth of origin. The fourth area, "Teachings on Karma," explains all the different aspects of karma: what the virtuous and nonvirtuous actions are, what gives them their karmic strength, and how their results are experienced. The fifth area, "Teachings on the Kernels," analyzes all the different aspects of the afflictions, focusing on the afflicted kernels, the subtle seeds of the afflictions within our beings that can flare up into full blown afflictions—the defilements, floods, yokes, and graspings also described in this chapter. This area describes in detail what the kernels focus on, how they tie us to samsara, how they develop into manifest afflictions, and so forth. As Vasubandhu says, "The root of existence is the kernels," so fully understanding them is critical to understanding why we remain in samsara and how we can free ourselves from it. For this reason, it is not uncommon to hear Tibetan scholars say that this is the most important area in the *Treasury.* The fifth area also discusses how to abandon the kernels and the result of abandoning them, the perfect knowings that are the truth of cessation.[2]

The truth of the path is taught in the first part of the sixth area, "Teachings on the Paths and Individuals," which describes the meditations one follows from the beginning stages of the ordinary individual through the paths of seeing and meditation. The four parts of the path of joining—the precursors to clear realization—and the path of seeing are described in particular detail. The area also describes the qualities and results that arise on the path, the results of the spiritual way, and the different types of noble individuals in the listener vehicle.

The last two chapters, "Teachings on Wisdom" and "Teachings on Absorption," describe the wisdom and deep meditation that arise in different individuals, presenting the qualities of the Buddha and arhats. Knowing about their qualities helps create enthusiasm for practicing the path: If we do not feel that there will be any benefit to listening, contemplating, and meditating, it will be hard to motivate ourselves to make the necessary effort. But if we understand what kinds of qualities we can attain, then we will have joy at the prospects of following the path to liberation.

Thus the eight areas collect the Buddha's teachings into a treasury that we can use and enjoy. It covers a vast scope—the natures of phenomena, the natures of our minds and bodies, why we exist as we do, and how we can free ourselves—but as Wangchuk Dorje says, Master Vasubandhu is "skilled in concise and simple words, and composed a text with few difficult words." Together with the Karmapa's clear explanations, it truly is what Wangchuk Dorje calls a "feast for those with intelligence and interest."

The translation of these works has occupied me intermittently over the last few years since 2005, a period one could argue is not really long enough to fully penetrate a topic some scholars spend decades studying. Yet I hope that by these efforts English speakers will be able to begin an exploration of the abhidharma. May they be able to bathe in the cooling waters of the oceans of abhidharma and cleanse themselves of the stains of misunderstanding and wrong view. May they develop the confident full knowing born of study and contemplation and then progress down the paths of meditation. May all who read these words soon be free of all the sufferings and difficulties of this life and live within the greatest ease and contentment. Sarva mangalam!

A Note on the Translation of the Root Verses

One of the peculiar qualities of Vasubandhu's *Verses on the Treasury of Abhidharma* is its extreme concision, both in the original Sanskrit and in the Tibetan translation. The root verses do not give full explanations of most points. Instead, they give short reminders—sometimes only a short phrase or a single word—that help the student organize and remember the large body of knowledge presented in the commentaries. As such, they are brilliant and helpful both during the process of studying the abhidharma and later for remembering it, but difficult to penetrate at first.

For this reason, many contemporary translators of texts such as this take the approach of filling in the root verses to make them more understandable—adding words or phrases from the commentaries so that it can be understood on the first pass. This can certainly be helpful, but if one were to insert enough extra language to make every line of this particular text immediately clear, the resulting translation would read more like a prose commentary than the original verses; it would lack the concision and rhythm that make the Tibetan so memorable.

This translation takes a different approach, following—albeit imperfectly—the example set by the Indian master Jinamitra and the great Tibetan translator Bande Kawa Paltsek in the Tibetan translation. It is an attempt to match both the structure and content of Vasubandhu's verses as closely as possible in English. Where Vasubandhu is concise, this translation is similarly concise. Where the antecedents of pronouns are not specified in the original, they are left unspecified here. Just as the original is metered verse, this translation is also set in meter in order to make it easier to remember and recite. In Vasubandhu's original and in the Tibetan translation there are many lines that only make sense after one looks at a commentary, and readers will find this English translation similar in this regard as well. That being said, I have also tried to avoid being too literal in the translation, as in many passages too strict an adherence to the Sanskrit and Tibetan grammar and versification would have rendered the English unnecessarily opaque. For this reason the meter of the English translation is less regular than the original, some stanzas have extra lines, and other liberties have been taken.

People reading abhidharma for the first time may find it helpful to compare the root text as they read it to Wangchuk Dorje's commentary, which explains all the words of the root in the order they appear in the verses. Students who are studying the text in-depth may want to recite the root verses aloud and consult the other commentaries available in English. I hope that as students grow more familiar with the verses and their explanations, they might have moments such as I had studying this text in Tibetan, when passages that had seemed inscrutable suddenly became clear and the beauty of Vasubandhu's argument and manner became apparent.

Acknowledgments

I am deeply grateful to Khenchen Thrangu Rinpoche, who has supported, encouraged, and helped me in all ways while I have been translating this, and to Khenpo Losal of the Vajra Vidya Institute, who taught the class in which I first studied these texts and later helped clarify many points. Especial thanks are due to Venerable Lodro Sangpo from Gampo Abbey, who reviewed the first draft, and Michele Martin, who reviewed the manuscript when it was almost finished. They both made dozens of helpful suggestions that improved this translation immeasurably. I would also like to thank the Tsadra Foundation for their generous support of this publication as well as for their general encouragement throughout the entire process of bringing this work to publication.

I pray that these people and all the numerous others who have helped and encouraged me in many ways have success in all they do and swiftly bring themselves and others to the enduring happiness of buddhahood.

Vasubandhu

Verses on the Treasury of Abhidharma

by Vasubandhu

In Sanskrit: Abhidharmakośakārikā

In Tibetan: chos mngon pa mdzod kyi tshig le'ur byas pa

In English: Verses on the Treasury of Abhidharma

I prostrate to youthful Manjushri.

FIRST AREA

Teachings on the Elements

1. It is he who has conquered entirely the darkness toward all
And guides sentient beings from the mire of samsara.
He teaches the meaning as it is: I prostrate to him,
Then fully explain this treatise, *The Treasury of Abhidharma.*

2. Abhidharma is stainless full knowing, along with its following;
That by which and treatises by which one gains it.
Since this collects them completely in meaning,
Or since they are its base, it's *The Treasury of Abhidharma.*

3. Without full discernment of dharmas, there is not
Any method to totally quell the afflictions.
Because of afflictions, the world wanders the seas of existence.
That is why the Teacher taught this, they claim.

4. Defiled and undefiled dharmas:
Except the truth of path, composites
Are defiled since defilements can
Develop in relation to them.

5. The undefiled is the truth of path
And the three noncomposites, too,
Which are space and the two cessations.
Space is that which does not obstruct them.

6. Cessation that is analytic
Is a removal. They are distinct.
The other cessation blocks arising
Forever; it's nonanalytic.

7. Composite dharmas are the five
Skandhas of form, et cetera.
Just these are time, the bases for talk,
Emancipatible, and grounded.

8. The defiled is the aggregates
Of grasping and is disputed, too.
They're suffering, origin, and the world,
Locus of views, existence, too.

9. The skandha of form: five faculties,
Five objects, the imperceptible.
Supports of consciousnesses are
The eye, et cetera—lucid forms.

10. Two types of form, or twenty types,
And there are the eight types of sound,
And taste is sixfold, scent is fourfold,
Touch is elevenfold in nature.

11. Distracted, and mind-free as well,
Virtue or non, continuous,
And caused by the great sources: this
Is called the imperceptible.

12. The sources are the elements
Of earth and water, fire and air.
Their functions are to hold, et cetera.
They are hard, wet, and hot, and moving.

13. According to the world's conventions,
Color and form are considered earth,
Water, and fire. The atmosphere
Is the element itself, and like those, too.

14. Only these faculties and objects
    Are called ten bases and elements.
Feeling's experience. Conception
    Is the perception of attributes.

15. Formation differs from four skandhas.
    These three and imperceptibles
And noncomposites are called the
    Sense base and element of dharmas.

16. Consciousness is distinctly knowing.
    The sense base of mind is also that,
And also seven elements—
    Six consciousnesses and the mind.

17. Six consciousnesses that have just
    Immediately past are mind.
To establish the support of the sixth,
    We posit eighteen elements.

18. One aggregate, one sense base, and
    One element include them all.
It's by their nature—they do not
    Possess another's entity.

19. Of course there are two eyes, et cetera,
    But since their type, sphere, consciousness
Are similar, they're just one element.
    To beautify, they come in pairs.

20. The meaning of aggregate is heaped,
    Sense base means the gate for arising,
And element means family.
    Delusions, faculties, and interests
Are threefold, so the three are taught:
    The aggregates, et cetera.

21. Because they are the root of quarrels
    And cause samsara and the order,
Feeling and conception are taught
    As different aggregates than factors.

22. Since noncomposites do not suit
Aggregate's meaning, they are not taught.
The order is by coarse, all-afflicted,
The pot, and so forth, the realms' meanings.

23. The object is present, so first five.
The object is source-derived, so four.
Since at great distance or since quickly,
Or else in order of location.

24. One is specific and the main,
And one has many dharmas, the highest,
So one is called sense base of form,
And one is called sense base of dharma.

25. The eighty thousand aggregates
Of Dharma the Sage taught are all
Words or are names, and thus they are
Included in form or in formation.

26. Some say their length equals the treatise,
Or depends on aggregates, et cetera.
But aggregates of Dharma taught
Correspond to antidotes for conduct.

27. Likewise the other aggregates,
Sense bases, or else elements:
Examine their own characters;
Include them in what has been explained.

28. Openings are the element
Of space—they're light and dark, it's claimed.
The element of consciousness
Is defiled consciousness, arising's basis.

29. The showable here is form alone.
The obstructive is the ten with form.
Eight neutral are just those except
For form and sound. The others are threefold.

30. They all are in the Desire realm.
    The Form realm has fourteen: except
The elements of scent and taste,
    And the nose and tongue consciousnesses.

31. The Formless realm has elements
    Of mind, dharma, mind consciousness.
Those three are defiled or undefiled.
    And those remaining are defiled.

32. Those which consider and examine:
    Five elements of consciousness.
The final three are of three types.
    Those which remain are free of both.

33. The nonconceptual have no thoughts
    That recognize or that remember.
These two distract the mind's full knowing
    Or are all memory in mind.

34. The seven elements of mind
    And half of dharma, too, have focus.
The nine are not appropriated:
    Those eight and sound. Nine others: twofold.

35. Touch has two types. The other nine
    With form and part of the element
Of dharmas, too, are source-derived.
    The ten with form, conglomerates.

36. The cutter and that which is cut
    Are four external elements,
As are the burnt and that which weighs.
    The burner and weighed are disputed.

37. The five internal are produced
    By ripening and development.
Sound is not ripened. The compatible
    And ripening produce eight unobstructive.

38. Others are threefold. One has substance.
    The last three are a moment. The eye
And element of consciousness:
    Gained singly or together, too.

39. Twelve are internal, except form,
    And so forth. Dharma must be active.
The remaining are inactive, too—
    That which does not perform its function.

40. Ten are discards of meditation.
    Five also. The last three, three types.
Seeing does not discard the unafflicted,
    Nor form, nor what is not born from the sixth.

41. The eye and part of the element
    Of dharma are views: they are eightfold.
Five minds concurrent with five consciousnesses,
    Not thoughts that recognize, are not view.

42. The eye sees form when it is active.
    Supported consciousness does not,
Because a form that is obstructed
    Cannot be seen, or so they claim.

43. Both of the eyes can see, as well,
    Because they both can clearly see.
The eye, ear, and mind do not meet
    Their objects. Three perceive elsewise.

44. The nose and other two perceive
    An object that in size is equal.
The last's support is past. The five
    Arise together with them, too.

45. Because when those change, they change, too,
    The eye and so on are the supports.
Because of that and being specific,
    Those indicate the consciousnesses.

46. The body can not have a lower eye.
    The eye can not see forms of higher.
Neither the consciousness. Their forms,
    And two of body, too, on any.

47. The ear is similar, as well.
    The three are all of their own level.
The consciousness of body is lower,
    Own level. Mind is indefinite.

48. Two consciousnesses, five external.
    Noncompound dharmas are permanent.
One part of dharmas and those taught
    As the internal twelve are faculties.

This completes the first area called "Teachings on the Elements" from the *Verses of the Treasury of Abhidharma*.

SECOND AREA

Teachings on the Faculties

1. Five exercise their power over
   Four meanings. Four over two, it's claimed.
The five and eight, over all-afflicted
   And over the utterly pure.

2. For power to focus on their own
   Or all objects, six faculties.
For power over femaleness and maleness:
   The body's female and male faculties.

3. For power to maintain one's likeness,
   The all-afflicted, and the pure;
Life, feelings, and five faculties
   Of faith and so forth are proposed.

4. To attain high, higher, and nirvana,
   Et cetera, there are faculties of
Producing all-knowing, all-knowing,
   And having all-knowing as well.

5. There are as many faculties as
   The mind's supports, distinctions, and
That which maintains, those which afflict,
   Gatherers, and the utterly pure.

6. Or as supports for entry, birth,
 Remaining, and enjoying there are
Fourteen, and likewise for the reverse
 There are the other faculties.

7. The faculty of suffering
 Is any unpleasant bodily feeling.
Pleasant is pleasure. On third dhyana
 The mind's is the faculty of pleasure.

8. On others, it is mental pleasure.
 Unpleasant feelings in the mind
Are unhappiness, and neutral feelings
 Are middling since both are thought-free.

9. On the paths of seeing, meditation,
 And of nonlearning, nine are three.
Three stainless. Those with form, life force,
 And suffering are defiled. Nine twofold.

10. Life force is fully ripened. Twelve
 Are twofold, except the last eight
And mental unhappiness. That one
 Must have full ripening. Ten twofold:

11. Mind, other feelings, faith, so forth.
 Eight virtuous. Unhappiness
Is twofold. Mind and other feelings
 Are threefold, and the rest are onefold.

12. Except the stainless, in Desire.
 Except male, female faculties,
And sufferings: in Form. In Formless
 There are none with form, nor any pleasures.

13. Mind and three feelings are threefold.
 The two discard unhappiness.
By meditation, nine. Five not
 Discarded, also. Three are not.

14. In Desire, at first one gains the two
Full ripened. Not miraculous birth—
With that, six, seven, or else eight.
There are six in Form and one above.

15. When dying in Formless, just life force
And mind and neutral feeling cease.
In Form, eight cease. With miraculous
Birth in Desire, ten, nine, or eight.

16. In gradual deaths, the four will cease.
In virtuous, add five to all.
Two outer results are gained with nine.
The two with seven, eight, or nine.

17. Because it's possible to attain
Arhat with eleven, it is taught.
One who possesses neutral feeling,
Life force, or mind must have the three.

18. Those who have pleasure or body, four,
And five have those who've eyes, et cetera,
Or mental pleasure. Those who have
Suffering, seven, and the female

19. Faculty and so forth have eight.
Those with the faculty of having
All-knowing have eleven. With
Producing all-knowing, thirteen.

20. Those without virtue who've the fewest
Have eight: life, body, feelings, mind.
The childish of the Formless likewise
Have neutral, life force, mind, and virtues.

21. The most that one could have is nineteen
Except the stainless, with two organs;
And nobles who are attached could have
All but one organ and two stainless.

22. In Desire, atoms without sound
Or faculties: eight substances.
With body faculty, nine substances.
Another faculty, ten substances.

23. The mind and factors must arise together.
All with the characteristics of composites.
Attainment, sometimes. Factors are fivefold,
Since there are different major grounds and so forth.

24. Feeling, volition, and conception,
Intention, contact, intelligence,
And mindfulness, attention, interest,
Samadhi are with all cognitions.

25. Faith, carefulness, and pliancy,
Equanimity, shame, modesty,
Two roots, and nonhostility,
And diligence are with all virtue.

26. Delusion, carelessness, and laziness,
Nonfaith, and torpor, agitation:
With all afflicted. With nonvirtue,
Immodesty and shamelessness.

27. Aggression, grudge, deceit, and envy,
Contentiousness, hypocrisy,
Stinginess, pretense, arrogance, and
Hostility: grounds of minor afflictions.

28. Minds in Desire, when virtuous, have
Considering and examining,
So they have twenty-two mental factors.
Some are augmented by regret.

29. With unmixed minds that are nonvirtuous
And have view, too, the twenty arise.
If the four afflictions; or aggression,
Et cetera; or regret, twenty-one.

30. In the obscured, eighteen. It's said
With other neutrals, there are twelve.
Since sleep does not preclude any other,
Whenever it occurs, it's added.

31. Of these, regret, sleep, and nonvirtues
Are not on the first dhyana's levels.
In special, no considering;
Above that, no examining, either.

32. Shameless is disrespect; immodesty is
To view the unwholesome without fear.
Affection's faith; respect is shame.
These two are in Desire and Form.

33. Considering and examining
Are coarse and fine. Pride is self-inflation.
Arrogance is clinging to one's features,
Which then consumes the mind completely.

34. Cognition, mind, and consciousness
Are equivalent. The mind and factors
Have a support, a focus, aspects,
Concurrence also that is fivefold.

35. Formations that are nonconcurrent
Include attainment, nonattainment,
Same class, Conception Free, absorptions,
And life force and the characteristics,

36. Collections of names and so forth, too.
Attainment is to get or have.
Attainment, nonattainment are of
What is in one's stream, or two cessations.

37. Attainment of three times is threefold;
Of virtue so forth, virtue so forth;
Of any realm is in that realm;
Of what's not in a realm is fourfold;

38. Of neither learner nor non, three;
    Of what is not abandoned, twofold.
Neutral attainment: at same time,
    Except clairvoyance, emanations.

39. Of form of the obscured, as well.
    In Desire, of forms does not precede.
Nonattainment is unobscured neutral;
    Of past and unborn, it is threefold.

40. Of Desire, et cetera, and the stainless, too.
    Path's nonattainment is asserted as
An ordinary being. It's forfeited
    When one attains that or shifts level.

41. Same status: sentient beings' resemblance.
    Conception-free stops mind and factors
Of beings in Conception Free.
    Full ripening. They're in Great Result.

42. Likewise conception-free absorption.
    Last dhyan. From wishing for release.
It's virtue. Experienced on birth only.
    Not nobles. Gained in one time only.

43. Cessation's like that, too. Its purpose
    Is staying. Born on Peak, it's virtue.
Experienced in two or indefinite,
    The nobles attain it by training,

44. The Sage by awakening. Not at first,
    Since it was gained by thirty-four moments.
Both have support of Desire and Form.
    Cessation is first among humans.

45. Life force is life. It is that which
    Supports one's warmth and consciousness.
The characteristics are birth,
    And aging, staying, impermanence.

46. They've birth of birth, et cetera, and
    Engage eight dharmas or else one.
Without the causes or conditions,
    Birth can't produce what is produced.

47. Collections of names and so forth are
    Collections of names, speech, and letters.
Desire and Form. Indicate beings.
    Compatible and neutral. Likewise

48. Same status. Fully ripened, too.
    Three realms, and its attainment is twofold.
Characteristics, too. Absorptions,
    Not having are compatible.

49. Enabling cause, the coemergent,
    Cause of same status, the concurrent,
The universal, and full ripening
    Are the six causes, it's proposed.

50. The enabling cause is other than self.
    The coemergent: mutual result,
Such as sources; mind and its followers;
    Characteristics and their base.

51. They're mental factors, two vows, and
    The mind's and their characteristics.
They follow mind in terms of time,
    Results, et cetera, virtue, et cetera.

52. Same status cause is similar,
    Own class and level, born before.
Nine levels' paths are mutual,
    Of equal or superior.

53. Produced by training is just those two.
    From listening, reflecting, so forth.
Concurrent cause is mind and factors
    With a support that is concurrent.

54. The universal, of afflicted.
Own level. Universal. Five.
Full-ripening cause can only be
Nonvirtue or a defiled virtue.

55. The universal and same status
Are in two times; three in three times.
Composites and removal are
Results. Noncompounds don't have those.

56. Full-ripened result is of the last;
The dominant result, of first.
Compatible: same status and
The universal. Personal, two.

57. Fully ripened is a neutral dharma,
Shows beings, not neutral, born later.
Compatible is like its cause.
Removal is to mentally

58. Extinguish, and the result born
From something's power is personal.
Composites that aren't previous are
The dominant of composites only.

59. The five hold a result in the present.
Two causes issue in the present.
Two present and past causes issue,
And one past cause issues results.

60. The afflicted, fully ripened, others,
And the first noble respectively
Arise from all except full ripening,
Universal, those two, and same status.

61. This is for mind and mental factors.
The rest are like; exclude concurrent.
There are four conditions, it is taught.
The one called causal is five causes.

62. The mind and factors that have arisen,
    But not the last, are immediate.
The objective is all dharmas, and
    The enabling is the dominant.

63. Two causes' function is directed
    Toward ceasing. The three toward arising.
The two conditions other than
    That are the opposite of those.

64. Four produce mind and mental factors,
    And three, the two absorptions. Others
Arise from two, not God and so forth,
    Since they're successive and so forth.

65. When sources cause the sources, twofold;
    When causing source-derived, fivefold.
Three ways the source-derived are mutual;
    They cause the sources in one way.

66. Minds in Desire: virtue, nonvirtue,
    Obscured, or else unobscured neutral.
In Form and Formless, those except
    Nonvirtue. Two are undefiled.

67. Nine minds arise from a virtuous mind
    Of Desire. It can arise from eight.
Nonvirtuous mind arises from ten.
    From it are four. Like that, the obscured.

68. The unobscured arises from five.
    Directly from it, seven minds.
In Form, from virtuous, eleven.
    That is directly after nine.

69. Obscured is from eight, and from it, six.
    The unobscured mind is from three.
From that one, six. In Formless, too,
    It's similar. From virtuous mind

70. Arise nine minds. That after six.
From obscured, seven. That is so.
The learner's from four. From it five.
Nonlearner's mind arises from five

71. And from it there arise four minds.
To make this dozen into twenty:
Divide the virtue of three realms
In what's attained on birth, from training.

72. Produced by ripening, the path
Of activities, crafts, emanations:
The neutral are fourfold in Desire.
In Form, the crafts must be excluded.

73. With the three realms' afflicted minds
One can acquire six, six, or two.
With virtuous in Form, it's three.
With learner, four. With others, those.

This completes the second area called "Teachings on the Faculties" from the *Verses of the Treasury of Abhidharma.*

THIRD AREA

Teachings on the World

1. Hells, hungry ghosts, and animals,
   And humans, and six types of gods
   Are the Desire realm. By dividing
   The hells and continents, there are twenty.

2. Above that there are seventeen
   Higher abodes of the Form realm.
   Each of the dhyanas has three levels,
   But the fourth dhyana has eight levels.

3. The Formless realm has no abodes.
   Because of birth, it has four types.
   There, likeness and life force as well
   Support the mind's continuum.

4. The names, the hells, and so forth, show
   Five wanderers. They're unafflicted
   And neutral. Sentient beings are called,
   But not those in the between state.

5. A different body and conception;
   A different body, same conception;
   Reverse; same body and conception;
   And the three places without form

6. Are seven places of consciousness.
   The others have that which destroys it.
With beings on Peak and Concept Free,
   They're said to be nine places for beings.

7. Since one remains against one's wishes,
   The others are not. Four more places:
Four aggregates that are defiled,
   On their own level. Consciousness

8. Alone is not explained as a place.
   Combined, there are four alternatives.
There sentient beings have four modes
   Of birth: from egg, et cetera.

9. Humans and animals have four.
   Hell beings have miraculous birth,
As do gods and the between states.
   From the womb as well are hungry ghosts.

10. In this, it is that which arises
   Between the states of death and birth.
It has not reached its destination,
   So the between state is not born.

11. Analogous to a grain's continuum,
   It is not born from interruption.
Since a reflection is not proven,
   Nor similar, it's not an example.

12. On one, no two are simultaneous.
   It's discontinuous, born from two.
Since mentioned, it exists. Scent-eaters,
   And five are taught, and Sutra of Wanderers.

13. Since it is propelled by the same karma,
   It has the body of the next.
The previous is prior to death
   But onward from the moment of birth.

14. They're seen by their class, divine eye.
    The miracles of karma have power.
Full facultied and unobstructive,
    They cannot turn back. They eat smells.

15. The mind mistaken, out of lust
    It goes into its destination.
Others from longing for a smell
    Or place. They fall head first to hell.

16. One enters wittingly, one stays,
    As well, and one emerges, too.
Others are ignorant of all,
    And always if oviparous.

17. The three—wheel wielding as well as
    Two self-awakened—enter the womb
Because their karma or their wisdom
    Or both are vast, respectively.

18. There is no self—mere aggregates.
    Continuums of between states
Assembled by afflictions and karma
    Enter the womb. It's like a lamp.

19. Just as propelled, the continuum
    Arose in stages, then from karma
And afflictions goes to the next world—
    Beginningless wheel of existence.

20. These are twelve links of interdependent
    Origination in three parts.
The previous and next, two each;
    The middle, eight, with all complete.

21. Previous afflictions: ignorance.
    Previous karma is formations.
The aggregates at linking: consciousness.
    And name-and-form is on from there

22. Until the six sense bases emerge.
Those are until three are assembled.
Contact is till one knows the causes
Of pleasure and of pain, et cetera.

23. Then feeling until sex. And craving
Is greed for possessions and for sex.
Close grasping is then chasing after
In order to obtain enjoyments.

24. Performing actions that result
In an existence is becoming.
Linking rebirth again is birth.
Up until feeling, aging and death.

25. They claim that this is periodic.
The link's called by the principal.
It's taught to reverse ignorance
About the previous, next, and middle.

26. Three are afflictions. Two are karma.
Seven are bases and results.
Cause and result of two is concise:
One can infer them from the middle.

27. Afflictions bear afflictions, action.
From that, the bases, and from those
Arise the bases and afflictions.
That is existence's progression.

28. Here what is arising is a cause;
What has arisen is a result.
An other dharma, opposite to knowing,
Ignorance is like untruth, unfriendly, et cetera.

29. Because of fetter and such words.
Not bad full knowing, since that is view.
Since it's concurrent with that view;
It's taught that it afflicts full knowing.

30. Skandhas that are not form are name.
    Six contacts happen from assembly.
Five are obstructive contact, and
    The sixth is designated contact.

31. Aware and unaware and other contact
    Are stainless and afflicted and the rest.
Malicious, lustful contact, and
    Three felt as pleasant and so forth.

32. From that, six feelings can arise:
    Five bodily, the other mental.
And that has eighteen types as well
    Because of movement of the mind.

33. In Desire, all focus on their own,
    And twelve can have Form in their sphere.
The three on higher. On two dhyanas
    Are twelve which can move toward Desire.

34. Eight focus on their own; the two
    On Formless. The two dhyans have six.
Six on Desire, the four on own,
    And one can focus on the higher.

35. On preparations for the Formless,
    Four move toward Form, one moves toward higher.
In actual, one with own object.
    All of the eighteen are defiled.

36. Others have been or will be explained.
    In this, afflictions are like seeds,
Like nagas, and like roots and trees,
    Like husks as well, it is proposed.

37. Karma's like rice within its husk,
    Like medicine and flowers. The bases,
Like food and drink that have been got.
    Among these four states of existence,

38. The state of rebirth is afflicted
By all the afflictions of its level.
The others, threefold. Three in Formless.
Wanderers abide from sustenance.

39. The sustenance food is in Desire.
Its nature is the three sense bases,
But not the sense base form, since that
Does not affect its organ or the freed.

40. Contact, volition, and consciousness are
Stained sustenance. They are in three.
It's born from mind, the searching state,
Scent-eater, and the between state,

41. And reestablishing. Two have the purpose
Of developing its base and the supported.
Two have the purpose to propel,
Establish the next life, in order.

42. To sever, to restore, and to
Detach, regress, die, and be born
Are the mind consciousness alone.
At death and birth, there's neutral feeling.

43. Not in one-pointed or no mind.
Nirvana in two neutral minds.
In gradual death, if low or human,
Divine or no rebirth, mind dies

44. In the feet, navel, or the heart.
Water, et cetera, severs the pith.
Nobles are destined for the correct;
The heinous deeds for the mistaken.

45. Now the container world is said
To have below a mandala
Of wind one million and six hundred
Thousands in depth, uncountable.

46. Then water to a depth of one
    Million one hundred twenty thousand.
Then it becomes eight hundred thousand
    In depth. The rest turns into gold.

47. The mandalas of water and gold
    Are in diameter one million
Two hundred and three thousand and
    Four hundred fifty leagues across.

48. They're thrice that in circumference.
    On that are Meru, the Yoke Holder,
Plow Holder, and Acacia Tree,
    And likewise Lovely to Behold,

49. And Horse's Ear and Bowing Down,
    Rim Holder Mounts, then continents.
Outside there is the Outer Ring.
    Seven are gold. That one is iron.

50. Mount Meru is four precious ores.
    Down eighty thousand into water
Plunges Mount Meru; above as well
    It lofts to eighty thousand leagues.

51. The eight are each half less in width.
    Their heights are equal to their widths.
Between them, seven Playful Seas;
    Across the first is eighty thousand.

52. This one is the Vast Inner Sea.
    Its sides are triple to its width.
The other seas are each half less.
    The rest is the Great Outer Ocean.

53. Across it is three hundred and
    Twenty-two thousand leagues. Therein
Is the Rose-Apple Land, two thousand
    Leagues on three sides, shaped like a cart,

54. With one of three and one half leagues.
Superior Body is half-moon like.
Three of its sides are like here; one
Is three and one half hundred leagues.

55. The Bountiful Cow Land is round,
Seven thousand and five hundred leagues.
Across its mid, twenty-five hundred.
Unpleasant Sound: eight, equal, square.

56. Between are eight subcontinents:
Deha, Videha, Kurava,
Kaurava, Chāmara, Avara,
And Śaṭhā and Uttaramantriṇa.

57. To the north of here, across the nine
Black Mounts is the Snow Mountain, then
On the near side of Perfume Mountain
Is a lake with waters fifty across.

58. Below this twenty thousand leagues,
The Incessant Hell is just that size.
Above that there are seven hells,
And all eight have an extra sixteen:

59. On each of their four sides there are
The Burning Ground and Rotten Corpse,
The Razor Road and those, the River.
Eight other cold hells—Blisters, et cetera.

60. The sun and moon are at mid Meru,
Fifty plus one in diameter.
So midnight, sunset, and mid-day
And sunrise are at the same time.

61. After the second rainy month's
Ninth day of waxing, nights grow longer
And then in the fourth month of autumn,
Grow shorter. Days are the reverse.

62. The days or nights by minutes lengthen.
 It's as the sun moves south or north.
From moving too close to the sun,
 Moon shades itself with its own shadow.

63. On that there are four terraces,
 The distance between which is ten thousand,
Extending sixteen thousand leagues,
 And eight, four, and two thousand leagues.

64. The Basin Holders, Garland Holders,
 The Always Intoxicated, and
The gods of the Four Great Kings' Realm
 Live there and in seven mountain ranges.

65. On Meru's peak is Thirty-Three,
 Each side of which is eighty thousand.
On peaks in each of its four corners
 There dwell the Vajra-Holder yakshas.

66. The central city Lovely to Behold,
 Twenty-five hundred leagues per side,
Has golden ground of one and half
 Leagues deep; it is soft and variegated.

67. Within is Utterly Conquering,
 With sides two hundred fifty leagues.
Outside are Colorful Chariots,
 Roughening, Mixing, and Joyous Grove.

68. To their four sides twenty leagues away,
 There are the four excellent grounds.
On the northeast corner is All-Gathering.
 On the southwest corner is Good Dharma.

69. The gods above that live in palaces.
 Six ways they act upon desire:
They couple in a pair, embrace,
 Or else hold hands or laugh or look.

70. The children born in those realms are
Like children aged from five to ten.
Those born in the Form realms are born
Full grown, with even their robes complete.

71. There are three ways desirables
Arise for Desire gods and humans.
Pleasure arises in three ways
On three of the dhyanas—thus nine levels.

72. There is as far above a realm
As there is below to the lowest realm.
Except through magic or another,
They cannot see what is above.

73. One thousand worlds, each with four lands,
A sun and moon, and a Great Mountain,
Desire god realms, and Brahma's World,
Are called a General Prime Thousand.

74. A thousand of those, the second thousand,
And that is called a Middle World Realm.
A thousand of those is the Three Thousands.
They are destroyed and formed together.

75. The ones on the Rose-Apple Land
Are four, or three and half cubits tall.
On the East, the Bountiful Cow, and North,
They're twice as tall as on the previous.

76. The bodies of Desire Gods grow
From a quarter earshot in height to
One and half earshots. In the first
Of Form, they are one-half league tall.

77. Above, a half league taller each.
Beyond the highest of Lesser Light,
Their bodies double on each level.
At Cloudless, though, discard three leagues.

78. Unpleasant Sound's life span, one thousand.
    On two, it is shorter by half each.
Here it's uncertain: from ten years
    At end; incalculable at first.

79. And fifty human years are just
    One day and night among the lowest
Of gods of Desire. Their life span is,
    Of such a day, five hundred years.

80. Above both day-length and span double.
    In Form, there's neither day nor night,
So their life span in aeons is
    Equal in number to their height.

81. In Formless each, by twenty thousand
    Aeons, is longer than the previous.
On Lesser Light and up, they are
    Great aeons. Below that, half aeons.

82. The Reviving and so forth, six hells,
    Have days that equal Desire Gods' lives.
Of such a day, their life spans equal
    The life spans of Desire realm Gods.

83. Extremely Hot, half aeon; the Incessant,
    An intermediate aeon. The longest life
For animals, an aeon. Hungry ghosts
    Live month-long days five hundred years.

84. If every hundred years one took
    A seed from a cart of sesame,
When that is empty is life in Blisters.
    In others, twenty times as long.

85. Untimely death except in Unpleasant.
    The units of form, name, and time
Are particles, letters, and instants.
    Called atoms, molecules, and iron,

86. And water, rabbit, sheep, and ox,
And particles of sunlight, nits,
What comes from that, and also knuckles—
Each seven times larger than the previous.

87. There are four and twenty fingers to
A cubit; four in every fathom.
Of those, five hundred make an earshot,
Which is a hermitage, it is said,

88. And eight of those are called a league.
One hundred twenty instants is
An instant of that. Sixty of those
Is a minute. Hours and days and months

89. Are thirty times as long as previous.
Including the impossible days
There are twelve months in every year.
The many types of aeon are explained.

90. An aeon of destruction lasts from when
There are no hell beings till the world's destroyed.
Formation is from primordial wind
Until a being exists in hell.

91. An intermediate aeon lasts
From when life is incalculable
Till it is ten years. Then another
Eighteen increasing and decreasing,

92. Then one increasing. During those,
Lives are as long as eighty thousand.
In this way this world that is formed
Lasts twenty intermediate aeons.

93. Forming, destroying, and remaining
After destruction are the same.
These eighty make up one great aeon.
Then after three uncountable

94. Of these appears a Buddha during
    The decrease to one hundred years.
In both, self-buddhas. Following
    One hundred aeons, a rhino appears.

95. Wheel-wielding emperors appear
    When life is not less than eighty thousand.
With wheels of gold, silver, copper, iron,
    They rule over one, two, three, or else

96. Four continents, in reverse order.
    At once, there are never two, like buddhas.
When their opponents welcome them,
    Or they themselves advance or gird
For battle or just brandish weapons,
    They triumph without causing harm.

97. The Sage's marks remain in place,
    Clear and complete, so they're superior.
The earliest beings are like Form gods.
    They gradually feel greed for tastes,

98. Grow lazy, and then gather and hoard.
    Land holders then appoint field chieftains.
Because of their strong karmic paths,
    Their life span shortens to ten years.

99. It's weapons, pestilence, and famine
    That bring an aeon to its end,
For seven days, then seven months,
    Then seven years respectively.

100. Then fire and water and then wind
    Bring three additional destructions.
These crest respectively at the
    Three dhyanas—second and so forth—

101. Because those correspond to their faults.
    But not the fourth, since it's immovable.
Not permanent, its palaces
    And beings arise, and then they perish.

102. There are seven by fire, then one by water.
When seven by water are thus finished,
Then seven by fire, and after that,
Finally wind will bring destruction.

This completes the third area called "Teachings on the World" from the *Verses of the Treasury of Abhidharma.*

FOURTH AREA

Teachings on Karma

1. From karma various worlds are born.
   Volition and what that creates.
   Volition is mental karma, which
   Creates the karma of body and speech.

2. Those two are percepts and impercepts.
   Bodily perceptible is shape.
   It is not movement, since composites
   Are momentary, as they perish.

3. Nothing can happen without cause.
   The cause would become the destroyer.
   Two would perceive it; not in particles.
   Perceptible speech is speech's sound.

4. Three kinds and stainless form are taught;
   Increase; and paths not done; et cetera.
   In subsequent moments, the impercepts
   Of Desire are born from the past sources.

5. Stained karmas of the body and speech
   Take their own sources as a cause.
   The undefiled, of where it arises.
   Impercepts aren't appropriated.

6. They are causally compatible
   And indicate a sentient being.
They arise from sources which must be
   Compatible, appropriated.
The ones born of samadhi arise
   From unappropriated sources
That are produced by development
   And are not separate.

7. There are no neutral imperceptibles.
   The others are threefold. Nonvirtue is
In Desire. There are impercepts in Form, too,
   And percepts where there is considering.

8. There's no obscured in Desire, either,
   Because there is no motivation.
Ultimate virtue is liberation;
   Inherent: roots, shame, modesty;

9. Concurrent with that is concurrent;
   Actions and such are motivated.
Nonvirtue is the opposite.
   The stable is the ultimate neutral.

10. Two motivations are the causal
   And the contemporaneous motives.
The first one is the instigator;
   The second is the executor.

11. The consciousness that seeing discards
   Is the instigator. And the mind
That is a discard of meditation
   Is both. The five are executors.

12. The executors from the virtuous
   And other instigators are threefold.
The Sage's are alike or virtuous.
   Those born of ripening are neither.

13. Three types of imperceptibles
Are vows, wrong vows, and neither. Vows
Are individual liberation
And dhyan-produced, and undefiled.

14. There are the eight called pratimokṣa,
But they are four in substance since
Name alone changes with the organ.
They're separate but not exclusive.

15. By swearing to hold five, eight, ten,
Or all the precepts, one becomes
A pursuer of virtue, or a faster,
Or else a novice, or a bhikshu.

16. This is called discipline, fine conduct,
Karma, and vow. The percept and
Impercept of the first are individual
Liberation and the path of action.

17. The eight have pratimokṣa vows.
When one has dhyana, one has that.
The nobles have the undefiled.
The latter two follow the mind.

18. The two, on Not Unable's paths
Of no obstacles, are called discarding.
Mindfulness and awareness are
Restraint of mind and faculties.

19. One who has pratimokṣa has
The present imperceptible
Until it's canceled. From the first
Moment and on, one has the past.

20. It's so for those with wrong vows, too.
Those who possess the vows of dhyana
Possess the past and future. Nobles
At first do not possess the past.

21. In equipoise, on noble paths:
    The present imperceptible.
If in between, at first the middle;
    From then on, one has the two times.

22. Those with wrong vows can have the virtuous,
    And those with vows can have nonvirtuous
Impercepts as long as they are
    Very sincere or strongly afflicted.

23. Those who are acting all possess
    The percept of the present time.
From the first moment until canceled,
    They have the past, but not the future.

24. There's no possession of the past
    Obscured, nor of the unobscured.
Wrong vows, and harmful conduct, and
    Immoral, karma, and its path.

25. As it's between, the mind is weak,
    Thus one who acts has just the percept.
When a noble's percept has been canceled
    Yet still is unborn, they have the impercept.

26. The dhyana vows are gained with the level
    Of dhyana itself. The undefiled
By nobles. Pratimokṣa is through
    The perceptible of others, et cetera.

27. The vows are taken for life or else
    The period of one day and night.
There is no one-day-long wrong-vow,
    Because there's no such oath, it's heard.

28. While kneeling low with no adornments,
    Recite the words. Till morrow's morn
One swears before another at dawn
    To all the precepts of the fast.

29. There are four, one, and three precepts
    Of discipline, and carefulness,
Austerity respectively.
    Those bring unmindfulness and arrogance.

30. Others may also fast, of course,
    But only after going for refuge.
By promising to pursue virtue
    The vow is made, it's taught, like bhikshus.

31. If that is so and all is thus bound,
    How is there single conduct, et cetera?
Hold that, and it is held, it's heard.
    They're weak, et cetera, like the mind.

32. All those who go for refuge to
    The three take refuge in the dharmas
That make the Buddha and the Sangha—
    No learning and both—and nirvana.

33. Since sexual misconduct is reviled,
    Since easy, since abstention is attained.
The vow's attained just as it's sworn;
    It is not total celibacy.

34. If one transgresses any precept,
    He would end up by telling a lie.
Of the prohibited unwholesome,
    Intoxicants, as one will hold the others.

35. The vows of Desire must be attained
    In relation to all, both, and present.
The dhyana and undefiled vows
    Relate to actual and all times.

36. Vows in relation to all beings;
    Distinctions in branches and cause.
Wrong vows are gained in relation to
    All and all branches; not to causes.

37. Wrong vows can be attained from action,
Or else they're gained through a commitment.
The other impercept is gained
From field, commitment, and respect.

38. The individual liberation
Is canceled by returning vows,
Or dying, or two organs arising,
Severing the roots, or passing the night.

39. Some say it's canceled by the downfalls;
By the True Dharma's decline, say others.
Kashmiris propose that when it happens,
There are both, like having debts and riches.

40. The virtue of dhyana can be canceled
By shifting level or regressing.
Formless is same; noble by gaining
A result, refining, or regressing.

41. Wrong vows are canceled by gaining vows
Or dying or two organs arising.
Mid-vows, when force or undertaking,
Act, object, life, or the roots cease.

42. The Desire realm's immaterial virtue,
By severing roots and rebirth higher.
The immaterial afflicted
Perishes when its anti arises.

43. Except sexless, neuters, hermaphrodites,
Unpleasant Sound, humans can have
Wrong vows. The vows are similar.
The gods as well. Humans have three.

44. The gods born in Desire and Form
Have dhyan-produced. Except for beings
In special dhyana and Concept Free,
They've undefiled—in Formless, too.

45. Pleasant, unpleasant, and other karma
 Are virtue, nonvirtue, and other.
Merit, nonmerit, and unmoving.
 The three experienced as pleasure, et cetera.

46. Merit is virtuous karma of
 Desire. Unmoving is of higher:
Because the karma fully ripens
 On just those levels, it does not move.

47. Virtue's experienced as pleasure
 Through the third dhyana. Above that
It's felt as neither pain nor pleasure.
 Nonvirtue is felt as suffering here.

48. Some say that in the lower, there
 Is middling, too, since there is ripening
In special dhyan, and since the three
 Can ripen without earlier or later.

49. Inherently, concurrently,
 Through focus, as full ripening,
Or else directly manifesting:
 Five ways that karma is experienced.

50. They're definite or indefinite.
 There are three definite because
There's visibly experienced,
 Et cetera. Some propose five types,

51. And others, four alternatives.
 Three karmas will propel a likeness.
In all realms, there are four propulsions.
 In hell, there are three virtuous.

52. A child detached stably from a realm
 Does none experienced on birth there.
Nobles do none experienced in others,
 Even those not stable toward Desire or Peak.

53. There are twenty-two propulsions in
    The between state of the Desire realm.
These are a visible result.
    These are one single likeness only.

54. An action done out of intense
    Afflictions or sincerity,
To the field of qualities, continuous,
    Or killing parents: that is definite.

55. Karma has visible results
    From excellence of field and intention,
From stable detachment from the level
    When it has definite full ripening.

56. To help or harm those risen from
    Cessation, unprovocative,
Love, seeing, or arhat's result,
    Brings swiftly experienced results.

57. Virtuous karma that is free of
    Considering will fully ripen
Only as feelings in the mind.
    Nonvirtue ripens on the body.

58. A distraught mind is mental mind.
    It's born from fully ripened karma,
From fear or harm, imbalance, sorrow
    Among the attached, not in the North.

59. The crooked, faulty, degenerate
    Are born of deceit, hate, desire.
Four types of karma are distinguished
    As white and black, et cetera.

60. Nonvirtue, virtue of Form realm,
    And of Desire, respectively
Are karma that is black, white, both.
    What douses them is undefiled.

61. Forbearance of dharmas and eight paths of
No obstacles that bring detachment:
These are the twelve volitions that
Are karma which destroys the black.

62. Volition of the ninth is what
Extinguishes the black and white.
The last path of no obstacles
To dhyan's detachment douses white.

63. Some say the two are what is felt
In hell and elsewhere in Desire.
Others call seeing's discards black;
The rest in Desire, black and white.

64. Nonlearners' karma of body and speech
And just their mind respectively
Are silence of the three. All three
Fine conducts are three purifiers.

65. Nonvirtue of the body, et cetera,
Is proposed as three harmful conducts.
To covet and so forth aren't action
But are three harmful mental conducts.

66. Fine conduct is the opposite.
Among them, to consolidate grossly,
The various virtues and nonvirtues
Are taught as the ten karmic paths.

67. Six nonvirtues are imperceptible.
The one is both. If done, they are as well.
The seven virtues are both. What samadhi
Produces is an imperceptible.

68. The preparations are perceptible.
They might be imperceptible, or not.
The aftermath is opposite of that.
The preparations come from the three roots.

69. They follow the three roots immediately,
So coveting and so forth come from them.
The virtues, preparation, aftermath,
Arise from nongreed, nonhate, nondelusion.

70. Hatred brings killing and harsh words
And malice to completion. Greed
Brings coveting, adultery,
And also stealing to completion.

71. Wrong view, completed by delusion.
The rest by three, it is proposed.
The bases, they are sentient beings,
Enjoyments, name-and-form, and words.

72. When killers die before or else
Together, there's no actual—
They've been born in another body.
In wars and so forth all of them
Have the same goal, so all possess
The karma, like the perpetrator.

73. To take life is to kill another
Intentionally, unerringly.
To steal is to make another's wealth
One's own by force or thievery.

74. To lie with one who shouldn't be lain with:
Four kinds of sexual misconduct.
To say one thing while thinking another,
When clearly understood, is lying.

75. That which is experienced by eye,
By ear, mind consciousness, and three,
Is seen, heard, cognized, and perceived
Respectively, it is explained.

76. Divisive speech is words said with
An afflicted mind to divide others.
Harsh speech is words that are unpleasant.
Any afflicted words are chatter—

77. Some say afflicted speech that's other
Than those, like flattery, song, shows,
Or else bad treatises. To covet
Is wrongly greeding for others' wealth.

78. Malice is hate for sentient beings.
Believing there's no virtue or
Nonvirtue is wrong view. Of these,
Three are paths and seven karma, too.

79. The nihilist view severs the roots
Of Desire that were attained at birth.
Denial of cause and result. All.
Gradual. By humans. They are cut

80. By men and women acting on views.
The severance is nonpossession.
Restored by doubt and view of existence;
Who've done a heinous deed, not here.

81. Up to eight nonvirtues and volition
Can simultaneously arise;
When they are virtuous, up to ten,
And yet not one, not eight, not five.

82. In hell, there is chatter and harsh words,
And malice in two ways; wrong view
And covetousness by possession.
There are three in Unpleasant Sound.

83. The seventh is manifest there, too.
Elsewhere in Desire, the ten nonvirtues.
Three virtues are in all by way
Of being possessed or manifest.

84. Beings in Concept Free and Formless
Have seven by possession, and
In the rest they're manifest as well,
Except in hell and Unpleasant Sound.

85. It's proposed these all give dominant,
Compatible, and ripened results.
Since it makes suffering, and kills,
And destroys vigor, three results.

86. Acting with body and speech from greed:
Wrong livelihood. It's hard to cleanse,
So it's taught separate. Saying it's greed
For sustenance contradicts the sutras.

87. The karma of stained discarding paths
Brings five results. The stainless, four,
As do the other defiled karmas,
Whether they're virtue or nonvirtue.

88. The remaining that are undefiled
Have three results, as does the neutral.
The virtue and so forth of virtue
Are four and two and likewise three.

89. Nonvirtue's virtue and so forth
Are two, three, four, respectively.
The virtue and so forth of neutral
Are two and three and likewise three.

90. Results of past in all three times
Are four, as are the middle's future.
The middle has two, and the unborn
Has three results that are unborn.

91. On its own level, four results.
On different levels, three or two.
Three learner and so forth of learner.
Results of karma of nonlearners,

92. The learners' dharmas and so forth,
Are one or three or otherwise two.
Results of karmas other than those
Are learner, et cetera, two, two, five.

93. Results of the discards of seeing,
 Et cetera, are three, four, and one.
Two, four, and three results of karmas
 That are discards of meditation.

94. Results of what is not discarded
 Are one, two, four, respectively.
Improper is afflicted action,
 Degenerate ways as well, some say.

95. One action propels one rebirth.
 There are multiple completing factors.
The two absorptions without mind
 Do not propel, nor does attainment.

96. The karma of the heinous deeds;
 Severe afflictions; lower realms,
Beings in Concept Free, and the North
 Are agreed to be three obscurations.

97. The heinous deeds are in three lands.
 The sexless and so forth do not
Since little benefit, no shame.
 Five wanderers have the remaining.

98. A schism of the Sangha is
 Discord by nature, nonconcurrent.
It's not afflicted; it is neutral.
 The Sangha does possess the schism.

99. The unwholesome act is telling lies;
 It is possessed by the schismatic.
It ripens for an aeon in Incessant.
 Additional bring additional pain.

100. A bhikshu acting upon views,
 Who is disciplined, divides. Elsewhere.
Childish. Accepting other teachers
 And paths divides. It does not last.

101. It is called a schism of the Wheel.
Rose-Apple Land. Not less than nine.
Ritual schisms happen in
Three continents, with at least eight.

102. At first, at end, before there are faults
Or a pair; or when the Sage has passed,
When boundaries are not established,
A schism of the Wheel can't happen.

103. Since fields of benefit and qualities
Are abandoned and annihilated.
Even if organs change, it is.
She whose menses bore one is the mother.

104. Intent to beat the Buddha is not,
Nor if they become an arhat later.
When one has prepared a heinous act,
Detachment is impossible.

105. To tell a lie in order to split
The Sangha is the gravest crime.
Of worldly virtues, the volition
Of Peak bears the greatest result.

106. To violate one's arhat mother,
To kill a certain Bodhisattva
Or learner, and to rob what has
Been gathered for the Sangha's purpose

107. Are similar to heinous deeds.
The fifth is to destroy a stupa.
Gaining forbearance, nonreturner,
And arhat totally blocks karma.

108. Since when is he the Bodhisattva?
Since doing the karma of the marks.
High realms, high caste, full faculties,
Male, recalls lifetimes, irreversible.

109. A male in Rose-Apple Land, when present,
With the volition to awaken,
Through contemplation, propels these
Over one hundred aeons more.

110. Each arises from one hundred merits.
The last of three uncountables,
Vipashyin, Dipa, Ratnashikhin
Appeared. The first was Shakyamuni.

111. Giving all to all compassionately
Perfected generosity.
While not detached, to cut his limbs
Did not perturb him: patience and discipline.

112. By praising Tiṣya, diligence.
Samadhi and mind, just prior to.
The three are merit, action, or
The basis, like the karmic paths.

113. What makes one gives is generosity,
Wishing to offer or to help.
It is body and speech karma, and
Intention, resulting in abundance.

114. Generosity brings benefit
To self or other, both or neither.
Distinctions of the donor and
Of things and field distinguish it.

115. Donors excel through faith, et cetera,
And make gifts with respect and such.
This brings them honor and abundance
In time and with no obstacles.

116. From excellently colored things
And so forth, there comes beauty, fame,
Affection, and most youthful flesh,
Pleasing to touch in all the seasons.

117. The fields of wanderers, suffering,
Benefit, qualities are highest.
The highest is from freed to freed
Or by the Bodhisattva. Eighth.

118. Although they are not noble, gifts
To parents, the ill, or Dharma teachers,
The Bodhisattva's last rebirth
Bring yields surpassing any measure.

119. Aftermath, field, base, preparation,
Volition, and intention, too:
When these are great or small in scope,
The karma, too, is great or small.

120. Intentional, complete, without
Regret, no anti, ripening,
Association: due to these
Karma is called accumulated.

121. Giving to stupas is merit caused
By giving: as with love, not taken.
Cause and result are infallible,
So bad fields, too, bear pleasant fruit.

122. Immoral is nonvirtuous form
That twofold discipline discards.
That which the Buddha barred as well.
Four qualities of the utterly pure:

123. Not sullied by immoral or
Its cause; based on the anti and peace.
Infusing the mind with meditation
Is the virtue of equipoise.

124. For high realms, discipline is prime,
And for removal, meditation.
Because one dwells in joy for aeons
In high realms, four are Brahma's merit.

125. To give the Dharma is teaching sutras,
Without affliction, as they are.
Precursors to merit and nirvana,
And realization are three virtues.

126. Threefold industrious karma with
Its motivation: writing letters
Or carving; poetry and counting;
Enumeration, in that order.

127. Obscured, bad, and unwholesome are
Afflicted dharmas. Stainless virtues
Are sublime. Practice compounded virtue.
And liberation is unexcelled.

This completes the fourth area called "Teachings on Karma" from the *Verses of the Treasury of Abhidharma.*

FIFTH AREA

Teaching on the Kernels

1. The root of existence is the kernels.
   They're six: desire, and likewise anger,
Pride, ignorance, and view, and doubt.
   These six are taught as seven when

2. Desire is split. That which arises
   In two realms is desire for existence
Since it looks inward. It is taught
   To rebut the idea it is freedom.

3. Five views are personality;
   Wrong view; and holding the extremes;
Overesteeming view; and discipline,
   Austerity. There are thus ten.

4. They're ten and seven, seven and eight,
   Excluding three or else two views.
When suffering and so forth of Desire
   Is seen, they are discarded in order.

5. Four are discards of meditation.
   Excluding anger, these same are
In Form. The Formless is like that.
   Thus they're proposed as ninety-eight.

6. The Peak's that forbearance destroys,
Are discards just of seeing. On others,
Of seeing and meditation. What forbearance
Does not destroy are just of meditation.

7. As me, mine; permanent and ceasing;
As nonexistent; overesteeming
The low; and viewing what is not cause
Or path as such: these are five views.

8. Since clinging to Ishvara, et cetera,
As cause, initially mistakes
Them to be permanent and self,
Just seeing suffering discards it.

9. Among three views, there are four errors,
Since they're mistaken, since they're thoughts
That judge, since they exaggerate.
Mind and conception, from their power.

10. The prides are seven. Nine types, three.
Destroyed by seeing, meditation.
Discards of meditation are
Entangled with killing and so forth.

11. Craving destruction, too. In nobles,
The prides, et cetera, that think "me"—
Developed by view—do not occur.
Nor does nonvirtuous regret.

12. The views and doubts that one discards
By seeing suffering and cause
And simultaneous and unmixed
Ignorance are the universals.

13. Of these, the nine can focus higher,
Excluding two views. What arises
Along with them is universal
As well, attainment not included.

14. Wrong views and doubts discarded by
  Seeing cessation and the path,
Concurrent and plain ignorance:
  These six take the undefiled as sphere.

15. Cessation that is of their level.
  Because paths can be mutual causes,
The paths of the six and nine levels
  Are objects of whose sphere they are.

16. Desire does not, since it's discarded.
  Nor hatred, since they do not harm.
Since they are peace, pure, and supreme,
  Pride does not, nor does overesteeming.

17. The universal kernels can
  Develop through a focus on
Any that is of their own level.
  Nonuniversal, on own class.

18. Not those whose sphere is high or stainless
  Since those are not made mine, since anti.
The ones concurrent with one, then
  Develop through concurrence with that.

19. In higher, all neutral. In Desire,
  The personality, extreme,
And simultaneous ignorance.
  The rest here are nonvirtuous.

20. Desire, aversion, and delusion
  In Desire are the roots of nonvirtue.
There are three roots of neutral: craving,
  And ignorance, intelligence.

21. Others act dually, loftily,
  So they are not. The Bāhyaka
Propose these four: craving, view, pride,
  Delusion. From ignorance, three dhyanists.

22. Categorical, distinguishing,
And questioning, and the declining
Responses answer queries on death,
Rebirth, superior, self or other.

23. One is tied down to things toward which
Desire and anger, pride as well,
Of both the past and present have
Arisen but not been abandoned.

24. The future mental tie to all.
The others tie in their own time.
The nonarising, to all times.
All that remain tie one to all.

25. The times always exist, it was said.
Since two, objects exist, result.
Because they say these all exist,
They're called Those Who Say All Exists.

26. They're four, called thing and character
And state and relative dependence.
The third is best, because the times
Are there presented through their action.

27. They'd block. What's it? Not different,
Not logical as time. If they
Exist, why don't they arise and perish?
So deep are the natures of dharmas.

28. Suffering is seen, they've been discarded;
Still other universals bind them.
The first has been abandoned, yet
Still tied by stains whose sphere it's in.

29. Those of Desire, discards of seeing
Suffering and cause, of meditation,
Are in the sphere of their own three,
Of one of Form, of stainless, too.

30. And those of Form are in their own,
Three low, one high, and stainless, too.
Those of the Formless, in the sphere
Of these three of three realms, of stainless.

31. Discards of seeing path and cessation,
Are in the same spheres, plus their own.
The undefiled are in the sphere
Of three realms' last three and the stainless.

32. Two ways the afflicted can have kernels;
The unafflicted, through development.
Out of delusion, doubt; from that,
Wrong view, then personality.

33. From that, extreme, then overesteeming
Discipline, overesteeming view.
For one's own view, there's pride, attachment,
And hate for others, in this order.

34. The kernels being not abandoned,
The object being present near,
And inappropriate attention
Fulfill the causes of afflictions.

35. In Desire, defilements are the afflictions
Except delusion, and the entanglers.
In Form and Formless, kernels alone
Are the defilements of existence.

36. Since they are neutral and look inward
On levels of equipoise, they're one.
The root is ignorance, so it
Is taught as a separate defilement.

37. The floods and yokes are like that, too,
But views are separate, since they're sharp.
Not as defilements—without helpers,
They do not tend to put, it's claimed.

38. Those just explained and ignorance,
With views divided into two,
Are grasping. Ignorance produces
No clinging, and it is combined.

39. Since they are subtle, since connected,
Since they develop in two ways,
Since they pursue, because of these,
They are explained to be the kernels.

40. Because they put and ooze, because
They carry away, attach, and grasp:
These are the explanations of
The words defilement and so forth.

41. When these are classified as fetters,
Et cetera, they're taught as five types.
Alike in substance, overesteeming,
The two views are a separate fetter.

42. Since they are both nonvirtuous only,
And are autonomous, it's taught
That jealousy and stinginess
Are fetters separate from those.

43. There are five that lead to the lowest.
The two prevent transcendence of
Desire. The three will send one back.
The three include the gates and roots.

44. Not having any desire to go,
Wrong path, and doubt about the path
Prevent one from arriving at
Liberation, so these three are taught.

45. There are just five that lead to higher:
The two desires of Form and Formless,
Excitement, pride, delusion, too.
Three bonds by force of the three feelings.

46. Those mental factors, different from
    Afflictions, in the aggregate of
Formations are near afflictions, too.
    They are not to be called afflictions.

47. Shamelessness and immodesty
    And jealousy and stinginess,
Excitement, regret, torpor, sleep:
    These are the eight types of entanglers.

48. Aggression and concealment. From desire
    Come shamelessness, excitement, stinginess.
Concealment is disputed. Ignorance
    Gives rise to torpor, sleep, immodesty.

49. From doubt, there comes regret. Aggression
    And jealousy are caused by anger.
There also are six filths of affliction:
    Pretense, deceit, and arrogance,

50. Contentiousness, resentment, and
    Hostility. Desire leads to
Pretense and arrogance. From anger,
    Resentment and hostility.

51. From overesteeming views, contentiousness.
    View motivates deceit. Of these,
Immodesty, and shamelessness,
    Excitement, torpor, sleep are twofold.

52. The rest, discards of meditation,
    Are autonomous, as are the filths.
They are nonvirtue in Desire.
    Three twofold. Above they are neutral.

53. Deceit and pretense are in Desire
    And on first dhyan, as Brahma deludes.
Torpor, excitement, arrogance
    Are in three realms. The rest in Desire.

54. Discards of seeing, sleep, and pride:
    On the level of mind consciousness.
Autonomous near afflictions, too.
    The others, in six consciousnesses.

55. Desire can be concurrent with
    The pleasures. Hate is the reverse.
Ignorance with all. The nihilist,
    With pleasure of mind, unhappiness.

56. Doubt with unhappiness. The others
    With happiness when in Desire.
And all with neutral. Higher levels
    Are with those which are on their level.

57. Regret, and jealousy, and anger,
    Hostility, resentment, and
Contentiousness, with unhappiness.
    But stinginess, with opposite.

58. Deceit, pretense, concealment, sleep
    Concur with both, while arrogance
Is with two pleasures. Neutral feeling
    With all. The other four with five.

59. The obscurations are in Desire.
    Their incompatibilities,
And nourishment and action are
    The same, so therefore two are one.
Because they harm the aggregates,
    Because of doubt, there are just five.

60. By knowing the focus perfectly,
    Extinguishing what focuses
On that, and discarding the focus.
    Extinguished by the anti's birth.

61. There are four types of antidotes:
    Discarding, base, and distancing,
Disgust, so called. Afflictions are
    Discarded through their focus, it's said.

62. Through different characteristics, and
    Through incompatibility,
Through separate place and time, like distance
    Of sources, discipline, region, times.

63. They are extinguished once. Removal
    Is then attained again and again
On birth of anti, attaining the
    Results, refining faculties.

64. Nine perfect knowings: in Desire,
    Upon exhausting the first two,
There's one. Exhausting two, there are two.
    And likewise just those three above.

65. What leads to lowest, Form, and the extinction
    Of all defilements: three more perfect knowings.
The six are the results of forbearance;
    The rest are the results of knowing.

66. They're all results of Not Unable.
    Five of the dhyanas, or else eight.
The one is of the preparations;
    One of three actual Formless, too.

67. They all are of the noble paths.
    Two of the worldly. Subsequent, too.
The three results of dharma knowing,
    Six of its similar kind, and five.

68. Since they are undefiled attainment
    Of a removal, weaken the Peak,
And utterly destroy two causes,
    They're perfect knowings. Transcending realms.

69. Not one. Those on the path of seeing
    May possess fully up to five.
Those on the path of meditation
    May possess six or one or two.

70. They are combined when one becomes
    Detached from realms or gains a result.
Some forfeit one, two, five, or six;
    But five cannot be gained.

This completes the fifth area called "Teachings on the Kernels" from the *Verses of the Treasury of Abhidharma*.

SIXTH AREA

Teachings on the Paths and Individuals

1. It's taught afflictions are discarded
 By seeing truth and meditating.
The path of meditation is twofold,
 But seeing, so called, is undefiled.

2. The truths are four, it is explained.
 Thus suffering and origin,
Cessation and the path. This is
 The order in which they are realized.

3. The attractive and the unattractive,
 And the defiled other than those
Are suffering without exception
 Because they have three sufferings.

4. If not engaged by mind when it's
 Destroyed or mentally excluded,
It's relative, like vases or water.
 Ultimate being is different.

5. With conduct, listening, contemplation,
 Completely train in meditation.
Full knowing of listening, et cetera,
 Are subjects of name, both, and meaning.

6. Those with two distances. Not the
Insatiable, dissatisfied.
To crave for more is insatiable;
To want what is not had, dissatisfied.

7. The opposite is their antidote.
These two are in three realms or stainless.
Nongreed, the noble family.
Of these, three are content by nature.

8. The three teach conduct; the last, action.
As anti for the arising of craving.
To quell desire for things one grasps
As mine or me, for a time, forever.

9. One enters that through the repulsive
And mindfulness of in, out breath,
For those with excess desire or thoughts.
The skeleton for all desirous.

10. At first imagine bones that spread
As far as the sea, then narrow down.
The trained discard bones from the foot
To half the skull. Perfect attention

11. Holding the mind between the eyebrows.
Repulsive is nongreed. It's on
Ten levels, focusing on the
Appearance of Desire. By humans.

12. The mindfulness of breath is full knowing.
It's on five levels; its sphere is wind.
Desire realm. Outsiders do not.
Six types are counting and so forth.

13. In and out breath, on those of the body,
Called beings, are not appropriated.
They arise from a compatible cause
And are not observed by lower mind.

14. After accomplishing tranquility
    Meditate on the founds of mindfulness
By examining two characteristics
    Of body, feeling, mind, and dharmas.

15. Full knowing from listening, et cetera.
    The others from connection, focus.
The order is as they arise,
    Four antis for the erroneous.

16. It is the foundation of dharmas
    That focuses on them combined.
They view them as impermanent,
    And suffering, empty, and selfless.

17. The warmth arises out of that.
    It has the four truths as its sphere
With sixteen aspects. Out of warmth
    Comes peak, which is like that as well.

18. Through dharma, they both aim at aspects,
    Develop through the others, too.
From that, forbearance. Two like that.
    Dharmas develops all of them.

19. The object of the great is suffering
    Of Desire realm. It is one moment.
So is supreme dharma. They are all
    Five aggregates, without attainments.

20. The four precursors to realization
    Must be produced by meditation
On Not Unable, special, and
    The dhyanas. Two below, perhaps.

21. Support of Desire realm, and women
    Gain supreme dharma on both supports.
The nobles forfeit them when leaving
    A level; nonnobles at death.

22. The first two by regressing, too.
The actual sees truth in this.
If one regresses, gained anew.
Both forfeitures are nonpossession.

23. When peak is gained, roots can't be severed;
Forbearance goes not to low realms.
Two can withdraw from the learners' family
And become buddhas. Others, third.

24. The Teacher and rhino, all on one
Seat and dhyan's end until awakening.
Before that, the precursor to freedom.
The swiftest in three lives are freed.

25. From listening and contemplation,
Three karmas are propelled by humans.
From the supreme of worldly dharmas
Comes undefiled dharma forbearance

26. Of suffering of Desire, from which
Arises dharma knowing of
Just that itself. And likewise for
The rest of suffering arises
The subsequent forbearance, knowing.
Three other truths are like that, too.

27. Thus clear realization of the truths
Is sixteen minds. There are three types,
Called seeing, focusing, and action,
On the same level as supreme.

28. Respectively, forbearance, knowing are
Paths of no obstacles and liberation.
From seeing the unseen, fifteen
Moments of these are the path of seeing.

29. During these, sharp and dull faculties
Are followers of faith and dharma.
They're entering the first result
If no discards of meditation

30. Or up to five have been destroyed.
    The second, till the ninth's extinguished.
One who is detached from Desire
    Or higher is entering the third.

31. Those who are entering a result
    Abide in it on the sixteenth.
Sharp and dull faculties are then
    Convinced through faith, attained through seeing.

32. To gain a result is not to gain
    The path of higher progress. Thus
Those dwelling in result, not striving
    To improve it, are not enterers.

33. Each level has nine kinds of faults,
    Likewise nine qualities, because
The lesser and so forth of lesser,
    Middle, and great are separate.

34. Those dwelling in result without discarding any
    Through meditation, at most seven times.
Those freed from three or four, with two or three
    More lives, from family to family.

35. If they have conquered up to five,
    They're also entering the second,
And when the sixth set is extinguished,
    At that time, they are a once-returner.

36. When they have extinguished seven or eight
    Classes of faults, one life, one obstacle.
They also are entering the third.
    When ninth has perished, nonreturner.

37. They pass into nirvana in between,
    On birth, with effort, without effort, or
They're bound for higher. If they alternate
    The dhyanas, they are bound for Below None.

38. They leap, half leap, or die in all
The realms, and others go to the Peak.
Four other types are bound for Formless.
Another transcends sorrow here.

39. Dividing the three in three more,
Nine bound for Form can be explained,
Distinguished by their different
Karma, afflictions, faculties.

40. Without dividing those bound higher,
There are seven holy wanderers,
They act on holy, not unholy;
They go without return, so holy.

41. Nobles who in Desire transform
Their lives don't go to other realms.
Both they and those born higher do not
Regress or refine faculties.

42. They alternate the fourth dhyan first,
Achieved by alternating moments
In order to take birth and dwell,
Also from fear of the afflictions.

43. Because there are five types of that,
Only five births in pure abodes.
Nonreturners who have gained cessation
Are called made manifest by body.

44. They are entering arhat until
The Peak's eighth blockage is extinguished,
And on ninth's path of no obstacles.
That is the vajra-like samadhi.

45. Attaining its extinction and
Knowing thereof, nonlearner arhat.
Transworldly brings detachment from
The Peak. Two kinds detach from others.

46. Nobles detached through worldly paths
    Attain removal that is twofold.
Some say through the transworldly, too,
    Since if they forfeit, no afflictions.

47. As when one's freed from half the Peak's
    Or born above, they're not possessed.
Undefiled Not Unable can
    Remove attachment to all levels.

48. In victory over the three levels
    The final path of liberation
Comes out of dhyan or preparation.
    Above, not from the preparations.
Eight nobles are victorious
    Over their own and higher levels.

49. The worldly paths of liberation
    And of no obstacles have peace
And coarse, et cetera, as their aspects,
    And as their sphere, the high and low.

50. From knowing extinction comes the nonarising
    Intelligence if they're unshakable.
If not, then knowing extinction or the view
    Of the nonlearner, which all arhats have.

51. The spiritual way is the stainless paths;
    Results are compound and noncompound.
They're eighty-nine: they are the paths
    Of liberation, with extinctions.

52. There are five reasons they are presented
    As four results: relinquishing
The previous path on the result,
    Acquiring another, and combining

53. Extinctions, gaining the eight knowings,
    And also gaining sixteen aspects.
Results of worldly paths are mixed,
    Supported by unstained attainment.

54. It is Brahma's method, Brahma's wheel,
Since Brahma is the one who turned it.
The Dharma Wheel is the path of seeing,
Since it goes fast, has spokes, et cetera.

55. Three gained in Desire, the last in three.
Above there is no path of seeing,
As there's no weariness, and scriptures say,
"Commence here; come to the end there."

56. It is said there are six arhats, five
Of whom come from the convinced through faith.
Their freedom is occasional.
Unshakable one cannot be shaken,

57. So that is nonoccasional freedom
Born out of the attained through seeing.
Some from the first are in their family,
And some become through purification.

58. The four regress from family,
Five from result. Not from the first.
Six families of learners and nonnobles.
There's no refining on the path of seeing.

59. Regression from attained, from not attained,
And from enjoyment: these are called three types.
The Teacher has the last; the unshakable,
The middle, too; and others have the three.

60. While they're regressed, they do not die.
They don't do what should not be done.
Nine paths of no obstacles and liberation
For unshakable from strong familiarity.

61. One each for the attained through seeing.
They're undefiled, refined by humans.
Nonlearners on support of nine,
And learners on six levels, since

62. Refinement forfeits the result
    And progress; the result is gained.
Two buddhas, seven listeners:
    Nine have nine different faculties.

63. The seven individuals
    Are made by training, faculties,
Absorption, liberation, both.
    They're six: the three paths each have two.

64. Those who have gained cessation, liberated
    By both; the others by full knowing.
From their absorption, faculties,
    And results, learners are called perfect.

65. Nonlearners are perfect through two.
    In brief, there are four types of path:
They're called distinctive, liberation,
    No obstacles, and path of joining.

66. The dhyanas' paths are easy; those
    Of other levels, difficult.
Dull minds are slow to clearly know;
    The other ones know clearly quickly.

67. Knowing extinction and nonarising
    Is enlightenment. They factor in it,
So the thirty-seven are its factors
    In terms of name. In substance, ten:

68. Faith, diligence, and mindfulness, full knowing,
    Samadhi, equanimity, and joy,
Considering, discipline, and pliancy.
    The mindfulness foundations are full knowing.

69. And diligence, called right endeavor.
    The feet of miracles, samadhi.
The main is mentioned. They are also
    All qualities produced by training.

70. Respectively, the seven groups
    Emerge among beginners and
Precursors to clear realization,
    On meditation, and on seeing.

71. The branches of bodhi and the path
    Are undefiled. The rest are twofold.
They all are on the first of dhyanas
    And Not Unable, except joy.

72. On second, all except considering,
    And on the two, except those two,
And special dhyan. On the three Formless,
    Not those, nor factors of discipline.

73. They're in Desire and on the Peak,
    Except enlightenment and path.
Seeing three truths gains discipline
    And faith in Dharma out of knowing;

74. In the Buddha and his Sangha, too,
    Upon the path's clear realization.
The Dharma is three truths and paths
    Of the self-buddhas and bodhisattvas.

75. In terms of substance, they are two:
    They're faith and discipline. They're stainless.
They're bound, so liberation is
    Not called a learner's branch. It's twofold.

76. Conquering afflictions, noncompound;
    While interest is composite.
That is the branch; two liberations.
    Enlightenment, as taught, is knowing.

77. Nonlearners' minds are liberated
    From obscurations of the future.
The path that is about to cease
    Fully discards its obscurations.

78. Just noncompound is called the elements.
Extinction of all attachment is detachment;
Of others, is the element of abandonment;
Of bases, called cessation's element.

79. Forbearance and knowing suffering
And cause can bring revulsion.
All that discard remove attachment.
There are thus four alternatives.

This completes the sixth area called "Teachings on the Paths and Individuals" from the *Verses of the Treasury of Abhidharma.*

SEVENTH AREA

Teachings on Wisdom

1. Stainless forbearances aren't knowing. Minds
 Of extinction, nonarising are not views.
The other noble minds than those are both.
 Others are knowing. Six are views as well.

2. The knowings are defiled and undefiled.
 The first is called the relative.
Two types of undefiled are only
 The subsequent and dharma knowings.

3. All is the object of the relative.
 The sphere of dharma is suffering, et cetera,
Of Desire realm. The sphere of subsequent
 Is suffering, et cetera, of the higher.

4. Through the distinctions of the truths,
 Just these are four—these four are knowing
Of nonarising and extinction.
 When these two first arise, they are

5. Subsequent knowing of suffering
 And cause. Four know another's mind.
That can't know higher levels, faculties,
 Or individuals, destroyed, unborn.

6. Dharma and subsequent don't know
Each other. Listeners know two
Moments of seeing. Rhinos, three.
The Buddha without training, all.

7. Knowing extinction is recognizing
The truths are fully known, et cetera.
"There is no more to know," et cetera,
Is nonarising mind, it's said.

8. From nature, antidote, or aspects,
Or aspects and the sphere, or training,
Or its work being done, or from
Development of cause, there are ten.

9. The dharma knowings of cessation
And path on meditation's path
Are antidotes for the three realms.
The subsequent is not Desire's.

10. The subsequent and dharma knowings
Have sixteen aspects. Relative
Knowing is like, or different, too.
They have four from aspects of their truths.

11. Undefiled knowing others' minds
Is like that, too. For stained, the aspects
Are the specifics of the known.
The sphere of each is a single substance.

12. The remaining possess fourteen aspects,
Except for empty and for selfless.
Unstained: no more than sixteen aspects,
But others say there are, from the *Treatise*.

13. In substance, there are sixteen aspects.
An aspect is full knowing. That
And that with focus can perceive.
All that exists is the perceived.

14. The first is threefold. Others, virtue.
    The first is on all of the levels.
The one called dharma is on six.
    The subsequent on nine. Six likewise.

15. Knowing others' minds is on four dhyanas.
    That has Desire and Form as support,
And dharma has support of Desire.
    The others, on three realms' support.

16. Cessation mind is one foundation
    Of mindfulness, and knowing minds
Is three. Those which remain are four.
    Nine are the sphere of dharma mind.

17. Nine of the path and subsequent mind;
    And two of suffering and cause.
Ten are of four, and none of one.
    There are ten dharmas to apply.

18. The three realms, and the stainless, and
    The noncompound are twofold each.
Just relative knows what is outside
    Its own collection to be selfless.

19. On the first of undefiled moments,
    Those who are attached possess one knowing.
On second, three. After on each
    Of four moments they have another.

20. As they arise on the path of seeing,
    Future forbearances and knowings
Like them are gained. On that upon
    Three subsequent, the relative, too.

21. Thus they are called clear realization's end.
    They are nonarising dharmas. On its own
And lower levels. Cessation's is the last.
    Their own truths' aspects. Born of effort.

22. Attached gain six on the sixteenth.
Those detached from Desire gain seven.
Later on paths of meditation,
The attached attain the seven knowings.

23. In victory over seven levels,
Gaining clairvoyance and unshakable,
Paths of no obstacles for alternating.
Eight paths of liberation from the highest.

24. On learner's liberation of refining,
One gains six or else seven knowings, or . . .
Six on paths of no obstacles.
Likewise on vanquishing the Peak.

25. On knowing extinction, there are nine.
Unshakable attains ten knowings,
Refining there, on the last as well.
Eight are attained on those not mentioned.

26. One gains them where one is detached,
On which is gained, and lower, too.
On knowing extinction, defiled, too; all levels.
Those previously gained are not attained.

27. Those called acquiring and maintaining
Are attainment of composite virtue.
Attainment of the antidote
And distancing are of defiled.

28. The Buddha's unshared qualities
Are eighteen: powers and so forth.
The possible and not, ten knowings,
Karma, result is eight. The dhyanas,

29. Et cetera, faculties, and interests,
Capacities, are nine. Path might
Be ten. The two are relative.
Extinction is six or else ten.

30. The powers of previous places and
    Of death and birth are on the dhyanas.
The others, on all levels. Why?
    Because his powers cannot be hindered.

31. His body has Nārāyaṇa power.
    Some say his joints. It is the power
Of elephants times ten seven times.
    This is the sensory base of touch.

32. There are four types of fearlessness.
    They're similar to the first, tenth,
Second, and seventh of the powers.
    The three are mindfulness, awareness.

33. The great compassion, relative mind,
    Is greater from its gathering,
Its aspect, sphere, and being equal.
    There are eight ways that it is different.

34. All buddhas are the equal in
    Accumulation, dharma body,
And acts for wanderers' benefit,
    But not in life span, caste, or size.

35. The dharmas common with the learners
    And ordinary beings are
The unprovocative, the knowledge from
    Aspiring, unhindered, clairvoyance, et cetera.

36. The unprovocative is relative
    Knowing on dhyana's end. Unshakable.
Human. Unborn afflictions of Desire,
    Including their basis, are its sphere.

37. The knowledge from aspiring is
    Similar, focusing on all.
Likewise unhindered knowledge of dharma,
    Meaning, expression, eloquence.

38. Three are, in order, knowing names,
Meaning, and speech without obstruction.
The fourth is logical and fluent
Clear speech, and mastery of path.

39. Its focus is on speech and path.
It is nine knowings, on all levels.
Knowledge of meaning, ten or six,
On all. The rest are relative.

40. Knowledge of dharma is in Desire
And dhyan; of speech, Desire and first.
If incomplete, they're not attained.
Those six are through the highest end.

41. It's sixfold: it is dhyana's end,
Gained by progressing through all levels,
Coming to highest development.
Other than Buddha, they are from training.

42. Sixfold clairvoyance manifests magic,
The ear, mind, knowing previous lives,
Death and rebirth, and knowing extinction.
These are the mind of liberation.

43. The four are knowing relative,
And knowing minds is the five knowings.
Clairvoyance of extinction is
Like power. Five are on four dhyanas.

44. Their object is own and lower level.
Familiar is attained by detachment.
The third one is the three foundations,
And magic, ear, and eye are the first.

45. Clairvoyance of ear and eye are neutral.
The rest are virtue. Three are knowledge,
Because they stop the ignorance
Of prior lives, et cetera.

46. The last one is nonlearner's. When two others
Arise in their mindstream, they are so called.
Although learners may have these, their streams
Have ignorance, so these are not called knowledge.

47. The first, third, sixth are miracles.
The miracle of teaching is best,
Since it is unconfused and brings
Benefit and a pleasant fruit.

48. The magical is samadhi. Motion
And emanations are from that.
The Teacher moves with mental speed;
Others: propulsion, interest.

49. In Desire, emanations are
Four external sense bases. Twofold.
In Form, two. Minds of emanation
Create them, too. These are fourteen

50. Results of dhyan, respectively,
From two to five, not lower's result.
It's gained like dhyan, arising from
The pure and self. Out of it, two.

51. They're emanated by own level,
But speech by lower levels, too.
With emanator, except the Teacher.
After it's blessed, another starts it.

52. There are blessings for the dead as well,
Not for the unstable. Some say not.
First, many emanate the one;
When mastered, it is opposite.

53. Produced by meditation, neutral;
But those produced by birth are threefold.
Magic from mantra, medicine,
And karma, for five types in all.

54. They are the divine eyes and ears,
Clear forms on levels of the dhyanas.
They're always active, nothing lacking.
Their sphere is distant, subtle, et cetera.

55. The arhat, rhino, and the Teacher
See a thousand squared or cubed or countless.
Others are gained on birth as well.
It cannot see the between state.

56. Knowing minds is three, created by
The intellect and mantra, too.
Hell beings know at first. With humans,
There are not any gained on birth.

This completes the seventh area called "Teachings on Wisdom" from the *Verses of the Treasury of Abhidharma.*

EIGHTH AREA

Teachings on the Absorptions

1. The dhyans are twofold. They are four.
   Rebirth there has been fully explained.
   Absorption is one-pointed virtue,
   Its following, five aggregates.

2. It has examining, joy, pleasure.
   The earlier branches are discarded.
   Formless are like. Four aggregates,
   Born of withdrawal from lower levels.

3. They are called, with three preparations,
   Destruction of conception of form.
   In Formless realms, there is no form.
   Then form arises from cognition.

4. They're called the Infinite Consciousness,
   Space, Nothing at All, from training so.
   Since it is feeble, no conception,
   But it's not nonconception, either.

5. Thus actual absorption is
   Eight substances. Seven are threefold:
   Concurrent with enjoyment, pure,
   And undefiled. The eighth is twofold.

6. The one concurrent with enjoyment
Has craving. Virtue of the worldly
Is pure, which is what that enjoys.
The undefiled transcends the world.

7. The first has five: considering,
Examining, joy, pleasure, and samadhi.
There are four branches on the second:
Serenity, joy, and so forth.

8. Five on the third: there's equanimity,
And mindfulness, awareness, pleasure, rest.
The last has four: mindful, equanimous,
Not pain nor pleasure, and samadhi.

9. In substance, they are eleven. Pleasure
On the first two is pliancy.
Serenity is faith, and two
Scriptures say joy is mental pleasure.

10. In the afflicted, there is no joy or pleasure;
Serenity; awareness, mindfulness;
Or equanimity, pure mindfulness;
Some say no pliancy, no equanimity.

11. The fourth is free from the eight faults,
So it's immovable. They are
Considering, examining, breaths,
And pleasure and the other three.

12. Dhyanas of birth have happiness,
And pleasure and the neutral feeling;
Neutral and happiness; and pleasure
And neutral; and the neutral feeling.

13. On second and so forth, the body,
Eye, and ear consciousnesses, and
What makes them perceive is of the first.
It's neutral; it is not afflicted.

14. Those who do not possess them gain
The pure through detachment or from birth;
The undefiled is through detachment;
Afflicted, by regressing, birth.

15. Right after undefiled, the virtue
Of levels up to two above
Or below can arise. From pure,
The same, or own level's afflicted.

16. From the afflicted, own pure, afflicted,
And one pure of the lower, too.
From pure at death, all the afflicted,
But from afflicted, not the higher.

17. Four types of pure tend toward regression,
Et cetera. Respectively,
They tend toward birth of the afflictions,
Of own, of higher, of undefiled.

18. Tendencies to regress, et cetera,
Are followed by two, three, three, one.
Going through eight levels up and down,
Both types in sequence, or skipping one,

19. Then going to the third of the
Different type is skipping absorption.
The dhyans and Formless, on their own
Or lower support. No use for lower.

20. On Peak, they manifest Nothingness
Of nobles, then extinguish defilements.
Enjoyment focuses on own existence.
All that exists is virtuous dhyan's sphere.

21. Defiled of lower is not the sphere
Of virtuous actual of Formless.
The undefiled discard afflictions,
As do pure preparations, too.

22. For those, there are eight preparations.
They're pure, not pleasure and not pain.
The first is also noble. Some say, threefold.
In special dhyan, there's no considering.

23. It's threefold, neither pain nor pleasure,
And has Great Brahma as result.
Below, samadhi has considering,
Examining. Above, there's neither.

24. The signless has aspects of peace,
And emptiness engages selfless
And emptiness. No wishing has
All other aspects of the truths.

25. They're pure or stainless. When they're stainless,
They are three gates of liberation.
There are three more samadhis, called
The empty of emptiness, et cetera.

26. Two focus on nonlearner's aspects
Of empty and impermanent.
The signlessness of signlessness,
On peace, nonanalyzed extinction.

27. Defiled, by humans, unshakable,
Except the seven preparations.
First dhyana's virtue is meditation
On samadhi which is happiness.

28. Clairvoyance of eye is that which sees.
Produced by training is discernment.
The vajra-like of the last dhyana
Extinguishes all the defilements.

29. Immeasurables are four, because
They're antidotes for malice, et cetera.
Love and compassion are nonhatred,
And joy is pleasure of the mind,

30. And equanimity is nongreed.
    Their aspects are thinking, "May they be
Happy! Not suffer! Joyous! Beings!"
    Their sphere is beings of Desire.

31. On the two dhyanas, there is joy.
    Others on six. Some say on five.
They don't abandon. They arise
    In humans. One must have the three.

32. Of eight emancipations, the first two,
    Repulsive, are on the two dhyanas.
The third, on the last, is nongreed.
    Virtuous Formless equipoise.

33. It is absorption of cessation
    That follows the subtlest of the subtle.
One rises from that through own level's
    Pure or the noble of the lower.

34. Sights of Desire are the first's object.
    The Formless' sphere is suffering
And such of own and higher levels,
    Compatible with subsequent knowing.

35. Eight overpowering sense bases.
    Two like the first emancipation;
Two like the second. Others are like
    Emancipation of the lovely.

36. Ten all-encompassing sense bases.
    Eight are nongreed on the last dhyana.
Their sphere is Desire. Two are pure Formless;
    Their sphere is their four aggregates.

37. Cessation has been explained. The rest
    Are gained through detachment or by training.
The Formless are supported by
    Three realms. The rest arise in humans.

38. In two realms, the power of cause and karma
Produces Formless equipoise.
Those two and also dharma nature
Produce the dhyanas in Form realm.

39. The Teacher's True Dharma is twofold:
In essence, scripture and realization.
These are upheld only by those
Who teach them and accomplish them.

40. I mostly have explained this abhidharma
According to the Kashmiri Exposition.
Any mistakes herein are solely ours;
The Sages are the authority in Dharma.

This completes the eighth area called "Teachings on the Absorptions" from the *Verses of the Treasury of Abhidharma.*

41. The Teacher, the eye of the world, has been closed;
The beings who were witness have mostly perished.
Those who haven't seen thatness, those who are bad logicians
And headstrong have confounded the teachings.

42. The one self-born, those who cherish his teachings,
Have passed into the supreme peace. There's no refuge
Or counsel for beings, and the stains that slay qualities
Run rampant in this at their pleasure.

43. And so, as we know that for the Sage's teachings,
It's as if the last breaths now rasp in the throat,
That this is a time when the stains have great strength:
All those who want freedom, be careful!

This completes the *Verses on the Treasury of Abhidharma* composed by Master Vasubandhu. Translated into Tibetan by the Indian Abbot Jinamitra and the Tibetan translator Bande Kawa Paltsek, and then corrected and finalized. Translated from the Tibetan into English by Karma Choephel, and then compared to the Sanskrit original and corrected.

The Commentary

The Ninth Karmapa Wangchuk Dorje

Youthful Play

An Explanation of the Treasury of Abhidharma

by the Ninth Karmapa Wangchuk Dorje

In Tibetan: chos mngon pa mdzod kyi rnam par bshad pa chos mngon rgya mtsho'i snying po mkhyen brtse'i zhal lung gzhon nu rnam rol legs bshad chos mig rnam 'byed grub bde'i shing rta zhes bya ba bzhugs so//

In English: An Explanation of the *Treasury of Abhidharma* called the Essence of the Ocean of Abhidharma, The Words of Those who Know and Love, Explaining Youthful Play, Opening the Eyes of Dharma, the Chariot of Easy Practice

I prostrate to the youthful Manjushri.

FIRST AREA

Teachings on the Elements

He displays many deeds that so marvelously appear
In the oceans of glorious realms;
The sunlight from his smallest marks, from his nails,
When it strikes even the tiniest of spots,
Destroys the unbearable gloom of three poisons.
He discerns with the light of full knowing
All dharmas, and manifestly shows to all wanderers
What he sees as it is: I bow to this guide.

They unite the intellect and courage of samsara and nirvana;
They are great ships of the transcendent full knowing
That frees one from the ocean of existence.
I laud the peerless Shariputra and the other arhats.

Many ascetic virtues directed their minds, and then
Kaśyapa and the others in the line of Second Teachers
Brought splendid glory to the Buddhist teachings:
I praise the elders of the teachings, the spiritual friends.

In order to thread the exquisite cloths of the heavens of knowables
Through even the eyes of the needles of students' faculties,
They distilled the essence of the compilations of teachings,
The oceans of specifics. I rejoice well in what they did.

Especially the Second Omniscient One, Vasubandhu,
Who had been learned in the five sciences for many lives,

Compiled the essence of the oceans of abhidharma
Into this *Treasury of Abhidharma*. I dedicate myself to this.

Here the fearless teacher Victorious Mikyö
Knew this without relying on others, and
From power of love, composed the detailed commentary.
With great respect I praise its words and meaning.

On a throne raised by the gods and all the world,
He conquers Mara's hordes in one sitting,
And radiates vast inexhaustible light.
He who wears the Red Crown shines clear on the lake of my mind.

He is the chariot who makes the sunlight,
Naturally bright, shine on the students' lands.
May Namgyal Drakpa, who has plumbed the depths
Of oceans of abhidharma, be pleased.

I who am the ninth rebirth called Karmapa,
Have sprinkled my heart with Manjushri's water.
By uttering the words of Saraswati,
I shall shine this lamp on abhidharma's basket.

Our Teacher, the unsurpassable, complete, perfect Buddha Shakyamuni himself, has liberated his mind from the two obscurations and their imprints. He clarified the right dharma, the unmistaken secret profound meaning that had not previously been evident to any being, even to the gods, through great knowledge mantras and light rays. In order to bestow benefit upon all beings, he turned all the Wheels of Dharma, which cannot be measured by numbers, topics, words, or measure.

As prophesied by the Thus-Gone-One himself, the eighth-level *bodhisattva-mahāsattva* Vasubandhu composed many treatises which teach the listener school's view, meditation, conduct, and result to help beings gradually enter the teachings. Because it is the root of all of the True Dharma and is the canon of the matrices,[3] he condensed the ocean of explanations from the Exposition school into this treatise, *The Treasury of Abhidharma*.

The explanation of this has two sections: I. History in terms of a reason to compose this, and II. The actual meaning of the treatise.

I. History in terms of a reason to compose this

For many inconceivable aeons in the past I have practiced merit at the feet of uncountable buddhas. From this merit, I have encountered the teachings of the Dakpo Kagyu, had the fortune to rely upon undisputed masters, and received instructions on the Three Baskets and so forth. For that reason, I have attained some slight bit of ability to comment on the thought of the buddhas, bodhisattvas, heroes, yoginis, and masters of practice.

Whether you classify the True Dharma as explaining, debating, and composing, or as listening, contemplating, meditating, as a cause to practice the Dharma it is necessary to have as one's master someone who has received the instructions passed down from the Lord Buddha in an unbroken stream through the liberated holders of the lineage. Without this, one can practice, but as the stream of the teachings has been broken, blessings will not arise. For this reason, one might say one is practicing the path, but realization will not arise in one's being, it is heard.

Therefore, I shall tell the manner in which I have listened to *The Treasury of Abhidharma*. According to the tradition passed down from the great Ngok Lotsawa, it is not necessary to explain the lineage from the perfect Buddha to the earlier masters. Why? you ask. Master Vasubandhu listened to all the vehicles of the dharma from his elder brother Noble Asanga, and he from Lord Maitreya, who listened to them from perfect Buddha—a very short lineage. From Master Vasubandhu, it was passed to Mahapandita Sthiramati, Master Pūrṇavardhana, Mahapandita Shāntipa, Lord Puṇyashila, Ngok Lotsawa, Chim Lhaje Gocha, Chim Tsondrü Senge, Chim Don Gyalwa, Chim Tsondrü Gyaltsen, Chim Loten, Chim Namkha Drak, Chim Lobsang Drak, Rongpa Chögyal, Nyangmang Rinchen, Martön Palden Rinchen, Rongton Shākya Gyaltsen, Sangwa Logyal, Jamchen Rabjampa, the great being Karma Trinleypa, and the omniscient Mikyö Dorje. He passed it on to my abbot, who, to indicate him by his name, is the lord of the complete and perfect teachings, the glorious great Konchok Shākya Tsowoy Bang.[4] Mikyö Dorje also taught it to the great Master Vijayakīrti. From these two, the lineage has passed to me.

II. The actual meaning of the treatise. This has three topics: A. Identifying and translating the name, B. The translator's prostration, and C. The explanation of the text.

A. Identifying and translating the name

In Sanskrit: Abhidharmakośakārikā
In Tibetan: chos mngon pa mdzod kyi tshig le'ur byas pa
In English: Verses on the Treasury of Abhidharma

There are four main languages of India—Apabhraṃśa, Piśaci, Prakṛit, and Sanskrit. Of these four, in Sanskrit this treatise is called *Abhidharmakośakārikā*. To translate that, *abhi* means manifest, *dharma* means dharma (phenomenon), *kośa* means treasury, and *kārikā* means verse. In English it is called *Verses on the Treasury of Abhidharma.*

B. The translator's prostration

I prostrate to youthful Manjushri.

As he is free of the roughness of the stains of body, speech, and mind, he is gentle and pleasant, or ***mañju.*** As he is the protector and glory of all wandering sentient beings, glory or ***shrī.*** Because he appears as if he were the age of fifteen, he is called **youthful. I prostrate** means that I bow down with body, speech, and mind.

C. The explanation of the text. This has four topics: 1. The homage and the pledge to compose, 2. Explanation of the treatise's name, 3. Teaching the necessity and purpose, and 4. Explaining the actual body of the treatise.

1. The homage and the pledge to compose

1. It is he who has conquered entirely the darkness toward all
   And guides sentient beings from the mire of samsara.
   He teaches the meaning as it is: I prostrate to him
   Then fully explain this treatise, *The Treasury of Abhidharma.*

"It is he" means the complete and perfect Buddha, the Bhagavan. There are four possibilities of buddha and bhagavan. First, a self-buddha[5] is a buddha but not a bhagavan. Second, a bodhisattva in his last existence[6] is a bhagavan but not a buddha. Third, the Buddha is both. Fourth, ordinary beings are neither.

The Buddha **has conquered entirely the darkness toward all** the internal **and** external sense bases[7] that does not know whether they are afflicted. By extending the hand that teaches dharma, he **guides sentient beings from the mire** of the three realms **of samsara. He** does this by unerringly **teaching**

the meaning that benefits sentient beings just **as it is**, not by displaying miracles or by bestowing holiness.[8] **I prostrate to him,** the Teacher who has such qualities, by composing this treatise and **then fully explain this treatise, *The Treasury of*** true ***Abhidharma.*** This is said as a pledge to compose the treatise.

Well, what sort of qualities does this Teacher have? you ask. He has the qualities of both the sublime benefit for self and the sublime benefit for others. The first of these is the qualities of abandonment and realization, which are both taught by the words, "It is he who has conquered entirely the darkness toward all." The qualities of benefit for others is taught by "And guides sentient beings from the mire of samsara."

There are four possibilities of being someone who explains the meaning as is and being a Teacher. Shariputra, for example, is the former but not the latter. The non-Buddhist Pūraṇa Kāśyapa, for example, is the latter but not the former. The Buddha, for example, is both, and those other than them are neither.

To say a few words to elaborate on this, there are three points: 1) Identifying the Teacher who is the object of homage; 2) Obscurations that hinder attaining buddhahood; and 3) The antidote to abandon those.

First, identifying the Teacher who is the object of homage: The one who is the Teacher here is the complete perfect Buddha. To recognize his nature, it is the dharma body alone, which is the truth of the path with the five undefiled aggregates. The schools[9] do not say that this body supports the form bodies of enjoyment or emanation. The schools also do not agree that the bodily support on which the *amṛita* nectar of enlightenment has been attained, such as the flesh of Prince Siddharta, is a Buddha, because it is the full ripening of karma and afflictions. Similarly, a bhikshu, too, is posited to be the bhikshu vows, not the individual who holds them. Likewise, learners, nonlearners, and nobles are said to be the truth of the path, not the individuals. To call the individual a buddha or bhikshu is to call that which is supported by the name of that which supports it. It is like, for example, the designations "goldsmith" and "horseman."

The Sutra school says that one can assert that the form body is characteristically the buddha. One does this optionally in situations where one does not wish to distinguish the path from the individual, or else when positing that the Buddha as he is generally thought of is merely the one to whom one goes for refuge. They do not, however, accept that this is the actual Buddha, because in their school the form body is posited as something to discard and as defiled.

Second, obscurations that hinder attaining buddhahood: The word "darkness" in the verse is a metaphor for the obscurations, because just as darkness hinders seeing, the obscurations also hinder seeing the correct meaning. There are two types of obscurations here: afflictive obscurations that primarily obscure liberation, and nonafflicted obscurations that primarily obscure omniscience. The first is held to be the six kernels[10] that are the root of existence, the cognitions that are concurrent with them, and their attainment. The Sutra school proposes that liberation is a no-negation,[11] the mere absence of that which creates suffering or obscures omniscience, but here it is presented as a thing. In this situation, it cannot be said to be either material or cognitive.

The second, nonafflictive obscuration, is primarily the mental factor delusion that is an impediment to all-knowing. It has the characteristic of cognitive obscuration and has four types: 1) not knowing because the Buddha's qualities are profound and subtle; 2) not knowing by being fully removed from the object; 3) not knowing by being fully removed from the time; and 4) not knowing because the classifications of meaning are infinite. Shariputra, for example, has the first and third; Maudgalyana, for example, has the second; and Noble Rahula has the fourth. From the commentary:[12]

> In this way, they are extremely removed from the Buddha's qualities, object, and time, and they have nonafflicted unknowing of the infinite classifications of meaning.

Well then, do the listeners and self-buddhas conquer the darkness taught here or not? If they do that darkness could not be proven to be something only the Buddha abandons. If they do not, they would not have made an end to suffering. This is because it is said in a sutra:

> If I did not clearly know, did not completely know one dharma, I would not say I have made an end to suffering… If I did not completely know and discard one dharma, I would not say I have made an end to suffering…

So you might say. These two faults cause no harm, because listener and self-buddha arhats conquer nonafflictive darkness, but do not conquer it entirely. This is because it is said in the commentary:

> Of course we agree that they conquer the darkness to all, but not entirely.

Here we do not assert the presentation of cognitive obscurations as the concept of perceived and perceiver explained in the Great Vehicle, but we must assert the designation cognitive obscuration because there are both scriptural and logical proofs. First, the scriptural proof: with regards to the verse, "At once, there are never two, like Buddhas,"[13] Pūrṇavardhana explains, "They are free of afflicted obscurations, so they are equal, but they are not equally equal because they are not free of cognitive obscurations." Second, the logical proof: holding the coarse and the continuum as substantial, obscurations that hinder refining faculties, holding dharmas of exclusion as not empty of their essence, holding the aggregates and so forth to be wholes, obscurations to the six perfections, obscurations to the attainment of final absorptions, and the four causes of unknowing are posited to be cognitive obscurations, because they are cognitions that are deluded about the nature but are not afflicted cognitions.

The schools also do not reject the selflessness of phenomena and thatness, because they assert the four seals that proclaim the view, and the thatness of things. However, they do not assert the selflessness of phenomena pervaded by emptiness of perceived and perceiver that is renowned in the Great Vehicle.

Third, analyzing the antidote: The actual antidote that discards the four causes of unknowing is asserted to be the nonlearners' wisdom of the ten powers, because previously on the learners' paths there is no full knowing that perceives in a way that is exclusive of their essence.[14]

Well then, the Buddha may have abandoned the four causes of unknowing, but he has not abandoned their attainment, which he must still possess, you say.[15] This is not a fault, because the arising of the future wisdom of the Buddha and the cessation of the present attainment of the four causes of unknowing are simultaneous—when the wisdom arises, the attainment of the four causes ceases, just as when you light a lamp, darkness is dispelled.

2. Explanation of the treatise's name

2. Abhidharma is stainless full knowing, along with its following;
 That by which and treatises by which one gains it.
Since this collects them completely in meaning,
 Or since they are its base, it's *The Treasury of Abhidharma.*

Ultimate **abhidharma is stainless**, or free of defiled stains, **full knowing**[16] that fully discerns dharmas, **along with its following,** the five aggregates. In the autocommentary:

> "Full knowing" is full discernment of dharmas. "Stainless" is undefiled. "Along with its following" includes what accompanies it, the five undefiled aggregates. This is what is taught as abhidharma. At this point, this is ultimate abhidharma.

Path abhidharma is **that by which** one attains it, the ultimate abhidharma, or that which is clearly directed toward its realization. From the autocommentary:

> Because it is clearly directed toward the characteristics of dharmas, it is abhidharma.

What is meant here by "that which" is the full knowing of nonnobles on the path: the defiled full knowing of listening, contemplating, and meditating, along with its following of the other aggregates that are associated with it. This can either arise from training or be attained upon birth.

The **treatises** that teach those topics **by which one gains it,** stainless full knowing, is textual abhidharma. In the Prince's commentary[17] it says, "Others say that what is called the 'Treatise' is *Jñānaprasthāna*… "

The meaning of the title: Why is this treatise called *The Treasury of Abhidharma?* **Since this** treatise **collects them,** the essential points of the seven treatises of abhidharma including the ocean of expositions, **completely in meaning, or** else **since they**, the seven treatises of abhidharma, **are its**, this treatise's, **base, it is** called ***The Treasury of Abhidharma.*** The meaning is taught here through the examples of a base and a treasury.

3. Teaching the necessity and purpose

> 3. Without full discernment of dharmas, there is not
> Any method to thoroughly quell the afflictions.
> Because of afflictions, the world wanders the seas of existence.
> That is why the Teacher taught this, they claim.

All treatises have a topic, necessity, vital necessity, and connection. The topic of abhidharma is explicitly taught by the word *dharmas,* which is explained as all that is defiled or undefiled. Alternatively the principal meaning of the topic is full knowing that is full discernment of dharmas. The necessity is to easily realize this full knowing that is full discernment of dharmas.

The text teaches the vital necessity in the negative; the actual, positive vital necessity is implied. **Without** what is necessary, the full knowing that is **full**

discernment of defiled and undefiled **dharmas,** there are afflictions which cannot be abandoned. Why is that? Because without that full knowing **there is not any method to totally quell the afflictions. Because of** the **afflictions, the worldly** beings accumulate karma and **wander the** great **seas of existence.** They do not achieve freedom, and **that,** helping them attain freedom, **is why the Teacher taught this** abhidharma.

And so here, from among the four of the topic, necessity, vital necessity, and connection, the first is principally full knowing that fully discerns defiled and undefiled dharmas. The second is to easily realize that full knowing on the basis of this treatise. The third is to attain nirvana on the basis of that realization. The fourth is that the latter are attained through the former. The way they are taught in the treatise is as follows: "Dharmas" teaches the topic. "Full discernment" teaches the necessity. "Without..." and "there are afflictions" teach the vital necessity obliquely. The connection is implicitly taught.

Well then, who first taught this abhidharma? you ask. In the tradition of the Great Exposition school, the seven treatises of abhidharma were first spoken in sections by the Teacher in various lands and to various individuals. Later, seven arhats collected them into treatises. For example, it is like the *Udānavarga,* a collection of verses spoken by the Teacher at different times and compiled by the monk Dharmatrāta. The seven treatises are *Jñānaprasthāna* by Kātyāniputra, *Prakaraṇapāda* by Vasumitra, *Vijñānakāya* by Devakṣema, *Dharmaskandha* by Shariputra, *Prajñāptiśastra* by Maudgalyāyana, *Dhātukāya* by Vasumitra, and *Saṃgītiparyāya* by Mahākauṣṭhila. Pūrṇavardhana lists it alternatively as "*Saṃgītiparyāya* by Shariputra." If the abhidharma were not the words of the Buddha, even though it says in the sutras, "Bhikshus, these are the three baskets," the three baskets would be incomplete.

The phrase "**They claim**" is a skeptical phrase from the Sutra school: in these treatises there are various wrong positions such as the proposition that noncomposites are substantial. As the Teacher did not say anything erroneous, these are the fabrications of the masters who assembled the abhidharma, they say.

4. Explaining the actual body of the treatise. This has two topics: a. Presenting the body, and b. Extensively explaining the limbs.

a. Presenting the body. This has two topics: i. An overview, and ii. An explanation.

i. Overview

4a Defiled and undefiled dharmas:

Having said that dharmas are the topic of this treatise, what are they? you ask. The presentation "**Defiled and undefiled dharmas**" teaches everything concisely as a mutual exclusion.[18] This is an actual exclusion, because there is no third possibility. Well then, it would be logical to recite, "Composite and noncomposite are dharmas" you say. This is not a fault, because saying "defiled" teaches what is to be rejected and "undefiled" teaches what should be mostly taken up, so it is recited in this way to teach that.

Here, the undefiled is not set forth as a no-negation, a mere absence of defilements, because a mere absence cannot be a thing, so it does not hold its own characteristics. Without holding those, it is not appropriate to be a dharma, because a dharma is characterized as that which holds its own essence. Dharmas are pervasively[19] things, and things must be either composite or noncomposite. Dharmas are pervasively things, because as it says in the autocommentary:

> The Sutra school says there are no noncomposites among things, and in the Abhidharma also it says, "What are dharmas that are not things, you say? They are noncomposite dharmas." But the Great Expositionists say that is not what this means. Well then, what does it mean? you say. There are five types of things: natural things, focused things, possessed things, causal things, and completely grasped things. In this passage, the term *causal thing* is meant. Therefore noncomposites are solely substantial, and they also have neither causes nor results.

This explains noncomposites to be things and substantial. Noncomposite dharmas are also able to perform a function, because although they cannot perform the function of producing a result, they are able to perform the function of supporting.

If something is composite, it is not pervasively arisen, because there are future composites. Not only that, it is not pervasively going to arise, because one must assert that there are future nonarising phenomena.[20]

ii. The explanation. This has two topics: (1) Explaining the defiled, and (2) Explaining the undefiled.

(1) Explaining the defiled

4b–d Except the truth of path, composites
Are defiled since defilements can
Develop in relation to them.

Except for **the truth of** the **path, composites are defiled.** Saying this eliminates the possibility that the Truth of the Path and noncomposites could be defiled. All that is other than those is only defiled. Why? you ask. **Since defiledments**[21] and near afflictions **can develop in relation to them,** the composites except for the path, in terms of either focus or concurrence.[22] Therefore, the characteristic of the defiled is a dharma on which defilements can develop through either focus or concurrence. Its character base[23] is composites except the truth of the path. If something is defiled the defilements do not pervasively develop in relation to it in those two ways. For example, even though arhats have abandoned defilements they still have a defiled body, but the defilements do not develop in relation to their bodies.

(2) Explaining the undefiled. This has two topics: (a) Overview, and (b) Specific explanation of noncomposites.

(a) Overview

5a–c The undefiled is the truth of path
And the three noncomposites, too,
Which are space and the two cessations.

The character base of **undefiled** dharmas **is the truth of the path and the three** types of **noncomposites.** Their characteristic is a dharma on which defilements cannot develop through either focus or concurrence. The word **"too"** means that just as composite has classifications and dharmas can be counted as either defiled or undefiled, noncomposite dharmas also can be counted as three: they **are space and the two cessations.**

Some say that this text does not teach that noncomposite dharmas are definitely divided into three. This is not logical: from the Prince's commentary:

> "What are the three types of noncomposites? you say," is a question posed because the answer is not universally known. To say "three types" is to identify them as just these three. Some—those in the school of Vatsīputra—say, however, that the only noncomposite is nirvana.

> The Particularists[24] propone noncomposite atoms and many such noncomposites. In order to refute their scriptural traditions, noncomposites are identified to be just these.[25]

(b) Specific explanation of noncomposites. This has three points.

(i) Space

5d Space is that which does not obstruct them.

Of these three types of noncomposites, according to the Exposition school the characteristic of **space is that which** is a noncomposite thing that **does not obstruct them,** those phenomena with form, and that opens the gate to the arising. Among the three, virtue and so forth, its essence is unobscured neutral.[26]

(ii) Analytic cessation

6ab Cessation that is analytic
Is a removal. They are distinct.

Cessation that is analytic is cessation attained by the power of analyzing suffering and the other noble truths with full knowing. Its essence is a cessation that **is a removal** of defiled dharmas.[27]

The classifications of analytic cessation: Is the cessation of all defiled dharmas one or separate? you ask. **They,** the different analytic cessations, **are distinct:** there are just as many substances of removal (cessations) as substances that had been possessed. There are five separate classes of discards[28] and there are five separate classes of antidotes. Therefore, there are five separate analytic cessations.

(iii) Nonanalytic cessation

6cd The other cessation blocks arising
Forever; it's nonanalytic.

The essence of nonanalytic cessation is a cessation that is **other** than analytic **cessation** and **blocks** the **arising** of the future composite that is negated **forever.** To explain the term, it is set forth as cessation attained by power that **is not analytic** full knowing: it is not attained by the power of individually analyzing the aspects of the four truths but rather is attained by the power of conditions not being met.

For example, when your mind is distracted by some other form, if there is a crow behind you where you cannot see it, a cognition that perceives the crow does not arise. Later when you are no longer distracted and the cognition could arise, the crow has flown off someplace else. Therefore the eye consciousness that sees the crow has become a future nonarising dharma base.

b. Extensively explaining the limbs. This has two topics: i. An overview of the eight areas, and ii. Teaching the meaning of each area.

i. An overview of the eight areas. This has three points.

(1) Establishing the number

The first two areas give a general presentation of defiled and undefiled dharmas. Following that, the middle three areas give specific explanations of defiled all-afflicted dharmas. The last three areas present specific explanations of undefiled perfectly pure dharmas. This presents everything defiled and undefiled that individuals must focus on as they progress through the paths, and whatever is not included in earlier chapters is taught in the later. These completely explain the necessary meaning, and thus the number of chapters is established as eight. Generally, by dividing the topics into eight chapters, the different topics can be combined into a coherent whole.

(2) Establishing the order

The order and connections between the areas was explained extensively by Narthangpa Sherdrag, who composed the verses that begin, "Just this desire for liberation," and continue until the lines, "The treasury that teaches absorption/Is taught after that."[29]

The order can be known from these, but to summarize in brief, the primary topic of abhidharma—the presentation of aggregates *(skandha),* elements *(dhātu)*, and sense bases *(āyatana)*—is explained first in the treasury that teaches elements. That ends with a mention of the word *faculties*, so next there follows an extensive explanation of those in the treasury that teaches faculties. That chapter mentions the names of the three realms, so an explanation of those follows in the treasury that teaches the world. One might wonder whether these various worlds arise without a cause. They do not. In order to explain that they arise out of karma, next comes the treasury that teaches karma. Karma can only produce a fully ripened result if there are afflictions, so to explain that, next comes the treasury that teaches the kernels. As Pūrṇavardhana says:

> The childish ride the chariot of birth,
> Which has the wheels of karma and afflictions,
> But without the one wheel of the afflictions,
> The single wheel of karma cannot turn.

This chapter also explains that when the afflictions are abandoned, perfect knowings arise. In order to explain that the afflictions are abandoned by paths and individuals, next is the treasury that teaches the paths and individuals. This chapter explains dharma knowing and subsequent knowing alone, so in order to give an extensive presentation of all ten knowings, next comes the treasury that teaches wisdom. That treasury explains the Buddha's unshared qualities, and so in order to explain the qualities of the absorptions and so forth shared in common with learners, next comes the treasury that teaches the absorptions. Elaborating on the final statement, "All those who want freedom, be careful,"[30] the *Commentary* then explains the logic refuting the individual self in a ninth area.

(3) What topic is taught in which area

This is known from each individual area. The establishment of order and number, which area teaches what, and so forth, are more extensively taught in the *Karṭīk*[31] and other commentaries, so refer there.

ii. Teaching the meaning of each area. There are eight areas. The first is "The Teachings on the Elements." This has an explanation of the text of the area and a presentation of the area's name.

The explanation of the text of the area. This has four sections: I. Presentation of composites, II. Presentation of the aggregates, elements, and sense bases, III. Teaching how everything is included in three dharmas, and IV. The complete classification of the aspects of elements.

I. Presentation of composites. This has three points.

A. The character base of composites

7ab Composite dharmas are the five
Skandhas of form, et cetera.

In the above verse, "Except the truth of path, composites," the character base for the composites mentioned is **composite dharmas** that are made by many causes and conditions coming together and meeting. They **are the five skandhas of form, et cetera**—the aggregates of feeling, conception,[32] formation, and consciousness.

B. Synonyms

7cd Just these are time, the bases for talk,
Emancipatible, and grounded.

All the teachers of abhidharma explained and systematized the sutras. In the sutras it says, "Bhikshus, the times are three... " and "The bases for talk are three... " and "Whatever is clearly composited and gathered is emancipation," and "What dharmas are grounded? you ask. All composites." What is the meaning of these? you ask.

Just these composites **are** called **time**, or *adhvā.* The word *adhvā* means either "time" or "path." In the meaning of "path," composites are like the paths by which an individual went, is going, or will go to the market. In the meaning of "time," the composites of the three times are called "time" because they have ceased, are ceasing, or will cease. Alternately, as they are consumed by impermanence, they are called "time."

Composites are either directly or indirectly the topic of speech, so they are called **the bases for talk**. They are called **emancipatible**, because if one transcends these composites, nirvana will be attained. **And** they are also called **grounded** because they have causes.

C. Specific explanation of the synonyms of composites.

8. The defiled is the aggregates
Of grasping and is disputed, too.
They're suffering, origin, and the world,
Locus of views, existence, too.

Among these composites, that which is explained as **defiled is the aggregates of grasping,** because grasping is afflicted, **and** the aggregates possess grasping in three ways: 1) Grasping is the afflictions, by which one accumulates karma out of which the aggregates arise, so calling them the aggregates of grasping is like saying "grass and a hay fire." 2) Because the aggregates produce the afflictions, it is like saying "flowering tree" or "fruit tree." 3) The aggregates are obtained by engaging objects under the power of afflictions, so it is like saying "the King's men."

They **are** called **disputed, too:** afflictions, just like worldly disputes, harm oneself and others, so they are disputes. Because the aggregates increase those, they are disputed.

As they possess the three sufferings and are incompatible with nobles, **they are** also called **suffering.** Nobles see that the third suffering, the suffering of formation that pervades all composites, is ultimately suffering.

As suffering originates from these, they are also called the **origin.** As they are supported on something that disintegrates, they are called **the** "disintegrating support" or **world.**[33] As views develop by focusing on them, they are called the **locus of views.** From beginningless time, in the way of causally compatible cause and result they have been born without interruption and arise again, they are also called **existence**, so they are called by these synonyms, **too.**

II. Presentation of the aggregates, elements, and sense bases. This has four topics: A. The individual natures of the aggregates, elements, and sense bases, B. The reason they are given the names aggregate, sense base, and element, C. The reason for teaching three dharmas, and D. The orders of the three dharmas.

A. The individual natures of the aggregates, elements, and sense bases. This has three topics: 1. Extensive explanation, 2. Teaching them in consolidation, and 3. Dispelling doubts.

1. Extensive explanation. This has three topics: a. The explanation of the aggregate, elements, and sense bases of form, b. The aggregates, sense bases, and elements of feeling, conception, and formation, and c. Those of consciousness.

a. The explanation of the aggregate, elements, and sense bases of form. This has three topics: i. Overview, ii. Explanation, and iii. How this is presented as elements and sense bases.

i. Overview

9ab The skandha of form: five faculties,
Five objects, the imperceptible.

Above where it says, "the five / Skandhas of form, et cetera," the **skandha of form** mentioned is the **five faculties** of eye and so forth, the **five objects** of form and so forth, and **the imperceptible** form[34] to make exactly eleven.

These dharmas, the eleven dissimilar things, are called form and characterized as the same with the characteristic of *appropriate for form*. The meaning of this is set forth as "able to be damaged." The meaning of that in turn is that they can be destroyed or conquered. This in turn means that through the internal collision of forms, they become dissimilar to the previous form—they are susceptible to the damage of production. Alternatively, the meaning of appropriate for form is obstructive.

Well then, should not atoms be inappropriate for form, you say? Atoms are either substance or sense base. Of these two, in the first case, the particles of the eight substances and so forth are not simultaneously assembled in a single atom. However, when they do assemble, being appropriate for form itself makes them into something that can be damaged, so they are included within form. Well then, if these atoms of substance are form, then are they not the object of eye consciousness and so forth, you say? In general, they are not, because as explained in the autocommentary:

> A single atom of the faculties or atom of an object does not produce a consciousness.

Therefore, if you include these atoms of substance in an aggregate, it has to be form. However, when they are considered a sense base, they are not included in the sense base of form, because they do not actually produce an eye consciousness that perceives them. This means the same as the passage in the *Compendium of Abhidharma*[35] that talks of "those of the five forms of the sense base of dharmas," so it is included in the forms of the sense base of dharmas. Therefore, not all the forms included in the sense base of dharmas are imperceptible, and the eleven classifications of form are not all included in the aggregate of form.

Well then, are they permanent or impermanent, you say? Some say that these are what is meant in the explanation of noncomposite empty particles from the Kalachakra, so they are permanent. Of course you might say so, but that is nothing more than talk that does not go anywhere. If that were so, our own position becomes the same as the assertion by the extremist[36] Particularists and others. Their assertion that atoms are permanent is a position that the Master[37] shreds. From the Prince:

> The Particularists propose many things such as noncomposite atoms and so forth, and this is to refute their scriptural tradition.

Because it has been established that there are only three noncomposites and because permanent composite particles have been refuted, you should be more careful. Therefore, in this Great Exposition presentation, atoms are proposed to be impermanent only. Otherwise, it would be logical to describe them as noncomposite substance, and they are not described as such.

In the second case of atoms as sense base, when they are combined, atoms become something showable that can obscure and obstruct made out of the particles of the eight substances. This can be demonstrated through the example of a vase.[38] As will be explained:

> In Desire, atoms without sound
> Or faculties: eight substances.[39]

ii. The explanation. This has three topics: (1) Explaining the five faculties, (2) Explaining the five objects, and (3) Explaining imperceptible form.

(1) Explaining the five faculties

> 9cd Supports of consciousnesses are
> The eye, et cetera—lucid forms.

The **supports of** the **consciousnesses** that perceive the five objects **are the eye, et cetera,** including the ear, nose, tongue, and body: the five internal **lucid forms.** The shapes of each of the faculties from the eye faculty to the body faculty are in succession flax, a knot of birch, a copper needle, a half-moon, and fur that is soft to the touch. The male and female faculties are like a thumb and the inside of a drum, respectively.

(2) Explaining the five objects. This has five points.

(a) Explaining form

> 10a Two types of form, or twenty types,

There is a concise classification **two types of form,** color and shape, **or** to classify it extensively, there are **twenty types:**

> They're blue and yellow, red and white;
> And light, dark, cloudy, smoky, dusty,
> As well as misty, sunny, and shaded;
> And long and short, square, round, high, low,
> As well as even and uneven.
> The first twelve are the colors, and
> Four colors are the primary;
> The other eight are secondary.
> The last eight are the forms of shape.

(b) Explaining sound

> 10b And there are the eight types of sound,

And to classify it concisely, **there are the eight types of sound.** The first is sound supported by appropriated sources[40] that indicates meaning to beings and is pleasant, such as lovely songs sung by sentient beings. The second is sound supported by appropriated sources that indicates meaning to beings and is unpleasant, such as scolding. The third is sound supported by appropriated sources that does not indicate meaning to beings and is pleasant, such as the sound of a drum or clapping. The fourth is sound supported by appropriated sources that does not indicate meaning to beings and is unpleasant, such as the sound of the body being struck. The fifth is sound supported by nonappropriated sources that indicates meaning to beings and is pleasant, such as magically emanated songs. The sixth is sound supported by nonappropriated sources that indicates meaning to beings and is unpleasant, such as emanated scolding. The seventh is sound supported by nonappropriated sources that does not indicate meaning to beings and is pleasant, such as the sound of wind-chimes in the wind. The eighth is sound supported by nonappropriated sources that does not indicate meaning to beings and is unpleasant, such as the sound of an avalanche.

(c) Explaining taste

> 10c And taste is sixfold,

And taste is sixfold: sweet, sour, bitter, pungent, salty, and astringent.

(d) Explaining scent

10c scent is fourfold,

Scent is fourfold: sweet smelling, foul smelling, strong, and weak.

(e) Explaining touch

10d Touch is elevenfold in nature.

For **touch**, the four sources of earth, water, fire, and air are causal touch, and soft, rough, heavy, light, cold, hunger, and thirst comprise resultant touch. These **eleven** are **in nature** touch only.

(3) Explaining imperceptible form. This has two topics: (a) Actual explanation, and (b) Its cause, the four sources.

(a) Actual explanation

11. Distracted, and mind-free as well,
Virtue or non, continuous,
And caused by the great sources: this
Is called the imperceptible.

The imperceptible form of a vow or so forth[41] follows the being who possesses it (i.e., the person who took the vow) even when he is **distracted** from the mind state that motivated him when he attained the vow. It also follows the stream of a being who is in one of the two **mind-free** absorptions. It follows the continuum of someone whose mind is not distracted **as well.** Imperceptible form is definitely only **virtue or non**virtue, because neutral minds are weak and so cannot motivate one to attain an imperceptible form. This excludes the eyes, ears, and so forth, which are neutral.

Continuous means that the imperceptible form remains in one's continuum until that which forfeits it arises. Therefore, it is continuously present in times of distraction and so forth. This distinguishes it from mere perceptible forms or perceptible speech. The continuum of the attainment[42] of a vow is also present both when the mind is present and not, is either virtuous or nonvirtuous, **and** is connected to a being's stream of being, but it is not an imperceptible form. Imperceptible form is distinguished from the mere attainment of a vow because it is **caused by the great sources**, the elements of earth and so forth.

Imperceptible form is by nature form and action, but whereas others can distinguish an individual's motivation when they perceive perceptible forms such as body and speech, others cannot discern an individual's motivation from imperceptible forms. **This is** what is **called the imperceptible,** to teach the Master's opinion.

The Master Saṅghabhadra says there are some faults in this presentation:

> It is incomplete and contradicts the treatise.
> It undermines, implies what is not must be,
> And states an extra "as well." It fails
> To distinguish where it should distinguish.

These six faults and their refutation are thoroughly explained in the *Karṭik,* so refer there.

(b) Its cause, the four sources. This has four points.

(i) The sources' classifications

> 12ab The sources are the elements
> Of earth and water, fire and air.

When it says above, "And caused by the great sources," what are these sources? you ask. **The sources**[43] **are the elements of earth and water, fire and air.** From beginningless time they have never been known not to arise and they are the source that makes the form of the result arise, so they are called *sources.* They are the greatest of the causes of the resulting forms and form the greater part of their functions, so they are *great.* As they hold their own characteristics and the form of the result, they are called *dhātu*[44] or elements.

(ii) Their functions

> 12c Their functions are to hold, et cetera.

The **function** of earth **is to hold** from falling down, **et cetera:** water has the function of cohering without spreading; fire, ripening without rotting or decaying; and air the function of making things increase further and further.

(iii) Their characteristics

> 12d They are hard, wet, and hot, and moving.

Earth is **hard** and solid. Water is **wet and** liquid. Fire is **hot and** burning, or heat. Air is **moving** a continuum from one place to another. Respectively, these are the characteristics of each of these elements.

(iv) Dispelling doubts

> 13. According to the world's conventions,
> Color and form are considered earth,
> Water, and fire. The atmosphere
> Is the element itself, and like those, too.

Well then, what is the distinction between earth and the element of earth? you ask. The elements of earth and so forth must fulfill the above characteristics, but earth and so forth do not, because **according to the world's conventions, color and form are considered earth.** For example, it is like saying earth is a yellow square. In the same way **water and fire** are too: water is said to be a white circle and fire a red triangle. **The atmosphere is** also in common parlance the **element** of wind **itself.**

Alternatively, earth and the others are **like those**, so their color and shape are called thus, **too**. It is said that the mandala of wind is a blue arc, but this last is said to be inconsistent with the *Treatise.*[45]

iii. How the form aggregate is presented as elements and sense bases

> 14ab Only these faculties and objects
> Are called ten bases and elements.

The Master is skilled in concise and simple words and composed a text with few difficult words. He teaches that this very aggregate of form itself is elements and sense bases. By saying the identifying words, "**Only these** five **faculties and** five **objects,**" he teaches that imperceptible forms are not included. When designating the five faculties and five objects as sense bases, they **are called** the **ten** sense **bases** that have form, **and** when designating them as elements, as the ten **elements** that have form.

b. The aggregates, sense bases, and elements of feeling, conception, and formation. This has four points.

i. Feeling

> 14c Feeling's experience.

The essence of the aggregate of **feeling is** to clearly **experience** in dependence by the manner of engaging help or harm. To classify feeling, there are the six from feeling that arises from contact assembled by eye up to feeling that arises from contact assembled by mind. Alternatively, there are also pleasant, suffering, neutral, mentally pleasant, and mental unhappiness.

ii. Conception

> 14cd Conception
> Is the perception of attributes.

The essence of the aggregate of **conception** is when one focuses on one of the six objects, to say, "These aspects are blue, and these are yellow," discerning the individual fine distinctions. Thus in essence, it **is the perception of attributes.** To classify, there are the six of conception that arises from contact assembled by eye and so forth.

iii. Formation

> 15a Formation differs from four skandhas.

The essence of the aggregate of **formation** is composites that **differ from** the **four skandhas** or aggregates: the previous three and consciousness that will be explained. Here, nonconcurrent formations[46] are proposed to be substantial. By saying "composites," noncomposites are excluded.

If you classify formations concisely, there are two types: mental factors and nonconcurrent formations. If you classify them extensively, there are 73 mental factors and 14 actual nonconcurrent formations and their compatibles. The *Teaching the Ten Areas*[47] also presents seven hundred classifications.

iv. Teaching these as the sense base and element of dharmas

> 15b–d These three and imperceptibles
> And noncomposites are called the
> Sense base and element of dharmas.

These three—feeling, conception, and formation—**and imperceptible** forms **and** the three **noncomposites,** when presented as sense bases, **are called the sense base** of dharmas, **and** when presented as elements, the **element of dharmas.**

c. The aggregate, elements, and sense base of consciousness. This has four topics: i. The essence of consciousness, ii. Presenting it as a sense base, iii. Presenting it as elements, and iv. A specific explanation of the element of mind.

i. The essence of consciousness

16a Consciousness is distinctly knowing.

The essence of aggregate of **consciousness is distinctly,** or by its own power, **knowing** the focus, object, and aspects, the bare meaning. By saying "its own power," mental factors are excluded, because they do not know by their own power, and by saying "knowing," the other three bases of the knowable[48] are excluded, because they are not cognition. Several methods of classifying consciousness are proposed, such the Great Vehicle's and so forth, but in this tradition only the six from the eye formation to the mind consciousness are proposed.

ii. Presenting consciousness as a sense base

16b The sense base of mind is also that,

When presenting it as a sense base, **the sense base of mind is also that,** these six very collections of consciousness.

iii. Presenting consciousness as elements

16cd And also seven elements—
Six consciousnesses and the mind.

Consciousness itself is not just presented as the sense base of mind, it is **also seven elements,** because it is proposed as the **six consciousnesses** from the eye consciousness to the mind consciousness **and the** element of **mind.**

iv. The specific explanation of the element of mind. This has two points.

(1) Identifying the character base

17ab Six consciousnesses that have just
Immediately past are mind.

What is this mind element that is different from the six collections of consciousness? you ask. Of course, there really is not any such thing. However, the **six** collections of **consciousness that have just immediately past,** without any other cognition occurring in between, provide the support for the next mind consciousness, so they **are** called the sense base of mind or the element of **mind**. Saying "six" indicates that it is in all six consciousness. Saying "past" makes the distinction with present consciousness: the present is taught as consciousness and the past as the faculty of mind or the element of mind. Saying "immediately past" indicates that it is the mind that has recently passed.

The explanation here of the mind element as immediately past is in relation just to the mind consciousness that it supports. It is not pervasively in the actual past, because it is said in the autocommentary that each of the eighteen elements has three times.[49] From the autocommentary:

> If that were not so, the element of mind would be past only and would not be either future or present, but all eighteen elements are also proposed to have three times.

(2) The proof

> 17cd To establish the support of the sixth,
> We posit eighteen elements.

Well then, the six elements of consciousness and the element of mind can each be included within the other, so in substance there are only seventeen or twelve, you say. In substance, it is so. However, in terms of characteristics, they are not the same. Just as the five sense consciousnesses each have a dominant condition as support,[50] the mind consciousness also needs a supporting dominant condition. The sixth mind consciousness has no other support, so in order **to** fully **establish the supporting** dominant condition **of the sixth** consciousness, the six consciousnesses are divided into past and present parts, and the past part is presented as the so-called mind element. Thus **we posit eighteen elements:** the six faculties as support, the six consciousnesses that are supported, and the focus of six objects.

2. Teaching them in consolidation. This has two points.

a. The actual consolidation

> 18ab One aggregate, one sense base, and
> One element include them all.

Is there also a consolidated presentation of the aggregates, elements, and sense bases? you wonder. There is. The **one aggregate** of form includes the ten sense bases that have form, the ten elements that have form, and imperceptible form. The **one sense base** of mind includes the aggregate of consciousness **and** the seven elements of cognition. The **one element** of dharma includes the aggregates of feeling, conception, and formation and the sense base of dharma. It also includes imperceptible form. Thus three categories **include them**, **all** dharmas.

b. The manner of consolidation

> 18cd It's by their nature—they do not
> Possess another's entity.

Is this consolidation a characteristic consolidation where what is included is the same as what includes, like made and impermanent, or is it a nominal consolidation like the four means of magnetizing[51] or the fourfold assembly,[52] where what is included is different from what includes?

It is not a nominal, but a characteristic consolidation where what is included is the same as what includes, because **it is by their** own **nature** that what is included is contained within that which includes. This is because that which is included possesses the specific characteristics of that which includes. **They do not possess** the characteristics of **other** dharmas' **entities**. Being included by something different is only an occasional or temporary inclusion, so that is only nominally an inclusion.[53]

3. Dispelling doubts

> 19. Of course there are two eyes, et cetera,
> But since their type, sphere, consciousness
> Are similar, they're just one element.
> To beautify, they come in pairs.

Well then, there are two eyes, two ears, and two nostrils, so should there not be twenty-one elements? you ask. **Of course there are two eyes, et cetera, but since their type**, being merely eyes and so forth, and **sphere**, or the type of object they perceive such as form and so forth, are similar; and because they produce and support the same type of eye **consciousness** and so forth, they **are similar**, so therefore **they are** proven to be **just one element.** The phrase "et cetera" means that the ears and nose should be known to be the same.

Well then, it is therefore unnecessary for two to arise, you say. Here in order **to beautify** the body support, **they come in pairs.** Well then, why is it that owls and so forth have two eyes but are not beautiful? you say. This is because they are by nature not beautiful; it is not that having two eyes makes them not beautiful. If they only had one eye, they would be even uglier, so for that reason two only is beautiful.

B. The reason they are given the names aggregate, sense base, and element

20a-c The meaning of aggregate is heaped,
Sense base means the gate for arising,
And element means family.

From a sutra:

> Any form at all, whether past or future or present, internal or external, coarse or subtle, base or sublime, that is far away or near, these are all included in one: they are counted within the form aggregate...

The sutra continues in the same way up to the aggregate of consciousness. As is said, **the meaning of** the term **aggregate is** many things of the same type such as form and so forth **heaped** together; **sense base means the gate for** the **arising** and expansion of mind and mental factors; **and element means** the origin of later things of the same **family.**[54]

Well then, noncomposites would therefore not be an element because they are permanent and produce no future noncomposites, you say. Noncomposites have no similar class, but because they are the source for mind and mental factors by way of being their focus, they are designated as an element.

C. The reason for teaching three dharmas. This has three points.

1. Actual

20d-f Delusions, faculties, and interests
Are threefold, so the three are taught:
The aggregates, et cetera.

Why did the Lord Buddha teach the three dharmas of aggregates, sense bases, and elements? you ask. The **delusions** of holding mental factors, form, and both form and mind to be a whole self, and the distinctions of the three sharp, middle, and dull **faculties, and** the three types of **interest** that seek concise, medium, and extensive explanations **are** all **threefold, so** the **three are taught: the aggregates, et cetera,** including sense bases and elements.

2. The reason for teaching feeling and conception as separate aggregates

21. Because they are the root of quarrels,
 And cause samsara and the order
Feeling and conception are taught
 As different aggregates than factors.

Why are both feeling and conception presented as separate aggregates from the other mental factors? you ask. **Because they are the root of** the **quarrels** among both householders and monastics, they are presented separately. Householders dispute water, fields, and so forth, and the root of these disputes is feelings: they want pleasure for themselves and suffering for others, so they quarrel. Monastics conceive of their own and others' views as good or bad and then prove and refute them. Because the root of these disputes is erroneous conceptions, the aggregate of conception is presented separately.

Alternatively, as they are the principal **cause** of **samsara**, they are presented separately. By clinging to feelings, out of mistaken conceptions one views egolessness as the self, and the four erroneous conceptions[55] become the support for many afflictions, so the wheel of samsara turns. This means that these aggregates are the root of all faults and problems, and therefore should be abandoned.

Alternatively, they are the cause of **the order** in which the five aggregates are taught, which will be explained below.[56] **Feeling and conception are taught as different aggregates than** the mental **factors.**

3. The reason for not teaching noncomposites as an aggregate

22ab Since noncomposites do not suit
 Aggregate's meaning, they are not taught.

Why are noncomposites presented as elements and sense bases but not as aggregates? you ask. There is a reason that noncomposites are not presented as an aggregate: **since noncomposites** cannot be destroyed, demolished, or so forth, they **do not suit aggregate's meaning.** A separate so-called "aggregate of noncomposites" is inappropriate: because they are not many things aggregated, **they are not taught** as aggregates.

This fault does not apply to presenting atomic substances as aggregates. From the autocommentary:

> In that case, if the meaning of aggregating were the meaning of aggregate, the aggregates would have nominal existence,[57] because they are many substances

> gathered together, like aggregating or an individual, you say. It is not so, because even a single atom of substance is an aggregate. In that way, as a single unit has no aggregating itself, do not say that the meaning of aggregating is the meaning of aggregate.

As this explains, the aggregates are not pervasively many things aggregated, but the aggregates are appropriate to be many things aggregated.

D. The orders of the three dharmas. This has three points.

1. The order of the five aggregates

> 22cd The order is by coarse, all-afflicted,
> The pot and so forth, the realms' meanings.

The order of the five aggregates **is** presented **by** the order of **coarseness**, the order in which the **all-afflicted** arise, the order of **the pot and so forth**, and the order of **the** three **realms' meanings**.

Because form is obstructive, it is the coarsest of all, so it is taught first. Next, feeling is coarse because it is variable. Next, conception is also coarser than the final two: it delineates attributes and so is easy to know. Next, formation is by nature to clearly formulate, "I must make myself happy; I must not make myself unhappy." As consciousness is merely focusing, it is the subtlest of all. This teaches the order from coarse to subtle.

Also the order can be taught through the order in which all-afflicted dharmas such as greed and so forth arise. First, males and females have lust for each others' bodily forms, and that creates desire for pleasant feelings. From that come mistaken conceptions, and from those, formation comes under the power of the all-afflicted. That makes consciousness afflicted as well.

Alternatively, they are comparable to the pot and so forth—food, flavorings, cook, and eater. Form is comparable to a pot, feelings to food, conceptions to flavorings, formation to the cook, and consciousness is comparable to the eater.

Alternatively, it is also taught by comparing it to the order of the Desire, Form, and Formless realms, and the Peak of Existence,[58] or the three realms. Desire is differentiated by form, the Form realm by feeling, the first three Formless realms by conception, and the Peak of Existence by formation. Consciousness is present in all, so it is taught last. This is like the order of a field, seeds, shoots, and so forth.

2. The order of the six faculties

> 23. The object is present, so first five.
> The object is source-derived, so four.
> Since at great distance or since quickly,
> Or else in order of location.

They are easy to realize as **the object** they perceive **is** in the **present**—the objects of form and so forth—**so first** the **five** that have form—the eye and so forth—are taught. Mind is the subject that perceives objects of the three times and noncomposites that are not included in the times, so it is difficult to realize, like for example realizing that all dharmas are egoless. For that reason, it is taught last.

Among the five, the four from eye up to tongue are subjects that perceive only **the object,** forms of **source-derived** that are results of the four sources,[59] **so** those **four** are taught first. Body is not necessarily like that because it is a subject that perceives both the sources and the source-derived.

Among these four, there is a reason that eye and ear are explained first, before the nose and tongue. **Since** the eye and ear perceive form and sound without contacting the object, they can engage an object **at** a **great distance**. Of these two, eye can engage an object at a much greater distance, so it is mentioned first. For instance, you can see a river from far off but not hear its sound. The nose and tongue both engage what is near, but **since** the nose engages the object more **quickly** than the tongue, it is explained first. It is like when the tongue does not yet taste the food, but the nose smells its aroma.

Or else the faculties are taught **in** the **order** of the height **of** their **location** or position. Mind is supported by them and does not stay in a location, so it is taught last.

Establishing the order of the six faculties also establishes the order of the objects and the consciousnesses. For example, it is just as when the ranks of six kings are established, the ranks of the queens and princes are also established.

3. An aside to dispel a doubt

> 24. One is specific and the main,
> And one has many dharmas, the highest,
> So one is called sense base of form,
> And one is called sense base of dharma.

If the first ten sense bases are all form, why is only the object of eye the sense base of form? And if all twelve sense bases are dharmas by nature, why is only the object of mental cognition the sense base of dharma? you ask.

The reason for the first is the **one** object of eye has no other name, so it **is** designated by applying the general name "form" to the **specific** sense base. One says, "This is it," to indicate something, and in common usage that is known as form. **And** others say that the sense base of form is **the main** or principal form for three reasons: 1) because form is coarse as it has twenty types; 2) because it is the sphere of the fleshly eye, the divine eye, and the eye of nobles' full knowing; **and** 3) because it is obstructive and showable.

The reason for the second is that the **one** object of mind **has** or includes **many dharmas**—the three middle aggregates, imperceptibles, and noncomposites—and that the sense base of dharma includes **the highest** of dharmas, the analytical cessation of nirvana. **So** in order, **the one** object of eye alone **is called** the sense base of form, **and** the **one** object of mind alone **is called** the sense base of dharma.

III. Teaching how everything is included in three dharmas. This has three topics: A. How the aggregates of Dharma are included, B. Including other dharmas in the aggregates, elements, and sense bases, and C. Additionally teaching the essence of two elements.

A. How the aggregates of Dharma are included. This has two topics: 1. Actual, and 2. The size of the aggregates of the Dharma.

1. Actual,

25. The eighty thousand aggregates
Of Dharma the Sage taught are all
Words or are names, and thus they are
Included in form or in formation.

In the sutras where it says, "The eighty thousand aggregates of Dharma," how are these included within the five aggregates? you ask. **The eighty thousand aggregates of Dharma** that **the Sage**, the Buddha, **taught are all**, according to the Sutra school, **words** or sound, **or** according to the Great Exposition, they **are names** that are the object of mind by nature. **Thus they are included in** the aggregate of **form or** in the aggregate of **formation** respectively, it is proposed.

2. The size of the aggregates of the Dharma. This has two points.

a. Refuting other positions

> 26ab Some say their length equals the treatise,
> Or depends on aggregates, et cetera.

What is the size of each of the aggregates of Dharma? you ask. **Some** schools **say** that **their length equals the** length of **treatise** composed by Shariputra, which has six thousand stanzas. Other schools propose that the size of each aggregate of Dharma **depends on** how long it takes to teach the **aggregates,** faculties, sense bases, **et cetera** completely, but there is not a fixed number of verses.

b. Presenting the Master's own position

> 26cd But aggregates of Dharma taught
> Correspond to antidotes for conduct.

But in the Master's own position, the size of the **aggregates of Dharma taught,** such as meditation on repulsiveness and so forth, **correspond to** the number of afflictions. They are taught as **antidotes for** sentient beings' **conduct** motivated by the three poisons and the eighty thousand afflictions of pride and so forth. The word "but" is explained as indicating that this is the Master's own position: there are twenty-one thousand as antidotes for each of the three poisons and twenty-one thousand as antidotes for conducted motivated by the three poisons mixed in equal parts for a total of eighty-four thousand. This is explained in the *Retention of the Jewel Tala*[60] and other texts, it is said.

B. Including other dharmas in the aggregates, elements, and sense bases

> 27. Likewise the other aggregates,
> Sense bases or else elements:
> Examine their own characters;
> Include them in what has been explained.

Just as the eighty thousand aggregates of Dharma are included in the five aggregates, **likewise the** various **other** dharmas named **aggregates, sense bases, or else elements** should be thoroughly **examined** on the basis of **their own characteristics.** Then **include them in what has been explained,** the five aggregates, eighteen elements, and twelve sense bases.

The five undefiled aggregates taught[61] are included in the five aggregates taught here as follows: the aggregate of discipline is included in form, and the last four are included in formation.

Among the ten all-encompassing sense bases,[62] the eight sense bases of earth, water, fire, air, blue, yellow, white, and red are also collected in nongreed, so they are included in the sense base of dharma. Including all that is associated with them, they are the five aggregates, and they are included in the sense bases of mind and dharma. The eight overpowering sense bases[63] are, as the above, included in the sense bases of mind and dharma. All-encompassing sky and consciousness, and the four sense bases of the Formless[64] have four aggregates, so they are included in the sense bases of mind and dharma.

Also in the sutras there are said to be the six elements of earth, water, fire, air, space, and consciousness. The first four are touch, the fifth is form, and the sixth is included in the seven elements of mind.

In brief, within the eighteen elements there are three groups of six, one group of four, six groups of three, and two groups of two: they are grouped in forty-four. The *Great Ṭīka*[65] explains this expanded manner of grouping them, so refer there.

C. Additionally teaching the essence of two elements. This has two points.

1. The element of space

28ab Openings are the element
Of space—they're light and dark, it's claimed.

The characteristics of earth and the other three have been explained, and the characteristics of space and consciousness have also been explained. But the characteristics of the elements of the latter two have not been explained. Are thus space and consciousness themselves those two elements? you ask.

They are not. They say that the **openings** in doorframes, smoke holes, mouths, and noses **are the element of space.** The Great Exposition school posits that this is because in the daytime **they are** mostly **light and** at nighttime they are mostly **dark.** "**It is claimed**" is a skeptical word from the Sutra school. The Sutra school posits that space itself is the element of space.

2. Consciousness

28cd The element of consciousness
Is defiled consciousness, arising's basis.

The element of consciousness is defiled consciousness because those six elements themselves provide the **basis** of **arising** from rebirth-linking (the moment of conception) to death and because undefiled consciousness is unsuitable for that.

Therefore earth and the other three are included in the element of touch. The element of space is included in the aggregate of form. The element of consciousness is included in the seven elements of consciousness.

IV. The complete classification of the aspects of elements. This has seven topics: A. Classifying in two categories, B. Classifying in three categories, C. Differentiating them by what they possess, D. Classification of those with form, E. Three modes of production, F. Distinctions of attainment, and G. Classifying as external, internal, and so forth.

A. Classifying in two categories. This has two points.

1. Showable and unshowable

> 29a The showable here is form alone.

Well then, among these eighteen elements, how many can be shown and how many cannot? you ask. **The showable here** in this discussion of the eighteen elements **is** the element of **form alone,** because phrases such as "It is here" or "Someone has it" indicate it to another. The remaining seventeen are not showable.

2. Obstructive and unobstructive

> 29b The obstructive is the ten with form.

How many of the eighteen elements are obstructive, and how many are unobstructive? you ask. **The obstructive are** those that block: only **the ten with form** are appropriate for form and are obscuring and obstructive.

There are three types of obstructiveness: resistance, contact of object, and contact of focus. In the first, when there is one obstructive thing in a particular location, that thing blocks the arising of another obstructive thing in that same location. For example, if there is a hand somewhere, another hand cannot arise there, or where there already is a stone, another stone cannot arise.

Contact of object is when the subject, the eye and so forth, contacts its object of form and so forth. *The Treatise on Designation* gives four possibilities of eyes that contact their object when in the water but not when out, and four possibilities of those that contact their object at night but not day.

Contact of focus is when the concurrent dharmas[66] contact their focus.

B. Classifying in three categories. This has two points.

1. Categories of virtue and so forth

29cd Eight neutral are just those except
For form and sound. The others are threefold.

Well then, of the eighteen elements, how many are virtuous, nonvirtuous, and neutral? you ask. Of the eighteen elements **eight** are solely **neutral**. They **are just those** that have been explained as obstructive **except for form and sound**. They are neutral by their very nature. **The** ten that are **other** than those eight **are threefold**—virtuous, nonvirtuous, and neutral. Form and sound can become virtuous or nonvirtuous by the power of virtuous or nonvirtuous motivation. The eight unobstructive elements—the seven of consciousness and the element of dharma—can be virtue, nonvirtue, or neutral.

2. Categories of the three realms

30. They all are in the Desire realm.
The Form realm has fourteen: except
The elements of scent and taste,
And the nose and tongue consciousnesses.

31ab The Formless realm has elements
Of mind, dharma, mind consciousness.

Well then, how many of the eighteen elements are in the realms of Desire, Form, and Formless? you ask. **They**, the eighteen, **are all in the Desire realm**, because in the Desire realm one is not detached from their nature and craves them, making them one's own.

The Form realm has fourteen. Which ones? you ask. All those **except the element of scent, and** the element of **taste, and** the element of **the nose** consciousness **and** the element of **tongue consciousness**. In the Form realm, there is no scent or taste because scent and taste are food and only those who are free of desire for food are born there. Therefore, there are neither nose nor tongue consciousness because their objects, scent and taste, do not exist.

Well then, there should not be an element of touch because there is no food, you say. There is no touch that is food, but the element of touch is presented because those in the Form realm wear clothes and so forth. Well then, there should not be faculties of nose or tongue either, you say. These two are presented because they beautify the bodily support.

The Formless realm has the three **elements of mind, dharma,** and **mind consciousness.** The remaining are not there, because one is free from craving for form, so the ten that have form do not exist there, and therefore the first five consciousnesses that arise from them do not exist either.

C. Differentiating them by what they possess. This has three points.

1. Whether or not they have defilements

31cd Those three are defiled or undefiled.
  And those remaining are defiled.

Well then, of these eighteen elements, how many are defiled and how are many undefiled? you ask. **Those** last **three** elements of mind, dharma, and mind consciousness have both **defiled or undefiled** aspects. The defiled aspect is that which is included in the first two truths. The undefiled aspect is that which is included in the truth of path **and** noncomposites. **Those** fifteen **remaining are** solely **defiled.** The ten with form are the truth of suffering, and the cognitions of the five sense gates look outward, so they are not on the level of equipoise and are thus discards of meditation. Also, "defilements can / Develop in relation to them."[67]

2. Whether or not they have consideration and examination

32. Those which consider and examine:
  Five elements of consciousness.
 The final three are of three types.
  Those which remain are free of both.

33. The nonconceptual have no thoughts
  That recognize or that remember.
 These two distract the mind's full knowing
  Or are all memory in mind.

Well then, of the eighteen elements, how many have both consideration and examination? How many have examination but not consideration? How many have neither consideration nor examination? you ask.

Of the eighteen elements, **those which consider and examine** are the first **five elements of consciousness**, because they are coarse as they look outward and because they are on levels that are connected with consideration and examination.

The final three elements of mind and so forth **are of three types**: they can have both consideration and examination, or no consideration and just examination, or neither consideration nor examination. The first type is the mental factors of the last three elements that are included in Desire and the mere first dhyana's actual practice except for consideration and examination themselves, because they are on levels that are not detached from consideration and examination. The second type is the mental factors of the last three elements that are in the special dhyana except for examination, because these have abandoned consideration and are on a level that is concurrent only with examination. The third type is the nonconcurrent of those three elements in Desire and the first dhyana, and the last three elements of the second dhyana and higher. In the second dhyana and higher, they may be concurrent, but they are on levels where consideration and examination have been abandoned.

Examination in Desire and the actual practice of the first dhyana does not fall within any of these three categories because it is concurrent with consideration but not with examination. That is because examination has no second examination.

Those elements **which remain**, the ten with form, **are free of both** consideration and examination, because they are not concurrent.

Well then, if the five collections of consciousness have consideration and examination, that contradicts the sutras' explanation of them as nonconceptual, you say. According to the Great Exposition school, there are three types of thoughts: essential thoughts, thoughts that recognize, and thoughts that remember.[68] The eye consciousness and other four do have essential thoughts, but they are **nonconceptual** because they **have no thoughts that recognize or** thoughts **that remember.** For example, it is like saying a horse with only one foot is a horse with no feet. Essential thoughts will be explained below. **These two**, thoughts that recognize and thoughts that remember, by their nature respectively 1) **distract the mind's full knowing** when the mind is not in equipoise, and 2) **are all memory in** association with **mind**, whether the mind is in equipoise or not.

3. Whether or not they have a focus

> 34ab The seven elements of mind
> And half of dharma, too, have focus.

Well then, how many of these eighteen elements have a focus, and how many do not? you ask. Of these eighteen elements, the **seven elements of mind** always have focus. **And** not only those but the mental factors that are **half of dharma, too, have** a **focus.** The remaining ten elements with form and the portion of the element of dharma that is nonconcurrent have no focus.

D. Classification of those with form. This has five points.

1. Classification of appropriated and nonappropriated

34cd The nine are not appropriated:
Those eight and sound. Nine others: twofold.

Well then, of these eighteen elements, how many are appropriated and how many are not? you ask. The meaning of *appropriated* is that which is suitable to be the support for the arising of pleasure or pain when helped or harmed by contact with something with form. The opposite is nonappropriated. In this context, of **the** eighteen elements, **nine are** solely **not appropriated.** They are **those eight** explained as having focus, with the second half of the element of dharma also added to make the whole element of dharma. These eight are not in the collection of faculties, so they cannot be either helped or harmed. **And sound** can be connected with the one's stream of being, but it is not in the collection of faculties, so it cannot be helped or harmed. Therefore it is not appropriated either.

The five of eye and so forth and the four of form and so forth—the **nine other** elements are different from those that are not appropriated. They are **twofold** because they can be either appropriated or nonappropriated. The five faculties of the present are appropriated. Form, scent, taste, and touch that are of the present and not separate from the faculties are appropriated. Those external elements that are separate from the faculties and not included in the stream of one's being—including hair, body hair, teeth, and nails with the exception of their roots—are not appropriated. All that is past or future is solely not appropriated.

2. Classification of source and source-derived

35a–c Touch has two types. The other nine
With form and part of the element
Of dharmas, too, are source-derived.

Well then, of the eighteen elements, how many are sources? How many are source-derived? you ask. The element of **touch has two types** of source and source-derived. Earth, water, fire, and air are the sources. Soft, rough, heavy, light, cold, hunger, and thirst are source-derived. **The other nine with form**—the eye and so forth—are source-derived, **and** likewise **part of the element of dharmas, too**—imperceptible form—**is** solely **source-derived**. These are source-derived because they are derived from the cause of the four sources, which act to produce them. The remaining that do not have form are proven to be neither sources nor source-derived.

3. Classification of conglomerated and nonconglomerated

35d The ten with form, conglomerates.

Well then, how many of the elements are accumulated, and how many are not? you ask. Of the eighteen elements, **the ten** elements **with form** are **conglomerates,** because they are solely collections or conglomerations of atoms. The definite article "the" is for emphasis: the elements that are unobstructive are proven not to be conglomerated.

4. Classification of cutter and that which is cut

36ab The cutter and that which is cut
Are four external elements,

How many of the elements can cut and how many can be cut? you ask. Of the eighteen elements, **the cutter**, such as an axe, **and that which is cut,** such as wood and so forth, **are** the **four external elements** of form, smell, taste, and touch. Thus it is determined that these four elements can be both cutter and cut; the others are proven to be neither.

5. Classifications of burning and weighing

36cd As are the burnt and that which weighs.
The burner and weighed are disputed.

Well, how many of the elements can be burned? How many are measurers? you ask. Just **as** the cutter and cut **are** the four elements, **the** wood and so forth which is **burnt and that which weighs,** scales and so forth, are also the four external elements. The faculties are neither because they are lucid, like light rays. Because it has no continuum, sound is also not that which is burnt, that which burns, that which is weighed, nor that which weighs. **The burner and** that which is **weighed are disputed** by earlier masters. Some say the four external elements only are that which burns and that which is weighed. Some say that which burns is the element of fire alone, and that which is weighed is heaviness alone.

E. Three modes of production. This has two points.

1. General

37. The five internal are produced
    By ripening and development.
Sound is not ripened. The compatible
    And ripening produce eight unobstructive.

38a Others are threefold.

Well, how many are produced by full ripening, development, and compatible cause? you ask. Of the eighteen elements, only **the five internal** faculties of the eye and so forth **are produced by** full **ripening and** produced by **development.** They can be produced by full ripening because the faculties of the lower realms are produced by the full ripening of nonvirtue and those of the higher realms are produced by the full ripening of virtue. They can also be produced by development through the four causes of food, sleep, fine conduct, and samadhi.

Sound can be either produced by development or produced by compatible cause but **is not** produced by full **ripening,** because it is the manifestation of one's desires. Well then, it says in the *Treatise on Designation:*[69]

Now listen well to how a Tathagata
Attains his qualities of voice and speech:
Fully abandoning harsh words and chatter
Will bring the marks of a Tathagata.

Is this not contradictory, you say? It is not contradictory. The meaning of this passage is that abandoning harsh words and chatter produces the fully ripened result of a fine throat. The throat produces the melody of Brahma,[70] but that melody is not itself a fully ripened result.

Those elements that **the compatible** cause **and** full **ripening produce** are the **eight unobstructive** elements. Of those eight, those that are produced by a cause of same status or universal cause are produced by compatible cause. Those that have are produced by a cause of full ripening are produced by full ripening.[71] They cannot be produced by development. By essence they are not aggregations of particles and they are unobstructive, so they cannot be developed.

The others, the four that remain—form, scent, taste, and touch—**are threefold:** they have all three modes of production.

2. Particulars

> 38ab One has substance.
> The last three are a moment.

Of the eighteen elements, noncomposite dharma **alone has** permanent, stable **substance.**

The last of the eighteen elements, the **three** undefiled elements of mind, dharma, and mind consciousness when assembled on the first moment of forbearance of knowing dharmas of suffering[72] **are a moment** that is not produced by compatible cause, because prior to that there is no undefiled path compatible with them.

This teaches particular points of the lines, "The compatible / And ripening produce eight unobstructive." The mind and so forth of the first undefiled moment and the noncomposite portion of the element of dharma are not produced by any of these three modes of production.

The mind concurrent with dharma forbearance of suffering is the element of mind and the element of mind consciousness. This presents it from the point of view of its function. All that is concurrent with this; its attainment; its arising, abiding, and perishing; and the undefiled vows attained at that moment are the element of dharma.

F. Distinctions of attainment

> 38b–d The eye
> And element of consciousness:
> Gained singly or together, too.

Does someone who newly attains the eye element also newly attain the eye consciousness? you ask. To distinguish how **the eye and** the **element of consciousness** can be **gained singly,** there are four alternatives. The four are 1) newly attaining the eye but not newly attaining the eye consciousness, 2) newly attaining the latter but not the former, 3) **or** attaining both **together** or simultaneously, and 4) not newly attaining either. The first is like dying in the Formless realm and taking birth in any one of the second, third, or fourth dhyanas.

The second is like taking rebirth in Desire from the second dhyana. The third is like taking birth in Desire from the Formless. The fourth is taking birth in the Formless from the Formless. The word "**too**" additionally includes these following:

The ear
And element of consciousness:
Gained singly or together, too.

The others are similar.

G. Classifying as external, internal, and so forth. This has seven topics: 1. Internal and external, 2. Active and inactive, 3. Discard of seeing and so forth, 4. Whether or not it is view, 5. Which element is the object of which consciousness, 6. Permanent/impermanent, and 7. Whether or not they are faculties.

1. Internal and external

39ab Twelve are internal, except form
And so forth.

Well then, of the eighteen elements, how many internal and external elements are there? you ask. Of the eighteen elements, **twelve are internal:** all **except** the external elements of **form and so forth.**

2. Active and inactive. This has two points.

a. Actual

39bc Dharma must be active.
The remaining are inactive, too—

Of these, how many are active and how many are inactive? you ask. Of the eighteen elements, the element of **dharma must be** solely **active,** because the object of the action of the mind consciousness of either nobles or ordinary individuals is definitely pervasively active.[73] This tradition, which does not assert a self-aware cognition, proposes that this is because the cognition that thinks, "All dharmas are egoless," has everything as its object except for itself and the assembly of mental factors that is coemergent with it. If one posits self-awareness, then the cognition itself also becomes its own object, but not positing that is a tenet of the Great Exposition school.

The remaining seventeen elements **are inactive.** The word "**too**" indicates that they can also be active.

b. The meaning of inactive

39d That which does not perform its function.

What is the distinction between active and inactive? you ask. Any element **which does not perform its own function** is inactive, and the opposite of that is active. The eye is active when it looked, looks, or will look at form. It is the same for the other faculties up to the body. The eye is said to be inactive in four instances: when it does not see form and has ceased, is ceasing, will cease, or is a nonarising dharma base. So say the Kashmiris, but the Westerners say that some nonarising dharma bases possess consciousness and some do not, so there should be five. The five external elements of form and so forth are also the same. The seven mind-elements can be either active or inactive.

The six elements from the eye up to the mind are specific to one individual—it is impossible that two individuals could look with the same eye and so forth. Therefore, whichever of those is active or inactive for one individual is active or inactive for all. The five elements from form to touch are common to multiple individuals. Furthermore, it is possible that one individual might watch a dance, for example, whereas another individual might not watch that dance. Therefore these five elements are active in relation to those who are watching or so forth, and inactive in relation to those who are not watching or so forth. Therefore, since the eye and so forth are specific to one being, they are presented as either active or inactive in relation to one being. Since form and the other four are common to many individuals, they are presented in relation to many beings.

The action of the six internal elements is to provide the subject of the object and the support for consciousness. The action of the six elements that are objects is to be the object of the faculties and the focused object of the consciousnesses. The action of the six elements of consciousness is to be supported by the faculties and to provide the subject for the objects. Therefore when these perform these functions, they are active, and when they do not, they are inactive. When these are nonarising dharma bases, they are inactive, and when they have arisen or will arise, they are active.

In the abhidharma tradition of the Great Vehicle, only the five faculties are divided into active and inactive; the others are not.

3. Discard of seeing and so forth. This has two points.

a. Actual

40ab Ten are discards of meditation.
Five also. The last three, three types.

Well then, how many of these are discarded by seeing? How many by meditation? How many are not discarded? you ask. The **ten** with form **are** solely **discards of meditation,** and the first **five** consciousnesses are **also** discarded by meditation. These fifteen are discards because they are defiled, but they are not discarded by seeing because the former ten have form, and the latter five look outward. **The last three** elements are all **three types,** because the eighty-eight afflicted kernels, what is concurrent with them, and their attainment are discarded by seeing; everything else that is defiled is discarded by meditation; and the undefiled parts are not discarded.

b. Refuting the Vatsiputrīya's position

40cd Seeing does not discard the unafflicted,
Nor form, nor what is not born from the sixth.

According to the Vatsiputrīyas,[74] ordinary individuals and the body and speech karma of the lower realms are discards of seeing, because when the path of seeing is attained, they are blocked, they say.

The path of **seeing does not discard** ordinary individuals, because they are **unafflicted,** unobscured neutral. Ordinary individuals are proven to be unafflicted neutral because they are neither virtuous nor afflicted. If they were virtuous, then there could be no nonvirtuous ordinary individuals and the roots of virtue could not be severed.[75] If ordinary individuals were afflicted, then someone who had become detached through a worldly path would not be an ordinary individual. Since neither of these are the case, ordinary individuals are proven to be unobscured neutral. Something that is unobscured neutral is pervasively not a discard of seeing, like a vase, for example. Discards of seeing are definitely afflicted.

Nor does the path of seeing discard the body and speech of those in the lower realms, because they have **form.**

Here there are four alternatives of being free of something and discarding it. The first, being free without discarding, is like the status of an ordinary individual when the path of seeing is attained. The second is like the arhat's faculties that have form—the arhat has abandoned them but is not free of them. The third is like discards of seeing when the path of seeing has been attained. Fourth is all the undefiled paths not included above and noncomposites.

Nor does seeing discard the consciousnesses of the five gates and their associations, because they are on a level that **is not born from the** sense base of mind, and because they look outward. They are not the **sixth** mental consciousness.

4. Whether or not it is view. This has a. Actual and b. Elaboration.

a. Actual

> 41ab The eye and part of the element
> Of dharma are views: they are eightfold.

Well then, how many of the elements are views? How many are not? you ask. **The** active part of the **eye and part of the element of dharma**—the five afflicted views, the correct worldly view, the learner's view, and the nonlearner's view—**are views: they are eightfold** types of view. The other sixteen elements, the inactive eye, and the remaining portions of the element of dharma are not views. The five afflicted views will be explained below.[76] The correct worldly view is presented as a virtuous, defiled full knowing that is concurrent with mental consciousness. The latter two are set forth as the undefiled views of learners and nonlearners.

b. Elaboration. This has six topics: i. Refuting the full knowing of faculties as view, ii. Proving that the eye is view, iii. Distinctions of the faculty perceiving the object, iv. Ascertaining the time of the support, v. The reason for supporter and supported, and vi. Ascertaining the levels of faculty, object, consciousness, and support.

i. Refuting the full knowing of faculties as view

> 41cd Five minds concurrent with five consciousnesses,
> Not thoughts that recognize, are not view.

Why is it that only the full knowing concurrent with mental consciousness can be view? you ask. The **five** virtuous **minds** or full knowings that arise in **concurrence with five consciousnesses** of the sense gates, since they are **not thoughts that** have the volition to **recognize** the object, **are not view.**

ii. Proving that the eye is view. This has two topics.

(1) Actual

42a The eye sees form

Well then, since the eye is also nonconceptual, it should not be a view, you say. Because **the** active **eye sees form**, it is view.

(2) Dispelling doubts. This has (a) Examining whether all eyes see, (b) Examining whether it is eye or eye consciousness that sees, and (c) Examining whether both eyes see.

(a) Examining whether all eyes see

42a when it is active.

Well then, do all eyes see? you ask. **When it is active,** the eye sees, but the inactive eye does not.

(b) Examining whether it is eye or eye consciousness that sees

42b–d Supported consciousness does not,
Because a form that is obstructed
Cannot be seen, or so they claim.

Well then, it is not the eye that sees, it is the eye consciousness it supports that sees, you say. That which sees is the eye. The **supported consciousness** that the eye supports **does not.** Why is this so? **Because** that consciousness is unobstructive. If it were to see, it would have to see **a form that is obstructed** by walls and so forth, and those **cannot be seen.**

"**Or so they claim**" is the Master's skeptical word for the Great Exposition school: Later Great Expositionists thought that the eye consciousness sees and that the faculties do not see. They spoke of many faults in the faculty of eye seeing and so forth.

The Sutra school explains that on the basis of eye and form, the eye cognition arises. There is a conventional label of "seeing form," and following this convention, one says, "The eye sees, the consciousness knows," as a manner of designation, but one should not be attached to this label, they explain.

(c) Examining whether both eyes see

43ab Both of the eyes can see, as well,
Because they both can clearly see.

Does one eye see, or do both see? you ask. **Both of the eyes see, as well, because** if one eye sees, it sees unclearly, but if one opens both eyes, **they both can see** more **clearly** than before. The phrase "as well" means that either one of them is capable of seeing.

iii. Distinctions of the faculty perceiving the object. This has two points.

(1) Meeting or not meeting

> 43cd The eye, ear, and mind do not meet
> Their objects. Three perceive elsewise.

Well then, do the six faculties perceive their objects by meeting them or not? you ask. Three—**the eye, ear, and mind—do not meet their objects** when they perceive them. This is because both the eye and ear see or hear forms or sounds that are far off, and as the mind has no form, it is impossible for it to meet anything. **The three**—nose, tongue, and body—**perceive elsewise** from not meeting: they perceive by meeting their object, because without inhaling, scent is not perceived, and it is proven that far-away tastes and touches are not perceived. The meaning of *meeting* and *not meeting* is proposed as particles striking and joining or not.

(2) Equal or unequal

> 44ab The nose and other two perceive
> An object that in size is equal.

Do the eye and so forth perceive objects that are equal or unequal to themselves in size? you ask. As **the nose and other two,** the tongue and body, perceive an object that they meet, it is proposed all three **perceive an object that in size is equal.** They perceive just as much of the object as meets the faculty. The eye, ear, and mind, however, do not necessarily perceive things that are their own size. The eye perceives things that are larger, equal to, and smaller than itself; the ear hears sounds that are large, medium, and small; and the mind is not corporeal, so there is no determination of its size.

iv. Ascertaining the time of the support

> 44cd The last's support is past. The five
> Arise together with them, too.

The object of the eye consciousness and so forth is always present, but the object of the mind consciousness can be in any of the three times. Are their supports the same? you ask. They are not. **The support** of the **last** of the six elements of consciousness, the mind consciousness, **is** the immediately **past** mind only; it is not the present or future mind. The supports of **the** first **five** elements of consciousness, the eye and so forth, are present because they **arise together with them,** the five consciousnesses. The word "**too**" means, "The immediately past mind supports them, too."

v. The reason for supporter and supported. This has two points.

(1) The reason for designating just the faculty as support

> 45ab Because when those change, they change, too,
> The eye and so on are the supports.

If the consciousnesses arise from both the faculties and the objects, why is it that only the faculty is designated as support? you ask. The reason for that is **because when those**, the eye and other faculties, **change, they,** the consciousnesses, **change, too.** Benefit or harm to the faculties, such as pain and so forth, can help or harm the consciousnesses, or create pain or pleasure in them, or make them clear or unclear. If form and so forth is changed, however, it is not definite that such a change will arise in the consciousness. Therefore, **the eye and so on are the supports** for mind consciousness.

(2) The reason the supports distinguish the consciousnesses

> 45cd Because of that and being specific,
> Those indicate the consciousnesses.

Well, if both the faculty and object produce consciousnesses, why do we say "eye consciousness" but not "form consciousness"? you ask. They are called the eye consciousness and so forth **because of that** reason given above that faculties alone are the supports of the eye consciousness and so forth, like saying, "The King's men."

In addition, within a single individual's continuum, form is a cause common to both the eye and mental consciousnesses, but the eye is the specific cause of the eye consciousness only. Form can also be the cause of eye consciousness in other individuals' streams of being, but the eye is the cause of consciousness for only one individual. Therefore, because they **are specific,**

those faculties form the basis on which we **indicate the** eye and so forth **consciousnesses.** It is like saying "a shoot of rice" or "the sound of a drum."

vi. Ascertaining the levels of faculty, object, consciousness, and support. This has four topics: (1) The levels of the eye, form, eye consciousness, and support, (2) Teaching that the ear is comparable to that, (3) Ascertaining the nose, tongue, and body, and (4) Teaching the mind as uncertain.

(1) The levels of the eye, form, eye consciousness, and support

> 46. The body can not have a lower eye.
> The eye can not see forms of higher.
> Neither the consciousness. Their forms,
> And two of body, too, on any.

Well, what body supports the consciousness? When the eye sees form, are the body, eye, form, and consciousness on the same level only or can they also be on different levels? you ask. When someone in the Desire realm looks with his own eye at a form of the Desire realm, all four are on the same level. When that same Desire-realm individual looks at form of the Desire realm with the eye of the first dhyana, the body and form are both on the level of Desire, but the consciousness and eye are on the level of the first dhyana. When he looks at forms of the first dhyana, the form is also on the level of the first dhyana.

When the Desire-realm individual looks at his own level's forms with the eye of the second dhyana, both the body and form are on the Desire-realm individual's own level, but the eye is on the level of the second dhyana, and the eye consciousness is on the level of the first dhyana, because there is no eye consciousness above the first dhyana.[77] When he looks at the form of the first dhyana, the eye consciousness and form are on the level of the first dhyana, the body is of the Desire realm and the eye is on the level of the second dhyana. In the same way, the others can be extensively known.

This is determined as follows: **The body** of a higher level **can not have** or support **a lower** level's **eye**, because one has the superior eye of their own level, so there is no need to manifest the inferior eye of a lower level. **The eye** of a lower level **can not** have the power to **see** the **forms of higher** levels, because the eye of the lower is coarse and the forms of the higher are subtle. **Neither** is **the** higher level's eye **consciousness** supported by a lower level's eye, because the superior consciousness of the higher is not supported by the inferior eye of the lower, just as a clay jug does not hold lion's milk.[78] **Their**—the higher, lower, and own levels'—**forms** of all types are visible to the eye consciousness of the first dhyana as its object. It is possible for the **two**, the form and eye consciousness, **of the body, too,** to be **on any** the levels—one's own level, the higher levels, and the lower levels.

(2) Teaching that the ear is comparable to that

47a The ear is similar, as well.

As has been explained for the eye, **the ear is similar, as well.** The verse could be modified:

> The body can not have a lower ear.
> The ear can not hear sounds of higher.
> Neither the consciousness. Their sounds,
> And two of body, too, on any.

(3) Ascertaining the nose, tongue, and body. This has two points.

(a) General

47b The three are all of their own level.

The object, body, and support of **the three**—the nose, tongue, and body consciousness—**are all of their own level.**

(b) Specifics

47cd The consciousness of body is lower,
Own level.

Are these three always like that? you ask. That is in general. In specific, when perceiving the touch of the second dhyana and above, **the consciousness of body is** that of the **lower** first dhyana. When someone in either Desire or the first dhyana feels a touch, they perceive it with the consciousness of their **own level.**

(4) Teaching the mind as uncertain

47d Mind is indefinite.

The **mind**'s object, body, and consciousness **are indefinite**, because sometimes they are all on a comparable level and sometimes they are on lower or higher levels. This will be explained extensively in the "Teachings on Absorption," so refer there.

5. Which element is the object of which consciousness

> 48a Two consciousnesses, five external.

Which of the six consciousnesses knows which of the eighteen elements? you ask. The **two consciousnesses** of faculty and mind take the **five external** elements from form to touch as their objects—form is the object of both the eye and mind consciousnesses, sound of both ear and mind consciousnesses, and so on. The internal twelve elements and dharmas are the objects of the mind consciousness only.

6. Classifying as permanent or impermanent

> 48b Noncompound dharmas are permanent.

Of the elements, how many are permanent? How many impermanent? you ask. Of the eighteen elements, there is none that is wholly permanent. However, a portion of the element of dharmas is permanent: **noncompound dharmas are permanent.** The remaining seventeen and a half elements have arising and disintegration, so they are proven to be impermanent.

7. Classifying by whether or not they are faculties

> 48cd One part of dharmas and those taught
> As the internal twelve are faculties.

Of these, how many are faculties? How many are not faculties? you ask. Of the eighteen elements, **one part of** the element of **dharma**—life force, the five feelings, faith and the other four, and the three undefiled faculties, making fourteen—**and those** of elements **taught as the internal twelve**—the eye and so forth—**are faculties.** The remainder are not faculties. One portion of the body is the male and female faculties. Those that remain, the five external elements of form and so forth, and the remainder of the dharma element, are proven not to be faculties.

The presentation of the area's name

> This completes the first area called "Teachings on the Elements" from the *Verses of the Treasury of Abhidharma.*

This completes the explanation of **the first area called "Teachings on the Elements" from** *The Explanation of* ***the*** **Verses of the Treasury of Abhidharma** called *The Essence of the Ocean of Abhidharma, The Words of Those who Know and Love, Explaining the Youthful Play, Opening the Eyes of Dharma, the Chariot of Easy Practice.*

A few words here:

> Through the analysis that knows all knowables,
> The dharma nature will be known just as it is.
> Since they are the base for both attachment and detachment,
> I have explained the presentation
> Of aggregates, sense bases, and the elements.

SECOND AREA

Teachings on the Faculties

You make the lotus of your students' intellect blossom
And expel the darkness of the night of ignorance.
To the great Master praised as the regent,
The friend, the sun, I prostrate, then

In this, rather than imposing my own concepts,
But by penetrating the depths of unchanging intelligence
Of the entire progression of schools of sutra and tantra,
I will release the mass of deep scriptural meaning.

The second area, the "Teaching on the Faculties," has an explanation of the text of the area and a presentation of the area's name. The explanation of the text of the area has three topics: I. The nature of the faculties, II. The manner in which composites arise, and III. The explanation of causes, conditions, and results.

I. The nature of the faculties. This has two topics: A. Identifying each faculty, and B. Understanding the aspects of the faculties' natures.

A. Identifying each faculty. This has three topics: 1. Explaining the names of each faculty, 2. Establishing the number of faculties, and 3. The individual characteristics of the faculties.

1. Explaining the names of each faculty. This has two points.

a. According to the Great Exposition tradition

1. Five exercise their power over
   Four meanings. Four over two, it's claimed.
   The five and eight, over all-afflicted
   And over the utterly pure.

In the first chapter, where it says "The internal twelve are faculties,"[79] what are the faculties? Where it says, "Composite dharmas are the five..."[80] what is the manner in which these composites arise? you ask. In order to explain the answers to these questions in depth, this second area is presented.

The meaning of the word *faculty* is as explained in the autocommentary:

> What is the meaning of faculty (*indriya*)? you ask. The root *idi* signifies supreme controlling power. Exercising power over that, they are faculties. For that reason, exercising power is the meaning of faculty.

There are twenty-two faculties: the five sense faculties of eye, ear, nose, tongue, and body; the mind faculty; the faculty of life force; the male and female faculties; the five feelings of pleasure, suffering, mental pleasure, mental unhappiness, and neutral; the five of faith, diligence, mindfulness, samadhi, and full knowing; and the three undefiled of producing all-knowing, all-knowing, and having all-knowing.

Of these twenty-two faculties, which faculty exercises power over what? you ask. Except for the inactive faculties,[81] the **five** faculties of eye and so forth **exercise their power over four meanings** each: beautifying the support, protecting the body, producing the consciousnesses and their concurrences, and exercising exclusive power over the perception of their own object.

The **four** faculties of male, female, life force, and mind each exercise power **over two** purposes. The first two differentiate sentient beings and differentiate their specifics, such as shape, whether they have large or small breasts, and whether they have high or low voices. The faculty of life force exercises power over rebirth-linking in a likeness[82] and correctly maintaining the likeness' continuum. The faculty of mind exercises power over rebirth-linking in the next existence and harmonizing the other faculties with the mind.[83] The meaning of life force exercising power over rebirth-linking is as said:

> If at that time, a scent-eater[84] has either of two minds—a mind associated with affection or a mind associated with anger—become manifest...

The meaning of the mind exercising power over rebirth-linking is extensively explained in the sutra that says, "This world is led by the mind… " "**It's claimed**" is a skeptical word from the Sutra school for the Great Exposition.

The five defiled feelings **and** the **eight** faculties of faith, diligence, mindfulness, samadhi, full knowing, producing all-knowing, all-knowing, and having all-knowing exercise respectively power **over** the **all-afflicted and over** the **utterly pure.** The five feelings produce greed, hatred, and delusion. During the paths of accumulation and joining, the five from faith to full knowing are the cause of the utterly pure, and in the paths of seeing, meditation, and nonlearning, the eight are utterly pure in essence.

b. According to the Sutra school tradition

2. For power to focus on their own
   Or all objects, six faculties.
   For power over femaleness and maleness:
   The body's female and male faculties.

3. For power to maintain one's likeness,
   The all-afflicted, and the pure;
   Life, feelings, and five faculties
   Of faith and so forth are proposed.

4. To attain high, higher, and nirvana,
   Et cetera, there are faculties of
   Producing all-knowing, all-knowing,
   And having all-knowing as well.

By saying, "It is claimed," the Sutra school said the Great Exposition tradition was illogical. Now to present their own tradition: There are six faculties from eye to mind. Of these, the five internal elements wield the **power to focus on their own** objects, and the mind wields power over focus on **all** six **objects** of form and so forth. For that reason, there are **six** distinct **faculties.**

For exercising **power over** that which defines **femaleness**, the female faculty is presented, **and** for power over that which defines **maleness**, the male faculty is presented. **The body's female and male faculties** are presented as a part of the body faculty, from which they are not separate.

For exercising **power to maintain one's own likeness,** over **the all-afflicted, and** over **the** utterly **pure,** respectively the faculty of **life** force, the faculties of the **feelings, and** the **five faculties of faith and so forth are proposed.**

This defines the faculties of producing all-knowing, all-knowing, and having all-knowing as faculties. To exercise the power **to attain** the **high** (all-knowing), the **higher** (having all-knowing), and **nirvana** without remainder, **et cetera,** in order **there are** the three **faculties of producing all-knowing, all-knowing, and having all-knowing**, which are presented. The words, "**as well**" mean that just as the eye and so forth are faculties, these three are also faculties. The words "et cetera" indicate that these three faculties also exercise power respectively to abandon the discards of seeing, to abandon the discards of meditation, and to reside blissfully in the visible—that is, in this lifetime.

2. Establishing the number of faculties. This has two points.

a. The Great Exposition tradition

> 5. There are as many faculties as
> The mind's supports, distinctions, and
> That which maintains, those which afflict,
> Gatherers, and the utterly pure.

If exercising power is a faculty, there are many powers such as creating karmic formations out of ignorance, speaking with the mouth, and so on, so fixing the number of faculties at twenty-two is illogical, you say. This is not a fault. Those exercise some small bit of power but do not exercise exclusive power, so they are not presented as faculties.

Therefore to provide **the mind's support,** there are the six faculties from eye to mind. To create **distinctions** in the bodily support, there are the female and male faculties. To **maintain** one's likeness in a similar body, there is the life force faculty. To make the consciousnesses all-**afflicted,** there are the feelings. Because they are the basis for **gathering** the utterly pure accumulations, there are the five of faith and so forth. **And** for power over the essence of **the utterly pure,** the last three faculties are presented. There are this many dharmas to exercise power over, and **there are as many faculties as** that, so their number is determined.

b. The Sutra school tradition

> 6. Or as supports for entry, birth,
> Remaining, and enjoying there are
> Fourteen, and likewise for the reverse
> There are the other faculties.

Or else one can alternatively establish the number of faculties as follows: **as**

they provide **support for entry** into samsara, there are the six from the eye to the mind. As they are the cause for **birth** in samsara, there are the male and female faculties. As it leads to **remaining** there, there is the life-force faculty. **And** as they are the cause of **enjoying** or making use of samsara, there are the feelings. Thus **there are** the **fourteen** faculties for the purpose of entering samsara.

And just as the entry into samsara has faculties for its support, birth, remaining, and enjoyment, **likewise for the reverse** of samsara as well, **there are the** faculties that exercise power over the support, birth, remaining, and enjoyment of the utterly pure. The support for the birth of the utterly pure is the five of faith and so forth. For power over the initial birth of the utterly pure, there is the faculty of producing all-knowing. For power over remaining in the utterly pure, there is the faculty of all-knowing, and for power over enjoying the utterly pure, there is the faculty of having all-knowing. These faculties are **other** than those that enter samsara; they are **faculties** that reverse samsara.

3. The individual characteristics of the faculties. This has two topics: a. The characteristics of the five faculties of feeling, and b. The characteristics of the three stainless faculties.

a. The characteristics of the five faculties of feeling. This has three topics: i. Bodily feelings of pleasure and suffering, ii. Mental feelings of pleasure and suffering, and iii. Neutral feelings.

i. Bodily feelings of pleasure and suffering. This has two points.

(1) Suffering

7ab The faculty of suffering
Is any unpleasant bodily feeling.

Among the twenty-two faculties, the seven faculties that have form and the faculty of mind have been explained. Life force and the five of faith and so forth will be explained below. Here the five faculties of feeling and the three undefiled faculties will be explained.

In this section, *body* is proposed to mean any of the faculties that have form. **The faculty of suffering is any unpleasant bodily feeling** associated with the five sense faculties, whatever it might be.

(2) Pleasure

7cd Pleasant is pleasure. On third dhyana
The mind's is the faculty of pleasure.

Any **pleasant** feeling associated with the sense faculties **is the faculty of pleasure.** Not only that, any pleasant feeling that arises in association with **the mind on** the **third dhyana is the faculty of** cognitive **pleasure.** This is because the five sense-gate consciousnesses are not present on that level, so there is no bodily feeling. The joy of the first two dhyanas is mental pleasure, but on the third level one is free of attachment to joy, so the pleasure felt on the third level is also not mental pleasure. Therefore, the faculty of pleasure combines the bodily pleasure of the sense faculties and the cognitive pleasure of the third dhyana.

ii. Mental feelings of pleasure and suffering. This has two points.

(1) Mental happiness

8a On others, it is mental pleasure.

On levels that are **other** than the third dhyana—Desire and the first two dhyanas—any pleasant feeling that is associated with the mental consciousness, whatever **it** might be, **is** the faculty of **mental pleasure,** because on those levels one is not free of attachment to joy. The distinction between cognitive pleasure and mental pleasure is that mental joy of the levels from Desire to the second dhyana is merely produced by thought and is unstable. That is mental pleasure. On the third dhyana, the pleasant feeling in the mind that remains stably is cognitive pleasure.

(2) Unhappiness

8bc Unpleasant feelings in the mind
Are unhappiness,

Any **unpleasant feelings** that arise **in** association with **the mind** consciousness **are** the faculty of mental **unhappiness.**

iii. Neutral feelings. This has two points.

(1) Characteristics

8cd and neutral feelings
Are middling

And the faculty of **neutral feeling is** a **middling** experience that is neither pleasant nor unpleasant.

(2) The reason neutral is not divided into bodily and of mental

8d since both are thought-free

Is this neutral feeling of body or of mind? you ask. Neutral is both bodily and mental **since** the middling neutral feelings of **both** body and mind **are thought-free** and born from within. The feelings of pleasure and suffering of both body and mind are not like that, so they are explained separately.

b. The characteristics of the three stainless faculties

9ab On the paths of seeing, meditation,
And of nonlearning, nine are three.

On the paths of seeing, meditation, and of nonlearning, the **nine** faculties of mind, pleasure, mental pleasure, neutral feelings, and the five including faith and so forth **are** called the **three** stainless faculties. This is because on the path of seeing these nine are the faculty of producing all-knowing; on the path of meditation they are the faculty of all-knowing, and on the path of no learning they are the faculty of having all-knowing.

B. Understanding the aspects of the faculties' natures. This has four topics: 1. Teaching the full classification of their aspects, 2. How they are acquired, 3. The number of faculties present when attaining a result, and 4. How the faculties are possessed.

1. Teaching the full classification of their aspects. This has six points: a. Whether they are defiled and undefiled, b. Whether they are fully ripened or not, c. Whether they produce fully ripened results, d. Aspects of virtuous, nonvirtuous, and neutral, e. Aspects of which realm they are in, and f. Whether they are discarded.

a. Whether they are defiled and undefiled

9cd Three stainless. Those with form, life force,
And suffering are defiled. Nine twofold.

How many of the faculties are defiled and how many are undefiled? you ask. The **three** faculties that were just explained are **stainless** or undefiled only. **Those** seven faculties **with form,** the faculty of **life force, and** the faculty of **suffering are** solely **defiled,** because they are discarded by meditation. The **nine** faculties including mind, pleasure, mental pleasure, neutral, and the five of faith and so forth are **twofold**—either defiled or undefiled—because when they are associated with the paths of seeing, learning, and no learning, they are undefiled, but otherwise they are defiled.

b. Whether they are fully ripened or not

10a–c Life force is fully ripened. Twelve
Are twofold, except the last eight
And mental unhappiness.

Well then, how many of these are fully ripened results, you ask. The faculty of **life force is fully ripened** only, because in the higher realms it is propelled by defiled virtue, and in the lower realms it is propelled by nonvirtue.

In the great *Ṭika* there is an extensive discussion of whether life force is fully ripened or not, the distinction between life force and life, proposals by Venerable Ghoṣaka and others, the necessity for the Teacher to prolong or forsake his life, and so forth. The Master's explanation is in agreement with Venerable Ghoṣaka. From the autocommentary:

> Therefore, that life force [of an individual who has extended his life through the power of meditation] is not fully ripened, but other than that, it [life force] is fully ripened.

The necessity for an arhat to prolong or forsake his life is as said:

> When one has acted well with Brahmic conduct
> And meditated fully on the path,
> There will be joy at extinguishing one's life,
> As if it were like being free of sickness.

Twelve faculties can **be** either of the **two**—either fully ripened or not. The twelve are the faculties **except** for **the last eight and mental unhappiness**: the seven that have form plus mind and four of the feelings. The seven that have form—eye, and so forth—are not fully ripened when produced by development, but are when produced by full ripening. Mental feelings that are virtuous or afflicted, that are associated with the paths of activity such as crafts, or that are associated with emanated minds, are not fully ripened. Those other than that are fully ripened.

The last eight of faith and so forth are only virtuous. Mental unhappiness is always either virtuous or nonvirtuous. For these reasons, these nine are proven not to be fully ripened.[85]

c. Whether they produce fully ripened results

10cd That one
Must have full ripening. Ten twofold:

11a Mind, other feelings, faith, so forth.

How many of these have full ripening? How many do not? you ask. **That one** faculty of mental unhappiness alone **must** always **have full ripening,** because it is always either nonvirtue or defiled virtue. **Ten** faculties are **twofold** as they can either have full ripening or not. These ten are the **mind** faculty, the **other** four **feelings** excluding mental unhappiness, and the five of **faith** and **so forth**. The nonvirtue of mind and the four feelings as well as the defiled virtue of all ten have full ripening; the neutral and undefiled of all ten have no full ripening. The seven that have form and life force are neutral, and the last three are undefiled, so they are proven not to have full ripening.

d. Aspects of virtuous, nonvirtuous, and neutral

11b–d Eight virtuous. Unhappiness
Is twofold. Mind and other feelings
Are threefold, and the rest are onefold.

How many of these are virtuous, nonvirtuous, and neutral? you ask. The last **eight** are always **virtuous.** Mental **unhappiness** is **twofold:** either virtue or nonvirtue. **Mind and** the **other** four **feelings are threefold,** because they can be concurrent with all three, **and the rest**, the seven that have form plus life force, are **onefold**—neutral only.

e. Aspects of which realm they are in

> 12. Except the stainless, in Desire.
> Except male, female faculties,
> And sufferings: in Form. In Formless
> There are none with form, nor any pleasures.

Among the faculties, how many are in the Desire, Form and Formless realms? you ask. **Except the** three **stainless** faculties, nineteen of the faculties are found **in** the **Desire realm. Except** the **male** and **female faculties, and** the mental and bodily **sufferings**, fifteen of the faculties are also found **in** the **Form realm.** Those four faculties are not found there for the following reasons: Because those in the higher realms are free of desire for sex, there are no male or female faculties. Because the body is extremely pure and the cause of bodily suffering, nonvirtue, is not present, there is no bodily suffering. Because one's continuum is moistened by tranquility meditation, and the nine causes of mental unhappiness[86] have been discarded, there is no mental unhappiness.

Of those fifteen faculties, **in** the **Formless** realm **there are none** of the five **with form, nor** are there **any** bodily and mental **pleasures,** so there are the eight faculties of life force, mind, neutrality, and the five of faith and so forth. The five with form are not in Formless because there is no form there. There is neither pleasure nor mental happiness there because one is detached from both of those.

It should be known that the three stainless faculties are in all instances outside of the realms.

f. Whether they are discarded

> 13. Mind and three feelings are threefold.
> The two discard unhappiness.
> By meditation, nine. Five not
> Discarded, also. Three are not.

How many of them are discarded by seeing? How many by meditation? How many are not discarded? The **mind and** the **three feelings** of pleasure, mental pleasure, and neutral feeling **are threefold**: one part is discarded by seeing, one part by meditation, and the third part is not discarded. Those that are concurrent with discards of seeing are discarded by seeing. Those that are defiled virtue are discards of meditation. Those that are undefiled are not discarded.

The two paths of meditation and seeing **discard** mental **unhappiness.** The faculties discarded **by meditation** only are the **nine**—the seven with form, life force, and suffering because they are defiled dharmas which are not discarded by seeing. The undefiled portion of the **five** faculties of faith and so forth are **not discarded.** The word "**also**" indicates that their defiled portion is discarded by meditation. The last **three are not** discarded because they are undefiled.

2. How the faculties are acquired. This has two topics: a. The actual way they are acquired, and b. Additionally, the way they cease.

a. The actual way they are acquired. This has three topics: i. Obtaining them in the Desire realm, ii. In the Form realm, and iii. In the Formless realm.

i. Obtaining them in the Desire realm. This has two points.

(1) General

> 14ab In Desire, at first one gains the two
> Full ripened.

In each realm, how many fully ripened faculties are acquired at first? you ask. **In Desire**, in the first three of the four modes of birth—birth from egg, warmth and moisture, and the womb—**at first one gains the two** faculties that are **fully ripened** by nature because the two faculties of body and life force are acquired.

Well then, is not the mind faculty also acquired? you ask. Of course it is acquired, but it is afflicted, as explained in the verse, "The state of rebirth is afflicted."[87] For that reason, it is not fully ripened.[88]

(2) Specific

> 14bc Not miraculous birth—
> With that, six, seven, or else eight.

Not just two fully ripened faculties are attained in **miraculous birth**. **With that**, miraculous birth, in the case of a miraculous birth of a being with no sexual organs, such as humans in the first aeon,[89] that being attains **six** fully ripened faculties: the first sense faculties of eye and so forth, and life force. Or if the being has one sexual organ, they also attain either one of the sexual faculties for a total of **seven. Or** if the being has two sexual organs, they attain both for a total of **eight** fully ripened faculties acquired. In the higher realms, there is no miraculous birth with two sexual organs, but there is in the lower realms.

ii. Obtaining them in the Form realm

14d There are six in Form

There are six faculties acquired **in Form**, because the five sense faculties and life force are acquired.

iii. Obtaining them in the Formless realm

14d and one above.

And only the **one** faculty of life force is newly acquired **above** that in the Formless realm, because there are no other fully ripened faculties in that realm.

b. Additionally the way the faculties cease. This has two topics: i. General, and ii. The particulars of when a virtuous mind is possessed.

i. General. This has three topics: (1) The manner of cessation in Formless, (2) The manner of cessation in Form, and (3) The manner of cessation in Desire.

(1) The manner of cessation in Formless

15ab When dying in Formless, just life force
And mind and neutral feeling cease.

When dying in the three realms, which of the faculties cease simultaneously? you ask. **When dying in** the **Formless** realms, **just** the three of **life force, and mind, and neutral feeling cease** simultaneously.

(2) The manner of cessation in Form

15c In Form, eight cease.

In Form, those three and the five sense organs, for a total of **eight** faculties, **cease** simultaneously.

(3) The manner of cessation in Desire. This has two points.

(a) The manner of cessation for miraculous birth

15cd With miraculous
Birth in Desire, ten, nine, or eight.

For beings born by **miraculous birth in Desire** who have two sexual organs, **ten** faculties stop simultaneously: the eight just mentioned plus the two sexual organs. For those with one organ, **nine, or** for those with no organs, **eight.**

(b) For birth from womb

16a In gradual deaths, the four will cease.

In gradual deaths, the four faculties of life force, mind, neutral feeling, and body **will cease** simultaneously.

ii. The particulars of when a virtuous mind is possessed

16b In virtuous, add five to all.

When dying **in** a **virtuous** mind-state, **add** the **five** faculties of faith and so forth **to all**, the faculties that cease in each of the six different types of death in the Three Realms discussed above. Therefore in the Formless realm, eight faculties stop simultaneously; in the Form realm, thirteen; and in the Desire realm fifteen or so forth stop simultaneously.

There is no gradual death in the two higher realms because one is born there by miraculous birth.[90] The undefiled faculties do not cease at death.

3. Number of faculties present when attaining a result. This has three points.

a. How many are present when the last two results are attained

16c Two outer results are gained with nine.

When counting either from the top or the bottom, the **two outer results** of arhat and stream-enterer **are** both **gained with nine** faculties each. The result of stream-enterer is attained with the six common faculties—mind and the five of faith and so forth—plus the faculties of neutral feeling, producing all-knowing, and all-knowing for a total of nine. Arhatship is attained by the same six common faculties; any one of the feelings of pleasure, mental pleasure, or neutral; and the faculties of all-knowing and having all-knowing for a total of nine.

b. Second, when the middle two results are attained

16d The two with seven, eight, or nine.

The two results of once-returner and nonreturner are attained **with seven, eight, or nine** faculties. If they are attained by successive results and the worldly path, then they are attained by the five of faith and so forth, mind, and neutral feeling. If it is a transworldly path, in addition to those there is the faculty of all-knowing for a total of eight. When attained by skipping results, they are attained by nine. The result of once-returner is attained by the same faculties as lead to stream-enterer, and nonreturner is attained by nine: the six common faculties, any one of the three feelings, producing all-knowing, and all-knowing.

c. Third, refuting a challenge

17ab Because it's possible to attain
Arhat with eleven, it is taught.

If it is possible to attain the state of arhat with nine faculties, then that is contradictory of the treatise *Jñānaprasthāna* where it states that arhat is attained with eleven faculties, you say. That explanation of attaining the state of arhat with eleven faculties and this explanation of attaining it with nine are not contradictory. This is **because it is possible** that some might **attain** the state of **arhat**, regress from the result over and over again,[91] and then re-attain it **with eleven** faculties, so **it is taught** there as eleven. Here it is taught as nine faculties in terms of attaining arhat a single time.

The manner in which it is possible to attain arhat by eleven is as follows: First one attains the state of arhat with the faculty of pleasure. Then one regresses from the result, and restores the result with the faculty of mental pleasure. Then one regresses again and restores again with the faculty of neutral feeling.

4. How the faculties are possessed. This has three topics: a. Must-haves, b. Minimum possessed, and c. Maximum possessed.

a. Must-haves. This has seven points: i. Three must-haves, ii. Four must-haves, iii. Five must-haves, iv. Seven must-haves, v. Eight must-haves, vi. Eleven must-haves, and vii. Thirteen must-haves.

i. Three must-haves

17cd One who possesses neutral feeling,
Life force, or mind must have the three.

If someone has any particular faculty, then how many faculties must they necessarily possess? **One who possesses** any one of the faculties of **neutral feeling, life force, or mind must have** all three of them. This pervades, because **the three** are must-haves.

Well then, when absorbed in the two mind-free states, because there is neither mind nor neutral feeling, therefore one must not have life force either, you say. Mind and neutral feeling are not manifestly present, but because they have been attained, it is logical that they are possessed.

ii. Four must-haves

> 18a Those who have pleasure or body, four,

Those who have either the faculty of **pleasure or** the **body** faculty, they must have four faculties, because that one is added to the three must-haves for a total of **four** which must necessarily be had.

iii. Five must-haves

> 18bc And five have those who've eyes, et cetera,
> Or mental pleasure.

Those who have any one of the faculties of **eye, et cetera**—ear, nose, and tongue—then they must **have five**, because in addition to that, they have the three must-haves and the body faculty. **Or** if they have **mind pleasure,** they must have five, because one has the three must-haves, pleasure, and mental pleasure.

Does someone who has been born in the second dhyana and who has not attained the third dhyana possess a faculty of pleasure? you ask. They possess the afflicted pleasure of the third dhyana.

iv. Seven must-haves

> 18cd Those who have
> Suffering, seven,

Those who have the faculty of **suffering** must have **seven**, because they must have body, life force, mind, and the four feelings excluding mental unhappiness.

v. Eight must-haves

18d and the female

19a Faculty and so forth have eight.

Those who possess either **the female faculty and so forth,** the male faculty, must **have eight** faculties, because they have that one in addition to the seven mentioned above. Not only that, one who possesses mental unhappiness must also have eight because they have mental unhappiness in addition to those seven. Those who possess the five faculties of faith and so forth must have the three must-haves in addition to those five for a total of eight.

vi. Eleven must-haves

19bc Those with the faculty of having
All-knowing have eleven.

Those with either of **the faculties of** all-knowing or **having all-knowing** must **have eleven** faculties because in addition to either of those, they must have the three must-haves, pleasure, mental pleasure, and the five of faith, and so forth.

vii. Thirteen must-haves

19cd With
Producing all-knowing, thirteen.

With the faculty of **producing all-knowing,** one must have **thirteen** faculties, because one must have mind, life force, body, the feelings with the exception of mental unhappiness, the five of faith, and so forth, and producing all-knowing. As this is the path of seeing, they must have either the male or the female faculty, but since it is not definite which of the two is possessed, neither is mentioned here.

b. Minimum possessed. This has two points.

i. The minimum possessed by those with no virtue

20ab Those without virtue who've the fewest
Have eight: life, body, feelings, mind.

What is the minimum number of faculties that one can have? you ask. In Desire, **those** who are at the moment of death and are **without virtue** from severing its roots are the ones **who have the fewest** faculties. They **have** the **eight** faculties of **life force, body,** five **feelings,** and **mind.**

ii. The minimum possessed by the childish in the Formless realm

> 20cd The childish of the Formless likewise
> Have neutral, life force, mind, and virtues.

The childish[92] beings **of the Formless realm likewise** have eight because they **have** the faculties of **neutral** feeling, **life force, mind, and** the five **virtues** of faith and so forth.

c. Maximum possessed. This has two points.

i. Ordinary individuals

> 21ab The most that one could have is nineteen
> Except the stainless, with two organs.

What is the maximum number of faculties that one can possess? you ask. **The most** faculties **that one** individual **could** possibly **have is nineteen,** as one can have all of them **except the** three **stainless** faculties. Who could possess all these? you ask. Some individuals **with two** sexual **organs** could possess them.

ii. Nobles

> 21cd And nobles who are attached could have
> All but one organ and two stainless.

And nobles who are stream-enterers or once-returners and **who are attached**[93] **could** also **have** nineteen faculties. As it is impossible for nobles to have two sexual organs, they can possess **all** the faculties **but one organ and** either the first and last or the last **two stainless** faculties. If they are detached from the Desire realm, they do not have mental unhappiness, so it specifies that they are attached.

II. The manner in which composites arise. This has two topics: A. Those with form, and B. Those without form.

A. Those with form. This has three points.

1. Those that arise with eight substances

> 22ab In Desire, atoms without sound
> Or faculties: eight substances.

In the Realm of **Desire, atoms,** the smallest agglomerated masses that appear to the mind to have parts but are **without** either **sound or faculties** of body and so forth, definitely arise simultaneously with the **eight substances,** because they arise simultaneously with the substances of the four sources and the four source-derived.[94]

2. Those that arise with nine substances

> 22c With body faculty, nine substances.

Those smallest masses **with** the **body faculty** have **nine substances,** because they have that faculty in addition to the previous eight, for a total of nine.

3. Those that arise with ten substances

> 22d Another faculty, ten substances.

If in addition they have **another faculty,** they have **ten substances,** because in addition to the previous nine they have any one of the eye and so forth.

Saying "agglomerated" above eliminates single partless particles that do not arise in a collection.

B. Those without form. This has two topics: 1. Overview, and 2. Explanation.

1. Overview

> 23a–c The mind and factors must arise together.
> All with the characteristics of composites.
> Attainment, sometimes.

The primary **mind and** its associated mental **factors must arise together** at the same time because they cannot mutually cannot arise without each other. As is said in a sutra:

> Without the mental factors,
> The mind cannot arise at all,
> Just like the sun and the sun's rays,
> It is always simultaneous with them.

All composites must arise simultaneously **with the characteristics of composites:** arising, staying, aging, and disintegrating. The **attainment** that is included within their stream of being arises at the same time as the dharma that is attained, like a body and its shadow. This is in terms of attainment that arises at the same time; attainment that arises earlier or later is not so.

The word "**sometimes**" is a word of inquiry. Its purpose is to inform that the attainment of the two cessations arises, but the cessations that are attained do not arise.

2. Explanation. This has two topics: a. An extensive explanation of those that are concurrent with mind, and b. An extensive explanation of nonconcurrent formations.

a. The extensive explanation of those that are concurrent with mind. This has two topics: i. Brief overview, and ii. Extensive explanation.

i. Brief overview

> 23cd Factors are fivefold,
> Since there are different major grounds and so forth.

Mental **factors are fivefold** groups, **since there are** the **different major grounds and so forth**.

ii. Extensive explanation. This has four topics: (1) The classification of the major grounds, (2) Which mental factors arise in association with which cognition, (3) Drawing distinctions between similar factors, and (4) Teaching synonyms.

(1) The classification of the major grounds. This has five topics: (a) The major ground of cognition, (b) The virtuous major ground, (c) The afflicted major ground, (d) The nonvirtuous major ground, and (e) The major ground of minor near afflictions.

(a) The major ground of cognition

24. Feeling, volition, and conception,
    Intention, contact, intelligence,
    And mindfulness, attention, interest,
    Samadhi are with all cognitions.

Feeling, which in essence is experience; **volition,** which makes the mind move to the object; **and conception** of attributes; **intention** which wishes to attain its aim; **contact** which, after the object, faculty and consciousness combine, determines whether an object is pleasant, unpleasant, or neutral; **intelligence** or full knowing which distinguishes defiled and undefiled dharmas; **and mindfulness,** which can hold the mind on its focus without forgetting it; **attention,** which aims the minds toward and engages the focus; **interest,** which is desire which perceives qualities in the focus; and **samadhi,** which makes the mind one-pointed, **are** the ten factors called the major ground of cognitions. They are called so because they arise in association **with all cognitions**.

(b) The virtuous major ground

25. Faith, carefulness, and pliancy,
    Equanimity, shame, modesty,
    Two roots, and nonhostility,
    And diligence are with all virtue.

Faith is the sincere purity of a mind that is free of the dirt of the afflictions and near afflictions. **Carefulness** is to value virtuous dharmas such as faith and to protect the mind from the defiled. **And pliancy** is workability of the mind that can withstand aiming toward its focus. Between immeasurable equanimity and the formation equanimity, **equanimity** here is the latter: it is the mind that spontaneously engages without dullness or agitation. **Shame** and **modesty** are both presented from the aspect of abstaining from the inherently un wholesome. They will be explained below.[95] The **two** virtuous **roots** of non-desire and nonhatred are the antidotes for greed and hatred. Nondelusion is designated as an aspect of full knowing, so it is included within the major ground of cognition **and** not mentioned here. **Nonhostility** is a loving heart, **and diligence** is a mind that is excited about virtuous actions. These ten are called the virtuous major ground because they **are** associated **with all virtuous** cognitions.

(c) The afflicted major ground

> 26a–c Delusion, carelessness, and laziness,
> Nonfaith, and torpor, agitation:
> With all afflicted.

Delusion is not knowing about karma, cause and effect, and so forth. Delusion and ignorance are equivalent. **Carelessness** is the opposite of carefulness: it is a mind not habituated to virtue. **And laziness** is the opposite of diligence: it is not being excited about virtue. **Nonfaith** is the opposite of faith: it is impurity in the mind. **And torpor** makes the mind unworkable and hazy. **Agitation** is disturbance in the mind. These six are the greater afflicted major ground because they arise **with all afflicted** cognitions.

(d) The nonvirtuous major ground

> 26cd With nonvirtue,
> Immodesty and shamelessness.

In association **with** all **nonvirtuous** cognitions, **immodesty and shamelessness** must always arise.

(e) The major ground of minor near afflictions

> 27. Aggression, grudge, deceit, and envy,
> Contentiousness, hypocrisy,
> Stinginess, pretense, arrogance, and
> Hostility: grounds of minor afflictions.

Aggression is to get angry with beings who might cause harm and fight with them. **Grudges** or resentment is to hold a grudge after getting angry. **Deceit** is a mind that does not accept faults to be faults and has the aspect of fooling, **and envy** or jealousy is not being able to bear it when someone else has something desirable. **Contentiousness** is to embrace misdeeds as truly fine. As it is explained, "Contentiousness is attachment to misdeeds." **Hypocrisy** is to hide one's faults and keep them secret. **Stinginess** is not giving dharma or material things to others out of greed for them. **Pretense** is to contrive that one has qualities that one really does not out of greed for goods, fame, or so forth. **Arrogance** will be taught below,[96] **and hostility** is to wish suffering upon sentient beings. These ten are called the **grounds of** the **minor** near **afflictions** because the only root affliction they are concurrent with is ignorance, because they are discarded only by meditation, and because they only arise in association with cognitions in the mental consciousness that are discarded by meditation. Thus the companions they are concurrent with, their class of discards, and the support they arise from are all minor.

Within these five groups there are thirty-eight mental factors. These do not include the indefinite factors, which Vasumitra and Pūrṇavardhana list in their commentaries:

> Considering, examining,
> Regret, and sleep, and anger, greed,
> And pride, and doubt, so called: these eight
> Are taught to be indefinite.

These eight are called indefinite because unlike the major grounds, they do not definitely arise with any particular cognition.

Including these eight indefinite, there are forty-six mental factors. Why are they not all mentioned here? you ask. Although they are not explained, they can be understood from the meaning. The definite ones are explicitly taught, and the indefinite are implicitly understood.

In the Great Vehicle abhidharma there are said to be fifty-one mental factors. Why are they condensed into forty-six here? you ask. As five of the Great Vehicle's factors have only nominal existence, they are not included in this enumeration of those with substantial existence. The virtuous factor of nondelusion, the root affliction view, and the near affliction of nonawareness are designations given to different aspects of full knowing. The near affliction of distraction is a designation given to one aspect of samadhi. Forgetfulness is a designation for one part of mindfulness.[97]

(2) Which mental factors arise in association with which cognition. This has two topics: (a) Which mental factors arise in association with cognitions in Desire, and (b) Which factors arise in association with cognitions in the upper realms.

(a) Which mental factors arise in association with the cognitions in Desire. This has four topics: (i) What is associated with virtuous cognitions, (ii) Nonvirtuous cognitions, (iii) Neutral cognitions, and (iv) Sleep added as a clarification.

(i) What is associated with virtuous cognitions. This has two points.

A. General

28a–c Minds in Desire, when virtuous, have
Considering and examining,
So they have twenty-two mental factors,

Minds in Desire, when virtuous, have or are accompanied by the associated mental factors of the first two major grounds, **considering, and examining, so** therefore **they have twenty-two mental factors** that arise.

B. Specific

28d Some are augmented by regret.

Some virtuous cognitions of Desire have twenty-three associated mental factors because it is possible that regret might arise in association with them, so the number of mental factors **is augmented by** one. **Regret** must be either virtuous or nonvirtuous.

(ii) What is associated with nonvirtuous cognitions

29. With unmixed minds that are nonvirtuous
And have view, too, the twenty arise.
If the four afflictions; or aggression,
Et cetera; or regret, twenty-one.

In association **with unmixed minds,** concurrent with unmixed ignorance, **that are nonvirtuous and have** the last three **views,**[98] **too, the twenty** mental factors **arise.** This is because the major ground of cognition, the afflicted major ground, the nonvirtuous major ground, consideration, and examination arise with these cognitions. **If** the cognition is associated with one of **the four** indefinite **afflictions** of greed, hatred, pride, or doubt; **or** one of the near afflictions such as **aggression, et cetera; or regret**, then there are **twenty-one**, because that affliction of greed or so forth is added to the previous twenty.

(iii) What is associated with neutral cognitions. This has two points.

A. Obscured neutral cognitions

30a In the obscured, eighteen.

In the obscured neutral cognitions that have personality and extreme views,[99] **eighteen** mental factors arise. The major ground of cognition, the afflicted major ground, consideration, and examination all arise. The distinction between obscured and unobscured is that although both are basically neutral, obscured neutral obscures or hinders liberation, but unobscured does not.

B. Unobscured neutral cognitions

30ab It's said
With other neutrals, there are twelve.

It is said that **with the other neutrals**, the unobscured neutral cognitions, **there are twelve** mental factors that arise, because in addition to the major ground of cognition, consideration and examination also arise.

(iv) Sleep added as a clarification

30cd Since sleep does not preclude any other,
Whenever it occurs, it's added.

Since sleep does not preclude any other, in that it can arise with all cognitions, whether virtuous, nonvirtuous, or neutral, **whenever it occurs,** associated with a principal cognition, **it is added.** If you added it to the verses, they would read as follows:

Minds in Desire, when sleepy and virtue,
Have considering and examining,
So there are twenty-three mental factors,
Some are augmented by regret.

With sleepy, unmixed, nonvirtuous minds
That have view, too, twenty-one arise.
If the four afflictions or aggression,
Et cetera, or regret, twenty-two.

In the obscured, nineteen. It's said
With other neutrals, there are thirteen.

(b) Which factors arise in association with cognitions in the upper realms. This has two topics: (i) Which are on the first dhyana, and (ii) Which are on the second dhyana and above.

(i) Which are on the first dhyana. This has two points.

A. Which are on the mere actual practice

> 31ab Of these, regret, sleep, and nonvirtues
> Are not on the first dhyana's levels.

Of these concurrent factors that have been proposed, **regret, sleep, and** the **nonvirtuous** cognitions—anger, shamelessness, immodesty, and the seven near afflictions other than deceit, pretense, and arrogance—**are not on the first dhyana's levels.** This is because regret and sleep are incompatible with samadhi, and one's continuum has been moistened by tranquility, so there is no nonvirtue.

B. On the special actual practice

> 31c In special, no considering;

In the **special** first dhyana not only are those factors absent, there is **no considering** because it has been abandoned.

(ii) Which are on the second dhyana and above

> 31d Above that, no examining, either.

Above that special dhyana on the levels from the second dhyana to the Peak of Existence there is **no examining**, because those levels transcend it. The word "**either**" teaches that deceit and pretense are also absent. In the first dhyana there is pretense and deceit, as will be explained below:

> Deceit and pretense are in Desire
> And on first dhyan, as Brahma deludes.[100]

(3) Drawing distinctions between similar factors. This has four topics: (a) The distinction between shamelessness and immodesty, (b) The distinction between affection and respect, (c) The distinction between consideration and examination, and (d) The distinction between pride and arrogance.

(a) The distinction between shamelessness and immodesty

> 32ab Shameless is disrespect; immodesty is
> To view the unwholesome without fear.

Well then, what is the distinction between shamelessness and immodesty? you ask. **Shamelessness is disrespect** for qualities and those who have qualities such as one's abbot, masters, and so forth. **Immodesty is to view the unwholesome**, such as killing and so forth, **without fear.**[101]

(b) The distinction between affection and respect. This has two points.

(i) Actual

> 32c Affection's faith; respect is shame.

Affection is faith in qualities and those who have qualities, and **respect is shame** that honors qualities and those who have qualities. Faith and respect in either qualities or individuals can also be presented as having four possibilities.

(ii) What realms these are in

> 32d These two are in Desire and Form.

Those two, affection and respect toward individuals, **are** found **in** the **Desire and** the **Form** realms, but they are not found in the Formless because in that realm individuals are not within each other's sphere of perception.

(c) The distinction between consideration and examination

> 33ab Considering and examining
> Are coarse and fine.

There is a distinction between **considering and examining**: they **are** respectively the **coarse and fine** mental factors that engage the aspects of the object's essence and particulars.

Well then, it is illogical that these both could arise simultaneously around a single cognition, you say. It is logical because by their combined power, the cognition becomes neither too coarse nor too fine. For example, if you were to put butter in cold water and then place it in the sun, by the power of both the water and the sun the butter would get neither too hot nor too cold. Some say that the explanation of both considering and examining arising in association with a single cognition is in terms of a continuum, but they are not simultaneous.

(d) The distinction between pride and arrogance

> 33b–d Pride is self-inflation.
> Arrogance is clinging to one's features
> Which then consumes the mind completely.

Pride and arrogance are separate because **pride is** the **self-inflation** of thinking that one is superior to others in terms social standing and qualities, while **arrogance is clinging to one's** own **features,** such as social standing or body, **which then consumes** or uses up **the mind completely.**

(4) Teaching synonyms. This has two points.

(a) Synonyms of cognition

> 34ab Cognition, mind, and consciousness
> Are equivalent.

In the sutras where it says, "Cognition, mind, and consciousness," what is the distinction between these three? There are many assertions of distinctions between these three in the Great Exposition, Sutra, and Yogic Conduct schools, but in our own tradition, the element of **cognition,** the sense base of **mind, and** the aggregate of **consciousness are equivalent.**

The Great Exposition school proposes that as they distinguish between virtue, nonvirtue, and so forth, they are presented as cognitions. As they know form and so forth, they are mind. As they know distinctions in the object, they are presented as consciousness.

(b) Parallels with mental factors

> 34b–d The mind and factors
> Have a support, a focus, aspects,
> Concurrence also that is fivefold.

The mind or mental **factors** are equivalent in **having** the eye and so forth as **support,** having **a focus** on form and so forth, and having an **aspect** such as thinking, "Blue!"

The **concurrence also** between mind and mental factors **is fivefold:** there is concurrence of support, focus, aspect, time, and substance.

b. The extensive explanation of nonconcurrent formations. This has three topics: i. Overview, ii. Explanation, and iii. Teaching other distinctions between dharmas as a summary.

i. Overview

> 35. Formations that are nonconcurrent
> Include attainment, nonattainment,
> Same class, Conception Free, absorptions,
> And life force and the characteristics,
>
> 36a Collections of names and so forth, too.

The fourteen **formations that are nonconcurrent** include 1) **attainment,** 2) **nonattainment,** 3) **same class,** 4) beings in the **Conception Free** abode, and the two **absorptions** of 5) the conception-free and 6) cessation, 7) **and life force and** 8-11) **the** four **characteristics** of composites, and **collections of** 12) **names and so forth** including 13) words, and 14) letters. The word "**too**" includes schism in the Sangha and the substance that is not wasted.

These are called nonconcurrent formations because they are in the aggregate of formations and not concurrent with mind.

ii. The explanation. This has seven topics: (1) The explanation of attainment and nonattainment, (2) Of same status, (3) Of nonconception, (4) Of the two absorptions, (5) Of life force, (6) Of the characteristics, and (7) Of names, words, and letters.

(1) The explanation of attainment and nonattainment. This has three topics: (a) Identifying their essence, (b) What they are of, and (c) Distinctions.

(a) Identifying their essence

> 36b Attainment is to get or have.

To classify **attainment,** there **is** the attainment of **getting** or acquiring **and** the attainment of **having** or possessing. The first has two: getting something anew, such as the first undefiled moment, and getting after regressing, such as getting what one had previously regressed from when attaining the actual practice of the dhyanas and formless absorptions. The attainment of having also has two: possessing the continuum, such as the second moment of the vows of individual liberation where one possesses the continuum of the first moment, and possession from the beginning, such as ordinary individuals who possess the afflictions of existence from the very beginning.

(b) What they are of. This has two points.

(i) General

> 36cd Attainment, nonattainment are of
> What is in one's stream

Attainment and **nonattainment are of** composites **that are** included **in one's** own **stream** of being, not of what is included in another being's continuum or not included in anyone's continuum.

(ii) Specifics

> 36d or two cessations.

The two noncomposite cessations are not connected with anyone's continuum, but since that which they negate can be connected to beings' continuums, there is attainment and nonattainment of the **two cessations.** Nonanalytic cessation is possessed by all sentient beings because it is said in the abhidharma:

> Who possesses undefiled dharmas? you ask. Answer. All sentient beings.

Analytic cessation is possessed by all nobles except those in the first moment who still have all the bonds.[102] It is also possessed by certain ordinary individuals. There is no possession of space, so therefore there is no attainment of it either. If something cannot be attained, there is no nonattainment of it either, it is said in this school.

The Great Exposition says that there are many scriptural and logical proofs that attainment and nonattainment are substantial. The Master makes many criticisms of this. From the commentary:

> Therefore this possession and nonpossession are in all aspects nominal dharmas, and they are not substantial dharmas.

Some Great Expositionists reply, "You make many harmful logical criticisms, but we will not give up the position that possession, nonpossession, attainment, and nonattainment are substantial because it is the position of our school." So they say, but such is the speech of someone who cannot distinguish whether he is querying or replying. In this land of Tibet, too, such fools who cannot bear losing a debate say, "Whether or not this position of mine is compatible with the sutras and tantras, it holds." Many such people turn their backs and listen to the echoes of their own voices.

The characteristic of attainment is a nonconcurrent formation that is the substance that makes one possess the dharma that is attained.

(c) Distinctions. This has two topics: (i) Distinctions of attainment, and (ii) Distinctions of nonattainment.

(i) Distinctions of attainment. This has six topics: A. Distinctions of time, B. Distinctions of essence, C. Distinctions of realm, D. Distinctions of learner and nonlearner, E. Distinctions of whether or not it is discarded, and F. The particulars of the distinction of time.

A. Distinctions of time

37a Attainment of three times is threefold;

The **attainment** of that which is attained, dharmas **of** the **three times, is threefold:** there are past, future, and present attainments. The attainments are like the supreme bull or garuda in the fore, like the body and its shadow, or like a calf pulled behind.

B. Distinctions of essence

37b Of virtue so forth, virtue so forth;

The attainments **of virtue** and **so forth**—neutral and nonvirtue—are themselves also those three, **virtue** and **so forth**.

C. Distinctions of realm

37cd Of any realm is in that realm;
Of what's not in a realm is fourfold;

The attainment of dharmas **of any** of the three **realms is** included **in that realm.** The attainment of a Desire-realm dharmas is itself included in the Desire realm. It is the same in the other realms.

The attainment **of what is not in a realm**—the two cessations and the truth of the path—**is fourfold.** It can be included in Desire, Form, Formless, and not included in any of the three realms. The attainment of nonanalytic cessation can be in any of three realms. The attainment of analytic cessation of Form or Formless attained by a worldly path is of either Form or Formless. The attainment of analytic cessation by a transworldly path and the attainment of the truth of the path are not included in any of the three realms.

D. Distinctions of learner and nonlearner

38a Of neither learner nor non, three;

Learner means the undefiled paths of seeing and meditation, and nonlearner means the undefiled path of no-learning. The attainment of these two is, in order, learner and nonlearner. What is **neither learner nor non**learner is either defiled or noncomposite. There are **three** types of attainment of these two: the attainment of defiled dharmas or nonanalytic cessation and the attainment of analytic cessation by the worldly path are neither learner nor nonlearner. The attainment of these through the path of the learner is learner, and their attainment through the path of the nonlearner is nonlearner. Although it is on the path of learning, the path of no obstacles of the vajra-like samadhi forms the support for the attainment of removal that is the nonlearner path of liberation, so it is designated as nonlearner's attainment.

E. Distinctions of whether or not it is discarded

38b Of what is not abandoned, twofold.

The attainment of the discards of seeing and meditation are in order discards of seeing and meditation. The attainment **of what is not abandoned** by either seeing or meditation is proposed to be **twofold:** it is either a discard of meditation or it is not a discard. The attainment of nonanalytic cessation and the attainment of analytic cessation through worldly paths are abandoned by meditation. The attainment of analytic cessation through noble paths and the attainment of the truth of the path are not discarded.

F. The particulars of the distinction of time. This has three points.

1. The particulars of unobscured neutral

38cd Neutral attainment: at same time,
Except clairvoyance, emanations.

The particulars of "Attainment of three times is threefold" are as follows: Well then, must attainment definitely arise in all three times or not? you ask. Not necessarily. Unobscured **neutral attainment** arises **at** the **same time** as the attained dharma. It does not arise earlier or later because it does not have manifest action and is weak.

However, not all attainments of unobscured neutral are simultaneous with the arising of the dharma. **Excepted** are the attainments of the two **clairvoyances** of divine eye and ear, and the neutral **emanated** mind. The attainment of these three arises in all three times because they are accomplished by specific training and therefore are strong.

2. The particulars of obscured neutral

> 39a Of form of the obscured, as well.

The attainment **of** the **form of the obscured** neutral, **as well**, such as the perceptible form of Great Brahma's lips moving when he deceives his entourage, does not arise earlier or later but arises simultaneously because the motivation is weak and the form is material.

3. The particulars of virtuous and nonvirtuous

> 39b In Desire, of forms does not precede.

In Desire, the attainment **of** the perceptible **forms** of virtuous and nonvirtuous conduct and of the imperceptible forms of vows and wrong vows[103] **does not** arise **preceding** the dharma that is attained but does arise at the same time as or later than it.

However, the attainment of the forms of the dhyana vows and the undefiled vows made manifest in the Desire realm is strong and follows the mind, so it is in all three times.

(ii) Distinctions of nonattainment. This has five points.

A. Distinctions of essence

> 39c Nonattainment is unobscured neutral;

Nonattainment is unobscured neutral only because those who have abandoned afflictions and those who have severed the roots of virtue both possess them, so they can be neither afflicted nor virtuous. Its characteristics are a nonconcurrent formation that is exclusive of attainment and unobscured neutral.

B. Distinctions of time

39d Of past and unborn, it is threefold.

The nonattainment **of past and unborn** future dharmas, **it is threefold** as it has aspects of all three times. Present dharmas have no present nonattainment, because it is impossible for the attainment and nonattainment of a particular dharma to coexist simultaneously.

C. Distinctions of realm

40a Of Desire, et cetera, and the stainless, too.

The nonattainment of dharmas **of Desire, et cetera,** the three realms, are included in those same realms. **And** the nonattainment of **the stainless,** undefiled dharmas can be in any of the three realms, **too,** because it is included within the continuum of the beings of those realms.

D. No undefiled nonattainment

40bc Path's nonattainment is asserted as
An ordinary being.

The undefiled **path's nonattainment is** nonattainment, and those who have it in their beings are **asserted as an ordinary being.** The reason is explained in the *Treatise*:[104]

> What is the ordinary individual itself? The nonattainment of the nobles' dharmas.

Another reason is because there is no undefiled nonattainment. Well then, is this nonattainment of the nobles' dharmas set forth as the nonattainment of nobles' dharmas in general or nonattainment of individual dharmas? you ask. It is set forth as nonattainment in general.

Here there are distinctions and disagreements between the Great Exposition and Sutra schools, and the Master's explanation is in accord with the tradition of the Sutra school. According to him, a stream of being in which noble dharmas have not arisen is an ordinary individual. A stream of being in which they have arisen is a noble individual. He does not present ordinary individual as a dharma distinct from individual.

E. Distinctions of the way they regress

40cd It's forfeited
When one attains that or shifts level.

It, that nonattainment, **is forfeited when one attains that,** a noble dharma, **or shifts level** from lower to higher, such as from Desire to Form.

Well then, is there the nonattainment of nonattainment and the attainment of attainment and so forth? you ask. Those do exist, but according to the Great Exposition tradition there is not an endless cycle of attainments of attainments of attainments, and so forth. From the autocommentary:

> Do the attainment and nonattainment of attainment and nonattainment exist? Reply. Both of both exist. Therefore, does it not follow that attainments become infinite? Because they possess each other mutually, they do not consequently become infinite. Included in the nature of dharmas, three arise: the dharma, its attainment, and the attainment of the attainment. Thus when the attainment arises, one possesses the attainment of the attainment, and when the attainment of attainment arises, only attainment is possessed, so for that reason it is not infinite.

Alas, says the Master, in this tradition of infinite attainments, the attainments are having a grand feast. Fortunately, they are unobstructive so there is room to move, but were it otherwise there would not be room for a second living being in all of space. So it is explained.

Nonattainment is finite.

(2) Same status

41a Same status: sentient beings' resemblance.

Same status is what makes **sentient beings** be comparable to or **resemble** one another in conduct, nature, thought, and so forth. Its characteristic is a non-concurrent formation that is the substance that makes sentient beings resemble one another. To classify it, there are two: not separate and separate. The first is like all sentient beings, who merely by being sentient beings are the same class. The second is like gods and humans, bhikshus and novices, and so forth, where the substances that create the similarity among them are separate from the beings themselves.

(3) The explanation of nonconception. This has three points.

(a) Identifying the character base

> 41bc Conception-free stops mind and factors
> Of beings in Conception Free.

Conception-free is the substance that **stops the mind and** mental **factors of beings in Conception Free,** gods who take birth there for five hundred great aeons.

(b) Which of the four results it is

> 41d Full ripening.

It is the **fully ripened** result of the conception-free absorption because it has no compatible cause with separate substance, and because it is not produced by development as they have no form.

(c) What level it is on

> 41d They're in Great Result.

They, these gods, live **in** one part of **Great Result**, the highest level of dhyana attainable by ordinary beings—their abode is not a different sort of place from Great Result. This is similar, for example, to the levels of Great Brahma and Brahma's Ministers, which are not different realms.

The characteristic of a being in Conception Free is the result of the conception-free absorption that is the substance of cessation in the continuum of the long-lived gods.

Do such gods have no consciousness at all? you ask. They do have some consciousnesses because consciousness arises at birth and death. The Master explains that because concurrences of body and mind have ceased, these are nominal, but they are not substantial.

(4) The explanation of the two absorptions. This has two topics: (a) Explaining their individual essences, and (b) Teaching their supports together.

(a) Explaining their individual essences. This has two topics: (i) The essence of conception-free absorption, and (ii) The essence of the conception-free absorption.

(i) The essence of the conception-free absorption

42. Likewise conception-free absorption.
Last dhyan. From wishing for release.
It's virtue. Experienced on birth only.
Not nobles. Gained in one time only.

Just as beings in Conception Free stop mind and mental factors, **likewise** the **conception-free absorption** also stops mental factors, because it is the cause of beings in Conception Free —it has such beings as its results.

Its level is the **last**, fourth **dhyana,** because its fully ripened result ripens in Great Result. It is the contemplation of entering absorption **from wishing for** the definite **release** of liberation—the individual who enters it conceives of the being in Conception Free as liberated and the absorption that achieves that as the path. That individual strives for pure conduct through the wrong path. **It,** the absorption, **is virtuous** in motivation. That virtue is **experienced on birth only**[105] because it causes one to take the existence of Conception Free in the next birth. The only ones who enter it are ordinary individuals; it is **not** entered by **noble** individuals, who see it as an abyss. It is never attained in the past or the future; it is **gained in** the **one time** of the present **only**, like the vows of individual liberation.

Its characteristic is an absorption that stops mind and mental factors and that is included in the level of the fourth dhyana.

(ii) The essence of the absorption of cessation. This has three points.

A. Actual

43. Cessation's like that, too. Its purpose
Is staying. Born on Peak, it's virtue.
Experienced in two or indefinite,
The nobles attain it by training.

The absorption of **cessation is** the cessation of mind and mental factors, **just like that,** the conception-free absorption, **too.** This absorption does not place attention on emancipation, but rather one enters **it** for the **purpose** of **staying** within the pacification of conceptions and feelings. The mental support it is

born on is the **Peak** of Existence, because it is easiest to stop the mind and concurrent mental factors right after that subtlest of subtle minds. What motivates **it is virtue.** Its karmic ripening is **experienced** either on rebirth or in other lifetimes because it can be experienced **in two** instances: in the next life one is either reborn on the Peak of Existence or in the Form realm and then in the lifetime after that on the Peak. **Or** it can be experienced **indefinitely** because one could attain nirvana on the same support as one attained the absorption. Its characteristic is an absorption that stops the concurrences and that is included in the level of the Peak of Existence. Only noble individuals can support it; the childish cannot. Even **the nobles** do not attain it merely by becoming detached; they **attain it by training**, which includes efforts that produce mental strength. Like the vows of individual liberation, it is only attained in the present; there is no past or future attainment of it.

B. The specifics of how it is attained

44a The Sage by awakening.

The Sage's absorption of cessation does not depend upon training; it is something that is attained **by** acquiring **awakening** or the enlightenment that is the knowing of extinction and nonarising. It does not depend upon training, because as is said in a sutra:

> You who are ultimate virtue
> Have nothing at all come from training.
> Whatever you wish for is certain:
> Just by the mere wish it's obtained.

C. The elaboration

44ab Not first,
Since it was gained by thirty-four moments.

Some Kashmiris in the Western school say that the Buddha sat under the Bodhi tree and produced the path of seeing. Then he arose from that absorption and entered the absorptions of the Peak of Existence and lower levels. Others respond that the Bodhisattva did **not** make those manifest **at first,** before he attained the knowledge of extinction. This is **since** he produced the sixteen moments of clear realization of truth, the nine paths of no-obstacles of the path of meditation that are the antidotes for the Peak and the nine paths of liberation without interruption. After that **it**, enlightenment, **was gained** by these **thirty-four moments.** Earlier when he was an ordinary individual studying with Ārāḍa and Udraka, the Bodhisattva had become detached from and abandoned all the discards of meditation of lower levels from Desire to Nothingness. In actuality, he did not need to abandon the lower level's afflicted discards of seeing.

In the tradition of the Foundation Vehicle, ordinary individuals cannot produce the absorption of cessation. However, the *Karṭīk* explains that according to the Highest Mantra ordinary individuals can have the samadhi of listeners' cessation of absorption.

(b) Teaching their supports together

> 44cd Both have support of Desire and Form.
> Cessation is first among humans.

Both of these absorptions **have** as bodily **support** the realms **of Desire and Form**, but they do not have the Formless as their support. This is because beings in Conception Free are the result of the fourth dhyana, and because the absorption of cessation is made manifest by the body, but there is no body in the Formless realm.

In general both of these absorptions have the two realms as support, but there is a distinction: when **cessation** has not previously arisen, it must **be** produced **first among humans,** because the concurrences there are coarse, so one grows weary with them. In the Form realm, the concurrences are pacified, so there is no weariness, and for that reason one does not meditate on it there first. If one has previously attained cessation but regressed from it, it is produced in the Form realm by the power of previous habituation. The conception-free absorption does not come from such weariness; rather one enters it by the wrong view that conceives of it as liberation.

Well then, if there is no mind while one is in these absorptions, where does the mind that arises from them come from? you ask. The Great Exposition proposes that the past mind also has substantial existence, so it arises from that. The Sutra school proposes that mind and body contain each others' seeds, so the body that has faculties also has the seeds of the mind, from which the mind arises. The Mind Only school proposes that when one is in either of these absorptions, the all-ground exists unceasingly, so the mind of arising is born from that.

(5) The explanation of life force

45ab Life force is life. It is that which
Supports one's warmth and consciousness.

The faculty of **life force is** the **life** of beings in the three realms. **It,** life, **is that which supports** or causes **one's warmth and consciousness** to remain continually. In the lower two realms, it provides the support for both of those, and in the Formless for consciousness only. Its characteristic is a nonconcurrent formation that is life.

(6) The explanation of the characteristics. This has two topics: (a) Classifications, and (b) Dispelling doubts

(a) Classifications

45cd The characteristics are birth,
And aging, staying, impermanence.

The characteristics of composites **are birth** that produces dharmas, **and aging** that makes things old, **staying** that makes things remain, and **impermanence** that makes things disintegrate—the suffix *-nence* means the condition of things.

Well then, it says in the sutras, "The characteristics of composites are threefold." Is this not contradictory? you say. There, in order to produce weariness among disciples, staying is taught only implicitly, which makes that teaching provisional. The abhidharma teaches four, so it is a characteristic, not a provisional, teaching.

(b) Dispelling doubts. This has three points.

(i) Teaching that the characteristics have characteristics

46a They've birth of birth, et cetera, and

Well then is there the birth of birth, the aging of aging, and so forth? you ask. **They**, birth and so forth, **have** the **birth of birth, et cetera**, including the aging of aging **and** so forth.

(ii) Refuting that it is endless

46b Engage eight dharmas or else one.

Well then, it becomes endless, you say. It does not become endless. This is because they **engage eight dharmas or else one** dharma: birth, for example, engages in the production of the three of aging, staying, and impermanence, the four of birth of birth and so forth, and one character base such as a vase, for a total of eight. The birth of birth engages in the production of the dharma of birth only. Aging and so forth are known to be the same.

The characteristics of the four are as follows. A nonconcurrent formation that is the substance which makes the composite that is its character base possess arising is the characteristic of birth. A nonconcurrent formation that is the substance which makes the composite that is its character base grow old is the characteristic of aging. A nonconcurrent formation that is the substance which makes the composite that is its character base remain is the characteristic of staying. A nonconcurrent formation that is the substance which makes the composite that is its character base disintegrate is the characteristic of impermanence.

(iii) Refuting the logical absurdity

46cd Without the causes or conditions,
Birth can't produce what is produced.

If future birth produces composites, then why do not the future composites arise all at once? you ask. According to this presentation, future composites will not arise at once, because **without the** assembly of **cause** and the **conditions, birth** alone **can not produce** that **which is produced.**

(7) The explanation of names, words, and letters. This has two topics: (a) Essence, and (b) Particulars.

(a) Essence

47ab Collections of names and so forth are
Collections of names, speech, and letters.

The "**Collections of names and so forth**, too… " mentioned earlier **are** the **collection of names,**[106] **speech, and letters.** The characteristic of a name is a nonconcurrent formation that tells merely the essence of the meaning. Its character base is like saying, "Vase," for example.

Speech and word are equivalent, because it is said in the *Commentary,* "Speech is words…" The characteristic of either speech or word is a nonconcurrent formation that indicates the combination of the essence and particulars of the meaning. Its character base is like saying, "Impermanent composite," for example.

The characteristic of letters is a noncomposite formation that is the basis for designating names and words. Its character base is like, for example the Sanskrit vowel *A* or consonant *Ka*.[107]

(b) **Particulars.** This has four points.

(i) Distinctions of level

47c Desire and Form.

These three collections are included only in **Desire and Form**, because they arise in dependence upon speech. Some say that there are words in Formless, but the Great Exposition says that is illogical. If you examine it further, however, the three collections of names, words, and letters that are formations, both that with which the mind speaks and that which the mind says, are in the Formless, because as is said, "The melodious banner is heard in all three worlds." So is it explained in the *Karṭīk*.

(ii) Distinctions of whether they indicate beings

47c Indicate beings.

They arise from beings' efforts and are in the collection of aggregates included within a stream of being, so they **indicate beings**; that is, they are included in a being's continuum.

(iii) Distinctions of sources

47d Compatible

As they are produced by a cause of same status,[108] they are causally **compatible** only. This is because they arise as all that is desired, so they are not produced by full ripening, and because they do not have form, so they are not produced by development.

(iv) Distinctions of virtue, nonvirtue, and neutral.

47d and neutral.

They are solely unobscured **neutral** because those who have severed the virtuous roots or gained detachment also possess them, so they are neither virtue nor nonvirtue in their essence. The *Commentary* explains it thus, but the Prince explains that these three have both virtuous and neutral aspects. From the Prince:

> Is this said because the Buddha's speech is virtuous, or is this said because the Buddha's speech is neutral? you ask. It is virtuous, and it is also neutral. Which is the virtuous? you ask. The perceptible speech of the Tathagata uttered with a virtuous mind. Which is the neutral? you ask. The perceptible speech of the Tathagata uttered with a neutral mind. Also, following this, "This which is called the Buddha's speech, what kind of dharma is it?" you ask. It is that which arranges the collection of names, the collection of words, and the collection of letters in order, and places them in order, and correctly joins them in order.

iii. Teaching other distinctions between dharmas as a summary

47d Likewise

48. Same status. Fully ripened, too.
    Three realms, and its attainment is twofold.
    Characteristics, too. Absorptions,
    Not having are compatible.

Just as names and so forth indicate beings, are produced by compatible cause, and are unobscured neutral, **likewise same status** is like that also. The part of that which is like full ripening is produced by **full ripening, too.** It is of the **three realms**: it is included in all three, **and its attainment is twofold**: produced by compatible cause and by full ripening. The **characteristics**, birth and so forth, **too**, are like attainment. The two **absorptions** and **not having** or nonattainment **are** produced by the causally **compatible.**

III. The explanation of causes, conditions, and results. This has four topics: A. The explanation of causes, B. The explanation of results, C. The explanation of dharmas common to causes and results, and D. The explanation of conditions.

A. The explanation of causes. This has three topics: 1. Classifying as an overview, 2. Explaining the nature of each cause, and 3. Identifying their times as a summary.

1. Classifying as an overview

> 49 Enabling cause, the coemergent,
> Cause of same status, the concurrent,
> The universal, and full ripening
> Are the six causes, it's proposed.

Above where it says, "Without the causes or conditions,"[109] what are the causes and conditions? you ask. That which abides in the essence that does not block the production of a result is the **enabling cause.** That which aids a result that is simultaneous with itself is **the coemergent** cause. That which aids results that are of similar realm or class is the **cause of same status.** That which aids the result that is concurrent through the five concurrences is **the concurrent** cause. That which aids the afflicted result is **the universal** cause. **And** that which aids the fully ripened result is the cause of **full ripening.** Thus these **are the six causes, it is proposed** by the Great Exposition school.

Well then, since the abhidharma is an explanation of the sutras, what sutra teaches the six causes? you ask. The Great Exposition says that the sutras that teach the six causes have mostly disappeared. However, they are explained in the treatise entrusted to Kātyāyana by the gods, they say.

2. Explaining the nature of each cause. This has six topics: a. Enabling cause, b. Coemergent cause, c. Same status cause, d. Concurrent cause, e. Universal cause, and f. Cause of full ripening.

a. Enabling cause

> 50a The enabling cause is other than self.

The enabling cause of a composite **is** all the dharmas that are **other** in meaning **than** the composite **itself,** because they do not prevent the composite from arising from the collection of its causes. The potent enabling cause, such as the eye producing the eye consciousness or a seed producing a stalk, is characteristic. The impotent is like noncomposite as the cause of a stalk, or hell as the cause of the Formless. The impotent enabling cause is a mere designation of that which does not block the arising of a result as a cause. It is, for example, as when a king does not oppress his subjects and they say, "This king makes us happy."

b. Coemergent cause. This has three topics: i. Identifying the essence, ii. Examples of character bases, and iii. Elaboration.

i. Identifying the essence

> 50b The coemergent: mutual result,

The **coemergent** cause is those dharmas that are a **mutual result** with the cause—they are one another's results.

ii. Examples of character bases

> 50cd Such as sources; mind and its followers;
> Characteristics and their base.

Examples of coemergent causes are **such as** the mutual relationships between the **sources**; between **mind and its followers;** or between the **characteristics** of composites, which are the characterized base's coemergent cause, **and their** characterized **base,** which is the coemergent cause of the characteristics.

iii. Elaboration. This has two points.

(1) Identifying the mind's followers

> 51ab They're mental factors, two vows, and
> The mind's and their characteristics.

They, the dharmas that follow primary mind, **are** the **mental factors;** the **two vows** of dhyana and undefiled vows; **and the mind's and their**—mind's followers including mental factors—**characteristics** of birth and so forth. These are presented as coemergent cause and result in terms of their mere isolate,[110] and will be discussed thoroughly, below.

(2) The manner in which they follow mind

> 51cd They follow mind in terms of time,
> Results, et cetera, virtue, et cetera.

The manner in which **they follow** the **mind** is **in terms of** being at the same

time as mind, having the same **results, et cetera,** and being the same in **virtue, et cetera.** In detail, there are ten ways in which they follow mind: 1) time in general; in particular, 2) arising, 3) staying, and 4) disintegrating; 5) the dominant, personal, or removal result; 6) causally compatible result, and 7) fully ripened result; 8) virtue, 9) nonvirtue, and 10) neutral. In these ten ways, they mutually follow each other and arise, making cause and result, it is said.

The word *same* does not mean they are the same substance: if the principal mind is virtuous, then because the mental factors are similarly virtuous and comparable, they are said to be the same. Saying here that they follow by ten causes is not in terms of substance, but in terms of type. This is because virtue, nonvirtue, and neutral do not follow the same mind because it is impossible for neutral and undefiled minds to either have a fully ripened result or be the same, and because it is impossible for birth, staying, and disintegrating to be the same.

There are many ways to count four possibilities or so forth of cause and caused, but I shall not say them.

A few words here:

Renowned as good, they cling to bad traditions of scholasticism;
Pretending to be learned, they are shrouded in dark ignorance.
While they've been sleeping in the darkness of a lesser mind,
They who presumed to be delighting in the heavens of the scriptures
Have now become old men, while those with young intelligence
Teach themselves their own wonders. Don't they shine?

c. Same status cause. This has two topics: i. Overview, and ii. Explanation.

i. Overview

52a Same status cause is similar,

The character base for the **same status cause** of **is** all past and present composites with the exception of the last aggregates of an arhat,[III] because earlier ones produce and make possible later, **similar** ones. The virtuous five aggregates arise from a virtuous cause of same status, but within virtuous dharmas, defiled virtue and undefiled virtue are separate classes. They are similar to virtues within their own class, but merely being virtues does not make them similar. Otherwise it would follow that the first undefiled moment would arise from a cause of same status.

Afflicted dharmas are similar to nonvirtue. The obscured neutral are similar to the afflicted. The obscured neutral and nonvirtue are mutually similar. The neutral is also similar to neutral.

ii. The explanation. This has four points.

(1) Similarities of the defiled

> 52b Own class and level,

The five classes of discards—four classes of discards of seeing, and one of discards of meditation—and the nine levels of the three realms produce results of their **own class and** own, same **level.** These are same status, but when the class and level are different, they are not, because their status is unequal.

(2) Distinction of time

> 52b born before.

Composites that are **born before**—the past and the present composites—are causes of same status of what has not been born, but the future composites are not, because there is no future cause of same status.

(3) Particular explanation of the undefiled

> 52cd Nine levels' paths are mutual,
> Of equal or superior.

Well then, must the cause of same status definitely be of the same level and class only? you ask. For the defiled, it definitely must be so, but **the nine levels'** undefiled **paths** the may **be mutual** causes of same status even if not comparable in level. This is because the paths happen to be on those levels only circumstantially and so do not crave the levels and make them their own. Therefore they are not included in the realms. However, they are not the same status cause of lower levels but **of** the **equal or superior** levels. Dharma forbearance of suffering is the same status cause for equal, later dharmas of its own class, the superior dharma knowing of suffering, and the paths of seeing, meditation, and no learning.

Similarly, the five faculties of faith and so forth, in terms of gradual purification, are the cause of same status for the six individuals: the pair of followers of faith and dharma, the pair of conviction through faith and attainment through seeing, and the pair of occasional and nonoccasional arhats.

Alternatively, they are the causes of followers of dharma, attainment through seeing, and nonoccasional arhats.[112]

(4) Teaching how the worldly produced by training is comparable

> 53ab Produced by training is just those two.
> From listening, reflecting, so forth.

Not only the undefiled, but worldly virtue **produced by training is** the same status cause of **just those two**, the equal and superior. For example, this is like qualities produced by training such as those arisen **from listening** and **reflecting** and **so forth**, those produced by meditation.

The characteristic of the cause of same status is a cause that produces a result of a similar class as itself.

d. Concurrent cause

> 53cd Concurrent cause is mind and factors
> With a support that is concurrent.

The **concurrent cause** is **mind and** the mental **factors with** concurrence only: they have **a support**, focus, aspect, time, and substance **that are concurrent.** Its characteristic is a cause that is included within either mind or mental factors.

e. Universal cause

> 54ab The universal, of afflicted.
> Own level. Universal. Five.

The universal cause is the common cause **of** its **afflicted** results. It produces results on its **own level.** The universal cause arises prior to its result. Its characteristic is a discard of seeing that which is the specific cause of its afflicted results. The character base is the thirty-three **universal** kernels[113] of the three realms and that which is associated with them except for their attainment. It is the common cause of the **five** classes of afflictions.[114]

f. Cause of full ripening

> 54cd Full-ripening cause can only be
> Nonvirtue or a defiled virtue.

The cause of full ripening has a strong essence and the moisture of craving.

Neutral dharmas have the moisture of craving, but are weak, like a rotten seed. Undefiled dharmas have strength but no moisture, without which they are like dried-up seeds. For that reason, the **full-ripening cause can only be** a **non-virtue or a defiled virtue.** Its characteristic is a nonneutral dharma that is a cause that produces the full ripening of its result.

3. Identifying their times as a summary

55ab The universal and same status
Are in two times; three in three times.

The universal and same status causes **are in** the **two times** of past and present only, and not in the future, because in the future there is no earlier or later. The **three** causes of coemergent, concurrent, and full ripening are **in** all **three times,** because they are recognized in all three. The enabling cause is in the three times. It can also be free of time because potent enabling causes are included in any one of the three times and impotent enabling causes are without time.

B. The explanation of results. This has two topics: 1. Overview, and 2. Explanation.

1. Overview

55cd Composites and removal are
Results. Noncompounds don't have those.

All **composites** are results that have causes because they must depend upon causes. Analytic cessations **and** the **removal** of what is abandoned by the antidote, **are results** that do not depend upon causes. Because they are neither clearly desired nor something to accomplish, space and nonanalytic cessation are not results. For that reason, from the *Treatise:*

> What dharmas are results? you ask. All composites and analytic cessation.

Here, because noncomposites are explained as results, they must have a cause, and because in the section on enabling causes they are explained as causes, they must also have a result. For that reason, it follows that they are composite, you say. There is a common ground between noncomposites and result, but **noncomposites** do not have a cause, because they **do not have** any of **those** six causes. This is because it is impossible for any of the six causes to be the cause of nonanalytic cessation, and it is impossible for the five results to be noncomposite. Well then, perhaps the path is the enabling cause of nonanalytic cessation? you think. It is not, because analytic cessation is noncomposite and has no birth, and because at the time that analytic cessation is arising and exists, the path is not something that does not block it.

2. Explanation. This has two topics: a. Which result is of which cause, and b. The essences of the five results.

a. Which result is of which cause

56 Full-ripened result is of the last;
The dominant result, of first.
Compatible: same status and
The universal. Personal, two.

Well then, what causes are these the results of? you ask. The **fully ripened result is** the result **of the last** cause, full ripening. **The dominant result** is the result **of** the **first,** the enabling cause.

How is it that an impotent enabling cause that merely does not hinder has power over a dominant result? you ask. It has the power of not hindering. For example, the five collections of consciousness have the ten sense bases as the enabling cause that produces them. The container of the world has karma as enabling cause. The ear also by continuum has the power to produce any eye consciousness, because from hearing something, the desire to look arises. Similarly, from grasping something, the desire to look arises and so forth.

The causally **compatible** result is the result of both the **same status and the universal** causes.

The **personal** result is the result of the **two** coemergent and concurrent causes. In the personal result, there is not necessarily a person who does the making; rather it is designating a mere dharma as a person, like calling a medicine "crowfoot." The actions and qualities of a mere dharma are not separate from the dharma itself, so its personal action is called merely *personal.* The result of that is the personal result.

b. The essences of the five results. This has five points.

i. The essence of the fully ripened result

57ab Fully ripened is a neutral dharma,
Shows beings, not neutral, born later.

The **fully ripened** result **is a** nonobscured **neutral dharma,** because if it were either virtuous or afflicted it would follow that neither individuals who have severed the roots of virtue nor arhats would possess them, and because if it were obscured neutral it would be illogical to enter the state without remainder from a mind produced by full ripening.

The phrase, "**shows beings**" means that it is included within the stream of an individual's being, because if it were not included, one's particular karmic actions would be wasted or fall upon those who did not do them. Some results produced by development and causally compatible results are also included within beings' continuums, but in contrast with those, the cause of the fully ripened result is **not neutral**. There are also absorptions in the dhyana and emanated minds produced by samadhi that are neutral, included in a being's continuum, and born from a not-neutral karma, but unlike those, the fully ripened result is **born later** than its cause—it is neither immediately following nor simultaneous.

ii. The essence of the causally compatible result

57c Compatible is like its cause.

The causally **compatible** result **is like** or similar to **its cause**, whether that cause is virtuous, afflicted, or unobscured neutral. If it is from a cause of same status, it must have a similar continuum and aspect. If it is from a universal cause, the aspect is not necessarily similar, but it must be similar in terms of its continuum, level, and whether it is afflicted. Therefore, there are four possibilities of things that have a cause of same status but not a universal cause, etc.

iii. The essence of the result of removal

57d Removal is to mentally

58a Extinguish,

Removal is attained by **mentally,** or through distinctive full knowing, **extinguishing** or abandoning discards. Extinguishing is equivalent to cessation. It is said to refute that mere nonattainment is removal, Pūrṇavardhana explains.

iv. The essence of the personal result

58ab and the result born
From something's power is personal.

And the result born from or attained through **something's power is** similar to what is made by persons, so it is **personal.** The character base is all composites that have arisen from causes in that manner. From the autocommentary:

> For example, from a lower level's mind of training, the samadhi of the higher; from defiled, undefiled; from the mind of dhyana the emanated mind.

There are four possibilities of causally compatible result and personal result.

v. The essence of the dominant result

58cd Composites that aren't previous are
The dominant of composites only.

Composites that have **not previously** arisen, prior to the cause itself—composites that arise at the same time or later than their cause—**are the dominant** result **of composite** causes. The causes are different from the result itself and arise either earlier or at the same time **only**. The word "only" indicates that composites that arise later and noncomposites do not have the power to hold or issue results, so they are not presented as having dominant results.

There is no result that is born prior to its cause, because that would render the cause meaningless. For example, it is impossible to first be a wheel-wielding emperor and later accumulate the karma that produces that result. Nor does one see shoots preceding seeds or other results preceding their cause.

The distinction between personal and dominant results is whether or not it is the result of a particular agent only. For example, a thing that is made is a personal result, and it is also the dominant result of all composites that are simultaneous or prior to it. There are also four alternatives of personal result and dominant result. The result of removal is a personal result but not a dominant result. Results whose cause has disappeared or been interrupted are dominant results but not personal. Simultaneous or immediately following composites are both. Space and nonanalytic cessation are neither.

C. The explanation of dharmas common to causes and results. This has two topics: 1. Times when causes hold and issue results, and 2. What results are produced by how many causes.

1. Times when causes hold and issue results. This has two points.

a. Holding

59a The five hold a result in the present.

The five latter causes not including the enabling cause **hold** and attain the power to produce **results in,** among the three times, **the present.** This is because they cease in the second moment, so there is no action of holding then, and the future is unborn, so there is no action in it. The enabling cause also holds its result in the same way, but as it does not necessarily produce a result, it is not mentioned.

b. Issuing

59b–d Two causes issue in the present.
Two present and past causes issue,
And one past cause issues results.

The **two** coemergent and concurrent **causes,** occur at the same time as their results, so they **issue** their result **in the present,** or *pra-* in Sanskrit, which is used in the meaning of *first.* As they issue their result from the first, holding and issuing are at the same time. **Two** types of **present and past** causes, the same status and universal **causes, issue** results.[115] Some Tibetans explain that it would be better to translate this line as, "And two through the present and past." **And** the **one past cause** of full ripening **issues** its **result** from the past only, because the full ripening does not arise either simultaneously with or immediately following its cause.

2. What results are produced by how many causes. This has two topics: a. The mode of production of concurrent, and b. Nonconcurrent results.

a. The mode of production of concurrent results. This has two points.

i. Explanation

60. The afflicted, fully ripened, others,
    And the first noble respectively
Arise from all except full ripening,
    Universal, those two, and same status.

Well, how many causes is a dharma produced by? you ask. Here there are four types of dharmas: 1) those that are **afflicted,** 2) those produced by **full ripening,** 3) the **others** not included in the other three categories—unobscured neutral not produced by full ripening such as the paths of conduct, crafts, emanated minds; and virtues other than the first undefiled moment—**and** 4) **the first noble** or first undefiled moment. **Respectively,** the first type **arises from all** the causes **except** the cause of **full ripening.** The second is born from all except the **universal.** The third is born from all except for **those two,** the full ripening and universal. **And** the fourth is born all except for the **same status.** They are born from the rest of the causes not mentioned.

They are not born from those causes for the following reasons. 1) The afflicted is not born from a cause of full ripening because it is afflicted. 2) The fully ripened result is not produced by a universal cause because it is not afflicted. 3) The third type is not produced by full ripening or universal cause because it is neither afflicted nor fully ripened. 4) The first noble moment is not born from same status because there is no prior undefiled of similar class.

ii. Summary

61a This is for mind and mental factors.

This is for how the **mind and mental factors** arise.

b. The mode of production of nonconcurrent results

61b The rest are like; exclude concurrent.

Dharmas that are nonconcurrent formations or have form that are 1) afflicted; 2) produced by full ripening; 3) the remaining—neutrals except the fully ripened and virtues except the first undefiled moment—and 4) the form of the first undefiled moment are born from **the rest** of the causes **like** that earlier manner of production, **excluding** the **concurrent** cause. 1) Discarding the full ripening and concurrent causes, the afflicted are born from four causes. 2) Discarding the universal and concurrent, the fully ripened are born from four causes. 3) Discarding the full ripening, universal and concurrent, the remainder are born from three causes. 4) The forms of the first undefiled moment are born from the two causes, the enabling and concurrent causes; they are not born from the remaining four.

Therefore, there is no dharma at all that is born from only one cause.

A few words here:

> The power to penetrate the depths of abhidharma's ocean
> With the sharp eye of mind that fully distinguishes dharmas
> According to Yangchen Gawa's thought—
> Does this not come out of the power of habitual imprints?

D. The explanation of conditions. This has two topics: 1. Brief overview, and 2. Explanation.

1. Brief overview

> 61c There are four conditions, it is taught.

Above where it says, "Without the causes or conditions," what are the conditions? you ask. **There are four conditions, it is taught** in the sutras: the causal condition, immediate condition, objective condition, and dominant condition.

2. The explanation. This has four topics: a. The essence of each of the four conditions, b. Which conditions operate at which time, c. Which things arise from how many conditions, and d. A specific explanation of the immediate condition.

a. The essence of each of the four conditions. This has four points.

i. Causal condition

> 61d The one called causal is five causes.

The one called the **causal** condition **is** any one of the **five causes** not including the enabling cause. It is something that benefits its result. Its character base is composite dharmas.

ii. Immediate condition

> 62ab The mind and factors that have arisen,
> But not the last, are immediate.

The concurrent immediate condition is **mind and** mental **factors that have arisen** in the past or present, **but not the last** mind and mental factors of an arhat. Other than that, all mind and mental factors **are** the concurrent **immediate** condition.

As for concurrence, in a single being's continuum, there can not be two simultaneous cognitions of the same substantial type, so the concurrences are comparable to each individual mental substance.[116] This condition may be separated from its result in terms of time, but it cannot be interrupted by another cognition. Thus it is the condition of immediate arising.

Form is not able to be a concurrent immediate condition because it arises in dissimilar classes interrupted by others. For example, right after the imperceptible form of Desire, the form of Desire realm's vow of individual liberation, the Form realm's vow of dhyana, or an undefiled dharma might all arise, which confuses the classes.

Here there are four alternatives between being the concurrent immediate result of a cognition and immediately following a cognition, and also four alternatives between being the concurrent immediate result of mind and immediately following absorption. These are discussed at length in the *Great Karṭik*, so refer there.

iii. Objective condition

> 62c The objective is all dharmas, and

The objective condition of an eye consciousness and so forth, including its concurrences, is its own object of defiled form and so forth, which is a present dharma. The objective condition of the mind consciousness **is all** defiled and undefiled **dharmas** of the three times, or that are not included in time. The objective condition's characteristic is a dharma that is suitable to be an object.

Why then, if all dharmas are the objective condition of mind consciousness, so are noncomposites. Therefore, noncomposites must be things, because they have the function of producing a result, you say.

The Great Exposition agrees that noncomposites are things, but if they produced a result, they would either produce it always or else they would never produce it because the school asserts they are permanent things. To sometimes produce and sometimes not produce is occasional, so they would become impermanent. This would be a fault, they say. Master Jampal Gegpay De states that because noncomposites have no essence, they are merely the object of observation but are not a condition that produces result. In the *Karṭīk*, this is stated to be untenable but I do not see any great discrepancy between the positions of the Great Exposition and Jampal Gegpay De. Those of you who have powers of reasoning, scrutinize this.

iv. Dominant condition

62d The enabling is the dominant.

The enabling cause **is** explained as **the dominant** condition. Its characteristics are not hindering the arising of the result and being suitable to be a condition.

Well then, if all dharmas are both objective condition and dominant condition, what is the distinction between the two? you ask. Those which are concurrent and coemergent are dominant conditions but not objective conditions.

Well then, above it explains all dharmas as the objective condition, but here it says that the coemergent and concurrent dharmas are not the objective condition. Is this not contradictory? Because this is in terms of general and specific, it is not contradictory.[117] Therefore, the dominant condition is all dharmas other than oneself: from the *Commentary*, "'All' is all composites except for its own essence."

b. Which conditions operate at which time. This has three points.

i. The time in which the coemergent and concurrent causes operate

63ab Two causes' function is directed
Toward ceasing.

In terms of the causal condition, the **two** coemergent and concurrent **causes** perform their **function** in the present, **directed toward** the **ceasing** of the result. Their function is threefold: holding the result, issuing the result, and making use of the object.

ii. The time in which the same status, full ripening, and universal causes operate

63b The three toward arising.

The three universal, same status, and full ripening causes perform their function in the future, directed **toward** the **arising** of the result.

iii. The time in which the immediate and objective conditions operate

> 63cd The two conditions other than
> That are the opposite of those.

First, **the two** concurrent immediate and objective **conditions** that are **other than that**, the causal condition, **are the opposite of those** above as they perform their function in the opposite order. The immediate condition performs its function at the arising that begins an action, and the objective condition is perceived by the present cognition and mental factors, so it performs its function on ceasing.

c. Which things arise from how many conditions. This has two topics: i. General teaching, and ii. Specific explanation of things with form.

i. General teaching. This has (1) Presenting our own tradition, and (2) Refuting other traditions.

(1) Presenting our own tradition. This has three points.

(a) From four conditions

> 64a Four produce mind and mental factors,

The causal condition of mind and mental factors is all five causes. The concurrent immediate condition is previous mind and mental factors that have not been interrupted by another cognition. The objective condition is any one of the five objects or all dharmas. The dominant condition is all dharmas except the cognition's own essence and dharmas that arise later. In this way, these **four** conditions **produce mind and mental factors**.

(b) From three conditions

> 64b And three, the two absorptions.

And three, the causal, immediate, and dominant conditions, produce **the two absorptions** of freedom from conception and cessation. As those two are not cognitions that focus, they do not arise from the objective condition. The causal condition in this context is the coemergent cause of birth and so forth and the same status cause of prior dharmas of comparable level. The mind of entry into absorption and its concurrences are the immediate condition, and the dominant condition is everything different from them that is previously or presently arisen.

(c) From two conditions

> 64bc Others
> Arise from two,

The **others**, the nonconcurrent formations other than the two absorptions and that which has form, **arise from** the **two** causal and dominant conditions. They do not arise from the concurrent immediate or objective conditions, because they are not concurrent.

(2) Refuting other traditions

> 64cd not God and so forth
> Since they're successive and so forth.

Some outsiders say all beings arise from the sole cause of God Indra, the self, the Person, the primal substance, or so forth. To refute that: all beings who are born are **not** born from **God**, a soul, the primal substance, **and so forth, since they are** born **successively, and so forth**—they are born intermittently in different locations, times, and substances. Additionally, it follows that all beings would arise at the same time, because their sole cause is permanent and single.

Here some say that the cause is permanent, but beings arise successively out of the power of God's wishes. If you say so, then it follows that the causes of beings are multiple, because the wishes that cause beings are separate and multiple.

ii. Specific explanation of things with form. This has four points.

(1) How the sources function as conditions for the sources

> 65a When sources cause the sources, twofold;

When the **sources cause** the **sources,** their function is **twofold** as the coemergent and same status cause.

(2) How the sources function as conditions for the source-derived

65b   When causing source-derived, fivefold.

When the sources function as **causes** of the **source-derived,** their function is **fivefold:** 1) because the sources produce the source-derived when it has not previously existed, arising; 2) because as a master does for his students, they support the source-derived that has arisen in correspondence with the sources, supporting; 3) like a wall with a drawing, because they are the support, remaining; 4) because if there are sources the continuum will not be interrupted, bearing; and 5) because they increase the source-derived, the increasing cause. With regard to this, Pūrṇavardhana says:

> Arise, and correspond, support,
> Uninterrrupted, and increase:
> Since they produce, support, remain,
> And bear, and make increase.

(3) How the source-derived function as mutual conditions

65c   Three ways the source-derived are mutual;

There are **three ways the source-derived** function as **mutual** causes: coemergent, same status, and full ripening causes.

(4) How the source derived function as conditions for the sources

65d   They cause the sources in one way.

They, the source-derived, function as a **cause** of **the sources in one way** as the cause of full ripening. Here, the previous life's perceptible and imperceptible defiled virtues and nonvirtue produce the sources in the next life's collection of faculties.

A few words:

> They've studied much but do not comprehend;
> With low capacities, they mistake the meaning.
> Out of unbearable compassion for them,
> I strive my utmost in this field of knowledge.

d. A specific explanation of the immediate condition. This has five topics: i. Classifying the mind in twelve, ii. The eight instances in which the twelve minds follow one another, iii. Which of the twelve minds is obtained from which, iv. Classifying the mind in twenty, and v. How afflicted minds and so forth are acquired.

i. Classifying the mind in twelve

66. Minds in Desire: virtue, nonvirtue,
 Obscured, or else unobscured neutral.
In Form and Formless, those except
 Nonvirtue. Two are undefiled.

All minds included in samsara and nirvana can be collected into twelve categories. **Minds** of nongreed and so forth **in** the realm of **Desire** are **virtue;** greed and so forth are **nonvirtue;** those that possess personality view and so forth are **obscured; or else** minds can be **unobscured neutral** for a total of four in Desire. **In Form and in Formless** there are three minds each—**those except** for **nonvirtue**—for six. **Two** minds **are undefiled:** learner and nonlearner. Altogether there is a total of twelve.

ii. The eight instances in which the twelve minds follow one another

There are known to be eight instances in which mind arises following upon another mind.

1) The instance of continuation is when virtuous minds and so forth arise in a continual stream of the same type.

2) The instance of comparable level is when minds of incompatible type but the same level arise following one another, such as when a nonvirtuous mind of Desire follows upon a virtuous mind and so forth of Desire.

3) The instance of entering absorption is when a higher level's virtue arisen from training or either of the undefiled minds arises from a lower level's virtue arisen from training.

4) The instance of arising from absorption is when Desire's virtue arisen either upon birth or from training, or an upper level's virtue arisen from training only, arise immediately after a higher level's virtue arisen from training or either of the undefiled minds.

5) The instance of rebirth-linking is when a defiled mind only arises upon dying with any of the minds of the three realms. The Prince explains that this mind of birth is in the between state.

6) The instance of being troubled by the afflicted is when an upper level's virtuous pure mind[118] becomes afflicted and one thinks, "May I arise with the virtue of a lower level." One casts that defiled mind aside and arises with a

virtuous mind. When arising from the afflicted samadhi of Form, either of the virtues of Desire can arise. When arising from the afflicted samadhi of Formless, only the virtue arisen from training of the Form realm can arise.

7) The instance of entering an emanation is when a mind of emanation of Desire or Form arises from Form's virtue arisen from training or from a mind of emanation itself.[119]

8) The instance of arising from an emanation is when a virtue arisen from training of the Form realm only arises from a mind of emanation.

These eight instances provide the reasons why it is possible or impossible for any one of the twelve minds to follow any of the other minds.

iii. Which of the twelve minds is obtained from which. This has five topics: (1) Minds of Desire, (2) Minds of Form, (3) Minds of Formless, (4) The learner's mind, and (5) The nonlearner's mind.

(1) Minds of Desire. This has three topics: (a) Virtuous minds, (b) Nonvirtuous minds, and (c) Neutral minds.

(a) Virtuous minds. This has two points.

(i) How many minds can arise right after a virtuous mind

> 67ab Nine minds arise from a virtuous mind
> Of Desire.

Nine minds can **arise** directly **from a virtuous mind of Desire:** In the instances of continuation and comparable level, the four of its own level can arise. In the instance of entering absorption, the virtue of form and the two undefiled can arise. In the instance of rebirth-linking from Desire to the two higher realms, the two obscured neutral of the higher realms can arise.

There is no entering absorption of the Formless from a mind of Desire, because the Formless is separated from Desire by the four distances of support, aspect, focus, and antidote.

(ii) How many minds a virtuous mind can immediately follow

> 67b It can arise from eight.

It, the virtuous mind of Desire, **can** only **arise from eight** minds: In the instances of continuation and comparable level, it arises from the four of its own level. In the instance of arising from absorption, it arises from the virtue of Form and the two undefiled. In the instance of being troubled by the afflicted, it arises from the obscured of Form for a total of eight. The word "only" indicates that it does not arise from the remaining four minds.

(b) Nonvirtuous minds. This has two points.

(i) How many minds a nonvirtuous mind can arise right after

> 67c Nonvirtuous mind arises from ten.

The **nonvirtuous mind** of Desire **arises from ten** minds. In the instances of continuation and comparable level, it arises from the four of its own level. In the instance of rebirth-linking from the two higher realms to Desire, it arises from the three minds of each of the upper realms. This is a total of ten.

(ii) How many minds arise right after it

> 67d From it are four.

From it, the nonvirtuous mind of Desire, there **are four** minds that can arise. In the instances of continuation and comparable level, only the four of its own level, with the exception of the emanated mind, can arise.

(c) Neutral minds. This has two topics: (i) Obscured neutral, and (ii) Unobscured neutral.

(i) Obscured neutral

> 67d Like that, the obscured.

Like that nonvirtuous mind, **the obscured** neutral mind of Desire also can arise from ten minds and immediately after it four minds can arise.

(ii) Unobscured neutral. This has two points.

A. How many it arises from

> 68a The unobscured arises from five.

The unobscured neutral mind of Desire **arises from five** minds. In the instances of continuation and comparable level, it arises from the four of its own level. In the instance of entering an emanation, the emanated mind of Desire, which is unobscured neutral, can arise from a virtuous mind arisen from training of Form.

B. How many arise from it

68b Directly from it, seven minds.

Directly from it, the unobscured mind of Desire, **seven minds** can arise. In the instances of continuation and comparable level, the four of its own level can arise. In the instance of rebirth-linking in the two higher realms, the obscured of the higher realms can arise. In the instance of arising from an emanation, the virtuous mind of Form can arise. Thus a total of seven can arise.

(2) **Minds of Form.** This has two topics: (a) Virtuous, and (b) Neutral.

(a) **Virtuous.** This has two points.

(i) How many minds arise right after it

68c In Form, from virtuous, eleven.

In the realm of **Form, from** a **virtuous** mind, **eleven** minds can arise. In the instances of continuation and comparable level, the three of its own level can arise. In the instance of entering absorption, the virtue of Formless and the two undefiled can arise. In the instance of arising from absorption, the virtue of Desire can arise. In the instance of rebirth-linking in the higher and lower realms, the obscured of Formless, the nonvirtue of Desire, and the obscured of Desire can arise. In the instance of entering an emanation, the unobscured of Desire can arise. This is a total of eleven.

(ii) How many minds it arises right after

68d That is directly after nine.

That virtuous mind of Form arises **directly after nine** minds. In the instances of continuation and comparable level, it arises from the three of its own level. In the instance of entering absorption, virtuous mind of Desire. In the instance of arising from absorption, it arises from the virtue of Formless and the two undefiled. In the instance of being troubled by the afflicted, it arises from the obscured of Formless. In the instance of arising from emanation, it arises from the unobscured of Desire. Thus it arises from a total of nine.

(b) Neutral. This has two topics: (i) Obscured, and (ii) Unobscured.

(i) Obscured. This has two points.

A. How many minds it arises right after

69a Obscured is from eight,

The **obscured** mind of the Form realm **is** arisen **from** the substances of **eight** minds. In the instances of continuation and comparable level, it arises from the three of its own level. In the instance of rebirth-linking from either the higher or lower realms, it arises from the three minds of Formless and the virtuous and unobscured of Desire, for a total of eight.

B. How many minds arise right after it

69a and from it, six.

And from it, the obscured mind of Form, **six** minds can arise. In the instances of continuation and comparable level, the three of its own level can arise. In the instance of rebirth-linking in Desire, the nonvirtuous and obscured of Desire can arise. In the instance of being troubled by the afflicted, the virtuous mind of Desire can arise, for a total of six.

(ii) Unobscured. This has two points.

A. How many it arises right after

69b The unobscured mind is from three.

The unobscured mind of Form **is** arisen **from** the **three** of its own level in the instances of continuation and comparable level.

B. How many arise from it

69c From that one, six.

From that one, the unobscured mind of Form, **six** minds can arise. In the instances of continuation and comparable level, the three of its own level can arise. In the instances of rebirth-linking in higher and lower realms, the three afflicted of the higher and lower levels can arise, for a total of six.

(3) Minds of Formless. This has three topics: (a) Unobscured, (b) Virtue, and (c) Obscured.

(a) Unobscured

69cd In Formless, too,
It's similar.

In Formless, too, it, the unobscured mind, **is similar** to that: just like the unobscured of Form, it arises from three minds, and right after it six minds can arise. In the instances of continuation and comparable level, the three of its own level can arise, and in the instance of rebirth-linking in the two lower realms, their three afflicted minds can arise.

(b) Virtue. This has two points.

(i) How many minds arise from it

69d From virtuous mind
70a Arise nine minds.

From the **virtuous** mind of Formless, there can **arise nine minds.** In the instances of continuation and comparable level, the three of its own level can arise. In the instance of entering absorption, the two undefiled can arise. In the instance of arising from absorption, the virtue of Form. In the instance of rebirth-linking in the lower two realms, the three afflicted minds of the lower levels can arise. Thus nine arise from it.

(ii) How many minds it arises from

70a That after six.

That virtuous mind of Formless arises **after six** minds: In the instances of continuation and comparable level, it arises from the three of its own level. In the instance of entering absorption, it arises from the virtue of Form. In the instance of arising from absorption, it arises from the two undefiled.

(c) Obscured. This has two points.

(i) How many minds arise from it

70b From obscured, seven.

From the **obscured** mind of Formless, **seven** minds can arise. In the instances of continuation and comparable level, the three of its own level can arise. In the instance of rebirth-linking in the lower two realms, the three afflicted minds of the lower levels can arise. In the instance of being troubled by the afflicted, the virtue of Form can arise.

(ii) How many minds it arises from

70b That is so.

That obscured mind of Formless **is so,** like the previous enumeration, in that it can arise immediately after seven minds. In the instances of continuation and comparable level, it arises from the three of its own level. In the instance of rebirth-linking from the two lower levels, it can arise of their two virtues and two unobscured minds for a total of seven.

(4) The learner's mind. This has two points.

(a) How many minds it arises from

70c The learner's from four.

The learner's mind arises **from four** minds: in the instance of continuation, from itself, and in the instance of entering absorption, from the virtuous minds of the three realms.

(b) How many minds arise from it

70c From it five.

From it, the learner's mind, **five** minds can arise. In the instance of continuation, itself and the nonlearner's can arise, and in the instance of arising from absorption, the three virtues of the three realms can arise.

(5) The nonlearner's mind. This has two points.

(a) How many minds it arises from

> 70d Nonlearner's mind arises from five

The **nonlearner's mind arises from five** minds. In the instance of continuation, it arises from itself. In the instance of entering absorption, it arises from the virtue of the three realms that is arisen from training only. It also arises from the learner's vajra-like samadhi.

(b) How many minds arise from it

> 71a And from it there arise four minds.

And from it, the nonlearner's mind, **there arise four minds**. In the instance of continuation, itself, and in the instance of arising, the three virtues of the three realms.

In that case, five minds can arise from the nonlearner's mind, because in the instance of regression from the result the learner's mind can arise right after the nonlearner's, you say. Without afflictions becoming manifest there is no regression from the state of nonlearner, and if afflictions do become manifest, it is interrupted by an afflicted mind. Therefore, the obscured minds of the three realms do not arise directly after the nonlearner's, because the minds of arising from the undefiled are the virtuous minds of the three realms. Any one of those three arises from the nonlearner's mind, and the afflicted mind arises from that.

iv. Classifying the mind in twenty

> 71b–d To make this dozen into twenty:
> Divide the virtue of three realms
> In what's attained on birth, from training.

> 72. Produced by ripening, the path
> Of activities, crafts, emanations:
> The neutral are fourfold in Desire.
> In Form, the crafts must be excluded.

To make more extensive classifications of **this dozen** minds **into twenty** categories, **divide the virtuous of** the **three realms, into** two: **what is attained upon birth** and what is arisen **from training.** In Desire, unobscured neutral is further classified: **produced by** full **ripening,** which arises from a cause of full ripening without effort and engages itself from within; **the path of activities** of going, walking, sitting, and standing; **crafts** that manufacture things; and

emanation minds that wish to make emanations first and then focus on the four objects during emanations. Thus, **the** unobscured **neutral are fourfold in** the **Desire realm. In** the **Form realm**, there is no manufacturing, so **the crafts must be excluded** and there are only the remaining three. In Formless, there is the arisen from full ripening alone. There are also the four afflicted minds of the three realms and the two undefiled minds. Therefore, in Desire there are eight, in Form six, in Formless four, and the two undefiled for a total of twenty. Alternatively, there are eight virtue, four afflicted, and eight unobscured for a total of twenty.

v. How afflicted minds and so forth are acquired. This has four topics: (1) How many minds are acquired from afflicted minds, (2) How many minds are acquired from the virtue of Form, (3) How many are acquired from the learner's mind, and (4) How many are acquired from the remaining minds.

(1) How many minds are acquired from afflicted minds. This has three points.

(a) How many are attained from afflicted minds of Desire

> 73ab With the three realms' afflicted minds
> One can acquire six,

Among the minds of **the three realms,** when the **afflicted minds** of Desire become manifest, **one can acquire six** minds. When taking birth in Desire from the two upper realms, one attains the two afflicted minds of Desire and virtue attained upon birth. When regressing from the state of arhat through nonvirtue, one acquires the two obscured of the higher realms and the learner's mind for a total of six.

(b) How many are attained from afflicted minds of Form

> 73b six,

From the afflicted of Form one acquires **six.** When taking birth in Form from Formless, one acquires the afflicted of Form and virtue attained upon birth and the two emanated minds of Desire and Form. When the entanglers[120] of Form make one regress from the state of arhat, one acquires the afflicted of Formless and the learner's mind, for a total of six.

(c) How many are attained from afflicted minds of Formless

73b or two.

Or one acquires **two** minds from the afflicted of Formless: when the entanglers of Formless make one regress from the state of arhat, one acquires the obscured of Formless and the learner's mind.

(2) How many minds are acquired from the virtue of Form

73c With virtuous in Form, it's three.

With virtuous minds born **in Form** first becoming manifest, that virtuous mind **is** acquired. When the mind of actual practice of dhyana becomes manifest, the two emanated minds of Desire and Form are acquired, for a total of **three**, as it is explained. However, it is impossible to acquire all three at once. Pūrṇavardhana states that at the time of attaining the actual practice of the first dhyana, three are acquired from absorption.

(3) How many are acquired from the learner's mind

73d With learner, four.

With the manifestation of the **learner's** mind of dharma forbearance of suffering, **four** are acquired: When entering the absorption of the first undefiled moment, that undefiled path itself is acquired. When it makes one detached from Desire, the emanated minds of Desire and Form are acquired. When it makes one detached from Form, the virtuous of Formless is acquired.

(4) How many are acquired from the remaining minds

73d With others, those.

With the **other** minds not just explained—the virtues of Desire and Formless, the nonlearner, and the three unobscured neutral—with these six minds, just **those** themselves are acquired, no others.

Second, presenting the area's name

This completes the second area called "Teachings on the Faculties" from the *Verses of the Treasury of Abhidharma.*

This completes the explanation of **the second area called "Teachings on the Faculties" from** *The Explanation of the "Verses of the Treasury of Abhidharma"* called *The Essence of the Ocean of Abhidharma, The Words of Those who Know and Love, Explaining the Youthful Play, Opening the Eyes of Dharma, The Chariot of Easy Practice.*

A few words here:

When my mind's seven horses[121] shine their hundred rays
Of acuity in expansive skies of knowables,
The minds of students yearning for emancipation
Will blossom in the lotus garden of abhidharma.
The *tirtikas* who arrogate that they are Brahma
Do not know the intent or meaning of the vast canon.
Audaciously they write their *ṭīkas* on
The surface meaning of sharp and clear words
Without a fine analysis of difficult points.
Alas! They pretend to know the meaning of the texts,
But are like bees trying to measure the sky's limits.
Unable to bear this, I strive to explain this text.

THIRD AREA

Teachings on the World

Unstained by ignorance, your wisdom sees
All that is knowable, directly and unhindered.
Lord of ten powers and all-knowing guru,
Jewel of the Shakyas, I bow to you respectfully.

The treasury that teaches the world from abhidharma's *Treasury,*
Is like a reflection in this mirror, taught clearly and precisely
Just as all-knowing Vasubandhu explained, without mistakes—
This is a feast for those with minds of intelligence and interest!

With these verses as a link between chapters, the third area, the "Teachings on the World," has an explanation of the text of the area and a presentation of the area's name. The explanation of the text of the area has two sections: I. The world of sentient beings, and II. The world that contains them.

I. The world of sentient beings. This has five topics: A. Classifications of wanderers who are born, B. The nature of interdependence, the manner of birth, C. Conditions for abiding after birth, D. The minds of staying and dying, and E. Categorizing beings in three groups.

A. Classifications of wanderers who are born. This has three topics: 1. Classifying in three realms. 2. Classifying wanderers in five, and 3. Classifying in the four modes of birth.

1. Classifying in three realms. This has three topics: a. Desire realm, b. Form realm, and c. Formless realm.

a. Desire realm. This has two points.

i. General classification

1a–c Hells, hungry ghosts, and animals,
And humans, and six types of gods
Are the Desire realm.

Just the names of the three realms have been mentioned, but what are the three realms? you ask. This area is intended to teach that. The connection between the chapters in terms of meaning is that individuals who wish for liberation should among the four truths internalize the characteristics and character bases of the truth of suffering first. This develops weariness with the world, it is said.

The actual meaning of this verse is as follows. Beings in the **hells** are led there by nonmeritorious causes that do not have even the slightest pleasant result and cannot find protection until extricated by the full ripening of karma. The **hungry ghosts** are overwhelmed by hunger and thirst. **And** there are the "bent-goers" or **animals** who bend as they go. **And humans** are predominantly mental. **And** the **six types of gods** of Desire have their palaces in the sky.[122] Including their environment or container, these **are the Desire realm.**

ii. Specific classification

1cd By dividing
The hells and continents, there are twenty.

To classify these further, **by dividing the** hot **hells** into eight **and** the humans into the four **continents, there are** ten lower realms and ten higher realms. Thus the Desire realm has **twenty.** The eight cold hells surround the Reviving Hell and so forth; the Occasional Hells are in indefinite location, number and size; the sub-continents surround the continents; and demigods are in the Desire realm, but are included within the other five types of beings. Therefore these are not counted separately.

b. Form realm. This has two points.

i. General classification

> 2ab Above that there are seventeen
> Higher abodes of the Form realm.

Above that Desire realm **there are seventeen higher abodes** from Brahma's Abode to Below None, which are called **the Form realm**, because they are realms where one is detached from desire but still attached to form.

ii. Specific classification. This has two points.

(1) The classification of the first three

> 2c Each of the dhyanas has three levels,

In that Form realm, of the four dhyanas, **each of the** first three **dhyanas has three levels**: the first has Brahma's Abode and so forth.[123] Each dhyana is divided into three levels because it can be caused by lesser, medium, or greater absorption.

(2) The classification of the fourth

> 2d But the fourth dhyana has eight levels.

On the fourth dhyana, there are the three levels of Cloudless and so forth[124] for ordinary individuals who have meditated on it. Nobles can have five levels of the absorption of alternation, such as the lesser, medium, and so forth absorptions of alternation.[125] Corresponding to these, there are five pure abodes.[126] Thus **the** level of the **fourth dhyana has eight levels.**

c. Formless realm. This has three points.

i. Teaching that there is no classification by abode

> 3a The Formless realm has no abodes.

In **the Formless realm,** the four name aggregates[127] of birth establish themselves in that very level on which the being died. There is **no** designation of other higher or lower **abodes.**

ii. Classifying in four by birth

3b Because of birth, it has four types.

Because of differences in **birth, it has** different **four types:** the sense bases of Infinite Space, Infinite Consciousness, Nothingness, and Neither Conception nor Nonconception. These absorptions are so called because of the way one trains to achieve them. First, when both the conception of form and the part of it that is perceived have disintegrated, one thinks, "Space is infinite." From transcending the negation of the existence of anything perceived in mere space, there is a not-negation[128] of it as a thing and one thinks, "Consciousness is infinite." Then one thinks, "This mere awareness cannot be proven to be any particular essence." Then one fears that conceptions are like results and pain, but the lack of conceptions is total stupidity, so one does not stop the subtle, unclear movement of conceptions. During the actual absorption, one attains a result similar to those trainings, so the absorptions are therefore named after them.

iii. How the continuum of mind is engaged

3cd There, likeness and life force as well
Support the mind's continuum.

In Desire and Form, the continuum of mind is supported by the bodily form, but what supports it here? you ask. **There** in the Formless realm, **likeness** of same status **and life force as well support the mind's continuum.** "As well" means that the continuum by mind is also supported by karma, nonpossession, attainment, birth, and so forth.

Well then, why do likeness and life force not support life in the realms of Desire and Form as well? you ask. That is because in those realms one is not free of the conception of form, and because life force and so forth are weak in comparison. The Formless realm arises from a particular absorption that has no conception of form, so the life force and so forth propelled by previous karma are strong.

In the philosophical school of the Great Exposition, these two support the mind, and the mind also supports them.

2. Classifying wanderers in five. This has three topics: a. Actual, b. Particulars of elements, and c. Elaboration on these points.

a. Actual

4ab The names, the hells and so forth, show
Five wanderers.

Saying **the names** in the three realms, **the hells and so forth,** animals, hungry ghosts, humans, and gods, **show five** types of **wanderers.**[129] These include all sentient beings of the previous state.[130]

The Levels[131] says that demigods are lesser gods. Others explain them as hungry ghosts. Gandharvas are gods. The Yaksha demons are probably gods but are also explained as hungry ghosts. Naga serpents, kinnaras, and garudas are animals. *Kumbhaṇḍas,* ghouls, banshees, and other demons are mostly hungry ghosts.

b. Particulars of elements

4b–d They're unafflicted
And neutral. Sentient beings are called,
But not those in the between state.

In terms of their self-isolate, **they,** the five wanderers, **are unafflicted, and** they are neither virtue nor nonvirtue, but unobscurerd **neutral** only. If that were not so and they were either afflicted or virtuous, the different beings would become mixed up, and those who have severed the roots of virtue and nobles would not be included among wanderers. As the environment of the world is not a wanderer, only **sentient beings are called** wanderers, **but those in the between state** are **not.** From the *Prajñāptiśastra:*

> The four modes of birth included the five wanderers, but the five wanderers do not include the four modes of birth. What is not included? you ask. The between state.

Therefore the Great Exposition proposes that beings are unobscured neutral only, because they are separate from the cause that establishes them, karmic becoming. This pervades because the full ripening propelled by karma is a wanderer.

c. Elaboration on these points. This has four topics: i. The seven places of consciousness, ii. The nine places for beings, iii. The four places of consciousness, and iv. Analyzing the four possibilities of the four places and seven places.

i. The seven places of consciousness. This has two points.

(1) Actual

5. A different body and conception;
   A different body, same conception;
   Reverse; same body and conception;
   And the three places without form

6a Are seven places of consciousness.

In these three realms of the five wanderers, seven places of consciousness are explained. 1) Gods and humans of Desire, and those who arise in the first dhyana in later epochs have **a different body and conception**. 2) Great Brahma and the assembly of gods around him have different robes, colors, and shapes, so they have **a different body**, but as they all conceive that, "Great Brahma created me," and Brahma also conceives that "I have created these beings," so they have the **same conception.** 3) In the **reverse** of the preceding, the gods of the second dhyana have bodies that are the same in that their nature is light, but their conception is sometimes pleasure and sometimes equanimity, so their conceptions arise differently. This is because the pleasure of this level is not stable. 4) The gods of the third dhyana are the **same** in having a **body** that is light by nature **and** the **conception** of pleasure, because the pleasure of this level is stable. These four places that have form **and the three places without form** of 5) Infinite Space, 6) Infinite Consciousness, and 7) Nothingness **are** the **seven places of consciousness**. These seven places are taught in the sutras. These are called the places of consciousness because in them the manner of craving supports and develops the consciousness.

(2) What is not that

6b The others have that which destroys it.

The others that were not mentioned—the three lower realms, the fourth dhyana, and the Peak of Existence—are not places of consciousness because the lower realms have suffering, the fourth dhyana has both the causal and resultant conception-free absorption, and on the Peak there is the absorption of cessation, so they **have that which destroys it**, consciousness.

ii. The nine places for beings. This has two points.

(1) Actual

6cd With beings on Peak and Concept Free,
They're said to be nine places for beings.

Along **with beings** on the **Peak** of Existence **and** in **Conception Free, they,** these seven places of consciousness, **are said to be** the **nine places for beings.** This is because sentient beings always remain there with pleasure.

(2) What is not that

7ab Since one remains against one's wishes,
The others are not.

Since their nature is that **one remains** in them **against one's wishes**—one is forced to stay by the demons of karma—**the other** three lower realms **are not** places for beings. They are, for example, like prisons.

iii. The four places of consciousness. This has two points.

(1) Actual

7b–d Four more places:
Four aggregates that are defiled,
On their own level.

There are **four more places** in another manner than the seven taught in a sutra:

> The places for consciousness are approaching form, and approaching feeling, conception, and formation.

Their nature is the **four aggregates** of form and so forth **that are defiled** and that are **on their own level,** but not those that are undefiled or on other levels. This is because the undefiled is the antidote for consciousness, and it is not logical that one level be the support of another level's consciousness.

(2) What is not that

7d Consciousness

8a Alone is not explained as a place.

Here, in differentiating the basis for staying and what stays, the Teacher says that the **consciousness,** which is what stays, **alone is not explained as a place** for consciousness. For example, it is like not mentioning the king himself.

iv. Analyzing the four possibilities of the four places and seven places

8b Combined, there are four alternatives.

Do the seven include the four, or do the four include the seven? you ask. If you examine how they can be **combined, there are four alternatives.** The first alternative (included in the seven but not in the four) is the consciousness on the seven places. The second alternative (included in the four but not the seven) is the defiled aggregates other than consciousness in the three lower realms, in the fourth dhyana, and on the Peak. The third alternative (included in both) is the first four defiled aggregates in the seven places. The fourth alternative (included in neither) is consciousness in the lower realms, fourth dhyana, and Peak; and undefiled dharmas.

3. Classifying in the four modes of birth. This has three topics: a. Where one enters: the classification of the modes of birth, b. What enters: the explanation of the between state, and c. The manner it goes to the place of birth.

a. Where one enters: the classification of the modes of birth. This has two topics: i. Actual classification, and ii. Examining which beings have which modes of birth.

i. Actual classification

8cd There sentient beings have four modes
Of birth: from egg, et cetera.

There, in those three realms, **sentient beings** are known to **have four modes of birth:** there is birth **from egg, et cetera,** including birth from womb, birth from warmth and moisture, and miraculous birth.

The so-called modes of birth are birth. They group together many different types of sentient beings who have their type of birth in common. For that reason, they are similar, and so these are the modes of birth.

ii. Examining which beings have which modes of birth. This has three points.

(1) Which are possessed by humans and animals

9a Humans and animals have four.

Which wanderers have how many modes of birth? you ask. **Humans and animals** can **have** any of the **four** modes. The elders Śaila and Upaśaila, for example, are humans born from eggs. Present humans are born from the womb. Māndhātar, Āmrapāli and so forth are born from warmth and moisture. Humans of the first aeon and Noble Aryadeva have miraculous birth.

Three of the modes of birth for animals are easy to understand; some nagas and garudas, for example, are born by miraculous birth.

(2) Which are possessed by hell beings, gods, and so forth

9bc Hell beings have miraculous birth,
As do gods and the between states.

Hell beings have miraculous birth only, **as do gods and** beings in **the between states.**

(3) Which are possessed by hungry ghosts

9d From the womb as well are hungry ghosts.

Most hungry ghosts are born by miraculous birth, but **from the womb as well are** some **hungry ghosts** born.

Among all the modes of birth, miraculous birth is the best, but the Teacher demonstrated birth from the womb in order not to fulfill the predictions of non-Buddhists, who had prophesied that a magician would appear and deceive the world. He also took birth from the womb to bring his Shakyan kinsfolk into the Dharma and leave relics of his body.

b. What enters: the explanation of the between state. This has two topics: ii. The essence and proof, and ii. Distinctions of bodily form and so forth

i. The essence and proof. This has three topics: (1) Essence, (2) Dispelling doubts, and (3) Proof.

(1) Essence

10ab In this, it is that which arises
Between the states of death and birth.

What is the essence of the between state? you ask. **In this** here, **it is that** continuum of the five defiled aggregates **which arises between** the cessation of **the** preceding **state of death and** the upcoming state **of birth.**

(2) Dispelling doubts

> 10cd It has not reached its destination,
> So the between state is not born.

What is the reason that it is arisen but not born? you ask. **It has not reached its destination,** the previous state with complete name-and-form and the six sense bases propelled by karma, **so the between state is not born.**

(3) Proof. This has (a) Logical proofs, and (b) Scriptural proofs.

(a) Logical proofs. This has three topics: (i) Actual proof, (ii) Teaching that the example is illogical, and (iii) Proving the reason for that.

(i) Actual proof

> 11ab Analogous to a grain's continuum,
> It is not born from interruption.

The Buddhist Mahāsāṃghika and Mahīśāsaka schools say that the birth state only happens immediately following the state of death, so there is no between state. This is the opponent's position.

Because the form of the birth state in Desire and Form is similar to a grain of seed, from which a shoot, from which a trunk, and so forth arise in an uninterrupted continuum, it is **analogous to a grain's continuum** and to the result of that continuum. Therefore, because the essence of the continuum of existence arises in a different place, **it is not born** solely **from** the continuation of a state of death that has been **interrupted**. This is a result reason of a prior cause[132] where the reason and the example are taught simultaneously.

(ii) Teaching that the example is illogical

> 11cd Since a reflection is not proven,
> Nor similar, it's not an example.

Well, one does see instances where the cause's continuum is interrupted but the result arises. For example, the reflection of a face that appears in a mirror is the result of that face, but it arises even though it is interrupted in space. For this reason, the birth state also arises from the interrupted state of death, you say.

This is not so, **since a reflection is not proven** to be a form. The word "**nor**" includes the alternatives: even if a reflection were proven to be a form, because it is not **similar** to an actual form, **it is not** suitable to be given as **an example.**

(iii) Proving the reason for that. This has two points.

A. The proof that it is not established as an obstructive form

> 12a On one, no two are simultaneous.

On the object of a mirror, the color of the mirror and the color of the reflection do not both arise simultaneously at one time, because **on one** object **no two** obstructive forms of similar type **are** able to arise **simultaneously.** A reflection is not an obstructive thing, but it is not logical for it to be any other type of thing either. If it were, the mirror would not be necessary as a support for the reflection. The Prince explains:

> Therefore, the state of birth is in the continuum of the state of death, but a reflection is not the same with respect to form, so the example of the reflection is not proof. The example of the essence that arises later in a grain's continuum is something that has its own continuum, thus it is a compatible example.

B. The proof that the example and meaning are dissimilar

> 12b It's discontinuous, born from two.

It, the reflection of a face's form in a mirror **is discontinuous** from the face's form because the reflection is connected to the continuum of the mirror and arises simultaneously as the face's form. The reflection is **born from** the **two** principal conditions of the mirror and the face's form, but here the state of birth is not born from two causes of the state of death and some other cause, because no principal cause other than the state of death can be observed. The primary cause of the state of birth can not be the semen, blood and so forth, because miraculous birth arises from space without any semen or blood.[133]

(b) Scriptural proofs

12cd Since mentioned, it exists. Scent-eaters,
And five are taught, and *Sutra of Wanderers.*

The Great Chim[134] summarized this thus:

> The Seven States, and Entering the Womb,
> Āśvalāyana, and nonreturners,
> Sutra of Wanderers, and other words
> Explain it, so the between state is taught to be.

To comment on this: From the *Sutra of Seven States:*[135]

> The states are seven: the state of hell, the state of animals, the state of hungry ghosts, the state of gods, the state of humans, the karmic state, and the between state.

Since it is actually **mentioned** in the Buddha's teachings, **it**, the between state, **exists.** We do not recite any sutra like that because it does not appear in our scriptures, you say. Well then, from the *Sutra of Entering the Womb:*[136]

> From the manifestation of three situations, the child is conceived in the mother's womb: a suitable mother who has a menstrual flow, the parents becoming lustful and joining, and the scent-eater also being nearby.

The **scent-eater** mentioned here is a just synonym for the between state. Also, it is also said in the *Āśvalāyana Sutra,* "Your scent-eater who is nearby… "

We do not recite any such sutras, you say. From another sutra:

> The nonreturners are five: complete nirvana in the intermediate, complete nirvana upon birth, complete nirvana without effort, complete nirvana with effort, and bound for higher.

Here **five** nonreturners **are taught. And** it is proven in the ***Sutra of the Seven Holy Wanderers.***[137] The word "**and**" means that in addition to the logical proofs, there are the above scriptures and many other scriptures that prove it, such as:

> Put dhyanas in four groups of ten,

The Formless in three groups of seven,
Conception in one group of six,
And all is put in categories.

Well, it is said that the demon named Criticism went directly to the Incessant Hell in one instant in his own body, so there is no between state. It is also said that if you commit a heinous deed, you will be born in hell immediately. So it is said, you say. These do not mean that there is no between state, but rather that while still alive the body is surrounded by the flames of hell, and then one dies and goes to hell in the between state. The latter also means that it is karma experienced on rebirth without any other intervening existence.

With regard to one sinful brahman:

Brahman, when youth has been carried away
There's aging and sickness: the demons approach.
Between there is no place for you,
There are no provisions for your journey.

Although this says there is no place in between, this means that between that life and the lower realms there is no place of birth in the higher realms; it does not teach that there is no between state.

However, when one is born from Desire or Form into Formless, there is no between state.

ii. Distinctions of bodily form and so forth This has five topics: (1) Distinctions of body, (2) Distinctions of miracles, (3) Distinctions of faculties, (4) Of manner of going, and (5) Of food.

(1) Distinctions of body. This has three points.

(a) Actual

13ab Since it is propelled by the same karma,
It has the body of the next.

Since it, the between state, **is** a corporeal sentient being **propelled by the** one **same** propelling **karma** as the upcoming previous state, **it has the body** shape and form **of the next** previous state that will arise.

(b) Identifying the previous state

> 13cd The previous is prior to death
> But onward from the moment of birth.

Well then, what is the previous state itself? you ask. **The previous** state **is** the continuum of the five aggregates of grasping themselves **prior to** the state of **death but onward from** the **moment of** the state of **birth.**

Therefore, among the four states, the between state and the previous state have been explained. The state of birth is the moment of rebirth-linking as a new being. The last moment of death is the state of death: it is what occurs before the between state for those who will take birth among sentient beings with form. Thus the states of birth and death are moments, and the other two states are continuums.

(c) What they are seen by

> 14a They're seen by their class, divine eye.

They, the between states of hell, **are seen** by hell beings, and the between states of gods are seen **by** gods of **their** comparable **class,** and they are seen by the clairvoyance of the **divine eye** that is produced by meditation and free of the eleven faults. They are not seen by the extremely pure divine eye attained upon birth. The eleven faults are as follows:

> They're doubt and inattention,
> A body that's unworkable,
> And torpor, sleep, and agitation,
> Harsh diligence, and crooked mind,
> Anxiety, and various conceptions,
> Too talkative, harsh meditation.

Some say that those in the between state of the gods can see the between states of all five wanderers, and those in the intermediates states of humans, hungry ghosts, animals, and the hells cannot see the higher ones.

(2) Distinctions of miracles

> 14b The miracles of karma have power.

They have **the miracles** of being able to fly in space and so forth out of the force **of karma.** These miracles **have power;** these are not emanated miracles. Not even the Buddha can block them because of the strength of karma.

(3) Distinctions of faculties

14c Full facultied

They have **full** and complete **faculties** of eye and so forth.

(4) Distinctions of manner of going

14cd and unobstructive,
They cannot turn back.

They cannot be blocked even by a vajra **and** so forth because they are **unobstructive.** For example, if you melt and smash a ball of iron, vermin can be seen inside it. Once the between state of a human, for example, is established, **it cannot turn back** into a god or other wanderer. In the higher abhidharma,[138] reversal to a higher between state is accepted.

(5) Distinctions of food

14d They eat smells.

They, the beings in the between state of Desire, **eat** the subtle **smells** of food; they do not eat coarse food. Those of lower classes with limited faculties eat smells that are not nice. Those with developed faculties eat nice smells.

How long does a being stay in the between state? you ask. There are many different propositions by Venerable Dharmatrāṇi of the Sutra school, the Second Teacher Vasubandhu, Venerable Vasumitra, the Great Exposition school, Saṅghabhadra, and so forth. To summarize them with verses from my own *Ṭīka:*[139]

> The venerable elders of the Sutra school
> Say the between state has indefinite duration.
> If a being with provisions for one hundred years
> Spends a year in between, once he has eaten that year's,
> He has only enough for some ninety-nine more
> In the previous state. By that logic it's known.
>
> Vasumitra says if the conditions are met,
> Within seven days. Or if not, after staying
> Seven days there's migration. And if the conditions
> Are still not met, one can remain seven weeks.
>
> Some certain proponents of the Sutra school

And Venerable Asanga and so forth say definitely
They will not stay longer than just seven weeks.

The Great Exposition says if the conditions
For one to be quickly reborn are not met—
For instance, if horses are not in mating season—
By karma, conditions will ripen and cause
Copulation, and they will link rebirth in there.

c. The manner it goes to the mode of birth. This has three topics: i. What frame of mind it enters with, ii. What shape it enters with, and iii. Explaining other distinctions of frame of mind.

i. What frame of mind it enters with. This has three points.

(1) The frame of mind in birth from the womb and egg

15ab The mind mistaken, out of lust
It goes into its destination.

With the eye that arises from the power of karma, a being in this period of the between state sees the place where he will be reborn from far off. When entering either of the modes of birth from womb or from egg, if the being will be male, he has lust for mother and hatred for the father, or if female, lust for the father and anger for the mother, and if neuter, he has the desire of either the male neuter or the female neuter. As the being has this particular desire, **the mind** is **mistaken** and **out of lust** goes between the organs during copulation. Then it wants to sleep, so **it goes** amongst the semen and blood **into its destination**, the uterus. Once it has gone into the womb, which is like a ball of yarn, it feels affection for the semen and blood as "mine," and it stays.

(2) The frame of mind in birth from warmth

15c Others from longing for a smell

Unlike the two just described, in birth from warmth **other** beings go to a clean or unclean place **from longing for a smell**, according to their karma.

(3) The frame of mind in miraculous birth

15d Or place.

In miraculous birth, they go out of longing for a **place.** This is entering the place of birth in a different manner than in either birth from the womb or the egg.

Well then, how is that one longs for hell? Because the mind is mistaken, one is tormented by cold rain and wind. Seeing fire in hell, one wants to get warm and rushes there. Alternatively, when suffering from and tormented by heat, one sees the cold hells as cool and rushes there. Thus is the link to the next rebirth made.

The between state of the gods is like arising from a cushion and going up. Humans, animals, and hungry ghosts go according to their situations.

ii. What shape it enters with

15d They fall head first to hell.

They, hell beings in the between state, **fall head first to hell.** This is because it is said:

All those who slander the austere
And fully restrained seers
Will tumble headlong into hell
And not to anywhere else.

The austerities are general, and the full restraint is abiding in the twelve purified qualities. The seers are buddhas and bodhisattvas.

iii. Explaining other distinctions of frame of mind. This has six points.

(1) What distinguishes wheel-wielding emperors

16a One enters wittingly,

When the being in the between state enters the womb, it is not always because the mind is mistaken at orgasm. The sutras tell of four instances of entry into the womb. In the first of these, **one** stays in and emerges from the womb without awareness, but **enters** it **wittingly.**

(2) What distinguishes self-buddhas

16ab one stays,
As well,

One not only enters, but **stays** knowingly **as well.**

(3) What distinguishes bodhisattvas

16b and one emerges, too.

And one not only both enters and stays, but **emerges** knowingly, **too.**

(4) What distinguishes ordinary beings

16c Others are ignorant of all,

Others are ignorant of all three: entering, staying, and emerging.

(5) Distinctions of birth from egg

16d And always if oviparous.

And the being is **always** deluded **if oviparous,** or born from an egg.

(6) Explaining the reason for the first three

17. The three—wheel wielding as well as
    Two self-awakened—enter the womb
    Because their karma or their wisdom
    Or both are vast, respectively.

First those who enter knowingly but stay and emerge unknowingly, and those who enter and stay knowingly but emerge unknowing, and those who are knowing in all three, are **the three**—respectively the **wheel-wielding** emperor **as well as** the **two self-awakened** individuals, self-buddhas and tathagatas—that **enter the womb** knowingly. This is **because their**—wheel wielding emperors'—**karma** or merit is vast, **or** because of **their**—self-buddhas'—**wisdom** from meditating for one hundred aeons is vast, **or** because of **both** of the buddha's accumulations **are vast, respectively.** When they enter the womb, they are not yet buddhas and so forth, but they are called by their future appellation.

But the self-buddha both entering and staying knowingly and birth from the egg always being deluded are contradictory, because the son of King Pañcāla was born from an egg and was a self-buddha, you say. This is not a fault, because entering and staying knowingly is in terms of the rhinolike, and birth from the egg is in terms of the congregating self-buddhas,[140] according to Pūrṇavardhana's explanation. Alternatively, entering and staying knowingly is in terms of birth from the womb.

B. The nature of interdependence, the manner of birth. This has three topics: 1. The manner the aggregates alone link rebirth, 2. The beginningless continuum of the aggregates, and 3. Understanding the nature of interdependence.

1. The manner the aggregates alone link rebirth

18. There is no self—mere aggregates.
    Continuums of between states
Assembled by afflictions and karma
    Enter the womb. It's like a lamp.

According to outsiders, it follows that there is a self because sentient beings transmigrate to different worlds, you say. This does not pervade, because **there is no self** that accepts or rejects in the internal aggregates that make up the being.

Well then, what provides continuity between the state of death and rebirth-linking? you ask. There is **merely** the continuum of the **aggregates** themselves. Labeling that continuum as the "self" is not refuted, because it is suitable to call it by any name. The aggregates alone have no power to transmigrate to new aggregates without stopping, because **continuums of** the **between states** that are fully ripened results and personally made results **assembled by afflictions and karma enter the womb. It is like a lamp** that is momentary but burns in a continuum of moments.

2. The beginningless continuum of the aggregates

19. Just as propelled, the continuum
    Arose in stages, then from karma
And afflictions goes to the next world—
    Beginningless wheel of existence.

Just as it was **propelled** by ignorance and formation, **the continuum arose in stages** of consciousness, name-and-form, six sense bases, contact and feeling. Here death in the womb, death as a small child, and death in the prime of life are propelled by the prior accumulation of the being's own specific karma. The order it develops is described in the scriptures:

At first it's mushiness.
From mushiness, the oval.
From the oval comes the oblong,
From the oblong comes the solid.
From the solid, the hands and feet move.
Hair, fur, and nails, and such;
The faculties with form;
And organs develop in sequence.

The faculties produced by sustenance and so forth mature, and **then from** accumulating **karma and** performing **afflicted** conduct itself the body disintegrates. Then just as before the continuum of the between state **goes to the next world** by aging and death and by birth. This is because from karma and afflictions comes birth, and from birth, too, karma and afflictions are accumulated, so it is a **beginningless wheel of existence.**

3. Understanding the nature of interdependence. This has four topics: a. The periodic links of interdependence, b. The essence of each link, c. Teaching the three all-afflicted through examples, and d. Teaching these links as the four states.

a. The periodic links of interdependence. This has two topics: i. Overview of the classifications, and ii. Extensive explanation of the links.

i. Overview of the classifications. This has two points.

(1) Classifying in twelve

20ab These are twelve links of interdependent
Origination

The continuum of the aggregates comes from another world to this next one and goes from here to the next—the period of three births. In order to refute that the entry into samsara happens either without a cause or incompatibly with its cause, it is taught that **there are twelve links of interdependent origination:** ignorance, formation, consciousness, name-and-form, six sense bases, contact, feeling, craving, grasping, becoming, birth, and aging and death.

(2) Condensing into three

> 20b in three parts.

These are **in** the **three parts** of previous, middle, and next lives, or the three times.

ii. Extensive explanation of the links. This has three topics: (1) How they are completed in three lifetimes, (2) Grouping them into afflictions, karma, and bases, and (3) Dispelling others' doubts.

(1) How they are completed in three lifetimes. This has four topics: (a) Explaining their individual natures, (b) Explaining the three periods that arise, (c) Teaching that these are periodic, and (d) Rebutting that this contradicts the sutras.

(a) Explaining their individual natures

> 20cd. The previous and next, two each;
> The middle, eight, with all complete.

Of these three lifetimes, in **the previous** lifetime **and next** lifetime there are **two each:** they are ignorance and formation, and birth and aging and death respectively. In **the middle,** the **eight** from consciousness to becoming are presented. This is intended in terms of **all** of the links **complete,** as in the first three modes of birth in Desire. In miraculous birth, the between state, and the two higher realms, it is not necessarily thus.[141]

(b) Explaining the three periods that arise. This has three points.

(i) Explaining what arises in the previous life

> 21ab Previous afflictions: ignorance.
> Previous karma is formations.

The **previous** period's five aggregates during **afflicted** conduct is the link of **ignorance.** In relation to this life, these are called the link of ignorance, because the afflictions act simultaneously with ignorance and the afflictions always arise by the power of ignorance. It is just as when the king arrives, the attendant also comes. The five aggregates in the **previous** lifetime at the time of accumulating meritorious and other **karma are formations.**

(ii) Explaining what arises in the middle

21cd The aggregates at linking: consciousness.
    And name-and-form is on from there

22. Until the six sense bases emerge.
    Those are until three are assembled.
  Contact is till one knows the causes
    Of pleasure and of pain, et cetera.

23. Then feeling until sex. And craving
    Is greed for possessions and for sex.
  Close grasping is then chasing after
    In order to obtain enjoyments.

24ab Performing actions that result
    In an existence is becoming.

The single moment of the five **aggregates at** the time of rebirth-**linking** in the mother's womb is the link of **consciousness. And** the link of **name-and-form is** the five aggregates **on from there**, the moment of rebirth-linking, **until** or before **the six sense bases emerge**. Name is the four aggregates—like names, they are unobstructive. Form is the fetal stages of mushiness and so on. The link of **those,** the six sense bases, **is** the five aggregates from the time when those have completely emerged **until** the **three** of object, faculty, and consciousness **are assembled.** The link of **contact is** the five aggregates from then **until** the object, faculty, and consciousness are assembled and **one knows the causes**—a pleasant, unpleasant, neutral, or other object—**of pleasure and of pain, et cetera,** including neutral feeling. **Then** the link of **feeling** is the five aggregates from the time one is able to discern the causes of the three feelings **until** the lust for **sex** arises. **And** the link of **craving is** the five aggregates during the period of especial **greed for** the **possession** of desirable things **and for sex** before one actively seeks the object. The link of **close grasping is** the five aggregates during the period when one begins actively seeking and **then chases after** everything **in order to obtain** the **enjoyments** of desirable objects such as horses, cattle, grain, treasures, and so forth as well as the pleasures of sex. The five aggregates that, in chasing after things, **perform actions** or karmas **that** accumulate virtue and nonvirtue and will later produce a happy or miserable **result** of **existence is** the link of **becoming.** As it will arise, becoming is a synonym for karma. If you examine it closely, it is not separate in essence from the interdependent link of formation.

(iii) Explaining what arises in the next life

> 24cd Linking rebirth again is birth.
> Up until feeling, aging and death.

When karma makes one die in this and migrate to the next, the five aggregates at the time of the **linking** of **rebirth again are** the link of **birth.** What is presented as the link of consciousness in this life is presented as the link of birth in the next lifetime. In order to instill world-weariness in disciples, the Bhagavan taught that the aggregates from birth **up until feeling** are the link of **aging and death.**

(c) Teaching that these are periodic. This has two points.

(i) Actual

> 25a They claim that this is periodic.

There are four ways to classify the links of interdependence: momentary, prolonged, connected, and periodic. The manner in which the twelve links are posited as a single moment is described in the autocommentary:

> How are they momentary, you ask? In a single moment there are all twelve links. This is how: that which is the delusion that kills out of the power of greed is ignorance. That which is the volition is formation. Individually knowing things is consciousness. The four aggregates that arise simultaneously with consciousness are name-and-form. The faculties that reside within name-and-form are the six sense bases. The six sense bases coming together is contact. Experiencing contact is feeling. That which is greed is craving. The entanglers that are concurrent with that are grasping. The actions of body and speech that those motivate is becoming. The arising of those actions is birth. Their complete ripening is aging. Their disintegration is death.

Thus among the four classifications of interdependence, the Bhagavan presented the continuum of the five aggregates over the period of three lifetimes as the twelve links. **They** of the Great Exposition **claim** here in this context **that this is** the teaching of the links to be **periodic.**

The word "claim" indicates that this is the Great Exposition's position: it is a skeptical word from the Sutra school, which says it is admissible to present the six sense bases and name-and-form as periods of the five aggregates, but how could ignorance and formation be a period of the five aggregates?

(ii) Dispelling doubts

> 25b The link's called by the principal.

If in all twelve links there are all five aggregates, why is the first link known simply as ignorance? you wonder. Because at that point ignorance is principal, **the link is called by** the name of **the principal**, like saying, "The king has come" when an army with four divisions[142] arrives. In the same way, the links from formation to aging and death are known by that which is principal at that point.

(d) Rebutting that this contradicts the sutras

> 25cd It's taught to reverse ignorance
> About the previous, next, and middle.

In the abhidharma, the links of interdependence are taught with regards to both sentient beings and all other composite phenomena. In the sutras, however, they are only taught with regard to sentient beings in order **to reverse** the doubt and **ignorance about** the self in the three times of **the previous, next, and middle** lives, such as the doubt, "Did it occur or not? Will it occur or not? What is it like here in the middle?"

(2) Grouping them into afflictions, karma, and bases. This has three points.

(i) Actual

> 26ab Three are afflictions. Two are karma.
> Seven are bases

Of the twelve links, **three are afflictions:** ignorance, craving, and grasping. Of these, ignorance is the cause of the current birth, and craving and grasping are the cause of future birth. The **two** links of formation and becoming **are karma.** These cause the present and future births. Because they are the support of karma and afflictions, **seven** links **are bases:** the five from consciousness to feeling, birth, and aging and death.

(ii) Teaching that seven are result

26b and results.

The seven branches that are the bases for karma and the afflictions are also **results,** because the result of ignorance and formation is the five from consciousness to feeling, and the result of craving, grasping, and becoming is the two links of birth and aging and death.

(iii) The reason for not explaining the previous and next lives in detail

26cd Cause and result of two is concise:
One can infer them from the middle.

Well, for this lifetime the five results from consciousness to feeling and both karma and the afflictions are explained in detail, so why in the future lifetime are they condensed into the two results of birth and aging and death? Why are they condensed in the previous lifetime into the cause ignorance only? you ask. The links of **cause and result of** the **two** past and future lives **is** taught **concisely**; the detailed explanations of the two causes in past lifetime and five results in future lifetime are not given. This is because **one can infer them from the** detailed explanation of cause and effect in the **middle.** There is no need to tire oneself pointlessly.

(3) Dispelling others' doubts. This has two points.[143]

(a) Dispelling doubts as to the quantity

27. Afflictions bear afflictions, action.
From that, the bases, and from those
Arise the bases and afflictions.
That is existence's progression.

Well, it follows that samsara has a beginning and an end, because ignorance has no cause and aging and death no result. If you agree, it follows that more links should be added, because those two need a cause and result. This would therefore become endless because of your assertion, you say.

Even if those two links have causes and results, it does not follow that more links need to be added. The Bhagavan said that the **affliction** of craving **bears** the **affliction** of grasping, and afflictions bear the karma of **action** itself: formation arises out of ignorance, and becoming arises out of grasping. **From that** karma of formation and becoming, **the bases** of consciousness and birth arise. **From those arise the bases** from name-and-form to feeling and aging and death, **and** from these bases of feeling and aging and death, the **afflictions** of ignorance, craving, and grasping arise. **This is** how the links of **existence progress.**

(b) The distinction between arising and arisen

> 28ab Here what is arising is a cause;
> What has arisen is a result.

Here in this presentation from the sutras, **what is arising** in interdependence **is** a link that is **a cause,** because something arises from it. **What has arisen** in interdependence **is** proposed as a link that abides, because it has arisen. Therefore all of the links are proven to be both arising and arisen, because they are both a cause and **a result.** Although this is so, cause and result do not get mixed up, because when they arise depending on something else, that something does not depend upon them. For instance, in relation to one's own father, one is the child and not the father.

b. The essence of each link. This has two topics: i. Actually explaining four links, and ii. Teaching that the other links are known from elsewhere.

i. Actually explaining four links. This has four topics: (1) An explanation of ignorance, (2) Of name, (3) Of contact, and (4) Of feeling.

(1) An explanation of ignorance. This has two topics: (a) Identifying its essence, and (b) Dispelling wrong conceptions.

(a) Identifying its essence

> 28cd An other dharma, opposite to knowing,
> Ignorance is like untruth, unfriendly, et cetera.

The meaning of ignorance: ignorance is **an other dharma** that is an unclear mental factor and is **opposite to** correct **knowing** of truth, karma and result, the jewels, and so on. As nonthings and matter are also the absence of knowledge or something that is not knowledge, **ignorance** is not merely either of those two. For example, it **is like untruth,** which is understood as a lie, **unfriendly** as enemies, nondharma as nonvirtue, "not its meaning" as "the incorrect meaning," wrong action[144] as unmindful action, **et cetera.**

Well then, from what do we know that ignorance is not merely the absence of knowing? you ask. It says in a sutra, "Through the condition of ignorance, formation arises."[145] It is also logically proven because the eye and so forth, which are not knowing, are not the condition for formations, and rabbits' horns and such, which are the nonexistence of awareness, also do not function as the causes for formations.[146]

(b) Dispelling wrong conceptions. This has two points.

(i) Refuting that ignorance is a mere absence because it is a name for an affliction.

29a Because of fetter and such words.

Ignorance is not presented as merely the absence of knowing or not knowing, **because** in teaching **fetter and such words** as the three bonds, four floods, and four yokes, it is taught as a separate mental factor.

(ii) Refuting calling bad full knowing "ignorance"

29b–d Not bad full knowing, since that is view.
Since it's concurrent with that view;
It's taught that it afflicts full knowing.

If that is so, then like saying a bad child is not your child, bad full knowing is ignorance, you say. Ignorance **is not** such **bad full knowing, since that is** an afflicted **view.** In that case, afflicted bad full knowing that is not a view is ignorance, you say. That is also not so, **since it,** ignorance, **is concurrent with that view,** and because views are full knowing, and it is never possible for two substances of full knowing to be concurrent with each other. Additionally, bad full knowing is not ignorance, because **it is taught that** ignorance **afflicts full knowing**, making it afflicted.

(2) An explanation of name

30a Skandhas that are not form are name.

The four **skandhas** or aggregates **that are not form**—feeling and so forth—**are name** in the link name-and-form because they engage their object by power of names, and because they are unobstructive, like names.

(3) An explanation of contact

30b–d Six contacts happen from assembly.
Five are obstructive contact, and
The sixth is designated contact.

31. Aware and unaware and other contact
Are stainless and afflicted and the rest.
Malicious, lustful contact, and
Three felt as pleasant and so forth.

The **six contacts** from eye to mind **happen from assembly,** because they arise from the assembly of object, faculty, and consciousness coming together.

Well then, the first five faculties and consciousness arise simultaneously, so they meet by assembly, but in contact assembled by mind it is not definite that all three will be assembled, because it is not logical that the mind faculty that has ceased, future dharmas that have not arisen, and the present mind consciousness could be assembled simultaneously, you say. This does not pervade, because the assembly of cause and result is called an assembly, even though they are not necessarily simultaneous. Alternatively, the single result itself has the meaning of assembly, because result is compatible with the production of a single contact. The many divergent opinions of earlier masters about contact appear in the *Great Ṭīka,* so refer there.

Of these contacts, the first **five are obstructive contact,** because they are contact that arises based upon obstructive faculties that have form. **And the sixth is** called **designated contact** because one meaning may be labeled with many names, so names are designations, and this is the contact that focuses on those. The eye consciousness knows blue, but does not know to think, "This is blue," whereas the mind consciousness does know to think, "This is blue"—it knows what the name of a given meaning is.

Also, these six can become three: **aware** contact, **and unaware** or ignorant contact, **and other contact** that is neither of those two. The first two are respectively **stainless,** undefiled contact **and afflicted** contact, because the aware mentioned here is undefiled full knowing, and ignorance in this context is afflicted full knowing, **and** these contacts are concurrent with those. The third is **the rest** other than those two: it is put forth as contact concurrent with virtuous defiled or unobscured neutral full knowing, because it is contact that is not concurrent with either of the two above full knowings. Within ignorant contact, **malicious** and **lustful contact**, which are labeled by the names of their companions, are especially harmful, so they are taught separately.

Alternatively, all contact can be included within the **three** categories of contact **felt** or experienced **as pleasant and so forth,** including contact experienced as unpleasant and contact experienced as neutral, because they are the compatible causes of the experiences of pleasure and so forth. In this way, there are sixteen types of contact.

(4) An explanation of feeling. This has two topics: (a) General classification, and (b) A specific explanation of mental feeling.

(a) General classification

> 32ab From that, six feelings can arise:
> Five bodily, the other mental.

From that contact, there are **six feelings** that **can arise**: feeling that arises from contact assembled by eye and so on. Of these, because the first **five** depend upon faculties with form, they are **bodily** feeling. **The** mental feeling is **other** than those five; it is feeling that arises from contact assembled by **mind.**

Does feeling arise after contact or together with it? you ask. Some Great Expositionists say they are together, because they are mutual coemergent causes. The Sutra school asks, if they arise simultaneously, how can the producer be proven to produce the thing that is produced? In response, the Great Exposition asks in return, why it would not be proven? The Sutra school replies that two coemergent dharmas cannot be proven to be producer and produced because after a dharma has arisen, there is no power to produce it again. There are many other such debates between the Exposition and Sutra schools which can be found in the great *Ṭīka* itself.

(b) A specific explanation of mental feeling. This has three topics: (i) Overview, (ii) Explanation, and (iii) Summary.

(i) Overview

> 32cd And that has eighteen types as well
> Because of movement of the mind.

And that mental factor of feeling itself is presented as **having eighteen types as well, because of the movement of mind**—mental pleasure, mental unhappiness, and neutral toward form and the other five objects.

The following appears in the Great Chim's commentary:

> The Great Exposition proposes that feeling moves to the object on the support of the mind as its mount. The Sutra school says mind moves to the object on the support of feeling.

(ii) Explanation. This has three topics: A. Explanation of feelings of the Desire realm, B. Of Form, and C. Of Formless.

A. Explanation of feelings of the Desire realm. This has three points.

1. Focusing on own level

33a In Desire, all focus on their own,

In the realm of **Desire**, there are all eighteen of those movements of mind. They **all focus on their own** level.

2. Focusing on Form

33b And twelve can have Form in their sphere.

And there are **twelve** movements of mind of Desire that **can have** the **Form** realm **in their sphere.** Since there is no scent or taste there, the six that focus on those two are not included.

3. Focusing on Formless

33c The three on higher.

The three feelings of Desire that focus on dharmas only can focus **on** the **higher** Formless, because the five objects of form and so forth do not exist there.

B. Of Form. This has two topics: 1. Explaining the feelings of the first two dhyanas, and 2. Of the higher two dhyanas.

1. Explaining the feelings of the first two dhyanas. This has three points.

a. Focusing on objects of Desire

33cd On two dhyanas,
Are twelve which can move toward Desire.

On the first **two dhyanas**, as there is no mental unhappiness nor its six movements, there **are** the remaining **twelve, which can move toward Desire** because they can focus on or perceive its six objects.

b. Focusing on Form

34a Eight focus on their own;

There are **eight** movements to the four objects (except the four that move to scent and taste) that **focus on their own** level of Form.

c. Focusing on Formless

34ab the two
On Formless.

Dharma alone is the object of **the two** feelings, mental pleasure and neutral, when focusing **on** the **Formless.**

2. Explaining the feelings of the higher two dhyanas. This has three points.

a. Focusing on Desire

34bc The two dhyans have six.
Six on Desire,

The higher **two dhyanas have** only the **six** movements of neutral feeling. The other, mental pleasure, is not present, because it has been abandoned. Those **six** focus **on** all six objects of **Desire**.

b. Focusing on Form

34c the four on own,

There are **the four** objects of its **own** Form realm, because there is neither scent nor taste.

c. Focusing on Formless

34d And one can focus on the higher.

And one, neutral feeling, **can focus on** the object of dharma only of **the higher** Formless realm.

C. Explaining the feelings of Formless. This has two topics: 1. Feelings of the preparations, and 2. Feelings of the actual absorption.

1. Feelings of the preparations. This has two points.

a. Focus on Form

35ab On preparations for the Formless,
Four move toward Form,

On the **preparations for** the **Formless** level of Infinite Space, the focus is on **four** objects, because they **move toward** the fourth dhyana of **Form,** so they focus on its form, sound, feeling, and dharma.

b. Focus on Formless

35b one moves toward higher.

On the preparation for Infinite Space, **one** movement of neutral feeling that focuses on the object dharma **moves toward** the **higher** Formless realm.

2. Feelings of the actual absorption

35c In actual, one with own object.

In the four **actual** absorptions of Formless and the preparations for the three higher levels, there is only **one** movement, because those levels do not focus on Desire or Form but focus only on their **own** level's dharma as **object**, with no other movement.

(iii) Summary

35d All of the eighteen are defiled.

All of the eighteen movements of the mind **are defiled** because they all propagate existence, so there are not any undefiled. The noble path is entered without effort and enters the expanse with no attributes, but the movements are the opposite of that.

ii. Teaching that the other links are known from elsewhere

36a Others have been or will be explained.

In that case, if this is a teaching on interdependence, why are only ignorance, name, contact, and feeling explained, and the others not? you ask. The **other** links of form, consciousness, and the six sense bases **have** already **been** explained, **or** formation, becoming, craving, and grasping **will be explained** in the fourth and fifth areas. The remaining links—birth, and aging and death—are not explained separately, because they are included within the others.

c. Teaching the three all-afflicted through comparisons. This has three points.

i. Teaching the all-afflicted afflictions through comparisons

36b-d In this, afflictions are like seeds,
Like nagas, and like roots and trees,
Like husks as well, it is proposed.

In this discussion, the **afflictions are like seeds:** just as trunks, branches, and leaves grow from seeds, afflictions, karma, and the bases grow out of the afflictions. They are **like nagas:** just as a lake will not dry up if there is a naga in it, the lake of birth will not dry up if there is the naga of afflictions. **And** they are **like** the **roots** of a thicket: just as if you do not pull those out, it will re-grow even if you cut off the branches, if you do not pull the afflictions out from the root, wanderers will be reborn. **And** they are like **trees:** just as trees produce flowers and fruit in season, afflictions are the cause of afflictions, karma, and the bases. They are **like** the thick **husks** of rice grains, **as well, it is proposed**: if there are husks, the grains produce a crop but without them do not. Similarly karma that has the husk of the attainment of afflictions leads to rebirth in the next lives, but without that, karma alone does not.

ii. Teaching the all-afflicted karma through comparisons

37ab Karma's like rice within its husk,
Like medicine and flowers.

Karma is like rice within its husk, because just as if there is a husk, the germ of a rice grain produces a fruit, karma that has the husk attained through the afflictions produces the result of birth. **Like medicine** that gives its power a single time, karma also produces a single fully ripened result, and does not produce any more. **And** like **flowers** that are the proximate cause for the arising of fruit, karma is the proximate cause of full ripening, and the afflictions are the distant cause.

iii. Teaching the all-afflicted bases through a comparison

37bc The bases,
Like food and drink that have been got.

The bases are **like food and drink that have been got.** For example, once food and drink has been obtained, it is no more than something to enjoy; it is not something that needs to be produced again. Similarly, the fully ripened bases also are merely something to enjoy and not to produce in other lifetimes, because after fully ripening they have no connection to other full ripening in other lifetimes.

d. Teaching these links as the four states

37d Among these four states of existence,

38a–c The state of rebirth is afflicted
By all the afflictions of its level.
The others, threefold. Three in Formless.

Among these four states of existence, the between state, the state of rebirth, the previous state, and the state of death, **the state of rebirth is** always **afflicted,** as there is neither virtue nor unobscured neutral in that state. Whatever level that state of rebirth is on, it is afflicted **by all the afflictions of its** own **level.** However, it is not afflicted by five autonomous entanglers: jealousy, stinginess, regret, aggression, and concealment.[147] **The** three states that are **other** than the state of rebirth, the between state, previous state, and state of death, are **threefold**—virtue, afflicted, and neutral. There are **three** states with the exception of the between state **in Formless,** which implies that all four states are in Desire and Form.

C. Conditions for abiding after birth. This has three topics: 1. Overview,

2. Explanation, and 3. As a summary, ascertaining that there are four types of sustenance.

1. Overview

38d Wanderers abide from sustenance.

Wanderers all **abide from sustenance.** There are four types of sustenance: food, contact, mental volition, and consciousness.

2. Explanation. This has three topics: a. Explaining food, b. Explaining the remaining kinds of sustenance, and c. Additionally, explaining the synonyms for the between state.

a. Explaining food. This has three points.

i. What level it is on

39a The sustenance food is in Desire.

The sustenance food is only **in Desire** and not in the two higher realms because one has no attachment to food there.

ii. What sense base it is

39b Its nature is the three sense bases,

Its nature is the three sense bases of smell, taste, and touch: the three faculties of nose, tongue, and body discern a bite of food, and then one swallows and eats it, so it is food.

iii. Dispelling a doubt

39cd But not the sense base form, since that
Does not affect its organ or the freed.

Doesn't it follow that the sense base form is food, because after discerning color, et cetera, as a bite of food, one eats? you ask. The **sense base form** is **not** food, **since** if it were, when swallowed it would have to benefit its faculty (the eye) and the sources that support that faculty, but it does not. If **that does not affect its** own **organ** or faculty, then it is impossible that it affect other faculties, and seeing the form of enticing food does not affect **the** nonreturners and arhats who are **freed** from desire for food.

b. Explaining the remaining kinds of sustenance. This has two points.

i. Identifying their essence

> 40ab Contact, volition, and consciousness are
> Stained sustenance.

Contact that arises from the assembly of object, faculty, and consciousness; the mental karma of **volition; and consciousness are,** between the two of defiled and undefiled, **stained** or defiled **sustenance;** they are not undefiled.

The Great Exposition says the undefiled contact, volition, and consciousness are not sustenance, because sustenance sustains existence by propelling what had not been propelled and completing what had been propelled, whereas those three exhaust existence and arise as its antidote.

ii. What realms they are in

> 40b They are in three.

They are in all **three** realms.

c. Additionally, explaining the synonyms for the between state

> 40cd It's born from mind, the searching state,
> Scent-eater, and the between state,

> 41a And reestablishing.

What seeks out existence? you ask. As it does not depend on future parents, warmth and moisture, and so forth, and arises from just mind, **it is** called **born from mind.** As its condition is to seek the state of rebirth, it is called **the searching state.** As it eats smells for sustenance, it is called a **scent-eater. And** it is called **the between state, and** as it is clearly directed toward taking birth in a body, it is called **reestablishing.**

3. As a summary, ascertaining that there are four types of sustenance

41a-d Two have the purpose
Of developing its base and the supported.
Two have the purpose to propel,
Establish the next life, in order.

If everything defiled maintains existence, why are only these four presented as sustenance? you ask. It is taught because they are of primary importance. Of the first **two** types of sustenance, food is presented as **having the purpose of developing its,** this life's, **base,** the body with its faculties, **and** contact is presented as having the purpose of developing **the supported** mental factors. The other **two** are sustenance of volition, which **has the purpose to propel** the next life, and the sustenance of consciousness, which has the purpose to actually **establish the next life** once it has been propelled. Thus they are presented **in** this **order.** In this way, the first two are like a wet nurse who takes care of someone after birth, and the latter two are like a mother who gives birth to someone who has not yet been born.

A few words here:

The wonderful acuity that purifies rebirth
Is not begrimed with filth from creatures of degenerate times.
Within this feast of explanations for those wanting freedom,
There is a great gate to inexhaustible nectar.

D. The minds of staying and dying. This has three topics: 1. Identifying the mind of death, 2. Where the consciousness stops, and 3. The cause of severing the pith.

1. Identifying the mind of death. This has two topics: a. General teaching, and b. Specific explanations.

a. General teaching

42a–c To sever, to restore, and to
Detach, regress, die, and be born
Are the mind consciousness alone.

To sever the roots of virtue through wrong views; **to restore** the virtuous roots through correct view or doubt; **and to detach** oneself from realms and levels, to **regress** from a result through malice or another inappropriate attention; to **die,** which is similar to the motion of the five faculties contracting and their continuum being cut; **and be born,** which is rebirth-linking through a mistaken mind, **are the mind consciousness alone,** not the others. The mention of birth also includes rebirth-linking in the between state.

b. Specific explanations. This has three points.

i. Distinctions of feeling

42d At death and birth, there's neutral feeling.

At death and at **birth there is neutral feeling** only, because pleasure and suffering are clear, but a clear consciousness is unsuitable for death or birth.

ii. Distinctions of mind

43a Not in one-pointed or no mind.

Those who were born in the Desire realm do not die or take birth while they are resting **in one-pointed** equipoise **or** in a state with **no mind.** This is because death and birth are not the same status as samadhi, because samadhi arises from effort and is beneficial, and because those who are in states with no mind cannot be harmed by fire, weapons, or so forth.

iii. The manner of entering the state without remainder

43b Nirvana in two neutral minds.

The mind of the state of death is explained to be virtuous, nonvirtuous, or neutral. Of these, an arhat passes into **nirvana in** one of **two neutral minds.** If one proposes that there is fully ripened neutral feeling in Desire, then it is either that of the path of conduct or full ripened. If one proposes there is not, it is either a virtuous mind of a path of conduct or an unafflicted neutral mind, it is said. In particular, those two are weak, which makes them consistent with severing the continuum of mind, whereas other minds are strong.

2. Where the consciousness stops

43cd In gradual death, if low or human,
Divine or no rebirth, mind dies

44a In the feet, navel, or the heart.

In that case, what part of the body does the consciousness cease in? you ask.

In dying a **gradual death, if** they are going to the **low or human** or **divine** god realms, **or** if they are arhats who have **no rebirth,** the **mind** is said conventionally to **die in the feet,** the **navel, or the heart,** because the body faculty ceases there. Some say that arhats exit through the crown of their heads. If one dies instantaneously, the body faculty stops in an instant along with the mind.

3. The cause of severing the pith

44b Water, et cetera, severs the pith.

In some of these instances, the *duḥkha* said to be of the **pith** being **severed** arises. The pith is that part of the body which harming will cause death. Severing is an intolerable feeling arising there. In cases when there is a lot of phlegm, this is caused by the element of **water** being disturbed. Included by the phrase "**et cetera,**" when there is a lot of bile, the element of fire is disturbed, and if there is a lot of wind, the element of wind is violently disturbed. It is not severed by the other source, earth: this is similar to the destruction of the environment, the world.[148]

These three are all in terms of gradual death. In the instantaneous death of those born by miraculous birth, the faculties are not discarded through a single part of the body, nor is the pith severed. The gods of Desire do not have their pith severed, but when the five near signs and five distant signs of death appear, they experience unfathomable suffering.

E. Categorizing beings in three groups

44cd Nobles are destined for the correct;
The heinous deeds for the mistaken.

From a sutra:

> Three groups of sentient beings are recognized: the group that is destined for the correct, the group destined for the mistaken, and the uncertain group.

Of these three groups that are taught, **nobles are destined for the correct** because they are certain to be born in the higher realms and not the lower, and then attain freedom, and those who have done **the heinous misdeeds are destined for the mistaken,** because immediately after dying they are certain to be reborn in hell. Everyone else is uncertain.

The explanation of sentient beings is thus completed. A few words:

In the full-knowing mirror of my mind,
The characters of what there is to know
From abhidharma are distinct,
Like brilliant stars, or gems in clear lake waters.

Alas! The teachings of this age's buddha
Are convoluted by those with evil minds!
Deceitfully they've criticized,
Sowing dissension, so I've tired myself.

But then, when I remember the great kindness
Of the translators, scholars, kings, and aides
Of olden times, my mind is seized
With excitement for the methods of this dharma!

II. The world that contains them. This has three topics: A. The nature of the supporting container, B. Additionally, the sizes of sentient beings, and C. Units of measure.

A. The nature of the supporting container. This has four topics: 1. A general teaching of the container's nature, 2. An explanation of particular places, 3. Identifying the world of three thousands, and 4. Teaching that the three thousands arise and are destroyed together.

1. A general teaching of the container's nature. This has two topics: a. An explanation of the three supporting mandalas, and b. An explanation of the mountains and seas they support.

a. An explanation of the three supporting mandalas. This has two topics: i. The size of the mandala of wind, and ii. The size of the other two mandalas.

i. The size of the mandala of wind

45. Now the container world is said
To have below a mandala
Of wind one million and six hundred
Thousands in depth, uncountable.

To explain the container, the world: in general, according to sutras of the Foundation and Great Vehicles, some world realms are upside down, some are sideways, some have no cover above, some have no sun and moon, in some a single sun and moon orbit the entire three thousands,[149] and in some the entire three thousands is the size of the Bodhi tree. Many such worlds that are said to exist, but in this presentation it is time to explain the Unbearable World Realm of our Teacher the Buddha Shakyamuni.[150] **Now the container,** this **world** realm of three great thousands, **is said to** exist as follows:

Through the power of sentient beings' karma, in the space that is the foundation **below** it, this world, there is **a mandala of wind.** That is **one million and six hundred thousand** leagues[151] **in depth** and **uncountable** leagues across in diameter. It is so hard that even a vajra of great power cannot destroy it.

ii. The size of the other two mandalas. This has two topics: (1) Explaining their depth individually, and (2) Explaining their diameter together.

(1) Explaining their depth individually. This has two topics: (a) Water, and (b) Gold.

(a) Water. This has two points.

(i) Its size at the time it coalesces

46ab Then water to a depth of one
Million one hundred twenty thousand.

By the power of the karma of sentient beings, sheets of rain the drops of which are the size of yokes **then** fall in space from clouds with golden essences. That becomes a mandala of **water to a depth of one million one hundred twenty thousand** leagues. The water does not immediately spill away because of the force of karma.

(ii) Its size when it abides

46cd Then it becomes eight hundred thousand
In depth.

Then a wind that arises from the karma of sentient beings churns all the water, and **it becomes eight hundred thousand** leagues **in-depth.**

(b) Gold

46d The rest turns into gold.

Just as when milk boils curd forms, **the rest turns into** the earth itself with a nature of **gold** and a depth of three hundred twenty thousand leagues.

(2) Explaining their diameter together. This has two points.

(a) Their diameter

47. The mandalas of water and gold
Are in diameter one million
Two hundred and three thousand and
Four hundred fifty leagues across;

The mandalas of water and gold that lie under each of the hundred million worlds of four continents **are** in diameter of **one million two hundred and three thousand four hundred fifty** leagues **across.** The diameters of these two mandalas are equal.

(b) Their circumference

48a They're thrice that in circumference.

They are thrice that in circumference, it is said, which means that their circumferences are 3,610,350 leagues.

b. An explanation of the mountains and seas they support. This has two topics: i. An explanation of the nine mountains, and ii. An explanation of the eight seas.

i. An explanation of the nine mountains. This has three topics: (1) Where they are, (2) What cause they are created from, and (3) Explaining their sizes.

(1) Where they are

48b–d On that are Meru, the Yoke Holder,
Plow Holder, and Acacia Tree,
And likewise Lovely to Behold,

49a–c And Horse's Ear and Bowing Down,
Rim Holder Mounts, then continents.
Outside there is the Outer Ring.

The mandala of golden earth is supported above the water, and **on that** in the middle there **is** Mount **Meru.** It is surrounded by **the** seven remaining mountain ranges: **Yoke Holder, Plow Holder, and Acacia Tree, and likewise** the **Lovely to Behold, and Horse's Ear and Bowing Down,** and the **Rim Holder Mountains. Then** there are the four **continents. Outside** the continents **there is the Outer Ring,** which surrounds it in a ring.

(2) What cause they are created from

49d Seven are gold. That one is iron.

50a Mount Meru is four precious ores.

The **seven** mountain ranges of Yoke Holder and so forth **are gold. That one** Outside Ring of mountains **is iron. Mount Meru is** created of **four precious ores:** its east is silver, the south vaidurya,[152] the west red crystal, and the north is gold. The color of the four faces of the Supreme Mountain[153] and the color of the sky of their corresponding continents appear similarly.

The reason for this is that the sheets of rain that fell from space and formed the mandala of water below the golden earth contained the elements of gold, various jewels, and so forth. When churned by the wind, these elements became the Supreme Mountain and the rest.

(3) Explaining their sizes. This has two topics: (a) Explaining how far they descend into the water together, and (b) Explaining how high each ascends above the water individually.

(a) Explaining how far they descend into the water together

50bc Down eighty thousand into water
Plunges Mount Meru;

Down eighty thousand leagues **into** the **water** that is on the golden earth **plunge Mount Meru** and the other eight mountain ranges.

(b) Explaining how high each ascends above the water individually. This has two topics: (i) The size of Mount Meru, and (ii) The sizes of the others.

(i) The size of Mount Meru

50cd above as well
It lofts to eighty thousand leagues.

Just as it descends into the water, **above as well, it lofts to eighty thousand leagues.** Combining the two, the height of the Supreme Mountain is 160,000 leagues.

(ii) The sizes of the others. This has two points.

(A) Width

51a The eight are each half less in width.

The eight including the seven mountain ranges and the Perimeter Circle **are each half less** than the previous mountain range **in width.** The Yoke Holder is the largest with a width of 40,000 leagues, and Plow Holder is half that width, or 20,000, and so on until the iron mountains which are 312½ leagues in width.

(B) Height

51b Their heights are equal to their widths.

Their, the mountains in these ranges, **heights are equal to their widths.**

i. An explanations of eight seas. This has two topics: (1) An explanation of the seven Playful Seas, and (2) An explanation of the Outer Ocean.

(1) An explanation of the seven Playful Seas. This has three points.

(a) The way the seven Playful Seas are

51c Between them, seven Playful Seas;

In the areas **between them,** the mountain ranges, are the **seven Playful Seas.** Their waters have the eight qualities.[154]

(b) The size of the innermost Playful Sea

> 51d Across the first is eighty thousand.
>
> 52ab This one is the Vast Inner Sea.
> Its sides are triple to its width.

Across the first Playful Sea **is eighty thousand** leagues. **This one is the Vast Inner Sea. Its sides** along the shores of the Yoke Holder Mountain **are triple to its width,** or 240,000 leagues.

(c) The size of the other six

> 52c The other seas are each half less.

The other Playful **Seas are each half less** in width than the previous.

(2) An explanation of the Outer Ocean

> 52d The rest is the Great Outer Ocean.
>
> 53ab Across it is three hundred and
> Twenty-two thousand leagues.

The rest of the water from the Rim Holder Mountains to the outer iron mountains **is the Great Outer Ocean.** It is filled with salt water. In its width, **across it is three hundred and twenty-two thousand leagues.**

2. An explanation of particular places. This has three topics: a. The places of humans, b. The places of hell, and c. The places of the gods.

a. The places of humans. This has two topics: i. Teaching of the twelve lands in general, and ii. A particular explanation of the Rose-Apple Land.

i. Teaching of the twelve lands in general. This has two topics: (1) Explaining the four continents, and (2) Explaining the eight subcontinents.

(1) Explaining the four continents. This has four points.

(a) The shape and size of the Rose-Apple Land

53b–d Therein
Is the Rose-Apple Land, two thousand
Leagues on three sides, shaped like a cart,

54a With one of three and one half leagues.

Therein, in that poisonous ocean, to the south of the Supreme Mountain **is the Rose-Apple Land,** which is **two thousand leagues on** its **three** long **sides.** It is **shaped like a cart,**[155] **with one** short side **of three and one half leagues.** Its perimeter measures 6,003½ leagues. Its depth extends eighty thousand leagues down—all four continents have an equal depth.

(b) The shape and size of Superior Body

54b–d Superior Body is half-moon like.
Three of its sides are like here; one
Is three and one half hundred leagues.

From the Rose-Apple Land, on the side of the supreme mountain is the eastern **Superior Body,** which **is half-moon like** in shape. **Three of its sides are like here,** the Rose-Apple Land, at a length of 2000 leagues each. **One** side **is three and one half hundred,** or 350, **leagues** long. Its perimeter measures 6,350 leagues. Because its level is seven *talas* above sea level, or alternatively, because the humans born there have bodies that are twice as large as humans here, it is called the Superior Body.

(c) The shape and size of the Bountiful Cow Land

55a–c The Bountiful Cow Land is round,
Seven thousand and five hundred leagues.
Across its mid, twenty-five hundred.

On the west face of the Supreme Mountain is **the Bountiful Cow Land.** It **is round,** and it is **seven thousand and five hundred** leagues in circumference. **Across its mid,** its diameter is **twenty-five hundred** leagues. It is bountiful with cows and jewels, and the river Sawaka flows through its middle.

(d) The shape and size of Unpleasant Sound

55d Unpleasant Sound: eight, equal, square.

On the north face of the Supreme Mountain is **Unpleasant Sound**, where they speak the language of ghosts, or where one's death is prophesied seven days prior to occurring. Its perimeter is **eight** thousand leagues, with four **equal** sides of two thousand leagues each and **square** in shape.

Humans' faces are similar in shape to the continents they live on.

(2) Explaining the eight subcontinents

56. Between are eight subcontinents:
Deha, Videha, Kurava,
Kaurava, Chāmara, Avara,
And Śaṭhā and Uttaramantriṇa.

Between them there **are eight subcontinents: Deha** and **Videha** on the sides of the eastern continent. **Kuruva** and **Kaurava** are on the sides of the northern continent. **Chāmara** and **Avaracāmara are** on the sides of the southern continent. **And Śaṭha and Uttaramantriṇa** are on the sides of the western continent.

ii. A particular explanation of the Rose-Apple Land

57. To the north of here, across the nine
Black Mounts is the Snow Mountain, then
On the near side of Perfume Mountain
Is a lake with waters fifty across.

To the north of here, the Rose-Apple Land, **across the nine Black Mounts,** there **is the** great **Snow Mountain. Then** further to the north of that is **Perfume Mountain,** and ten leagues away **on** its **near** south **side**, there **is a lake with waters fifty** leagues **across.** This is the Unheated Lake, whose waters have the eight qualities. It is difficult for people who do not have miraculous powers to get there.

On the shore of the Unheated Lake there is a rose-apple tree with sweet fruit. When its clay-pot sized fruit ripens, the nagas emanate as fish and eat it, and what is not eaten becomes the gold of the Rose-Apple River, it is heard. Based on this tree, this continent is called the Rose-Apple Land. There were some trees of this type around the ancient city of Kapilavastu, because it is told that the Bodhisattva achieved dhyana under the shade of such a tree.

b. The places of hell. This has two topics: i. An explanation of the hot and neighboring hells, and ii. An explanation of the locations of the cold hells.

i. An explanation of the hot and neighboring hells. This has three topics: (1) An explanation of the location of the Incessant Hell, (2) An explanation of the locations of Extremely Hot and the other six, and (3) An explanation of the locations of the neighboring hells.

(1) An explanation of the location of the Incessant Hell

58ab Below this twenty thousand leagues,
The Incessant Hell is just that size.

Below this Rose-Apple Land **twenty thousand** leagues, there is **the Incessant Hell**, so called, which is the largest of the hells. It **is just that size:** twenty thousand leagues in width and depth.

(2) An explanation of location of Extremely Hot and the other six

58c Above that there are seven hells,

Above that Incessant Hell **there are** the **seven hells** of Extremely Hot, Hot, Great Wailing, Wailing, Crushing, Black Line, and Reviving, one above another.

(3) An explanation of the locations of the neighboring hells. This has two points.

(a) The number of neighboring hells

58d And all eight have an extra sixteen:

And all eight of the hot hells **have an extra sixteen** perils.

(b) The location of the neighboring hells

59a On each of their four sides

They are **on each of their,** the eight hot hells', **four sides.**

(c) The names of each class

59a-c there are
The Burning Ground and Rotten Corpse,
The Razor Road and those, the River.

There are the Burning Ground, where you sink into a burning ground up to your knees; **and Rotten Corpse,** a filthy mire; **Razor Road and those** others: the forest of trees with sword-like leaves and the grove of iron *shalmali* trees with sharp thorns sixteen fingers in length, all three of which are similar to weapons and thus grouped together; and **the** Unfordable **River** of boiling, ashy water.

ii. An explanation of the locations of the cold hells

59d Eight other cold hells—Blisters, et cetera.

There are also **eight** more hells that are **other** than the hot hells in both type and location. These are the **cold hells** of **Blisters, et cetera**: Bursting Blisters, Chattering Teeth, Whimpering, Howling, Cracked Like an Utpala, Cracked Like a Lotus, and Greatly Cracked Like a Lotus.

It says of the occasional hells in the autocommentary:

> Their location is uncertain: they are in rivers, mountains, wastelands, other places and also below.

The animals have as their sphere land, water, and the sky. The hungry ghosts, whose king is named Yama, mainly live five hundred leagues below the city Rajgir in this Rose-Apple Land.

c. The places of the gods. This has two topics: i. Actual, and ii. Additionally, distinctions of their inhabitants.

i. Actual. This has two topics: (1) Those connected to the earth, and (2) Those not connected to the earth.

(1) Those connected to the earth. This has two topics: (a) The Realm of the Four Great Kings, and (b) The Realm of the Thirty-Three.

(a) The Realm of the Four Great Kings. This has two topics: (i) Palaces, and (ii) Places on mountains.

(i) Palaces. This has four topics: A. Measuring the sun and moon, B. The way they function, C. Distinctions of season that depend upon them, and D. The reason the moon waxes and wanes.

A. Measuring the sun and moon. This has two points.

1. The altitude of the sun and moon

60a The sun and moon are at mid Meru,

The sun and moon are **at** the **middle** of Mount **Meru**: they orbit at the same altitude as the peaks of the Yoke Holder mountains.

2. The sizes of the sun and moon

60b Fifty plus one in diameter.

The orb of the moon is **fifty** leagues and the orb of the sun is fifty **plus one,** or fifty-one, leagues **in diameter**. They are $6\,{}^{1}/_{18}$ leagues in-depth. The moon is made from water crystal, and the sun from fire crystal. Their shapes are fine and lovely to behold, and they are inhabited by the divine children Sun and Moon, who have great wealth, and their entourages.

The largest of the stars are eighteen earshots[156] and the smallest are one earshot in size.

B. The way they function

60cd So midnight, sunset, and midday
And sunrise are at the same time.

So the way a single sun and single moon function in all four continents is that **midnight** in Northern Unpleasant Sound, **sunset** in Eastern Superior Body, **and midday** in the Rose-Apple Land, **and sunrise** in Bountiful Cow **are** all **at the same time.** In the same way, when it is midnight in the east, it is sunset in the south, noon in the west, and dawn in the north, and so forth; the order of times is related in this way.

C. Distinctions of season that depend upon them. This has three points.

1. When day length changes

61. After the second rainy month's
    Ninth day of waxing, nights grow longer
And then in the fourth month of autumn,
    Grow shorter. Days are the reverse.

From a commentary:

> The seasons, for Buddhists, are first autumn, second spring, and third rains.

The autumn, spring, and summer mentioned here each have four months. The four autumn months are Āṣvina, Kārttika, Mārgaṣīrṣa, and Paiṣa. The four spring months are Māgha, Phālguṇa, Caitra, and Vaiṣakha. The four rainy months are Jyeṣṭha, Āṣādha, Śravaṇa, and Bhādra.

The first autumn month, Āṣvina, begins on the day following the full moon of the eighth month of the Tibetan calendar,[157] and continues one month until the next full moon. It is followed by the second autumn month, Kārttika, and then Mārgaṣīrṣa and so forth in order. In this tradition, the waning phase is presented as the first half of the month, and the waxing phase the second.

The month of Jyeṣṭha begins from day after the full moon of the middle Tibetan summer month (May-June) and continues until the full moon of the last Tibetan summer month. From the day after that full moon until the full moon of the first Tibetan month of autumn is the second month of rains or the rains, the month of Āṣādha. On the eighth day of its last half or waxing phase, the days are eighteen hours long and the nights twelve hours long.[158] **After the second rainy month's ninth day of** the **waxing** phase of the moon, the **nights grow longer** and the days grow shorter. From the commentary:

> The nights grow longer from the ninth day of the waxing phase of the second rainy month Āṣādha.

And then on the eighth day of the last half **in the fourth month of autumn,** the sun reverses, and from the ninth day nights **grow shorter.** The **days are the reverse** of that and grow longer. From the commentary:

> From the ninth day of the last half of the fourth of the winter months they grow shorter, it is said: this is from the ninth day of the waxing phase of the second spring month.

2. The amount it changes by

62a The days or nights by minutes lengthen.

The days or nights by the duration of **minutes lengthen.** The duration of a minute is 1/900th of the length of a day and night. According to the Kalachakra, it is the duration of the inhalation, holding, and exhalation of twenty-four breaths. That is explained as four moments, so in each moment there are six breaths.

3. Position of the sun in the sky

62b It's as the sun moves south or north.

It is as the sun moves to the **south** that the nights lengthen **or** as it moves **north** that the days lengthen.

D. The reason the moon waxes and wanes

62cd From moving too close to the sun,
Moon shades itself with its own shadow.

What causes the moon to wane? you ask. **From** the house of the moon **moving too close to the** house of the **sun,** the light of the sun falls on the **moon** and the moon's own shadow falls on the opposite side, so it appears as if the mandala **shades itself with its own shadow** and wanes, it is said, like a candle and a pillar.

(ii) Places on mountains. This has two topics: A. An explanation of the terraces on the Supreme Mountain, and B. Which gods live on which mountains.

A. An explanation of the terraces on the Supreme Mountain

63. On that there are four terraces,
The distance between which is ten thousand,
Extending sixteen thousand leagues,
And eight, four, and two thousand leagues.

On this Supreme Mountain **there are four terraces, the distance between which is ten thousand** leagues. As for the distance they extend out, the first **extends** out **by sixteen thousand leagues, and** the second by **eight** thousand, and also the third by **four** thousand, **and** the fourth by **two thousand leagues.**

The terraces start from the base, so they come up to the middle of the Supreme Mountain.

B. Which gods live on which mountains. This has two points.

1. Which live on the Supreme Mountain

> 64a-d The Basin Holders, Garland Holders,
> The Always Intoxicated, and
> The gods of the Four Great Kings' Realm
> Live there

On the first of these terraces live the yakshas called the **Basin Holders.** On the second live the **Garland Holders,** on the third the **Always Intoxicated, and the gods of the Four Great Kings' Realm live there** on the fourth: Dhritarashta in the East, Virudhaka in the South, Virupaksha in the West and Vaishravana in the North, along with the gods in their retinues.

2. Which live on the seven gold mountains

> 64d and in seven mountain ranges.

The cities **and** villages of these gods are also **in** the **seven mountain ranges** of Yoke Holder and so forth. The class of gods of the Four Great Kings is much more numerous than the other classes either individually or together.

(b) The Realm of the Thirty-Three. This has three topics: (i) General teaching, (ii) Describing the location of the Vajra-Holders, and (iii) An extensive explanation of the Realm of the Thirty-Three.

(i) General teaching

> 65ab On Meru's peak is Thirty-Three,
> Each side of which is eighty thousand.

On Mount **Meru's peak is** the Heaven of the **Thirty-Three, each side of which,** just like Mount Meru, **is eighty thousand** leagues, for a perimeter of 320,000 leagues.

(ii) Describing the location of the Vajra Holders

65cd On peaks in each of its four corners
There dwell the Vajra-Holder yakshas.

On four **peaks** that have a height of 500 leagues **in each of its**—the Supreme Mountain's—**four corners, there dwell the Vajra-Holder yakshas** in order to protect the careless gods.

(iii) An extensive explanation of the Realm of the Thirty-Three. This has two topics: A. The city, and B. The groves.

A. The city. This has two points.

1. The city in general

66. The central city Lovely to Behold,
Twenty-five hundred leagues per side,
Has golden ground of one and half
Leagues deep; it is soft and variegated.

In the center of the ground on the top of the Supreme Mountain is the **city** of the god Śakra called **Lovely to Behold**. It has **twenty-five hundred leagues per side**, and **has golden ground of one and** one **half leagues deep. It is soft** to the touch **and variegated** with one hundred hues.

2. Indra's palace

67ab Within is Utterly Conquering,
With sides two hundred fifty leagues.

Within the center of that city **is** the palace of Śakra,[159] **Utterly Conquering.** It is made out of various precious substances and is lovely to behold. Elevated four and one half leagues, its glory is greater than any other's and it overwhelms all. Each of its **sides** are **two hundred fifty leagues**, for a perimeter of one thousand leagues.

B. The groves. This has four points.

1. The actual groves

67cd Outside are Colorful Chariots,
Roughening, Mixing, and Joyous Grove.

On the **outside** of the city's four sides there **are** four groves, the grove of **Colorful Chariots,** the grove of **Roughening,** the grove of **Mixing, and** the **Joyous Grove.**

2. The grounds

68ab To their four sides twenty leagues away,
There are the four excellent grounds.

To their—the four groves'—**four sides twenty leagues away, there are** four **excellent** and pleasant **grounds** that rival the groves, as it were.

3. The tree

68c On the northeast corner is All-Gathering.

On the outside of **the northeast corner** of the city Lovely to Behold **is** the **All-Gathering** Earth-Piercing wish-fulfilling tree. Its roots are explained to penetrate five, or according to the *Prajñāptiśastra,* fifty leagues into the ground, and it reaches one hundred leagues into the sky. Its branches spread fifty leagues. The scent of its blooming flowers and petals carries one hundred leagues downwind and fifty leagues upwind.

4. The gathering place

68d On the southwest corner is Good Dharma.

On the southwest corner of that city **is** the gathering place **Good Dharma,** where the gods gather and discuss what to do or not to do. Good Dharma is round in shape with a circumference of 900 leagues and is made of crystal.

This is where the gods of Thirty-Three live.

(2) Those not connected to the earth

69a The gods above that live in palaces.

The gods above that Heaven of the Thirty-Three **live in palaces.** The heavens from Conflict Free to Mastery over Others' Emanations are here in order.[160]

ii. Additionally, distinctions of their inhabitants. This has five topics: (1) Acts of desire, (2) Birth of children to the gods, (3) The arising of desirables and pleasure, (4) The distance between the higher and lower levels, and (5) The way of ascending.

(1) Acts of desire

> 69b–d Six ways they act upon desire:
> They couple in a pair, embrace,
> Or else hold hands or laugh or look.

From the Realm of the Four Great Kings to Mastery over Others' Emanations, there are **six ways they act upon desire.** Those of the lower two realms that are connected to the earth, **they couple in a pair** with their male and female faculties touching, like humans. As there is no flow of sperm or water, there is nothing unclean. The gods of Conflict Free couple by **embracing, or else** the gods of Joyous by **holding hands, or** the gods of Joy of Emanations by **laughing, or** the gods of Mastery over Others' Emanations by **looking.** This is because just that is enough to free them from the throes of desire.

When a boy or girl appears in the lap of either a god or goddess, that is their son or daughter.

(2) Birth of children to the gods. This has two points.

(a) Children of gods of Desire

> 70ab The children born in those realms are
> Like children aged from five to ten.

The children born in those god **realms are like children aged from five** in the Realm of the Four Great Kings, the age of six in the Thirty-Three, and so on in a similar fashion up **to ten**-year-old children in Mastery over Others' Emanations. This is in comparison to the size of children in this land at a time when the life span is one hundred years.

(b) Children of Form

> 70cd Those born in the Form realms are born
> Full grown, with even their robes complete.

Those gods **born in the Form realm are born full grown** with all parts of their body perfect, **with even their robes complete.**

(3) The arising of desirables and pleasure. This has two points.

(a) Actual

71ab There are three ways desirables
Arise for Desire gods and humans.

In the sutras, the three ways desirable objects arise are explained as a distinction among beings. **There are three ways desirable** things **arise for Desire** realm **gods and humans.** It is like this: first, humans and four classes of gods enjoy what arises from the power of previous karma. Second, out of the power of karma, the gods of Joy of Emanation emanate whatever they themselves desire and then enjoy it. Thirdly, out of the power of karma, the gods of Mastery over Other's Emanation enjoy whatever they or others emanate in common just as they desire.

(b) Additionally the arising of the pleasure of Form

71cd Pleasure arises in three ways
On three of the dhyanas—thus nine levels.

The sutras explain that **pleasure arises in three ways**: pleasure that arises from solitude, the joyous pleasure that arises from samadhi, and pleasure without joy. These are all three **on** the first **three of the dhyanas, thus** they are explained as **nine levels.**

(4) The distance between the higher and lower levels

72ab There is as far above a realm
As there is below to the lowest realm.

There is as far above a realm up to the next higher realm **as there is below to the lowest realm** of the Rose-Apple Land. Just as there are eighty thousand leagues from the Thirty-Three down to the Rose-Apple Land, there is the same number from it up to Conflict Free. Just as there are one hundred sixty thousand leagues from Conflict Free down to the Rose-Apple Land, there is the same number from it up to the Joyous. Continuing in that way, finally just as it is eighty trillion leagues from Great Vision down to the Rose-Apple Land, it is equally distant from there up to the realm of Below None.

(5) The way of ascending

> 72cd Except through magic or another,
> They cannot see what is above.

Can beings born in lower realms go to higher realms and see them? you ask. **Except through the magic** of higher realms that one has attained **or** the help of **another** individual who has attained it, **they** who are in lower realms **cannot** go to higher realms and **see what is above.** Individuals from higher realms can easily descend to lower realms, and when they have descended it is possible for those of similar level to see them, but those of dissimilar level do not see them.[161]

3. Identifying the world of three thousands. This has three points.

a. The General Prime Thousand

> 73. One thousand worlds, each with four lands,
> A sun and moon, and a Great Mountain,
> Desire god realms, and Brahma's World,
> Are called a General Prime Thousand.

One thousand worlds, each single world **with four lands** of the Rose-Apple Land and so forth, **a sun and a moon, and a Great** Supreme **Mountain,** the six **Desire God Realms, and Brahma's World, are called a General Prime Thousand.**

b. The middle second thousand

> 74ab A thousand of those, the second thousand,
> And that is called a Middle World Realm.

A thousand of those General Prime Thousands is **the second thousand, and that is called a Middle World Realm.** The middle is a thousand of the lesser thousands, or a million Rose-Apple Lands.

c. Identifying the Great Thousands of Three Thousands

> 74c A thousand of those is the Three Thousands.

A thousand of those second thousands **is** the **Three Thousands.** It has a billion of the four continents.

4. Teaching that the three thousands arise and are destroyed together

74d They are destroyed and formed together.

When those are destroyed, **they are** all **destroyed** together, **and** when they are formed, they are **formed together.**

B. Additionally, the sizes of sentient beings. This has two topics: 1. Bodily height, and 2. Life span.

1. Bodily height. This has three topics: a. Height of humans, b. Height of gods of Desire, and c. Height of gods of Form.

a. Height of humans. This has two points.

i. Humans on the Rose-Apple Land

75ab The ones on the Rose-Apple Land
Are four, or three and half cubits tall.

The human **ones on the Rose-Apple Land are four** cubits **or three and half cubits tall.**

ii. Humans on the other three continents

75cd On the East, the Bountiful Cow, and North,
They're twice as tall as on the previous.

On the East, the Bountiful Cow, and the **North, they are twice as tall as on the previous,** as it is said. Therefore, if the inhabitants of the Rose-Apple Land when the life span is one hundred years are four cubits tall, the inhabitants on the other three lands are eight, sixteen, and thirty-two cubits tall respectively.

b. Height of gods of Desire

76a–c The bodies of Desire Gods grow
From a quarter earshot in height to
One and half earshots.

The heights of the **bodies of** the six **Desire Gods grow from a quarter earshot in height** in Four Kings **to one and half earshots** in Others' Emanations.

c. Height of gods of Form

76cd   In the first
Of Form, they are one-half league tall.

77. Above, a half league taller each.
    Beyond the highest of Lesser Light,
Their bodies double on each level.
    At Cloudless, though, discard three leagues.

In the first of the realms of **Form,** Brahma's Realm, **they,** the gods there, **are one-half league tall. Above** Brahma's Realm on Brahma's Ministers, Great Brahma, and Lesser Light, they are **a half** league **taller** on **each** level, or one league, one and a half leagues, and two leagues respectively. **Beyond highest of Lesser Light,** on Immeasurable Light and higher, **their bodies double** in size **on each level. At Cloudless, though, discard three leagues** from the doubled size. In this way, the height goes from four leagues on Immeasurable Light to sixteen thousand on Below None.

In Formless there is no body, so there is no body height.

2. Life span. This has two topics: a. Actual, and b. Examining whether there is premature death.

a. Actual. This has two topics: i. Life span in the higher realms, and ii. Life span in the lower realms.

i. Life span in the higher realms. This has three topics: (1) Life span of humans, (2) of Desire gods, and (3) of Form and Formless.

(1) Life span of humans. This has two points.

(a) Life span on the other three continents

78ab Unpleasant Sound's life span, one thousand.
    On two, it is shorter by half each.

On **Unpleasant Sound,** the **life span** is **one thousand** years. **On** the **two** continents of Bountiful Cow and Superior Body, **it,** the life span on **is shorter by half** of the previous **each**, or five hundred and two hundred fifty years.

(b) Life span on the Rose-Apple Land

78cd Here it's uncertain: from ten years
At end; incalculable at first.

Here on the Rose-Apple land, **it,** the life span, **is uncertain**—sometimes it is long, and sometimes it is short. The shortest is **ten years at** the **end,** and the longest is the **incalculable** life span of the humans of the **first** aeon.

(2) Life span of Desire gods. This has two points.

(a) Life spans in the Realm of the Four Great Kings

79. And fifty human years are just
One day and night among the lowest
Of gods of Desire. Their life span is,
Of such a day, five hundred years.

And fifty human years are just one day and night among the lowest of gods of Desire, the gods of the Four Great Kings. **Their life span is, of such a day,** counting thirty such days as a month and twelve months as a year, **five hundred years.** This is nine million human years.

(b) Life spans in the other five

80a Above both day-length and span double.

In the five god realms **above** that, **both** the **day-length and** the life **span double:** therefore in the Thirty-Three, there are one hundred human years per day and they live for one thousand of their own years, and so on up to Others' Emanations, where the life span is sixteen thousand years with a day-length of sixteen hundred human years.

(3) Life span of Form and Formless. This has three points.

(a) In the Form realm

80b–d In Form, there's neither day nor night,
So their life span in aeons is
Equal in number to their height.

In the **Form realm there is neither day nor night, so** one cannot count years, but there is a life span: **their life span in aeons is equal in number to their** bodies' **height** in leagues.

One could recite the verse as follows:

In the first
Of Form, they live one half aeon long.

Above each lives a half aeon longer.
Beyond the highest of Lesser Light,
Their life spans double on each level.
At Cloudless, though, discard three aeons.

(b) In the Formless realm

81ab In Formless each, by twenty thousand
Aeons, is longer than the previous.

In the **Formless** level of Infinite Space, the life span is twenty thousand aeons. **Each** of the higher levels **by twenty thousand aeons is longer than the previous** or lower level. On Infinite Consciousness, Nothingness, and the Peak of Existence, the life spans are forty, sixty, and eighty thousand aeons respectively.

(c) As an elaboration, examining the length of the aeons

81cd On Lesser Light and up, they are
Great aeons. Below that, half aeons.

On the divine abode of **Lesser Light and up, they,** the aeons used to measure life spans here, **are great aeons.**[162] **Below that** on Great Brahma and so forth, they are **half** of a great **aeon**, or forty intermediate aeons that are presented as an aeon. In the world, in the space of three spans of twenty intermediate aeons the world forms, and then it stays, and then is destroyed. Thus these sixty intermediate aeons are explained as the one and half aeon life span on Great Brahma.

ii. Life span in the lower realms. This has four topics: (1) Hot hells, (2) Animals, (3) Hungry ghosts, and (4) Cold hells.

(1) Hot hells. This has three points.

(a) Life span in the upper six

82. The Reviving and so forth, six hells,
    Have days that equal Desire Gods' lives.
    Of such a day, their life spans equal
    The life spans of Desire realm Gods.

The Reviving Hell **and so forth,** the first **six** hot **hells, have days that** are **equal** in length to the six **Desire realm gods' life spans. Of such a day,** there are thirty days to a month and twelve months to a year, and **their life spans** in such years are five hundred, one thousand, two thousand, four thousand, eight thousand, and sixteen thousand years, **equal** in number of years to **the life spans of the Desire realm gods.**

(b) Life span in Extremely Hot

83a Extremely Hot, half aeon;

In the **Extremely Hot** hell, the life span is a **half** intermediate **aeon.**

(c) Life span in the Incessant Hell

83ab the Incessant,
    An intermediate aeon.

The life span in **the Incessant** Hell is **an intermediate aeon.**

(2) Animals

83bc The longest life
    For animals, an aeon.

The longest life span **for animals** is **an aeon,** as garudas and the lord of the nagas live for an intermediate aeon. The shortest is just an hour.

(3) Hungry ghosts

83cd Hungry ghosts
    Live month-long days five hundred years.

Hungry ghosts live month-long days that are equal in length to a human month. Of such days, they live **for five hundred** years. That is fifteen thousand human years.[163]

(4) Cold hells. This has two points.

(a) Life span in the Blisters

84a–c If every hundred years one took
A seed from a cart of sesame,
When that is empty is life in Blisters.

If every one hundred years one took a single **seed from a cartful of sesame** seeds, which in the land of Magadha contains eighty bushels, **when that is empty is** the **life** span of those **in Blisters.** Some say it is twenty times that.

(b) Life span in the other seven

84d In others, twenty times as long.

In the **other** seven, the life spans are each **twenty times as long** as the life span of the next higher.

b. Examining whether there is premature death

85a Untimely death except in Unpleasant.

There is **untimely death except in Unpleasant** Sound, so life span is uncertain.

C. Units of measure. This has two topics: 1. What is combined, and 2. Units that measure what has been combined.

1. What is combined

85bc The units of form, name, and time
Are particles, letters, and instants.

The smallest **units of** aggregated **form, name, and time are particles, letters, and instants** respectively. Particles in this context are aggregated particles that are objects of the faculties and perform the functions of obscuring and obstructing. The particles of substance[164] are not meant here, because they are too small for the faculties to perceive and have no parts.[165]

The letters that are the units of name are the letters in names and words, which are the vocal sounds that are the basis for forming names.

2. Units that measure what has been combined. This has two topics: a. Units of distance, and b. Units of time.

a. Units of distance. This has three topics: i. Units from atoms to knuckles, ii. Units up to earshots, and iii. The size of the actual unit, the league.

i. Units from atoms to knuckles

85d Called atoms, molecules, and iron,

86. And water, rabbit, sheep, and ox,
And particles of sunlight, nits,
What comes from that, and also knuckles—
Each seven times larger than the previous.

The units **called atoms, molecules, and iron and water, rabbit, sheep, and ox, and particles of sunlight, nits, what comes from that** or lice, **and also knuckles** are **each seven times larger than the previous.**

ii. Units up to earshots. This has two points.

(1) Actual

87a–c There are four and twenty fingers to
A cubit; four in every fathom.
Of those, five hundred make an earshot,

There are four and twenty fingers to a cubit, and **four** cubits **in every fathom. Of those** fathoms, **five hundred make an earshot.**

(2) Hermitage

87d Which is a hermitage, it is said.

One earshot outside of town **is a hermitage, it is said.**

iii. The size of the actual unit, the league

88a And eight of those are called a league.

And eight of those earshots **are called a league.**

b. Units of time. This has two topics: i. The length of a year, and ii. The length of an aeon.

i. The length of a year. This has two points.

(1) The length of the months used to measure

88b–d One hundred twenty instants is
An instant of that. Sixty of those
Is a minute. Hours and days and months

89a Are thirty times as long as previous.

One hundred twenty instants of the limit of time **is an instant of that. Sixty of those is a minute.** Thirty of those is an hour. **Hours and days and months are thirty times as long as** the **previous.**[166]

(2) The actual year

89bc Including the impossible days
There are twelve months in every year.

Including the six **impossible days, there are twelve months in every year.** The way impossible days are discarded is described in the commentary:

> When one and one half months of autumn,
> Of rains, and of the spring have passed,
> The wise from the half month remaining,
> Discard one impossible day.

ii. The length of an aeon. This has three topics: (1) Identifying aeons, (2) The way the long beginning diminishes, and (3) Destructive aeons.

(1) Identifying aeons. This has two topics: (a) Overview, and (b) Explanation.

(a) Overview

89d The many types of aeon are explained.

In the sutras and treatises, **the many types of aeon are explained:** intermediate aeons, aeons of destruction, aeons of formation, and great aeons.

(b) Explanation. This has three topics: (i) Explaining aeons of destruction and formation, (ii) Explaining aeons of abiding, and (iii) Explaining great aeons.

(i) Explaining aeons of destruction and formation. This has two points.

A. Aeons of destruction

90ab An aeon of destruction lasts from when
There are no hell beings till the world's destroyed.

An aeon of destruction lasts from the time at end of an aeon of abiding **when** the life span is eighty thousand years, **there is no** birth of a new **hell being** in the Incessant Hell and its prior inhabitants have all died, so that it is empty. Then in the same way, the other hells, hungry ghost, and animal realms are also gradually destroyed. Then the humans of the Rose-Apple Land, without any teacher, attain the first dhyana by the dharma nature, gradually die and are reborn in the Brahma's World. The eastern and western continents are the same. The humans of Unpleasant Sound are reborn as Desire gods, and the Desire gods are then successively reborn in the first dhyana. Those in the first dhyana attain the second dhyana by dharma nature and are born in the second dhyana and so forth. In this way the destruction of sentient beings lasts for nineteen intermediate aeons.

Then seven suns that are four times as hot as our sun appear, and all the brooks, rivers, the four great rivers, the Unheated Lake, and the great oceans up to the Supreme Mountain dry up. Smoke billows and fires burn: the container of the world becomes one great fire and everything up **until** Brahma's World is burnt without even a trace left over and **the** container **world is destroyed.** This lasts one intermediate aeon, which makes a total of twenty intermediate aeons. In the same way everything up to the second dhyana is destroyed by water, and everything up to the third dhyana is destroyed by wind.

B. Aeons of formation

90cd Formation is from primordial wind
Until a being exists in hell.

The aeon of **formation is** after the destruction by fire, water, and air. It lasts one intermediate aeon **from** the **primordial** formation of the **wind** mandalas that are the ground first under Full Virtue, Radiant Light, Great Brahma, and then in order down to Conflict Free, until the previously described formation of the mandala of wind and so on.

After that, in the same order, from the first rebirth of one being from the fourth, third, or second dhyana into Full Virtue, Radiant Light, or Great Brahma, beings are reborn in the god realms in descending order. Humans are born successively in the north, west, east, and southern continents, and as a result of humans in the Rose-Apple Land acting nonvirtuously, they are reborn in the animal, hungry ghost, and hell realms, **until a being** attains the **existence** of the prior state **in** the Incessant **Hell**. This lasts nineteen intermediate aeons.

(ii) Explaining aeons of abiding. This has A. Explanation, and B. Summary.

A. Explanation. This has four points.

1. The long beginning

91a–c An intermediate aeon lasts
From when life is incalculable
Till it is ten years.

The aeon of abiding is twenty intermediate aeons. Of these, **an intermediate aeon lasts from when** the **life** span of humans **is incalculable,** then decreases to eighty thousand years, and then **until it is** a life span of **ten years.** This one intermediate aeon is called the long beginning.

2. The eighteen intermediate cycles

91cd Then another
Eighteen increasing and decreasing,

Then after that there are **another eighteen** intermediate aeons that have life spans that **increase** to eighty thousand **and decrease** to ten years. These are known as the intermediate cycles that are different from the long beginning.

3. The long ending

92a Then one increasing.

The word **then** links this to the previous verse. At the end of all these there is **one** intermediate aeon known as the long ending that has life spans that lengthen or **increase.** Therefore, there are twenty intermediate aeons of abiding.

4. The maximum increase of the life span

> 92ab During those,
> Lives are as long as eighty thousand.

During those periods of increase, the **life** span increases to **as long as eighty thousand** years.

B. Summary. This has two points.

1. Actual

> 92cd In this way this world that is formed
> Lasts twenty intermediate aeons.

In this way this world that is formed lasts twenty intermediate aeons.

2. Teaching that destruction and formation are also equal

> 93ab Forming, destroying, and remaining
> After destruction are the same.

Aeons of **forming, destroying, and** the empty aeons that **remain after destruction are** all of **the same** duration, twenty intermediate aeons.

(iii) Explaining great aeons. This has two topics: A. Actual, and B. Additionally, the way the three individuals appear.

A. Actual

> 93c These eighty make up one great aeon.

These eighty such intermediate aeons **make up one great aeon.** As explained by the words "Just these are time,"[167] the nature of an aeon is the five aggregates.

B. Additionally, the way the three individuals appear. This has three topics: 1. How buddhas arise, 2. How self-buddhas arise, and 3. How wheel-wielding emperors arise.

1. How Buddhas arise. This has two points.

a. The cause of the buddhas

93d Then after three uncountable

94a Of these appears a Buddha

Then after three uncountable of these great aeons of gathering accumulations **appears a Buddha.** Here so-called uncountable is a novemdecillion (10^{60}), a number described in *Short Discourses;* it is the name of a number that exists, not something that cannot be counted.

Well, what are the numbers? you ask. They are:

One, ten, hundred, thousand,
Ten thousand, hundred thousand,
Million, ten and hundred million,
These are the common numbers.
Billion, ten and hundred billion,
Trillion, ten and hundred trillion,
Quadrillion, ten and hundred quadrillion,
Quintillion, ten and hundred quintillion,
Sextillion, ten and hundred sextillion,
Septillion, ten and hundred septillion,
Octillion, ten and hundred octillion,
Nonillion, ten and hundred nonillion,
Decillion, ten and hundred decillion,
Undecillion, ten and hundred undecillion,
Duodecillion, ten and hundred duodecillion,
Tredecillion, ten and hundred tredecillion,
Quattuordecillion, ten and hundred quattuordecillion,
Quindecillion, ten and hundred quindecillion,
Sexdecillion, ten and hundred sexdecillion,
Septendecillion, ten and hundred septendecillion,
Octodecillion, ten and hundred octodecillion,
And novemdecillion: that is one uncountable.

b. The time when they appear

> 94ab during
> The decrease to one hundred years.

The Buddhas appear **during the decrease** of beings' life spans **to one hundred years.** They do not appear during the period of increase or when the life span is less then one hundred years, because it is difficult for beings to develop weariness during the former, and because the latter is a bad and lowly time of the five degenerations of life, time, afflictions, views, and sentient beings.

2. How self-buddhas arise. This has two points.

a. The time when self-buddhas appear

> 94c In both, self-buddhas.

In both times when the life span is increasing and when it is decreasing, **self-buddhas** appear. The eighty thousand attendants of King Given by Fire became self-buddhas during a period of increase, and Excellent White Tip appeared on earth during a period of decrease, at which time there were five hundred self-buddhas who appeared in the Deer Park of the Fallen Sages.

b. Their cause

> 94cd Following
> One hundred aeons, a rhino appears.

Following one hundred aeons of the three trainings, the accumulations of enlightenment, as the cause of awakening, **a rhinoceros**-like self-buddha attains self-enlightenment and **appears.**

3. How wheel-wielding emperors arise. This has three topics: a. The time they appear, b. Classifications of their types, and c. Distinctions in qualities.

a. The time they appear

> 95ab Wheel-wielding emperors appear
> When life is not less than eighty thousand

Wheel-wielding emperors, who wield political power through their all-powerful weapons, wheels, **appear** during a time **when** human **life** ranges from uncountable to **not less than eighty thousand** years. When the life span is shorter than that, there is not sufficient wealth for one to appear.

b. Classifications of their types. This has four points.

(1) Actual classification

95c With wheels of gold, silver, copper, iron,

They have **wheels of gold, silver, copper,** and **iron:** the supreme, nearly supreme, middle, and least.

(2) Which continents they have power over

95d They rule over one, two, three, or else

96a Four continents, in reverse order.

They rule over one continent, **two** continents, **three continents,** or **else four continents, in reverse order.**

(3) Elaboration

96b At once, there are never two, like buddhas.

There is only one wheel-wielding emperor at a time: **at one** time, **there are never two.** It is **like buddhas,** for example, of whom there are never two that appear in the world at the same time.

(4) How they achieve victory

96c–f When their opponents welcome them,
Or they themselves advance or gird
For battle or just brandish weapons,
They triumph without causing harm.

The way the four wheel-wielding emperors are victorious over all is respectively **when their opponents welcome them, or they themselves advance, or** merely **gird for battle, or** after preparing **just brandish** their **weapons. They triumph without** taking life or **causing** any other **harm.**

c. Distinctions in qualities

97ab The Sage's marks remain in place,
Clear and complete, so they're superior.

Wheel-wielding emperors also have the major marks, so what is the difference between their marks and the Sage's? you ask. **The Sage's marks remain in** their **place** without moving. They are more radiant and their parts are **clear and complete** with a thousand spokes and so on, **so they are superior.**

(2) The way the long beginning diminishes. This has three topics: (a) The particulars of the first aeon, (b) How it diminishes, and (c) What happens at the end of the diminishing.

(a) The particulars of the first aeon

97c The earliest beings are like Form gods.

Just after the formation of the world, **the earliest** human **beings are** born miraculously, do not eat food, have radiant bodies, perform miracles, and live for incalculable numbers of years, **like** the **Form** realm's **gods.**

(b) How it diminishes. This has three points.

(i) How the Age of Threefold Qualities arose[168]

97d They gradually feel greed for tastes,

Then **they gradually** ate the three foods of honey-like nectar of the earth, yellow dust, and the grove of reeds, so their bodies became heavy and their radiance weakened and became dark. By the force of karma, the sun, moon, and so forth then provided light. Those who ate a lot of those foods developed a bad color, and those who ate a little had good color. Because of this, those with good color scorned those with bad, and acted nonvirtuously, so those foods disappeared. Then they began to **feel greed for** the **taste** of the *salu* rice crops that grew without toil, so filth and so forth appears. They developed male and female faculties, and their shapes and colors became different. When they saw each other, desire arose, and they acted indecently. Others criticized this, and they built houses and such for propriety.

(ii) How the Age of Twofold Qualities and the Age of Strife arose[169]

98ab Grow lazy, and then gather and hoard.
Land holders then appoint field chieftains.

When they wanted to take the salu rice, they **grew lazy, and then** some started to **gather and hoard,** so they began threshing the rice and also reaping it. When that happened, it did not grow, so then those beings became unfriendly. Each took full possession of his own, and they divided the fields. The **land holders** stole from each other, and a man who was good by nature was **then appointed** and installed as the **field chieftain.** He was granted a sixth of the crop and called the King Respected by Many.

(iii) How the life span becomes ten years

98cd Because of their strong karmic paths,
Their life span shortens to ten years.

Because of acting out of **their strong** nonvirtuous **karmic paths, their life span shortens to ten years** for humans, and they are not able to live any longer than that.

(c) What happens at the end of the diminishing. This has two points.

(i) Teaching how the three ages of calamities happen

99ab It's weapons, pestilence, and famine
That bring an aeon to its end,

When the human life span is ten years, **it is** ages of **weapons, pestilence, and famine that bring an** intermediate **aeon to its end.**

(ii) The duration of those three

99cd For seven days, then seven months,
Then seven years respectively.

Those sentient beings are killed by weapons **for seven days, then** by pestilence for **seven months** and seven days, and **then** by famine for **seven years,** seven months, and seven days **in succession.** The plural of the word *days* in the root indicates that the seven days also follow the latter two. When these happen in the Rose-Apple Land, something somewhat similar also happens on the other two continents.

(3) Destructive aeons. This has three topics: (a) How levels up to the third dhyana are destroyed, (b) How the fourth is destroyed, and (c) The number of destructions by fire, water, and wind.

(a) How levels up to the third dhyana are destroyed. This has three points.

(i) What destroys what

> 100ab Then fire and water and then wind
> Bring three additional destructions.

Then when all sentient beings have been gathered in one dhyana, there is destruction by **fire** for seven days, **and** then by **water** from rain and floods, **and then** destruction by extremely violent **wind,** so these **bring three additional destructions:** not even an atom remains.

(ii) The crests that remain undestroyed

> 100cd These crest respectively at the
> Three dhyanas—second and so forth—

These three additional destructions **crest respectively at the three dhyanas** because those dhyanas remain after destruction. The crest of destruction by fire is the **second** dhyana. The phrase "**and so forth**" indicates that the crest of destruction by water is the third dhyana, and the crest of destruction by wind is the fourth dhyana. This is because the first dhyana and below are destroyed by fire, the second and below by water, and the third and below are destroyed by wind.

(iii) The reasons for those

> 101a Because those correspond to their faults.

This is **because those,** fire, water, and wind, **correspond to their,** the three dhyana's internal **faults:** considering and examining are like fire; joy and pleasure are like water; and the inhalation and exhalation are like wind. They are destroyed by fire, water, and wind, respectively.

(b) How the fourth is destroyed. This has two points.

(i) Teaching that it is not destroyed by fire, water, or air

> 101b But not the fourth, since it's immovable.

But there is **not** an external cause for destruction on **the fourth** dhyana **since it is immovable** by the eight faults, as will be explained in the eighth area.[170]

(ii) The actual way it is destroyed

> 101cd Not permanent, its palaces
> And beings arise, and then they perish.

The container of the fourth dhyana is **not permanent,** because **its palaces and beings arise, and then they perish.**

(c) The number of destructions by fire, water, and wind

> 102. There are seven by fire, then one by water.
> When seven by water are thus finished,
> Then seven by fire, and after that,
> Finally wind will bring destruction.

There are seven times when there are destructions **by fire.** After those, there is **the one** destruction **by water.** Then after a succession of seven destructions by fire, there is another destruction by water, and **when seven** destructions **by water are thus finished, then** there is a sequence of **seven** destructions **by fire, and after that** at the end of every sixty-four great aeons, **there is finally destruction by wind.**

Second, presenting the area's name

> This completes the third area called "Teachings on the World" from the *Verses of the Treasury of Abhidharma.*

This completes the explanation of **the third area called "Teachings on the World" from** *The Explanation of the "Verses of the Treasury of Abhidharma"* called *The Essence of the Ocean of Abhidharma, The Words of Those who Know and Love, Explaining the Youthful Play, Opening the Eyes of Dharma, The Chariot of Easy Practice.*

A few words here:

Because of the second Vasubandhu, Vijayakīrti's
Full explanation of these signs and meanings
And the development of my intelligence,
I have explained the *Treasury* of the world.

May the great masses of virtue greatly please
The mighty guides appearing in all three times.
May their one hundred peals of laughter
Pacify the tumult of false teachers.

FOURTH AREA

Teachings on Karma

The illumining master, the Karmaka, skilled
In shining in the playful, ocean-like skies
Of the Land of Snows, playing in vibrant compassion:
I prostrate to him who's omniscient. And then
    From love and compassion for those
    Whose six-legged, wingèd intelligence
    Could go to the ends of the skies
    Of his unexcelled explanations,
    This short commentary of mine
Whose cool rays make clear the Karmapa's intent
Comes from the great ocean of the abhidharma.

The fourth area, the "Teachings on Karma," has an explanation of the text of the area and a presentation of the area's name. The explanation of the text of the area has three topics: I. How everything arises from karma, II. Understanding karma itself, and III. Teaching the synonyms of dharmas as a summary.

I. How everything arises from karma

1a From karma various worlds are born.

What created the environment of the world and its inhabitants, sentient beings, described above? It was not created out of forethought by Ishvara or some other god. Instead, **from** various virtuous and nonvirtuous **karmas** the environments and inhabitants of **various** happy and wretched, good and bad **worlds are born.**

II. Understanding karma itself. This has three topics: A. Identifying karma, B. The presentation of karma, and C. The meaning of karma as explained in the sutras.

A. Identifying karma. This has three points.

1. Classifying karma in two

1b Volition and what that creates.

What is karma like? you ask. If you classify it, there are two types: **volitional** karma **and what that** volition **creates,** intended karma. This is because it is said in the sutras, "Karma is twofold: volitional and intended karma." Intended karma is also classified in two, so there are three types.

2. Their individual essences

1cd Volition is mental karma, which
Creates the karma of body and speech.

Of those three, the mental factor **volition is** the **mental karma.** That **which** volition **creates**, intended karma, is **the karma of body and** the karma of **speech.**

3. Perceptible or imperceptible karma

2a Those two are percepts and impercepts.

Those two, karma of body and speech, **are** the **perceptible** karma of body, the imperceptible karma of body, and the perceptible **and imperceptible** karmas of speech.

B. The presentation of karma. This has three topics: 1. Classifying karma in two, 2. The presentation of general features of the three karmas, and 3. The presentation of imperceptible karma.

1. Classifying karma in two. This has two topics: a. Perceptible, and b. Imperceptible.

a. Perceptible. This has two points: i. Perceptible of body, and ii. Perceptible of speech.

i. Perceptible of body. This has three points.

(1) Identifying its essence according to the Great Exposition tradition

2b Bodily perceptible is shape.

When the mind thinks, "I will prostrate," **bodily perceptible** action, such as prostrating and joining one's palms, **is** proposed to be **shape.**

(2) Refuting the doubts of the Vatsiputrīya school

2cd It is not movement, since composites
Are momentary, as they perish.

3ab Nothing can happen without cause.
The cause would become the destroyer.

Followers of the Vatsiputrīya school agree that some composites such as rainstorms or flames are momentary but mostly do not assert momentary impermanence. Therefore perceptible actions of body are not impermanent because they are actions that move the body from one location to another. They are not unmoving actions, they say.

This is illogical. **It,** karma or action of the body, **is not movement** to another location without ceasing **since** it is composite, like cognition and so forth. To prove that this is pervasively true, all **composites are** without a doubt **momentary** phenomena that are destroyed immediately upon arising, **as** without a doubt **they** immediately **perish** independent of other causes or conditions. The disintegration of composites does not depend upon some other cause because **nothing** that depends upon a cause **can happen without** a **cause,** but lightning and so on are directly seen to perish without any cause at all.

In that case, some things such as lightning are like that, but we can see that hammers and such are the cause of the destruction of clay jugs and so forth, you say. If that were so, **the cause** of the red color of a clay jug that is heated, fire, **would become the destroyer** of the red color of the heated jug: it would follow that the creator was also the destroyer.

(3) The tradition of the Sutra school

> 3c Two would perceive it; not in particles.

The Sutra school holds that shape does not exist substantially, because when it is destroyed, there is no mind that perceives it, just as with a vase. If shape were to exist, the **two** faculties of body and eye **would** both **perceive it**, because the eye would see shape directly and know it, and also when the body faculty touches it, a cognition that thinks "long" or so forth would occur. One cannot agree, because then it would be senseless to have multiple faculties, and the correspondence between the sense bases and substances would be weakened.

Any existing obstructive form at all must exist in the atoms that are aggregated. Long and other such shapes do not substantially exist, because there is **not** any such thing **in** the **particles**, because atoms have no parts.

At this point, there are many arguments and counter-arguments between the Great Exposition and Sutra schools, but I shall not go into them here.

ii. Perceptible of speech

> 3d Perceptible speech is speech's sound.

The **perceptible** karma of **speech is speech's sound**—sound that has the nature of speech—because it makes the desire that motivates the speaker to talk perceptible to others.

b. Imperceptible forms. This has two topics: i. Proof they exist substantially, and ii. Presentation of their features.

i. Proof they exist substantially

> 4ab Three kinds and stainless form are taught;
> Increase; and paths not done; et cetera.

The Sutra school says that imperceptible forms do not substantially exist. This is because they are merely promises not to do something any more from this time forward until forfeited which are merely given the label imperceptible form; because they are designated based upon the past sources, but the past sources do not exist in essence; and because they do not fulfill the characteristics of form.

The Great Exposition school says that imperceptible forms exist substantially. As proof of this, a sutra says:

> The three types of form include all forms. There is form that is showable and obstructive. There is also form that is not showable but is obstructive. There is also form that is neither showable nor obstructive.

Thus imperceptible forms exist because **three kinds** of form are taught. A sutra also says:

> These forms for which greed or anger do not arise are called undefiled dharmas.

Thus it is also proven because **stainless form is taught,** and without imperceptible forms it would not be logical for there to be such forms.

If it is one of the seven material merits or the seven immaterial merits, the merit **increases** greatly.[171] The seven material merits are:

> To give a monastery or a temple,
> A bed, or sustenance continuously,
> A passing guest, or nursing for the sick
> Or generosity in times of darkness:
> These are the seven material merits.

The seven immaterial merits are:

> To hear he[172] dwells or plans to come or else
> Has embarked upon the road, arrived; to see him,
> To hear the Dharma, hold the basic precepts:
> If these should make true faith and joy arise,
> These are the seven immaterial merits.

Additionally, it would follow that the karmic **paths not done** by oneself but that one incites others to do would not exist because there is no imperceptible form. The phrase "**et cetera**" means that imperceptible forms exist also because it is taught that there is form in the sense base of dharmas, because the eightfold noble path is taught, and because it is taught that vows obstruct immorality like a dike and water. There are many additional proofs, so imperceptible form is proven to exist.

At this point, there are many refutations, presentations, and positions from others, including the Yogic Action, Sutra school, Dārṣṭāntika, earlier masters, the venerable elders of the Great Exposition, the Master, and so forth. These appear in the *Ṭīka.*

ii. Presentation of their features. This has four topics: (1) The features of their cause, (2) of their level, (3) of their essence, and (4) Other attributes of their cause.

(1) The features of their cause. This has two points.

(a) Attributes of the cause of the first moment

A small number of the present and future forms that act as causes arise from the past sources. In the first moment of an imperceptible form of Desire—at the time of swearing a vow or so forth—the sources of the basis and the sources of the support are both coemergent sources of the present imperceptible.

(b) Attributes of the cause of subsequent moments

4cd In subsequent moments, the impercepts
Of Desire are born from the past sources.

In subsequent moments, the imperceptible forms **of Desire are born from the** sources of the basis, **past sources,** and the present sources of the bodily support.

(2) The features of their level. This has two points.

(a) Attributes on the defiled levels

5ab Stained karmas of the body and speech
Take their own sources as a cause.

The sources of which level function as their cause? you ask. The imperceptible forms of **stained** or defiled **karmas of the body and speech** from the Desire realm up to the fourth dhyana **take their own** level's **sources as a cause.**

(b) Attributes on the undefiled levels

5c The undefiled, of where it arises.[173]

Undefiled forms take the four sources **of** the support of the level **where they arise.** If the undefiled vow is attained on the support of a Desire-realm body, its great sources also must arise or originate out of the sources of the Desire realm. If the undefiled vow is attained on a support of the first dhyana, its great sources also must be from the first dhyana.

(3) The features of their essence

5d Impercepts aren't appropriated.

6ab They are causally compatible
And indicate a sentient being.

Imperceptible forms are unobstructive, so they **are not appropriated,** and as they are always either virtuous or nonvirtuous, it is impossible for them to be neutral. As they are not produced by development, by implication **they are** produced by **compatible cause.** They **indicate a sentient being** because they are included within the continuum of one.

(4) Other attributes of their cause. This has two points:

(a) Attributes of the causes of imperceptible forms of Desire

6cd They arise from sources which must be
Compatible, appropriated.

They, imperceptibles of Desire, **arise from** the cause of the great **sources** in the continuum of the assemblage of the body, **which must be** causally **compatible** and **appropriated.**

(b) Attributes of the causes in the dhyanas and undefiled levels

6e-h The ones born of samadhi arise
From unappropriated sources,
That are produced by development
And are not separate.

Since they follow the mind, the **ones born of samadhi**—undefiled and dhyana vows—**arise from** the cause of **unappropriated sources.** Because they are developed by samadhi, they **are produced by development.** They are born from one set of four sources, as the four sources that produce all seven different abandonments **are not separate.**[174]

Here there are different assertions made by the Great Exposition, Sutra school and Mind Only school.

2. The presentation of general features of the three karmas. This has two topics: a. Presenting the actual meaning, and b. Explaining motivation in detail.

a. Presenting the actual meaning. This has three topics: i. Distinctions of virtue and so forth, ii. What is in which realm, and iii. The individual classification of the three dharmas.

i. Distinctions of virtue and so forth

7ab There are no neutral imperceptibles.
The others are threefold.

Among the three types of karma explained above,[175] **there are no neutral imperceptible** karmas that are neither virtuous nor nonvirtuous. **The** perceptible and volitional karmas that are **other** than that **are threefold.** For example, there are virtuous perceptibles such as joining palms in prayer, nonvirtuous such as taking life, and neutral such as the crafts and so forth—all three are possible. Likewise volition can be all three.

ii. What is in which realm. This has four points:

(1) Which realm nonvirtue is in

7bc Nonvirtue is
In Desire.

Nonvirtuous karma **is** only **in** the **Desire** realm. It is not in the higher realms, because beings in those realms have discarded shamelessness and immodesty.

(2) Which realms imperceptibles are in

7c There are impercepts in Form, too,

There are the **imperceptibles** of dhyana and undefiled vows **in Form, too.** The word "too" indicates they are also in Desire. They are not in Formless.

(3) Which realm mere perceptibles are in

7d And percepts where there is considering.

And there are **perceptibles,** including action, in those levels **where there is**

considering—Desire and the first dhyana. They are not in the second dhyana and higher, because there is neither the motivation of consideration and examination, nor obscured neutral.

(4) Which realm obscured perceptibles are in

8ab There's no obscured in Desire, either,
Because there is no motivation.

Not only in the levels without consideration, but **there is no obscured** neutral perceptible **in** the **Desire** realm **either**. What is the reason? **Because there is no motivation** for it: in Desire, the obscured is only associated with personality and extreme views, and these are always discards of seeing only, so they directed inward. For that reason they are not suitable as the motivation for perceptible karma.

iii. The individual classification of the three dharmas. This has three topics: (1) The classification of virtue, (2) of nonvirtue, and (3) of neutral.

(1) The classification of virtue. This has four points.

(a) Ultimate virtue

8c Ultimate virtue is liberation;

What is called **ultimate virtue is** the **liberation** of nirvana, because it is both exalted and truly virtuous. That is because it is the supreme happiness that is free of suffering, like freedom from illness, for example.

(b) Inherent virtue

8d Inherent: roots, shame, modesty;

Inherent or intrinsic virtue is the three virtuous **roots** of nongreed, nonhatred, and nondelusion; **shame**; and **modesty**, because they do not depend upon concurrence or motivation, like beneficial medicine, for example.

(c) Concurrent virtue

9a Concurrent with that is concurrent;

Dharmas that are **concurrent with that,** inherent virtue, **are concurrent** virtue, because there are no virtues in a mind that is not concurrent with the roots of virtue, like drink that is mixed with medicine.

(d) Virtue of motivation

9b Actions and such are motivated.

The **actions** or karmas of body and speech motivated by those **and such** things, including birth, attainment, cessation, the absorption of the conception-free **are motivated** virtue, like the milk from a mother who has drunk a beverage mixed with beneficial medicine.

(2) The classification of nonvirtue

9c Nonvirtue is the opposite.

Nonvirtue, which also has four types, **is the opposite** of the four virtues. All that is in the end samsaric is ultimate nonvirtue. The three nonvirtuous roots, shamelessness, and immodesty are inherent nonvirtue. Dharmas that are concurrent with those are concurrent nonvirtue. The karmas of body and speech that these motivate, as well as the characteristics of birth and so forth and the attainment of nonvirtue, are motivated nonvirtue. An example to illustrate this would be milk from a mother who has drunk a beverage mixed with harmful drugs.

(3) The classification of neutral

9d The stable is the ultimate neutral.

That which is **stable is the ultimate neutral:** space and nonanalytic cessation among the noncomposites. The inherent neutral is that which is obscured by personality and extreme view in the Desire realm and by all afflictions in the higher realms. The concurrent neutral is that which is concurrent with the mind of crafts, et cetera. Motivated neutral is the perceptibles of body and speech in the path of conduct and so forth, birth and so forth, and attainment.

b. Explaining motivation in detail. This has three topics: i. Classification of motivation, ii. The nature of each classification, and iii. Examining the four possibilities of their dharma bases.

i. Classification of motivation

> 10ab Two motivations are the causal
> And the contemporaneous motives.

Well then, if the cognition of a discard of seeing cannot motivate a perceptible, then it contradicts the sutra that says, "From that wrong view come wrong thought, wrong speech, and extreme actions," you say.

It is not a contradiction. In general, there are **two** types of **motivations,** which are called **the causal and the contemporaneous** (with the action) **motivations.**

ii. The nature of each classification

> 10cd The first one is the instigator;
> The second is the executor.

The first one of the two motivations **is the instigator** because it is both cause and motivation and because it impels the karma. **The second** one, the contemporaneous motive, **is the executor** because one engages in action according to it at the time of the action. Without the contemporaneous motivation, there might be the causal motivation, but the action will not be brought to a perceptible end. For example, it is like someone who resolves to go to the market but dies in the interim and does not reach the market.

iii. Examining the four possibilities of their dharma bases. This has five topics: (1) The possibility of being only the instigator, (2) The possibility of being both, (3) The possibility of only being the executor, (4) The possibility of analyzing the way they mutually engage, and (5) The possibility of being neither.

(1) The possibility of being only the instigator

> 11ab The consciousness that seeing discards
> Is the instigator.

The consciousness that **seeing discards is the** perceptible's **instigator** only, because the causal motivation is a motivation that is the basis for the consideration and examination. At the time that the executor is looking outward, the six groups of consciousness arise in succession, so the earlier motivation that looked inward does not exist and thus cannot be the executor.

(2) The possibility of being both

11b–d And the mind
That is a discard of meditation
Is both.

And of **the** different kinds of **mind** consciousness, those **that are a discard of meditation are both** instigator and executor, because they engage when focused outward and inward.

(3) The possibility of only being the executor

11d The five are executors.

The five sense consciousnesses **are** only **executors** because they are thought-free consciousnesses.

Undefiled consciousness is neither because it rests in equipoise, looks inward, and is exclusive of engagement.

(4) The possibility of analyzing the way they mutually engage. This has two points.

(a) General

12ab The executors from the virtuous
And other instigators are threefold.

Additionally, it is not definite that the instigator and executor are similar. **The executors** that come **from the virtuous and other,** nonvirtuous and neutral, **instigators are** also **threefold:** these executors can be either virtuous, nonvirtuous, or neutral, so there are a total of nine combinations. For example, the vows of individual liberation have a mental factor of virtuous intention as their causal motivation. For the contemporaneous motivation at the time of the ceremony, however, either the continuation of that intention, hatred, or the mind of the path of activities[176] might be manifest, so the attainment of the vow could be any one of these.

(b) Specific

12c The Sage's are alike or virtuous.

The Sage's instigator and executor **are alike** because his virtue engages out of virtue and neutral engages out of neutral. The word "**or**" is a conjunction.

Alternatively, following a neutral instigator, the executor, is **virtuous,** but after a virtuous instigator there can only be a virtuous executor and never a neutral one because it is impossible that the Buddha's powers could decrease.

(5) The possibility of being neither

12d Those born of ripening are neither.

Those cognitions that are **born of** full **ripening are neither** instigator nor executor, because they are born naturally without effort.

3. The presentation of imperceptible karma. This has two topics: a. An overview of the classifications, and b. The extensive presentation.

a. An overview of the classifications

13ab Three types of imperceptibles
Are vows, wrong vows, and neither.

There are said to be **three types of imperceptibles.** They **are vows** that bind the continuum of immorality; their opposite, **wrong vows** that arise as extremely harmful conduct of body and speech; **and** the mid-vow that is **neither** of those two.

b. The extensive presentation. This has two topics: i. Explaining vows in particular, and ii. Explaining the three types of karma together.

i. Explaining vows in particular. This has two topics: (1) Overview, and (2) Explanation.

(1) Overview

13b–d Vows
Are individual liberation
And dhyan-produced and undefiled.

The discipline that a dharma practitioner maintains in Desire is called the **vow of individual liberation. And** the discipline that **dhyana** primarily **produces** and that is effective in the Form realm is called the vow of dhyana. **And** undefiled discipline is called the **undefiled** vow.[177]

(2) Explanation. This has three topics: (a) The explanation of vows of individual liberation, (b) The explanation of the undefiled vows and vows of dhyana, and (c) Additional points.

(a) The explanation of vows of individual liberation. This has two topics: (i) Teaching them together, and (ii) Teaching them separately.

(i) Teaching them together. This has three points.

A. Classifying in eight in terms of name

14a There are the eight called *pratimokṣa*,

There are the eight vows **called** vows of ***pratimokṣa***, individual liberation: the vows of the bhikshu or "almsman," the vows of the bhikshuni, the vows of the *śikṣamāṇa* or "nun postulant," the vows of the male and female *śramanera* or novices, the male and female *upāsaka* lay precepts or "pursuer of virtue," and the vows of fasting or *upavāsastha*. The vows of fasting can be held by the sexless and neuters as well as males and females, so the male and female fasting vows are not counted separately.

B. Combining in four in terms of substance

14bc But they are four in substance since
Name alone changes with the organ.

The vows are eight in terms of name, but **they are four in substance:** the bhikshu vows, novice vows, fasting vows, and pursuer of virtue vows. The reason for this is **since** just the **name alone changes** to bhikshuni **with the** change of sexual **organs** of a bhikshu.[178] As there is no cancellation, attainment, or shift in the essence of the vows, they are proven to be the same continuum as before.

C. How they relate

14d They're separate but not exclusive.

When a single individual has all three vows, **they are** definitely, solely **separate** in their characteristics because otherwise, if one should forfeit the bhikshu vows, one would also forfeit the other two, which is not the case.

In that case, because they abandon the same class **but** are substantially separate, they should be simultaneously exclusive[179] in the stream of a single being, you say. They are **not** simultaneously **exclusive** of each other in that way because taking a later vow is not the cause of forfeiting the previous.

(ii) Teaching them separately. This has four points.

A. Their individual essences

15. By swearing to hold five, eight, ten,
 Or all the precepts, one becomes
A pursuer of virtue, or a faster,
 Or else a novice, or a bhikshu.

What makes someone a pursuer of virtue and so forth? you ask. **By swearing** (1) **to hold** for the rest of one's life the **five** precepts of abandoning taking life, taking what is not given, sexual misconduct, lying, and intoxicants; (2) to hold for one day the **eight** precepts of abandoning the root four plus intoxicants; refraining from dancing, ornaments, and so forth counted as one; no high beds; or food after noon; (3) to hold for the rest of one's life the **ten** precepts of those eight with dancing and ornaments counted separately to make nine, plus abandoning taking gold and silver for a total of ten; **or** (4) to hold for the rest of one's life **all the precepts** of abandoning all the harmful conducts of body and speech, is how **one becomes** respectively (1) **a pursuer of virtue,** (2) **or a faster, or** (3) **else a novice, or** (4) **a bhikshu.**

B. Synonyms

16ab This is called discipline, fine conduct,
 Karma, and vow.

This is called discipline as it correctly settles one and is the attainment of cool relief from the torments of immorality.[180] As it is praised by the wise, it is called **fine conduct.** As its nature is action, it is **karma. And** as it binds the body and speech, it is called the **vow** of individual liberation.

C. Explaining their names

16b–d The percept and
Impercept of the first are individual
 Liberation and the path of action.

At the time of correctly taking a vow, **the perceptible and imperceptible of**

the first moment **are** called **individual liberation** because they liberate the individual from misdeeds. They are also called the vow of individual liberation because they bind the harmful conduct of body and speech. **And** they are also called **the** actual **path of action,** because they are not the aftermath but part of the actual basis.[181]

The perceptibles and imperceptibles of the second moment are similar to individual liberation and are born from individual liberation, so they are called a vow of individual liberation only. However, they are not actually individual liberation, because one has already been liberated by the first moment alone.

D. The individuals who possess them

> 17a The eight have pratimokṣa vows.

The eight individuals from bhikshu to faster **have pratimokṣa vows** of individual liberation.

(b) The explanation of the undefiled vows and vows of dhyana. This has three points.

(1) Who possesses them

> 17bc When one has dhyana, one has that.
> The nobles have the undefiled.

When one has dhyana—when dhyana has arisen—**one** definitely **has that,** the vow of dhyana. In the preparations[182] as well there are vows of dhyana and undefiled vows, so the preparations are also taught as dhyanas, just as when we say, "There is a rice field in this town," the area surrounding a town is called the town.

The nobles, individuals who are learners and nonlearners, **have the undefiled** vows.

(2) Teaching how they follow the mind

> 17d The latter two follow the mind.

During the discussion of the coemergent cause, it was mentioned that the two vows follow the mind. Of these three vows, **the latter two,** vows of dhyana and undefiled vows, **follow the mind.**[183] The vows of individual liberation do not follow the mind because they follow one even when one has a different cognition or is in a mind-free state such as the absorption of cessation.

(3) Teaching how they are vows that discard

18ab The two, on Not Unable's paths
Of no obstacles, are called discarding.

The two, vows of dhyana and undefiled vows, if supported **on** the level of **Not Unable,**[184] and produced as the essence of the **path of no obstacles,** discard immorality and the afflictions that motivate it, so they **are called discarding** vows. Therefore there are four possibilities between dhyana or undefiled vows and discarding vows.

(c) Additional points

18cd Mindfulness and awareness are
Restraint of mind and faculties.

The sutras say:

> Restraint of body is excellent.
> Restraint of speech is excellent.
> Restraint of mind is excellent.
> Restraint in all is excellent.

They also say, "Whoever binds the faculty of the eye abides by a vow." What is the nature of the vows or restraint of the mind and faculties explained there? you ask. They do not have the nature of an imperceptible. Well then, what are they? you ask. **Mindfulness,** which does not forget what to do and what not to do, **and awareness,** which knows what that is, **are both** also said to be **restraint of** the **mind and** restraint of the **faculties** because these two prevent the mind and faculties from acting incorrectly toward the object and bind them.

ii. Explaining the three types of karma together. This has four topics: (1) How long they are possessed, (2) How they are attained, (3) Causes that cancel them, and (4) What support possesses them.

(1) How long they are possessed. This has four topics: (a) How imperceptibles are possessed, (b) How perceptibles are possessed, (c) Synonyms of wrong vows, and (d) Explaining their four possibilities.

(a) How imperceptibles are possessed. This has three topics: (i) How vows that are not equipoise are possessed, (ii) How vows of equipoise are possessed, and (iii) How mid-vows are possessed.

(i) How vows that are not equipoise are possessed. This has two points.

A. Vows

19. One who has pratimokṣa has
The present imperceptible
Until it's canceled. From the first
Moment and on, one has the past.

One who has pratimokṣa or vows of individual liberation **has the present imperceptible** as long as they have the vows **until it is canceled** by that individual returning the vows and so forth. **From the first moment and on** until the vows are canceled, **one** also **has** the **past.**

B. Wrong vows

20a It's so for those with wrong vows, too.

It is so for those individuals **who have wrong vows, too,** as they possess their wrong vows similarly.

(ii) How vows of equipoise are possessed

20b–d Those who possess the vows of dhyana
Possess the past and future. Nobles
At first do not possess the past.

21ab In equipoise, on noble paths:
The present imperceptible.

Those who possess vows of dhyana, from the moment they arise until they are canceled, must always **possess** both **the past and** the **future** imperceptible. **Noble** individuals, **at** the time of the **first** undefiled moment, **do not possess the past** undefiled vow, since it has not previously arisen. This is because the vow has never arisen before the dharma forbearance of knowing suffering, so the past imperceptible cannot have been possessed. Those who abide **in** the **equipoise** of the worldly paths and possess the vows of dhyana and those in the equipoise of the **noble path** who possess undefiled vows have **the present imperceptible**, so they have all three times.

(iii) How mid-vows are possessed. This has two points.

A. Actual

21cd If in between, at first the middle;
From then on, one has the two times.

If there is the imperceptible of a mid-vow that is **in between** a vow and a wrong vow, in the **first** moment, the imperceptible of **the middle** time between the past and future, the present, is possessed. **From then**, the first moment, **on** until the mid-vow is canceled, **one** also **has the** past, so one possesses **two times.**

B. As an elaboration, how those who have vows or wrong vows possess mid vows.

22. Those with wrong vows can have the virtuous,
And those with vows can have nonvirtuous
Impercepts as long as they are
Very sincere or strongly afflicted.

When **those with wrong vows** do something virtuous such as a prostration out of great sincerity, they **can have the virtuous** mid-vow, **and** when **those with vows** do something nonvirtuous, such as killing or beating someone out of the force of afflictions, they **can have** the **nonvirtuous** mid-vow's **imperceptible.** These remain with them **as long as they are very sincere or strongly afflicted.**

(b) How perceptibles are possessed

23. Those who are acting all possess
The percept of the present time.
From the first moment until canceled,
They have the past, but not the future.

24ab There's no possession of the past
Obscured, nor of the unobscured.

Those who abide by vows, wrong vows, or mid-vows and **are** actually, perceptibly **acting, all possess the perceptible** of body and speech **of the present time. From the first moment until** the action is **canceled** by the cause of cancellation, **they** also **have the past. But** there is **not** any possession of **the future** perceptible because it does not follow the mind.

There is no possession of the past obscured, nor of the unobscured neutral perceptibles, because they are extremely weak and thus are unable to create past or future attainment.

(c) Synonyms of wrong vows

24cd Wrong vows, and harmful conduct, and
Immoral, karma, and its path.

The body and speech are not bound, so they are **wrong vows. And** they are criticized by the exalted and produce an unpleasant result, so they are **harmful conduct. And** they are the opposite of discipline, so they are **immorality.** They are karma of body and speech, so they are **karma.** When the actual taking of life is completed, they are included in the actual basis, **and** so for that reason they are **its** karmic **path.**

(d) Explaining the four possibilities of possessing perceptibles and imperceptibles.

25. As it's between, the mind is weak
Thus one who acts has just the percept.
When a noble's percept has been canceled
Yet still is unborn, they have the impercept.

The first possibility: **as it,** a mid-vow **is between** a vow and a wrong vow, **the mind is weak. Thus one who** performs a virtuous or nonvirtuous **act has just the perceptible** only. The second possibility is **when a noble** individual's **perceptible** from their previous lifetime **has been canceled** and **yet** their perceptible for this life **still is unborn;** that noble has no perceptible but does **have the imperceptible.**[185] The third possibility is such as when someone who has vows prostrates. The fourth possibility is such as an ordinary individual in the Formless realm. Because the last two possibilities are easy to understand, they are not mentioned in the root text.

(2) How they are attained. This has three topics: (a) How vows are attained, (b) How wrong vows are attained, and (c) How mid-vows are attained.

(a) How vows are attained. This has two topics: (i) Actual, and (ii) What vows are attained in relation to.

(i) Actual. This has three topics: A. How vows of dhyana are attained, B. How undefiled vows are attained, and C. How the vows of individual liberation are attained.

A. How vows of dhyana are attained

26ab The dhyana vows are gained with the level
Of dhyana itself.

The dhyana-produced **vows are gained** by attaining the actual practice and preparations of the mind of **the level of dhyana itself** because they arise simultaneously with the mind of dhyana. Not Unable is attained by training. The actual practice is attained by detachment. If the first dhyana arises out of the higher second dhyana, it is attained when either the preparations or the actual practice arise.

B. How undefiled vows are attained

26bc The undefiled
By nobles.

The undefiled vows are attained **by** the arising of the **noble** levels: any one of the six levels of undefiled dhyana.

C. How the vows of individual liberation are attained. This has two topics: 1. General overview, and 2. Specific explanations.

1. General overview

26cd Pratimokṣa is through
The perceptible of others, et cetera.

Those vows called **pratimokṣa** individual liberation **are** attained **through the perceptible** speech and prayers to the Sangha **of others** including abbots, masters and so forth, because others can perceive that the vow has been born in one's being, and one can also perceive for oneself the proof that it is born within one's continuum. The phrase "**et cetera**" includes the desire to take the vow, the knowledge of attaining it, and renunciation.

The vows of the bhikshu and bhikshuni are attained from the Sangha. The novice monk, novice nun, and male and female pursuer of virtue vows are attained from an individual. The phrase "et cetera" is mentioned in order to include the ten ways the Great Exposition vinaya says the bhikshu vows may be taken. The ten ways the vows are taken are taught in the autocommentary:

> (1) The buddhas and self-buddhas take bhikshu vows spontaneously. (2) The five supports, by developing certainty.[186] (3) Ājñāta and the others, by being summoned, "Bhikshu, come hither." (4) Mahākāshyapa, by accepting the Buddha as Teacher. (5) Sodāyin, by delighting the Buddha with his response to a question. (6) Mahāprajapatī, by accepting the dharmas of respect.[187] (7) Dharmadinnā, by messengers.[188] (8) People in remote lands, by five upholders of the vinaya. (9) People in central lands, by an assembly of ten. (10) The assembly of the good group of sixty took bhikshu vows by repeating three times that they go for refuge.

At this point, the glorious Shakya Chokden explains that the Buddha taking vows spontaneously refers to him renouncing his household and so forth, but this is an imaginary fabrication. It is thoroughly and completely refuted in the Great Karṭīk *The Springtime Cow of Easy Accomplishment* itself, so I shall not beat that dead thing over again.

> Philosophies one's own mind imagines,
> Not heard of in the Noble Land,
> May delight all the fools in Tibet,
> But alas, can they bring true relief
> To all those who want liberation?

2. Specific explanations. This has four topics: a. The time vows are taken for, b. Ascertaining the time period of wrong vows, c. Specifics of fasts, and d. Specifics of the five lay precepts.

a. The time vows are taken for

27ab The vows are taken for life or else
The period of one day and night.

The seven classes of **vows** of individual liberation **are taken for** the rest of this

life, or else the fasting vows are taken for **the period of one day and night.** The end of the period of the vows of individual liberation is either the end of life or the end of a day and night.

Here the Great Exposition proposes that fasting vows can only last one day and night. The Sutra school says there is no harm in fasting vows lasting for many days. The Master explains there is no logical problem with fasting vows lasting many days, but fasting vows are taken for a single day only because that is how it was established by the Buddha. The modern tradition of taking fasting vows for every month, where one takes a vow today, for example, and maintains it on the eighth or some other day of every lunar month, is said to be Lord Atisha's tradition.

Some scholars say that this is illogical. If one were to take fasting vows for one particular day of every month, would such a vow arise or not? In the first instance, one would have to maintain the fasting vow continually from that day on. In the second instance, there would be no possibility of maintaining the vows on the eighth day or full moon of the subsequent months, so they say.

Well then, it follows that one can take the eight precepts of fasting for the rest of one's life, because you have explained that the individual who swears to uphold the eight precepts of fasting for the rest of his life is a righteous pursuer of virtue.[189] You cannot deny the proof, and the pervasion holds. If you agree, it contradicts your position that the fasting vows cannot last longer than one day and night.

Our own position is that when one promises to maintain the fasting vows on the full moon or eighth day of the following lunar months, the vow arises out of the power of resolve in the mind. Extensive proofs and rebuttals of this appear in the great *Ṭīka.*

b. Ascertaining the time period of wrong vows

> 27cd There is no one-day-long wrong-vow,
> Because there's no such oath, it's heard.

There is no one-day-long wrong vow. What is the reason? you ask. **Because there is no such oath** where one says, "May I possess a wrong vow for one day and night," **it is heard.**

c. Specifics of fasts. This has three topics: i. General presentation, ii. Establishing the quantity of precepts, and iii. The need to begin by going for refuge.

i. General presentation

28. While kneeling low with no adornments,
 Recite the words. Till morrow's morn
One swears before another at dawn
 To all the precepts of the fast.

How does one swear to the day-long fast? It is taken **while** the person who is taking the vow is **kneeling** on one or both knees with their palms joined **lower** than the preceptor. One should adorn oneself **with no** new **adornments.** One **recites the words,** repeating after the preceptor. The period for which the vow is taken is **until** the sun rises on the **morrow** or next day**'s morn,** one complete day and night. The time when one commits is when **one swears before another at dawn** before eating any food **to all the precepts of the fast.**

ii. Establishing the quantity of precepts. This has two points.

(1) Actual

29a–c There are four, one, and three precepts
 Of discipline, and carefulness,
Austerity respectively.

There are four root precepts, **one** precept of abandoning alcohol, **and** the last **three** precepts. These are the **precepts of discipline,** which abandon the inherently unwholesome; **and** the precept of **carefulness**, remaining in mindfulness; and the precepts of **austerity,** which are compatible with those precepts, **respectively.**

(2) Dispelling doubt

29d Those bring unmindfulness and arrogance.

Those, drinking alcohol and eating food after noon, respectively **bring unmindfulness** of what to do and what not to do **and** weaken the mindfulness of the fast. High seats, song, dance, and so forth not only weaken mindfulness, they make one **arrogant.**

iii. The need to begin by going for refuge

30ab Others may also fast, of course,
 But only after going for refuge.

Can only people who hold the lay precepts take the fasting vows, or may others as well? you ask. **Others** than just those who have the pursuer of virtue vows **may also fast, of course, but only after** first **going for refuge** to the Three Jewels on that day. Otherwise the vow will not arise.

d. Specifics of the five lay precepts. This has five topics: i. Explaining the meaning of a quotation from a sutra, ii. Rebutting that it is contradictory of the sutras, iii. Distinctions between lesser and greater vows, iv. Explaining the sources of refuge, and v. Specifics of the precepts.

i. Explaining the meaning of a quotation from a sutra

30cd By promising to pursue virtue
The vow is made, it's taught, like bhikshus.

From the *Mahānāman Sutra*:[190]

> Mahānāman, thus if a householder dressed in white clothes who possesses the male faculty of a man goes for refuge in the Buddha and goes for refuge to the Dharma and Sangha, and then also says the words, "Accept me as a pursuer of virtue," by that alone he becomes a pursuer of virtue.

Can one become a pursuer of virtue who holds the lay precepts merely by going for refuge? you ask. The Aparāntakas say one can. The Kashmiris say that alone does not make one a pursuer of virtue, but **by promising** after going for refuge, "Accept me as a **pursuer** of **virtue** for the rest of my life," **the vow is made** and arises—one becomes a pursuer of virtue.

Well then, reciting the liturgy "Just as the noble Arhats... "[191] then become meaningless, you say. It does not, because **it is taught** not as a way to attain something that has not yet been attained but as a way to know what limits have been attained and must be upheld. For example, it is **like** reciting the precepts of a **bhikshu** or a novice after attaining the vows.

ii. Rebutting that it is contradictory of the sutras

31a–c If that is so and all is thus bound,
How is there single conduct, et cetera?
Hold that, and it is held, it's heard.

If that is so and all five precepts of a pursuer of virtue **are thus bound, how is** it that the Buddha spoke of four types of pursuers of virtue: those who abandon taking life alone as **single conduct, et cetera,** including those who hold two precepts as partial conduct, those who hold three or four as majority conduct, and those who hold all five as complete pursuers of virtue?

In response, the Great Exposition says that the intent of this is that at first all of these attain all five precepts completely. Later one violates some precepts, but one **holds that,** another of the precepts, without violation. **And** that is how **it,** single conduct or any of the others, **is held, it is heard.**

iii. Distinctions between lesser and greater vows

31d They're weak, et cetera, like the mind.

The cause for **them,** vows, **being weak, et cetera,** middling and strong, is that although there are differences in how many precepts are held, one's motivation is primary, so the vow is stronger or weaker, **like the** stronger or weaker faith in one's **mind.**

iv. Explaining the sources of refuge

32. All those who go for refuge to
 The three, take refuge in the dharmas
That make the Buddha and the Sangha—
 No learning and both—and nirvana.

What are the Three Jewels to which we go for refuge? you ask. **All those who go for refuge to the Three** Jewels, **take refuge in** the Buddha: they go for refuge in **the dharmas that make the Buddha,** the truth of the path of no more learning. **And** going for refuge in the Sangha is going for refuge in the dharmas that make **the Sangha,** the truth of the path of **no learning and** learning **both. And** going for refuge to the Dharma is going for refuge in the dharma that makes the jewel of the Dharma, **nirvana,** which is the cessation of all afflictions and suffering without exception.

The Great Exposition proposes that the dharma body alone is the Buddha who is the source of refuge, and the form body is not the Buddha. Likewise, the Sangha that is the source of refuge is the truth of the path only, while the Sangha that is its support is not the Sangha that is a source of refuge. The Sutra school proposes that both the support of the form body and the dharma body it supports are the Buddha who is the source of refuge, and both the support of the Sangha and the truth of the path it supports are the Sangha that is the source of refuge.

v. Specifics of the precepts. This has three topics: (1) The meaning of presenting sexual misconduct as a precept, (2) The meaning of presenting lying as a precept, and (3) The meaning of presenting intoxicants as a precept.

(1) The meaning of presenting sexual misconduct as a precept. This has two points.

(a) Actual

> 33ab Since sexual misconduct is reviled,
> Since easy, since abstention is attained.

In all the other vows, abandoning sexual activity in its entirety is presented as a precept. Why in the lay precepts is abandoning sexual misconduct presented as a precept? you ask. The reason for this is **since** lustful **sexual misconduct** dishonors another's spouse, because it is on its own a cause for rebirth in the lower realms, because it **is** utterly **reviled** in the world, and because not all sexual activity is like that. It is also **since** it is **easy** for householders to vow to abandon lustful misconduct, whereas abandoning sexual activity is difficult because of habituation from beginningless time. In addition, it is **since abstention** from lustful misconduct in other lifetimes as well **is** a vow that the nobles have **attained.**

(b) Dispelling a doubt

> 33cd The vow's attained just as it's sworn;
> It is not total celibacy.

If a pursuer of virtue should subsequently take a bride, that alone does not violate his vow. **The vow is attained just as it is sworn,** so one promises not to commit sexual misconduct. **It is not** saying, "I will not act out of desire and will practice **total celibacy.**"

(2) The meaning of presenting lying as a precept

> 34ab If one transgresses any precept,
> He would end up by telling a lie.

Why is lying presented as a precept? you ask. It is because **if** some**one** should **transgress any precept,** when asked about it they might possibly say, "I did not do that." **He would** possibly **end up by telling a lie** on top of their previous violation. Abandoning lying is presented as a lay precept in order to prevent that.

(3) The meaning of presenting intoxicants as a precept

34cd Of the prohibited unwholesome,
Intoxicants, as one will hold the others.

Of the prohibited unwholesome acts,[192] why is only abandoning **intoxicants** presented as a precept? you ask. The reason is that if one abandons drinking intoxicating beverages, **one will hold** the **other** precepts.

(ii) What vows are attained in relation to. This has two topics: A. Individual explanations, and B. Combined explanation.

A. Individual explanations. This has two points.

1. Where the vows of individual liberation are attained from

35ab The vows of Desire must be attained
In relation to all, both, and present.

When one attains any one of the vows of individual liberation, dhyana, or undefiled from one basis,[193] does one also attain the remaining from that basis? you ask. No. **The vows** of individual liberation **of Desire must be attained in relation to all** three aspects of karma: the preparation, the actual act, and the aftermath. They are attained in relation to **both** inherently unwholesome acts and prohibited unwholesome acts, and in relation to both that which indicates and does not indicate sentient beings. **And** because they engage the mind's support, they are attained in relation to the **present** aggregates, sense bases, and elements. They are not attained from the future or past because these are not counted as sentient beings.

2. Where the vows of dhyana and the undefiled vows are attained from

35cd The dhyana and undefiled vows
Relate to actual and all times.

If **the dhyana and undefiled vows** are attained in **relation to** the **actual** basis but not the preparation and aftermath, what need is there to mention the prohibited unwholesome? These vows are attained in relation to the aggregates, elements, **and** sense bases of **all** three **times.**

B. Combined explanation

36ab Vows in relation to all beings;
Distinctions in branches and cause.

Are these **vows** attained in relation to all sentient beings, precepts and cause, or are they attained in relation to specific ones? The **vows** are attained **in relation to all** sentient **beings,** but there are **divisions in branches and cause.** The bhikshu vows are attained from all seven branches, and the lesser vows from four.[194] If you propose the three virtuous roots as a cause, the three arise together, and if you propose greater, middling, and lesser volition as cause, they do not arise together, so there is division. They are attained if one is free of the five qualifications.[195]

(b) How wrong vows are attained. This has two points.

(i) Where they are attained from

36cd Wrong vows are gained in relation to
All and all branches; not to causes.

Wrong vows are attained in relation to all sentient beings and **all** the **branches** of karmic paths. Because it is impossible to have all three roots of nonvirtue simultaneously, they are **not** attained in relation **to** all **causes,** the Great Exposition proposes.

The Master explains that vows have the intention to help all sentient beings, so it is logical to attain vows with regard to all sentient beings, but butchers and so forth do not have wrong intentions with regards to their parents, so how could they attain their wrong vows in relation to all sentient beings? He considers that illogical.

(ii) How they are attained

37ab Wrong vows can be attained from action,
Or else they're gained through a commitment.

Wrong vows can be attained from being born in a particular caste and beginning the preparations for the **action** of killing and so forth, **or else they are gained through a commitment**: "I will pursue this for my livelihood."

(c) How mid-vows are attained

37cd The other impercept is gained
From field, commitment, and respect.

After vows and wrong vows, **the other** virtuous or nonvirtuous **imperceptible** of a mid-vow **is gained from** the **field,** such as with the seven material merits of offering a monastery and so forth.[196] It can also be attained by making promises and **commitments** such as, "I will not eat until I have prostrated to the Buddha" or "I will donate food for one month or half a month," or from the opposite of such commitments. **And** it is gained from paying **respect.** The imperceptible of the mid-vow is attained through a strong afflicted or sincere intent.

(3) Causes that cancel them. This has four topics: (a) Causes that cancel vows, (b) Causes that cancel wrong vows, (c) Causes that cancel mid-vows, and (d) Causes that cancel other dharmas.

(a) Causes that cancel vows. This has three topics: (i) Causes that cancel vows of individual liberation, (ii) Causes that cancel vows of dhyana, and (iii) Causes that cancel undefiled vows.

(i) Causes that cancel vows of individual liberation. This has two points.

A. General teaching

38. The individual liberation
Is canceled by returning vows,
Or dying, or two organs arising,
Severing the roots, or passing the night.

With the exception of fasts, **the** vows of **individual liberation are canceled by** going in front of a cognizant person and resolutely **returning vows** because this produces a perceptible that is exclusive of the previous complete commitment. **Or** they are canceled by **dying** and leaving that class of beings because one has cast away the support with which one made the commitment. **Or** they are canceled by the **two** male and female sexual **organs arising** simultaneously because that weakens the male or female body that was the support for taking the vows. They are also canceled by **severing the roots** of virtue completely because the basis of the vows, the roots of virtue, have been severed.

The fasting vows are canceled by those causes **or** by the **passing** of **the night** because they had only been resolved for a single day and night. These five are the causes that cancel the taming of individual liberation.

The vows of individual liberation are called taming because they make the faculties tame.

In the Vinaya, the sexual organs changing three times, and the person taking the vow not being twenty and knowing that he is not twenty, are explained as causes of cancellation.

B. Presenting different proposals. This has three points.

1. Proposing the root downfalls as a cause of cancellation

> 39a Some say it's canceled by the downfalls;

Some say if **it**, either the bhikshu or novice vow, **is canceled by** any one of **the** four root **downfalls** happening.

2. Proposing the disappearance of dharma as a cause of cancellation

> 39b By the True Dharma's decline, say others.

The vows are canceled **by the True Dharma's decline** because there would be no *poṣadha*[197] or similar rituals, **say** the **others**, the red-robed Dharmaguptas

3. The Kashmiri proposal that root downfalls do not cause cancellation

> 39cd Kashmiris propose that when it happens,
> There are both, like having debts and riches.

The **Kashmiris propose** that **when it**, one of the root downfalls, **happens**, it is **like** a person who **has debts and** also has **riches**, for example. Similarly, whichever root downfall has happened is canceled and broken, but the other ones remain unviolated, so **there are both** immorality and maintained discipline. This is because otherwise when you take one you would take all, they say. They also say there is scriptural proof.

(ii) Causes that cancel vows of dhyana. This has two points.

A. Actual

40ab The virtue of dhyana can be canceled
By shifting level or regressing.

All of **the virtue of dhyana can be canceled by shifting one's level** by both shifting from a lower to a higher level, which cancels the virtue of the lower level, and by shifting from a higher to a lower level, which cancels the virtue of the higher level. **Or** it can also be canceled by **regressing** from absorption. It is possible that the virtue of the preparations for both dhyana and the undefiled can be canceled by death, it is explained.

B. Supplementary point

40c Formless is same;

Just as the virtue of the dhyanas is canceled by shifting levels and regressing, the virtue of **Formless** is canceled **like that, too.**

(iii) Causes that cancel undefiled vows

40cd noble by gaining
A result, refining, or regressing.

The **noble** or undefiled vow is canceled **by gaining a result** or by **refining** faculties. The first cancels those included in the path of entering, and the second those included in the paths of dull faculties. Some that are included in the two higher paths are also canceled by **regressing.**

(b) Causes that cancel wrong vows

41ab Wrong vows are canceled by gaining vows
Or dying or two organs arising.

Wrong vows are canceled by gaining either of the two **vows, or** they are canceled by **dying, or** by **two organs arising** simultaneously, because the body is discarded and the support weakened.

(c) Causes that cancel mid-vows

41cd Midvows, when force or undertaking,
Act, object, life, or the roots cease.

The imperceptible of the **midvow** is canceled **when** the **force** of the sincerity or afflictions that propelled the imperceptible ceases, like a potter's wheel or the flight of an arrow.[198] It is also canceled by giving up on what has been properly undertaken, saying, "**Undertaking** this is enough," and by the **action** ceasing when one does not do the action as one had undertaken. It is also canceled by the cessation of the **object:** stupas, monasteries, temples, beds, seats, snares, traps, weapons, and poison.[199] It is canceled by the cessation of **life.** It is also canceled by **the roots** of virtue **ceasing** or being severed. If one frees oneself from the desire of the Desire realm, the roots of nonvirtue are severed and the nonvirtuous mid-vow is canceled.

(d) Causes that cancel other dharmas. This has two points.

(i) The cause for canceling immaterial virtue

42ab The Desire realm's immaterial virtue,
By severing roots and rebirth higher.

The Desire realm's immaterial virtue is canceled **by severing the roots** of virtue **and** by **rebirth** in the **higher** Form and Formless realms.

(ii) The cause for canceling the immaterial afflicted

42cd The immaterial afflicted
Perishes when its anti arises.

All that is **immaterial** and **afflicted** of the three realms **perishes** and is canceled **when its** own **antidote's** path **arises.**

(4) What support possesses them. This has two topics: (a) How wrong vows are possessed, and (b) How vows are possessed.

(a) How wrong vows are possessed

43a–c Except sexless, neuters, hermaphrodites,
Unpleasant Sound, humans can have
Wrong vows.

Except for the **sexless, neuters, hermaphrodites** with two sexual organs, and those who live on **Unpleasant Sound, humans can have wrong vows.**

(b) How vows are possessed. This has two topics: (i) General overview, and (ii) Which support possesses which vow.

(i) General overview

> 43cd The vows are similar.
> The gods as well.

The vows are just like or **similar** to wrong vows: they can be possessed only by men and women of the three continents. Not only that, **the gods** can possess them **as well.** Other wanderers cannot possess them because their minds are unclear since they cannot forbear the antidote of discrimination; because they have very little modesty and shame; or because they have the obscurations of full ripening.[200]

(ii) Which support possesses which vow. This has two topics: A. Which vows humans possess, and B. Which vows gods possess.

A. Which vows humans possess

> 43d Humans have three.

Humans can **have** the **three** vows: individual liberation, dhyana, and undefiled.

B. Which vows gods possess. This has two points.

1. Who possesses the dhyana vow

> 44ab The gods born in Desire and Form
> Have dhyan-produced.

The gods born in the realms of **Desire and Form have dhyana-produced** vows, but the gods of Formless do not because there is no form on their level and those attained on lower levels have been canceled when they shifted levels.

2. Who possesses the undefiled vow

44b–d Except for beings
In special dhyana and Concept Free,
They've undefiled—in Formless, too.

Undefiled vows can be possessed in Desire. **Except beings in** the **special dhyana** level of Great Brahma **and** beings born in **Conception Free, they,** the gods born in Desire and Form, can **have undefiled** vows. Gods born **in Formless, too,** can have them in terms of possession. They are not manifest in Formless because there is no form there.

C. The meaning of karma as explained in the sutras. This has two topics: 1. General teachings, and 2. Specific explanations.

1. General teachings. This has four topics: a. Classifying in terms of cause and result, b. Teaching the many enumerations of karma, c. Which karma has how many results, and d. Other presentations of karma.

a. Classifying in terms of cause and result. This has three topics: i. Classifying in terms of result, ii. Classifying in terms of cause, and iii. Classifying in terms of both cause and result.

i. Classifying in terms of result. This has four topics: (1) Classifying in three as virtue, etc., (2) Classifying in three as merit, etc., (3) Classifying in three by experience, and (4) The explanation of the latter two.

(1) Classifying in three as virtue, etc.

45ab Pleasant, unpleasant, and other karma
Are virtue, nonvirtue, and other.

The sutras say, "Karma is threefold." Karma that produces **pleasantness,** and that does not produce pleasantness but produces **unpleasantness, and other karma** that does not produce either pleasantness or unpleasantness **are** in succession **virtue, nonvirtue, and** the **other,** neutral.

(2) Classifying in three as merit, etc.

45c Merit, nonmerit, and unmoving.

The sutras also say that there are the three types of **meritorious, nonmeritorious, and unmoving** karma.

(3) Classifying in three by experience

> 45d The three experienced as pleasure, et cetera.

Additionally, there are another **three** types of karma that are taught: karma **experienced as pleasure, et cetera,** including karma experienced as suffering and karma experienced as neutral.

(4) The explanation of the latter two. This has two topics: (a) Explaining merit and so forth, and (b) Explaining the three ways it is experienced and additional points.

(a) Explaining merit and so forth. This has two points.

(i) Meritorious karma

> 46ab Merit is virtuous karma of
> Desire.

Because it is the antidote for nonmerit, **merit is virtuous karma of** the **Desire realm.**

(ii) Unmoving karma

> 46b–d Unmoving is of higher:
> Because the karma fully ripens
> On just those levels, it does not move.

Unmoving karma **is** virtuous karma **of** the **higher** Form and Formless levels. Well then, a sutra says, "In this first dhyana, there is analysis and examination, so the nobles move…" Does this not explain that the three dhyanas are moving? you ask. This is said because those levels have the faults of samadhi; it is not in terms of unmoving karma.

Completing karma[201] of the Form and Formless realms cannot fully ripen on another level. What is the reason? **Because the karma fully ripens on just those levels.** This pervades because it is unmoving: **it does not move** to other levels in dependence upon conditions.

Well then, in Desire as well the full ripening does not move to other levels because in Desire there are no separate levels, you say. This is not a fault. There are no separate levels there, but wanderers of the higher realms and lower realms are separate. In the higher realms it definitely ripens in one type of wanderer only.

These are taught solely in terms of the defiled.

(b) Explaining the three ways it is experienced and additional points. This has three topics: (i) The actual explanation of the three ways karma is experienced, (ii) Additionally, teaching the five ways karma is experienced, and (iii) Understanding the particulars of experience.

(i) The actual explanation of the three ways karma is experienced. This has two points: A. The essence of each individually, and B. Presenting others' positions.

A. The essence of each individually. This has three points.

1. Karma experienced as pleasure

47ab Virtue's experienced as pleasure
Through the third dhyana.

Defiled **virtue** from the Desire realm **through the third dhyana is** karma **experienced as pleasure** because the beings in those three levels have the pleasure of body and mind. The feeling of pleasure in Desire and on the first dhyana is bodily pleasure. On the second dhyana, it is mental pleasure. On the third dhyana, it is cognitive pleasure.[202]

2. Karma experienced as neutral

47bc Above that
It's felt as neither pain nor pleasure.

Above that third dhyana **it,** virtuous karma, **is felt** or experienced **as neither pain nor pleasure** because in those levels there are feelings of neither pleasure nor suffering.

3. Karma experienced as suffering.

47d Nonvirtue is felt as suffering here.

The **nonvirtuous** karma **is** karma **felt** or experienced **as suffering here** in the Desire realm. "Here" indicates that the feeling of suffering is only in Desire. Not only is the feeling itself the result of nonvirtue, but the faculty and object including the characteristics of consciousness in the assembly of sense bases is also its result.

B. Presenting others' positions

48. Some say that in the lower, there
    Is middling, too, since there is ripening
    In special dhyan, and since the three
    Can ripen without earlier or later.

Some say that in the lower levels of the third dhyana and lower, **there is middling,** the karma experienced as neutral, **too**. Why? you ask. It is **since** in the actual practice of the first dhyana, **there is** fully **ripened** feeling **in special dhyana, and** that is a level where there is only neutral feeling.

Additionally, the *Treatise* says:

> In this way, can the full ripening of the three karmas fully ripen without any earlier or later? you ask. They can.

This is **since** it is proposed that **the three** karmas **can** fully **ripen without earlier or later** in the Desire realm, which is impossible in the other realms.

(ii) Additionally, teaching the five ways karma is experienced

49. Inherently, concurrently,
    Through focus, as full ripening,
    Or else directly manifesting:
    Five ways that karma is experienced.

Inherent experience is feeling. **Concurrent** experience is contact: the contact that is compatible with the experience of pleasure is experienced as pleasure. Objects are experienced **through** the **focus** on them. Karmas are experienced **as full ripening** of the result. **Or else** experience through **directly manifesting** is feeling, because it is said:

> At the time that the feeling of pleasure is experienced, at that time the two feelings cease.[203]

The karma experienced in these ways can be experienced as pleasure, suffering, or neutral, so thus there are **five ways that karma is experienced.**

(iii) Understanding the particulars of experience. This has two topics. A. Overview, and B. Explanation

A. Overview

> 50a They're definite or indefinite.

They, the three ways karma is experienced, **are** twofold: the **definitely** experienced and the **indefinitely** experienced.

B. Explanation. This has three topics: 1. General classification, 2. Their individual attributes, and 3. Teaching on karma that will definitely be experienced.

1. General classification. This has two points: a. Own tradition, and b. Others' traditions.

a. Own tradition

> 50b–d There are three definite because
> There's visibly experienced,
> Et cetera.

There are three types of **definitely** experienced karma **because there is** karma that is **visibly experienced** in this lifetime, **et cetera,** including karma experienced on birth and karma experienced in other lifetimes.

b. Others' traditions. This has two points.

i. The tradition that proposes it as five

> 50d Some propose five types,

Some earlier masters **propose** that the indefinitely experienced karma is divided into indefinite full ripening and the indefinite period, so that there are **five types** of karma. The way this is counted is that there are two indefinite: karma with definite ripening but indefinite time frame, and karma with both indefinite. Adding the three definite of visibly experienced and the others, this makes a total of five. Alternatively, in addition to the three (visibly experienced and the other two) whose time frame is definite, there is karma whose essence will be definitely experienced as something four, and both essence and time frame indefinite for five.

Visibly experienced karma ripens in the very same life in which it is committed. Karma experienced on birth is experienced in the next life. Karma in other lifetimes is experienced after that.

ii. The tradition that proposes it as four possibilities

51a And others, four alternatives.

And others, the Dārṣṭāntikas, say there are **four alternatives:** definite period but indefinite full ripening, definite full ripening but indefinite period, both definite, and both indefinite. Examples can be found in the *Ṭīka.*

2. Their individual attributes. This has two topics: a. Which karmas propel likeness, and b. How many karmic propulsions there are for the realms and beings.

a. Which karmas propel likeness

51b Three karmas will propel a likeness.

In one moment, can all four of the visibly experienced and so forth be propelled? you ask. They can. Of those four karmas, visibly experienced does not propel a likeness, but experienced on birth and **the** other **three karmas will propel a likeness.**[204] The former does not propel likeness, but because it occurs in a likeness that has been propelled by another karma, it produces its result in that very one.

b. How many karmic propulsions there are for the realms and beings. This has two topics: i. General, and ii. Specific.

i. General

51c In all realms, there are four propulsions.

How many propulsions are there for each realm and wanderer? **In all realms** and for all beings **there are four** virtuous and nonvirtuous **propulsions.** The intent here is that nonvirtuous propulsions occur in Desire only.

ii. Specific. This has two topics: (1) How many propulsions there are in the state of birth, and (2) How many propulsions there are in the between state.

(1) How many propulsions there are in the state of birth. This has three points.

(a) How many there are in the birth state of hell

51d In hell, there are three virtuous.

"For all beings" above was in general, but in specific, **in hell,** while there are four nonvirtuous propulsions, **there are** the **three virtuous** karmas of karma experienced on birth, karma experienced in other lifetimes, and indefinitely experienced karma. There is no visibly experienced virtuous karma because there is no pleasant full ripening in hell.

(b) How many there are in the birth state of superior ordinary individuals

52ab A child detached stably from a realm
Does none experienced on birth there.

A childish ordinary individual with sharp faculties who is **detached stably from a realm** and who does not regress in that lifetime **does no** karma that is **experienced on birth there** in that level, but does perform the others.

(c) How many there are in the birth state of Nobles

52cd Nobles do none experienced in others,
Even those not stable toward Desire or Peak.

Nobles who are stably detached from a particular level not only perform no karma experienced on birth in that level, they also **do not** accumulate karma **experienced in other** lifetimes, because they will not return to that level. They do perform visibly experienced and indefinitely experienced karma. **Even those** who are **not stably** detached from **Desire and the Peak** of Existence do not perform any karma experienced on birth or in other lifetimes because when they regress from those, they regress from either the result of a nonreturner or arhat, and if one regresses from those results, it is impossible to die without first restoring them.[205]

(2) How many propulsions there are in the between state. This has two points.

(a) Classifications

53ab There are twenty-two propulsions in
The between state of the Desire realm.

Can karma be propelled in the between state? you ask. **There are twenty-two propulsions in the between state of the Desire realm.** When one will take birth in an egg or from the womb only, there is one propulsion into the between state itself, five into the periods of the womb explained above, and five into the period after birth,[206] for a total of eleven. By distinguishing between definite and indefinite propulsions, this makes twenty-two types. In Form there are no propulsions into the womb.

(b) Proving that the eleven definite are visibly experienced

53cd These are a visible result.
These are one single likeness only.

These eleven definite propulsions **are** karma that has **a visibly** experienced **result,** because **these** aggregates at the time of performing the karma and the aggregates at the time of experiencing the result **are** the continuum of **one single likeness only** that is propelled by a single karma.[207]

3. Teaching on karma that will definitely be experienced. This has three topics: a. General explanation, b. Explaining visibly experienced in particular, and c. Teaching other ways karma and result can be experienced.

a. General explanation

54. An action done out of intense
Afflictions or sincerity,
To the field of qualities, continuous,
Or killing parents: that is definite.

How is karma definitely experienced? you ask. **A** nonvirtuous **action** that is **done out of** a motivation that is **intensely afflicted, or** virtuous actions performed with a motivation that is intensely **sincere,** help or harm that may be performed without intense motivation but is done **to the field of qualities**—the three jewels and five individuals who will be explained below—and those virtuous or nonvirtuous preparations that are done **continuously, or,** like the Persians, **killing parents** with a meritorious intention:[208] **that,** any of these karmas, **is definitely** experienced.

b. Explaining visibly experienced in particular. This has three points.

i. Visibly experienced by power of the karma

55ab Karma has visible results
From excellence of field and intention

Karma has visibly experienced **results from** the **excellence of** the **field,** like the bhikshu named Defeated by Quarreling who once called some Sangha members women during an argument **and** later became a woman. It is also from excellence of **intention,** like the blind eunuch of King Kaṇika who gave a gift that saved five hundred bulls from castration and then regained his manhood.

ii. Visibly experienced by the power of the antidote

55cd From stable detachment from the level
When it has definite full ripening.

From stable detachment from the level of Desire or another level, **when it,** the karma, **has** a **definitely** experienced result, it is visibly experienced. What is this karma like? you ask. This is karma whose period is indefinite, but whose **full ripening** is definite.

iii. Distinctions of the field

56. To help or harm those risen from
Cessation, unprovocative,
Love, seeing, or arhat's result,
Brings swiftly experienced results.

What is karma that is visibly experienced like? you ask. **To** give **help or** bring **harm** to the Sangha of the Buddha's bhikshus or to the five individuals—**those** who have just (1) **risen from** the absorption of **cessation** that is like going to nirvana, (2) aroused from the **unprovocative** samadhi,[209] (3) aroused from the samadhi of **loving**-kindness that has the supreme pure intention, (4) aroused from new transformation of abandoning all the discards of seeing that is the stainless path of **seeing, or** (5) aroused from the new transformation of abandoning all the discards of meditation that is the **arhat's result—brings swiftly experienced results.** Others on the path of meditation do not have these causes, so help or harm to them is not necessarily visibly experienced.

c. Teaching other ways karma and result can be experienced. This has four points.

i. The way feelings are experienced

57. Virtuous karma that is free of
    Considering will fully ripen
Only as feelings in the mind.
    Nonvirtue ripens on the body.

Full ripening is primarily feeling, so is there any type that is only mental feeling and not bodily feeling? you ask. There is. **Virtuous karma that is free of considering,** from the levels of the special dhyana to the Peak of Existence, **will fully ripen only as feelings in the mind,** or mental feelings, because bodily feeling is always accompanied by considering. This implicitly teaches that the full ripening of virtuous karma on the first dhyana and below is both mental and bodily feeling. **Nonvirtuous** karma fully **ripens on the body** as bodily feeling only. It is not mental, because the suffering of mind is mental unhappiness, which is not a fully ripened result, as was explained in the "Teaching on Faculties."[210]

ii. Where the distracted mind is

58a A distraught mind is mental mind.

Well then, where does a distraught mind come from, and what is its cause? you ask. **A distraught** and crazed **mind is** in the **mental mind** or consciousness. It is not in the consciousnesses of the five gates, because these do not think with thoughts that recognize and thoughts that remember.

iii. What results produce that

58bc It's born from fully ripened karma,
From fear or harm, imbalance, sorrow

It, the distraught mind, **is born from** being confused by others through substances or mantras, from being given intoxicants, and from other **full ripenings of karma.** The mind is also made distraught **from** the conditions of the mind being adversely affected by **fear** from seeing the ugly form of a nonhuman, and when angering it, the **harm** of being stricken with illness, an **imbalance** of the elements when agitated by wind, bile, or phlegm, and **sorrow** at the death of a beloved child.

iv. What beings can have that

58d Among the attached, not in the North.

Which sentient beings can become distraught? It happens **among the** sentient beings who are **attached,** but **not in the Northern** Unpleasant Sound, because if gods can be crazed, what need is there to speak of humans, hungry ghosts, hell beings, and animals? Except for the Bhagavan, nobles can be distraught because of imbalances of the elements, but they cannot be distraught by other causes or karma, because definite karmas ripened earlier when they were ordinary individuals, and the indefinite ones do not ripen when they are nobles.

ii. Classifying in terms of cause

59ab The crooked, faulty, degenerate
Are born of deceit, hate, desire.

As taught in a sutra, there is **the** karma of body, speech, and mind that is said to be **crooked, faulty** or harmful, and **degenerate.** These are respectively karma **born of deceit** that is dishonest, **hate** that is most extremely harmful, and **desire** that is hard to separate from.

iii. Classifying in terms of both cause and result. This has two topics: (1) Overview, and (2) Explanation.

(1) Overview

59cd Four types of karma are distinguished
As white and black, et cetera.

The sutras teach **four types of karma** that **are distinguished as white** karma that has a white full ripening, **and black** karma that has a black full ripening, **et cetera,** including mixed white-and-black karma that has a mixed white-and-black full ripening, and that which is neither white nor black and has no full ripening but extinguishes karma.

(2) Explanation. This has three topics: (a) General teaching, (b) Specific explanation of the extinguisher, and (c) Presenting other traditions.

(a) General teaching

60. Nonvirtue, virtue of Form realm,
    And of Desire, respectively
Are karma that is black, white, both.
    What douses them is undefiled.

Nonvirtuous karma is always afflicted only and produces only unpleasant full ripening. **Virtue** itself **of** the **Form realm** is not mixed with nonvirtue **and** produces only pleasant full ripening. The virtue **of Desire** is not mixed in its essence, but appears mixed with nonvirtue in one person's being, so its full ripening can be mixed with unpleasant full ripening of nonvirtue. For that reason, **respectively** these **are** the **karma that is** taught in a sutra:

> **Black** karma that fully ripens as black, **white** karma that fully ripens as white, black and white karma that ripens as **both** black and white...

That **which** does not have full ripening, is not afflicted, and discards or **douses them,** the other three karmas, **is undefiled** karma, which is described as:

> Karma that is neither white nor black, has no full ripening, and extinguishes other karma.

(b) Specific explanation of the extinguisher. This has three topics: (i) That which extinguishes the black, (ii) That which extinguishes the white-and-black, and (iii) That which extinguishes the white.

(i) That which extinguishes the black

61. Forbearance of dharmas and eight paths of
    No obstacles that bring detachment:
These are the twelve volitions that
    Are karma which destroys the black.

Not all undefiled karmas or paths extinguish all three karmas. The four **forbearances of** knowing **dharma** of suffering and the other truths that are part of the path of seeing **and** first **eight** undefiled **paths of** meditation of **no ob-**

stacles that bring detachment from the Desire realm **are the twelve volitions that are karma which destroys the black,** because they abandon Desire's dharmas of nonvirtuous misdeeds. The four dharma knowings and the eight detached paths of liberation are not, because the paths of no obstacles have already extinguished the black. The four subsequent forbearances and four subsequent knowings are not antidotes for the black because they are only antidotes for the higher realms.[211]

(ii) That which extinguishes the white-and-black

> 62ab Volition of the ninth is what
> Extinguishes the black and white.

The **volition of the ninth** path of no-obstacles that detaches one from the Desire realm **is what extinguishes the black-and-white** karma, because it abandons the ninth black afflicted karma of Desire by severing the attainment of its essence, and it also abandons the white of Desire by freeing one from intentional desires.

(iii) That which extinguishes the white

> 62cd The last path of no obstacles
> To dhyan's detachment douses white.

The last to arise of the four **paths of no obstacles to detachment** from the essence of the four **dhyanas**—the volition that abandons the ninth meditation discard—**douses** or extinguishes **white** karma. As long as that ninth discard has not been discarded, when it focuses on something, it is possessed as a discard. When discarded, it is discarded in terms of removing the desire of intention.

(c) Presenting other traditions

> 63. Some say the two are what is felt
> In hell and elsewhere in Desire.
> Others call seeing's discards black;
> The rest in Desire, black and white.

Some masters **say the two,** black karma and black-and-white karma, are as follows: karma **which is felt** or experienced **in hell** is black karma that fully ripens as black, **and** karma experienced by other wanderers **elsewhere in Desire** is logically both black and white. Some limited completing karmas are said to be neutral. **Others** say that the karmas of **seeing's discards** are not mixed with virtue, so they are only **black. The rest** produced **in Desire,** the discards of meditation, are **black-and-white** karma, because it is possible for them to be either virtuous or nonvirtuous.

b. Teaching the many enumerations of karma. This has two topics: i. Classifying in terms of function, and ii. Explaining karmic paths in particular.

i. Classifying in terms of function. This has five points.

(1) Explaining the silence of the three

> 64a–c Nonlearners' karma of body and speech
> And just their mind respectively
> Are silence of the three.

Nonlearners' undefiled **karma of body and speech and just their** undefiled **mind, respectively are** said in the sutras to be the **silence of the three,** body, speech, and mind. These have in the ultimate sense silenced and abandoned all the impediments of the three gates, and are free of everything afflicted.

(2) Explaining the three cleansers

> 64cd All three
> Fine conducts are three purifiers.

The sutras tell of the three cleansers of body, speech, and mind. **All three fine conduct** of body, speech, and mind, **are** respectively the **three purifiers** of body, speech, and mind, because defiled fine conduct temporarily and undefiled fine conduct permanently abandon the stains of harmful action. The purpose of this is to rebut the non-Buddhist views that merely sitting without talking or falsely cleansing by washing on a river bank could cleanse or purify the stains.

(3) Three types of harmful conduct

> 65ab Nonvirtue of the body, et cetera,
> Is proposed as three harmful conducts.

What are the three harmful actions the sutras teach? you ask. The three **nonvirtuous** karmas **of body, et cetera,** including speech and mind, produce unpleasant full ripening, so they are **proposed as** the **three harmful conducts** of the three gates.

(4) Three types of harmful mental conduct

65cd To covet and so forth aren't action
But are three harmful mental conducts.

To covet and so forth, to have malice and wrong views, **are not** inherently **action but are** the **three harmful conducts of mind.** The reason is that they are greed, hatred, and delusion, so they are not karma, because they are afflictions contained within the six root afflictions.[212] The Dārṣṭāntikas say the *Conceived for That Purpose Sutra*[213] teaches that covetousness and so forth only are mental karma.

(5) Three types of fine conduct

66a Fine conduct is the opposite.

Fine conduct is the virtues that are the **opposite** of those three types of harmful conduct of the three gates. These are the virtuous karma of the three gates, the absence of covetousness, the absence of malice, and the correct view.

ii. Explaining karmic paths in particular. This has two topics: (1) Overview, and (2) Explanation.

(1) Overview

66b–d Among them, to consolidate grossly,
The various virtues and nonvirtues
Are taught as the ten karmic paths.

Among them, fine conduct and harmful conduct, **to consolidate grossly** or present very coarsely the actual basis, **the various virtuous** and **nonvirtuous** karmas **are taught** in the sutras **as the ten** virtuous and nonvirtuous **karmic paths** in order to know what to take up and what to give up. Saying "various" indicates that this is a coarse consolidation that does not include everything. What is not included? you ask. The preparations and aftermaths of the seven karmas of body and speech, and the mental karma of volition are not included. Additionally, many nonvirtues such as destroying stupas or beating sentient beings, and many virtues such as abandoning drinking alcohol, generosity, and pleasant speech are not included.

(2) Explanation. This has four topics: (a) Classifications of perceptible and imperceptible, (b) The three virtuous and three nonvirtuous roots, (c) Teaching the three completing factors, and (d) Teaching the individual karmas.

(a) Classifications of perceptible and imperceptible. This has two topics: (i) Actual and (ii) Additionally, ascertaining which are the preparation and the aftermath.

(i) Actual. This has two points.

A. Ascertaining which nonvirtue is

> 67ab Six nonvirtues are imperceptible.
> The one is both. If done, they are as well.

The **six nonvirtues** of body and speech excluding sexual misconduct **are** solely **imperceptible** when they arise from ordering somebody to do something. **The one,** sexual misconduct, cannot be completed by ordering someone else and must be done oneself, so it **is both** perceptible and imperceptible. **If** one **does** them oneself, **they**—the previous six—**are** both perceptible and imperceptible **as well** when completed at the time that the perceptible has not ceased, but imperceptible only when completed at the time that the perceptible has ceased.

B. Ascertaining which virtue is

> 67cd The seven virtues are both. What samadhi
> Produces is an imperceptible.

The seven virtuous, material karmic paths **are both** perceptible and imperceptible because correct discipline is without a doubt dependent upon the perceptible. The dhyana and undefiled vows **which samadhi produces are** only **imperceptible** because they are dependent on just the mind.

Previously it said in the *Ṭīka* that undefiled vows have both perceptible and imperceptible aspects, but I cannot find the source and wonder whether it might be a typographical error.

Here some say that the verse, "The percept and/Impercept of the first"[214] presents the four possibilities of individual liberation and the vows of individual liberation, so the first moment of taking the vow correctly is individual liberation but not a vow. This is not harmed by the root text and commentary on the lines, "If done, they are as well./The seven virtues are both..." because this teaches that there are both perceptibles and imperceptibles at the time of the actual basis of the seven karmic paths of body and speech. The perceptible of the first moment of taking a vow is not an actual karmic path, so they explain that a vow of individual liberation is not pervasively imperceptible.

Such twisted explanations appear to make many contradictions of both the root verses and the commentary, so it is like the chatter of common beings who have eaten thorn apple[215] and is not worthy of being spoken by wise exalted beings such as yourselves. Modern students of the abhidharma, look at the entire root and commentary and choose your words carefully!

(ii) Additionally, ascertaining which are the preparation and the aftermath

68a–c The preparations are perceptible.
They might be imperceptible, or not.
The aftermath is opposite of that.

The preparations for the seven virtuous and seven nonvirtuous karmic paths have without a doubt a **perceptible** nature. If they are undertaken out of intense entanglers[216] or sincerity, **they might be imperceptible, or** if with a weak mind, **not. The aftermath** of the karmic path **is** the **opposite of that,** the preparations. Until it is canceled, there is definitely an imperceptible. If one performs an action that is in accord with the actual basis, there is also a perceptible, but if not, there is none.

Well then, what is the distinction between preparation, actual basis of the karmic path, and aftermath? you ask. When someone wishes to kill a living creature, the actions from getting up off the seat, approaching that being, taking a weapon, and striking the creature once or twice, until actually taking the life of that being, are the preparations. The perceptible and imperceptible moment of striking the creature and taking its life is the actual karmic path. The following imperceptible moments and the perceptible skinning the animal, selling, cooking, eating its meat, and so forth are the aftermath. It is similar with the other six.

Covetousness, malice, and wrong view do not depend upon the actual basis or the aftermath, but become a karmic path by merely manifesting.

(b) The three virtuous and three nonvirtuous roots. This has two topics: (i) Nonvirtuous, and (ii) Virtuous.

(i) Nonvirtuous. This has two points.

A. Roots of nonvirtue of body and speech

68d The preparations come from the three roots.

From a sutra:

> Bhikshus, taking life is threefold: that produced by greed, hatred, and delusion…

The others up to wrong view are taught similarly. The meaning of this is that **the** motivation of the **preparations** for the seven karmic paths of body and speech **come** or arise **from the three** nonvirtuous **roots.** Taking life produced by desire is killing out of craving for meat and so forth; that produced by hatred is killing for revenge; and that produced by delusion is animal sacrifice, or the Persians killing their elderly parents or those who are extremely ill, and so on. Stealing and so forth are similar.

B. Roots of nonvirtue of the mind

69ab They follow the three roots immediately,
So coveting and so forth come from them.

They follow the three roots, the three poisons, **immediately, so coveting and so forth** also **come from them.**

(ii) Virtuous

69cd The virtues, preparation, aftermath,
Arise from nongreed, nonhate, nondelusion.

The virtuous karmic paths, their **preparations, and** their **aftermath, arise from nongreed, nonhate,** and **nondelusion,** because they are motivated by a virtuous mind and such virtuous minds are concurrent with nongreed and so forth. These discard the nonvirtuous aftermaths.

For example, the perceptible and imperceptible karmas of a novice who wishes to take full ordination up until they complete the actual basis are the preparation. The perceptible and imperceptible attained during the phrase "For that purpose, if the Sangha grants full ordination…" on the third repetition of the motion is the actual basis, and those from then on are the aftermath.[217]

(c) Teaching the three completing factors. This has three topics: (i) Actual, (ii) What their bases are, and (iii) Delineating what is or is not the actual basis.

(i) Actual. This has four points.

A. The three completed by hatred

70ab Hatred brings killing and harsh words
And malice to completion.

Hatred brings killing and harsh words and malice to completion, because killing eradicates life, and a harsh mind is manifest in the other two.

B. The three completed by desire

70b–d Greed
Brings coveting, adultery,
And also stealing to completion.

Greed brings coveting, adultery or sexual misconduct, **and also stealing to completion.**

C. The one completed by delusion

71a Wrong view, completed by delusion.

Wrong view is brought to its **completion by delusion,** because it is confused about dharma.

D. The three completed by all three

71b The rest by three, it is proposed.

The rest—the three that remain, lying, divisive speech, and idle chatter—are brought to completion **by** any one of the **three**—greed, hatred, or delusion—**it is proposed.**

(ii) What their bases are

71cd The bases, they are sentient beings,
Enjoyments, name-and-form, and words.

The basis or object for taking life **is sentient beings.** The basis for lying with someone else's spouse and so forth is **enjoyments.** The basis for wrong view is feeling and the other four aggregates of **name and** the aggregate of **form, and** the basis for the other four of lying and so forth is a collection of **words,** because speech engages words.

(iii) Delineating what is or is not the actual basis. This has two points.

A. Those which seem to be but are not

> 72a–c When killers die before or else
> Together, there's no actual—
> They've been born in another body.

If a killer and his victim should die together or the killer should die first, is there an actual basis of karma or not? you ask. **When killers die before or else together** with their victims, **there is no actual** karmic path, because at the time that the taking of life is completed, **they,** the killer, **have been reborn in another body** than the one in which they performed the preparations.

B. Those that do not seem to be but are

> 72d–f In wars and so forth all of them
> Have the same goal, so all possess
> The karma, like the perpetrator.

Well then, when many people gather and agree to make war or so forth, if one person actually deprives another sentient being of life, do the others also have the misdeed of taking life or not? you ask. **In wars,** hunts, **and so forth, all of those** sentient beings **have** the preparations for **the same goal** and so forth, **so all** those who are not actually killers **possess the** actual **karmic** path of taking life, **like the perpetrator** who did the actual killing. Those who were conscripted against their will possess it if they later develop a mind intent upon the same goal, but if they do not wish to do harm even at the cost of their own life, they do not possess it.

(d) Teaching the individual karmas. This has four topics: (i) The characteristics of each karma, (ii) How many can simultaneously engage volition, (iii) Which wanderers have how many karmic paths, and (iv) Teaching the results of the karmic paths.

(i) The characteristics of each karma. This has two topics: A. Identifying each one, and B. Explaining wrong view in particular.

A. Identifying each one. This has four points: 1. Karma of the body, 2. Karma of speech, 3. Karma of mind, and 4. The distinction between karma and karmic paths.

1. Karma of the body. This has three points.

a. Taking life

> 73ab To take life is to kill another
> Intentionally, unerringly.

What is the nature of taking life and the other karmic paths? you ask. **To take life is to kill another** being—someone other than oneself—**intentionally**, thinking "I will kill him." It is **unerringly** killing the one whom the killer intended to kill. Thus it has three aspects, otherwise it possesses merely the harm of the preparation.

Life is a nonconcurrent formation or the distinctive wind that occurs based on the support of the body and mind. Taking it is merely preventing it from continuing.

b. Taking what is not given

> 73cd To steal is to make another's wealth
> One's own by force or thievery.

To steal or take what's not given **is to make another's wealth one's own** either **by force** through actually robbing **or** by **thievery**, taking without being detected. Here also it must be intentional and unerring. Merely taking without the intention to make it one's own does not constitute a fault, and taking Yajñadatta's things when one wanted to take Devadatta's merely produces the fault of preparation, not that of the actual basis.

Well then, if one takes what has been offered to a stupa, an unowned treasure, or the wealth of a dead monk, from whom is one taking without being given? you ask. In the first instance, one is taking from the Buddha, in the second, from the king of that region, and in the third from the Sangha, which are extremely grave faults.

c. Sexual misconduct

74ab To lie with one who shouldn't be lain with:
Four kinds of sexual misconduct.

To lie with someone who should not be lain with and so forth are the **four kinds** of **lustful sexual misconduct:** lying with someone who should not be lain with, with the wrong part of the body, in the wrong place, and at the wrong time. The first is with someone who has been taken as another's spouse and so forth. The second is in the mouth, the anus, and so forth. The third is in the open or near stupas, and so forth. The fourth is with pregnant or nursing mothers, and so forth.

2. Karma of speech. This has four points: A. Lying, B. Divisive speech, C. Harsh speech, and D. Idle chatter.

a. Lying. This has two points.

i. Actual

74cd To say one thing while thinking another,
When clearly understood, is lying.

To say one thing while thinking another about the subject that is being spoken of, **when** the meaning is **clearly understood, is lying.** If the words are not understood, it becomes merely idle chatter.

ii. The meaning of seeing, hearing, and so forth

75. That which is experienced by eye,
By ear, mind consciousness, and three,
Is seen, heard, cognized, and perceived
Respectively, it is explained.

What are seeing, hearing, consciousness, and realizing? you ask. **That which is experienced by** the **eye** consciousness, and likewise **by** the **ear** consciousness, the **mind consciousness, and** by the **three** consciousnesses of nose, tongue, and body **is seen, heard, cognized, and perceived respectively, it is explained.** The reason that scent, taste, and touch are taught in a single group is that they are similar in being only neutral, or in Master Saṅghabhadra's presentation, they are similar in terms of being perceived upon contact.

b. Divisive speech

76ab Divisive speech is words said with
An afflicted mind to divide others.

What is **divisive speech?** you ask. It is **words** whose meaning can be understood, that are unerringly **said with** or motivated by **an afflicted mind** in order **to divide others.** It is not intended to help.

c. Harsh speech

76c Harsh speech is words that are unpleasant.

Harsh speech is words of an afflicted mind **that are unpleasant,** understandable, and unerring, which one actually says to another out of a desire to speak.

d. Idle chatter. This has two points.

i. Actual

76d Any afflicted words are chatter—

Any afflicted words, spoken with an afflicted motivation, **are** idle **chatter.** Lying and the others are all three idle chatter, but because they are more harmful, they are classified separately.

ii. Others' proposals

77a–c Some say afflicted speech that's other
Than those, like flattery, song, shows,
Or else bad treatises.

Some others **say** that **afflicted speech that is other than those** previous three are idle chatter, **like,** for example, **flattery** spoken sweetly out of a desire for personal gain, honor, and fame; singing **songs** out of desire; **shows** intended to make people laugh and so forth. **Or else** it is also like reciting **bad treatises** out of attachment to their erroneous views. Other words intended to bring fame and so forth are also idle chatter.

3. Karma of mind. This has three points.

a. Covetousness

77cd To covet
Is wrongly greeding for others' wealth.

Coveting is wrongly or inappropriately **greeding for others' wealth**—wealth that belongs to another. It is the desire to take something by force or thievery.

b. Malice

78a Malice is hate for sentient beings.

Malice is hate for sentient beings that has the aspect of wanting to harm others.

c. Wrong view

78bc Believing there's no virtue or
Nonvirtue is wrong view.

Believing there is no virtue or nonvirtue is like this: saying that there is no generosity, no burnt offerings, no offerings, and no fine conduct is denial of cause. Saying there is no fully ripening of the result of fine conduct and harmful conduct is denial of result. Saying that this world, the next world, fathers, mothers, and miraculous birth of sentient beings do not exist is denial of function. Saying there are no arhats in the *loka* is a view that destroys existing things. Such views are **wrong views.** The root teaches the denial of cause explicitly as an illustration of the others.

4. The distinction between karma and karmic paths

78cd Of these,
Three are paths and seven karma, too.

Of these nonvirtues, the **three** of mind are the gates to enter karmic volition, so they **are** karmic **paths,** but they are not karma. **And** the **seven** karmic paths of body and speech are karma of body and speech, so they are karmic paths and are **karma, too.**

B. Explaining wrong view in particular. This has two topics: 1. How the roots of virtue are severed, and 2. How they are restored.

1. How the roots of virtue are severed. This has six points.

a. What severs them

79a The nihilist view severs the roots

The nihilist view that there is no cause and result from the ten nonvirtues **severs the roots** of virtue. The others are exclusive of virtue but do not sever the roots.

However, the *Treatise* says:

> Well then, what are the great roots of nonvirtue? you ask. The roots of nonvirtue are that which severs the roots of virtue and that which is discarded first of all by those who attain detachment from Desire.

Is this not contradictory? you say. It is not contradictory. The intent of this is that the roots of nonvirtue lead to wrong view. Therefore it is like saying that the thief who set the fire burned the town down even though he is not himself the actual combustion.

b. What is severed

79b Of Desire that were attained at birth.

Which roots of virtue are severed? you ask. The roots of virtue **of Desire that were attained at birth** are completely severed, because the person who has the wrong view that severs the roots of virtue does not have the virtue or nonvirtue of the two higher realms, and because the attainment of those that were attained by training in listening, contemplating, and meditating was previously severed when he had the lesser of lesser wrong views.

c. What the views that sever them focus on

79c Denial of cause and result. All.

What is the focus of views that cut the virtuous roots? you ask. Wrong views that are a **denial of cause**, saying there is no fine or harmful conduct, **and result,** saying there is no full ripening of result, sever the roots.

Some say those that focus on the defiled and realms of the same status sever the roots, but those that focus on the undefiled and realms of different status do not sever them. Here the Great Exposition explains that denial of cause and effect and **all** that focuses on the same or different status or on defiled or undefiled sever them.

d. How they are severed

79d Gradual.

Some say that like the discards of seeing, the roots of virtue are severed at once. Here, however, similar to the afflictions discarded by meditation, the nine roots of virtue are **gradually** severed by the nine wrong views from the least of lesser wrong view, middling of lesser wrong view, and so forth up to the greatest of greater wrong views, which severs the smallest of small roots of virtue. This is also the Master's explanation.

e. What support they are severed on

79d By humans. They are cut

80a By men and women acting on views.

They are severed **by humans** but not by other wanderers, because in the lower realms afflicted and unafflicted full knowing are not stable, the gods perceive karma and result directly, and in Unpleasant Sound there is no intention to perform misdeeds, so they are not severed there. Thus **they are cut** or severed **by** the **men and women** of the three continents. The sexless, neuters, and so forth, do not sever them. Among them craving is very powerful, so they do not cut them, because they have unstable intentions, like beings in the lower realms. The roots are severed by those who **act on** strong **views,** because they have stable, sinful intentions and are ensnared by nonvirtue.

f. Its essence

80b The severance is nonpossession.

When **the** roots of virtue have been **severed**, the attainment of the virtuous roots also does not arise, so it **is** said that if the **nonpossession** or nonattainment of the virtuous roots arises, they have been severed.

2. How they are restored. This has two points.

a. Actual

80c Restored by doubt and view of existence;

How are the virtuous roots restored? you ask. What was severed is **restored** when **doubt** about cause and effect arises **and** when the correct **view** that believes in the **existence** of cause and effect arises. At that time, their attainment arises, which is called their restoration. When that arises, the attainment of the nine attained upon birth arises simultaneously, but they become manifest gradually, just as a patient recovers his strength gradually.

b. How they are restored in those who have committed a heinous deed

80d Who've done a heinous deed, not here.

If one has not done a heinous deed, the roots can be restored in the very same lifetime. The virtuous roots of individuals **who have done a heinous deed** can **not** be restored **here,** in this lifetime. If they were severed by conditions, they will be restored in the between state before birth in hell, and if severed by causes, they are restored when about to die and transmigrate from hell. There are four possibilities of those who have severed the roots of virtue and those who are destined for the mistaken:[218] the first is Pūraṇa Kāśyapa and the other five logicians. The second is King Ajātaśatru. The third is Devadatta. The fourth is people other than those.

(ii) How many karmic paths can simultaneously engage volition. This has two points.

A. How many nonvirtues can simultaneously engage volition

81ab Up to eight nonvirtues and volition
Can simultaneously arise;

To analyze how many karmic paths and one volition can arise simultaneously: as far as the nonvirtues, because it is possible for any one of the three of mind and the seven of body and speech—either done by oneself or by ordering others—to be completed simultaneously, from one **up to eight nonvirtues and volition can simultaneously arise.** Nine or ten cannot arise, because it is impossible for the three of mind to arise simultaneously, and sexual misconduct cannot be completed by ordering another.

B. How many virtues can simultaneously engage volition

81cd When they are virtuous, up to ten,
And yet not one, not eight, not five.

When they, the karmic paths, **are virtuous, up to ten** can arise with a single volition in general, **and yet** in particular, there is **not** only **one** single karmic path and volition, because the absence of covetousness and absence of malice come together with a virtuous mind, and there is no vow that has the nature of only abandoning one discard.

Volition does **not** arise simultaneously with only **eight,** because a bhikshu who has abandoned seven has seven when he has an afflicted or neutral contemporaneous motivation, and when he has a virtuous mind of the five sense consciousnesses, nongreed and nonhatred both arise, so there are nine, and if it is mental consciousness, there is also the correct view for ten.

It does **not** arise simultaneously with only **five,** because if one is a novice or holds the lay precepts it is impossible to have a single virtue of mind in addition to the four discards: if it is one of the five sense consciousnesses, in addition to the four discards there are nongreed and nonhatred, which both arise for a total of six, and if it is mental consciousness, in addition to those there is correct view for a total of seven.

(iii) Which wanderers have how many karmic paths. This has two topics: A. Which have nonvirtue, and B. Which have virtue.

A. Which have nonvirtue. This has three points.

1. How many there are in hell

> 82a–c In hell, there is chatter, and harsh words,
> And malice in two ways; wrong view
> And covetousness by possession.

How many of the virtuous and nonvirtuous paths are there, both manifest and in terms of possession? you ask. **In hell,** as there is lamentation and wailing, **there are** idle **chatter, and** the **harsh words** of quarrels with one another, **and** the **malice** that motivates them. These three exist **in** the **two ways** of being manifest and by possession. There is **covetousness and wrong view by possession,** as they have not been abandoned by an antidote, but they are not manifest, because there are no things to desire and karma and result are directly perceived.

In the hells, killing someone does not make them die, there is no ownership of sexual partners or things, there is no need to lie, and there is no one who is near to one's heart so everyone is already divided. For that reason, the five from taking life to divisive speech are not manifestly present, nor is there any attainment of them.

2. How many there are in Unpleasant Sound

82d There are three in Unpleasant Sound.

83a The seventh is manifest there, too.

There are three of mind that are possessed **in Unpleasant Sound**, but they are not manifest, because there is no clinging to mine, their beings are gentle, there is nothing cruel, and they do not have sinful intentions. **The seventh,** idle chatter of singing songs out of desire and so forth, **is manifest there,** in Unpleasant Sound, **too.** The other six of taking life and so forth are not manifest, because they do not have sinful intentions, the lifespan is definite, and there is no ownership of sexual partners or things. Whoever wishes to behave impurely takes the hand of the woman he desires and goes near a tree. If she is someone who may be lain with, the tree screens them and they lie together, and if not, the tree does not screen them and they do not.

3. How many there are in the Desire realm other than those two

83b Elsewhere in Desire, the ten nonvirtues.

Elsewhere in other **Desire realm**s excluding the hells and Unpleasant Sound, **the ten nonvirtuous** karmic paths are present both manifestly and by possession. Among animals, hungry ghosts, and gods, they are included in the nonvirtuous mid-vows, and among humans they can also be included in wrong vows.

Gods do not kill gods, but do kill hungry ghosts and other wanderers. Others say that gods do kill gods, because when the gods and demigods battle, if the limbs or torso are cut they rejuvenate, but if the head or neck is cut, it cannot be healed and they die.

B. Which have virtue. This has two topics: 1. Where the three of mind are, and 2. Where the seven of body and speech are.

1. Where the three of mind are

83cd Three virtues are in all by way
Of being possessed or manifest.

The **three virtues** of mind—the absence of covetousness and so forth—**are** present **in all** realms and all five wanderers **by way of being possessed or** being **manifest.**

2. Where the seven of body and speech are. This has two topics: a. How many there are in Formless and Conception Free, and b. How many there are among other wanderers.

a. How many there are in Formless and Conception Free

84ab Beings in Concept Free and Formless
Have seven by possession, and

Sentient **beings in Conception Free and Formless have** the **seven** karmic paths of body and speech **by possession.** They have either the dhyana or the undefiled vows, because nobles born in the Formless possess the past and future undefiled vows, and because beings in Conception Free have the vows of dhyana. "**And**" is a conjunction with the next line.

b. How many there are among other wanderers. This has two points.

i. General

84c In the rest they're manifest as well,

In the rest, the realms and wanderers other than the Formless and Conception Free, **they,** the seven virtuous karmic paths, **are manifest as well.** Among animals and hungry ghosts, there are those except for the ones included in vows. In the Form realm, there are those included in the vows of dhyana, and except for the gods and the Northern Unpleasant Sound, there are both those in vows and those in mid-vows. There might be any of the three vows.

ii. Exceptions

84d Except in hell and Unpleasant Sound.

However, this is **except** for **in hell and Unpleasant Sound,** because there is no correctly undertaken discipline there.

(iv) Teaching the results of the karmic paths. This has two topics: A. Actual, and B. Additional points.

A. Actual. This has two points.

1. The position

> 85ab It's proposed these all give dominant,
> Compatible, and ripened results.

It is proposed that **these** virtuous and nonvirtuous karmic paths are **all give dominant** results, causally **compatible** results, **and** fully **ripened results.** To illustrate this through the example of taking life, the dominant result of the karmic path of taking life is that one does not have any beautiful external things and so forth. The causally compatible result is that one is born as a human but has a short life and so forth. The fully ripened result is to be born in the hells.

2. The reason

> 85cd Since it makes suffering, and kills,
> And destroys vigor, three results.

Why do these karmic paths create the three results? you ask. To illustrate with taking life, **since** one **makes** another being **suffer,** there is the fully ripened result of enduring the suffering of the hells, **and** because **killing** prevents life from continuing, the causally compatible result is a short life. Because it **destroys vigor** in the region of the heart, the dominant result is to be born with little vigor or power. There are these **three results.** The remaining, taking what is not given and so forth, are similar.

The lesser, medium, and greater results of the virtues are respectively birth among humans, gods of Desire, and the gods of the higher realms. The causally compatible and dominant results are the opposite of the nonvirtues' results: a long life in a place with great vigor, power, and so forth.

B. Additional points. This has three topics: 1. Identifying wrong livelihood of speech, 2. The reason for presenting it separately, and 3. Refuting other traditions.

1. Identifying wrong livelihood of speech

> 86ab Acting with body and speech from greed:
> Wrong livelihood.

The Bhagavan taught about wrong speech, wrong action, and wrong livelihood. The first two of these are the karma of speech and the karma of body produced by hatred and delusion. **Acting with body and speech from greed** is not only wrong speech and wrong action, it **is** also **wrong livelihood.**

2. The reason for presenting it separately

86bc It's hard to cleanse,
So it's taught separate.

The dharma of greed is subtle and also seizes the mind, it is not easy even for the extremely wise to guard themselves from the karmas it motivates, and **it is hard to cleanse** or purify for the rest of one's life. Therefore **it is taught separately** from wrong speech and wrong action.

3. Refuting other traditions. This has two points.

a. Presenting their position

86cd Saying it's greed
For sustenance

It is **said** that if **it is** body and speech karma aroused by **greed for sustenance,** that alone is wrong livelihood. It is not logical for the dancing and singing that please us to be wrong livelihood.

b. Refuting it

86d contradicts the sutras.

Because this proposal **contradicts the** ***Discipline Sutra,***[219] it is not logical. It is said in that sutra:

> Watching elephant fights and so forth is presented as wrong livelihood. What is the reason? you ask. Because it is enjoying a wrong object.

c. Which karma has how many results. This has six topics: i. How many results defiled and undefiled have, ii. Virtuous and so forth, iii. Karma of the three times, iv. Karma of one's own level and other level, v. Learner, nonlearner, and so forth, and vi. How many results discards of seeing and so forth have.

i. How many results defiled and undefiled have. This has four points.

(1) How many results defiled paths that abandon have

87ab The karma of stained discarding paths
Brings five results.

Of the five results explained above, which karmas have how many results? you ask. **The karma of stained** or defiled **discarding paths,** paths of no obstacles, **bring** all **five results.** Their fully ripened result is the pleasant full ripening included in their own level. The causally compatible result is the later similar dharmas that arise from samadhi. The result of removal is only removal: it is not that which has abandoned. The personal result is the dharmas it brings forth: the path of liberation, that which is coemergent with that, what is attained in the future, and also that which has abandoned. The dominant result is all composites different from its own essence, except for those that arise earlier.

(2) How many results undefiled paths that abandon have

87b The stainless, four,

The karmas of the **stainless** paths that abandon have **four** results. As there is no full ripening of the undefiled, this does not include the fully ripened result. The other four are as above.

(3) How many results the defiled that are not paths that abandon have

87cd As do the other defiled karmas,
Whether they're virtue or nonvirtue.

As do the stainless, **the other defiled** karmas except for the paths that abandon, **whether they are virtue or nonvirtue,** have four results: those except for the result of removal.

(4) How many results the undefiled that are not paths that abandon and the neutral have

88ab The remaining that are undefiled
Have three results, as does the neutral.

The remaining karmas **that are undefiled,** other than the paths that abandon, **have** the **three results** excluding the fully ripened result and result of removal, **as do the** karmas that are **neutral.**

ii. How many results virtuous and so forth have. This has three results.

(1) How many results virtuous karma has

88cd The virtue and so forth of virtue
Are four and two and likewise three.

The virtuous and so forth results **of virtuous** karma **are,** if they are virtuous, the **four** excluding the fully ripened result, **and** if nonvirtuous, the **two** personal and dominant results, **and likewise** if they are neutral, the **three** results discarding the causally compatible and result of removal.

(2) How many results nonvirtuous karma has

89ab Nonvirtue's virtue and so forth
Are two, three, four, respectively.

Nonvirtue's virtuous results **and so forth**—nonvirtuous and neutral results—**are** the **two** of personal and dominant, the **three** excluding the result of removal and fully ripened result, and the **four** excluding only the result of removal **respectively**.

How is it that nonvirtue, which has full ripening, and neutral, which does not, can be causally compatible even though they are dissimilar? you wonder. This is not a problem, because nonvirtue and obscured neutral are similar in being afflicted. They are suitable as a cause of same status, because nonvirtue can also be the causally compatible result of the neutral, and the unobscured neutral personality view and extreme view are the causally compatible results of the nonvirtuous universal desire and so forth[220] discarded by seeing suffering and origin.

(3) How many results neutral karma has

89cd The virtue and so forth of neutral,
Are two and three and likewise three.

The virtuous and so forth results **of** karma that is just **neutral,** if they are virtuous, **are two:** the personal result that arises immediately after and the dominant result. This excludes the other three. **And** the nonvirtues produced by neutral karmas are the **three** excluding the result of removal and, as there is no nonvirtuous full ripening, the fully ripened result. As it is actually produced, there is the personal result. There are also dominant results. When neutral produces nonvirtue, they are similar in being afflicted, so there is a causally compatible result, because the five classes of nonvirtue from the discards of seeing suffering to the discards of meditation are the causally compatible result of the neutral personality and extreme views. **And likewise** the neutral results of neutral are only the **three** excluding the fully ripened result and result of removal.

iii. How many results karma of the three times has. This has three points.

(1) Results of the past

> 90ab Results of past in all three times
> Are four,

The **results of past** karma **in all three times are** the **four** excluding the result of removal.

(2) Results of the present

> 90bc as are the middle's future.
> The middle has two,

As the results of the past **are** four, **the future** results of karma that is in the **middle** between the past and future—that is, the present—are four as well. The present results of the **middle** present karma are the **two** personal and dominant results.

(3) Results of the future

> 90cd and the unborn
> Has three results that are unborn.

And the unborn or future karma also **has three results that are unborn** or in the future, excluding the causally compatible result and result of removal.

iv. How many results karma of one's own level and other level have

> 91ab On its own level, four results.
> On different levels, three or two.

When the results of karma are dharmas that are **on its,** the action's, **own level,** there are **four results** excluding the result of removal. If the result is an undefiled dharma **on a different level,** there are **three** results, excluding full ripening and the result of removal, which is not included in any realm. **Or** else if the result is defiled, it is the **two** personal and dominant results.

v. How many results learner, nonlearner, and so forth have. This has three points.

(1) Results of learners' dharmas

> 91c Three learner and so forth of learner.

There are **three** results that are **learner and so forth**, nonlearner and neither of those two, **of learner's** dharmas. They are the same in number. The first two (results that are learner and nonlearner) exclude full ripening and removal, the last excludes full ripening and causally compatible.

(2) Results of nonlearner's dharmas

> 91d Results of karma of nonlearners,
>
> 92ab The learners' dharmas and so forth,
> Are one or three or otherwise two.

The **results of** the **karma of nonlearners,** if they are **the learner's dharmas and so forth, are** the **one** dominant result. **Or** if they are nonlearner itself, the **three**, excluding full ripening and removal. **Or otherwise** if they are neither, the **two** of personal and dominant.

(3) Results of dharmas other than those two

> 92cd Results of karmas other than those
> Are learner, et cetera, two, two, five.

Results of karmas which are **other than those** learner and nonlearner, **are** if they are **learner, et cetera,** the **two** personal and dominant; if nonlearner, also those **two;** and if neither, all **five** results.

vi. How many results discards of seeing and so forth have. This has three points.

(1) How many results discards of seeing have

93ab Results of the discards of seeing,
Et cetera, are three, four, and one.

Results of the karma **of the discards of seeing,** if they are discards of seeing, **et cetera, are** the **three** excluding full ripening and the result of removal. If they are discards of meditation, they are the **four,** excluding the result of removal. **And** if they are not discards, they are the **one,** dominant result only.

(2) How many results discards of meditation have

93cd Two, four, and three results of karmas
That are discards of meditation.

There are **two, four, and three results of karmas that are discards of meditation.** If they are discards of seeing, they are the two dominant and personal. If they are discards of meditation, they are the four excluding the result of removal. If the result is a discard, they are the three excluding full ripening and causally compatible.

(3) How many results karmas which are not discarded have

94ab Results of what is not discarded
Are one, two, four, respectively.

Those **results of** karmas **that are not discarded are,** if the results are discards of seeing, the **one** dominant result. If they are discards of meditation, they are the **two** personal and dominant, and if they are not discards, they are the **four** excluding full ripening. These are presented **respectively.**

d. Other presentations of karma. This has two topics: i. Which karmas are caused by which cause, and ii. The distinction between propelling and completing karma.

i. Which karmas are caused by which cause

94cd Improper is afflicted action;
Degenerate ways as well, some say.

From the *Treatise:*

> The treatises teach action that is improper, proper, and neither proper nor improper. What are the characteristics of these? you ask.

Some say that **improper** karma **is afflicted** karma, because of inappropriate attention itself. Alternatively, actions that have **degenerated** from the abandonment of the five wrong **ways** of acting are improper actions **as well, some say,** because the way the person walks, sits, eats, dresses are improper or not in accord with custom, so it is called improper action. Proper action is virtuous karma. Others say it is ways that are not degenerate. Karma other than those two is neither.

ii. The attributes of propelling and completing karma. This has three points.

(1) The attributes of propelling karma

95a One action propels one rebirth.

Does one action propel only one rebirth or does it propel multiple rebirths? Likewise, do multiple actions propel one rebirth or do they propel multiple rebirths? you ask. This is the position of this school: **one action propels** only **one rebirth.** One action does not propel multiple rebirths, and multiple actions do not propel one rebirth.

Well then, in a sutra, Elder Aniruddha said to the monks:

> By that one merit fully ripening, I was born seven times among the gods of the Thirty-Three, until I was born now in the clan of the rich Shakyas.

Is this not contradictory? you ask. It is not. The meaning of this is that when he was born in the higher realms, he remembered his previous birth and out of enthusiasm performed more virtue, which led him to be reborn there again. For example, it is like when one finds a single coin, uses it to make a profit, becomes rich, and then says, "I got rich from a single coin."

(2) The attributes of completing karma

95b There are multiple completing factors.

If many karmas propelled a single birth, many similar likenesses would be propelled, which is not logical. It is proposed that **there are multiple completing factors** for a likeness propelled by a single karma. Beings born as human from a single propelling karma are similar in being born as humans, but some have beautiful bodies and so forth because of virtuous completing factors, and some have ugly bodies and so forth because of nonvirtuous completing factors. It is like, for example, a single artist drawing the outlines and several other artists filling in the color.

(3) Dispelling doubts about propulsion

> 95cd The two absorptions without mind
> Do not propel, nor does attainment.

There are other things with full ripening than just propelling karma. **The two absorptions without mind do not propel** a likeness, because they do not arise simultaneously with action. **Nor does attainment** of propelling karma propel a likeness, because what is attained and the result are separated. Not only that, all *Āryan* karma and worldly beings' precursors to clear realization[221] are not propelling karma, because they are directed against the karma of becoming.

2. Specific explanations. This has three topics: a. Explanation of the three obscurations to discard, b. Explanation of the three bases of meritorious action to rely upon, and c. Explanation of the three virtuous precursors.

a. Explanation of the three obscurations to discard. This has three topics: i. The essence of the three obscurations, ii. Which obscurations are where, and iii. Explaining karmic obscurations in particular.

i. The essence of the three obscurations

> 96. The karma of the heinous deeds;
> Severe afflictions; lower realms,
> Beings in Concept Free, and the North
> Are agreed to be three obscurations.

Those who kill their own father or commit **the** other **karma of the heinous deeds** have karmic obscurations. Neuters, et cetera, **and** the **severely** afflicted in whom **afflictions** continually arise have afflicted obscurations. Those in the **lower realms,** sentient **beings in Conception Free and** humans of **the North,** Unpleasant Sound, have obscurations of full ripening. Because these obscure the Āryan paths, they **are agreed to be three obscurations.**

Well then, karma that definitely ripens in places with no leisure such as the lower two realms, the first two modes of birth, and so forth should also be a karmic obscuration, you say. It should not. Here it is easy to show the basis, result, wanderer, birth, individual, and five causes of heinous karma, and easy to label it conventionally, so only heinous karma is taught and the others are not. This means that heinous karmas are taught because they are extremely powerful and the most important.

ii. Which obscurations are where. This has three points.

(1) The heinous deeds in general

97ab The heinous deeds are in three lands.
The sexless and so forth do not

First of all, **the heinous deeds are** found **in three lands** or continents, but because they are not found in Northern Unpleasant Sound or among other wanderers, what need is there to mention other realms? In those three, they are found only among men and women. **The sexless and so forth,** neuters and hermaphrodites, **do not** have them.

(2) The specifics of the heinous deed of killing one's parents

97c Since little benefit, no shame.

If the sexless and so forth should kill their parents, it is not a heinous deed **since** their parents gave them bodies that are not conducive to liberation, so there is **little benefit, and** because although their births depended upon their parents, they have very little or **no shame** and modesty.

(3) Where the other two obscurations are found

97d Five wanderers have the remaining.

All **five wanderers have the remaining** afflictive and fully ripened obscurations, because among humans, those on Unpleasant Sound and among gods, the beings in Conception Free have them.

Killing an arhat or killing one's father or mother is the karmic path of taking life. Drawing blood from the Tathagata with harmful intent is the preparation for taking life, and creating a schism in the Sangha is the karmic path of lying.

iii. Explaining karmic obscurations in particular. This has two topics: (1) Heinous deeds, and (2) The near heinous deeds.

(1) Heinous deeds. This has three topics: (a) Actual heinous karma, (b) Its karma and result, and (c) Additional points on karma and result.

(a) Actual heinous karma. This has two topics: (i) An extensive explanation of the heinous deed of creating a schism, and (ii) Explaining all five heinous deeds together.

(i) An extensive explanation of the heinous deed of creating a schism. This has three topics: A. Essence, B. Its result, and C. Explaining it in terms of its aspects.

A. Essence. This has two topics: 1. The schism that is the division, and 2. The schism that is that which divides.

1. The schism that is the division. This has two points.

a. Essence

98a–c A schism of the Sangha is
Discord by nature, nonconcurrent.
It's not afflicted; it is neutral.

A schism of the Sangha is a dharma that **is discord** between two camps of the Sangha **by** its **nature.** It is substantially existent and **nonconcurrent** with mind. Because **it is not afflicted** and not virtuous, **it is** unobscured **neutral,** so it is not a heinous karma.

b. Who possesses it

98d The Sangha does possess the schism.

The Sangha does possess the schism; but the schismatic Devadatta does not possess it.

2. The schism that is that which divides. This has two points.

a. Essence

99a The unwholesome act is telling lies;

The perceptible and imperceptible **unwholesome act** of speech of the schism **is telling lies.**

b. Who possesses it

99b It is possessed by the schismatic.

It, the lie, **is possessed by the schismatic** Devadatta who split the Sangha.

B. Its result. This has two points.

1. Actual

99c It ripens for an aeon in Incessant.

It ripens for the schismatic of the Wheel[222] as **an** entire intermediate **aeon in** the **Incessant** Hell because there is no longer lifespan than that in the Desire realm. The other heinous deeds are not definitely destined for the Incessant.

2. Dispelling doubts

99d Additional bring additional pain.

If heinous karma cannot be experienced in other lifetimes and must be experienced on rebirth only, how can the results of multiple heinous karmas ripen on someone who has committed several? Multiple **additional** heinous karmas **bring** two, three, four, or five times as much suffering. The being is born with a huge body that has especially tender flesh, so they experience an immense amount of extremely unbearable **additional pain.**

C. Explaining it in terms of its aspects. This has three topics: 1. Aspects of a schism of the Wheel, 2. Explaining a ritual schism, and 3. Identifying times when a schism of the Wheel does not arise.

1. Aspects of a schism of the Wheel. This has eight points: a. Who is the schismatic, b. Where the schism occurs, c. Who is divided, d. What they are divided by, e. How long it lasts, f. Explanation of the term, g. Which continents it is on, and h. The number of bhikshus.

a. Who is the schismatic

100ab A bhikshu acting upon views,
Who is disciplined, divides.

The schism is perpetrated by **a bhikshu**, and not by a householder, who would not be an equal in the body of bhikshus that is divided, or a bhikshuni and so forth who would not have such power of persuasion over the bhikshus. The bhikshu who creates the schism **acts upon** and enters into the five **views** of personality view and so forth. Only such a one can uphold another Teacher or path through his ability to analyze and discern, because he is ensnared in stable wicked intentions. It is not someone who acts out of craving because such a person does not have stable intentions toward the all-afflicted and utterly pure. A bhikshu **who is disciplined divides** the Sangha: someone with weak discipline does not have enough power behind his words to be able to create a schism.

b. Where the schism occurs

100b Elsewhere.

The schism happens **elsewhere** than where the Bhagavan actually is. Because it is difficult to overcome his splendor and his words are potent, it is not possible to create a schism where he actually resides.

c. Who is divided

100c Childish.

Only **childish** ordinary beings can be divided. Āryans cannot be divided because they have directly perceived the dharmas of scripture and realization and because they have undivided faith.

d. What they are divided by

100cd Accepting other teachers
And paths divides.

Accepting other teachers than the Tathagata **and paths** other than the one he taught, such as the five bases of not drinking milk, not eating meat, not using salt, wearing uncut robes, and staying in monasteries in towns, is enough to **divide** the Sangha.[223]

e. How long it lasts

100d It does not last.

It, the schism, **does not last** longer than from sun-down to sun-up, because the Sangha will definitely be reunited before daybreak.

f. Explanation of the term

101a It's called a schism of the Wheel.

This schism of the Sangha **is called a schism of the Wheel,** because it breaks the Dharma Wheel of the Tathagata and creates an obstacle to entering the path.

g. Which continents it is on

101b. Rose-Apple Land.

It happens in **Rose-Apple Land,** not the other continents, because there is no Teacher there, so there is no rebellious person such as Devadatta who wishes to be the Teacher's equal.

h. The number of bhikshus

101b Not less than nine.

In number, there are **not less than** four bhikshus on each side and the schismatic in the middle, so it is completed by **nine** or more, but not by fewer. This sets the minimum.

2. Explaining a ritual schism

101cd Ritual schisms happen in
Three continents, with at least eight.

Ritual schisms are created by sowing discord among two groups who perform poṣadha and other rituals within a single boundary. This is **in** any of the **three continents** where the Teachings are. The ritual schism does not need a schismatic, so it is completed **with at least** four bhikshus on each side, or **eight** or above.

3. Identifying times when a schism of the Wheel does not arise

102. At first, at end, before there are faults
Or a pair; or when the Sage has passed,
When boundaries are not established,
A schism of the Wheel can't happen.

At first, immediately after the Wheel of Dharma has been turned, everyone is happy, overjoyed, and harmonious, and **at** the **end** immediately after the parinirvana, everyone is focused on impermanence and they are united in grief, so schisms do not arise. Or in between **before there are faults** in *śīla* or views; **or** before the **one** supreme **pair** who quickly reunite the Sangha appears; **or** as there is no one to compete with, **when the Sage has passed;** as the schism is disunity within the boundaries of one monastery, **when boundaries are not** yet **established:** in these times, **a schism of the Wheel cannot happen.**

(ii) Explaining all five heinous deeds together. This has two topics: A. Establishing the quantity of the five heinous deeds, and B. As an elaboration, refuting a doubt.

A. Establishing the quantity of the five heinous deeds

103ab Since fields of benefit and qualities
Are abandoned and annihilated.

Why is it that among the karmic paths of taking life and so forth, only killing one's mother and so forth are heinous deeds? you ask. **Since** parents produce a body that is suitable for attaining freedom, they are the **field of benefit, and** the other three are a supreme field of **qualities.** These **are abandoned** in one's mind. In the first three life is **annihilated,** and in a schism the Sangha's harmony is destroyed. The Tathagata cannot be killed by anyone, but one makes the preparations to do so.

B. As an elaboration, dispelling doubts. This has three topics: 1. Dispelling doubts about killing one's mother, 2. Dispelling doubts about drawing blood with an evil intent, and 3. Dispelling doubts about killing arhats.

1. Dispelling doubts about killing one's mother. This has two points.

a. Examining when sex changes

103c Even if organs change, it is.

Even if their sexual **organs change** to the other sex, **it is** a heinous deed to kill one's parents. From the *Treatise:*

> If one kills a man who is neither his father nor an arhat, can it become a heinous unwholesome act? you ask. It can. If one kills his mother whose organ has changed...

Murdering one's father whose sex has changed is comparable.

b. Dispelling the doubt about when the fetus is transplanted into another womb

103d She whose menses bore one is the mother.

If one is conceived in one woman's womb and then transplanted into another, murdering which of the two is a heinous deed? you ask. **She whose menses bore one is the mother,** so murdering her is a heinous deed. The other is similar to a mother so of course she deserves respect, but murdering her is not actually a heinous deed.

2. Dispelling doubts about drawing blood with an evil intent

104a Intent to beat the Buddha is not,

Drawing blood from the Buddha becomes a heinous act because of the intention to kill the Buddha, but if one draws blood when **intending to beat** up **the Buddha,** it **is not** a heinous deed, because there is no intention that he die.

3. Dispelling doubts about killing arhats

104b Nor if they become an arhat later.

Nor is the killing a heinous deed **if** one strikes someone who is not an arhat with a weapon and **they become an arhat later,** after being struck. This is because one did not make the preparations with regard to the arhat.

(b) Its karma and result. This has two points.

(i) General teaching

104cd When one has prepared a heinous act,
Detachment is impossible.

If one has made preparations for a heinous karma, is it possible to attain a result of detachment without stopping them? you ask. **When one has** done **preparations** for **a heinous act** and not stopped them, attaining the result of **detachment** that transcends the world, the *loka,* **is impossible.**

(ii) Explaining the specifics

105ab To tell a lie in order to split
The Sangha is the gravest crime.

Among these heinous deeds, which is the most harmful? you ask. **To tell a lie in order to split the Sangha** even while knowing the difference between dharma and nondharma **is** proposed to be **the gravest** of **crimes,** because it pierces the Tathagata's dharma body and because it hinders worldly ones on the path to the higher realms and the freedom of enlightenment. Among the heinous deeds, killing one's mother, killing an arhat, and drawing blood from the Tathagata with an evil intent are each successively heavier than the previous; killing one's father is lighter.

(c) Additional points on karma and result

105cd Of worldly virtues, the volition
Of Peak bears the greatest result.

Among the fine conducts, which has the greatest result? you ask. **Of** all **worldly virtuous** karmas, the **volition of** the **Peak** of Existence **bears the greatest** fully ripened **result,** because it ripens as eighty thousand great aeons in the higher realms. In terms of results of removal, among all virtues, there is none greater than the vajra-like samadhi, and in terms of personal results, supreme *loka* dharma[224] has the greatest.

(2) The near heinous deeds. This has three topics: (a) Actual, (b) Additionally, explaining what blocks the three paths, and (c) Particular explanation of the certain bodhisattva.

(a) Actual

106. To violate one's arhat mother,
 To kill a certain Bodhisattva
Or learner, and to rob what has
 Been gathered for the Sangha's purpose

107ab Are similar to heinous deeds.
 The fifth is to destroy a stupa.

Not only the five heinous deeds lead to birth in hell; the five that are near to them also lead to birth in hell. What are they? you ask. **To violate one's arhat mother** through sexual misconduct, **to kill a certain Bodhisattva or** killing an Āryan **learner, and to rob** food for one day or more **that has been gathered for the Sangha's purpose.** These four **are similar to** the first four **heinous deeds** of killing one's mother and so forth so they are near it. The one near **the fifth is to destroy a stupa,** the place of offering to the body, speech, and mind. Here killing a certain bodhisattva is far more harmful than killing one's father, so it is difficult to understand why it is given as a near heinous deed.

(b) Additionally, explaining what blocks the three paths

107cd Gaining forbearance, nonreturner,
 And arhat totally blocks karma.

Gaining forbearance on the path of joining, **nonreturner, and arhat** respectively **totally blocks** the definite **karma** for rebirth in the lower realms, Desire and the two upper realms, because that karma can only be experienced in those realms. It is like when you quit a country and free yourself from debt.

(c) Particular explanation of the certain bodhisattva. This has two topics: (i) General teaching, and (ii) In particular the deeds of the Teacher

(i) General teaching. This has three topics.

A. Threshold

108ab Since when is he the Bodhisattva?
 Since doing the karma of the marks.

Since when is he the certain **Bodhisattva?** you ask. **Since** the time of **doing**

the deeds that accumulate **the karma** that has as its full ripening **the** thirty-two major **marks,** he attains buddhahood in one hundred aeons.

B. Dharmas that are his qualities

108cd High realms, high caste, full faculties,
Male, recalls lifetimes, irreversible.

From that time on he is free of the four faults, so he is born in the **high realms** of gods and humans. He has **high caste** birth in the Great Sala Tree House of the Kshatriya caste and so forth. He is born with **full faculties** and as a **male** only. He has the two qualities of **recalling** his **lifetimes** and being **irreversible** or unable to be turned away from attaining awakening. In order to benefit all sentient beings, he is not discouraged by any aspect of suffering or any misunderstanding.

C. Explaining his aspects

109. A male in Rose-Apple Land, when present,
With the volition to awaken,
Through contemplation, propels these
Over one hundred aeons more.

110a Each arises from one hundred merits.

Only a being on the support of **a male in Rose-Apple Land** can propel the karmas that will ripen as the marks; inhabitants of other continents or females cannot. He accumulates them **when** a Teacher who is the object for accumulating the karma **is** actually **present**. Whether the volition of, "May I become a buddha in this way" is manifest or hidden, he performs the karmas only **with the volition** that focuses on **awakening.** Karma born of listening is low, and that born of meditation does not ripen in Desire, so this is born **through contemplation.** He **propels these over one hundred** great **aeons more,** so they are not visible results. From his diligence in praising the Buddha Tiṣya, our Teacher shortened that by nine aeons, and propelled the karma through more than ninety-one aeons. As it says in a sutra, "Village chief, I remember from ninety-one aeons to now completely… " so he naturally remembers his lifetimes. **Each** of the fully ripened thirty-two major marks that are thus propelled **arises from one hundred merits** or volitions. As far as the quantity counted as one hundred, some say that it is the same as all the merit from generosity of all sentient beings. There are many other such proposals.

(ii) In particular the deeds of the Teacher. This has two topics: A. How he accumulated merit, and B. How he perfected the transcendences.

A. How he accumulated merit

110b-d The last of three uncountables,
Vipashyin, Dipa, Ratnashikhin
Appeared. The first was Shakyamuni.

When our Teacher was a bodhisattva, how many buddhas did he pay respects to in each of the incalculable aeons? you ask. In the first incalculable aeon, he paid respects to seventy-five thousand buddhas, in the second, seventy-six thousand, and in the third, to seventy-seven thousand buddhas. Among them, the **last** buddhas **of** the first **three uncountable** aeons respectively were the buddhas **Vipashyin, Dipankara,** and **Ratnashikhin,** who had **appeared.** Before all of those, **the first** buddha to appear **was** called the Sage of the Shakyas, or **Shakyamuni.** He appeared in a time of strife, and his life span, the duration of his teachings, his mother, and so on, were all similar to our Teacher's. During his time, our Teacher was a potter named Illumination who offered him sweet water, massages with ointment, and service, and then prayed, "May I, too, awaken in the same fashion as him."

B. How he perfected the transcendences. This has four topics: 1. How he perfected transcendent generosity, 2. How he perfected transcendent discipline and patience, 3. How he perfected transcendent diligence, and 4. How he perfected transcendent dhyana and full knowing.

1. How he perfected transcendent generosity

111ab Giving all to all compassionately
Perfected generosity.

Giving all from his eyes to his feet **to all** who needed it, not from hope for a high state but **compassionately,** he completely **perfected** transcendent **generosity.**

2. How he perfected transcendent discipline and patience

111cd While not detached, to cut his limbs
Did not perturb him: patience and discipline.

While he was **not detached** at the time, **to cut his limbs did not** even **perturb him.** At that time he perfected the transcendence of **patience and discipline.**

3. How he perfected transcendent diligence

112a By praising Tiṣya, diligence.

When the Bhagavan was a bodhisattva, he saw the Tathagata Tiṣya in a mountain cave in the absorption of the all-encompassing fire element and stood on one foot praising him for seven days with a single verse. **By** reciting **praises** of **Tiṣya** in this way, he gathered nine aeons' merit and completed the perfection of transcendent **diligence.**

4. How he perfected transcendent dhyana and full knowing

112b Samadhi and mind, just prior to.

He produced the vajra-like **samadhi** and at that time completed the transcendences of dhyana **and mind** or full knowing **just** immediately **prior** to enlightenment.

Because these six go beyond in terms of their own excellence, they are transcendences.

b. Explanation of the three bases of meritorious action to rely upon. This has three topics: i. Explaining the terms in general, ii. The nature of each classification, and iii. Specific explanation of the generosity of dharma.

i. Explaining the terms in general

112cd The three are merit, action, or
The basis, like the karmic paths.

From a sutra:

> The bases of meritorious action born from generosity,
> born of discipline, and born of meditation…

The three are either **merit** that has an attractive full ripening, **actions** with the nature of karma, **or the basis** for engaging the intention that is both, so they are said to be the bases of meritorious actions. For example, it is **like** was explained with the ten **karmic paths:** some are both karma and karmic path, and some only karmic paths. To illustrate this with the merit born of generosity first, the karmas of generosity of body and speech are all three, the volition is both merit and action, and the dharmas simultaneous with that are merit only. The other two follow the same pattern. The reason these three are explained is that achieving possessions, karma, and liberation, or alternatively achieving possessions, a human or divine body, and a body in one of the higher two realms depend upon these.

ii. The nature of each classification. This has two topics: (1) Explaining merit born of generosity, and (2) Explaining the other two merits.

(1) Explaining merit born of generosity. This has three topics: (a) The essence of generosity, (b) Classifications, and (c) Distinctions.

(a) The essence of generosity. This has two points.

(i) Actual

113a–d What makes one give is generosity,
Wishing to offer or to help.
It's body and speech karma, and
Intention,

That **which makes one give** itself **is** called **generosity.** Clothes and so forth that are given are called by that name, but they are not actually generosity because they are neutral. Likewise, giving without the motivation of virtuous volition, such as out of fear, a wish for a response, desire, or so forth, is not virtuous, so it is not giving that is generosity. Thus generosity is giving with a **wish to offer or to help**, which are distinguished in terms of the recipient.[225] **It is** the **body and speech** virtuous **karma, and** motivating **intention** that is concurrent with nongreed along with its associations. From the commentary:

When beings make gifts of their own
Possessions with virtuous minds,
At that time, the virtuous aggregates
Are said to be called generosity.

(ii) Its result

113d resulting in abundance.

The basis of meritorious action born from generosity **results in** great **abundance.** It is abundance's nature that it should arise from this source.

(b) Classifications

> 114ab Generosity brings benefit
> To self or other, both or neither.

When nobles who are not detached or ordinary individuals who are detached give to a stupa, that is **generosity** that **brings benefit to** one's **self** only, because it does not benefit another. **Or** when nobles who are detached give to another sentient being, with the exception of visibly experienced results, it is generosity that is only for the benefit of the **other**, because it benefits the others. It is not for the nobles' own benefit, because they have transcended the level where it fully ripens. When nobles who are not detached or ordinary individuals who are detached give to another sentient being, that is generosity for the benefit of **both** self and other. **Or** when nobles who are detached give to a stupa, it is generosity for **neither**'s benefit: it is no more than offering to pay respect and to repay kindness.

(c) Distinctions. This has two topics: (i) Overview, and (ii) Explanation

(i) Overview

> 114cd Distinctions of the donor and
> Of things and field distinguish it.

Distinctions of the donor and of the **things** given **and** the **field** of the recipient, **distinguish it,** generosity.

(ii) Explanation. This has five topics: A. Distinctions of donor, B. Distinctions of what is given, C. Distinctions of field, D. Identifying superior generosity, and E. Elaborations.

A. Distinctions of donor. This has three points.

1. Actual

> 115a Donors excel through faith, et cetera,

Donors are **excellent** when they give with **faith, et cetera**—qualities such as discipline, learning, and so forth. Included in the phrase "and so forth" is giving with charity, full knowing, few desires, and so forth.

2. Distinctions in the manner of giving

> 115b And make gifts with respect and such.

When one **makes gifts with** the preparation of **respect** for the recipient **and such,** including giving with one's own hand, at a good time, and without harming anyone else, the generosity becomes superior.

3. Its result

> 115cd This brings them honor and abundance
> In time and with no obstacles.

From these four causes of generosity, there are four distinctions, respectively. **This** first will **bring them honor, and** the second will bring vast **abundance.** The third brings the abundance **in** a **timely** manner, **and** from the fourth, one will receive the abundance **with no obstacles.**

B. Distinctions of what is given. This has two points.

1. Actual

> 116ab From excellently colored things
> And so forth,

From excellently colored things and so forth, including fragrance, taste, and touch, gifts are superior.

2. Their result

> 116b–d there comes beauty, fame,
> Affection, and most youthful flesh,
> Pleasing to touch in all the seasons.

From these ways of being generous, respectively **there comes beauty;** one will have **fame** that spreads in all directions, like fragrance; one will have **affection,** like delicious taste, **and** one's body will have the **most youthful flesh** that, like a precious queen, is **pleasing to touch in all the seasons** of the year. During the cold seasons, it will be warm; during the hot seasons, it will be cool; and during normal seasons, it will be natural.

C. Distinctions of field

> 117ab The fields of wanderers, suffering,
> Benefit, qualities are highest.

There are **the** four superior **fields.** Of these, the one that is superior in terms **of wanderers** is, for example, as is said:

> If you give to those born in the places of animals, hope for one hundred times the full ripening. If you give to humans with faulty *śīla,* hope for one thousand times the full ripening.

The superior field of **suffering** is such as among the seven material merits,[226] giving nursing, or giving during cold seasons. The superior field of **benefit** is giving to parents and other benefactors. When it is through **qualities** that the field **is highest** or superior, it is as is said:

> If one gives to those who have discipline, one can hope for one hundred thousand times the result.

D. Identifying superior generosity. This has two topics: 1. Supreme generosity, and 2. Immeasurable generosity.

1. Supreme generosity. This has two points.

a. Actual

> 117cd The highest is from freed to freed
> Or by the Bodhisattva.

The highest of all the different types of generosity **is from** one who is **freed** and has no desire **to** one who is **freed** and has no desire, **or** generosity given **by the Bodhisattva** in order to benefit all sentient beings. That is giving by one who is not freed to those who are not freed, but it is also supreme, because it is generosity given in order to benefit all sentient beings.

b. Identifying the supreme of the eight types of generosity

117d Eighth.

Likewise, from a sutra:

> Generosity is eightfold: giving to the near; giving out of fear; giving because someone has given to you; giving so that someone will give to you; giving because your parents gave before; giving for the purpose of the higher realms; giving out of desire for fame; and giving in order to attain the mind's ornament, the mind's necessities, the collection of yogas, and the supreme purpose.

Of these, the **eighth,** giving for the purpose of attaining the mind's ornament and so forth, is supreme.[227]

2. Immeasurable generosity

118. Although they are not noble, gifts
    To parents, the ill, or Dharma teachers,
The Bodhisattva's last rebirth
    Bring yields surpassing any measure.

It is said in the sutras that giving to stream-enterers and other nobles brings great and immeasurable merit. In addition, **although they are not nobles** but ordinary individuals, **gifts to parents, the ill, or Dharma teachers,** or **the Bodhisattva** in his **last birth**[228] **bring yields surpassing any measure** in terms of result.

Well then, the others are in the fields of benefit, suffering, and qualities, but what are the Dharma teachers included in? you ask. They give all beings who are blinded by ignorance the eye of full knowing, teach what is Dharma and what is not, and accomplish the undefiled dharma body, and in brief, accomplish the activity of the buddhas, so they are spiritual friends. For that reason, they are the field of benefit.

E. Elaborations. This has three points.

1. Distinctions in size

119. Aftermath, field, base, preparation,
Volition, and intention, too:
When these are great or small in scope,
The karma, too, is great or small.

What makes the distinction between heavy and light karma? you ask. The **aftermath** of completing the karmic path, the **field** to which help or harm is done, the **base** of any of the karmic paths of the three gates, the **preparation** that begins the karmic path, the **volition** that motivates karmic paths of body and speech, **and** the **intention, too,** that thinks, "I will do this in this way." **When these** six causes **are great or small in scope, the karma, too, is great,** that is, heavy, **or small,** that is, light.

2. The distinction between accumulated and not accumulated

120. Intentional, complete, without
Regret, no anti, ripening,
Association: due to these
Karma is called accumulated.

When we say that we have done and accumulated karma, what is accumulated karma? It is karma that is neither unwitting nor involuntary but that is done after consideration, or **intentionally;** that is **completed,** by which it will have full ripening, and that is done **without regret** after the karma is completed; that has **no antidote;** that is karma that has a definitely experienced **full ripening;** and that has all the corresponding **associations.**[229] **Due to these, karma is called accumulated.**

3. Dispelling doubts

121. Giving to stupas is merit caused
By giving: as with love, not taken.
Cause and result are infallible,
So bad fields, too, bear pleasant fruit.

When someone who is detached gives to a stupa, there is no enjoyment of the gift, so how is it meritorious? you ask. There are two types of merit: merit that is caused by giving, and merit that is caused by enjoyment. The merit of **giving to stupas is merit** caused not by enjoyment, but merit that is **caused by giving.** For example, it is **as with** meditation on **loving**-kindness or the others of the four immeasurables, or like the correct worldly view, which are meritorious, even though it is **not taken** or does not benefit another.

Well then, if it is logical that being generous with gifts to a good field produces a pleasant result, how is it that giving to a bad field brings a pleasant result? Because whatever type a **cause** might be, the **result** born from it **is infallibly** of the same type, **so** it is logical that giving to a **bad field, too,** should **bear** a **pleasant fruit** or result. For example, grape seeds produce sweet fruits, and neem seeds produce bitter fruits.

(2) Explaining the other two merits. This has three topics: (a) The nature of each, (b) The result of both, and (c) Additionally, an explanation of the four merits of Brahma.

(a) The nature of each. This has two topics: (i) Merit born of discipline, and (ii) Merit born of meditation.

(i) Merit born of discipline. This has three points.

A. Identifying what is discarded

122ab Immoral is nonvirtuous form
That twofold discipline discards.

Immorality is the **form** of unwholesome **nonvirtues** from taking life to idle chatter. The four or seven abandonments of nonvirtuous form is discipline. **That** discarding is the **twofold discipline** of the perceptible by which one **discards** immorality and the imperceptible that is the discarding.

B. Its antidote, discipline

122c That which the Buddha barred as well.

Discipline is not pervasively the antidote for immorality. There are things that may be done in particular times or circumstances but in other times and circumstances become the causes of the inherently unwholesome. This is because **that which** not immoral by nature but which **the Buddha's** word **barred**, such as swearing not to eat at wrong times, has both perceptible and imperceptible forms and is discipline **as well.** Having sworn to the precept of abandoning something, if one does it, it becomes immoral, because it is disrespectful of the Bhagavan's word. This teaches implicitly that it is not immoral for those who have not sworn to the discipline.

C. The merit of purifying it

122d Four qualities of the utterly pure:

123ab Not sullied by immoral or
Its cause; based on the anti and peace.

There are **four qualities of the utterly pure** discipline, because the opposite of that is impure. What are the four? you ask. It is **not sullied by immoral** nonvirtue—it does not arise as a fault; it is not sullied by **its,** nonvirtue's, **cause,** the root and near afflictions; it is **based on** its, immorality's, **antidote,** the four foundations of mindfulness; **and** as it is dedicated toward freedom, it is based on **peace.**

(ii) Merit born of meditation

123cd Infusing the mind with meditation
Is the virtue of equipoise.

Meditation **infuses the mind with meditation,** the qualities of samadhi, and makes it similar to samadhi, so it **is** called **the virtue of** the samadhi of **equipoise** and what is associated with it. For example, it is like infusing oil with the scent of flowers.

(b) The result of both

124ab For high realms, discipline is prime,
And for removal, meditation.

Well then, if it is logical that generosity produces abundance, what comes from discipline and meditation? you ask. Of course generosity can be the cause of the high realms, but **for** the sake of attaining a body in the **high realms,** maintaining **discipline is primary, and for** the sake of **removal** of desire, what is principal is **meditation,** because these and just these are their primary causes.

(c) Additionally, an explanation of the four merits of Brahma

124cd Because one dwells in joy for aeons
In high realms, four are Brahma's merit.

Because building a stupa for the Tathagata's relics in a place where there was not one before, offering a monastery for the Sangha of the four directions and building a temple there, reconciling a split among the listeners of the Tathagata, and meditating on immeasurable love are four causes for **one** to **dwell,** living **in joy, for** forty intermediate **aeons** one after the other **in** the **high realms,** they are similar to the merit of Brahma's Ministers, so the merit of these **four is** called **Brahma's merit.** This is said in the sutras and explained by earlier masters. The Great Exposition explains that these are equal to what was explained as the size of each of the merits that fully ripens as a major mark.

iii. Specific explanation of the generosity of dharma

125ab To give the Dharma is teaching sutras,
Without affliction, as they are.

To give the Dharma is teaching the **sutras,** et cetera, including the rest of the twelve precepts, with a mind **without afflictions** that does not desire rewards and fame, not teaching them wrongly but correctly and just **as they are.**

c. Explanation of the three virtuous precursors

125cd Precursors to merit and nirvana,
And realization are three virtues.

Of the three precursors, the **precursor to merit** propels an attractive full ripening included in existence. **And** the precursor to freedom is something that, once it has arisen, becomes a dharma base that attains **nirvana.**[230] As a sign of its presence, when one hears about the faults of samsara and qualities of nirvana, one's hair stands on end out of faith. **And** the four of warmth and so forth that will be explained are the precursors to clear **realization.**[231] Thus **are** the **three virtues** of the precursors taught.

III. Teaching the synonyms of dharmas as a summary. This has three points.

A. The synonyms of the three worldly karmas

126. Threefold industrious karma with
Its motivation: writing letters
Or carving; poetry and counting;
Enumeration, in that order.

The **threefold,** engaged through the **industrious** learner's method, **karma** of body, speech, and mind **with its motivation** is **writing letters or carving** them into stamps; reciting **poetry, and counting;** and tallying **enumerations** with the mind, and vows. These are presented **in that order.**

B. Synonyms of the afflicted

> 127ab Obscured, bad, and unwholesome are
> Afflicted dharmas.

They **obscure** freedom, they are **bad** since they are solely something to reject, and they are **unwholesome** since they are disparaged by the exalted. These three **are** synonyms of **afflicted dharmas.**

C. Synonyms of the virtuous

> 127b–d Stainless virtues
> Are sublime. Practice compounded virtue.
> And liberation is unexcelled.

The undefiled or **stainless virtues are** the ultimate of purity, so they are called **sublime. Practice compound virtues,** because they produce an attractive result and are something to be familiar with. Because other things lack these two reasons, they are not something one practices. All other dharmas are excelled by something, but there is no dharma at all that is superior to the **liberation** of nirvana, so it **is** also called **unexcelled,** because it is virtuous and permanent. This is the supreme dharma that is superior to all other dharmas.

Second, presenting the area's name

> This completes the fourth area called "Teachings on Karma" from the *Verses of the Treasury of Abhidharma.*

This completes the explanation of **the fourth area called "Teachings on Karma" from** *The Explanation of the "Verses of the Treasury of Abhidharma"* called *The Essence of the Ocean of Abhidharma, The Words of Those who Know and Love, Explaining the Youthful Play, Opening the Eyes of Dharma, The Chariot of Easy Practice.*

A few words here:

> The behavior of unruly beings, the poisonous nightshade
> Of millions of manifestations of black piled on black—
> My mind had been sickened by distractions and clamor,
> And so at that time I climbed up into one-pointed solitude.

And then out of faith in the buddhas and bodhisattvas,
Unbearably great fervor opportuned tears,
And now day and night by transcending through dharma,
I've sworn in my mind to discard life's distractions.

With the good eye medicine of *prajñā* I've purified
The cataracts of ignorance, no more to arise.
I've gained the mind's eye of the Wheel of the teachings
To explain and debate and compose in these times.

And thus I'm emboldened with complete sincerity
To explain the Tathagata's intent as it is
In all of the Sugata's scriptures, particularly
The *Treasury* of Dharma's matrix, abhidharma.

In the stainless space of examining, the radiant
White treasury that teaches on karma is completed.
With all of the branches of scriptures and words,
In White Cave, this place so delightful to dwell,

The monk of the Shakya, Vajreshvara composed this.
By the power of virtue that's gained in three times
By the tenth emanation to enter Karma's teachings,
May these teachings flourish to the end of four times.

FIFTH AREA

Teachings on the Kernels

Your wisdom itself, from its origin truly awake,
Makes gifts that illumine all wanderers with help and
with happiness
By tearing away all the darkness of the fleeting stains—
You great precious Kagyupas, grant us your blessings.

The thicket of suffering and origin's faults not ripped out,
We have not arrived in complete freedom's happiest place,
So in order to cut out its radix, the kernels,
I'll open the door to the *Treasury* that teaches the kernels.

The fifth area, the "Teachings on the Kernels," has an explanation of the text of the area and a presentation of the area's name. The explanation of the text of the area has three topics: I. The nature of the kernels, II. What discards the kernels, and III. The results of discarding the kernels.

I. The nature of the kernels. This has two topics: A. Teaching the kernels as the root of existence, and B. Understanding the kernels.

A. Teaching the kernels as the root of existence

1a The root of existence is the kernels.

"From karma are various worlds born," it is explained. That karma is accumulated by the power of the afflicted kernels: without the kernels, existence would not be able to be manifestly established, so for that reason, know that **the root of existence is the kernels.**

B. Understanding the kernels. This has three topics: 1. Classifications of the kernels, 2. How the kernels arise, and 3. Enumeration of the kernels.

1. Classifications of the kernels. This has three topics: a. Classifications of the essence, b. Classifications of the aspects, and c. Classifications of what has the kernels.

a. Classifications of the essence. This has two topics: i. General classification, and ii. Specifically classifying views and pride.

i. General classification. This has four topics: (1) Classifying as six, (2) Classifying as seven, (3) Classifying as ten, and (4) Classifying as ninety-eight.

(1) Classifying as six

1bc They're six: desire, and likewise anger,
Pride, ignorance, and view, and doubt.

To classify the kernels concisely, **there are six.** What are the six? They are **desire, and likewise anger, pride, ignorance, and view, and doubt,** because they are ascertained to be six in their focus. The word "likewise" means that anger and the others can likewise develop in relation to anything that desire focuses on.

(2) Classifying as seven. This has two points.

(a) Actual classification

1d These six are taught as seven when

2a Desire is split.

These six kernels **are taught as seven** kernels **when desire is split** into the desire for Desire and the desire for existence, because then there are desire for Desire, anger, desire for existence, pride, ignorance, view, and doubt.

Here the meaning of what are called *kernels* is proposed by the Great Exposition to be manifest afflictions, by the Vatsiputrīyas to be attainment, and by the Sutra school to be seeds.

(b) Identifying desire for existence

2a–d That which arises
In two realms is desire for existence
Since it looks inward. It is taught
To rebut the idea it is freedom.

That desire **which arises in** the **two** Form and Formless **realms is** explained to be **desire for existence since they**, the two desires of Form and Formless, are attachment to absorption and its support, so they are similar in **looking inward.** The reason **it is taught** that these are desire for existence is **to rebut the** wrong **idea** that **it,** existence in those two realms, **is freedom.**

(3) Classifying as ten

3. Five views are personality;
Wrong view; and holding the extremes;
Overesteeming view; and discipline,
Austerity. There are thus ten.

In the abhidharma, the kernels are also classified as ten by dividing view into **five views.** These **are** the view of **personality,** and **wrong view, and** the view of **holding the extremes,** the view of **overesteeming view, and** the view of overesteeming **discipline** and **austerity. There are thus** five views and five non-views, for a total of **ten** kernels.

(4) Classifying as ninety-eight. This has two topics: (a) Actual, and (b) Additional point.

(a) Actual. This has three topics: (i) Explaining the thirty-six included in the level of Desire, (ii) Explaining the sixty-two included in the levels of the higher realms, and (iii) Summary.

(i) Explaining the thirty-six included in the level of Desire. This has two points.

A. Explaining the thirty-two discarded by seeing

4. They're ten and seven, seven and eight,
 Excluding three or else two views.
When suffering and so forth of Desire
 Is seen, they are discarded in order.

The *Sutra of Abhidharma* explains the kernels as ninety-eight. To summarize, they are the discards of seeing and meditation of all three realms. Of these, **they**, the discards of seeing of the Desire realm **are** thirty-two: from the previously explained ten, they are all **ten** of suffering, **and seven** of origin, **seven** of cessation, **and eight** of path. For origin and cessation, there are these ten **excluding** the **three** views of personality, extreme, and overesteeming discipline and austerity, **or else** for the path, the first **two** personality and extreme **views,** because a discard must mistakenly engage the truths either directly or indirectly, and those views do not mistakenly engage those truths.

When the nature of the truths of **suffering and so forth**—origin, cessation, and path—**of Desire is seen, they are discarded in order.**

B. Explaining the four discarded by meditation

5a Four are discards of meditation.

The **four** that cannot be discarded by seeing the truth—desire, anger, pride, and ignorance—are **discards of meditation**, because they are discarded by meditating on the path.

In summary, there are twelve views, four types of doubt, five types of desire, five types of anger, five types of pride and five types of ignorance for a total of thirty-six kernels that function in Desire.

(ii) Explaining the sixty-two included in the levels of the higher realms

5bc Excluding anger, these same are
In Form. The Formless is like that.

In the higher realms, one's being is moistened by tranquility, the bodily support is clear, and the basis for anger's development, the feeling of suffering, is absent. Therefore **excluding anger, these same** thirty-one kernels function **in** the **Form** realm. **The Formless is like that** Form realm with thirty-one kernels. Thus for the higher realms one should recite the verses thus:

They're nine and six and six and seven,
 Excluding anger, three, two views.

When suffering and so forth of Form
Is seen, they are discarded in order.
Three are discards of meditation.

(iii) Summary

5d Thus they're proposed as ninety-eight.

Thus by classifying the six kernels in terms of aspect, class, and realm, **they,** the kernels **are proposed as ninety-eight** by the masters of the abhidharma.

Here in the *Compendium of Ascertainments*,[232] the view of overesteeming discipline and austerity is said to mistakenly engage all four truths, so there are ninety-four discards of seeing. The discards of meditation are explained similarly to this explanation. In the *Compendium of Abhidharma*,[233] all five views as explained to mistakenly engage all four truths, so there are 112 discards of seeing, and the views of personality and holding extremes also have instinctive types that are discards of meditation, for a total of sixteen discards of meditation. Drangti explains that the former is the tradition of the Sutra school and the latter of the Mind Only school. The Great Chim says that both are the Mind Only tradition, but the first is in terms of actually exclusive aspects and the latter in terms of mere exclusion.

(b) Additional point

6. The Peak's that forbearance destroys,
Are discards just of seeing. On others,
Of seeing and meditation. What forbearance
Does not destroy are just of meditation.

Well then, are the discards of seeing definitely discarded by seeing? It is not definite. There are two types of discards that are destroyed: those destroyed by forbearance and those destroyed by knowing. The first is equivalent to the discards of seeing and the second to the discards of meditation. **The** discards born on the **Peak** of Existence **that forbearance destroys are** definitely **discards just of seeing,** but **those on** the **other** eight levels that forbearance destroys can be discarded **by** both the path of **seeing and** the path of **meditation.** When nobles discard them, they are discarded by the path of seeing, and when the childish discard them, by the path of meditation. Those discards of meditation **that forbearance does not destroy are** discards **just of** the path of **meditation,** because it is impossible for the path of seeing to abandon a discard of meditation.

The path of meditation can be either defiled or undefiled. Of these two, the former is the eight preparations for the levels from the first dhyana to the Peak, which take coarseness and purity as their aspects. The second, the undefiled path of meditation, is the subsequent knowing of path and so forth.[234]

ii. Specifically classifying views and pride. This has two topics: (1) Classifying views, and (2) Classifying pride.

(1) Classifying views. This has three topics: (a) The nature of each of the five views, (b) The reason the fifth is not a discard of seeing the origin, and (c) Classifying as the four erroneous.

(a) The nature of each of the five views

7. As me, mine; permanent and ceasing;
   As nonexistent; overesteeming
The low; and viewing what is not cause
   Or path as such: these are five views.

What is the nature of the five views? you ask. When focusing on the aggregates of grasping, viewing them **as me** and **mine** is personality view. Viewing that me itself as **permanent** or **ceasing** is extreme view. Viewing the truth of suffering and so forth **as nonexistent** is wrong view. **Overesteeming the low,** personality view, and the others, is overesteeming the view. **And viewing what is not** the **cause**—Indra, the Lord of Living Creatures Brahma, and so forth—as the cause, viewing what is not the cause of high realms—entering fire and water and so forth[235]—as the cause of high realms, **or** viewing what is not the **path**—mere *śīla* and austerity—**as such** is overesteeming discipline and austerity. **These are** the natures of each of the **five views.**

(b) The reason the fifth is not a discard of seeing the origin

8. Since clinging to Ishvara, et cetera,
   As cause, initially mistakes
Them to be permanent and self,
   Just seeing suffering discards it.

If viewing as a cause what is not a cause is overesteeming discipline and austerity, why is it not also a discard of seeing origin? you ask. This is **since clinging to** or holding **Ishvara, et cetera**—things that are not causes—**as causes**

initially engage by power of **mistaken** views of them as **permanent and** as a **self.** Directly seeing the characteristics of the truth of suffering eliminates clinging to permanence and a self. When that has been abandoned, viewing Ishvara and so forth who are not causes to be causes is also discarded. For that reason **just seeing suffering discards it,** clinging to Ishvara and so forth as causes.

(c) Classifying as the four erroneous. This has two points.

(i) Actual

9a–c Among three views, there are four errors,
Since they're mistaken, since they're thoughts
That judge, since they exaggerate.

Well then, must the errors necessarily be just the two errors of self and permanence? you ask. Not necessarily. From **among** the **three views** of personality, extreme, and holding view supreme, **there are four errors** presented as one set. Clinging to a self is presented from personality view. The view of permanence is presented out of extreme view. Views of the clean and blissful are presented out of holding views supreme.

Well then, other afflictions are not presented as errors, so why are these three presented as errors? you say. They are presented as errors because of three reasons: **because they are** solely **mistaken** about their focus, **since they are thoughts that judge,** and **since they exaggerate.** Other afflictions do not fulfill one or more of those reasons, so they are not presented as errors.

(ii) Additional point

9d Mind and conception, from their power.

Well then, both mind and conception must not be errors, because they do not make one have thoughts that judge. If you agree, it is contradictory of the sutras which tell of both erroneous mind and erroneous conception, you say. This is not contradictory, because **mind and conception** are concurrent with those erroneous views and so are presented as erroneous **from their power.**

Well then, the feelings that are concurrent with those three also become erroneous, you say. In common parlance, feelings are not called erroneous, so they do not become so.

(2) Classifying pride. This has three points.

(i) Actual classification

10a The prides are seven. Nine types, three.

There are not only classifications of views: pride can be classified as well. There are **seven** types of **pride:** pride, superior pride, more proud than pride, pride in thinking me, pride of exaggeration, pride in thinking almost, and mistaken pride. The first is the conceit of thinking one is better than an inferior, and that one is equal to his equals. The second is thinking one is superior to his equals. The third is thinking one is superior to his betters. The fourth is the conceit of thinking, "That's me" when focusing on the aggregates of grasping. The fifth is the conceit of thinking one has attained clairvoyant powers when one has not. The sixth is the conceit of thinking one is almost as good as his superiors. The seventh is thinking one has qualities he does not.

In the treatise *Jñānaprasthāna,* there are nine aspects of pride that are taught. The **nine types** are included in **three:** pride, superior pride, and pride in thinking almost.

(ii) What antidotes discard them

10b Destroyed by seeing, meditation.

Those seven prides are **destroyed by** either the path of **seeing** or the path of **meditation,** because those concurrent with discards of seeing are extinguished by seeing and those concurrent with discards of meditation are extinguished by meditation.

(iii) Why discards of meditation do not manifest themselves in nobles' beings even though they have not been discarded

10cd Discards of meditation are
Entangled with killing and so forth.

11. Craving destruction, too. In nobles,
The prides, et cetera, that think "me"—
Developed by view—do not occur.
Nor does nonvirtuous regret.

The nobles have not abandoned the discards of meditation, but do they act upon them? you ask. Kernels that are **discards of meditation are entangled with** the seven nonvirtues of **killing and so forth** and with what focuses on those. They have not been abandoned but they do not become manifest among nobles, because they are developed through the condition of wrong views, which nobles have abandoned. Similarly both **craving destruction** by thinking, "What would be wrong with ceasing to exist?" and craving birth, **too,** by thinking, "What would be wrong with becoming the lord of the gods?" do not manifest themselves in nobles, because they are developed by extreme views, which nobles have discarded.

In nobles, the nine types of **pride, et cetera,** and the pride **that thinks "me"** that are included among the discards of meditation **do not** manifestly **occur,** because they are **developed by** personality **view,** which nobles have abandoned. **Nor does nonvirtuous regret** become manifest because it is developed by doubt, which the nobles have discarded.

b. Classifications of the aspects. This has five topics: i. Classification of universal or not, ii. Distinctions of focusing on the undefiled or not, iii. Developed by concurrence and by focus, iv. Classification as nonvirtuous and neutral, and v. Which kernels tie one down in the three times.

i. Classification of universal or not. This has three points.

(1) Universals of same status realm

12. The views and doubts that one discards
 By seeing suffering and cause
And simultaneous and unmixed
 Ignorance are the universals.

Among the kernels, how many are universal, and how many are not universal? you ask.[236] There are eleven universal kernels of same status: seven views—**the** five **views** discarded by seeing the truth of suffering plus the two discarded by seeing the truth of origin, wrong view **and** overesteeming view—two **doubts that one discards by seeing** the truths of **suffering and cause; and** the ignorance that is **simultaneous** with those; **and unmixed ignorance** that is not mixed with other kernels. These **are the universal** kernels of same status because they focus on all five classes of discards of their own level.

(2) Universals of realms of dissimilar status

13ab Of these, the nine can focus higher,
 Excluding two views.

Of these eleven universals, **the nine** kernels **can focus** on **higher** levels and realms, so they are universals of realms of dissimilar status. This is **excluding** the **two of** personality and extreme **views,** because these view only the aggregates of one's own being mistakenly. The way these nine focus is that sometimes they focus on one realm of dissimilar status and sometimes on two, as is stated in the *Treatise.*

(3) Explaining other universals than those

13b–d What arises
Along with them is universal
As well, attainment not included.

Are only kernels universal? you ask. **What arises along with** and at the same time as **them,** the kernels—feelings, etc., and arising, etc.—**is universal as well.** However, **attainment** is **not included,** because the kernels and attainment have dissimilar results, attainment does not produce full ripening, and their compatible causes are also dissimilar.

Here there are four alternatives between universal kernels and universal causes.

ii. Distinctions of focusing on the undefiled or not. This has two topics: (1) Those that focus on the undefiled, and (2) Those that do not focus on the undefiled.

(1) Those that focus on the undefiled. This has two points.

(a) Overview

14. Wrong views and doubts discarded by
Seeing cessation and the path,
Concurrent and plain ignorance:
These six take the undefiled as sphere.

How many of them focus on the defiled? How many focus on the undefiled? you ask. The two **wrong views and** two **doubts discarded by seeing cessation and the path,** the ignorance that is **concurrent** with them, **and plain,** unmixed **ignorance: these six take the undefiled** cessation and path **as** their **sphere;** those two are their object. In aspects, they engage them through denial, through being of two minds or other doubt, or through unclear aspect.

The mistaken engagements that focus on mistaken engagement of cessation and path and the mistaken engagements of suffering and origin focus on the defiled.[237]

(b) Explanation

15. Cessation that is of their level.
    Because paths can be mutual causes,
The paths of the six and nine levels
    Are objects of whose sphere they are.

The object of the wrong views discarded by seeing cessation is the antidote, **cessation that is of their** own **level. Because paths can be mutually causes** of same status, **the paths** compatible with the dharma knowing **of** the **six** levels of dhyana are objects of the three of wrong views, et cetera, of Desire that have those paths as their sphere. **And** all the paths compatible with the subsequent knowing of the **nine** undefiled **levels are** the **objects of** wrong view, et cetera, of the eight higher levels **whose sphere they,** the paths, **are** in, because these paths are definitely in the family of antidotes of those levels.

(2) Those that do not focus on the undefiled

16. Desire does not, since it's discarded.
    Nor hatred, since they do not harm.
Since they are peace, pure, and supreme,
    Pride does not, nor does overesteeming.

Desire does not focus on cessation and path **since its** focus **is** that which is **discarded** only. Otherwise it would be like intention toward virtuous dharmas. Hatred focuses on things that generate hostility, so **nor** does **hatred** focus on cessation and path, **since they do no harm.** Additionally, **since they are** both **peace,** because they are **pure** and purifying, and because they are **supreme,** respectively, **pride does not** focus on the peaceful, **nor** are they the object of the views of **overesteeming**—the fifth view that holds what is not a purifier to be so, and the view of holding view supreme, which holds the inferior to be supreme. In this way, those that focus on the undefiled are direct mistaken engagements. Those that focus on the defiled of those two classes are mistaken engagements of mistaken engagements.

iii. Developed by concurrence and by focus. This has two points.

(1) Those which develop through focus

17. The universal kernels can
 Develop through a focus on
Any that is of their own level.
 Nonuniversal, on own class.

18ab Not those whose sphere is high or stainless,
 Since those are not made mine, since anti.

Among the kernels, how many develop in terms of their focus? How many develop in terms of concurrence? you ask. **The universal kernels can develop through a focus on any** of the afflicted five classes **that is of their own level.** The **nonuniversal** develop through focus **on** their **own class.** This is in general.

Specifically, the kernels that do **not** develop through focus are **those** universal kernels **whose sphere is** the **higher** levels and the nonuniversals whose sphere is the **stainless.** This is **since** the kernels develop in relation to things that are divided into sets by craving and made into "mine" through self-view, whereas **those are not made mine.** It is also **since** the undefiled and higher levels are in the class of their **antidotes,** so they are overwhelmed. For example, a burning stone is not a place where one can rest the sole of one's foot.

(2) Those which develop through concurrence

18cd The ones concurrent with one, then
 Develop through concurrence with that.

The ones, kernels, which are **concurrent with one** cognition, feeling, or other dharma, **then develop through concurrence with that** dharma. The word "then" draws the distinction that this is as long as it has not been abandoned. Kernels, such as the two concurrences with pleasure and greed, that have been abandoned when past are on the past level, and when future, they are simultaneously on the future level. However, they do not develop, as in the example of Shariputra.[238]

Therefore, all kernels that focus on the undefiled and all those which focus on the higher realms' defiled develop only through concurrence. The remainder develop through either focus or concurrence. There are none which develop solely through focus.

iv. Classification as nonvirtuous and neutral. This has three topics: (1) Actual, (2) Specifics of the roots, and (3) An elaboration.

(1) Actual

19. In higher, all neutral. In Desire,
    The personality, extreme,
    And simultaneous ignorance.
    The rest here are nonvirtuous.

How many of the kernels are nonvirtuous? How many are neutral? you ask. The kernels that arise **in** the **higher** Form and Formless realms are **all neutral,** because the full ripening of afflicted dharmas is suffering, and that is in neither of those two as there is no cause for harming another. **In Desire, the** view of **personality,** the view of holding **extremes, and simultaneous ignorance**—ignorance concurrent with them—are neutral, because they are not exclusive of generosity and other such virtuous dharmas, and because they look inward so they are unable to motivate harmful conduct. **The rest,** kernels other than those three, **here** in the Desire realm **are nonvirtuous.**

(2) Specifics of the roots. This has two topics: (a) The roots of nonvirtue, and (b) The roots of the neutral.

(a) The roots of nonvirtue

20ab Desire, aversion, and delusion
    In Desire are the roots of nonvirtue.

How many of them are roots of nonvirtue? How many are not? you ask. All **desire, aversion, and delusion in** the **Desire** realm, except those concurrent with personality view and extreme view, **are the roots of nonvirtue.** Only those that are both nonvirtues and also the roots of nonvirtue are agreed to be the roots of nonvirtue. The remaining kernels of doubt and pride are nonvirtuous, but they are not the roots of nonvirtue.

(b) The roots of the neutral. This has two points.

(i) Kashmiri tradition

20cd There are three roots of neutral: craving,
    And ignorance, intelligence.

21ab Others act dually, loftily,
    So they are not.

How many of them are roots of the neutral? How many are not? you ask. The Kashmiris say that **there are three roots of** the **neutral.** They, the roots, are **craving, and ignorance,** and **intelligence** or full knowing. The latter can be arisen from full ripening, but those that are slightly neutral are the roots of the neutral.[239] **Others**, doubt and pride, which are other than those kernels, **act** in doubt's case **dually** and unstably, and in pride's case **loftily,** they do not deserve to be called roots. In common parlance, roots are said to be things that are stable and underneath. **So** thus **they**, doubt and pride, **are not** roots, because they are dissimilar to roots, it is said.

(ii) Aparāntakas' tradition

21b–d The Bāhyaka
Propose these four: craving, view, pride,
Delusion. From ignorance, three dhyanists.

The Bāhyaka (Aparāntakas) **propose these four** roots of the neutral: **craving, view, pride,** and **delusion.** What is the reason? you ask. **From** the power of **ignorance,** there arise the **three** meditators of **dhyana**, who have excessive craving, view, and pride.

(3) An elaboration

22. Categorical, distinguishing,
And questioning, and the declining
Responses answer queries on death,
Rebirth, superior, self or other.

What are the fourteen neutral, indeterminate dharmas mentioned in the scriptures? you ask. They are questions whose answer was not actually indicated, so they are called neutral or indeterminate. Giving a **categorical** response, **distinguishing** response, **and questioning** response, and **the declining response** are four ways to **answer queries.** The first of these is like when asked, "Will all beings die?" answering, "They will **die.**" The second is like when asked, "Will all who die be **reborn**?" answering, "Those who have not extinguished the afflictions will be reborn, but those who have will not." The third is like when asked, "Is this person inferior or superior?" responding with the question, "In relation to whom? In relation to gods he is inferior. In relation to the lower realms, he is **superior.**" The fourth is like when asked, "Is the **self other** than the aggregates **or** not?" This is asking about nonexistent attributes, like whether the child of a childless woman is blue or white, so it is something to put aside only. The fourteen indeterminates are similar.

v. Which kernels tie one down in the three times. This has four topics: (1) The things to which one is tied, (2) Examining the three times, (3) Discarded yet possessed, and (4) Which dharmas are the objects of which cognitions.

(1) The things to which one is tied. This has two topics: (a) How specific afflictions bind, and (b) How general afflictions bind.

(a) How specific afflictions bind.[240] This has two points.

(i) How they bind in the past and present

23. One is tied down to things toward which
  Desire and anger, pride as well,
Of both the past and present have
  Arisen but not been abandoned.

One is tied down to any **thing** that is an object, **toward which** object **desire,** **and anger,** and **pride as well, of both the past and present have arisen but not been abandoned.** The individual is tied down to them because they are specific afflictions. For example, it is like when a calf is tied to a stake with a rope, the calf cannot leave the area where it is tied.

(ii) How they bind in the future

24a–c The future mental tie to all.
  The others tie in their own time.
The nonarising, to all times.

The future desire, anger, and pride associated with the **mental** consciousness that has arisen but not been abandoned **tie** one **to all** things of the three times, because all three times are the object of mind. Desire and anger that are future arising dharma bases of the five groups of consciousness **other** than the mental **tie** one down **in their own time**, the future focus. **The** desire and anger of the five groups of consciousness that are **nonarising** dharma bases tie one down **to** the things they focus on **in all** three times, like flax.[241]

(b) How general afflictions bind

24d All that remain tie one to all.

As long as they have not been discarded, **all that remain**—view, doubt, and ignorance of all three times—**tie one to all** things that are objects of focus of all three times in all five classes, because they are general afflictions[242] as they are tied to all five aggregates.

(2) Examining the three times. This has two topics: (a) Presenting the position of this school, and (b) Rebutting criticism.

(a) Presenting the position of this school. This has three topics: (i) The position that all three times exist substantially, (ii) Presenting the proof, and (iii) Teaching that this is the tradition of the Great Exposition.

(i) The position that all three times exist substantially

25a The times always exist,

Well then, do past, present, and future composites exist substantially or not? If so, they must be permanent. If not, one cannot be tied to them in the present, you say. The position is that **the times always,** at all times, **exist.**[243]

(ii) Presenting the proof. This has two points.

A. Scriptural proof

25ab it was said.
Since two,

The times exist because **it was taught** in a sutra:

> Bhikshus, if there were no past form, the well-versed noble listeners would not view past forms, but because past form exists, the well-versed noble listeners view past form…

So it was said. It is also **since** it was said that consciousness arises from the **two,** object and faculty.

B. Logical proof

25b objects exist, result.

The past and future exist in their own time because if the focused **object exists,** consciousness arises, but if it does not exist, consciousness does not arise. Since the past and future can be objects of the mind consciousness, they must therefore exist. Also because there is production by past karma of a later fully ripened **result,** we know the past exists.

(iii) Teaching that this is the tradition of the Great Exposition. This has three points: A. Actual, B. Divisions of schools, and C. Analyzing which of the four traditions is best.

A. Actual

25cd Because they say these all exist,
They're called Those Who Say All Exists.

Someone who claims to be a Sarvāstivādin must certainly hold this position, it is known. **Because they say these** three times **all exist, they are called Those Who Say All Exists,** or Sarvāstivādin. Those who distinguish and say the present and past karma that has not yet produced a result exist, but the future and the past that has produced a result do not exist, are called Vibhajyavādin, those who say there is a distinction.

B. Divisions of schools

26ab They're four, called thing and character
And state and relative dependence.

They, the Sarvāstivādins, have **four** traditions, **called** transforming **thing,** transforming **characteristics,** transforming **state, and relative dependence.**

The first of these is the tradition of the Venerable Dharmatrāta. He says that as dharmas progress through time, the thing transforms, but the substance does not transform. For example, if you destroy a gold vessel and make it into something else, the shape has changed but the gold's color and nature do not change.

The second is the tradition of Venerable Ghoṣaka. He says that as dharmas progress through time, in the past it possesses the characteristics of the past, but it does not *not* possess the characteristics of the other two times. The others times are similar. For example, when one man feels manifest lust for one woman, he is not free of desire for others.

The third is the tradition of Venerable Vasumitra. He says that as dharmas progress through time, when the action has not been done, they are future. When the action is being done, they are present. When the action has been done and ceased, they are past. When they go from one time period to another, they are different in terms of being in a different state, but not in terms of substance. For example, if you put a token in the ones column it is called "one," but if you put it in the hundreds column it is called "one hundred."

The fourth is the tradition of Venerable Buddhadeva. He says that as dharmas progress through time, in relation to earlier and later they are called differently. For example, one woman can be both a mother and a daughter.

C. Analyzing which of the four traditions is best

26cd The third is best, because the times
Are there presented through their action.

The first tradition is subsumed within the non-Buddhist Saṃkhya tradition because it says that dharmas completely transform. In the second, since everything has the characteristics of all the times, the times would get mixed up. The fourth is illogical as well, since at any one time all three times would be present. Therefore of all these traditions, **the third,** transforming state, **is** the **best** position, **because the times** of past and so forth **are there presented through** or in terms of **their action.** Any dharma that has not yet performed its action is future. When it is doing its action, it is present. When the action is done and ceased, it is past, so it is heard.

(b) Rebutting criticism. This has two points.

A. The criticism

27a-c They'd block. What's it? Not different,
Not logical as time. If they
Exist, why don't they arise and perish?

They, the two times, **would block** the action from happening because they have action and exist substantially. Additionally, **what is it,** so-called action—is it different from time or not? If it is different from time, then it is noncompound, and so action would be permanent. However, if it is **not different**, all the times would have action, so it would **not** be **logical** for the action not to be performed in the past and the future **times** as well.

If the action exists, then it is not separate from time, but in the two times the action has not arisen or it has destroyed, so it does not exist, you say. That also does not make sense. **If** you propose that just as they are in the present, **they,** actions, also **exist** in the other two times, one must ask **why do they not arise and perish** in them? It would follow that action should not be arisen and should have perished in the present.

B. Its rebuttal

27d So deep are the natures of dharmas.

The Great Exposition says that the past and future must exist. To those who cannot be convinced, they say, "**So deep are the natures,** the inherent essences, **of dharmas,** which without a doubt are not the sphere of sophists."

(3) Discarded yet possessed. This has two points.

(a) Discards of seeing

28ab Suffering is seen, they've been discarded;
Still other universals bind them.

When one has discarded a thing, has it been removed—that is, is one free of it? Has everything one has removed been abandoned? you ask. When one has removed something, one has abandoned it, but it is possible to abandon something without removing it. When **suffering is seen, they,** all **those** kernels, **have been discarded** upon seeing suffering, but **still the other** remaining **universals** that are discarded by seeing the origin **bind them.**

(b) Discards of meditation

28cd The first has been abandoned, yet
Still tied by stains whose sphere it's in.

Among the nine types of discards of meditation, **the first,** the greater of greater, may **have been abandoned** and removed,[244] **yet** one is **still tied** to it **by** the focus of **the** remaining **stains whose sphere it is in,** the middle greater, lesser greater, and so forth afflictions that focus on it.

(4) Which dharmas are the objects of which cognitions. This has two topics: (a) Which cognitions focus on the five dharmas of each of the three realms, and (b) Which cognitions focus on the undefiled.

(a) Which cognitions focus on the five dharmas of each of the three realms. This has two topics: (i) Which cognitions focus on the first two discards of seeing and the discards of meditation, and (ii) Which cognitions focus on discards of seeing cessation and path.

(i) Which cognitions focus on the first two discards of seeing and the discards of meditation. This has three points.

A. Which cognitions focus on those on the level of Desire

29. Those of Desire, discards of seeing
  Suffering and cause, of meditation,
 Are in the sphere of their own three,
  Of one of Form, of stainless, too.

In order to easily understand with few words how many kernels develop through focus on the different classes of things, this is taught in brief. To briefly categorize all dharmas that are objects, there are the five classes of discards in each of the three realms plus undefiled dharmas, for a total of sixteen classes. The perceiving subjects, cognitions, are likewise also sixteen. The word *cognition* is used as an illustration—it includes all the concurrences.

Among these, **those of Desire** that are **discards of seeing suffering and** its **cause,** the origin, and those which are discards **of** the path, **meditation**—three dharmas—**are in the sphere of** the five subjects each: **their own three** cognitions of Desire, **of one** virtuous cognition, the preparation for the first dhyana included within meditation discards **of** the **Form realm**, and also the consciousness that is compatible with **stainless** dharma knowing.

B. Which cognitions focus on those on the levels of Form

30ab And those of Form are in their own,
  Three low, one high, and stainless, too.

And those same three classes of dharmas[245] **of** the **Form** realm **are in** the sphere of eight cognitions. They are the objects of the three of **their own** cognitions in the Form realm, **three** from the **lower** Desire realm—the two universals of dissimilar status and virtuous discards of meditation—**one** cognition from the preparation for Infinite Space from the **higher** Formless, **and** the consciousness that is compatible with **stainless** subsequent knowing, **too.**

C. Which cognitions focus on those on the levels of Formless

30cd Those of the Formless, in the sphere
Of these three of three realms, of stainless.

Those same three classes of dharmas **of the Formless** are the focus of ten cognitions. They are **in the sphere of these three** classes of cognitions **of three realms,** or nine cognitions, plus the sphere **of stainless** cognition.

(ii) Which cognitions focus on discards of seeing cessation and path

31ab Discards of seeing path and cessation,
Are in the same spheres, plus their own.

The dharmas of the three realms that are **discards of seeing path and cessation are** the **in the same sphere** of all the previous minds, **plus** the cognitions of **their own** class.

(b) Which cognitions focus on the undefiled

31cd The undefiled are in the sphere
Of three realms' last three and the stainless.

The **undefiled are in the sphere of** each of the **three realms' last three** of the five classes of discards—they are in the sphere of the direct mistaken engagements of cessation and path, and of virtuous discards of meditation—**and** also **the stainless** undefiled cognition. Thus they are the sphere of ten cognitions.

c. Classifications of what has the kernels

32ab Two ways the afflicted can have kernels;
The unafflicted, through development.

If the fifteen dharmas and cognitions are put forth as defiled, do they have kernels only through the development of the kernels? you ask. First of all, it is presented that there are **two ways** or reasons by which **the afflicted** cognitions **can have kernels.** When their companions, the kernels, have not been abandoned, the kernels develop in them, so they are presented as having the kernels. Kernels that have been abandoned do not develop in but do coexist with afflicted minds, which are thus presented as having those kernels.

If the kernels have been abandoned, how can they coexist with an afflicted mind? you ask. When abandoning the kernels, they are not separated from the afflicted mind and then discarded. Instead they are abandoned together with it. Since this merely makes it so that they will not arise in the future, they still coexist in the period of the past, it is said.

All defilements of **the unafflicted** minds, such as defiled virtue, are presented as having them, the kernels, **through** the **development** of the kernels through focus.

2. How the kernels arise. This has two points.

a. The order in which they arise

> 32cd Out of delusion, doubt; from that,
> Wrong view, then personality.
>
> 33. From that, extreme, then overesteeming
> Discipline, overesteeming view.
> For one's own view, there's pride, attachment,
> And hate for others, in this order.

First **out of** total **delusion** about the truths comes **doubt,** and then **from** hearing or contemplating wrongly, **wrong view** arises. From that denial of the selfless nature of the aggregates **then** comes the view of **personality. From that** comes holding the **extremes** of oneself as permanent or ceasing, and **then,** from that extreme view, comes the belief in the purifying power of discipline and austerities, the view of **overesteeming discipline** and austerities, and then **overesteeming** that inferior **view** itself. Next, **for one's own view, there is pride and attachment** that arise, **and** out of excessive attachment to one's own view, there is **hate for others.** Thus they arise **in this order.**

b. The causes of their arising

> 34. The kernels being not abandoned,
> The object being present near,
> And inappropriate attention
> Fulfill the causes of afflictions.

There are three principal causes that produce the afflictions: **The kernels being not abandoned**—if one has not severed the attainment of the origin of the kernels, they have not been abandoned; **the object** that is compatible with the arising of the afflictions **being present near; and** by the immediate condition of being mistaken about the appearance of the object, **inappropriate attention.**

These produce the afflictions. These three are the power of cause, object, and training. These **fulfill the** principal **causes of** the **afflictions.**

However, they do not necessarily all have to be fulfilled, because from the power of the object alone arhats can regress, it is heard. The Sutra school is skeptical of this: it says that arhats cannot regress from abandonment.

3. Enumeration of the kernels. This has three topics: a. The actual enumeration, b. What the kernels are concurrent with, and c. Teaching the five obscurations.

a. The actual enumeration. The first has two topics: i. Points from the sutras, and ii. Points from the treatises.

i. Points from the sutras. This has two topics: (1) Actual, and (2) Explaining terms.

(1) Actual. This has three topics: (a) Defilements, (b) Floods and yokes, and (c) Grasping.

(a) Defilements. This has three topics: (i) Defilements of Desire, (ii) Defilements of existence, and (iii) The reason ignorance is taught separately as a defilement.

(i) Defilements of Desire

> 35ab In Desire, defilements are the afflictions
> Except delusion, and the entanglers.

In the **Desire** realm, the **defilements are the afflictions except** the five **delusions**—the twelve views, four doubts, and five each of desire, anger, and pride for thirty-one—**and** the ten **entanglers** of shamelessness and so forth that will be explained below.[246] Thus there are forty-one defilements of Desire.

(ii) Defilements of existence. This has two points.

A. Identifying the character base

35cd In Form and Formless, kernels alone
Are the defilements of existence.

In Form and in **Formless,** excluding ignorance, there are the twelve views, four doubts, five desires, and five prides for twenty-six that function in Form and also twenty-six that function in Formless. These fifty-two **kernels alone are the defilements of existence.**

B. The reason the two higher realms' are defilements of existence

36ab Since they are neutral and look inward
On levels of equipoise, they're one.

Since they, the kernels of both of the higher realms **are neutral, and** since they do not primarily act on an object but mainly engage by **looking inward,** and since they are **on levels of equipoise,** for those three comparable reasons **they are** combined into **one** and called the defilements of existence.

(iii) The reason ignorance is taught separately as a defilement

36cd The root is ignorance, so it
Is taught as a separate defilement.

The root of the defilements of Desire, etc., and of samsara **is ignorance, so it** is especially harmful. For that reason, the fifteen types of ignorance of the three realms **are taught as a separate defilement.**

(b) Floods and yokes

37. The floods and yokes are like that, too,
But views are separate, since they're sharp.
Not as defilements—without helpers,
They do not tend to put, it's claimed.

The floods number four: except for the views, the defilements of Desire are the floods of Desire. The defilements of existence themselves are the floods of existence. There are the floods of views **and** the floods of ignorance. The **yokes** should **be** known **like that, too. But** the **views are** by nature full knowing, so they are taught **separately** as floods and yokes **since they are sharp,** it is heard. Why are they not taught as separate defilements? you ask. The views are **not** taught **as** separate **defilements,** as the meaning of defilement is "that which puts one in samsara," but **without helpers,** the views are sharp so **they do not tend to put** one into samsara. The aside "**it is claimed**" is said in order to teach that ignorance should not be taught as a separate floods or yoke because it is also stable and unclear, explains Purṇavardhana.

Thus there are twenty-nine floods of Desire, twenty-eight of existence, thirty-six of views, and fifteen of ignorance. The first is the fifteen floods of desire, anger, and pride; four types of doubt; and ten entanglers for a total of twenty-nine. The second is five types each of desire and pride for each of the two realms plus eight types of doubt for a total of twenty-eight. The third is twelve views for each of the three realms, or thirty-six. The fourth is the fifteen types of ignorance of the three realms. The yokes are the same.

(c) Grasping

38. Those just explained and ignorance,
    With views divided into two,
Are grasping. Ignorance produces
    No clinging, and it is combined.

Among **those just explained,** the twenty-nine substances of the yokes of Desire **and** the five types of **ignorance,** or thirty-four substances only, are grasping at Desire: five each of desire, anger, pride, and ignorance; four doubts; and ten entanglers. The thirty-eight substances of the floods of existence, including ignorance, are grasping at belief in a self: five each of desire, pride, and ignorance for each higher realm; and eight doubts. However, it is not that this does not make four[247] because **the views** are **divided into** the **two** of grasping at views and grasping at discipline and austerity.

Grasping at discipline and austerity has one each for both suffering and path in each of the three realms, for a total of six. Why are these pulled out separately from view? you ask. They are enemies of the path and deceive both householders and those who have gone forth, so they **are** taught separately as **grasping.**

Well then, why is ignorance explained as combined with the other graspings and not taught separately? you ask. The reason for this is because the meaning of grasping is clinging to existence, but unmixed **ignorance** is not strong and **produces no clinging** to existence, **and it,** mixed ignorance, **is combined** with the afflictions other than view and taught as grasping.

(2) Explaining terms. This has two points.

(a) Explaining the meaning of *kernels*

39. Since they are subtle, since connected,
    Since they develop in two ways,
Since they pursue, because of these,
    They are explained to be the kernels.

What is the reason to teach the afflictions as kernels and so forth? you ask. **Since they are subtle** causes or engagements, **since** they are **connected** with attainment, **since they develop in two ways** through focus and concurrence, and **since** until they are discarded **they pursue** not secretly but manifestly, **because of these** four reasons, **they are explained to be the kernels.** The first and third are the actual explanation of the word, and the other two explain the meaning.[248]

(b) Explaining the meaning of *defilements* and so forth

40. Because they put and ooze, because
    They carry away, attach, and grasp:
These are the explanations of
    The words defilement and so forth.

Also, **because they,** the afflictions, **put** and yoke one into samsara in an unmoving way **and ooze** and flow through the wounds of the six sense bases;[249] **because they** lead or **carry** one **away** to other wanderings and other lands; because they yoke and **attach** one to places and things; **and** because they cling to the body of existence, or closely hold and **grasp** the consciousness of Desire and so forth, **these are the explanations of the words defilement and so forth,** including floods, yokes, and grasping.[250]

ii. Points from the treatises. This has two topics: (1) Overview, and (2) Explanation.

(1) Overview

41ab When these are classified as fetters,
    Et cetera, they're taught as five types.

When these afflictions **are classified as** the **fetters, et cetera,** including bonds, kernels, near afflictions, and entanglers, **they are taught as five types.**

(2) Explanation. This has four topics: (a) Fetters, (b) Bonds, (c) Near afflictions, and (d) Entanglers.

(a) Fetters. This has three topics: (i) Explaining the nine fetters, (ii) Those which lead to the lowest, and (iii) Those which lead to the higher.

(i) Explaining the nine fetters. This has three points.

A. Identifying the nine fetters

From a sutra:

> The fetters are nine: the fetters of greed, anger, pride, ignorance, view, holding supreme, doubt, jealousy, and stinginess.

B. The reason that views are divided into two different fetters

> 41cd Alike in substance, overesteeming,
> The two views are a separate fetter.

Among the fetters, why are three views taught separately as the fetter of view and two views taught separately as the fetter of holding supreme? you ask. The first three and last two views are **alike in** having eighteen **substances** each, and because the last two views **overesteem** the first three—the first three are what is overesteemed and the last two are similar in overesteeming the inferior—so **the** latter **two views are** said to be **a separate fetter** from the first three.

C. The reason jealousy and stinginess are explained separately as fetters

> 42. Since they are both nonvirtuous only,
> And are autonomous, it's taught
> That jealousy and stinginess
> Are fetters separate from those.

Among the eight entanglers, why are jealousy and stinginess explained as separate fetters? you ask. **Since they,** jealousy and stinginess, **are both nonvirtuous only and,** as they **are** concurrent only with ignorance, **autonomous, it is**

taught that jealousy and stinginess only **are fetters separate from those**—the other six entanglers—which are not like that.

(ii) Those which lead to the lowest. This has two points.

A. Actual

43a–c There are five that lead to the lowest.
The two prevent transcendence of
Desire. The three will send one back.

The sutras explain that **there are five** fetters **that lead to the lowest:** personality view, overesteeming discipline and austerity, doubt, pleasure seeking, and malice. *Lowest* means the lowest of the three realms, the Desire realm: the inferior is indicated by the word "lowest." These five are precursors to that.

Because they are consistent with Desire, **the two** guards of pleasure-seeking and malice **prevent** one from **transcending** the prison **of Desire**. If the guards are careless and one should escape, **the three** of personality view and so forth **will send one back.**

The Mind Only school says that the first three lead to the lowest of sentient beings, ordinary individuals, and the latter two lead to the lowest of the realms, the Desire realm.

B. Dispelling a doubt

43d The three include the gates and roots.

44. Not having any desire to go,
Wrong path, and doubt about the path
Prevent one from arriving at
Liberation, so these three are taught.

Why is it that when stream-enterers have discarded all the discards of seeing without exception, they are said to have only abandoned personality view, overesteeming discipline and austerity, and doubt? you ask.

These three are taught to **include the gates and** the **roots** of the afflictions discarded by seeing. The gates of the afflictions are onefold, twofold, and fourfold. Personality view includes one gate, discards of seeing suffering. Overesteeming includes the two outside gates, discards of seeing suffering and path. Doubt includes all four, discards of seeing the four truths.

The Master explains that these teach the blocks to discard that prevent stream-enterers from entering liberation. In order, they are inherently **not having any desire to go** to liberation, entering the **wrong path, and doubt about path.** These three alone **prevent one from arriving at liberation, so these three are taught** as an illustration of the primary obstacles.

(iii) Those that lead to the higher

45a–c There are just five that lead to higher:
The two desires of Form and Formless,
Excitement, pride, delusion, too.

Just as the Bhagavan explained that five fetters that lead to the lowest, **there are just five** fetters that are explained to **lead to** the **higher** Form and Formless—**the two desires of Form and Formless, excitement, pride,** and **delusion** or ignorance, **too**—because without discarding them one cannot transcend the higher realms.

(b) Bonds

45d Three bonds by force of the three feelings.

The **three bonds** of desire, hatred, and delusion develop toward pleasant, unpleasant, and neutral feelings **by the force of the three feelings.** Desire and hatred can develop on neutral feelings, but do not develop as much as delusion does. Because delusion corresponds to neutrality in being lacking intensity, it develops greatly.

(c) Near afflictions

46. Those mental factors, different from
Afflictions, in the aggregate of
Formations are near afflictions, too.
They are not to be called afflictions.

Those mental factors that are **different from** the root **afflictions** in meaning and are afflicted dharmas included **in the aggregate of formations are** near to the root afflictions, so they are the **near afflictions, too. They are not to be called** the root **afflictions,** because they are not roots. These are the entanglers and the filths, as well as the displeasure and yawns mentioned in the *Minor Topics.*[251]

(d) Entanglers. This has three topics: (i) Actual meaning, (ii) A supplementary explanation of the filths, and (iii) Explaining the distinctions among entanglers.

(i) Actual meaning. This has two topics: A. Identifying their essence, and B. What they are causally compatible with.

A. Identifying their essence. This has two points.

1. Those taught in the treatise Prakaraṇapāda

47. Shamelessness and immodesty
And jealousy and stinginess,
Excitement, regret, torpor, sleep:
These are the eight types of entanglers.

How many entanglers are there? you ask. They are **shamelessness, immodesty, jealousy, stinginess, excitement, regret, torpor,** and **sleep: these are the eight types of entanglers.** Virtuous regret and sleep are not included among these.

2. Those proposed by the Great Exposition

48a Aggression and concealment.

The Great Exposition proposes that in addition to those, **aggression and concealment** are also entanglers, for a total of ten.

B. What they are causally compatible with

48a-d From desire
Come shamelessness, excitement, stinginess.
Concealment is disputed. Ignorance
Gives rise to torpor, sleep, immodesty.

49ab From doubt, there comes regret. Aggression
And jealousy are caused by anger.

The near afflictions are the causally compatible results of the root afflictions, so this verse teaches which root afflictions they arise out of. **From desire come** three: **shamelessness, excitement,** and **stinginess.** Some say **concealment** is causally compatible with craving, but some say it is causally compatible with ignorance, so it **is disputed. Ignorance gives rise to** the causally compatible results of **torpor, sleep,** and **immodesty. From doubt, there comes regret. Aggression and jealousy are** results **caused by anger.**

(ii) A supplementary explanation of the filths. This has two points.

A. The classification of the filths

49cd There also are six filths of affliction:
Pretense, deceit, and arrogance,

50ab Contentiousness, resentment, and
Hostility.

Just as filth comes out of the body, **there are also six filths** that come out of the root **afflictions: pretense, deceit, and arrogance, contentiousness, resentment, and hostility.** The natures of these have already been taught above.[252]

B. Their individual causes

50b–d Desire leads to
Pretense and arrogance. From anger,
Resentment and hostility.

51ab From overesteeming views contentiousness.
View motivates deceit.

Of the six filths, **desire leads to pretense and arrogance. From anger** arise **resentment and hostility. From overesteeming views** comes **contentiousness.** The affliction wrong **view motivates deceit.**

(iii) Explaining the distinctions among the entanglers. This has three points.

A. Distinctions of whether they are discarded by seeing or by meditation

51b–d Of these,
Immodesty, and shamelessness,
Excitement, torpor, sleep are twofold.

52ab The rest, discards of meditation,
Are autonomous, as are the filths.

Of these ten entanglers that have been explained, the five of **immodesty, and**

shamelessness, excitement, torpor, and **sleep are twofold:** they are discarded by both seeing and meditation. Those concurrent with discards of seeing are abandoned by seeing, and those concurrent with discards of meditation are abandoned by meditation. Other than those five, **the rest**—the five of jealousy and so on included among the near afflictions—are only **discards of meditation** and **are autonomous,** because those five are concurrent only with ignorance. Just **as** the five of jealousy and so forth **are** autonomous discards of meditation, likewise **the** six afflicted **filths** are discards of meditation and autonomous.

B. Distinctions between nonvirtuous and neutral

> 52cd They are nonvirtue in Desire.
> Three twofold. Above they are neutral.

They, the seven entanglers that have been explained, excluding torpor, excitement, sleep, deceit, and so forth, **are nonvirtue in** the **Desire** realm. The **three** of torpor, excitement, and sleep are **twofold:** either nonvirtue or neutral. **Above** that Desire realm, **they,** the near afflictions that can possibly be found there, **are neutral.**

C. Distinctions of realm and level

> 53. Deceit and pretense are in Desire
> And on first dhyan, as Brahma deludes.
> Torpor, excitement, arrogance
> Are in three realms. The rest in Desire.

Both **deceit and pretense are in Desire and on the first** two **dhyanas.** When noble Aśvajit asked Great Brahma where the four sources cease, even though he did not know, Brahma replied saying, "I am Brahma, I am Great Brahma." **As Brahma** tried to **delude** Aśvajit with such inappropriate answers as these, there is pretense, which also proves that there is deceit.

Torpor, excitement, and **arrogance are in three realms.** Excluding those three, pretense, and deceit, **the rest**—the eleven that remain—arise **in** the **Desire** realm only.

b. What the kernels are concurrent with. This has two topics: i. Which cognitions they are concurrent with, and ii. Which feelings they are concurrent with.

i. Which cognitions they are concurrent with

54. Discards of seeing, sleep, and pride:
On the level of mind consciousness.
Autonomous near afflictions, too.
The others, in six consciousnesses.

All the root and near afflictions that are **discards of seeing** and the discards of meditation, **sleep, and pride** are all only **on the level of mind consciousness.** The eleven **autonomous near afflictions** are like that, **too. The** ones contained among discards of meditation **other** than those, including the three poisons, shamelessness, immodesty, torpor, excitement, carelessness, laziness, and faithlessness, are supported **in** all **six consciousnesses.**

ii. Which feelings they are concurrent with. This has two topics: (1) Which root afflictions are concurrent with which feelings, and (2) Which near afflictions are concurrent with which feelings

(1) Which root afflictions are concurrent with which feelings. This has two points.

(a) In Desire

55. Desire can be concurrent with
The pleasures. Hate is the reverse.
Ignorance with all. The nihilist,
With pleasure of mind, unhappiness.

56a–c Doubt with unhappiness. The others
With happiness when in Desire.
And all with neutral.

Desire can be concurrent with the pleasures of body and mind. **Hate is the reverse,** concurrent with duḥkha of body and mind. **Ignorance** is concurrent **with all** five feelings. **The nihilistic** view is concurrent **with** nonvirtuous **pleasure** of mind **and** for those with meritorious karma, with **unhappiness. Doubt** is concurrent **with unhappiness. The other** five kernels are on the mental level and have a joyous aspect only, so they are concurrent **with happiness.** This is in terms of strong instances **when** they arise **in Desire.** When they are directed toward ceasing, they are weak, so they are **all** ascertained to be concurrent **with neutral** and all afflictions.

(b) In the higher realms

56cd Higher levels
Are with those which are on their level.

The afflictions of **higher levels** of Form and Formless **are,** according to their level, concurrent **with those** consciousnesses and faculties of feelings **that are** present **on their** own **level.** Which consciousnesses and feelings are present on which levels has already been explained.[253]

(2) Which near afflictions are concurrent with which feelings.

57. Regret, and jealousy, and anger,
Hostility, resentment, and
Contentiousness with unhappiness.
But stinginess, with opposite.

58. Deceit, pretense, concealment, sleep
Concur with both, while arrogance
Is with two pleasures. Neutral feeling
With all. The other four with five.

Because **regret, and jealousy, and anger, hostility, resentment, and contentiousness** engage with the aspect of discontent and are on the level of mind, they are concurrent **with unhappiness. But stinginess** is concurrent **with** the **opposite,** mental pleasure, because it arises from the cause of greed and engages with the aspect of joy. **Deceit, pretense, concealment,** and **sleep** are **concurrent with both** mental pleasure and mental unhappiness, because sometimes one deludes another out of mental pleasure, and sometimes out of mental unhappiness. It is similar for pretense, concealment, and sleep, **while arrogance is** concurrent **with** the **two pleasures,** the pleasure of mind of the second dhyana and below and the pleasure of the third dhyana. **Neutral feeling,** as it goes with all the near afflictions, is concurrent **with all,** just as above. **The other four,** the entanglers of shamelessness, immodesty, torpor, and excitement, are concurrent **with** the **five** faculties of feeling, because the first two are the nonvirtuous major ground and the other two are the afflicted major ground.

c. Teaching the five obscurations. This has two topics: i. Their essences, and ii. Establishing their quantity.

i. Their essences

59a The obscurations are in Desire.

From a sutra:

> Pleasure-seeking, malice, torpor and sleep, excitement and regret, and doubt are the five obscurations.

Of these that are taught, torpor, excitement, and doubt are in all three realms, so are those of all three realms obscurations, or just those of Desire? you ask. It is the latter. From a sutra:

> These are an unmixed, complete, and total heap of nonvirtue. They are thus: the five obscurations.

This says that they are solely nonvirtue. **The obscurations** of the dhyanas and absorptions **are in Desire** but not in the other realms.

ii. Establishing their quantity. This has two points.

(1) The reason this is not contradictory with the explanation of them as seven

59b–d Their incompatibilities,
And nourishment and action are
The same, so therefore two are one.

Why are both torpor and sleep and both excitement and regret taught as one obscuration each even though they are separate mental factors? you ask. The reason is because **their incompatible** antidotes, **and** cause or **nourishment, and** karmic **action are the same, so therefore** both sets of **two are** made into **one.**

Thus the antidote for both torpor and sleep is the conception of light. Their nourishment is lethargy, displeasure, yawning, the heaviness of undigested food, and depression. Their action is to depress the mind. Likewise, the antidote for both excitement and regret is tranquility. Their nourishment is thoughts of those dear to one, thoughts of one's homeland, thoughts of immortality, and remembering exciting games and so forth from the past. Their action is to distract the mind.

(2) The reason they are established as five

59ef Because they harm the aggregates,
Because of doubt, there are just five.

Because they, pleasure-seeking and malice, **harm the aggregate** of discipline; torpor and sleep harm the aggregate of full knowing; and excitement and regret harm the aggregate of samadhi; and **because** without samadhi and full knowing one will have **doubts** about the truth, it is explained that **there are just these five** obscurations.

II. What discards the kernels. This has five topics: A. How they are discarded, B. Classifications of the antidotes that discard, C. What they are divided from and discarded, D. What distances one from what has been discarded, and E. Teaching that the abandonment is attained over and over.

A. How they are discarded. This has two points.

1. How discards of seeing are abandoned

60a–c By knowing the focus perfectly,
Extinguishing what focuses
On that, and discarding the focus.

There are three ways that discards of seeing are abandoned. They are discarded **by knowing the focus perfectly,** by **extinguishing** the afflicted subject **that focuses on that, and** by **discarding the focus.**

The first method discards the first two classes, discards of seeing suffering and origin of all three realms, with the exception of the nine universals that focus on higher realms, or thirty-eight kernels. It also discards the twelve types of wrong view and doubt of the three realms discarded by seeing cessation and path, for a total of fifty kernels. In addition, it discards the portion of the six ignorances from those two classes that focuses on the undefiled and the portion of the nine universals of Desire that focuses on its own level. Just as knowing something is a scarecrow blocks the perception of it as a human, these kernels are discarded by simply seeing the actual characteristics of the four truths.

The second method discards the portion of the nine universals of Desire that focus on higher realms. Even though one does not know the truths of the higher realms, when the subject that focuses on these truths, the universals of same status of the kernels' own level, is extinguished, they are blocked.

The third method discards all twenty-three discards of seeing cessation and path that focus solely on the defiled, and the portion of their six ignorances that focus on the defiled. When their focus, the subjects of the undefiled, are discarded, they have no objects, so they also do not arise.

These three methods of discarding happen at the same time with separate isolates: there is no order of earlier or later.

2. How discards of meditation are abandoned

60d Extinguished by the anti's birth.

The discards of meditation in one's own being are extinguished not by completely knowing the focus and so forth. Rather, the nine lesser, medium, and so forth discards are **extinguished by the** nine lesser, medium, and so forth **antidotes' birth.** They are discarded by severing the attainment of the essence. Those in others' beings are discarded through becoming free of the desire of interest, because one does not have the attainment of them and because when the afflictions in one's own being have been discarded through severing the attainment, they will also be abandoned.

B. Classifications of the antidotes that discard

61a-c There are four types of antidotes:
Discarding, base, and distancing,
Disgust, so called.

There are four types of antidotes: the **discarding** antidote, the path of no obstacles that completely severs the attainment of the discard; the **base** antidote, the path of liberation consolidates the abandonment; **and the distancing** antidote, the distinctive path distances one from what has been discarded; **and** the antidote of **disgust, so called,** which is any path that sees a realm as deficient and creates disgust.

C. What they are divided from and discarded

61cd Afflictions are
Discarded through their focus, it's said.

When the afflictions are discarded, what are they proposed to be discarded through? you ask. They cannot be divided from the concurrences, because they cannot be detached from their own group. Therefore **the afflictions are to be discarded through** their **focus, it is said,** because if that is discarded they cannot arise through a focus on it.

D. What distances one from what has been discarded

62. Through different characteristics, and
    Through incompatibility,
Through separate place and time, like distance
    Of sources, discipline, region, times.

There are four ways of being distant: being far apart **through** having **different characteristics** even within one assemblage; being far apart **through** being **incompatible** with the antidote; being far apart **through separate places, and** being far apart in **time.** In order, these are **like the distance of** the four **sources,** the distance between immorality and **discipline**, the distance between the two **regions** of east and west, or, in the *Treatise's* explanation, the distance between the two **times** of past and future.

E. Teaching that the abandonment is attained over and over

63. They are extinguished once. Removal
    Is then attained again and again
On birth of anti, attaining the
    Results, refining faculties.

Is the attainment of the removal of abandonment by the previously explained methods of discarding only caused by abandoning the discards with the antidote? you ask. It is not. When the antidotes have discarded what **they** abandon, those **are extinguished once.** Their **removal is then attained again and again,** becoming better. It improves in this way **upon** the **birth of** the **antidote,** the path of liberation; upon **attaining the** four **results** of the spiritual way;[254] and upon **refining faculties** from dull to sharp. This is a total of six instances. This teaches all of the causes for obtaining improved attainments of removal.

III. The results of discarding the kernels. This has five topics: A. The classification of the results, B. Which perfect knowings are the result of what, C. Establishing their quantity, D. How they are possessed by individuals, and E. Forfeiting and attaining.

A. The classification of the results

64. Nine perfect knowings: in Desire,
  Upon exhausting the first two,
 There's one. Exhausting two, there are two.
  And likewise just those three above.

65ab What leads to lowest, Form, and the extinction
  Of all defilements: three more perfect knowings.

Well then, is the abandonment of all discards presented as a single perfect knowing? you ask. It is not. There are **nine perfect knowings** of abandonment. Firstly, **in** the realm of **Desire, upon exhausting the first two** discards by seeing suffering and origin, **there is one** perfect knowing. In the Desire realm only, upon **exhausting two** discards by seeing cessation and path, **there are two** perfect knowings, one each, for a total of three perfect knowings in Desire. **And** just as there are three perfect knowings of the abandonment of discards of seeing in Desire, **likewise** there are **just those three above** in Form and Formless: the first upon abandoning those discarded by seeing suffering and origin, the second upon abandoning those discarded by seeing cessation, and the third upon abandoning the discards of seeing the path. Thus the abandonment of the discards of seeing of the three realms is six perfect knowings.

On the path of meditation, there is one perfect knowing of the abandonment of the discards **that lead to** the **lowest.** It is called by that term because it has extinguished all the defilements of the Desire realm. In the abandonment of the defilements of **Form,** there is the perfect knowing of the extinction of desire for Form, its primary fetter. **And the extinction of all defilements** is also one: the perfect knowing of the total elimination of all fetters. Thus there are **three more perfect knowings** on the path of meditation.

B. Which perfect knowings are the result of what. This has three points.

1. Which are the results of the knowings and forbearances

65cd The six are the results of forbearance;
  The rest are the results of knowing.

Among them, **the six** perfect knowings of the abandonment of discards of seeing **are the results of forbearance,** and **the rest,** perfect knowing of the abandonment of that which leads to lowest, etc., **are results of** the **knowings:** results of the path of meditation, because the path of meditation is pervasively knowing and has no forbearances.[255]

2. Which are the results of what levels

66. They're all results of Not Unable.
    Five of the dhyanas, or else eight.
The one is of the preparations;
    One of three actual Formless, too.

They, the nine perfect knowings, **are all results of** the preparations for the first dhyana, **Not Unable,** as that level can act as the antidote for all discards:

> Undefiled Not Unable can
> Remove attachment to all levels.[256]

In the tradition of the Great Exposition, there are **five** perfect knowings that are results **of the** actual **dhyana:** the three of the abandonment of the discards of seeing of the two higher realms and the latter two perfect knowings of the abandonment of discards of meditation of the two realms. If on the basis of the dhyanas, nonreturners previously detached produce the path of seeing, they attain the three perfect knowings of the abandonment of the two higher realms' discards of seeing, and when they produce the path of meditation, they also attain the last two perfect knowings. The four perfect knowings of the abandonment of Desire's discards have already been attained earlier by the level of Not Unable, so they are not attained, they say.

The phrase "**or else**" indicates the position of Venerable Ghoṣaka. According to him, if nonreturners previously detached produce the path of seeing on the actual practice of dhyana, the three isolates of the perfect knowings of the abandonment of Desire's discards of seeing are individually obtained at that time, so there are **eight** results of the dhyanas. They also, of course, obtain the isolate of the perfect knowing of the abandonment of that which leads to the lowest, but that is only attained incidentally with the perfect knowing of the abandonment of the higher realms' discards of seeing the path, so it is not counted separately, he says.

Of **the** Formless, there is **one** perfect knowing that **is** a result **of the preparations** for Infinite Space: the extinction of desire for Form. That is a worldly path, but only nobles are presented as having perfect knowings as result, so it is possible to attain undefiled removal. The **one** perfect knowing of the total elimination of all fetters is the only result **of three** undefiled **actual Formless, too.**

3. Which are the results of what paths

67. They all are of the noble paths.
Two of the worldly. Subsequent, too.
The three results of dharma knowing,
Six of its similar kind, and five.

They, the nine perfect knowings, **all are** results **of the noble paths,** because they are results revealed by the dharma and subsequent knowing of the paths of seeing and meditation. The **two** perfect knowings of that which leads to the lowest and extinction of desire for Form are the results **of the worldly** paths in nobles' beings. The results of **subsequent** knowing on the path of meditation are two perfect knowings, **too:** extinction of attachment to Form and the total elimination of the fetters.

The three perfect knowings of abandonment of that which leads to the lowest and so on are **results of dharma knowing** contained in the path of meditation, because dharma knowing is the antidote for the discards of meditation of all three realms. The **six** perfect knowings, excluding the perfect knowings of the abandonment of the higher realms' discards of seeing, are the results of **its similar kind**, dharma knowing including dharma forbearance, **and** the perfect knowings similar in kind to subsequent knowing are **five:** the three perfect knowings of the abandonment of the higher realms' discards of seeing that are the results of subsequent forbearance and knowing, and the last two perfect knowings.

C. Establishing their quantity. This has two points.

1. Establishing the quantity of the six of the abandonment of discards of seeing

68a-d Since they are undefiled attainment
Of a removal, weaken the Peak,
And utterly destroy two causes,
They're perfect knowings.

Well then, of those two types of discards, there are eight, twelve, or eighty-one abandonings, so should there not be the same number of perfect knowings? you ask. First of all, **since they,** the removals that **are** results of the forbearances, gain **undefiled attainment of a removal, weaken** the afflictions of **the Peak** of Existence, **and** discard and **utterly destroy** the universals of the **two causes,** suffering and origin, they are superior through three causes, so **they are** presented as **perfect knowings.**

2. Establishing the quantity of the three of the abandonment of discards of meditation

68d Transcending realms.

The abandonment that is the result of the knowing of the path of meditation attains the name *perfect knowing* through those three causes and from completely **transcending** any one of the three **realms.**

D. How they are possessed by individuals

69. Not one. Those on the path of seeing
May possess fully up to five.
Those on the path of meditation
May possess six or one or two.

70ab They are combined when one becomes
Detached from realms or gains a result.

Ordinary individuals do **not** have even **one** perfect knowing, because they do not have any undefiled attainment of removal. **Those** nobles **on the path of seeing** do not possess any up through the fifth moment, but **may possess fully** one from the sixth moment, two from the eighth, three from the tenth, four from the twelfth, and **up to five** on the fourteenth and fifteenth moments.[257]

Those nobles **on the path of meditation** who are attached or who have regressed from detachment **may possess** the first **six, or** if they have previously been or later become detached from Desire, they possess the **one** perfect knowing of the abandonment of that which leads to the lowest. **Or** if they are detached from Form, they possess the **two** perfect knowings of abandonment of the afflictions of Form and that which leads to the lowest. Arhats possess the last, single perfect knowing of the exhaustion of all defilements.

Why are nonreturners who are not detached from Form and arhats presented as having one perfect knowing? you ask. The reason for that is **they,** the individual abandonments, **are combined when one becomes detached from** a **realm or** has newly **gained a result.** When these two are combined, the individual attainments of removal for each abandonment are forfeited and a single one is acquired, so the individual abandonments are combined and presented as a single perfect knowing.

E. Forfeiting and attaining

70cd Some forfeit one, two, five, or six;
But five cannot be gained.

How many perfect knowings can one forfeit and attain? you ask. **Some forfeit one** perfect knowing: if one regresses from the state of arhat or detachment, one perfect knowing is forfeited. Nonreturners who are detached from Form forfeit **two** if they regress from detachment from Desire. Nonreturners previously detached forfeit **five** when abiding in subsequent knowing of path, **or** some forfeit **six** in instances when the successive nonreturner[258] has gradually detached himself from Desire.

Likewise, there can be attainment of one, two, or six, but **five cannot be gained,** because it is impossible to regress from the state of a previously detached nonreturner. There is attainment of one in instances such as when a nonreturner attains arhatship. There is attainment of two in instances such as when an arhat regresses through the afflictions of Formless. There is attainment of six in instances such as when an arhat or nonreturner regresses through the afflictions of Desire.

Second, presenting the area's name

This completes the fifth area called "Teachings on the Kernels" from the *Verses of the Treasury of Abhidharma.*

This completes the explanation of **the fifth area called "Teachings on the Kernels" from** *The Explanation of the "Verses of the Treasury of Abhidharma"* called *The Essence of the Ocean of Abhidharma, The Words of Those who Know and Love, Explaining the Youthful Play, Opening the Eyes of Dharma, the Chariot of Easy Practice.*

A few words here:

The trunk of rebirth and stained karma's great tree
Is the kernels, two types of discards, and if you
Should wish to uproot their attainments, their seed,
As the lord of twice-drinkers,[259] when scorched by the sun,
Dives into the lake spread with full lotus blossoms,
All those who have freedoms and riches and zeal
Should plunge into dharmas that classify kernels.

When satisfied sippling this nectar that is drunk
From the ladle of listening, contemplate well.
In a place that is peaceful, one-pointedly meditate—
How wondrous these victuals of undefiled bliss!

SIXTH AREA

Teachings on the Paths and Individuals

To the all-seeing Teacher, the physician for wanderers,
To the unequaled Gautam I prostrate.
This sixth part, the treasury that tells of individuals—
The focus of two paths, the truths,
The manner to train in abiding in discipline,
And listening, reflecting, meditating,
How five paths arise, those who enter and dwell,
Results of the spiritual, factors—
The treasury that fully classifies these
Is what I shall now explain.

The sixth area, the "Teachings on the Paths and Individuals," has an explanation of the text of the area and a presentation of the area's name. The explanation of the text of the area has three topics: I. Explanation of the paths, II. Explanation of individuals, and III. A specific explanation of paths.

I. Explanation of the paths. This has four topics: A. The link between chapters, B. The essence of the paths, C. The focus of the paths, and D. How the paths arise.

A. The link between chapters

1ab It's taught afflictions are discarded
By seeing truth and meditating.

In the fifth area, abandonment is given the name *perfect knowing*. With regards to that abandonment, **it is taught** above **that afflictions** of the kernels **are discarded by seeing truth,** the path of seeing, **and** by **meditating** on the truths, the path of meditation. Here it is those paths that abandon that are explained.

B. The essence of the paths

1cd The path of meditation is twofold,
But seeing, so called, is undefiled.

Which of those paths are defiled and which are undefiled? you ask. **The path of meditation is twofold:** the defiled worldly path and the undefiled transworldly path. **But** the path of **seeing, so called, is** transworldly **undefiled** only, because it is the antidote for all three realms including the Peak of Existence, because it discards the nine sets of discards of seeing of the three realms at one time, and because the worldly paths do not have such power to discard.

C. The focus of the paths. This has two topics: 1. Explaining the four truths, and 2. Explaining the two truths.

1. Explaining the four truths. This has three points.

a. Essence

2a The truths are four, it is explained.

The truths mentioned in the line, "By seeing truth," **are four, it is explained.** The line "The undefiled is the truth of path"[260] explicitly teaches the truth of the path. The line "Cessation that is analytic"[261] explains the truth of cessation. The line "They're suffering, origin, and the world... "[262] explains the truths of suffering and origin.

b. Order

2b–d Thus suffering and origin,
Cessation and the path. This is
The order in which they are realized.

Is that the only order in which they must be known? you ask. It is not. Well then, what is the order? you ask. **Thus** they are the truths of **suffering and**

origin, cessation and the path. This is the order. The word "thus" means that their essences are just as has been already described. They are presented in the order **in which they are realized,** because on the path of seeing, one clearly realizes duḥkha first and then origin, cessation, and path. The reason for that is that on the paths of accumulation and joining, the truths are fully realized in that order. For example, when you see illness, you think of its cause, and then out of the desire to eliminate the illness you look for the method, which is medicine. Because only nobles see the truths from suffering to path as something that is just as it is, they are called the noble truths. Because ordinary individuals see the truths and so forth incorrectly, they are not called ordinary individuals' truths.

c. Elaboration

3. The attractive and the unattractive,
   And the defiled other than those
   Are suffering without exception
   Because they have three sufferings.

There are three types of suffering: **the attractive** are the suffering of change, **and the unattractive** are the suffering of suffering, **and the defiled other than those** two **are** the **suffering** of formation. Everything defiled **without exception** is suffering due to any one of the three sufferings, **because they,** the defiled composites, **have** the **three sufferings.**

The three of attractive and so forth appear in an order that is compatible with the three feelings, so pleasant feeling is the suffering through change. From a sutra: "Pleasant feeling is pleasant when it arises. It is pleasant while it stays. When it changes, it is suffering." Unpleasant is by its very nature suffering. From a sutra: "The feeling of suffering is suffering when it arises. It is suffering while it stays." Feeling that is neither pleasant nor unpleasant is manifestly formed by conditions so it is suffering only through formation, because it is said, "Whatever is impermanent is suffering."

2. Explaining the two truths

4. If not engaged by mind when it's
   Destroyed or mentally excluded,
   It's relative, like vases or water.
   Ultimate being is different.

The sutras teach the four truths, but they also teach relative and ultimate truth. What are those two? you ask.

If a thing is **not engaged by mind when it is destroyed** by a hammer or so forth, **or** when it is **mentally excluded** through full knowing, **it** exists **relatively, like vases or water.** They are true merely in conventional terms.[263]

Ultimate being or existence **is different** from such relative things that may be damaged. It is dharmas such as form, subtle particles, instants, and non-composites that the mind can engage even when they are destroyed or when a dharma is excluded by mind.[264] As that is the highest meaning of wisdom, it is ultimate, and as it is also truth, it is the ultimate truth.

The respective characteristics of the two truths are those things that when destroyed or disintegrated the mind that perceives them is discarded or not discarded.

Here the explanation in the *Ṭīka* of "permanent subtle particles of substance" means merely that they do not disintegrate through destruction by force; it seems not to mean permanent as in the context of permanent and impermanent, I would think.

D. How the paths arise. This has two topics: 1. An overview of how to enter the paths, and 2. An explanation of how to meditate.

1. An overview of how to enter the paths. This has two points.

a. Actual

> 5ab With conduct, listening, contemplation,
> Completely train in meditation.

Those who wish to see the truth should first abide in the disciplined **conduct** of definite renunciation, retain the meaning from **listening** that is compatible with seeing the truths and then, by knowing the meaning they have listened to, **contemplate** appropriately. Possessing both of these qualities, then they should **completely** and unerringly **train in** the samadhi **meditation** on the meaning they have contemplated. Contemplation arises from listening, and meditation arises from contemplation.

b. The essence of the three full knowings make one enter

> 5cd Full knowing of listening, et cetera,
> Are subjects of name, both, and meaning.

Some members of the Great Exposition say that the natures of the three **full knowings** born out **of listening, et cetera,** contemplation and meditation, **are** respectively conscious **subjects** that take the **name** only, **both** the name and meaning, **and** the **meaning** only as their object, like beginner, intermediate, and expert swimmers grabbing onto a float when learning to swim, it is heard.

The Master says that if that is so, there is no contemplation separate from listening or meditation. Therefore he explains that the three are the full knowings born respectively from credible scriptures, analyzing with logic, and samadhi.

2. An explanation of how to meditate. This has two topics: a. Attributes of the support, the meditator, and b. The stages of the path one meditates upon.

a. Attributes of the support, the meditator. This has three topics: i. The support that will complete the path, ii. The support that will not complete the path, and iii. As an elaboration, an explanation of the noble families.

i. The support that will complete the path

6a Those with two distances.

How can meditation be completed? you ask. **Those** who first are **with** or possess the **two distances** from bodily distractions and mental negative thoughts will entirely complete meditation.

ii. The support that will not complete the path. This has two topics: (1) What is to be discarded, and (2) The antidote.

(1) What is to be discarded

6a–d Not the
Insatiable, dissatisfied.
To crave for more is insatiable;
To want what is not had, dissatisfied.

Those two distances are easy for those who have few desires and who are satisfied. They are **not** easy for **the insatiable** or the **dissatisfied.** The proponents of the abhidharma say that when one has received an excellent dharma robe and so forth, **to crave for more is** to be **insatiable,** and **to want what is not had** is to be **dissatisfied,** it is heard. The Master explains that mental displeasure at getting only a few, poor things is insatiability, and not getting many good things but wanting to is dissatisfaction.

(2) The antidote

> 7ab The opposite is their antidote.
> These two are in three realms or stainless.

The opposite of insatiability and dissatisfaction **is their antidote:** it is contentment and satisfaction. **These two,** contentment and satisfaction, **are in the three realms, or** they are **stainless,** for four types. They are both nongreed by nature.

iii. As an elaboration, an explanation of the noble families. This has two points.

(1) Overview

> 7c Nongreed, the noble family.

Among these types of **nongreed,** those that produce nobles are called **the noble family.**

(2) Explanation

> 7d Of these, three are content by nature.

> 8. The three teach conduct; the last, action.
> As anti for the arising of craving.
> To quell desire for things one grasps
> As mine or me, for a time, forever.

Of these four **noble** natures, **the** first **three,** satisfaction with having a dharma robe, alms, and a bed, are **content by nature.** The fourth noble family is joy for being without what has been abandoned and for meditating. This is also nongreed by nature, because it is directed against existence and the desire for existence.

The four noble natures explained by the Bhagavan teach both method and action to students who yearn for liberation. Of these, **the** first **three teach** the **conduct,** and **the last** teaches **action.** As it says in a sutra, "If you do this action by these methods, before long you will attain liberation." They are taught **as an antidote for the arising of craving.** The four cravings are taught in a sutra:

> Bhikshus, if craving arises, it arises for a dharma robe, for alms, for a bed, and a seat. If it stays, it stays. If it is manifest attachment, it is attachment. Bhikshus, if craving arises, it arises thus for birth and destruction.

The first three are **desire for things one grasps as mine** such as dharma robes and so on, and the fourth is to desire or crave for the thing grasped as **me,** the body. The conduct **quells** craving for things grasped as mine **for a time** or temporarily, and action quells craving for both the things grasped as mine and those grasped as me **forever.**

b. The stages of the path one meditates upon. This has two topics: i. Methods for tranquility meditation, and ii. Methods for insight meditation.

i. Methods for tranquility meditation. This has two topics: (1) The order in which to begin, and (2) The actual methods of samadhi meditation.

(1) The order in which to begin

9a–c One enters that through the repulsive
And mindfulness of in, out breath,
For those with excess desire or thoughts.

How should someone who is thus a suitable vessel enter meditation? you ask. **One** first **enters that by** the meditation on **the repulsive and** meditation on **mindfulness of in**-breath and **out-breath,** as these will tame the mind. Whose mind? you ask. This is **for those with** greatly **excessive desire or** excessive **thoughts.**

(2) The actual methods of samadhi meditation. This has two topics: (a) Methods for meditation focused on the repulsive, and (b) Methods for meditation focused on the breath.

(a) Methods for meditation focused on the repulsive. This has three topics: (i) Overview, (ii) Explanation, and (iii) Particular attributes.

(i) Overview

9d The skeleton for all desirous.

There are four types of desire: greed for color, shape, touch, and respect. The antidote for the first is to meditate upon the bluishness, foulness, and redness of a corpse. The antidote for the second is to think of it wasting and being torn apart. The antidote for the third is to meditate on it being eaten by bugs, and the bones being just barely held together. The antidote for the fourth is to meditate on an unmoving corpse. Meditating on **the skeleton** is the antidote **for all** the **desirous,** because it does not allow for any of the four types of greed.

(ii) Explanation. This has three points.

A. The method for beginners

10ab At first imagine bones that spread
As far as the sea, then narrow down.

At first, the beginner yogi who is meditating on repulsiveness at first turns their attention to their forehead or any other suitable body part and imagines that the flesh gradually rots and falls off, visualizing their body as a skeleton. Then they **imagine bones that spread** and fill everything **as far as the sea,** and **then narrow** the visualization **down** to only their own body. This is the yoga for the beginner.

B. The method for the trained

10cd The trained discard bones from the foot
To half the skull.

In order to enhance this gathering of the mind, the completely **trained** yogi **discards bones from** the body, starting with the **foot,** and directs their attention on the remainder. Then one discards or casts away all the bones up **to half** of **the skull** and focuses the attention on half the skull.

C. The method to perfect the attention

10d Perfect attention

11a Holding the mind between the eyebrows.

When honing in the meditation, yogis who have **perfected attention** on the repulsive discard half the skull as well, and **hold the mind** on a bone that is just the size of a thumb **between the eyebrows,** it is heard.

(iii) Particular attributes

> 11b–d Repulsive is nongreed. It's on
> Ten levels, focusing on the
> Appearance of Desire. By humans.

The nature of the **repulsive** meditation **is nongreed. It is on** the **ten levels:** nine of the four dhyanas, their four preparations and special dhyana, plus the level of Desire. In Desire there is no equipoise, but this is meant in terms of similarity. Its **focus** is **on the appearances of Desire,** which are color and shape. Because it focuses on color and shape, it is proven that it does not focus on names, it focuses on meaning. Its support: if it is not even among other wanderers, what need is there to mention other realms? It is only produced **by humans.** However, it is not in Northern Unpleasant Sound, because there is no path to detachment there.

(b) Methods for meditation focused on the breath. This has two topics: (i) Common overview, and (ii) Particular explanation.

(i) Common overview

> 12a–c The mindfulness of breath is full knowing.
> It's on five levels; its sphere is wind.
> Desire realm. Outsiders do not.

The mindfulness of in-**breath** and out-breath **is** the **full knowing** that knows the two just as they are. However, because it is produced by and arises out of the power of mindfulness, it is called mindfulness. It is concurrent only with neutral feeling. As it focuses on just the in-breath and out-breath, **it is** only **on** the **five levels** where those two are: the lower three preparations, special dhyana, and Desire. Some say neutral feeling is also present in the actual practice of the three lower dhyanas, so according to their proposal, there are eight levels. **Its sphere is wind,** and it has the gods and humans of **Desire realm** as its support. It is practiced only among practitioners of this Dharma; **outsiders do not** practice it.

(ii) Particular explanation. This has three points.

A. Classifications of the methods of meditation

> 12d Six types are counting and so forth.

The **six types** of causes that perfect it **are counting and so forth:** following, placing, closely considering, modifying, and completely purifying.

In the first, *counting,* if one tries to count too many, they will become distracted, and if too few, discouraged, so one counts from one to ten only. If two are counted as one, then it is incomplete, or if one is counted as two, there are extra. If the in-breath is perceived as the out-breath or the out-breath perceived as the in-breath, the count is confused: these three faults must be avoided.

In *following the breath,* pay attention as the in-breath goes from the throat, heart, navel, and calves down to the feet, and then as the out-breath goes out the nostrils out to a hand's width or arm span.

In *placing,* consider that it is like a string of jewels from the tip of the nose to the feet that is beneficial and warm.

In *closely considering,* the object of the wind is a form comprised of the eight substances, and the perceiving subject of full knowing includes the four name aggregates, so consider it as the five aggregates.

In *modifying,* the mind that focuses on the breath engages higher and higher along the path as far as supreme dharma, and in *completely purifying,* up to the path of seeing and so forth. Alternatively, some say that modifying is from the four foundations of mindfulness to vajra-like samadhi, and completely purifying is the knowing of extinction, et cetera.

As a summary of these, the autocommentary says:

> The mindfulness of breathing in
> And breathing out is counting, following,
> Placing, considering, modifying,
> And purifying: these six types.

B. The essence of the object

> 13a–c In and out breath, on those of the body,
> Called beings, are not appropriated.
> They arise from a compatible cause

What level are the **in**-breath **and out-breath** on? They are **on those** levels that have a body from Desire to the third dhyana, because they both are a part **of the body.** Both the in-breath and out-breath are **called** or counted as a sentient **being,** because they can be attained, not attained or possessed, and because they are imagined as one's being. Because they are engaged separately from the faculties, they **are not appropriated.** As they are produced by a cause of same status, **they arise from compatible cause** and not from development or full ripening, because they can diminish even if the body grows, and when cut, they can be restored.

C. Distinctions in the subject

> 13d And are not observed by lower mind.

The mind of one's own level and higher levels realizes the in-breath **and** out-breath, but if the in-breath and out-breath of a higher level **are not observed by** even the **lower mind** of conduct and emanated minds, what need is there to mention the virtuous or afflicted?

ii. Methods for insight meditation. This has three topics: (1) The path of accumulation, (2) The path of joining, and (3) The path that directly realizes the truths.

(1) The path of accumulation. This has two topics: (a) Overview, and (b) Explanation.

(a) Overview

> 14ab After accomplishing tranquility
> Meditate on the founds of mindfulness

Through the two gates of entry, meditation on repulsiveness and on the breath, the samadhi of tranquility has been accomplished, but without the full knowing of insight, the afflictions cannot be discarded from their root, because as a sutra says, "The afflictions are what is conquered by wisdom." For that reason, having pacified the afflictions or distractions, **after accomplishing** the **tranquility** of a mind that remains within, then **meditate on the foundations of mindfulness** in order to generate the full knowing of insight that discards the afflictions from their root. By meditating on them, insight will be accomplished, as it says in a sutra: "Bhikshus, the one path to go down is this one. It is this: the four foundations of mindfulness."

(b) Explanation. This has two topics: (i) Common features, and (ii) The method for meditating on the mindfulness of dharmas in particular.

(i) Common features. This has four points:

A. Method of meditation

14cd By examining two characteristics
Of body, feeling, mind, and dharmas.

The foundations of mindfulness are known **by examining** the **two** specific and general **characteristics of body, feeling, mind, and dharmas.** The specific characteristics of the body are the sources and source-derived; of feeling is experience; of mind is focus; and of dharmas are the conceptions, formations, and noncompound dharmas other than body, feeling, and mind. The general characteristics are that composites are impermanent; defiled dharmas are suffering; and all dharmas are empty and selflessness. The characteristic of suffering is incompatibility with the nobles.

B. Essence

15ab Full knowing from listening, et cetera.
The others from connection, focus.

The essence of the four foundations of mindfulness is **full knowing.** From a sutra: "The viewing of body in the body is the foundation of mindfulness." This is full knowing that is born **from listening**, **et cetera,** contemplating and meditating, but not that attained upon birth. The word *mindfulness* is used because these are produced by the power of mindfulness, or in the Master's explanation, this simultaneously applies mindfulness, so it is explained as thus.

Thus full-knowing is the natural foundation of mindfulness. Its companions, **the others** that are concurrent with it, **from** their **connection** with it are called connected foundations of mindfulness. Their focus—body, feeling, mind, and dharmas—are the **focus** of both, so they are called the focused foundation of mindfulness. For this reason, a sutra says, "Bhikshus, that which we call 'all dharmas' is a synonym for the four foundations of mindfulness."

C. Order

15c The order is as they arise,

The order of earlier and later **is,** according to some from the Great Exposition, the same **as** the order in which **they arise,** because the earlier ones are coarser and easier to realize, so that is how they are seen, they say. The Master says it is because on the basis of the body desire arises, which is attached to or manifestly desires feeling, which disturbs the mind, and because of that afflictions are not abandoned.

D. Establishing their quantity

> 15d Four antis for the erroneous.

The body is like feces, so it is unclean. Feelings are suffering. The mind changes quickly, so it is impermanent. Dharmas have no independent single self, so these **four** foundations of mindfulness are taught as **antidotes for the erroneous** ideas of cleanliness, bliss, permanence, and the self. More than that are unnecessary, but fewer would not include everything.

(ii) The method for meditating on the mindfulness of dharmas in particular

> 16. It is the foundation of dharmas
> That focuses on them combined.
> They view them as impermanent,
> And suffering, empty, and selfless.

Having familiarized oneself with the foundations of mindfulness that focus on body and so forth, **it,** that familiarization, **is the foundation of dharmas that** rests **focusing on them** in general or **combined. They,** the yogis, generally combine all the foundations of body and so forth and **view them as** the four aspects of **impermanence, suffering, emptiness, and selflessness.**

(2) The path of joining. This has four topics. (a) How it arises, (b) Essence, (c) Features, and (d) Preliminaries.

(a) How it arises. This has five topics: (i) Warmth, (ii) Peak, (iii) Forbearance, (iv) Supreme dharma, and (v) Common features.

(i) Warmth

> 17a–c The warmth arises out of that.
> It has the four truths as its sphere
> With sixteen aspects.

The warmth of virtuous roots gradually **arises out of that** meditation on the dharma foundation of mindfulness. Just as when you rub two sticks, warmth arises as a sign of forthcoming fire, this is called warmth. **It,** warmth, **has the four truths as its sphere:** it focuses on the truths of the higher and lower realms in succession, since it cannot focus on them in a single moment. As training for dharma knowing and forbearance, it meditates in a general way on the four truths of the Desire realm as the sixteen aspects.[265] As training for subsequent knowing and forbearance, it meditates on the four truths of the two higher realms as sixteen aspects. Thus it is the near training for the path of seeing, so it is the path of joining in the sense of training. It is meditation **with** the **sixteen aspects** of impermanence and the others.

(ii) Peak. This has two points.

A. The actual peak

17cd Out of warmth
Comes peak, which is like that as well.

Out of the gradual increase of **warmth** through the lesser, medium, and greater **comes** the **peak, which is like that,** warmth, **as well** in focus and aspects: it focuses on the four truths and views them as the sixteen aspects. Because it is the peak of unstable roots of virtue, it is called the peak.

B. Common features of both warmth and the peak

18ab Through dharma, they both aim at aspects,
Develop through the others, too.

Through the foundation of mindfulness of **dharma, they, both** warmth and the peak, first **aim at** and engage the **aspects** in the four truths. They are also **developed** or familiarized and refined **through the others**—those other than the foundation of mindfulness of dharma—all four foundations of mindfulness.

(iii) Forbearance. This has two points.

A. Actual

18cd From that, forbearance. Two like that.
Dharmas develops all of them.

What arises **from that** development of the lesser, middle, and greater peak is called **forbearance.** When one is childish, one fears for oneself and cannot bear to see the truth. When one has attained warmth and the peak, one can bear the lesser and medium truth but one falls away from that. Because at this stage one has great forbearance for seeing the truth without falling away from it at all, it is called forbearance.

The **two**, lesser and middle forbearance, are **like that,** the peak, in the way they aim at the aspects of the truths. The foundation of mindfulness of **dharmas develops all of them,** lesser, middle, and greater forbearance. The first two each have individual aims and development, so they are also like that, but greater forbearance is a single instant, so it is not like that. This is said in terms of how it engages the truths. It does not engage them through the other foundations because it is near supreme dharma and the path of seeing. Thus it is the mindfulness of dharmas, which is close to those.

B. Explaining the particular features of greater forbearance

> 19ab The object of the great is suffering
> Of Desire realm. It is one moment.

Because it is near supreme dharma, **the object of the greater** forbearance **is** the **suffering of Desire realm:** it focuses on that in any one of its four aspects. **It is one moment;** it does not have a continuum.

(iv) Supreme dharma

> 19c So is supreme dharma.

So is supreme dharma similar to greater forbearance: it focuses on the suffering of Desire and is one moment. It is worldly, but it is the supreme of worldly dharmas, or alternatively its power leads to the path of seeing, which has no cause of same status, so it is the supreme of all that is worldly. For these reasons, it is called supreme dharma.

(v) Common features

> 19cd They are all
> Five aggregates, without attainments.

> 20a The four precursors to realization

They, the four, **are all** inherently the foundations of mindfulness, so they are primarily full knowing and its associations. They are also equipoise, so they have an imperceptible form. For that reason, they are the **five aggregates.** They are **without attainments,** which are not included as warmth and the others, because the nobles have the attainments in a manifest way. Otherwise it would follow that nobles would also manifestly have warmth and the others.[266] In this way, warmth, the peak, forbearance, and supreme dharma are **the four precursors to** clear **realization.**

(b) Essence

> 20b Must be produced by meditation

All four of the precursors to clear realization **must be produced by meditation:** they do not arise from listening or contemplating.

(c) Features. This has five topics: (i) Distinctions of level, (ii) Distinctions of support, (iii) Distinctions in how they are forfeited, (iv) Distinctions in qualities, and (v) Distinctions in family.

(i) Distinctions of level

> 20cd On Not Unable, special, and
> The dhyanas. Two below, perhaps.

These are **on** the levels of the preparation for the first dhyana **Not Unable,** the **special** dhyana, **and** the four actual practices of **the dhyanas,** or six levels. As these are contained in those six levels, there are no precursors to clear realization on the levels of Formless. This is because clear realization is the practice of the path of seeing, which is not present on the levels of Formless. The reason there is no path of seeing there is because the path of seeing focuses on the Desire realm, and Formless does not focus on the Desire realm.

In the tradition of Venerable Ghoṣaka, the **two,** warmth and the peak, are also **below** in the Desire realm. The word "**perhaps**" indicates that this is a separate tradition in which those two would be on seven levels: the six levels of dhyana and Desire. In that case, since they could be supported on a level of Desire, they would not necessarily be meditation-produced.

(ii) Distinctions of support

> 21ab Support of Desire realm, and women
> Gain supreme dharma on both supports.

The first three can be newly produced in those men and women of the three continents who have not previously had them. Those that have already arisen can become manifest among the gods, and the fourth can be produced among the gods, so they all have the **support of Desire realm, and women** can **gain**

supreme dharma on both male and female **supports.**[267] Men can only attain it with a male support, because they also attain a nonanalytic cessation of becoming female.

(iii) Distinctions in how they are forfeited. This has two topics: A. How the nobles forfeit them, and B. How ordinary individuals forfeit them.

A. How the Nobles forfeit them

> 21cd The nobles forfeit them when leaving
> A level;

The nobles forfeit them, the paths of joining attained on the support of a particular level, **when** they **leave a level** and are born in a higher. Because their roots of virtue are greatly increased by the path of seeing, unlike ordinary individuals they do not forfeit them through regression or death.

B. How ordinary individuals forfeit them. This has two points: 1. Actual, and 2. Elaboration.

1. Actual

> 21d nonnobles at death.
>
> 22a The first two by regressing, too.

Nonnoble ordinary individuals who are detached forfeit them when they transmigrate from one level to be reborn in a higher **at death,** and by discarding their likeness. Those not detached also forfeit them by discarding their likeness, even when not transmigrating to a new level. **The first two,** warmth and the peak, are forfeited during the period of an ordinary individual, **by regressing, too,** through the afflictions that are incompatible with them. Even ordinary individuals cannot regress from forbearance or supreme dharma.

2. Elaboration. This has three points.

a. The particulars of forfeiture through death

> 22b The actual sees truth in this.

Someone who has produced the precursors to clear realization of the level of

the actual practice of the first dhyana will definitely **see** the **truth in this** very lifetime, because they have great revulsion. The explanation of forfeiture through regression and death is for those on Not Unable, so there is no contradiction.

b. How they are re-attained

22c If one regresses, gained anew.

If one who has **regressed** from the precursors to clear realization later attains them again, one **gains** them **anew**, like the vows of individual liberation. One does not re-attain the same ones previously forfeited, because they are something that is unfamiliar and created through effort.

c. The essence of the two types of forfeiture

22d Both forfeitures are nonpossession.

What are the natures of forfeiture and regression? you ask. All loss of attainment is called forfeiture, and in particular, forfeiture because of an incompatible affliction is called regression. **Both forfeitures are** in essence **nonpossession:** nonattainment from forfeiting the attainment.

(iv) Distinctions in qualities

23ab When peak is gained, roots can't be severed;
Forbearance goes not to low realms.

When peak is gained, if one regresses, one might commit heinous misdeeds and go to the lower realms, but the **roots** of virtue **cannot be severed,** because one has attained sincere faith in the Three Jewels through training in their qualities. When lesser **forbearance** is attained, there is also the attainment of the freedom of **not going to lower realms.** When greater forbearance is attained, one also attains freedom from being reborn in certain modes of birth, births, bodies, and so forth.

(v) Distinctions in family. This has two points.

A. The families that can change

23cd Two can withdraw from the learners' family
And become buddhas. Other, third.

Two, those who have attained warmth and the peak, can **withdraw from the learner's family** of listeners, develop the mind of great enlightenment, **and become buddhas,** but those who have attained forbearance cannot, because from then on there is no birth in the lower realms, but a bodhisattva takes birth there for others' benefit. Those **other** than the Buddha, self-buddhas, on the **third** stage of the path of joining, forbearance, can also change because they do not go to the lower realms even for others' benefits. Once supreme dharma has been attained there is no changing family.

B. The families that cannot change

24ab The Teacher and rhino, all on one
Seat and dhyan's end until awakening.

The Teacher, the Buddha, **and** the **rhino**like self-buddha cannot change family at any time after reaching warmth, because **all** the paths from the precursors to clear realization arise **on one seat** and only on **dhyana's** upper **end**, the fourth dhyana, **until awakening** to enlightenment.

(d) Preliminaries

24cd Before that, the precursor to freedom.
The swiftest in three lives are freed.

25ab From listening and contemplation.
Three karmas are propelled by humans.

Do the precursors to clear realization arise right from the beginning, or must something precede them? you ask. **Before that** precursor to clear realization, one must produce the virtuous roots of **the precursor to freedom.**[268] **The** absolutely **swiftest** of all **in three lifetimes are liberated.** For example, just as one plants a seed, the fruit forms and the fruit ripens: in the first lifetime one produces the virtuous roots of precursor to liberation, in the second the precursor to realization, and in the third produces the noble path. The being gradually enters, ripens, and is completely liberated in this dharma.

The precursors to liberation arises **from listening and contemplation;** they do not arise from meditation. They are primarily karma of mind, but because they are embraced by prayers, they are also karma of speech, so they are the **three karmas** of body, speech, and mind. They **are propelled by humans** of the three continents only, and not by others, who lack either full knowing or world-weariness.

(3) The path that directly realizes the truths. This has four topics: (a) How the sixteen moments of cognition arise, (b) Teaching the three types of clear realization, (c) Which levels support it, and (d) Classifying the cognitions as sixteen.

(a) How the sixteen moments of cognition arise

25cd From the supreme of worldly dharmas
Comes undefiled dharma forbearance

26. Of suffering of Desire, from which
Arises dharma knowing of
Just that itself. And likewise for
The rest of suffering arises
The subsequent forbearance, knowing.
Three other truths are like that, too.

27ab Thus clear realization of the truths
Is sixteen minds.

From the supreme of worldly dharmas, the **undefiled dharma forbearance** immediately arises. That focuses **on suffering of Desire.** It is forbearance for the sake of the dharma knowing of duḥkha, so it is called exactly that, like saying "flowering tree" or "fruit tree." Immediately after or **from** that forbearance, there **arises** the **dharma knowing of just that itself,** the suffering of Desire. This is given the designation *dharma knowing of suffering* in the *Treatise.* This is in all respects an undefiled moment, so it is called undefiled dharma knowing.

Just as forbearance of dharma knowing of suffering and the dharma knowing arise, **likewise** forbearance of subsequent knowing **for the rest of suffering** of Form and Formless **arises** immediately following the dharma knowing of suffering. It focuses on general characteristics and is called **the subsequent forbearance,** or the forbearance of subsequent knowing of suffering. Then the so-called subsequent **knowing** of suffering arises.

Just as the four forbearances and knowings of the truth of suffering arise, the four forbearances and knowings of each of the other **three other truths** of origin, cessation and path arise **like that, too. Thus** in this way, through this progression, the **clear realization of truth is sixteen** moments of **mind.**

(b) Teaching the three types of clear realization

27bc There are three types,
Called seeing, focusing, and action,

There are three types of clear realization. Directly realizing the truth with undefiled full knowing is **called** the clear realization of **seeing.** The feelings and so forth that are concurrent with that full knowing and also the full knowing itself focus on the truth, so they are called the clear realization of **focusing.** The clear realization of the **action** is knowing, discarding, making manifest, and meditating during the path. It is the five aggregates of a single assembly: discipline that is not concurrent with full knowing, arising and so forth, attainment and so forth, and that which is concurrent with full knowing. This is because these all perform those actions. Thus there are said to be three clear realizations of truth.

(c) Which levels support it

27d On the same level as supreme.

The sixteen cognitions of clear realization explained above are **on the same level as supreme** dharma. These are the six levels explained earlier.[269]

(d) Classifying the cognitions as sixteen. This has two points.

(i) Classifying them as paths of no obstacles and paths of liberation

28ab Respectively, forbearance, knowing are
Paths of no obstacles and liberation.

Respectively the eight **forbearances** and eight **knowings** here **are,** presented in this order, the **paths of no obstacles** that discard the four classes of discards of Desire and the four classes of discards contained in the higher realms **and** the paths of **liberation,** for a total of sixteen.

(ii) Explaining the term *path of seeing*

28cd From seeing the unseen, fifteen
Moments of these are the path of seeing.

These sixteen cognitions are not all the path of seeing. **From seeing** what had been **the unseen, fifteen moments of these** sixteen cognitions, from forbearance of dharma knowing of suffering to forbearance of subsequent knowing of path, **are the path of seeing.** The sixteenth moment of cognition is the path of meditation only. This is because there is no previously unseen truth to see; instead it familiarizes one with seeing the truth.

II. Explanation of individuals. This has three topics: A. Explaining the four pairs of individuals, B. Classifying into seven enumerations, and C. Combining them into six substances.

A. Explaining the four pairs of individuals. This has three topics: 1. Explaining entering stream-enterer, 2. Explaining those previously detached, and 3. Explaining successive results.

1. Explaining entering stream-enterer. This has two points.

a. Classifications of mind

> 29ab During these, sharp and dull faculties
> Are followers of faith and dharma.

During the period when they are abiding in **these** fifteen moments of the path of seeing, the two types of individuals with **sharp and dull faculties are** called, if of dull faculties, **followers of faith and** if of sharp faculties, followers of **dharma.** This is because those of dull faculties clearly realize the truth because of the spiritual advice of other masters during their previous period as ordinary individuals, whereas those of sharp faculties did not rely on other masters during their previous time as ordinary individuals. They realize the meaning of the scriptures on their own through full knowing and clearly realize the truth.

b. Distinctions in abandonment and realization

> 29cd They're entering the first result
> If no discards of meditation
>
> 30a Or up to five have been destroyed.

They, those two individuals, **are entering the first** of all **results** to be attained and are called entering the result of stream-enterer **if no discards of meditation** have been discarded previously by a worldly path and they possess all the bonds. **Or** if **up to five** discards of meditation **have been destroyed** by the worldly path, they are entering the first result, just as they were when they still possessed all the bonds. The phrase "up to" includes one, two, three, four, or five discards.

2. Explaining those previously detached. This has two topics: a. Enterers, and b. Abiders in result.

a. Enterers. This has two points.

i. Entering once-returner

> 30b The second, till the ninth's extinguished.

They are entering **the second** result of once-returner if any one of the sixth, seventh, eighth, or up **until the ninth** discard of meditation **is extinguished.**

ii. Entering nonreturner

> 30cd One who is detached from Desire
> Or higher is entering the third.

One who **is detached from Desire or** a **higher** level up to Nothingness **is entering the third** result of nonreturner.

b. Abiders in result. This has two points.

i. Actual

> 31ab Those who are entering a result
> Abide in it on the sixteenth.

Those, whether follower of faith or dharma, **who are entering a result abide in it,** that result, **on the sixteenth** moment. Arhatship is not attained at first, because the path of seeing does not abandon discards of meditation, and because it is impossible to have previously detached oneself from the Peak of Existence by the worldly path.

ii. The names they are called

> 31cd Sharp and dull faculties are then
> Convinced through faith, attained through seeing.

Between those with **sharp and** those with **dull faculties,** those with dull faculties **are then,** at the time one abides on the sixteenth moment, called **convinced through faith, and** those with sharp faculties are called **attained through seeing,** because they are respectively brought about by great faith and full knowing.

3. Explaining successive results. This has four topics: a. Entering and abiding in stream-enterer, b. Entering and abiding in once-returner, c. Entering and abiding in nonreturner, and d. Entering and abiding in arhat.

a. Entering and abiding in stream-enterer. This has two topics: i. Entering, and ii. Abiding.

i. Entering. Entering has already been taught above.

ii. Abiding. This has (1) General teaching, and (2) Individual explanations.

(1) General teaching. This has two points.

(a) Teaching that the mere abider in result is not an enterer

32. To gain a result is not to gain
    The path of higher progress. Thus
Those dwelling in result, not striving
    To improve it, are not enterers.

When stream-enterers have abandoned the fifth discard and are on the sixteenth cognition, why are they not entering the result of once-returner? you ask. At that time, they have **gained a** mere **result** of stream-enterer, but that **is not to gain the path of higher progress. Thus those** stream-enterers are **dwelling in result, not striving to** attain the second result that **improves it.** Those who are not making efforts to attain a result **are not enterers** in that result.

By this logic one can also know the reason why someone who has abandoned the eighth discard of Desire and abides on the sixteenth moment is not called entering the result of nonreturner, and the reason why someone who is detached from Nothingness and abides on the sixteenth moment is not entering the result of arhat.

(b) Classifications of the path of enterer and discards of meditation

> 33. Each level has nine kinds of faults,
> Likewise nine qualities, because
> The lesser and so forth of lesser,
> Middle, and great are separate.

The nine sets of afflictions of Desire have been taught, and likewise **each level** from the first dhyana to the Peak of Existence **has nine kinds of faults** each. **Likewise,** in the same way as the faults, each of the levels also has **nine** sets of **qualities**—the antidotes, the paths of no obstacles—and also the paths of liberation. This is **because the lesser and so forth,** middle, and greater **of lesser**—the lesser, middle, and greater of **middle,** and the lesser, middle, **and** greater of **greater—are** all **separate.** The lesser of lesser path discards the greater of greater afflictions, and the greater of greater path discards the lesser of lesser afflictions. This is because at the very beginning the greater path is impossible and when the greater path arises, the greater afflictions are impossible.

(2) Individual explanations. This has two topics: (a) Seven-timer, and (b) From family to family.

(a) Seven-timer. This has two points.

(i) Ascertaining the seven-timer

> 34ab Those dwelling in result without discarding any
> Through meditation, at most seven times.

Those who **dwell in** a **result without discarding any** of Desire realm's afflictions which are discarded **through meditation,** if they reach the uppermost limit, will be reborn in **at most** seven more lives—they are a **seven-timer.** Since not all stream-enterers are seven-timers, this is the lowest of all results.

Stream-enterers are so called because they have entered the stream of the path to nirvana.

Some proponents of the Great Exposition say that "seven more lifetimes" means seven more births each in the prior state of gods and the prior state of humans plus their between states, for twenty-eight, but as they are similar in having sets of seven, it is called "seven times." It is like for example calling a plant seven leaved, they say. Others say it is seven rebirths combining the rebirths as gods and humans. The noble Master's explanation is consistent with the former.

Well then, does this not contradict *The Sutra of Many Realms*,[270] which states:

> There is no occasion and no opportunity for an individual with excellent view to produce an eighth existence. There is no place for that.

It is not contradictory, because this is about not producing existence in one class of beings in Desire. Otherwise it would be impossible to die and be reborn in all places.[271]

(ii) The family of seven-timers

Seven-timer is the longest, but it is possible to make nirvana manifest before the seventh birth. Additionally, ordinary individuals on the paths of accumulation and joining whose beings have been ripened are also seven-timers.

(b) From family to family

> 34cd Those freed from three or four, with two or three
> More lives, from family to family.

Those stream-enterers who have three causes—in terms of discarding, being **freed from three or four** of the afflictions; in terms of faculties, attainment of their antidote, the undefiled faculties; and in terms of birth, **with two or three more lifetimes** remaining—are stream-enterers who are born **from family to family.**

b. Entering and abiding in once-returner. This has two topics: i. Entering, and ii. Abiding in result.

i. Entering

> 35ab If they have conquered up to five,
> They're also entering the second,

If they, stream-enterers abiding in the distinctive result, **have conquered up to five** sets of the discards of meditation of the Desire realm, **they are also entering the second** result.

ii. Abiding in result. This has two points.

(1) Mere abiding in result

35cd And when the sixth set is extinguished,
At that time, they are a once-returner.

And when the sixth set of Desire's discards of mediation **is extinguished, at that time they** have attained the second result of **once-returner.** It is possible that they will be reborn once more in Desire, but twice or more is impossible.

(2) Distinctive abiding in result

36ab When they have extinguished seven or eight
Classes of faults, one life, one obstacle.

The distinction in terms of abandonment is that **they** who are abiding in the result of once-returner **have extinguished** the **seventh or eighth class of faults** of Desire that are discarded by meditation and have attained the undefiled path that is its antidote. The distinction in terms of birth is that they have one intervening lifetime before attaining nirvana. Alternatively, they have only one aspect of affliction preventing them from attaining the result of nonreturner. Thus for that reason, they are called **one lifetime, one obstacle.**

This is explained to rebut the doubt that the three lesser afflictions together make one take rebirth in Desire, but perhaps only one or two might not have that power to cause rebirth. The reason that one set of afflictions cannot prevent the attainment of the result of once-returner in this lifetime but can prevent the attainment of nonreturner is that for the former one does not need to transcend the Desire realm, but for the latter one does.

c. Entering and abiding in nonreturner. This has two topics: i. Entering, and ii. Abiding in result.

i. Entering

36c They also are entering the third.

They, one-obstacle once-returners who have discarded the seventh and eight sets, **also are entering the third** result of nonreturner.

ii. Abiding in result. This has two topics: (1) Overview, and (2) Individual explanations.

(1) Overview

36d When ninth has perished, nonreturner.

Those who abide in the result of nonreturner, **when** the **ninth** set of discards of meditation of Desire **has perished**, are **nonreturners,** because they will not return to the Desire realm even once. The essence of this result is a combination of the composite ninth liberation and the noncomposite extinction of the discards. The continuum that possesses those two is an individual who abides in the result.

(2) Individual explanations. This has five topics: (a) Explanation of those bound for Form, (b) Explanation of those bound for Formless, (c) Explanation of visible peace, (d) Explaining the many classifications of nonreturners, and (e) Explanation of those made manifest by body.

(a) Explanation of those bound for Form. This has two topics: (i) General classifications, and (ii) Particular explanation of the classifications of those bound for higher.

(i) General classifications

37a–c They pass into nirvana in between,
On birth, with effort, without effort, or
They're bound for higher.

Of the many different nonreturners, **they,** the nonreturners bound for Form, are fivefold. There are those who **pass** beyond sorrow **into nirvana** without remainder **in** the **between** state, those who pass into nirvana **on birth, with effort, without effort; or they are** those who are **bound for the higher.**

The first of these dies here, makes the path manifest in the between state for any of the sixteen abodes other than Great Brahma, and attains the state of arhat. By their dharma nature, they do not remain long in the between state, and as they do not have the afflictions of birth, they immediately enter the state without remainder.

The second passes into nirvana with remainder not long after birth in Form because of effort and the path appearing naturally.

The third makes efforts, but the path does not appear naturally, so they pass into nirvana with effort a somewhat long time after taking birth.

The fourth attains nirvana without effort, but not immediately after birth:

they do not actually make efforts, but the path appears naturally, so they pass into complete nirvana without great efforts.

The fifth does not make efforts and the path does not appear naturally. They do not attain arhat in the lower abodes, but transmigrate to higher realms and pass into nirvana in any one of them.

The first of these has discarded the fetters of birth and so attains nirvana solely without remainder. Those who attain nirvana immediately after birth are not asserted to attain it without remainder, because those who have not attained the highest end of dhyana[272] on the support of a human body on the three continents do not have the power to cast off life, and the karma that makes one remain in the previous state is also very strong.

As for the order they are presented, the sutras explain nirvana without effort before nirvana with effort, and the Master also explains it thus. The Great Exposition, however, says that as their path arises naturally, if they are mentioned first there would be no distinction between them and those who pass into nirvana immediately upon birth, and so list it later.

(ii) Particular explanation of the classifications of those bound for higher. This has two points.

A. Those who will go to Below None

> 37cd If they alternate
> The dhyanas, they are bound for Below None.
>
> 38ab They leap, half leap, or die in all
> The realms,

There are two types of those bound for higher in terms of cause and result. In terms of cause, there are those who train in insight and those who train in tranquility. **If they alternate the** defiled and undefiled **dhyanas** and meditate mixing them, those who train insight **are** ultimately **bound** to go as far as **Below None** in terms of result. **They** are also threefold: **leapers, half leapers, or** those who **die in all the realms.**

A leaper is someone who alternates dhyanas as a human but regresses through the afflictions of the first dhyana and is reborn in Brahma's Abode, et cetera. There they meditate on the great alternation, and so are born in Below None, where they make nirvana manifest.

A half leaper is unable to produce the great alternation in Brahma's Abode and so forth and meditates only on the lesser or medium alternation. Through that they are reborn in Not Great or Without Pain, where they meditate on the great alternation, and then they are born in Below None and make nirvana manifest.

One who dies in all realms is born in all the sixteen abodes, with the exception of Great Brahma, in succession and then makes nirvana manifest.

B. Those who will go to the Peak of Existence

38b and others go to the Peak.

Those **other** than the ones who alternate the dhyanas and go to Below None are those who enjoy tranquility and neither meditate on alternation nor go to Below None. They **go** from the first dhyana through all levels with the exception of the fourth dhyana's pure abodes and ultimately **to the Peak** of Existence. They can also be similar to leapers and so forth. They do go to the Formless realms later, but since they first go to the dhyanas, they are called bound for Form.

Can they pass into nirvana in the meantime? you ask. It is possible. Here Below None and the Peak of Existence are taken as the upper limit, but there can be attainment of nirvana without going to them, similar to the seven-timers, it is explained.

These are nobles who prefer samadhi and train in tranquility. The former who are ultimately bound for Below None prefer full knowing and train in insight.

(b) Explanation of those bound for Formless

38c Four other types are bound for Formless.

Additionally there are **four other types,** different from the previously explained nonreturners, who have attained the mind of Formless in Desire and not regressed. They **are** the four types **bound for Formless.** There is no between state, so they are the four types of nirvana upon birth and so on. It is also suitable to give them the designations of leaper and so on. Thus this is the sixth type of nonreturner.

(c) Explanation of visible peace

38d Another transcends sorrow here.

Another nonreturner, different from those bound for Form and Formless, **transcends sorrow** by attaining nirvana **here** in the Desire realm itself in the very same lifetime as they attain nonreturner. This is the seventh nonreturner, called visible peace.

Thus the five bound for Form can each be born in the sixteen abodes, with the exception of Great Brahma. They have six families,[273] nine detachments,[274] and three faculties. By multiplying these, there are 12,960 bound for Form. The four bound for Formless have four supports, six families, nine detachments, and three faculties, which when multiplied makes 2,592 bound for Formless. Visible peace has nine supports, six families, seventy-two detachments, and three faculties, which when multiplied makes 11,664 who are visible peace.

(d) Explaining the many classifications of nonreturners. This has four topics: (i) Classifying those bound for Form as nine, (ii) Explaining the holy wanderers, (iii) Identifying nobles whose lives have been completely transformed, and (iv) Methods for meditating on alternation of the dhyanas.

(i) Classifying those bound for Form as nine. This has two points.

A. Actual

> 39ab Dividing the three in three more,
> Nine bound for Form can be explained,

Dividing the three nonreturners who achieve nirvana in the between state, upon birth, and bound for higher **in three more** each, the **nine bound for Form can be explained.** The way they are classified is that the first category has those who attain nirvana quickly, not quickly, and after a long time. The second category has those who attain nirvana immediately after birth, with effort, and without effort. The third category has leapers, half-leapers, and those who die in all realms. Alternatively it is explained that it is possible to classify all three as those who attain nirvana quickly, not quickly, and after a long time.

B. Their distinctions

> 39cd Distinguished by their different
> Karma, afflictions, faculties.

The nine are **distinguished by their different karma, afflictions,** and **faculties.** They are individually classified through karma that produces manifest results, that is experienced on rebirth, or that is experienced in other lifetimes; through lesser, medium, and greater afflictions that are harder or easier to discard; and through faculties that are sharp, medium, or dull.

(ii) Explaining the holy wanderers. This has two points.

A. Actual

40ab Without dividing those bound higher,
There are seven holy wanderers,

The seven holy wanderers taught in the sutras are the three who pass into nirvana in the intermediate, three who pass into nirvana upon birth and **without dividing those bound** for the **higher,** one bound for the higher. Thus **there are seven holy wanderers,** it is proposed. Pūrṇavardhana explains that the reason for not dividing those bound for higher is its classifications are so confusing. The Prince explains that it depends upon the disciples' interests.

B. Elaboration

40cd They act on holy, not unholy;
They go without return, so holy.

Why are only these, and not the attached learner stream-enterers and once-returners, presented as holy wanderers? you ask. Between the two types, holy and unholy beings, **they,** the former, only **act upon** virtuous, **holy** conduct, whereas the latter merely do **not** act on the nonvirtuous or **unholy.** This is the meaning of *holy.* **They** are also called holy from **going** to the higher realms **without return** either to that or a lower level. That is the meaning of *wanderer.* **So** therefore only the nonreturners are **holy.** Because the learners who are stream-enterers and once-returners do not fulfill those two criteria, they are not.

However, it says in a sutra:

> What is a holy being? you ask. One who has the correct view of the learners…

Additionally, attached learners have attained vows to never do five misdeeds and have mostly discarded nonvirtue, for which reason they are qualifiedly holy. Here the explanation is for the unqualifiedly holy, so there is no contradiction.

(iii) Identifying nobles whose lives have been completely transformed. This has two points.

A. Actual

41ab Nobles who in Desire transform
Their lives don't go to other realms.

Are there such classifications of the nobles whose lives are completely transformed in Desire? you ask. There are not. Well, what are they like? you ask. **Nobles who in Desire** completely **transform their lives do not go to other realms,** because in that very life they attain the result of nonreturner and then completely pass into nirvana.

Those whose lives are completely transformed in the Form realm can also enter into the Formless realms, such as those bound for higher that are going to the Peak of Existence.

Well then, a sutra says:

> Śakra said, "If after I die here, I am born as a human and attain nirvana, that would be excellent. If I do not attain nirvana then, may I then be reborn in Below None."

What does this mean? The Great Exposition says that Śakra merely does not know the abhidharma and the Teacher did not refute him in order to please him.

B. Dharmas connected with it

41cd Both they and those born higher do not
Regress or refine faculties.

Both they, nonreturners whose lives are completely transformed in Desire, **and those** nobles **born** in the **higher** realms have familiarity with the path through continuous lifetimes and have attained superior supports that cannot regress. For these reasons, they **do not regress,** and because that in itself fully ripens their faculties, they also do not **refine faculties.**

(iv) Methods for meditating on alternation of the dhyanas. This has four points.

A. The alternated dharma

42a They alternate the fourth dhyan first,

Where it says, "If they alternate/The dhyanas, they are bound for Below None..."[275] what is alternated first? you ask. **They alternate** both **the** defiled and undefiled **fourth dhyana first,** because that is the most workable of all levels and because it is the supreme of the easy paths. The dhyanas arise in order from the first up, and the one that is alternated first is the fourth. Later the third, second, and first are also alternated. The support is that at first one can alternate only as a human in one of the three continents, and then later one can alternate in the Form realm as well.

B. The measure of accomplishment in alternating meditation

42b Achieved by alternating moments

Great Expositionists say that right after an undefiled moment a defiled moment is manifested, and then right after that defiled moment another undefiled moment is manifested. In that way alternation is **achieved by alternating** the defiled and undefiled **moments,** like flowers on a garland. The undefiled and defiled moments are like the path of no obstacles, and the third undefiled moment is like the path of liberation, so they say.

The Master says that no one except for the Buddha can alternate three single moments, so alternation is performed by entering the three equipoises in succession for as long as they wish.

C. The reason to perform alternating meditation

42cd In order to take birth and dwell,
Also from fear of the afflictions.

What is the purpose of alternating dhyana? you ask. Nonreturners with sharp faculties alternate **in order** to not pass into nirvana here but **to take birth** in the pure abodes **and** to **dwell** in bliss in the visible.[276] Those with dull faculties **also** meditate **from fear of the afflictions,** in order to keep from regressing from the result by distancing themselves from the samadhi that is concurrent with enjoyment.[277] Those nonreturners with dull faculties alternate for all three reasons (birth, abiding, and fear), the sharp for the former two, dull arhats for the latter two, and sharp arhats for only the second reason.

D. The cause for the pure realms being definitely five

43ab Because there are five types of that,
Only five births in pure abodes.

Why are there only five births in pure abodes? you ask. It is **because there are five types of that** alternating meditation. In the lesser, there is one defiled between two undefiled moments—three minds are manifest. In the middle, it is doubled for six minds; in the greater it is tripled for nine alternations. In the very great another three are added for twelve alternations, and in the extremely great there are fifteen alternations. As results of these types, there are **only five births in** the **pure abodes** from Not Great to Below None out of the power of their defiled aspects

(e) Explanation of those made manifest by body

43cd Nonreturners who have gained cessation
Are called made manifest by body.

Nonreturners who have gained the absorption of **cessation are** explained in the sutras as being **called made manifest by body,** it is proposed. The reason is because like liberation, the peace of cessation arises on the support of a body with no mind, the Great Exposition explains. The Master states that there is mind at the times when one arises from or enters the absorption of cessation.

d. Entering and abiding in arhat. This has three topics: i. Entering, ii. Abiding in result, and iii. The classifications of arhat enterers and abiders.

i. Entering

44. They are entering arhat until
The Peak's eighth blockage is extinguished,
And on ninth's path of no obstacles.
That is the vajra-like samadhi.

They, nonreturners, are in the state of **entering arhat** from the time of abandoning the first dhyana's greater of greater discards **until the Peak** of Existence's **eighth blockage is extinguished** or abandoned, **and** those who are **on** the **ninth** obstacle's **path of no obstacles** that abandons it are also enterers. **That** path of no obstacles **is the vajra-like samadhi,** because like a diamond vajra, it is the greatest of all the paths of no-obstacles, so it has the power to conquer all the kernels.

ii. Abiding in result. This has two topics: (1) Actual, and (2) Supplementary topics.

(1) Actual

> 45ab Attaining its extinction and
> Knowing thereof, nonlearner arhat.

When a noble has **attained its,** the ninth's, **extinction** or abandonment **and** the simultaneously arising **knowing thereof,** the knowing of extinction that is the ninth path of liberation, then that noble is called a **nonlearner,** because there is no more learning for the purpose of another result. For that reason, they have attained the ultimate benefit for themselves, so they are capable of performing benefit for others. Because they are worthy of respect from all ordinary individuals and from attached learners, they are an **arhat.**

(2) Supplementary topics. This has two topics: (a) Analyzing methods of detaching from desire, and (b) Explaining the results of the spiritual way.

(a) Analyzing methods of detaching from desire. This has four topics: (i) An overview of detachment, (ii) How the attainment of removal arises, (iii) Which levels discard attachment, and (iv) Analyzing the focus and aspects of the paths.

(i) An overview of detachment from desire

> 45cd Transworldly brings detachment from
> The Peak. Two kinds detach from others.

When it says, "The path of meditation is twofold,"[278] which learner path detaches one from the desire of which levels? you ask. Only the **transworldly** path **brings detachment from the Peak** of Existence. The worldly paths cannot, for there is nothing worldly above that and because they are not antidotes for their own levels. Both of the **two kinds** of paths—the worldly paths of preparation for higher levels and the transworldly path—can **detach** one **from** levels **other** than the Peak of Existence.

(ii) How the attainment of removal arises. This has two topics: A. Worldly, and B. Transworldly.

A. Worldly

46ab Nobles detached through worldly paths
Attain removal that is twofold.

Well then, what is the distinction between the removal caused by those two paths? you ask. **Noble** stream-enterers who practice tranquility, for example, and become **detached through worldly paths attain removal that is twofold:** the attainment of both worldly and transworldly removal arises.

B. Transworldly. This has two points.

1. Presenting others' propositions

46cd Some say through the transworldly, too,
Since if they forfeit, no afflictions.

Some schools say there can be double attainment through the transworldly paths, too, since if a nonreturner who has been detached only through the distinctive undefiled path from all levels up to Nothingness refines their faculties, they forfeit the distinctive path of the dull and attain the mere result of the sharp, yet they have none of the higher level's afflictions.

2. Refuting them

47ab As when one's freed from half the Peak's
Or born above, they're not possessed.

The Master says that although such nonreturners do not have the attainment of worldly removal, they do not have those levels' afflictions. For example, it is just **as when one** has no worldly attainment of **freedom from half of the Peak** of Existence's afflictions, if one forfeits the transworldly paths by refining faculties, those afflictions would not be possessed. **Or** for example, when an ordinary individual is **born above** in a level of the first dhyana or higher, they forfeit the attainment of removal of the afflictions of Desire but do **not possess** them. Thus the opponents' position is not convincing. Therefore, those nonreturners do not possess the afflictions since there is their nonattainment.

(iii) Which levels discard attachment. This has two topics: A. Not Unable, and B. The other eight levels.

A. Not Unable. This has two points.

1. Actual

47cd Undefiled Not Unable can
Remove attachment to all levels.

Which levels can detach one from the desire for which levels? you ask. The **undefiled** preparations for the first dhyana **Not Unable can remove attachment to all** the higher and lower **levels** from Desire to the Peak of Existence. The other preparations are definitely defiled, so they can only detach one from the desire of lower levels.

2. Dispelling a doubt about its freedom

48a–d In victory over the three levels
The final path of liberation
Comes out of dhyan or preparation.
Above, not from the preparations.

Do all paths of liberation arise out of the preparations, like the paths of no obstacles? you ask. They do not. Well, how is it? you ask. **In victory over the three levels** of Desire and the first two dhyanas, if the faculties are sharp, one can switch feelings and as there is little affection for the preparations, the dhyana or essence of the actual practice arises. **The final path of liberation** thus **comes out of dhyana** or the actual practice. **Or** if the faculties are dull, one cannot switch feelings, so the final path of liberation arises from the essence of the **preparations.**[279]

In victory over the higher levels of the third dhyana and **above,** the preparations and actual practices of the fourth and so forth have compatible feelings. Because of that, and because there is respect for the actual practice, the path of liberation is **not** born **from the** last **preparations for** these higher realms, but from the essence of the actual practice.

B. The other eight levels

48ef Eight nobles are victorious
Over their own and higher levels.

The **eight noble** or undefiled absorptions—the four actual, special samadhi, and first three Formless—**are victorious over their own and higher levels** and remove the desire for those levels. They do not detach one from lower levels, because if one is not detached one cannot manifest the actual practice, so one has already detached from lower levels.

(iv) Analyzing the focus and aspects of the paths. This has two points.

A. Actual

49. The worldly paths of liberation
    And of no obstacles have peace
And coarse, et cetera, as their aspects,
    And as their sphere, the high and low.

Well then, if transcendent paths of no obstacles and liberation have the truths as their focus and also have their aspects, what do the worldly paths have? you ask. **The worldly paths of liberation and of no obstacles have peace,** et cetera, sublimity and emancipation, as aspects, **and coarse, et cetera,** like rigidity and thick walls, **as their aspects,** respectively. **And as their sphere,** the paths of liberation focus on **the higher** level **and** the paths of no obstacles on the **lower** level.

B. What arises immediately following the knowing of extinction

50. From knowing extinction comes the nonarising
    Intelligence if they're unshakable.
If not, then knowing extinction or the view
    Of the nonlearner, which all arhats have.

What cognitions can arise immediately after knowing extinction? you ask.

From knowing extinction comes the nonarising intelligence if they, arhats, **are unshakable** ones who will not regress. **If** they are **not** unshakable, **then** only **knowing extinction or the** correct **view of the nonlearner** arise from the knowing of extinction. As there is no regressing from knowing nonarising, that knowing does not arise in those who are not unshakable. That correct view of the nonlearner is something **which all arhats have** or produce. For even the unshakable, sometimes only the knowing of nonarising arises from the knowing of nonarising, and sometimes the nonlearners' correct view arises.

(b) Explaining the results of the spiritual way. This has two topics: (i) Classifications of the results of the spiritual way, and (ii) Explaining the spiritual way itself.

(i) Classifications of the results of the spiritual way. This has four points: A. Classifying in brief, B. Classifying extensively, C. Establishing the number of the four results, and D. Rebutting that not all are included.

A. Classifying in brief

51ab The spiritual way is the stainless paths;
Results are compound and noncompound.

What are the four results that have been explained? you ask. They are results of the spiritual way. What is the so-called spiritual way? you ask. **The spiritual way is the** eighty-nine **stainless paths** of no obstacles. Its **results are** the same number of **compound** paths of liberation **and noncompound** results of removal. In the sutras, these are said to be fourfold.[280] Because ordinary individuals have not produced lasting peace, they are not ultimately spiritual.

B. Classifying extensively

51cd They're eighty-nine: they are the paths
Of liberation, with extinctions.

They, the spiritual ways and their results, if classified extensively, **are eighty-nine** each. How? you ask. There are the eight classes of discards of seeing for Desire and the higher realms. There are the eighty-one discards of meditation, nine for each of the nine levels, for a total of eighty-nine. The paths of no obstacles that discard these are the ways. **They**, the results of the ways, **are the** eighty-nine composite **paths of liberation,** along **with** the eighty-nine cessations that are the **extinction** of those discards.

C. Establishing the number of the four results

52. There are five reasons they are presented
As four results: relinquishing
The previous path on the result,
Acquiring another, and combining

53ab Extinctions, gaining the eight knowings,
And also gaining sixteen aspects.

Well then, does the Buddha's presenting the results to be four have the fault of being too few? It does not. In any given period, **there are five reasons they are presented as four results.** For that reason, the results are presented as four.

What are the five causes? you ask. They are 1) **relinquishing the previous** entering **path** when abiding **on the result,** 2) **acquiring** the path of abiding in **another** result, **and** 3) **combining extinctions** or discards and acquiring an attainment of removal, and 4) **gaining the** complete set of **eight knowings**—four dharma knowings and four subsequent knowings—**and also** 5) the complete attainment of **gaining** all **sixteen aspects** of impermanence and so forth. In brief, each of the four results has these five causes.

D. Rebutting that not all are included

> 53cd Results of worldly paths are mixed,
> Supported by unstained attainment.

Well then, if only the undefiled paths are spiritual ways, how is it logical for the two results attained by worldly paths to be results of the spiritual way? you ask. Because the two **results**, once-returner and nonreturner, are not attained by the **worldly path** alone but are also attained by the undefiled path, they are results of the spiritual path. With the two types of result for individuals who were previously detached, it is because the previous defiled attainment of removal and the later removal of the undefiled path of seeing **are mixed** into one and attained together. Or if it is a successive result, the abandonment is **supported by** the previous **unstained attainment** of removal.

(ii) Explaining the spiritual way itself. This has three topics: A. Explanation of Brahma's wheel of the path, B. Explaining the path of seeing in particular as the wheel of dharma, and C. How many results of the spiritual way are attained in which realms.

A. Explanation of Brahma's wheel of the path

> 54ab It is Brahma's method, Brahma's wheel,
> Since Brahma is the one who turned it.

It, that which is explained as the spiritual way, itself **is Brahma's method,** because it discards many types of nonvirtuous dharmas of afflictions and misdeeds. The Bhagavan is the Brahma of the unexcelled undefiled path, the method of Brahma, so it is **Brahma's Wheel, since Brahma,** the Bhagavan, **is the one who turned it.** It says in a sutra:

> The Bhagavan is called Brahma. He is also called peaceful and cool.

B. Explaining the path of seeing in particular as the Wheel of Dharma

54cd The Dharma Wheel is the path of seeing,
Since it goes fast, has spokes, et cetera.

What is the essence of the Wheel of Dharma? you ask. The essence of **the Dharma Wheel is the path of seeing, since it** is comparable to the wheel of a wheel-wielding emperor. Just as the precious wheel spins quickly, vanquishes the unvanquished, brings the vanquished to natural ease, flies up to high levels, and then descends, the fifteen moments of the path of seeing **go fast** and so on. They cast off the previous truths and enter the later. The paths of no obstacles vanquish personality view and the other unvanquished afflictions by severing their attainment. The paths of liberation bring the vanquished to natural ease. It flies up to the truths of the higher realms and, focusing on the truths of the lower, descends.

The Venerable Ghoṣaka says that the noble eightfold path is comparable to **spokes, et cetera,** so it is called a wheel. Right view, thought, effort, and mindfulness are like spokes. Right speech, action, and livelihood are like the hub. Right samadhi is like the rim.

Where does the saying that the path of seeing is the Wheel of Dharma come from? you ask. When the path of seeing arose in noble Kauṇḍinya, the yakshas above the earth exclaimed, "The Bhagavan has turned the Wheel of Dharma." This was repeated three times. There is a repetition for the essence of the truth: "These are the noble truths of duḥkha, origin, cessation, and path." There is a repetition for their actions: "I shall respectively know them, discard them, manifest them, and meditate on them." There is a repetition for their completions: "I have known them, discarded them, manifested them, and meditated on them." For each of the twelve aspects, "Upon appropriate attention, the eye, knowledge, awareness, and mind arose," dividing them each into four. If you multiply these, there are twelve repetitions and forty-eight aspects, but they are similar in being sets of three and sets of twelve, so that is what they are called. For example, there are twelve sense bases, but because they are similar in being sets of two, a sutra combines them in a like way:

> Bhikshus, I will show you two. Listen to them well, retain them in your mind, and explain them. What are the two? you ask. The eye and form… [and so forth up to] and mind and dharma.

The three repetitions teach the paths of seeing, meditation, and no more learning respectively, the Great Exposition says. The Master asks, if that is so, how can the path of seeing alone be the Wheel of Dharma, since it does not fulfill all three repetitions? Therefore, that enumeration of dharmas itself is the Wheel of Dharma, and the three repetitions are also the twelve. It is also *turned* because their meaning is taught fully and made understood in another's being.

Alternatively, all noble paths are Wheels of Dharma, and the three repetitions of the twelve aspects as before are from the specifics of repeating the four truths. Turning is producing it in another's being. Where the sutra says, "When the path of seeing arose in Kauṇḍinya, he had turned the Wheel of Dharma..." this means the first turning, it is explained.

C. How many results of the spiritual way are attained in which realms. This has two points.

1. Actual

55a Three gained in Desire, the last in three.

Well, how many results of the spiritual path are attained in which realms? you ask. Of the four results, the **three** results of stream-enterer, once-returner, and nonreturner are **gained in Desire** but not in the other realms. **The last** result is arhat itself, which can be attained **in** all **three** realms.

2. Dispelling a doubt

55b–d Above there is no path of seeing,
As there's no weariness, and scriptures say,
"Commence here; come to the end there."

In that case, it is logical that the results of stream-enterer and once-returner, which are attained by those not detached from Desire, are not attained in the higher realms, but why is not the result of nonreturner attained there? you ask. **Above** the realm of Desire **there is no path of seeing.** Without that, there is no attainment of the result of detached nonreturner. That is the proof.

Why is there no path of seeing there? you ask. In the Formless realm, there is no listening and one does not focus on the lower realms. In the Form realm, one never grows weary because there is attachment to the bliss of absorption and because there is no feeling of suffering, and if **there is no** world-**weariness** one cannot attain the noble path. Thus there is no path of seeing there. This is the logical proof.

And it is also because *The* ***Scripture*** *that Teaches the Ten Groups of Ten*[281] **says,** "The five individuals from those who pass into nirvana in the between state to those bound for higher **commence here** and **come to the end there.**"

In this, "here" is Desire and "there" is the higher realms. "Commence" means to enter the gate to the path of liberation.

iii. The classifications of arhat enterers and abiders. This has two topics: (1) Classifying in six, and (2) Classifying in nine.

(1) Classifying in six. This has two topics: (a) Actual classification, and (b) Methods for refining faculties.

(a) Actual classification. This has two topics: (i) Overview, and (ii) The explanation.

(i) Overview

56a It is said there are six arhats,

The verse says, "From knowing extinction comes the nonarising / Intelligence if they're unshakable… "[282] so are there also classifications of arhats? you ask. There are, because in the sutras **it is said there are six arhats:** the regressed one, the one with volition for death, the protected one, unshaken from abiding, capable to realize, and the unshakable one.

(ii) The explanation. This has five topics: A. Condensing into two, B. The families and results from which one regresses, C. Applying the classification of families to others, D. On which paths faculties can be refined, and E. The complete classification of regression.

A. Condensing into two. This has three points.

1. Teaching the five families as occasional liberation

56a–c five
Of whom come from the convinced through faith.
Their freedom is occasional.

Five of whom, these six arhats except for the unshakable one, **arise out of the convinced through faith** that precedes them. **Their,** those five's, **freedom** or liberation of mind **is occasional,** so it should be known as contingent, because it must always be protected. For just that reason, they are called occasional liberation. They depend upon occasion and are liberation, so they are occasional liberation, like saying butter dish. Because they depend upon specifics of provisions, good health, and place to manifest samadhi, they depend upon occasion.

2. Teaching the sixth family as nonoccasional liberation

56d Unshakable one cannot be shaken,

57ab So that is nonoccasional freedom
Born out of the attained through seeing.

Because the liberation of the **unshakable one** cannot be moved through regression, it **cannot be moved. So** for that reason **that is** called **nonoccasional freedom.** Because it directly manifests the samadhi of all that is desired, it is not dependent upon occasion and is liberation.

Alternatively, of these two results, it is possible for one to regress and impossible for the other, so the one is liberated until another occasion and the other is liberated forever. For this reason they are occasional and nonoccasional liberation.

The unshakable is definitely preceded by attainment through seeing, so it should be known as **born out of the** cause of the **attained through seeing.**

3. Elaboration on these points

57cd Some from the first are in their family,
And some become through purification.

Are these six arhats in one family only from the very first, or can they change later? you ask. Of the six arhats, **some from the** very **first are in their family** of those with volition for death, **and some become** it **through purification** of their faculties from regressed one to one with volition for death. Know that it is thus up to the unshakable one, it is taught.

Regressed ones without a doubt regress from their result. Those with volition for death think, "If I do not kill myself, I will regress from my result, but if I kill myself, I will not regress." Protected ones will regress from the result if they do not protect their mind from desirable things, but if they protect it, they will not regress. Those unshaken from abiding will not regress from visible bliss whether or not they protect their mind, but they do not have the capability to purify their faculties. Those capable to realize will not regress from visible bliss whether or not they protect their mind and have the capability to purify their faculties from dull to sharp. Unshakable ones will not regress from the result whether or not they protect their mind and do not need to purify their faculties, because from the beginning they have been in the family of those with sharp faculties.

B. The families and results from which one regresses

58ab The four regress from family,
Five from result. Not from the first.

Well then, can these all regress from their result or family? you ask. The four—one with volition for death and so on—can completely regress from their family, and the five—regressed one and so on—can regress from the result because they have dull faculties. However, there is not any regression from the first family, because there is no lower family than that, and it is made stable by the learner, nonlearner, worldly, and transworldly paths. There is no regression from the first result, stream-enterer, because the first result is distinguished by the abandonment of discards of seeing, and the discards of seeing have no basis. For that reason, there is no complete regression from the result of stream-enterer.

Well then, why is it possible to regress from the higher three results but not from stream-enterer? you ask. It is because the discards of seeing have no basis since they are rooted in personality view. They engage the basis of the self, and that self does not exist.

The three results delineated by the abandonment of discards of meditation can regress. The afflictions discarded by meditation may have been discarded once, but their object, mere things themselves that are attractive and so forth, do exist, so by that condition it is possible that the afflictions might arise again. For that reason, the discards of meditation do have a basis.

From a sutra:

> Gain and respect make obstacles even for arhats, I declare.

From the *Sutra like a Heap of Ashes:*[283]

> Noble listeners who are well versed, for those who act in this way and dwell in this way, thoughts of nonvirtuous misdeeds will occasionally arise out of weakened mindfulness.

In another sutra, Venerable Godhika also regressed many times, it is explained. These are the reasons, it is said.

The Sutra school says there is no regression from any result attained through an undefiled path, because that conquers afflictions from their root, so it is impossible that the afflictions could arise again. Also, from a sutra:

> Whatever has been discarded through noble full knowing, that has been discarded.

It is possible to regress from what has been attained through a worldly path, because that cannot conquer the seed of afflictions from its roots.

Therefore, the first and last results are definitely only attained by undefiled paths, so regression is impossible, but the middle two both can be attained by either of the paths, so they are possibly both regressable and nonregressable. It is in terms of this that, "I say to the learners, 'Be careful!'" was said, while that was not said to the nonlearners.

Well then, if all arhats thus become only unshakable, why are they explained as six? you ask. They are unshakable from the result only, but they can be divided into six in terms of regression some qualities such as samadhi. This is the intent behind saying that gain and respect make obstacles. The latter two scriptures are intended in terms of learners.

C. Applying the classification of families to others

> 58c Six families of learners and nonnobles.

Do only the arhats have six families, or do others also have six families? you ask. Not only arhats, **there are six families of learners and nonnoble** ordinary individuals in the same way, because the families of arhats precede the attainment of arhat.

D. On which paths faculties can be refined

> 58d There's no refining on the path of seeing.

On the paths other than seeing, the faculties can be refined, but **there is no refining** faculties while **on the path of seeing,** because training is impossible. Some refine their faculties while ordinary individuals. Some refine while they are in the state of interest through faith.

E. The complete classification of regression. This has three points.

1. Actual

59ab Regression from attained, from not attained,
And from enjoyment: these are called three types.

From a sutra:

> I declare that those who have attained bliss in the visible, the four that arise from the superior training in mind, can regress from any one of them, but I declare that in no way at all can one regress from this one unshakable liberation of mind made manifest by body.

So it is said, but how can an unshakable one who abides in bliss in the visible regress from the attainment of the four dhyanas? you ask. In general, there is **regression from** what has been **attained** by losing qualities, regression **from** what has **not** been **attained** by not attaining what is to be attained, **and** regression **from enjoyment** by not manifesting what has been attained. **These are called** the **three types** of regression.

2. Which individuals regress in which way

59cd The Teacher has the last; the unshakable,
The middle, too; and others have the three.

Of those types of regression, **the Teacher,** the Buddha, **has** only **the last,** regression from enjoyment: he possesses all qualities but does not make them all manifest. He does not have the other types of regression. **The unshakable** one **has** that and the **middle,** regression from what is not attained, **too,** because they have not attained the dharmas of the superior individual. **And** because the **other** arhats can also regress from what is attained, they **have the three** regressions. For that reason, because unshakable ones can completely regress from enjoyments, this does not contradict the sutra.

3. The reason there is no death while regressed from result

60ab While they're regressed, they do not die.
They don't do what should not be done.

Is an arhat who has regressed from the result reborn? you ask. There is no such thing, because **while they,** all those who have regressed, **are regressed, they do not die** before they have restored the result. From a sutra:

> Bhikshus, noble listeners who are well-versed might have some slight regression in mindfulness, but that will disappear very quickly and be completely extinguished and completely eliminated.

If that were not so, it would not be logical for their minds to be stable with regards to celibacy. **They,** those who have regressed from a result, **do not do** anything **that should not be done** that is exclusive of the result, such as sexual conduct, just as a great hero who has slipped cannot be struck.

(b) Methods for refining faculties. This has four topics: (i) Refining faculties while on the path, (ii) The essence of those paths, (iii) What the support for refining is, and (iv) On which levels one refines faculties.

(i) Refining faculties while on the path. This has two points.

A. Nonlearner

60cd Nine paths of no obstacles and liberation
For unshakable from strong familiarity

How many paths of no obstacles and liberation are there for refining faculties? you ask. Someone who is capable of realization has **nine paths** each **of no obstacles and liberation** to refine to the state of the **unshakable** one. The reason is **from strong familiarity** with the dull family: they have been accustomed to it for a long time and it has been stabilized by the leaner and nonlearner paths. For example, if someone is accustomed to bad grammar, it is difficult to correct it.

B. Learner.

61a One each for the attained through seeing.

One can train with **one** path of no obstacles and liberation **each** to refine one's faculties from convinced through faith into **the attained through seeing,** because it has not been stabilized by both the learner and nonlearner paths so it is easy to change. Both only have one path of training.

(ii) The essence of those paths

61b They're undefiled,

They, all of those paths of no obstacles and liberation, **are undefiled,** because defiled paths cannot refine the faculties of noble individuals. Ordinary individuals refine their faculties through the defiled aspects of peaceful and coarse.

(iii) What the support for refining is

61b refined by humans.

On what support does one refine faculties? you ask. They are **refined by humans,** not on other supports, because nobles born in higher realms cannot regress, as is said:

> Both they and those born higher do not
> Regress or refine faculties.[284]

Nobles born as gods of Desire develop renunciation for great and fine objects and then see the truth, so their faculties are naturally sharp and they do not regress, the Prince explains.

(iv) On which levels one refines faculties. This has two points.

A. Nonlearner

61c Nonlearners on support of nine,

On what levels can one refine faculties? you ask. **Nonlearners** refine their faculties **on** the **support of nine** levels: Not Unable, special dhyana, the four dhyanas, and the first three Formless levels, because the result of refinement is contained within any one of these nine levels.

B. Learner

61d And learners on six levels, since

62ab Refinement forfeits the result
And progress; the result is gained.

And attached **learners** refine their faculties on Not Unable, and if they are detached, **on** any of the **six levels** of dhyana that they have attained. If they have attained the three levels of Formless, why do they not refine faculties on its support? It is **since refinement** of faculties **forfeits** both **the** mere **result** of the dull **and** the path of higher **progress** even if it has been attained, because **the** mere **result** of sharp faculties **is** always **gained.** Therefore, since there is no mere nonreturner result on the levels of Formless, these levels do not support refinement.

(2) Classifying in nine. This has two points.

(i) Actual classification

> 62c Two buddhas, seven listeners:

There are nine arhats by distinctions in their faculties. The buddha and self-buddha are instances of unshakable only, because these **two buddhas** are both included within those liberated through both parts.[285] The five of regressed one, etc., and the two unshakable ones—those who became unshakable through purification and those who were unshakable from the first—are the **seven listeners.**

(ii) The reason for this classification

> 62d Nine have nine different faculties.

Those **nine** noble individuals are presented as nine since there are dull, medium, and sharp faculties, each of which is divided into three, so they **have nine different faculties.** The regressed one, the one with volition for death, and the protected one are the three lesser, medium, and greater dull faculties. The one unshaken from abiding, the capable to realize, and the unshakable one from purification are the lesser, medium, and greater medium faculties. The unshakable from the first, self-buddha, and buddha are the lesser, medium, and greater sharp faculties.

B. Classifying into seven enumerations

> 63a–c The seven individuals
> Are made by training, faculties,
> Absorption, liberation, both.

Noble individuals can also be classified as seven: followers of faith and dharma, convinced through faith and attained through seeing, made manifest by body, freed through full knowing, and liberated through both aspects. Of these **seven individuals,** the distinctions in the first two **are made by training,** because they trained in the meaning by relying on others from the first or by following the meaning of the sutras and so forth. Interest through faith and attained through seeing are distinguished by dull or sharp faculties, because the **faculties** are dull with strong conviction through faith and sharp through strong full knowing. Made manifest by body is distinguished through **absorption,** because those in that state can make the absorption of cessation manifest through their bodies. Liberated through full knowing is distinguished by **liberation** from the afflictions, and liberated through both aspects is distinguished **both** by liberation from the afflictions and by absorption. The former are liberated from the afflictive obscurations through full knowing and the latter are liberated from those and the obscurations to the absorptions respectively. As they have attained absorption, they are liberated from the obscurations to absorption or liberation.

C. Combining them into six substances. This has two topics: 1. Actual, and 2. Elaboration.

1. Actual

> 63d They're six: the three paths each have two.

In terms of their names, there are seven individuals, but **they are six** in substance. It is like this: **the three paths** of seeing and so forth **each have two** substances. On the path of seeing there are followers of faith and followers of dharma. On the path of meditation, there are convinced through faith and attained through seeing. On the path of no learning, there are occasional and nonoccasional liberation.

To classify them extensively, followers of faith alone can be classified in terms of faculty, family, path, detachment, and support for a total of 147,825 classifications. Followers of dharma and so forth can all also be calculated in the same way. The detailed method of classification appears under this topic in the *Ṭīka.*

2. Elaboration. This has two points.

a. Identifying the two liberations

> 64ab Those who have gained cessation, liberated
> By both; the others by full knowing.

Well then, what are liberation through both aspects and liberation by full knowing? you ask. **Those who have gained** the absorption of **cessation** through the actual dhyana have been **liberated by both,** because they are liberated from afflictive obscurations by full knowing and from the obscurations of liberation by samadhi. The obscurations of liberation are the five obscurations of forgetting the focus, torpor, agitation, effort, and lack of effort. The obscurations of absorption are the inability to produce the actual first dhyana even when detached from the three realms because the mind is not workable and so forth.

The others—those other than those who are liberated through both aspects—are liberated **by full knowing** from the afflictive obscurations only on the basis of the preparation for the first dhyana Not Unable. This is liberation through the aspect of full knowing. These two are known as ornamented arhat and unornamented arhat.

b. Distinctions in perfection of qualities

> 64cd From their absorption, faculties,
> And results, learners are called perfect.
>
> 65a Nonlearners are perfect through two.

From a sutra:

> All those who have discarded five afflictions
> And have the unlosable dharmas are perfect.

What is it that makes learners and nonlearners perfect? you ask. **From their** perfection of **absorption** (attainment of cessation, the dharma which is similar to liberation) the perfection of **faculties** (sharp faculties which cannot be lost through conditions) and the perfection of **results** (nonreturner who has abandoned the five afflictions that lead to the lowest) **learners are called perfect.**

There are four alternatives of **nonlearners** who **are perfect** and those who are not **through** the **two** aspects of faculty and absorption. There is none whose result is not perfect.

III. A specific explanation of paths. This has three topics: 1. Qualities of the different paths, 2. Presentation of the factors of enlightenment, and 3. Liberation attained through the path.

1. Qualities of the different paths. This has two points.

a. Distinctions of the four paths of joining and so forth

65b–d In brief, there are four types of path:
They're called distinctive, liberation,
No obstacles, and path of joining.

Many paths have been explained, but to put it concisely, how many paths are there? you ask. **In brief, there are four types of** all the **paths: they are** the paths **called** the **distinctive** path, the path of **liberation,** the path of **no obstacles, and** the **path of joining.** In the text they are presented from top down, but to explain them in accord with the way they arise, there are the path of joining, which is the cause of the path of no obstacles; the path of no obstacles, which for the most part is what actually discards obscurations; the path of liberation, which is the first arising of freedom from obscurations; and the distinctive path, which is the continuum of liberation following that. To illustrate with the path of seeing, for example, the precursors to realization, eight forbearances, eight knowings, and that which follows subsequent knowing of path are these four respectively.

Why are these called paths? you ask. As one goes from there to nirvana, or one finds nirvana by these, they are called paths.

b. Distinctions of difficult, easy, slow, and fast

66. The dhyanas' paths are easy; those
Of other levels, difficult.
Dull minds are slow to clearly know;
The other ones know clearly quickly.

From a sutra:

> There are paths that are slow to know clearly and difficult. There are paths that are quick to know clearly and difficult. Likewise there are also two that are easy.

What are these? you ask. **The** four **dhyanas' paths are easy** because they are fully embraced by the branches of dhyana and arise naturally through equal parts of tranquility and insight, without need for effort. **Those** paths **of** the **other levels,** Not Unable, special dhyana, and the Formless, are **difficult** because they are not embraced by the branches and must be produced by making efforts at the path as tranquility and insight are not equally balanced. On the first two there is less tranquility, and in Formless there is less insight. Those with **dull minds** or full knowing, whether on an easy or difficult path, are **slow to clearly know** and realize, because they direct themselves toward an object and then come to know it slowly. **The other ones,** those with sharp faculties, **know clearly quickly,** whatever level they are on, because their minds are quick.[286]

2. Presentation of the factors of enlightenment. This has five topics: a. Classifications and groupings of the factors of enlightenment, b. During which periods one meditates on them, c. Examining whether they are defiled or undefiled, d. Examining which levels they are on, and e. When faith from knowing is attained.

a. Classifications and groupings of the factors of enlightenment. This has two topics: i. The result, enlightenment, and ii. The cause, dharmas of the path.

i. The result, enlightenment

67ab Knowing extinction and nonarising
Is enlightenment.

The path is given the name factors of enlightenment. The thirty-seven factors are the four foundations of mindfulness, four complete abandonments, four feet of miracles, five faculties, five powers, seven branches of enlightenment, and the noble eightfold path.[287]

Knowing extinction and nonarising is called **enlightenment** because it is the ultimate abandonment and realization. To classify it in terms of individuals, there are three: the enlightenment of the listeners, that of the self-buddhas, and complete enlightenment.

ii. The cause, dharmas of the path. This has three topics: (1) Explaining the term as an overview, (2) The actual classification and grouping, and (3) The proof of the grouping in ten.

(1) Explaining the term as an overview

67b–d They factor in it,
So the thirty-seven are its factors
In terms of name.

They factor in it, so the thirty-seven of enlightenment, the four foundations of mindfulness, et cetera, **are** called **its,** enlightenment's, **factors.** They are classified **in terms of** their **names.**

(2) The actual classification and grouping

67d In substance, ten:

68a–c Faith, diligence, and mindfulness, full knowing,
Samadhi, equanimity, and joy,
Considering, discipline, and pliancy.

In substance, they are **ten: faith, diligence, and mindfulness, full knowing, samadhi, equanimity, joy, considering, discipline, and pliancy.**

(3) The proof of the grouping in ten. This has two points.

(a) Actual

68d The mindfulness foundations are full knowing.

69ab And diligence, called right endeavor.
The feet of miracles, samadhi.

How are these thirty-seven grouped as ten? you ask. **The** four **mindfulness foundations are full knowing,** because as it is said, "He views the body as the body and rests."[288] **And diligence** is **called right endeavor** or the four complete abandonments, because as it is said, "Arouse interest, make efforts, be diligent." The nature of **the** four **feet of miracles** is **samadhi.** The faculties and powers are, as told by their names, faith, diligence, mindfulness, samadhi, and full knowing in substance.

The four foundations of mindfulness; the branch of enlightenment, the right full discernment of dharmas; and right view are full knowing only. The four right endeavors, the branch of enlightenment right diligence, and right effort are solely diligence. The four feet of miracles, the branch of enlightenment samadhi, and right samadhi are solely samadhi. The branch of enlightenment mindfulness and right mindfulness are solely mindfulness. Three branches of enlightenment, joy, pliancy, and equanimity as well as right thought are indicated by their names. Right speech, right action, and right livelihood are discipline in substance.

(b) Elaboration

69cd The main is mentioned. They are also
All qualities produced by training.

In the explanation of the four foundations of mindfulness and so forth as full knowing, discipline, and samadhi by nature, **the main** substance **is mentioned,** but if their associated factors are included, **they,** the foundations of mindfulness and the others, not including faith and so forth that are attained upon birth, **are also all qualities** of listening, contemplation, and so forth that are **produced by training.**

b. During which periods one meditates on them

70. Respectively, the seven groups
Emerge among beginners and
Precursors to clear realization,
On meditation, and on seeing.

During which stages do which factors of enlightenment emerge? you ask. The Great Exposition says that **respectively these seven groups** of the foundations of mindfulness, complete abandonments, feet of miracles, faculties, powers, branches of enlightenment, and the noble eightfold path, **emerge among beginners, and** on the four **precursors to clear realization, on** the paths of **meditation, and on** the path of **seeing.**[289] Others present the seven branches of enlightenment as the path of seeing and the noble eightfold path as the path of meditation.

c. Examining whether they are defiled or undefiled

71ab The branches of *bodhi* and the path
Are undefiled. The rest are twofold.

How many of the factors of enlightenment are defiled and how many are undefiled? you ask. **The branches of bodhi,** or enlightenment, **and the** eightfold **path are** solely **undefiled** because they are contained within the paths of seeing, meditation, and no learning. **The rest are twofold,** both defiled and undefiled, because they can be present during the equipoise and post-meditation of all five paths.

d. Examining which levels they are on

71cd They all are on the first of dhyanas
And Not Unable, except joy.

72. On second, all except considering,
And on the two, except those two,
And special dhyan. On the three Formless,
Not those, nor factors of discipline.

73ab They're in Desire and on the Peak,
Except enlightenment and path.

How many factors of enlightenment are there on each of the levels? you ask. **They all are** able to be **on** the actual practice of **the first of** the **dhyanas, and** on **Not Unable** there are thirty-six with the **exception** of **joy. On** the **second** dhyana, there are **all, except** for thought, which is **considering,** for thirty-six. **And on the two,** the third and fourth dhyanas, there are thirty-five **except those two,** joy and thought. **And** on the **special dhyana,** too, there are likewise thirty-five. **On the** first **three Formless,** too, there are **not those** two, joy and thought, **nor** are there the three **factors of discipline,** right speech, and so forth, so there may be thirty-two. **They,** twenty-two, **are in Desire and on the Peak, except** for fifteen: the branches of **enlightenment and** the noble eightfold **path.** These may be included in the substance of either the paths of accumulation or the nobles' training or post-meditation.

e. When faith from knowing is attained. This has two topics: i. Actual, and ii. Elaboration.

i. Actual

73cd Seeing three truths gains discipline
And faith in Dharma out of knowing;

74ab In the Buddha and his Sangha, too,
Upon the path's clear realization.

At what point are the factors of enlightenment known to be the attainment of faith from knowing? you ask. Upon **seeing** the **three truths** of suffering, origin, and cessation, one **gains** or attains the **discipline** that pleases the nobles **and faith in** the **Dharma out of knowing.** One attains faith from knowing **in the Buddha and his Sangha** of listeners, **too, upon** the truth of **the path's clear realization.** Faith in these two is faith in the nonlearner dharmas that make the Buddha and faith in the learner dharmas that make the Sangha. The word "too" indicates that faith in discipline and Dharma from knowing are also attained.

ii. Elaboration. This has three points.

(1) Identifying the essence of the Dharma

> 74cd The Dharma is three truths and paths
> Of the self-buddhas and bodhisattvas.

What is thought of as Dharma here? you ask. **The Dharma** in this context **is** the clear realization the first **three truths, and** the learner and nonlearner **paths of the** rhinolike **self-buddhas, and** truth of the path of **bodhisattvas,** and the seventeen antidotes for the Peak of Existence. Within these, there is not a gathering of four bhikshus, so they are not the Sangha. As they hold their own essence, they are dharma.

(2) How many substances it has

> 75ab In terms of substance, they are two:
> They're faith and discipline.

In terms of substance they are two: they are faith in the Three Jewels from knowing, which is **faith, and** discipline that pleases the nobles, which is **discipline.**

(3) Essential features

> 75b They're stainless.

They, the faiths from knowing, **are** solely **stainless.** The meaning of *faith through knowing* is that *knowing* means realizing the truths correctly as they are through full knowing and *faith* means belief.

3. Liberation attained through the path. This has three points: a. Right liberation, b. Right knowing, and c. A particular explanation of liberation.

a. Right liberation. This has two points.

i. The reason liberation is not a learner's branch

75cd They're bound, so liberation is
Not called a learner's branch.

From a sutra:

> The learners possess eight branches. The nonlearners possess ten branches.

Why are learners not explained as having liberation and right knowing? you ask. **They,** the learners, **are bound** by any one of the bonds of the afflictions, **so liberation is not called a learner's branch.** Without liberation, there can hardly be right knowing, because that is inherently the knowing of extinction and nonarising.

ii. Classifications of liberation

75d It's twofold.

76a–c Conquering afflictions, noncompound;
While interest is composite.
That is the branch; two liberations.

It, liberation, **is twofold:** the cessation of **conquering afflictions** is **noncompound, while** the nonlearner's mental factor **interest is composite. That** composite liberation **is the branch** of the path, because it is not logical for a noncomposite to be a branch. Composite liberation itself is said in the sutras to be the **two liberations** of liberation of the mind from desire and liberation of full knowing from ignorance.

Others say that mind and full knowing are also taught as liberation, so therefore liberation can be other things than just interest. It is primarily the liberation itself of the mind from afflictions.

b. Right knowing

76d Enlightenment, as taught, is knowing.

That which is **enlightenment, as** previously **taught, is** known as right **knowing.** It is this: the knowing of extinction and nonarising.

c. A particular explanation of liberation. This has four topics: i. Which paths are freed from obscurations, ii. Which paths discard obscurations, iii. Distinctions of liberation and so forth, and iv. The four possibilities of revulsion and so forth.

i. Which paths are freed from obscurations

77ab Nonlearners' minds are liberated
From obscurations of the future.

What is this mind that is liberated? The **nonlearners' minds are liberated from obscurations of the future,** it is said in the *Treatise.* The nonarising dharma bases and worldly cognitions in their mind are also liberated for the same reason.

ii. Which paths discard obscurations

77cd The path that is about to cease
Fully discards its obscurations.

At what time does the path discard the obscurations of the nonlearner's mind? you ask. **The** present **path that is** directed toward and **about to cease fully discards its** present **obscurations.**

iii. Distinctions of liberation and so forth

78. Just noncompound is called the elements.
Extinction of all attachment is detachment;
Of others, is the element of abandonment;
Of bases, called cessation's element.

Just the liberation taught as **noncomposite is** classified in the sutras as three, **called the elements** of abandonment, detachment, and cessation. The features of these three are that the **extinction of all attachment is** the element of **detachment.** The extinction **of** all **other** afflictions than desire **is the element of abandonment**. The complete extinction of the **bases** of all the afflictions is **called cessation's element.** That basis is the defiled aggregates excluding the afflictions.

iv. The four possibilities of revulsion and so forth

> 79. Forbearance and knowing suffering
> And cause can bring revulsion.
> All that discard remove attachment.
> There are thus four alternatives.

Does a thing by which one develops revulsion free one from desire? you ask. There are four possibilities. The **forbearances and knowings** of **suffering and cause,** the origin, **can bring revulsion,** because they focus on things for which one feels revulsion. Forbearance and knowing of cessation and path do not, because they focus on things that are supremely pleasing. **All** the forbearances and knowings of suffering, origin, cessation, and path **that discard remove attachment,** because they are what discards the afflictions.

Thus there are four alternatives between revulsion and detachment. The first, that which is revulsion but not freeing from desire, is the paths that focus on suffering and origin that do not discard. The second possibility is discarding paths that focus on cessation and path. The third is discarding paths that focus on suffering and origin. The fourth is paths other than discarding paths that focus on cessation and path.

Second, presenting the area's name

> This completes the sixth area called "Teachings on the Paths and Individuals" from the *Verses of the Treasury of Abhidharma.*

This completes the explanation of **the sixth area called "Teachings on the Paths and Individuals" from** *The Explanation of* **the** ***"Verses of the Treasury of Abhidharma"*** called *The Essence of the Ocean of Abhidharma, The Words of Those who Know and Love, Explaining the Youthful Play, Opening the Eyes of Dharma, The Chariot of Easy Practice.*

A few words here:

The only refuge of all those who yearn for peace,
Is the supreme protector, the great and perfect Buddha.
I followed with respect the Glorious Jewel,
Disciple of the Shakyan King,[290] and Vajrakīrti,

The great master, and received all levels of the teachings.
I became unafraid to explain the meaning as it is
Of the three baskets and four classes of tantras.
In this, the Buddha's teachings were exalted.

At that time I awakened to all knowledge,
And so while dwelling in White Cave I wrote
This treasury on paths and individuals,
The sixth part of my explanation of the *Treasury.*

The stainless waxing moon of virtue
Destroys the darkness that besmirches
The Victor's teachings in this Land of Snow.
May the teachings of the Karma Kagyu blaze!

SEVENTH AREA

Teachings on Wisdom

On my mind's clean white *dukūla*[291] cloth, the many hues
Of all dharmas I distinguish clearly are so bright!
At that time if I do not forget my glorious lama,
Youthful Manju, then how could I wander in samsara?

The Ganges' current, explanations
Of the paths of three baskets, washes
Away all stains of faulty views.
This is the cleanser I release.

The seventh area, the "Teachings on Wisdom," has an explanation of the text of the area and a presentation of the area's name. The explanation of the text of the area has four topics: I. The knowings, II. Explanation of possession, III. How the knowings are attained, and IV. Qualities of the knowings.

I. The knowings. This has three topics: A. Distinctions between forbearances, knowings, and views, B. Identifying the ten knowings, and C. Examining distinctions among the knowings.

A. Distinctions between forbearances, knowings, and views. This has two points.

1. Undefiled

1a–c Stainless forbearances aren't knowing. Minds
Of extinction, nonarising are not views.
The other noble minds than those are both.

In the abhidharma, the terms *forbearance, knowing, correct view,* and *right knowing* all appear. Is there anything that is a forbearance but not a knowing, or right knowing but not a view? you ask.

The eight **stainless forbearances** of the path of seeing **are** views but **not knowing,** because knowing is inherently recognition, but the forbearances are paths of no obstacles, so at that point the kernels they discard have not been abandoned and there is doubt with regard to their object. Because they are inherently right thought, they are view. Saying they are not knowing does not mean that they are not cognition but means that they are not included among the ten knowings.

Although the undefiled forbearances are views but not knowing, in contrast the **minds** or knowings **of extinction** and **nonarising** have no right thought and do not have the intention to thoroughly investigate, so they **are** knowings but **not views.**

The undefiled full knowing of **other noble minds than those,** the undefiled forbearances and the knowings of extinction and nonarising, **are both** view and knowing, because they are right consideration and complete recognition, so they have discarded doubt.

2. Defiled

1d Others are knowing. Six are views as well.

Those which are **other** than the undefiled, all that are defiled worldly full knowing, **are knowing.** This relative knowing does not have to be solely free of doubt. **Six** of these—personality view and the rest of the five views and the correct worldly view—are not only knowing, they **are views as well.** In particular, some full knowings of the precursors to clear realization are all three,[292] because they are an instance of the correct worldly view and are also forbearances that are compatible with seeing the truth. Other worldly knowings are knowing but not view.

B. Identifying the ten knowings. This has two topics: 1. The actual classification, and 2. Teaching knowing others' minds in particular.

1. The actual classification. This has two topics: a. Overview, and b. An explanation.

a. Overview

2. The knowings are defiled and undefiled.
 The first is called the relative.
Two types of undefiled are only
 The subsequent and dharma knowings.

How many knowings contain them all? you ask. They are contained in ten: 1) dharma knowing, 2) subsequent knowing, 3) relative knowing, 4) knowing others' minds, 5–8) knowing of the four truths, and 9–10) knowing extinction and nonarising. Knowing death, rebirth, individuals, samsara, and so forth are all contained within just these.

In brief, there are **the** two **knowings,** which **are defiled** knowing **and undefiled** knowing. **The first** can be perception of either general or self-characteristics but is mostly perception of relative things such as vases, blankets, men, women, and so forth, so it **is** labeled with the name of the majority of its objects and **called the relative** knowing. To condense the undefiled, there are **two types of undefiled** as well: they **are only the subsequent and dharma knowings.** Since there is no undefiled knowing not comprised within those two, the word "only" is said.

b. An explanation

3. All is the object of the relative.
 The sphere of dharma is suffering, et cetera,
Of Desire realm. The sphere of subsequent
 Is suffering, et cetera, of the higher.

4. Through the distinctions of the truths,
 Just these are four—these four are knowing
Of nonarising and extinction.
 When these two first arise, they are

5ab Subsequent knowing of suffering
 And cause. Four know another's mind.

Well then, what are the objects of these knowings? you ask. **All** dharmas, whether compound or noncompound, **are the object of the relative** knowing. **The sphere of dharma** knowing **is** the four truths of **suffering, et cetera, of** the **Desire realm. The sphere of subsequent** knowing **is** the four truths of **suffering, et cetera, of the higher** realms.

Through the distinctions of the four **truths, just these,** dharma and subsequent knowing, **are** the **four** knowings of suffering, origin, cessation, and path because they focus on suffering and so on. **These four** from suffering to path, when they are dharma and subsequent knowing that is not by nature view, **are knowing of nonarising and** knowing **extinction. When these two first arise, they are the subsequent knowing of suffering and cause,** origin, because without a doubt they focus on the aspects of subsequent knowing of suffering and origin that are on the Peak of Existence.

Well, does not vajra-like samadhi have the same focus as those two? you ask. If vajra-like samadhi focuses on suffering or origin, it is the same, but if it focuses on cessation or path, it does not have the same focus. For example, when struck by a poisoned arrow, the deadly poison spreads to all parts of the body, but at the time of death it collects in the area of the wound only and is not in the other parts.

Four knowings, dharma, subsequent, path, and relative knowing, can **know another's mind,** because that is the nature of those knowings. To speak similarly of the other knowings:

> Dharma and subsequent are known by seven each.
> The relative by two, and the three truths
> By four each. Knowing path is by five.
> Extinction, nonarising are each known by six.

2. Teaching knowing others' minds in particular. This has two topics: a. Features of knowing others' minds, and b. The distinction between knowing extinction and knowing nonarising.

a. Features of knowing others' minds. This has two points.

i. General teaching

> 5cd That can't know higher levels, faculties,
> Or individuals, destroyed, unborn.

Knowing others' minds should be recognized in this way: **That,** knowing others' minds, knows minds that are equal or inferior to it. A superior mind is not the object of the inferior. For that reason the mind of a lower level **cannot know** the minds of **higher levels** that surpass it; the mind of dull faculties, interest through faith, cannot know higher **faculties** that surpass it, **or** an inferior individual can not know the minds of superior **individuals** that surpass them, because these all surpass what that mind can know. Because it is a subject that perceives the present mind only, it does not know the **destroyed** past or **unborn** future.

ii. During the time of the path

> 6. Dharma and subsequent don't know
> Each other. Listeners know two
> Moments of seeing. Rhinos, three.
> The Buddha without training, all.

The knowing of others' minds that is **dharma** mind or **subsequent** mind knows only those minds of its own class. Those two knowings of mind **do not** mutually **know each other**, because they focus on the separate antidotes of the Desire and the higher realms. It is like looking at the ground or looking at the sky.

There is no knowing of others' minds on the path of seeing, but that path can be its object. If they train, those **listeners** who can know others' minds and wish to know the path of seeing can **know** through knowing others' minds **two moments of seeing:** forbearance of dharma knowing of suffering and dharma knowing. As far as focusing on subsequent knowing, because it is something that is accomplished through the effort of other trainings, subsequent knowing is not known.

Because their faculties are sharper, the **rhino**like self-buddhas[293] have at that point completed two trainings and can know **three** moments: the first two moments of dharma forbearance of suffering and dharma knowing plus the eighth moment of subsequent knowing of origin. Some say they can know the first two and the fifteenth moment: in either case, they only know three moments and not more. **The buddha, without** any **training,** knows **all** fifteen moments of the path of seeing.

b. The distinction between knowing extinction and knowing nonarising

> 7. Knowing extinction is recognizing
> The truths are fully known, et cetera.
> "There is no more to know," et cetera,
> Is nonarising mind, it's said.

What is the distinction between knowing extinction and knowing nonarising?

you ask. The Kashmiris say the two are similar during equipoise, but the distinction is in terms of the recognition by post-meditation cognitions. **Knowing extinction is** knowing that **recognizes** for each of **the truths** of suffering and so forth, "I have **fully known** suffering...," **et cetera:** "I have discarded the origin. I have made cessation manifest. I have meditated on the path." Saying "I have completely known suffering: **there is no more to know," et cetera** up to "I have completely meditated on the path; there is no more to meditate on" **is** the **nonarising mind** or knowing, **it is said.**

Unlike the Kashmiris who assert that undefiled equipoise can only have sixteen aspects, the Aparāntakas assert twenty-eight undefiled aspects, so they say this difference is known by equipoise as well as post-meditation.

C. Examining distinctions among the knowings. This has four topics: 1. Distinctions of the ten knowings, 2. Distinctions of antidote, 3. Distinctions of aspect, and 4. Explaining other distinctions.

1. Distinctions of the ten knowings

8. From nature, antidote, or aspects,
Or aspects and the sphere, or training,
Or its work being done, or from
Development of cause, there are ten.

If there are the three knowings—dharma, subsequent, and relative—why are they presented as ten? you ask. The ten knowings are presented because of seven causes, it is heard. Relative knowing is presented **from** its **nature** and essence because it does not know the ultimate. Dharma and subsequent knowing are presented as the **antidote**, because they are antidotes for Desire and the higher realms. **Or** knowing suffering and origin are presented from their **aspects,** because their focuses are not separate. **Or** knowing cessation and path are presented from **aspects and the** focus, because they have separate aspects and **sphere. Or** knowing others' minds is presented from **training**: it is not as if it does not know mental factors of course, but because it arises from training in order to know others' minds, it is called knowing others' minds. **Or** knowing extinction is presented **from its work being done** because at first it arises from the cause of its action being completed.[294] Knowing nonarising comes from the **development of** its **cause,** because it has all undefiled knowings as its cause. Thus **there are** determined to be **ten** knowings.

2. Distinctions of antidote

9. The dharma knowings of cessation
And path on meditation's path
Are antidotes for the three realms.
The subsequent is not Desire's.

Dharma knowing is explained as the Desire realm's antidote, and subsequent knowing as the higher realms' antidote. The distinction between them is this: **The dharma knowings of cessation and path on meditation's path** first achieve victory over Desire. Because it then is possible that very continuum of the path of familiarization will also achieve victory over the higher realms, they can also **be antidotes for the three realms.**

The subsequent cannot possibly **be** the **Desire** realm's antidote, because subsequent knowing only arises after dharma knowing, so when it arises, dharma knowing has already achieved victory.

Thus if it is logical for subsequent knowing not to be explained as the antidote for the Desire, why is dharma knowing not taught as the antidote for the higher? you ask. That is because it is impossible for all dharma knowing on the path of seeing and dharma knowing of suffering and origin on the path of meditation to act as the antidote for the higher realms.

3. Distinctions of aspect. This has two topics: a. The aspects of each knowing, and b. The essence of each aspect.

a. The aspects of each knowing. This has five topics: i. Through which aspects dharma knowing and subsequent knowing engage, ii. Relative knowing, iii. The knowings of the four truths, iv. Knowing others' minds, and v. Through which aspects knowing of extinction and nonarising engage.

i. Through which aspects dharma knowing and subsequent knowing engage

10ab The subsequent and dharma knowings
Have sixteen aspects.

From those ten knowings, **the subsequent and dharma knowings have sixteen aspects,** because the four truths each have four aspects. The sixteen aspects will be explained below.[295]

ii. Relative knowing

10bc Relative
Knowing is like, or different, too.

Relative knowing is like dharma and subsequent knowing, with sixteen aspects on warmth, peak, and so forth, **or** it is **different** with aspects of revulsion, the in-breath and out-breath, loving-kindness, and so forth, **too,** because it perceives the specific and general characteristics of all dharmas. The phrase "and so forth" includes things which are not specific or general characteristics, including commands such as "Make!" "Drink!" or "Go!" or things such as vases and blankets.

iii. The knowings of the four truths

10d They have four from aspects of their truths.

They, the knowings of the four truths, **have four** aspects each **from** the **aspects of their** own individual **truths.**

iv. Knowing others' minds. This has two points.

(1) How the stainless engage

11ab Undefiled knowing others' minds
Is like that, too.

Undefiled knowing others' minds is like that—knowing path—**too,** in having the aspects of the truth of the path as its aspects, because it is also knowing of the truth of path.

(2) How the stained engage

11b–d For stained, the aspects
Are the specifics of the known.
The sphere of each is a single substance.

For stained knowing of minds, the perceived **aspects are the specific** characteristics **of the known,** mind and mental factors. Both the stained and the stainless cannot perceive the two substances of mind and mental factors simultaneously, so for that reason **the sphere of each is a single substance.**

v. Through which aspects knowing of extinction and nonarising engage

12ab The remaining possess fourteen aspects,
Except for empty and for selfless.

The two **remaining** from the eight previously explained, knowing extinction and knowing nonarising, **possess fourteen aspects** of impermanence and so forth, **except for empty and for selfless.** They do not have the aspects of empty or selfless because these knowings designate the self in conventional labels, thinking, "I have extinguished rebirth. I shall know no existence beyond this one." However, when meditating on the empty and selfless, such conventional designations become illogical through the power of that meditation.

b. The essence of each aspect. This has four points: i. Examining whether the undefiled have specific characteristics as aspects, ii. Proving that the sixteen aspects are substantial, iii. The essence of the aspects, and iv. The distinction between perceiver and perceived.

i. Examining whether the undefiled have specific characteristics as aspects. This has two points.

(1) Own tradition

12c Unstained: no more than sixteen aspects.

Do the undefiled knowings have self-characteristics as aspects? you ask. The Kashmiris propose that the **unstained** have **no more than** the **sixteen aspects** of impermanence and so on.

(2) Other tradition

12d But others say there are, from the *Treatise.*

But others, the Aparāntakas, **say** that **there are** also aspects of specific characteristics. The reason comes **from the *Treatise, Jñānaprasthāna:***

> Does the mind that does not possess know dharmas? you ask. It knows. In terms of being produced logically, it knows impermanence, suffering, empty, selflessness, cause, origin, fully arising, condition, that this is the place, and that this is the basis.[296]

ii. Proving that the sixteen aspects are substantial

13a In substance, there are sixteen aspects.

The Aparāntakas say that **in substance** there are the four aspects of suffering and one each for origin, cessation, and path, for a total of seven aspects. The others are synonyms. The Great Exposition proposes that **there are sixteen** substantially established **aspects.**

The aspects of the truth of suffering are as follows: because it depends upon conditions, *impermanent.* Because it is inherently harmful, *suffering.* As it is incompatible with the view of "mine," *empty.* As it is incompatible with viewing "me," *selfless.*

The aspects of the truth of origin are: In the manner of a seed, *cause.* In the manner of arising, *origin.* In the manner of connection, *production.* Through the meaning of manifestly establishing, *condition.*

The aspects of the truth of cessation are: Because the aggregates have been destroyed, *cessation.* Because the three fires[297] are pacified, *peace.* Because there is no hostility, *sublime.* Because it is free of all faults, *emancipation.*

The aspects of the truth of path are: Through the meaning of going, *path.* Because it has proof, *reasoning.* Through the meaning of completely accomplishing, *accomplishing.* Because it makes one transcend utterly and completely, *deliverance.*

iii. The essence of the aspects

13b An aspect is full knowing.

What is a so-called aspect itself? you ask. The Sutra school posits that an aspect is cognition's manner of perception, but Great Exposition proposes that **an aspect is full knowing.**[298]

iv. The distinction between perceiver and perceived

13b–d That
And that with focus can perceive.
All that exists is the perceived.

Well then, does only full knowing perceive? you ask. No. **That** full knowing **and that with** a **focus can perceive. All that exists** as knowable phenomena **is** what is **perceived.** Thus full knowing is proposed to be all three—full knowing, perceiver and perceived. All other dharmas with focus are perceiver and perceived, and all that does not have a focus is only perceived.

4. Explaining other distinctions of the knowings. This has five topics: a. Distinctions of essence, b. Distinctions of level, c. Distinctions of support, d. Distinctions of foundations of mindfulness, and e. Distinctions of focus.

a. Distinctions of essence

14a The first is threefold. Others, virtue.

Of the ten knowings, **the first,** relative knowing, **is threefold**—virtuous, nonvirtuous, and neutral—and the **other** nine are **virtuous** only.

b. Distinctions of level

14b–d The first is on all of the levels.
The one called dharma is on six.
The subsequent on nine. Six likewise.

15a Knowing others' minds is on four dhyanas.

For distinctions of levels, **the first** of the knowings **is on all the levels** from Desire to the Peak of Existence. The **one called dharma** knowing **is on** only the **six** levels of dhyana.[299] As that is the antidote for Desire in particular, it is not on the Formless levels. **The subsequent** knowing is **on** any of the **nine** undefiled levels.[300] The portion of **six**—knowing the four truths, knowing extinction, and nonarising—that is included within subsequent knowing is **likewise** also on nine. The portion included within dharma knowing is on six levels. **Knowing others' minds is** difficult to produce, so only the easy paths of the actual practices of the **four dhyanas** support it.

c. Distinctions of support

15b–d That has Desire and Form as support,
And dharma has support of Desire.
The others, on three realms' support.

What supports are they on? you ask. **That** knowing others' minds is supported only by the dhyanas, so it definitely **has Desire** and **Form as** its bodily **support. And dharma** knowing, as it is primarily weariness with Desire, **has** the **support of Desire** only. The higher two realms are detached from Desire, so they are no longer weary of it. **The** eight knowings **other** than those two have any of the **three realms** as **support.**

d. Distinctions of foundations of mindfulness

16ac Cessation mind is one foundation
Of mindfulness, and knowing minds
Is three. Those which remain are four.

Well then, which of the foundations of mindfulness do these knowings have as their essence? you ask. The essence of **cessation mind** focuses only on noncomposites, so it **is** only the **one foundation of mindfulness** of dharmas. **And** because minds that **know** others' **minds** only perceive concurrences,[301] they **are** the **three** foundations other than mindfulness of body. **Those** eight knowings **which remain are** any of the **four** foundations of mindfulness.

e. Distinctions of focus. This has three points.

i. How many knowings does each knowing have as its focus.

16d Nine are the sphere of dharma mind.

17a–c Nine of the path and subsequent mind;
And two of suffering and cause.
Ten are of four, and none of one.

How many knowings are the focus of each knowing? you ask. **Nine** knowings **are the sphere of dharma mind**, because relative knowing is the object of dharma knowing of suffering and origin, and the eight undefiled except for subsequent knowing are the object of dharma knowing of path. **Nine** knowings other than relative knowing are the sphere **of the** knowing of **path**, because that only takes an undefiled object. **And** the object of **subsequent** knowing is the nine other than dharma knowing, as above. **And two**, relative knowing and defiled knowing of others' minds, **are** the object **of** both knowing **suffering and** knowing its **cause**, origin. All **ten** knowings in order **are** the object **of four** knowings—relative, others' minds, extinction, and nonarising. This is because the object of relative knowing is all dharmas, the object of knowing others' minds is all concurrences, and knowing extinction and nonarising are partially dharma knowing and partially subsequent knowing. **And none** of the knowings at all are the object **of** the **one** knowing cessation, because that does not know composites and focuses on noncomposites.

ii. Which subjects focus on many dharmas

17d There are ten dharmas to apply.

18ab The three realms, and the stainless, and
The noncompound are twofold each.

There are ten dharmas into which knowables can be divided. **To** know how many are the object of each of the knowings, **apply** them. The way the dharmas are divided into ten is that **the** defiled **three realms and the stainless** dharmas are each divided into concurrent and not concurrent, **and the noncompound** has virtue and neutral, so they **are twofold each** or divided in two.

iii. How much one knowing knows

18cd Just relative knows what is outside
Its own collection to be selfless.

Can one knowing know all dharmas? you ask. It cannot. However, **just** the **relative** knowing **knows** all dharmas **that are outside its own collection to be selfless.** Here, its "own collection" is its essence and the dharmas that are simultaneous with it. Because their object is separate from their subject, because they are separate from their focus, and because they are extremely close, these do not see each other, just as the eye cannot perceive the eyebrows.

II. Explanation of possession

19. On the first of undefiled moments,
Those who are attached possess one knowing.
On second, three. After on each
Of four moments they have another.

Which individuals possess how many knowings? you ask. An ordinary individual who is attached possesses relative knowing alone, and if detached they also possess defiled knowing of mind.

Of nobles who are **on the first of** the **undefiled moments, those who are attached possess** the **one** relative **knowing. On** the **second** moment dharma knowing and duḥkha knowing are added, so they have **three. After** that **on each of four moments**, the fourth, sixth, tenth, and fourteenth, **they have another** knowing—subsequent knowing, knowing of origin, knowing of cessation, and knowing of path respectively. On the path of meditation, they possess those seven.

If they are detached, knowing minds is added to all of these: they would possess two on the first moment and so on up to eight on the path of meditation. A nonlearner possesses the first nine if of dull faculties, and all ten if sharp.

III. How the knowings are attained. This has four topics: 1. Attained during the path of seeing, 2. Attained on other paths, 3. How many are attained from each path, and 4. Classifications of their attainment.

1. Attained during the path of seeing

20. As they arise on the path of seeing,
    Future forbearances and knowings
Like them are gained. On that upon
    Three subsequent, the relative, too.

21. Thus they are called clear realization's end.
    They are nonarising dharmas. On its own
And lower levels. Cessation's is the last.
    Their own truths' aspects. Born of effort.

At what points are how many knowings attained? you ask. **As they,** the eight forbearance and seven knowings, **arise on the path of seeing,** when they arise the **future** similar **forbearances and knowings like them are gained** in their own time. Thus when dharma forbearance of duḥkha arises, the attainment of a future dharma forbearance with similar focus and aspects arises and so forth. For the attached, the level is only Not Unable, **and** for those detached, any of the six levels. One attains the forbearance of two times for the level of one's bodily support. One attains only the future forbearance of other levels, but it does not become manifest because multiple paths of seeing do not arise.

On that path of seeing itself **upon three subsequent** knowings of suffering, origin, and cessation, **the relative** knowing is attained, **too.** It is not attained on dharma knowing, because the truth has not been clearly realized to its full extent. Why not on subsequent knowing of path? you ask. The truth of the path itself is not clearly realized by the previous worldly path, and the truth has not been clearly realized to its full extent. **Thus they**—the relative knowings that arise out of the subsequent knowings of suffering, origin, and cessation—**are called** "arisen from **clear realization's end**" because they arise after the clear realization of each truth. Well, do not these relative knowings that are arisen from the end of clear realization sometimes become manifest? you ask. Because **they are nonarising dharmas,** they do not become manifest.

The relative knowings of how many levels are attained? you ask. Relative knowings are attained **on** the level that is **its,** the path of seeing's, **own and** on

lower levels. If the path of seeing is on Not Unable, relative knowings of that level and the lower level of Desire are attained.

The relative knowing arisen from the end of clear realization of **cessation is the last** of the four foundations of mindfulness, mindfulness of dharmas. The other two are all are foundations of mindfulness. These relative knowings arisen from the end of clear realization have **their own truth's aspects,** attained on the level of the clear realization of that truth. Because they are attained by the path of seeing, they are **born of effort,** not through detachment.

2. Attained on other paths. This has two topics: a. Explaining those with different counts individually, and b. Explaining those similar counts together.

a. Explaining those with different counts individually. This has two topics: i. How many are attained on the path of learning, and ii. How many are attained on the path of no learning.

i. How many are attained on the path of learning. This has five topics: (1) How many are attained on the sixteenth moment, (2) On most of the path of meditation, (3) On the eight paths of liberation from the Peak of Existence, (4) On the learner's paths of liberation when purifying faculties, and (5) On the paths of no obstacles of the Peak of Existence.

(1) How many are attained on the sixteenth moment. This has two points.

(a) Attached

22a Attached gain six on the sixteenth.

Those who are **attached** to Desire **gain six** knowings—the four knowings of the four truths, dharma knowing, and subsequent knowing—when abiding **on the sixteenth** moment, subsequent knowing of path. This is knowing that is liberated from discards of seeing, but it is not liberated from discards of meditation because it is mere abiding in the result. Because subsequent knowing of path is by nature both path knowing and subsequent knowing, those are attained in the present, but the four other knowings are attained in the future only. Because these individuals are attached, it is on the level of Not Unable. It is produced by completing seeing, so it is attained from the expansion of a cause of similar status.

They do not attain knowing others' minds because they are attached to

Desire. Relative knowing is not attained because "what has already been acquired is not acquired": it has already been acquired. Knowing extinction and nonarising are not acquired because they are learners.

(b) Detached

22b Those detached from Desire gain seven.

Those detached from the **Desire realm gain seven:** knowing others' minds in addition to the previous six.

(2) How many are attained on most of the path of meditation. This has two points.

(a) Attached

22cd Later on paths of meditation,
The attached attain the seven knowings.

Later, after the sixteenth moment, the subsequent knowing of path, **on** the **paths of meditation**—all **the** paths of joining, no obstacles, liberation, and distinction—those **attached** to Desire **attain the seven knowings:** dharma knowing, subsequent knowing, four knowings of four truths, and relative knowing. If it is a worldly path of meditation that views the aspects of peaceful and coarse, the present relative knowing arises. However if the path is transworldly, since subsequent knowing is not the antidote for Desire but dharma knowing is, dharma knowing and knowing of one of the four truths arises in the present. The remaining knowings are attained in the future, because they develop the cause of same status of their own class. As the individuals are attached and learners, the other three knowings are not attained.

(b) Detached

23a–c In victory over seven levels,
Gaining clairvoyance and unshakable,
Paths of no obstacles for alternating.

In the **victory over** the **seven levels** of the four dhyanas and three Formless that detaches one from desire, and in **gaining** the five **clairvoyances** other than extinction of defilements, learners attain seven knowings: dharma knowing, subsequent knowing, knowings of the four truths, and relative knowing.

And on realizing and attaining the status of **unshakable**, seven knowings, the six undefiled that go with all and knowing extinction, are attained. Relative knowing, knowing others' minds, and knowing nonarising are not attained. The first is not attained because the paths of refining are always undefiled and there is no cause to attain anything else. The latter two are not attained because they are paths of liberation.

On any of the **paths of no obstacles for the alternating** meditation as well, the six undefiled and relative knowing are attained. The other three are not attained because these are not nonlearner, so the latter two are not attained, and it is not a path of liberation, so knowing others' minds is not attained.

(3) How many are attained on the eight paths of liberation from the Peak of Existence

23d Eight paths of liberation from the highest.

On the first **eight paths of liberation** that vanquish the level of **the** Peak of Existence that is **higher** than the other seven levels, seven knowings are attained: the six undefiled and knowing others' minds.

(4) How many are attained on the learner's paths of liberation when purifying faculties

24a–c On learner's liberation of refining,
One gains six or else seven knowings, or…
Six on paths of no obstacles.

On attached **learner's** paths of **liberation of refining** faculties, **one gains six** knowings: dharma knowing, subsequent knowing, knowing suffering, origin, cessation, and path. **Or else** if detached, knowing others' minds is added for a total of **seven knowings** attained. The word "**or**" indicates that there is another tradition that says that both attached and detached also attain relative knowing. On the paths of joining, they both also attain relative knowing.

Whether the learner is attached or detached, **six** knowings are attained as above **on paths of no obstacles** for refining faculties. Relative knowing is not attained because this is similar to the path of seeing. Knowing others' minds is also not attained, because it is blocked on all paths of no obstacles. Why is it blocked? you ask. Because it is not an antidote.

(5) How many are attained on the paths of no obstacles of the Peak of Existence

24d Likewise on vanquishing the Peak.

As with the previous, **likewise on** the path of no obstacles that **vanquishes the Peak** of Existence, only those six are attained.

ii. How many are attained on the path of no learning. This has three points.

(1) Dull faculties

25a On knowing extinction, there are nine.

Upon attaining **knowing extinction, there are nine** knowings that those with dull faculties attain. Knowing nonarising is excluded because it is possible they might regress.

(2) Sharp faculties

25b Unshakable attains ten knowings,

The **unshakable** one, who also attains the knowing of nonarising, **attains ten knowings.**

(3) How many are attained on paths of refining faculties

25c Refining there, on the last as well.

When **refining there,** to unshakable, all ten are attained **on the last** path of freedom **as well.**

b. Explaining those similar counts together

25d Eight are attained on those not mentioned.

Eight knowings excluding knowing extinction and nonarising **are attained on those** remaining paths that were **not** previously **mentioned**—the nine paths of liberation from desire for Desire, the paths of liberation from desire for seven levels, the paths of liberation for the five clairvoyances and the meditation of alternating the dhyanas, the first eight paths of liberation that create realization of the unshakable, paths of joining for detachment, and the distinctive paths.

On the nonlearners' paths of joining, liberation, and distinction for clairvoyance, occasional nonlearners attain nine knowings excluding knowing nonarising. Nonoccasional nonlearners attain all ten. On the paths of no-obstacles for the clairvoyances and alternating meditation, the occasional attain the eight that exclude knowing of nonarising and of others' minds. The nonoccasional attain the nine excluding the knowing of nonarising.

3. How many are attained from each path

26. One gains them where one is detached,
    On which is gained, and lower, too.
    On knowing extinction, defiled, too; all levels.
    Those previously gained are not attained.

On which paths are how many levels' knowings attained? you ask. To consider relative knowing first, when attaining a level, one attains future relative knowings that are on the level of the path and the level that has been attained for the very first time.[302]

Undefiled knowings are attained not just on the levels of the paths. Well, how is it then? you ask. **One gains them,** undefiled knowings, on the levels **where one** has become **detached** through both the defiled and undefiled paths of joining and so on, and **on** that level **which is gained. And** the **lower** levels' undefiled knowings are attained, **too.**[303]

On knowing extinction, the **defiled** qualities attained by knowing extinction are attained, **too.** The qualities of **all levels,** repulsive meditation, mindfulness of the in-breath and out-breath, and so on are attained in a way similar to cutting the cords that bind a basket[304] or releasing one's breath. Just as when a king gains a large kingdom, the people of the country welcome him with offerings of gifts, when the kingdom that is not under the control of the afflictions is gained in the mind, one is welcomed with gathering of all the qualities of virtuous dharmas. How many are attained? you ask. Only those not previously acquired are attained; **those** that have **previously** been **gained are not attained.** One also does not attain those from which one has regressed, because one has forfeited the attainment.

4. Classifications of their attainment

27. Those called acquiring and maintaining
Are attainment of composite virtue.
Attainment of the antidote
And distancing are of defiled.

Is attainment only acquisition? you ask. It is not. There are four types of attainment: acquiring attainment, maintaining attainment, attainment of antidote, and distancing attainment. **The** one **called acquiring** attainment is newly acquiring compound virtue, **and maintaining** attainment **is** the **attainment of** manifesting already attained **composite virtue** over and over again. Present dharmas can have both acquiring and maintaining attainments, but future dharmas can only have acquiring attainment, and past dharmas have neither.

As far as the **attainment of the antidote and** the attainment of **distancing,** the first **is** the attainment **of** the antidote for **defiled** dharmas, and the second, distancing, is having abandoned them. Respectively these are making oneself detached from body and mind, and cutting the attainment of the afflictions. Therefore, undefiled attainment can be the first two, defiled virtuous attainment can be all four, and the remaining defiled attainments can be the last two.

The Aparāntakas posit that there are six attainments by adding the attainment of vows, which bind the gates of the faculties, and the attainment of disintegration, which destroys clinging to a whole by analyzing the body into its parts. The Kashmiris, however, say that these two are contained within the last two of the previous four attainments.

IV. Qualities of the knowings. This has two topics: A. Unshared qualities, and B. Shared qualities.

A. Unshared qualities. This has three topics: 1. Overview, 2. Explanation, and 3. Summary.

1. Overview

28ab The Buddha's unshared qualities
Are eighteen: powers and so forth.

Generally it is explained that all individuals attain the qualities of knowing extinction, but what is it that only the Buddha acquires? you ask. The qualities only **the Buddha** acquires at the time of knowing extinction are not common to listeners, self-buddhas, or others, so they are **unshared qualities.** They **are**

eighteen: the ten **powers and so forth** including the four fearlessnesses, three foundations of mindfulness, and great compassion.

2. Explanation. This has four topics: a. Explanation of the ten powers, b. Explanation of the four fearlessnesses, c. Explanation of the three foundations of mindfulness, and d. Explanation of great compassion.

a. Explanation of the ten powers. This has two topics: i. Powers of wisdom, and ii. Powers of the body.

i. Powers of wisdom. This has three points: (1) Distinctions of essence, (2) Distinctions of level, and (3) Explanation of the term.

(1) Distinctions of essence

28cd The possible and not, ten knowings,
Karma, result is eight. The dhyanas,

29. Et cetera, faculties, and interests,
Capacities, are nine. Path might
Be ten. The two are relative.
Extinction is six or else ten.

The possible and the **not** possible is fact and nonfact, such as that it is impossible to become a buddha as a woman but possible as a man and so forth.[305] In brief, it is composites and noncomposites. Knowing the possible and impossible is in general the **ten knowings:** if one divides dharmas into ten,[306] all ten are objects of relative knowing. Dharma knowing knows five; subsequent knowing seven; knowing suffering and origin, six; knowing cessation knows noncomposite virtue alone; path knowing knows the two undefiled; knowing others' minds knows three; and knowing extinction and nonarising knows nine dharmas, excluding neutral noncomposites.

The power of knowing **karma** and the full ripening of its **result is** the power of knowing the defiled contained within suffering and origin. In that, there are the **eight** knowings with the exception of knowing cessation and path.

There are also the powers of knowing **the dhyanas, et cetera,** including the eight emancipations, three samadhis, two absorptions, and the nine absorptions of final repose; knowing through the differences in lesser, medium, or greater faculties of faith and so forth whether someone is principal or not principal, which is the power of knowing whether the **faculties** are supreme or not; **and** the power of knowing the various **interests** of individuals who have interest in listeners, self-buddhas, or buddhas; and the power of knowing various **capacities.** Master Saṅghabhadra says that capacities are the intentions completely created by previously habituated imprints. Here it is proposed as knowing the many different distinctions in mind and mental factors. These four powers focus only on composites, so they **are** the **nine** knowings excluding knowing cessation.

The power of knowing the **paths** that lead everywhere from hell to cessation, if held to be knowing the path and its result, **might be ten** knowings. The word "might" indicates that if you hold it to be knowing only the path, it is the nine that exclude cessation.

Knowing many of one's own and others' previous births and their particulars is the power of remembering previous places. The power of knowing death and rebirth is seeing death, transmigration, and the good and bad colors and so forth of the between state through the utterly pure divine eye and knowing that the causes of virtuous and nonvirtuous karma make beings wander to the high or low realms. These **two,** as they must definitely perceive the aspects of specific characteristics, **are relative** knowing.

The power of knowing the **extinction** of defilements, if you hold the extinction of defilements to be cessation only, **is** the **six** knowings of dharma knowing, subsequent knowing, knowing cessation, knowing extinction and nonarising, and relative knowing. **Or else** if you hold it to be cognition in the being of one who has extinguished defilements, it is all **ten** knowings.

(2) Distinctions of level

30a–c The powers of previous places and
Of death and birth are on the dhyanas.
The others, on all levels.

The two **powers of** remembering **previous places and of** knowing **death and rebirth are on the** four actual **dhyanas,** because these are something that is generated by samadhi that is the union of tranquility and insight, whereas the other powers are not. **The other** eight powers are **on all levels**—Desire, the six levels of dhyana, and the four Formless—because they are easy to generate. The undefiled ones are supported by any of the undefiled levels, and those powers contained within relative knowing are supported by all levels, it is proposed. The bodily support is a male on Rose-Apple Land only.

(3) Explanation of the term

30cd Why?

Because his powers cannot be hindered.

Why are only the Buddha's ten knowings called powers? The listeners and self-buddhas also have them, so why are theirs not called powers? you ask. **Because** theirs are hindered, they are not called powers. Therefore, only **his,** the Buddha's, are presented as **powers.** The reason they are said to be powers is because they engage all knowable phenomena and **cannot be hindered.** The others' knowings are not like that, but the Buddha's are.

ii. Powers of the body

31. His body has Nārāyaṇa power.
Some say his joints. It is the power
Of elephants times ten seven times.
This is the sensory base of touch.

Well then, if his powers of mind are infinite, how much power does his body have? **His,** the Buddha's, **body has Nārāyaṇa power.** *Nārāyaṇa* is the name of a power, like for example calling a number with sixty digits *uncountable*. Therefore, Nārāyaṇa is the power, and one who has that is called Nārāyaṇa. Alternatively, the power of people of the first aeon is also called Nārāyaṇa power.

Some say that he has the Nārāyaṇa power in each of **his** bones' **joints.** Some venerable Dārṣṭāntika elders say that the power of his body is infinite, like the power of his mind, because if that were not the case, the body would not be able to bear the infinite power of his mind. If it could not bear that, the Buddha would not have inner nature of forbearance. The Master also gives the same explanation. The joints of buddhas, self-buddhas, and wheel-wielding emperors are respectively as strong as the most exalted knot of nagas, a chain, and driven nails.

As for the measure of what **it,** Nārāyaṇa power **is, the power of** ten ordinary **elephants** is one elephant chief. Likewise there are the seven powers of great quantity, completely overcoming, supreme limbs, supreme power, and Nārāyaṇa power.[307] The power of the previous **times ten** is the power of the next in succession, so it is multiplied **seven times.** Some say that ten supreme powers are half of Nārāyaṇa power.

The essence of **this** sort of power **is the sensory base of touch.** This is a feature of only the great sources; it is not source-derived. Some say that power is an eighth touch that is different from the seven that were explained before.[308]

b. Explanation of the four fearlessnesses. This has two points.

i. Overview

32a There are four types of fearlessness.

There are four types of fearlessness: the Tathagata proclaimed aloud, "I myself have completely, perfectly awakened. I have extinguished the defilements." When teaching the listeners, he proclaimed "These obstruct liberation. These are the paths that definitely deliver one from samsara." As he sees no true reason that anyone could say, "It is not like that," and defeat him in accord with the Dharma, he has attained fearlessness.

ii. Explanation

32bc They're similar to the first, tenth,
Second, and seventh of the powers.

What are their natures? you ask. **They are similar to** the powers. The fearlessness to proclaim the benefit for himself of perfect realization is like **the first** power of knowing the possible and impossible. The fearlessness to proclaim the benefit for himself of perfect abandonment is just like the **tenth** power of knowing the extinction of defilements. The fearlessness of teaching the dharmas that obstruct for benefit of others is just like the **second** power of knowing karma and its fully ripened result. **And** the fearlessness of teaching the dharmas of emancipation for the benefit of others is just like the **seventh of the powers,** knowing the paths that lead everywhere.

c. Explanation of the three foundations of mindfulness

32d The three are mindfulness, awareness.

There are **three** foundations of mindfulness taught in the sutras. When the Tathagata teaches the Dharma, if the beings gathered are respectful and wish to listen, he is neither pleased nor attached; if they are not respectful and do not wish to listen, he is neither displeased nor angry; and if some are respectful and some not, he does not become in part pleased and in part displeased, but abides in equanimity with mindfulness and awareness. The essence of these **is mindfulness** and **awareness,** but they are taught as three because of distinctions in the gathering.

Well then, the listeners and self-buddhas also have this quality, so it is not appropriate to be unshared, you say. That is not the case, because the listeners and self-buddhas have not abandoned the imprints, but the buddhas have. In this context, imprints are features that out of the power of prior training in afflictions have the ability to move the body and speech. These are in the mind, the authors of the *ṭīkas* explain.[309] Some others say they are features of a neutral mind.

d. Explanation of great compassion

> 33. The great compassion, relative mind,
> Is greater from its gathering,
> Its aspect, sphere, and being equal.
> There are eight ways that it is different.

The great compassion is inherently **relative** knowing or **mind.** If it were not, not only would it be proven not to focus on all sentient beings, it would be proven not to have as aspects the three sufferings, as compassion does.

Why is it called great compassion? you ask. It **is greater** because it is perfectly created by the great **gathering** accumulation of merit and wisdom, because **its aspect** is consideration of the three sufferings, because its focus and **sphere** are the focus on all sentient beings of the three realms, and because it **is equal** in the way it engages beings, remembering that all sentient beings of the three realms have the suffering of formation, and because it is full knowing by nature, so it is extremely sharp, and there is nothing greater than that.

How many things make compassion and great compassion different? you ask. **There are eight ways they are different** in essence and so forth. The eight are:

> In essence, nonhatred, nondelusion.
> In focus, one realm or three realms.
> In aspect, one suffering or three.
> In level, four dhyanas, the fourth.
>
> In beings, the listeners, the Victor,
> Attainment, detached or Peak.
> In meaning, don't fully protect, fully.
> In deed, partial, or impartial.[310]

3. Summary. This has two points.

a. How the buddhas are equal in some features

34a–c All buddhas are the equal in
Accumulation, dharma body,
And acts for wanderers' benefit,

Are all buddhas equal in all aspects? you ask. **All buddhas are the equal in** three ways: the excellent cause, having completed gathering the two **accumulations**; the excellent result, acquiring the transformation of the undefiled accumulations, the **dharma body; and** the excellent benefit, **acting for wanderers' benefit** to place them in the higher realms and the liberation of enlightenment. Otherwise some buddhas would be better or worse, which is impossible.

b. How they are unequal

34d But not in life span, caste, or size.

But however, they are **not** equal or comparable **in** their **life span, caste,** or body **size,** because they display those variously in accord with those who need taming.

Three qualities' classifications:
Four each, gathered in sets of four.
Four causes: all of two accumulations,
Familiarized for a long time

With no interruptions, respectfully.
Four results are of wisdom and also
Abandonment, power, Form Body.
Four wisdoms: knowing everything,

All aspects, untaught, without effort.
Four abandonments: all the afflictions,
Forever, all imprints as well,
And all obscurations of absorption.

Four powers are mastery to emanate
And bless and transform outside objects;
And mastery to bless or discard life;
And mastery to go where obscured,

To the sky or far off, or make smaller;
And constant display of amazements.
Four of Form Body: marks major, and signs;
The powers, relics hard as a vajra.

Four benefits: deeds of emancipating
From three lower realms and samsara;
Three vehicles and bringing to high realms.
As proofs and rebuttals are prominent,
These last are in two sets of four.

These are just in brief: no one other than the Buddha could possibly recite them in full, because the tathagatas possess infinite marvelous qualities. Those without merit could not hear of his qualities, and even if they heard of some, fools measure things against themselves and feel neither sincerity nor belief. Whoever has great sincerity and belief in the Buddha and his features, such a being is wise.

B. Shared qualities. This has two topics: 1. Overview, and 2. Explanation.

1. Overview. This has two points.

a. Brief teaching

35ab The dharmas common with the learners
And ordinary beings

Not including **the** eighteen unshared qualities, other **dharmas** are held in **common with** listener and self-buddha **learners, and** some dharmas of qualities are common **with ordinary beings.**

b. Short explanation

35b–d are
The unprovocative, the knowledge from
Aspiring, unhindered, clairvoyance, et cetera.

What are those dharmas? you ask. They **are the unprovocative** samadhi, **the knowledge from aspiration,** the four **unhindered** knowledges, six **clairvoyances, et cetera,** including four dhyanas, four immeasurables, eight emancipations, eight overpowering sense bases, ten all-encompassing sense bases, samadhis, and so on. The first five clairvoyances, four dhyanas, four Formless, four immeasurables, the first seven emancipations, the ten all-encompassing sense bases, the eight overpowering sense bases, and three samadhis are common to ordinary individuals. The others are common to noble listeners, self-buddhas, and bodhisattvas.

2. Explanation. This has two topics: a. Those common to nobles, and b. Those common to both noble and ordinary individuals.

a. Those common to nobles. This has two topics: i. Explaining the features of each of the six qualities, and ii. Explaining the features common to all six qualities.

i. Explaining the features of each of the six qualities. This has three topics: (1) The unprovocative samadhi, (2) Knowledge from aspiration, and (3) The four unhindered knowledges.

(1) The unprovocative samadhi

36. The unprovocative is relative
    Knowing on dhyana's end. Unshakable.
    Human. Unborn afflictions of Desire,
    Including their basis, are its sphere.

Some arhats produce a cognition such as, "The suffering of sentient beings arises from the afflictions, so when they know me to be a superior field of qualities, may they not produce any of the afflictions sentient beings have, such as desire and so forth, when they observe me." Because that path does not provoke afflictions in anyone, it is called unprovocative samadhi.

The unprovocative is by nature **relative knowing.** It is **on** the support of the fourth **dhyana's end**, because that is the supreme of the easy paths. It is produced by arhats who are **unshakable,** but not by others, because occasionally afflictions arise in others' beings as well, so they cannot abandon the afflictions. It is produced by **humans** of the three continents. The **unborn** future **afflictions of Desire including their basis are its sphere** or focus, because it has the aspect of thinking, "May future afflictions not arise in others." It cannot discard afflictions that do not have a basis.[311]

(2) Knowledge from aspiration

> 37ab The knowledge from aspiring is
> Similar, focusing on all.

The knowledge from aspiring is similar to the unprovocative: it is relative knowing in essence, on the level of the last dhyana, among the unshakable ones, and on human support of three continents. However, knowledge from aspiration **focuses** not just on the afflictions and their bases, but **on all,** form and all other dharmas.

Knowledge from aspiration is knowledge that comes after having made a previous aspiration. After aspiring, "I will know this and that," one enters the equipoise of the highest end fourth dhyana and knows it as the object just as it is. Therefore, since higher levels are not the object, it does not know the Formless realms directly, says the Great Exposition. Others propose that the Buddha knows even the Formless directly through knowledge from aspiration.

(3) The four unhindered knowledges. This has three topics: (a) Teaching their common features by way of classification, (b) Explaining their individual features, and (c) Their manner of attainment as a summary.

(a) Teaching their common features by way of classification

> 37cd Likewise unhindered knowledge of dharma,
> Meaning, expression, eloquence.

The two previous[312] are produced by unshakable arhats on the support of humans of the three continents, and **likewise** the **unhindered knowledge of dharma, meaning, expression,** and **eloquence** are also similar in those respects.

(b) Explaining their individual features. This has six points: (i) The nature and focus of the first three, (ii) The four dharmas of the fourth, (iii) The two dharmas of the second, (iv) The essence of the first and third, (v) The level of the first, and (vi) Distinctions of the level of the third.

(i) The nature and focus of the first three

> 38ab Three are, in order, knowing names,
> Meaning, and speech without obstruction.

Their other features are different from the unprovocative and knowledge from aspiration. The first **three** unhindered knowings **are, in order, knowing names, meaning, and speech without obstruction.** The word *dharma* applies to many different meanings, but in terms of the unhindered knowledge of dharmas, it refers to unobstructedly knowing the collection of names, words, and letters. Unhindered knowledge of meaning is proposed as unobstructedly knowing either all dharmas that can be known or the supreme meaning, nirvana. Unhindered knowledge of speech or the expression of words is unobstructedly knowing gender, tense, usage, and other aspects of syntax.

(ii) The four dharmas of the fourth

> 38cd The fourth is logical and fluent
> Clear speech; and mastery of path.
>
> 39ab Its focus is on speech and path.
> It is nine knowings, on all levels.

The fourth, unhindered knowledge of eloquence, **is** the **logic** of the contradictions and connections between meanings, **and fluent, clear speech** itself, **and** through attention on oneself, having unobstructed knowledge of **mastery of path** by not forgetting the samadhi of tranquility and insight. The first of these is skill in articulate speech, and the second is skill in attention on oneself. These are eloquence and also unhindered knowledge, so they are the unhindered knowledge of eloquence.

Its, unhindered knowledge of eloquence's, **focus is on speech and** the defiled and undefiled **paths. Its** nature **is** the **nine knowings** excluding knowing cessation. When focused on speech, it is in Desire and the four dhyanas, or five levels, and when focused on the path, it is **on all** nine of **the levels.**

(iii) The two dharmas of the second

> 39cd Knowledge of meaning, ten or six,
> On all.

Of the four unhindered knowledges, unhindered **knowledge of meaning** is **ten** knowings if the meaning that is spoken of is all dharmas, **or** if the meaning is nirvana, **six** knowings: dharma, subsequent, cessation, extinction, nonarising, and relative. The unhindered knowledge of meaning is **on all** the levels.

(iv) The essence of the first and third

> 39d The rest are relative.

The rest, unhindered knowledge of dharma and expression, **are relative** knowing by nature, because they focus on dharma—the collection of names and so forth—and speech.

(v) The level of the first

40ab Knowledge of dharma is in Desire
And dhyan;

Unhindered **knowledge of dharma is in Desire and** on the four **dhyanas** but not above that, because there is no collection of names, words and letters there.

(vi) Distinctions of the level of the third

40b of speech, Desire and first.

The unhindered knowledge **of speech** or expression is in **Desire and** on the **first** dhyana but not above, because speech is inherently motivated by consideration, and on the second dhyana and above there is neither consideration nor examination.

The order of the four is as follows: On the basis of dharma or names, the meaning is realized. On the basis of the meaning, expression is known. On the basis of realizing those, eloquence is attained.

(c) Their manner of attainment as a summary

40c If incomplete, they're not attained.

Whoever has one must definitely have all four, because **if** any one is **incomplete, they,** the other three, **are not attained.**

ii. Explaining the features common to all six qualities. This has four points.

(1) Teaching the mental support in general

40d Those six are through the highest end.

Those six qualities of unprovocative and so forth **are** attained **through** the training of dhyana of **the highest end,** but they are not necessarily included within the highest end, because as is said "Speech in Desire and on first" and so forth.

(2) The distinctions between what is and what is not the actual highest end

41a It's sixfold:

The fourth dhyana's highest end is unprovocative samadhi, knowledge through aspiration, three of the unhindered knowledges, and the highest end alone: **it is sixfold** in nature. Although unhindered knowledge of expression is attained through the power of the fourth dhyana, it is not on the level of the fourth dhyana, just as the emanated mind of Desire is attained by the actual dhyana but is not the actual dhyana.

(3) Identifying the highest end of the fourth

41a–c it is dhyana's end,
Gained by progressing through all levels,
Coming to highest development.

It is dhyana's especial upper **end,** because it is **gained by progressing through all levels** from Desire to the Peak of Existence, entering the absorption of each level in forward and reverse order,[313] so that it is compatible with the highest end of all levels. It has **come** through the lesser, medium, and greater, or **to** the **highest development**, and is even higher than that. It has arrived at the extreme upper limit of the fourth dhyana: it is like a fourth alternative.[314]

(4) The particulars of its training

41d Other than Buddha, they are from training.

When they are in the continuum of those who are **other than** the **Buddha, they**, these six, **are** arisen **from training:** they are not attained by mere detachment. The Buddha accomplishes them without depending on training but by merely wishing, because he is the master of all qualities.

b. Those common to both noble and ordinary individuals. This has two topics: i. Distinctions of their qualities, and ii. Understanding their features.

i. Distinctions of their qualities. This has four topics: (1) Classifications, (2) Essence, (3) Distinctions of dharmas, and (4) How they are attained.

(1) Classifications

42a–c Sixfold clairvoyance manifests magic,
The ear, mind, knowing previous lives,
Death and rebirth, and knowing extinction.

Sixfold clairvoyance manifests the **magic** of emanating objects and knowing how to move; **the** divine **ear** that through relative knowing associated with the ear consciousness hears all sounds whether near or far; knowing others' **minds** discussed above;[315] **knowing previous** places or **lives;** knowing **death and rebirth; and knowing extinction.**

(2) Essence

42d These are the mind of liberation.

In general, **these,** all six clairvoyances, **are the mind** of the path **of liberation.**

(3) Distinctions of dharmas. This has three points.

(a) What knowings they are

43a–d The four are knowing relative,
And knowing minds is the five knowings.
Clairvoyance of extinction is
Like power.

In particular, **the four** other than the third and sixth **are knowing** only the **relative,** because they are always defiled. **And** the clairvoyance **knowing of** others **minds is five knowings:** dharma knowing, subsequent knowing, path knowing, knowing others minds, and relative knowing. The **clairvoyance of** knowing the **extinction** of defilements **is like** the **power** of knowing the extinction of defilements: it is either six or ten knowings and is on all eleven levels.

(b) What levels they are on

43d Five are on four dhyanas.

The first **five** clairvoyances **are on** each of the **four** actual **dhyanas.** Clairvoyance of divine eye[316] and ear are only of the level of the first dhyana, but in terms of how they are attained and their support, they are explained to be on four.

(c) What their spheres are

44a Their object is own and lower level.

Their, five clairvoyances's, **object is** on their **own and lower levels,** but the higher levels are not their object, because the superior is not the object of the inferior. Therefore the object of clairvoyance of magic is knowing how to go or make emanations on its own or lower levels, but not on higher. The others are similar.

(4) How they are attained

44b Familiar is attained by detachment.

As far as the manner of attainment of the clairvoyances, those that are not familiar from previous close paths must be attained through training, but the **familiar is attained** merely **by detachment.** In either case, manifesting them depends upon training.

ii. Understanding their features. This has two topics: (1) Understanding common features, and (2) Understanding their particular features.

(1) Understanding common features. This has four topics: (a) Their intersection with the foundations of mindfulness, (b) Their intersection with virtue and so forth, (c) Their intersection with the three knowledges, and (d) Their intersection with the three miracles.

(a) Their intersection with the foundations of mindfulness

44cd The third one is the three foundations,
And magic, ear, and eye are the first.

Because it focuses on mind and mental factors, **the third one,** clairvoyance of knowing minds, **is** contained within **the three foundations** of mindfulness of feeling, mind, and dharmas. **And** the three clairvoyances of **magic, ear, and eye are the first** foundation of mindfulness of body, because they focus on form. The focus of the clairvoyance of magic is the four external sense bases excluding sound. The focuses of the consciousnesses of divine ear and divine eye are the sense bases of sound and form.

(b) Their intersection with virtue and so forth

45ab Clairvoyance of ear and eye are neutral.
The rest are virtue.

The **clairvoyances of** divine **eye and** divine **ear are** not afflicted, nor are they included within the four virtues, so they are unobscured **neutral.** These two are full knowing that is concurrent with the eye or ear consciousnesses. **The** four **rest are virtuous.**

(c) Their intersection with the three knowledges. This has two topics: (i) Overview, and (ii) Explanation.

(i) Overview

45b–d Three are knowledge,
Because they stop the ignorance
Of prior lives, et cetera.

The **three** clairvoyances of knowing previous places, death and rebirth, and extinction of defilements **are** called the three nonlearners' **knowledges.** Why is it only these three and not the others? you ask. The reason is **because** respectively **they stop the** totally deluded **ignorance of prior lives, et cetera,** including future lives and the present.

(ii) Explanation. This has three points.

A. Identifying the ultimate nonlearners' knowledge

46a The last one is nonlearner's.

Of those three, **the last one,** clairvoyance of extinction of defilements, since it is undefiled, **is** both **nonlearner** and also nonlearner's knowledge.

B. The reason the other two are called by that term

46ab When two others
Arise in their mindstream, they are so called.

The defiled first and second are not nonlearner by essence, but **when** these **two others arise in their,** the nonlearner's, **mindstream,** they are **so called,** nonlearners' knowledge.

C. Elaboration

46cd Although the learners may have these, their streams
Have ignorance, so these are not called knowledge.

Why are those clairvoyances not called learners' knowledge? you ask. **Although the** detached **learners may** also **have these** two, **their mindstreams have ignorance, so these are not called knowledge** in the sutras.

(d) Their intersection with the three miracles. This has two points.

(i) General teaching

47a The first, third, sixth are miracles.

Of these clairvoyances, **the first,** magic, **third,** knowing others' minds, and **sixth,** extinction of defilements, **are** the three **miracles.** This is because they are respectively miracles of magic, addressing, and teaching.[317]

(ii) Identifying the supreme among these

47b–d The miracle of teaching is best,
Since it is unconfused and brings
Benefit and a pleasant fruit.

Of these three, **the miracle of teaching is best, since it** arises only from the extinction of afflictions and thus from its good cause, since **is unconfused, and** since it **brings** the **benefit** of freeing beings from afflictions in this life, **and** since in the future it brings **a pleasant fruit** or result that is entirely free of duḥkha. The other two are not like that.

(2) Understanding their particular features. This has three topics: (a) Understanding the clairvoyance of magic, (b) Understanding the clairvoyances of eye and ear, and (c) Understanding the natures of those attained by birth, etc.

(a) Understanding the clairvoyance of magic. This has five topics: (i) Magic's features, (ii) Identifying the mind of emanation, (iii) How that emanates, (iv) The essence of the mind of emanation, and (v) Classifications of magic.

(i) Magic's features. This has two topics: A. General explanation of magic, and B. Its actual features.

A. General explanation of magic

48ab The magical is samadhi. Motion
And emanations are from that.

What is the essence of magical clairvoyance? you ask. **The** essence of **magical** clairvoyance **is samadhi** because that is what creates it. What is created? you ask. The three **motions** through the body, interest, and mental speed **and emanations** that did not previously exist **are** created **from that** samadhi.

B. Its actual features. This has two topics: 1. The distinctions between the three motions, and 2. Distinctions of the two emanations.

1. The distinctions between the three motions

48cd The Teacher moves with mental speed;
Others: propulsion, interest.

The Teacher, the Buddha, **moves with mental speed,** because he can go long distances by merely thinking. Others cannot do this. Those **other** than the Buddha have motion through bodily **propulsion,** because their body propels them like birds. They have motion of **interest,** because by imagining what is far to be close, they can go there quickly.

2. Distinctions of the two emanations. This has two points.

a. Emanations that act in Desire

49ab In Desire, emanations are
Four external sense bases. Twofold.

In general, there are two types of mind of emanation: emanations of Desire and Form. Of these, **in Desire emanations are** the **four external sense bases** of form, scent, taste, and touch by nature. They are **twofold:** connected to one's own being and connected to another being.[318]

b. Emanations that act in Form

49c In Form, two.

Because in Form there is neither scent nor taste, emanations **in Form** are the **two** sense bases of form and touch. These can also be connected to one's own or another's body.

(ii) Identifying the mind of emanation. This has four topics: A. What emanates, B. Classifications of the mind of emanation, C. What it is acquired through, and D. What arises from which.

A. What emanates

49cd Minds of emanation
Create them, too.

Does only clairvoyance create emanations? you ask. No. The result of clairvoyance, the **mind of emanation, creates them**—emanations—**too.**

B. Classifications of the mind of emanation

49d These are fourteen

50ab Results of dhyan, respectively,
From two to five, not lower's result.

These minds of emanation also **are fourteen.** What are the fourteen? you ask. The **results of** levels of **dhyana, respectively. From** the first dhyana, there are **two** minds of emanation on the levels of Desire and the first dhyana. The results of the second dhyana are three—those of the two lower levels and its own level. The results of the third dhyana are four—those of the three lower levels and its own level. This continues **to** the fourth dhyana that has **five,** the four lower levels and its own in succession.

Here there is something that must be known: emanating an object in Desire is the action of the emanating mind of Desire, but that emanating mind itself is contained within the levels of dhyana. Therefore, emanating minds that are results of dhyana are of their own and lower levels, but those emanating minds born from the higher levels are **not** the **lower** levels' **result**, because if one has not attained the higher level, one cannot produce its emanating mind. If one has attained the higher level, the emanating mind is the result of that level itself.

C. What it is acquired through

50c It's gained like dhyan,

How is the mind of emanation acquired? you ask. **It is gained like dhyana** by detaching from lower realms. One can also acquire the emanating mind of the first dhyana by being born from the second dhyana into the first.

D. What arises from which. This has two topics: 1. What the mind of emanation arises from, and 2. What arises from the mind of emanation.

1. What the mind of emanation arises from

50cd arising from
The pure and self.

There is no arising directly from the mind of emanation itself. When first manifesting a mind of emanation—that is, in entering a mind of emanation—the emanating mind **arises from the pure** dhyana[319] **and** later also from **itself.**

2. What arises from the mind of emanation

50d Out of it, two.

When abiding in a mind of emanation, there is no arising without entering samadhi, so **out of it,** a mind of emanation, **two** cognitions can arise: in the instance of arising from the mind of emanation there is a pure dhyana upon arising, and in the instance of continuation, there is the mind of emanation itself. There are no others that arise. When abiding in an emanating mind that is the result of samadhi, there is no arising from samadhi without first re-entering it.

(iii) How that emanates. This has three topics: A. Which minds of emanations emanate, B. Minds that emanate speech, and C. Whether minds of emanation are more or less numerous than emanations.

A. Which minds of emanations emanate

51a They're emanated by own level,

They, all emanations, **are emanated by** their **own level's** emanating minds: emanating minds of one level do not create emanations on other levels.

B. Minds that emanate speech. This has three topics: 1. What mind supports emanations speaking, 2. Distinctions in how emanations speak, and 3. The manner of speaking through blessings.

1. What mind supports emanations speaking

51b But speech by lower levels, too.

But in particular, when emanations of the second dhyana and higher engage in **speech**, they speak only **by** the speaking mind of the **lower level** first dhyana, because above that there is no consideration or examination on their own level, and speech depends upon the motivation of consideration and analysis. The word "**too**" means that in Desire and on the first dhyana, only the mind of its own level engages in speech.

2. Distinctions in how emanations speak. This has two points.

a. Actual

51c With emanator, except the Teacher.

Emanations speak along **with** the **emanator, except** if they are **the Teacher's** emanations. The Teacher, the Buddha, can make multiple emanations speak. From *The Long Discourses:*[320]

> If one speaks, then all
> The emanations speak.
> If one doesn't speak,
> Then none of them do.

b. Dispelling a doubt

51d After it's blessed, another starts it.

Well then, when there is a mind that speaks, there is no mind of emanation, so for that reason the emanation would disappear and who would speak? you ask. This is not a problem, because **after it,** the emanation, **is blessed** to be able to stay, **another** mind, a speaking mind, **starts it** speaking.

3. The manner of speaking through blessings

52ab There are blessings for the dead as well,
Not for the unstable. Some say not.

Are blessings only for the living, or are there also blessings for the dead? you ask. **There are blessings for the dead as well,** which allow them to remain for a long time, because through his own blessings, the skeleton of Noble Mahākaśyapa remained after his death. There are blessings for bones and other stable body parts, but **not for the unstable** flesh, blood, and so forth, because Noble Mahākaśyapa did not bless his flesh and so forth. **Some say** there are **not** any blessings for the dead, and that Noble Mahākaśyapa's skeleton was caused to remain by the power of the gods of the pure realms.

C. Whether minds of emanation are more or less numerous than emanations

52cd First, many emanate the one;
When mastered, it is opposite.

At **first, many** minds of emanation **emanate the one** emanation. **When** clairvoyance has been **mastered,** then **it is** the **opposite:** one mind creates many emanations.

(iv) The essence of the mind of emanation

53ab Produced by meditation, neutral;
But those produced by birth are threefold.

Are all minds of emanation neutral? you ask. Minds of emanation **produced by meditation** are always **neutral,** because they arise on lower levels, so the lower level's mind of emanation is manifest. **But those** minds of emanation that **produced by** attainment upon one's **birth,** such as those of gods, nagas, flesh-eaters,[321] or so forth, **are threefold:** virtuous, nonvirtuous, and neutral, because they are produced to help or harm another, or for a neutral reason. Emanations created by gods and so forth, whether connected to their own or others' bodies, are the nine sense bases as they have eyes, etc., and the sense bases of form excluding sound. Emanations not connected to one's own or others' bodies are only four sense bases.

(v) Classifications of magic

53cd Magic from mantra, medicine,
And karma, for five types in all.

Is magic just the two produced by meditation and attained upon birth? you ask. **Magic** is produced by meditation; attained upon birth; produced **from mantra,** such as flying in the sky because of the GHANDHARI mantra and so forth; produced by **medicine** such as turtle's mane or peacock feather; **and** produced by **karma,** such as the miracles of Māndhātar or beings in the between state, **for** a total of **five types in all.**

(b) Understanding the clairvoyances of eye and ear. This has three points.

(i) What their essence is

54ab They are the divine eyes and ears,
Clear forms on levels of the dhyanas.

Are the divine eye and ear only for the gods, or when the Bodhisattva, wheel-wielding emperors, or precious householders see many leagues, which is like the divine eye, is this called the divine eye or ear? you ask. **They,** the Desire realm gods' eyes and ears, **are the** actual **divine eye and** divine **ear.** When in the equipoise of dhyana, if one trains to direct the attention to appearances in the arena of the eye and ear, this creates the causes for seeing the form and hearing the sound of **clear forms** caused by the sources **of** the **levels of the dhyanas,** so they are on the level of dhyana.

(ii) Distinctive features

54cd They're always active, nothing lacking.
Their sphere is distant, subtle, et cetera.

Both the divine eye and ear always accompany consciousness, so **they are always active** and never inactive.[322] As there is never any deficiency or fault, that is to say, no distortion or deafness, there is **nothing lacking,** just as with the eyes and ears of sentient beings of the Form realm. **Their sphere is** forms and sounds that are **distant, subtle, et cetera,** including hidden. As it is said:

> The fleshly eye, it cannot see
> The distant, hidden, subtle forms,

Or everything. So for that reason
This is what's called the sight of gods.

"Everything" means that not only things in front, but things that are behind and so on are also seen.

(iii) How the three individuals see with the divine eye

55ab The arhat, rhino, and the Teacher
See a thousand squared or cubed or countless.

Seeing lower levels with the divine eye of the first dhyana and so forth has been explained. The listeners and self-buddhas see the thousand worlds, two thousands, and three thousands with their divine eyes.[323] In particular, **the** listener **arhats,** the **rhino**-like self-buddhas, **and the Teacher** of gods and humans **see** through the strength of effort **a thousand squared** (a million) worlds, **or** a thousand **cubed** (a billion), **or countless** world realms respectively. The Teacher's depends upon merely thinking of it.

(c) Understanding the natures of those attained by birth, etc. This has two topics: (i) General teaching, and (ii) Distinctions in support.

(i) General teaching. This has three points.

A. Teaching that the other four can also be attained upon birth

55c Others are gained on birth as well,

Is magic the only clairvoyance attained upon birth, or can the others be as well? you ask. Not only magic, the **others,** including the divine ear and so forth, can **be gained on birth as well,** but since those are not produced by meditation, they are not called clairvoyance.

B. How the divine eye attained upon birth sees

55d It cannot see the between state.

It, the divine eye attained upon birth, **cannot see the between** state, which can only be seen by the divine eye produced by training.

C. Detailed explanation of knowing minds

56ab Knowing minds is three, created by
The intellect and mantra, too.

Knowing others' **minds** attained upon birth, depending upon its intention, **is threefold,** virtue and so forth. Knowing others' minds that is **created by the intellect** from perceiving the attributes of someone's body and speech, **and** that created by **mantra** are virtuous, nonvirtuous, or neutral, **too.** These are not like the result of meditation, which is solely virtuous.

(ii) Distinctions in support

56cd Hell beings know at first. With humans,
There are not any gained on birth.

Hell beings both **know** others' minds and remember previous places **at first** from the time they are born until they are agonized by the feelings of suffering. Once they are agonized, they no longer know because they are oppressed by suffering. Those who live among other wanderers know permanently. Of the clairvoyances that have been taught, **with humans there are not any gained on birth,** but there is magic that is attained by detachment, intellect, mantras, medicine, and karma.

Well then, how is it that some humans naturally remember their previous births? you ask. That is not attained upon birth but produced by previous karma. From the *Precious Garland:*[324]

> For purpose of Dharma and likewise
> Remembering the meanings of scriptures,
> And stainless generosity of Dharma,
> Remembrance of lifetimes is attained.

Second, presenting the area's name

This completes the seventh area called "Teachings on Wisdom" from the *Verses of the Treasury of Abhidharma.*

This completes the explanation of **the seventh area called "Teachings on Wisdom" from** *The Explanation of* **the** ***"Verses of the Treasury of Abhidharma"*** called *The Essence of the Ocean of Abhidharma, The Words of Those who Know and Love, Explaining the Youthful Play, Opening the Eyes of Dharma,* the *Chariot of Easy Practice.*

A few words here:

The moon of speech who has perfected fully
The all-knowing wisdom and compassion of
The master of ten powers, my glorious master,
Melts in my heart into a drop whose pureness

Then rises to my throat as Manju's riches.
Thus have I gained some independent courage
In all the scriptures of the infinite victors—
I have no fear to teach, write, or debate.

By excellently bringing to a finish
The seventh section of this explanation
Of abhidharma, the treasury on wisdom,
While staying in retreat in solitude

In the White Cave on the side of the mountain
On the full moon of winter's second month
When the moon rose among the Pleiades,
May the teachings of the Sage remain for ages!

EIGHTH AREA

Teachings on the Absorptions

From the fields that bring happiness to great cooling groves
He went at his leisure, the glorious lama,
And then gave the gift of this feast that's supreme
To beings of this fortunate aeon: I prostrate to him.

The causal, resultant pure dhyanas, the Formless,
The eight emancipations, all-encompassing, et cetera—
The eighth part, the treasury that teaches absorption—
If you wish to know these all with ease, enjoy this.

The eighth area, the "Teachings on the Absorptions," has first an explanation of the text of the area and second, an explanation of the branch that completes the composition, the summary of the treatise. The explanation of the text of the area has three topics: I. Explanation of the dhyanas and the Formless, II. Classifications of samadhi, and III. Explanation of the qualities supported by samadhi.

I. Explanation of the dhyanas and the Formless. This has two topics: A. Individual explanations, and B. Understanding them in common.

A. Individual explanations. This has three topics: 1. An explanation of the dhyanas, 2. An explanation of the Formless, and 3. Summary of both.

1. An explanation of the dhyanas. This has two topics: a. Classifications, and b. Individual natures.

a. Classifications

1a The dhyans are twofold. They are four.

The qualities of the knowings have been explained in the section on the knowings. Now the other qualities must be told. Because they support all the qualities, first we must begin with the explanation of the dhyanas.

The support of the qualities, **the dhyanas, are** in brief **twofold** through the distinctions between the resultant birth and the causal absorption. **They are** each the **four** of the first dhyana and so forth.

b. Individual natures. This has two topics: i. The reason the resultant dhyanas of birth are not explained here, and ii. Understanding the causal dhyanas of absorption.

i. The reason the resultant dhyanas of birth are not explained here

1b Rebirth there has been fully explained.

Rebirth in the dhyanas will not be further discussed here because the dhyanas of birth **there have been fully explained** in the Treasury that teaches the world. How were they explained? you ask. They were explained in the verses:

> Each of the dhyanas has three levels,
> But the fourth dhyana has eight levels.[325]

ii. Understanding the causal dhyanas of absorption. This has two topics: (1) Their general essence, and (2) Their individual essences.

(1) Their general essence. This has two points.

(a) Actual

1c Absorption is one-pointed virtue.

The causal **absorption** of dhyana **is** without differentiation **one-pointed virtue** because it is samadhi by nature. By saying "virtue," afflicted and nonobscured neutral one-pointed minds are excluded.

(b) Including what is associated with it

1d Its following, five aggregates.

Including **its following** or associated dharmas, it is known as **five aggregates** by nature, because they include imperceptible forms and so forth, the rest of the five aggregates.

What is so-called one pointedness? you ask. It is called that because the mind rests one-pointedly on the focus of equipoise. The Great Exposition says that the dharma that is the mental factor of samadhi that makes the cognition rest in equipoise is samadhi, and that itself is one-pointedness. The Sutra school says that cognitions with the same focus only are samadhi, and other dharmas such as the mental factors are not. The Great Exposition and Sutra schools both make many propositions. The term is explained as meaning that it makes the mind contemplate.

(2) Their individual essences. This has two points.

(a) The essence of the first dhyana

2a It has examining, joy, pleasure.

It, the one-pointed virtuous first dhyana, **has examining, joy,** and **pleasure.** Saying "examining" explains that considering is also present, because they function together, like fire and smoke. Without considering, there is no examining that possesses joy and pleasure.

(b) The essence of the remaining dhyanas

2b The earlier branches are discarded.

The remaining dhyanas are one-pointed virtue in which **the earlier branches** of considering, examining, and so on **are discarded.** The second dhyana has discarded examination but possesses joy and pleasure. The third has discarded examination and joy but possesses pleasure. The fourth has abandoned examination, joy, and pleasure.

2. An explanation of the Formless. This has three topics: a. Their general essence, b. Their individual essences, and c. Elaboration.

a. Their general essence. This has two points.

i. Comparing similar features

2c Formless are like.

The **Formless are like** those dhyanas, in that they have the resulting Formless of birth and the causal Formless of absorption. They are also the four of Infinite Space and so on. Their births have been explained.[326]

ii. Dissimilar features.

2c Four aggregates,

Including their associations, they are **four aggregates,** because there is no form that accompanies them.

b. Their individual essences

2d Born of withdrawal from lower levels.

The one-pointed virtue **born of withdrawal from** the **lower level** of the fourth dhyana is the sense base of Infinite Space. What is born from withdrawal from that is the sense base of Infinite Consciousness. What is born from withdrawal from that is the sense base of Nothingness. What is born from withdrawal from that is the sense base of Neither Conception nor Non-Conception. Thus there are the four Formless. What is withdrawal? you ask. It is the path that separates completely from the lower level, because one becomes detached from it.

c. Elaboration. This has two topics: i. Distinctions in conceptions, and ii. Explanations of terms.

i. Distinctions in conceptions

3ab They are called, with three preparations,
Destruction of conception of form.

They, the Formless, **are called with** the **three** higher **preparations,** by the name **destruction of conception of form,** because there is no form on their own level and they do not focus on the defiled form of lower levels. The preparation for Infinite Space is a conception that views the form of the fourth dhyana as coarse and so forth, so it is not given the name *destruction of conception of form.*

ii. Explanations of terms. This has two topics: (1) Explaining the term *Formless realm,* and (2) Explaining the names of each of the four.

(1) Explaining the term *Formless realm.* This has two points.

(a) Actual

3c In Formless realms, there is no form.

The Majority school and others say that the Formless is not entirely without form, but as the form there is subtle, it is said to be Formless. Such a proposal is illogical. If its form is subtle by aspect, tiny aquatic creatures would also be present there, and if it is subtle by nature, the Form realm would also be Formless. If it is by extreme subtlety and clarity, you should only propose that the Peak of Existence is that.

Well then, merely the forms of vows of body and speech are there, you say. They are not, because there are neither body nor speech, nor any sources there. It is also not acceptable to say that they are not on their own level but are born from other levels, similar to undefiled vows, because the forms of vows of body and speech are bound by the bonds of existence and thus cannot exert power over another level.

From the *Sutra of the Great Welcome:*[327]

> Those dharmas that are life and that are warmth are mixed; they are not unmixed...

Also:

> Name and form are mutually supporting.

And in teaching interdependence:

> By the condition of consciousness, name-and-form...

These quotations are said with the lower two realms in mind. If you propose that they apply to all situations, it would follow that external warmth would also be mixed with life and all external forms would depend upon name and arise from consciousness itself. Because of this, these quotations are not proof that there is form in Formless.

From a sutra:

> The Formless are emancipation from form. Whatever is one of the four peaceful Formless emancipations transcends form…

Also:

> There are sentient beings who do not have form.

Also:

> Having transcended the conception of form in all aspects…

These quotations contradict the proposition, so the name Formless is not arbitrary. Therefore, **in** the **Formless** realm **there is no form**, not even the slightest bit, which is why it is called Formless.

(b) Dispelling a doubt

3d Then form arises from cognition.

Well then, when one is born from the Formless in a lower realm, for more than a few aeons the continuum of form has been broken, so how does form arise again? you ask. **Then** at that time **form arises from** acquiring entry into the **cognition** that is stained with the cause of its full ripening. The grasping cause is the four sources in Desire and Form.

The Sutra school says that there is a seed of form in the mind's continuum, from which form arises. The Yogic Conduct school says form arises from its seeds, which are in the all-ground.

(2) Explaining the names of each of the four. This has two points.

(a) Explaining the names of the first three

4ab They're called the Infinite Consciousness,
Space, Nothing at All, from training so.

Are the sense bases of infinite consciousness and so forth called that because they only focus on space and so on? you ask. No. Well then, what are they like? you ask. **They are called** by those names because during the training for them, one views the lower levels as having faults and thinks, "**Consciousness** is **infinite. Space** is infinite. There is **nothing at all.**" **From training so** with such attention, they are called by the names Infinite Consciousness and so forth because of the training. However, any of them can focus on other dharmas.

(b) Explaining the names of the last

4cd Since it is feeble, no conception,
But it's not nonconception, either.

Since it, the motion of conception, **is feeble,** there is **no** clear **conception, but it is not** total **nonconception, either.** Alternatively, during the training one views both coarse conception and nonconception as faulty and generates the absorption through the attention that thinks, "This which is neither conception nor nonconception is peace." This is the highest level of samsara, so it is also called the Peak of Existence.

3. Summary of both

5ab Thus actual absorption is
Eight substances.

Thus actual absorption is eight substances: four dhyanas and four Formless.

B. Understanding them in common. This has six topics: 1. Examining their essence, 2. Identifying the branches of dhyana, 3. The manner in which absorptions are attained, 4. What support manifests them, 5. What sphere they focus on, and 6. Identifying what discards afflictions.

1. Examining their essence. This has two topics: a. Classifying in terms of their essence, and b. The meaning of each classification.

a. Classifying in terms of their essence. This has two points.

i. Classifications of the seven lower absorptions

5b–d Seven are threefold:
Concurrent with enjoyment, pure,
And undefiled.

The **seven** absorptions other than the Peak of Existence **are threefold.** Absorptions of those with the lowest faculties where there is great craving, view, pride, and doubt are **concurrent with enjoyment,** the absorptions of those with medium faculties are **pure, and** the absorptions of those with the highest faculties are **undefiled.**

ii. Classifications of the Peak of Existence

> 5d The eighth is twofold.

The eighth, the Peak of Existence, **is twofold:** it can be concurrent with enjoyment or pure. There is no undefiled Peak of Existence.

b. The meaning of each classification

> 6. The one concurrent with enjoyment
> Has craving. Virtue of the worldly
> Is pure, which is what that enjoys.
> The undefiled transcends the world.

The one called **concurrent with enjoyment has** concurrence with **craving.** It is also concurrent with other afflictions, of course, but the reason that only craving is taught here is because craving is realized to be the greatest hindrance to emancipating oneself onto higher levels. The **virtue of the worldly** absorptions **is** called **pure** because it is concurrent with nongreed and other positive dharmas.

What does the concurrent with enjoyment enjoy? you ask. Pure absorption passes, immediately after **which is what,** the experience, **that** concurrent with enjoyment **enjoys.** It is regression from that which it experiences.

The undefiled absorption **transcends the world** and takes the truths as aspects.

2. Identifying the branches of dhyana. This has three topics: a. Correlating the branches to each absorption, b. Teaching three branches in particular, and c. Teaching the distinctions among the absorptions.

a. Correlating the branches to each absorption. This has two points: i. Classifying in terms of name, and ii. Summarizing in terms of substance.

i. Classifying in terms of name

7. The first has five: considering,
   Examining, joy, pleasure, and samadhi.
   There are four branches on the second:
   Serenity, joy, and so forth.

8. Five on the third: there's equanimity,
   And mindfulness, awareness, pleasure, rest.
   The last has four: mindful, equanimous,
   Not pain nor pleasure, and samadhi.

The first dhyana **has five** branches: through abandoning such impediments as desire of the Desire realm, malice, hostility, and so on, there are the two antidotal branches of **considering** and **examining.** Having discarded the impediments through considering and examining, there is **joy** and **pleasure** born of withdrawal, which are the branches of benefit. These former are accomplished through the power of one pointedness, so there is the supporting branch of **samadhi.** Samadhi is both a branch and also dhyana. The others are only branches, it is heard. The Master explains that, "The dhyana of five branches is just like an army with four branches."

There are four branches on the second dhyana: the antidotal branch that abandons the impediments of consideration and examining, true inner **serenity;** and the branches of benefit and support, **joy, and so forth,** pleasure and one-pointedness itself.

There are **five** branches **on the third** dhyana: the three antidotal branches that discard the impediment of the lower levels' joy: the formation **equanimity,** which by not striving for joy has the characteristic of spontaneity in relation to the focus; **and mindfulness,** which does not forget the continuum of sequanimity; and **awareness,** which does not forget mindfulness. The branches of benefit and support are respectively **pleasure** and the samadhi of a mind that **rests.**

The last, fourth dhyana, **has four** branches: completely pure **mindfulness,** the formation **equanimity** that is free of the eight faults of lower levels, and neutral feeling that is **not pain nor pleasure, and** completely pure **samadhi.**

In terms of names, the branches of dhyana are eighteen, because the first and third have five branches each, and the second and fourth each have four.

ii. Summarizing in terms of substance

9a In substance, they are eleven.

In substance, they are eleven. The first dhyana has five substances. The second's true inner serenity, and the third's equanimity, mindfulness, awareness, and pleasure make ten. The fourth's neutral feeling makes eleven. For that reason, there are four alternatives of branches that are on the first dhyana but not on the second, etc.

b. Teaching three branches in particular. This has three points.

i. Explaining distinctions in pleasure

9ab Pleasure
On the first two is pliancy.

Why is the pleasure of the third dhyana said to be a different substance than the pleasure of the first two dhyanas? you ask. What is called the branch of **pleasure on the first two** dhyanas **is pliancy**; it is not a feeling. Because the pleasure of the third is the feeling of pleasure, it is logical to say that it is a different substance than the pleasure of the first two levels.

The pleasure of those two levels is not the feeling of pleasure because the dhyanas of absorption block the sense consciousnesses, so it is not bodily pleasure. Joy is taught as a branch, and that is mental pleasure, which cannot arise simultaneously with cognitive pleasure, the Great Exposition proposes.

The Dārṣṭāntikas do not assert pleasure born of cognition and so present only bodily pleasure as a branch. The branch is not pliancy called by the name of pleasure. Otherwise it would follow that the pliancy of the fourth dhyana would be pleasure. If one needs a pliancy that is compatible with the feeling pleasure, it follows that the pliancy of the third would also be that. It also says in a sutra:

> At the time that noble listeners have manifested through their bodies the pleasure born from complete withdrawal and perfected it, dwelling within it, at that time the five dharmas of this are discarded. The meditation of the five dharmas, great serenity, joy, pliancy, pleasure, and samadhi, is completely perfected.

Here pliancy and pleasure are said to be separate, and that would be contradicted, they say.

ii. Explaining complete serenity in particular

9c Serenity is faith,

True inner **serenity is** confident **faith** that having attained the second dhyana, one is emancipated from the first dhyana.

iii. Explaining the distinctions of mental pleasure

9cd and two
Scriptures say joy is mental pleasure.

Some other schools say that joy is a different mental factor **and** mental pleasure is taught as the branch of pleasure of all three dhyanas. This is not correct, because if it were, it would contradict the **two scriptures.** In the *Viparītasūtra,*[328] after **saying**, "The third dhyana," the Bhagavan said:

> On this, the arising of all faculties of mental pleasure without exception cease...

Also:

> On the fourth dhyana, all faculties of pleasure without exception cease.

From the *Sutra which Teaches the Branches of Dhyana:*[329]

> And pleasure is also discarded. Previously suffering has also been discarded, and mental pleasure and mental suffering have also previously disappeared...

Because it would not be proven that mental pleasure had previously been discarded, on the third dhyana there can be no faculty of mental pleasure. Therefore, the **joy** of the first two dhyanas **is** only **mental pleasure** and is not pleasure.

c. Teaching the distinctions among the absorptions. This has three topics: i. Distinctions between the afflicted and unafflicted, ii. Features of the fourth dhyana, and iii. Distinctions in feeling between causal and resultant absorptions.

i. Distinctions between the afflicted and unafflicted

10. In the afflicted, there is no joy or pleasure;
    Serenity; awareness, mindfulness;
    Or equanimity, pure mindfulness;
    Some say no pliancy, no equanimity.

Are those same branches previously explained also present in afflicted dhyana? you ask. They are not. Which of them are not? you ask. **In** the **afflicted** first dhyana, **there is no joy or pleasure** born of withdrawal, because it is not withdrawn from the afflictions of that level. On the second dhyana, there is no great **serenity,** because it is sullied by the afflictions of its own level. On the third dhyana, there is no **awareness** or **mindfulness** because it has been made completely deluded by afflicted pleasure. On the fourth, there is no **equanimity** or **pure mindfulness,** because those two have been stained by the afflictions. **Some say** there is **no pliancy** on the afflicted first or second dhyana, and on the third and fourth there is **no equanimity,** because these are virtuous major grounds, they say.

ii. Features of the fourth dhyana

11. The fourth is free from the eight faults,
    So it's immovable. They are
    Considering, examining, breaths,
    And pleasure and the other three.

The Bhagavan said, "Because the three dhyanas have faults, they are movable." **The fourth** dhyana **is free from eight faults** explained below, **so it is immovable. They,** the eight faults, **are considering, examining,** the in-**breath** and out-breath, **and pleasure and the other three,** suffering, mental pleasure, and mental unhappiness.

iii. Distinctions in feeling between causal and resultant absorptions. This has two points.

(1) Actual

12. Dhyanas of birth have happiness,
    And pleasure and the neutral feeling;
    Neutral and happiness; and pleasure
    And neutral; and the neutral feeling.

Are those feelings that are in the causal dhyanas of absorption also present in the resultant dhyanas of birth? you ask.

The first **dhyanas of birth have happiness** of the level of mind consciousness, **and pleasure** of the three consciousnesses,[330] **and the neutral feeling** of the four consciousnesses. On the second dhyana, there are both **neutral and** mental **happiness; and** on the third there is also **pleasure and neutral. And** on the fourth there is only **the neutral feeling.**

Of these, the pleasure of the first dhyana is solely bodily feeling supported by eye, ear, and body, and its neutral feeling is both bodily and mental. From the second dhyana and above, they are all only mental feelings. Bodily feeling is always accompanied by considering and examining, and because there is no considering and examining on the second and above, there can be no bodily feelings, either.

(2) Dispelling a doubt

13. On second and so forth, the body,
 Eye, and ear consciousnesses, and
What makes them perceive is of the first.
 It's neutral; it is not afflicted.

On the second dhyana, et cetera, if there is no considering and examination, how can they see, hear, or touch, and how is the act of knowing motivated? you ask. Those who are born there are not without eye consciousness and so forth, but they are not of their own level. **On** the **second** dhyana **and so forth,** the third and fourth dhyanas, **the body** consciousness, **eye** consciousness, **and ear consciousness, and** that which is the considering and examining **that makes them perceive is** only manifested through those **of the first** dhyana. **It,** the consciousness on the second or higher dhyana, **is** unobscured **neutral;** because it is detached, **it is** also **not afflicted.** Because it is inferior, it is also not pure absorption.

3. The manner in which absorptions are attained. This has three topics: a. The actual manner in which they are attained, b. What arises following which, and c. The manner in which the skipping absorption arises.

a. The actual manner in which they are attained. This has three points.

i. How the pure is attained

14ab Those who do not possess them gain
The pure through detachment or from birth;

How are the absorptions of dhyana and the Formless attained? you ask. **Those who do not possess them,** the dhyanas and Formless, from before **gain** any of **the** three **pure** with the exception of tendency toward the undefiled[331] **through detachment or,** except for the Peak of Existence, **from birth** from a higher into a lower. The Peak is not attained by birth because there is no level above it.

ii. How the undefiled is attained

14c The undefiled is through detachment;

The undefiled actual absorptions, if one has not previously possessed them, **are** only attained **through detachment** from the lower levels. If previously possessed, they can also be attained through training such as the distinctive actual practices of the nonlearners and those with sharp faculties, but are not attained through birth or regression.

iii. How the afflicted is attained

14d Afflicted, by regressing, birth.

Afflicted absorption, when not previously possessed, is attained **by regressing** such as when one regresses from detachment from the first dhyana and attains the afflicted first dhyana. Except for the Peak, it is also attained by **birth** from a higher realm into a lower realm. For example, when one is born from the second or higher dhyana into the first dhyana, one can attain the afflicted first dhyana. The afflicted Peak is only attained through regression. Afflicted absorption is not attained through training or detachment.

b. What arises following which. This has two topics: i. General teaching, and ii. Specifics of the latter two.

i. General teaching. This has three points.

(1) What arises right after the undefiled

15a–c Right after undefiled, the virtue
Of levels up to two above
Or below can arise.

Right after which substances of absorption can how many arise? **Right after the** substance of **undefiled** absorption of dhyana and Formless, **the** pure and undefiled **virtue of** its own **level** and **up to two** levels **above or** two levels **below can arise,** because when doing skipping absorption, one cannot skip more than one level.[332]

(2) What arises right after the pure

15cd From pure,
The same, or own level's afflicted.

From the **pure** absorption, the pure and undefiled arise, which should be known to be the **same** as what has just been explained. **Or** in addition, just after the pure, its **own level's afflicted** can also arise. The afflicted cannot arise right after the undefiled, because that is totally exclusive of entry into the afflicted.

(3) What arises right after the afflicted

16ab From the afflicted, own pure, afflicted,
And one pure of the lower, too.

From the afflicted absorption, in the instance of taking hold of it with mindfulness and awareness and then arising from it, the **pure** of its **own** level can arise directly. In the instance of continuation, the **afflicted** arises. Not only that, when greatly tormented by the afflictions, one gains affection for the pure of the lower level, **and** so the **one pure of the lower** can arise, **too.**

ii. Specifics of the latter two. This has two topics: (1) At the time of death, and (2) Particulars of the four tendencies.

(1) At the time of death. This has two points.

(a) Pure

16c From pure at death, all the afflicted,

It has been explained that during the period of absorption only their own level's afflicted can follow directly upon the pure or afflicted absorptions, but other levels' cannot. However, **from** a **pure** absorption that was attained upon birth, **at** the time of **death** it is possible to be reborn in any of the levels above or below, so at the time of rebirth-linking, **all the afflicted** of the nine levels can possibly arise.

(b) Afflicted

> 16d But from afflicted, not the higher.

But from afflicted absorptions at the time of death, the afflicted of their own level or lower arise, but **not the** afflicted of **higher**, because if the afflicted of the lower level has not been discarded, there is no birth in the higher. This is because the lower afflicted is exclusive of rebirth-linking in the higher.

(2) Particulars of the four tendencies. This has three points.

(a) Classifying the pure in four

> 17ab Four types of pure tend toward regression,
> Et cetera.

Not all pure absorptions produce the undefiled. In general, there are **four types of pure** absorption: the **tendency toward regression, et cetera,** the tendency to staying, the tendency toward the superior, and the tendency toward the undefiled. On the Peak of Existence, there is no tendency toward the superior, because there is no higher level.

(b) The meaning of each classification

> 17b–d Respectively,
> They tend toward birth of the afflictions,
> Of own, of higher, of undefiled.

In essence, **respectively, they tend** in the instance of continuation **toward** the **birth of the afflictions,** toward the birth of virtue **of** their **own** level, toward the birth of virtue **of** a **higher** level, and toward the birth **of undefiled.** The meaning of *tend* here is "directed toward its birth."

(c) What arises after which of the four

> 18ab Tendencies to regress, et cetera,
> Are followed by two, three, three, one.

What arises right after each of the four? you ask. **The** four **tendencies** toward **regression, et cetera,** may **be followed** immediately **by** the first **two** right after the first, and the first **three** right after the second. Right after the third, the last **three** arise, and right after the last, only the last **one** itself arises.

c. The manner in which skipping absorption arises. This has two topics: i. Training, and ii. Actual practice.

i. Training. This has two points.

(1) Distant training

> 18cd Going through eight levels up and down,
> Both types in sequence,

How does one produce skipping absorption? you ask. One **goes through** the **eight levels,** going **up** in ascending order **and down** in descending order. One enters each of the four dhyanas and four Formless, **both** defiled and undefiled **types in sequence.** In order, one enters the absorption of the defiled first samadhi. Then one enters the absorptions going up in ascending order as far as the Peak of Existence, and then coming back down in descending order to the first dhyana. Then one enters the absorption of the undefiled first samadhi. Then one enters the absorptions going up in ascending order as far as undefiled Nothingness, and then coming back down in descending order to the undefiled first dhyana. This is the initial training for skipping absorption.

(2) Near training

> 18d or skipping one,

Then one enters the defiled absorption of the first dhyana, skips one level, and enters the absorption of the third dhyana. Then by **skipping** every other level **one goes** up as far as the Peak in ascending order, and then skipping every other level one comes back down as far as the defiled first dhyana in descending order. Then one enters the undefiled absorption of the first dhyana and skipping one level enters the undefiled absorption of the third. Then skipping every other level, one enters the undefiled absorption of Nothingness and then comes down to the undefiled first dhyana skipping every other level. This is the advanced training for skipping absorption.

ii. Actual practice

> 19ab Then going to the third of the
> Different type is skipping absorption.

Following that, one **then** enters the defiled absorption of the first samadhi and then skips one and **goes to the third** dhyana **of the different,** undefiled **type.** Discarding the fourth, one enters defiled Infinite Space, and discarding another, enter undefiled Nothingness. Then one discards every other level down to the first dhyana. In this way, skipping every other level and alternating between the incompatible defiled and undefiled dhyanas and Formless **is** the actual practice of **skipping absorption.**

The explanation here that one cannot skip more than one level is in terms of listeners with dull faculties. The explanation in the *Ornament of Clear Realization*[333] that it is possible to skip eight is in terms of bodhisattvas with sharp faculties.

Only nonoccasional, totally liberated arhats on the support of the three continents can produce this, because they have no afflictions and have mastery over samadhi.

4. What support manifests them. This has two points.

a. General

> 19cd The dhyans and Formless, on their own
> Or lower support. No use for lower.

The dhyanas and the Peak and the other **Formless** absorptions are manifested **on** the support of **their own** level **or lower** levels down to Desire. When one is born in a higher level, the absorption of the lower level is not manifested, because there is absolutely **no use for** the substance of the **lower** absorption. Producing the samadhi of the lower has the function of producing the full ripening of the lower, but the higher level has transcended the full ripening of the lower, because the samadhi of the lower level is inferior.

b. An exception on the Peak of Existence

20ab On Peak, they manifest Nothingness
Of nobles, then extinguish defilements.

That was in general, but there is an exception: when born **on** the **Peak, they,** nobles, **manifest** the undefiled sense base of **Nothingness of nobles,** and **then** they **extinguish defilements** of the Peak of Existence, because there is no undefiled path on the Peak and the undefiled sense base of Nothingness is close to the Peak.

5. What sphere they focus on. This has three points.

a. What afflicted dhyana focuses on

20c Enjoyment focuses on own existence.

Absorptions with craving that are concurrent with **enjoyment focus on** their **own** level's **existence,** defiled things. They do not focus on the lower because they are detached from it. They do not focus on the higher, because they are completely separated from the higher by craving. They do not focus on the undefiled, either, because then it would follow that they were virtuous.

b. What pure and undefiled dhyanas focus on

20d All that exists is virtuous dhyan's sphere.

All that is composite and noncomposite and **exists is** the pure and undefiled **virtuous dhyana's sphere** or object.

c. What the actual Formless focuses on

21ab Defiled of lower is not the sphere
Of virtuous actual of Formless.

The **defiled of lower** levels **is not the sphere of** the **virtuous actual** practices **of Formless.** Their sphere is either the defiled or undefiled of their own and higher levels, and also the lower level's undefiled paths of subsequent knowing.

6. Identifying what discards afflictions. This has two topics: a. What discards what, and b. Distinctions in the discarding antidotes.

a. What discards what. This has two points.

i. What the undefiled actual practice discards

21c The undefiled discard afflictions,

Of the dhyanas and Formless that are pure, undefiled, and concurrent with enjoyment, **the undefiled discard** the **afflictions** of their own and higher levels. There's no need to mention the concurrent with enjoyment—even the pure does not discard. Because the preparations have detached one, the pure does not discard the afflictions of lower levels. Because it is not their antidote, it does not discard afflictions of its own level. Because they are greatly superior, it does not discard the higher level's afflictions.

ii. What the preparations discard

21d As do pure preparations, too.

As do the undefiled, the **pure preparations** for higher levels of dhyana and form discard the afflictions of the level below them, **too.** The word "too" means that Not Unable is included within the undefiled. It has already been explained that it can discard the afflictions of every level.[334]

Therefore, the defiled actual practices do not discard any afflictions at all because the lower level's have already been discarded and they cannot discard the afflictions of their own or higher levels.

b. Distinctions in the discarding antidotes. This has two topics: i. Distinctions of the preparations, and ii. Identifying special dhyana.

i. Distinctions of the preparations. This has two topics: (1) Classifications, and (2) Their essences and the feelings they are concurrent with.

(1) Classifications

22a For those, there are eight preparations.

For entering **those** eight actual practices, **there are** also **eight preparations.** As far as the manner of entering absorption, each of the preparations has seven aspects through which one can enter the absorption: attention on thorough knowledge of the characteristics, attention produced by interest, attention on complete withdrawal, attention on taking delight, attention on examination, attention on the end of training, and attention on the result of the end of training. The first six of these are preparations, and the last is the actual practice.[335]

(2) Their essences and the feelings they are concurrent with. This has four points.

(a) General essence

22b. They're pure,

On the first two dhyanas, there is the feeling joy. On the third, pleasure, and on the fourth, neutral. Do their preparations have similar feelings? you ask. They do not. **They,** the preparations, **are pure** in essence. They are not concurrent with enjoyment because they are not free of revulsion for the lower level and because they are a path that brings detachment.

(b) Which feelings they are concurrent with

22b not pleasure and not pain.

They, the feelings on the preparations, are **not pleasure** and are **not pain** or suffering, so they are only neutral. This is because the preparations must be induced by exertion, so they arise out of effort. The pervasion holds because the paths that arise without effort are concurrent with joy and pleasure.

(c) Particulars of the essence

22c The first is also noble.

The first of the preparations, Not Unable, **is** not solely pure; it can **also** be **noble** or undefiled.

(d) Others' assertions

22c Some say, threefold.

Some say Not Unable can be all **three,** including concurrent with enjoyment. The reason is because it is clear, or according to Master Saṅghabhadra, because it pursues and competes with the actual practice.

ii. Identifying special dhyana. This has four points.

(1) Identifying its essence

22d In special dhyan, there's no considering.

Well then, there is the term *preparations* and also the term *special dhyana*. Are these two the same or different? you ask. They are different. The former is the path that brings detachment. The **special dhyan** is an actual practice in which **there is no considering,** but in which there is examining. Thus the first dhyana has the classifications as the mere actual practice that has both considering and examining, and the special that has examining only. There is no such distinction in the second and so forth, so there is no classification of them as mere or special.

(2) Classifications

23a It's threefold,

It, the special dhyana, **is threefold:** concurrent with enjoyment, pure, and undefiled.

(3) Which feelings it has

23a neither pain nor pleasure,

Because the special dhyana is a difficult path that must be created by exertion, it only has neutral feeling that is **neither pain nor pleasure.**

(4) Result

23b And has Great Brahma as result.

And what is the particular result of the special dhyana? you ask. It **has** the **Great Brahma** realm **as result,** because those who meditate on it will be reborn in Great Brahma.

II. Classifications of samadhi. This has two topics: A. Classifying samadhi in three, and B. Classifying samadhi in four.

A. Classifying samadhi in three. This has three topics: 1. Classifying in terms of level, 2. Classifying in terms of path, and 3. Classifying in terms of the mode of engaging the object.

1. Classifying in terms of level

> 23cd Below, samadhi has considering,
> Examining. Above, there's neither.

The sutras teach that there are three types of samadhi. Of these, on special dhyana there is samadhi that has no considering but does have examining alone. **Below** it, on the first dhyana and Not Unable, there is **samadhi** that **has considering** and **examining. Above** it, from the preparations for the second to the Peak, **there is** samadhi that has **neither** considering nor examining.

2. Classifying in terms of path. This has three points.

a. Identifying the essences of the three samadhis

> 24. The signless has aspects of peace,
> And emptiness engages selfless
> And emptiness. No wishing has
> All other aspects of the truths.

The sutras speak of the three samadhis: the samadhi of emptiness, samadhi of no wishing, and samadhi of signlessness. Of these, **the signless** samadhi is a samadhi that is free of the ten attributes—the five objects, the four characteristics of composites, and male and female attributes—and from focusing on noncomposites **has aspects of peace,** the four aspects of the truth of cessation. **And** the samadhi of **emptiness** is samadhi that, for any focus, **engages** only **the** two aspects of **selfless and emptiness.** The samadhi of **no wishing** is a samadhi that focuses on composites and only **has** the aspects of the truths that create revulsion, so it is concurrent with **all** the **other aspects of the truths** than those six previously mentioned. It is a samadhi that is concurrent with the ten remaining aspects: four of the truth of origin, four of path, and suffering's aspects of impermanence and suffering. Because the other six do not create revulsion, it does not have them.

b. Classifications of their internal categories

> 25a They're pure or stainless.

They, these three samadhis, can **be pure** worldly **or stainless,** transworldly undefiled. The pure are on the eleven levels of Desire, Not Unable, special dhyana, the four dhyanas, and the four Formless. The stainless are on the nine undefiled levels.

c. Examining their names

25ab When they're stainless,
They are three gates of liberation.

When they, these three, **are stainless,** they are gates to liberation, so **they are** the **three** stainless **gates of liberation** of emptiness, no wishing, and signlessness.

3. Classifying in terms of the mode of engaging the object. This has two topics: a. Teaching the classification in general, and b. Explaining their features in detail.

a. Teaching the classification in general

25cd There are three more samadhis, called
The empty of emptiness, et cetera.

Also in the sutras, **there are three more samadhis** in addition to the previous three. They are the samadhis **called emptiness of emptiness, et cetera,** including no wishing of no wishing and signlessness of signlessness.

b. Explaining their features in detail. This has five points.

i. Distinctions of focus and aspect

26. Two focus on nonlearner's aspects
Of empty and impermanent.
The signlessness of signlessness,
On peace, nonanalyzed extinction.

Of those three, the first **two focus** respectively **on** the **nonlearner's aspect of** emptiness while viewing the **empty, and** focus on the nonlearner's no wishing while viewing the aspect of **impermanent.** As for **the signlessness of signlessness,** if one arises from the nonlearner's signlessness while viewing the aspect of **peace,** the conditions for the continuation of signlessness are not met, so signlessness of signlessness focuses on the **nonanalytic extinction** or the attainment of nonanalytic cessation. Of these three, the first two look at liberation itself. The third focuses on its cessation and is thus diminished, so it is diminished liberation.

ii. Distinction of essence

27a Defiled,

These three are solely **defiled.**

iii. Distinctions of support

27a by humans,

Where are they produced? you ask. They are only produced **by humans,** not by gods or others.

iv. Distinctions of individual

27a unshakable.

Who produces them? you ask. They only arise for **unshakable** arhats, not for others.

v. Distinctions of level

27b Except the seven preparations.

Except the seven latter **preparations,**[336] they are on the eleven levels previously explained.

B. Classifying samadhi in four

27cd First dhyana's virtue is meditation
On samadhi which is happiness.

28. Clairvoyance of eye is that which sees.
Produced by training is discernment.
The vajra-like of the last dhyana
Extinguishes all the defilements.

The Bhagavan said:

> There are four meditations on samadhi: if you always remain in meditation on samadhi and do this many times, you will also dwell in happiness in the visible…

Of these the first, the **first dhyana's virtue**—pure or undefiled—**is** the **meditation on samadhi which is** dwelling in **happiness** in the visible. The other dhyanas are also known to be the same. There is no certainty of dwelling in happiness in future lifetimes, because it is possible to regress, and those who are reborn in higher realms or pass into complete nirvana do not have the first dhyana's happiness. The **clairvoyance of** divine **eye** that knows death and rebirth, and the knowing concurrent with the mind consciousness that arises after that, **are** proposed as **that** samadhi **which** knows and **sees.** The defiled or undefiled qualities of the three realms that are **produced by training** and everything undefiled are the meditation on samadhi of **discernment** or full knowing. **The vajra-like** samadhi that has the support **of the last** fourth **dhyana** is samadhi meditation that **extinguishes all the defilements.**

Thus these four samadhis are taught just as the Bhagavan himself manifested them in the past. At the very first, he produced the first dhyana in the shade of a Rose-Apple tree. Later he sat beneath the Bodhi Tree, and just after taming the Maras he saw with the divine eye the miserable deaths and births of sentient beings. In order to give them refuge, he produced the dhyanas, emancipations, and so forth during the night session. At dawn, on the basis of the fourth samadhi, he manifested the paths up to the vajra-like samadhi, the Great Exposition says.

III. Explanation of the qualities supported by samadhi. This has two topics: A. Teaching the immeasurables, and B. Teaching the other qualities.

A. Teaching the immeasurables. This has two topics: 1. Classifications, and 2. Distinguishing features.

1. Classifications. This has three points.

a. Actual classification

29a Immeasurables are four.

As they focus on immeasurable sentient beings and have immeasurable merit, they are called **immeasurables.** In focusing on immeasurable sentient beings, there **are four:** loving-kindness, compassion, joy, and equanimity.

b. Establishing their quantity

29ab because
They're antidotes for malice, et cetera.

Why are there four of them? you ask. **Because they are antidotes for** excessive **malice and so forth,** including hostility, dislike, and the attachment of the Desire realm, their number is established as four.

c. The essence of each classification

> 29cd Love and compassion are nonhatred,
> And joy is pleasure of the mind,
>
> 30a And equanimity is nongreed.

Love and compassion are the virtue of **nonhatred, and joy is pleasure of the mind** at others' happiness, **and equanimity is** the virtue of **nongreed.** Therefore they are the antidotes for malice preceded by greed and so forth. Alternatively, the Master explains that they are nongreed and nonhatred both, so they are suitable as antidotes for both greed and hatred.

2. Distinguishing features. This has six topics: a. Distinctions of aspects, b. Distinctions of object, c. Distinctions in levels, d. Distinctions in how they function as antidotes for the levels, e. Distinctions in support, and f. Distinctions in how they are possessed.

a. Distinctions of aspects

> 30bc Their aspects are thinking, "May they be
> Happy! Not suffer! Joyous! Beings!"

Their aspects are thus: the aspect of love is **thinking,** "O! **may they,** sentient beings, **be happy!**" The aspect of compassion is thinking, "May they **not suffer!**" The aspect of joy is thinking, "May they have **joyous** minds!" The aspect of equanimity is thinking, "Without attachment to those near or hatred for the distant, I will treat all sentient **beings** equally." One reflects with such an intention and enters absorption. One rests in the middle, without any prejudice, and without any attachment or animosity either.

b. Distinctions of object

> 30d Their sphere is beings of Desire.

What do they focus on when they meditate on these aspects? you ask. **Their** focus or **sphere is** sentient **beings of Desire,** because the immeasurables are the antidote for malice and so forth that focus on beings of Desire.

c. Distinctions in levels. This has two points.

i. Actual

31ab On the two dhyanas, there is joy.
Others on six.

How many levels are they on? you ask. **On the** first **two dhyanas, there is joy** because it is produced by meditation and is mental pleasure. The **other** three immeasurables are **on six** levels: the four dhyanas, special dhyana, and Not Unable.

ii. Others' assertions

31b Some say on five.

Some say that they are **on** the **five** excluding Not Unable. Others say that they are on ten, adding Desire and the four preparations.

d. Distinctions in how they function as antidotes for the levels.

31c They don't abandon.

It is explained that "They're antidotes for malice, et cetera… " Do the immeasurables discard the afflictions? you ask. The explanation of them as antidotes for malice and the others is through distinctions in power either in terms of suppressing or distancing. **They,** the four, **do not** actually **abandon**, because they are the pure actual practice so they do not discard afflictions, and because they all focus only on sentient beings, so they are merely interested attention.

e. Distinctions in support

31cd They arise
In humans.

As far as their bodily support, because a clear mind and the power of familiarization produce them, **they arise in humans,** excluding those on Unpleasant Sound. Others do not produce them.

f. Distinctions in how they are possessed

31d One must have the three.

If one possesses one immeasurable, must one also without a doubt possess all of them? you ask. It is not definite that one will possess them all. However, if one possesses any of the three excluding joy, they also have the other two, so **one must have the three.** Joy is mental pleasure, so it is not possessed on the third or fourth dhyana. This is intended in terms of attainment. In terms of their manifestation, they are possessed individually because their aspects are exclusive.

B. Teaching the other qualities. This has four topics: 1. The essence of the qualities attained, 2. How they are attained, 3. Distinctions of support, and 4. How samadhi arises.

1. The essence of the qualities attained. This has three topics: a. The emancipations, b. The overpowering sense bases, and c. The all-encompassing sense bases.

a. The emancipations. This has three topics: i. Classifications of the emancipations, ii. Their individual natures, and iii. The spheres of the first seven.

i. Classifications of the emancipations

32a Of eight emancipations,

As they are directed away from their focus, they are emancipations. The **eight emancipations** are, according to the sutras, viewing external form while conceiving of internal form, viewing external form while conceiving of no internal form, the emancipation of loveliness, the four Formless, and the emancipation of cessation.

ii. Their individual natures. This has four topics: (1) Explanation of the first two emancipations, (2) Of the third, (3) Of the Formless emancipations, and (4) Of the emancipation of cessation.

(1) Explanation of the first two emancipations. This has two points.

(a) Actual

32ab the first two,
Repulsive,

Because **the first two** of the emancipations have the aspects of bluishness and so forth, they have the nature of meditation on the **repulsive.**[337]

(b) Distinctions of level

32b are on the two dhyanas.

These two emancipations are antidotes for desire for color, so they **are on the** first **two dhyanas,** but they are absent from the third and higher, because above that there is no desire for color. That is because there is no eye consciousness above the second dhyana.

(2) Explanation of the third

32c The third, on the last, is nongreed.

The third, the emancipation of the lovely, is **on the last** of the dhyanas, the fourth. As its essence is the antidote for greed, it **is** primarily **nongreed,** but since it has the lovely as its aspect, it is not repulsiveness meditation. Thus one emanates an attractive form and views it as lovely. As that itself is manifested by the body of samadhi, it is so called. Including their associations, the first three are the five aggregates by nature.

The need for the emancipation of the lovely is that by meditating on the repulsive, one's mind is depressed, so one uplifts it with intense joy. Also, if attachment to a lovely emanation arises, the first two emancipations have not been completed, but if it does not arise, they have, so this is in order to examine that.

The emancipation of the lovely is not taught in the first three dhyanas because there is joy on those levels, so if one pays attention to the lovely and has joy and craving for that object, nongreed will not be accomplished. Alternatively, it is not taught there because they are dhyanas that have faults, so nongreed is not accomplished there.

(3) Explanation of the Formless emancipations

32d Virtuous Formless equipoise.

Only the four **virtuous**—pure or undefiled—**Formless equipoises** are emancipations; the afflicted and the states of beings not in equipoise such as the state of death are not. On the preparations, the paths of liberation are emancipation, but the paths of no obstacles are not because they focus on the lower level.

(4) Explanation of the emancipation of cessation. This has three points.

(a) Identifying its essence

33a It is absorption of cessation

It, the eighth emancipation, **is** the **absorption of cessation** of conception and feeling. This was explained in the second area.[338]

Why are these called emancipations? you ask. It is because the first two are directed away from greed; the third, away from being discouraged and attached; the four Formless, from the conception of form; and cessation is directed away from conceptions and feelings, or alternatively all formations.

(b) The mind of entry

33b That follows the subtlest of the subtle.

Regarding entering the absorption of cessation, the conception of the Peak of Existence is the subtlest in the three realms, but focusing on cessation is by far the subtlest of all, so one enters **that** absorption of cessation immediately **following that subtlest of the subtle** minds.

(c) The mind of arising

33cd One rises from that through own level's
Pure or the noble of the lower.

When arising, **one rises from that** cessation, as one has resolved to do, **through** one's **own level**—the Peak's—**pure, or** through **the noble** undefiled mind **of the lower** sense base of Nothingness. In this way, the absorption of cessation and the mind that enters it are on the level of the Peak, so they are defiled only. The mind of arising can be either defiled or undefiled.

iii. The spheres of the first seven. This has two points.

(1) The sphere of the first three

34a Sights of Desire are the first's object.

The **sights** of the sense base of form **of Desire are** the **object** of **the first** two of the eight emancipations, and the third has an attractive object. Well then, are these not emanations on the basis of samadhi? you ask. Of course they are, but they are emanations contained in Desire.

(2) The sphere of the Formless

> 34b–d The Formless' sphere is suffering
> And such of own and higher levels,
> Compatible with subsequent knowing.

The sphere of the four emancipations of **Formless is** the **suffering and such,** including origin and all paths, **of** their **own and higher levels** that is **compatible with subsequent knowing.** It is possible that the Formless emancipations can be the samadhi of no attributes of no attributes, so they can also be nonanalytic cessation. Noncomposite space is also the object of the sense base of Infinite Consciousness.

Why is there no emancipation presented on the third dhyana? you ask. Because it has no desire for the colors of the level of second dhyana and because it is produced by absorption of pleasure, it is not presented. Well then, if on the third dhyana also there is no desire for color, why is the emancipation of the lovely produced on the fourth dhyana? you ask. As one is discouraged by repulsiveness, it is to make oneself intensely joyous or else to analyze whether or not the repulsive emancipations have been accomplished. If when paying attention to the lovely, afflictions do not arise, those two have been accomplished.

b. The overpowering sense bases. This has two topics: i. Classifications, and ii. Explanation of their characteristics.

i. Classifications

> 35a Eight overpowering sense bases.

According to the sutras, while conceiving of internal form, viewing small external forms with good and bad colors and viewing large external forms with good and bad colors are the first two overpowering sense bases. While conceiving that there is no internal form, viewing the same two are the third and fourth. While conceiving only that there is no internal form, viewing external forms that are blue, yellow, red, and white are the last four. When these eight all have overpowered those forms, the sort of conception that arises is the first through the **eighth overpowering sense bases.**

Conceiving of internal form and *that there is no internal form* is the conception of the form of the viewer himself being destroyed or not. *Small* and *large* are forms of sentient beings and the world. *Good and bad colors* are attractive and unattractive. *Overpowering them* is gaining mastery. *Knowing* and *seeing* are explained as paths of no obstacles and liberation, or tranquility and insight according to Master Ārya.[339] In the sutra, for the four colors there are four phrases using the words blue and so forth that are repeated twice each, once for the example and once for the meaning. The first mention is an overview, the second the natural, the third the fabricated, and the fourth the dharmas common to both. The flax, *karṇikāra* flowers,[340] *bandhujīvaka* flowers, and the planet Venus are examples of the natural, and the cloth is an example of the fabricated.[341]

ii. Explanation of their characteristics. This has three points.

(1) Explanation of the two overpowering sense bases of that with form viewing form

35b Two like the first emancipation;

Of those, the first **two** overpowering sense bases are **like the first emancipation** in the particulars of their nature, level, and aspects.

(2) Explanation of the two overpowering sense bases of that without form viewing form

35c Two like the second.

Two of the overpowering sense bases, the third and fourth, are views **like the second** emancipation.

(3) Explanation of the four overpowering sense bases of color

35cd Others are like
Emancipation of the lovely.

The **others,** the four emancipations of color, **like emancipation of lovely** are on the level of fourth dhyana, focus on attractive forms of the Form realm, are nongreed by nature, and are the five aggregates, it should be understood.

c. The all-encompassing sense bases. This has two topics: i. Classifications, and ii. Their individual natures.

i. Classifications

36a Ten all-encompassing sense bases.

The sutras teach of the **ten all-encompassing sense bases,** which have the meaning of making the visualized aspect pervade the focus uninterruptedly. To classify them, there are the ten of earth, water, fire, air, blue, yellow, red, white, space, and consciousness.

ii. Their individual natures. This has two points.

(1) Explaining the first eight

36bc Eight are nongreed on the last dhyana.
Their sphere is Desire.

Of these, the first **eight are** in essence the virtue of **nongreed.** They are **on** the level of **the last** fourth **dhyana. Their sphere is** the sense base form of **Desire,** similar to how the four sources are known as color and shape in the world.[342] According to some, since it says, "The atmosphere/Is the element itself... "[343] the object of the all-encompassing sense base of wind is touch.

(2) Explaining the last two

36cd Two are pure Formless;
Their sphere is their four aggregates.

It is explained in the *Levels*[344] that the other sense bases are not set forth as all-encompassing, since sound is discontinuous; and since the five faculties do not pervade the world, and scent and taste do not pervade the Form realm.

The last **two** all-encompassing sense bases **are** in nature the **pure** virtue of the first two **Formless** equipoises. **Their sphere is their** own level's **four aggregates** only, unlike the Formless emancipations described above, because here it is in terms of focus on particulars, the learned ones have said.

The last two Formless are not set forth as all-encompassing sense bases since they are unclear and thus incompatible with expanding and contracting, or according to some, since they are the result of the all-encompassing. It is explained in the *Great Compendium:*[345]

> ... because the all-encompassing of Infinite Space and Consciousness is infinitely and immeasurably accomplished, so there is no enhancement of that.

The distinctions among the emancipations, overpowering sense bases, and all-encompassing sense bases is that their qualities gradually increase. First the emancipations are directed away from the discards. Then the discards are overpowered. Then it is made pervasive, so as the earlier are perfected and purified, the latter arise, and they are each superior to the previous. For that reason, they are lesser, medium, and greater, or cause, both cause and result, and result only.

2. How they are attained

> 37ab Cessation has been explained. The rest
> Are gained through detachment or by training.

Of these twenty-six, the support and attainment of the emancipation of **cessation have** already **been explained** in the second area.[346] **The rest,** the remaining twenty-five, **are gained** merely **through detachment** if familiar—that is, if they have ever arisen before—**or** if unfamiliar, **by training** and effort, because they arise from the power of habituation or nonhabituation.

3. Distinctions of support. This has two points.

i. Actual

> 37cd The Formless are supported by
> Three realms. The rest arise in humans.

The four emancipations called **Formless** and two of the all-encompassing **are supported by three realms. The rest,** the other nineteen, **arise in humans,** so they are only on the support of humans. This is because they must be produced by the power of scripture, and the gods and other wanderers do not have the scriptures.

ii. Elaboration

> 38ab In two realms, the power of cause and karma
> Produces Formless equipoise.

Well then, since there are no scriptures there, how do the absorptions of dhyana and the Formless of higher levels arise in the higher two realms? you ask. The absorptions of dhyana and the Formless are produced by the power of four things: scripture, cause, karma, and dharma nature. **In** the higher **two realms,** there is no scripture, but **the power of** both **cause and karma produces**

Formless equipoise. Production by power of cause is when previously on a human support one has meditated on the samadhi of the Peak of Existence and regressed from that. After being born either on one of the lower Formless levels or in the Form realm, through the cause of same status of previous meditation, the samadhi of the Peak arises. Production by force of karma is also when in a previous human life one performs karma that will definitely ripen as birth in the Peak in a future life. After regressing, one is born in one of the previously mentioned lower levels, and since one must definitely be reborn on the Peak, at that point the absorption of the Peak will be attained. This also has a causal aspect, but since karma is primary it is explained to be called produced by the power of karma.

4. How samadhi arises

38cd Those two and also dharma nature
Produce the dhyanas in Form realm.

Those two powers of cause and karma, **and also** the power of the **dharma nature produce the dhyanas in** the **Form realm.**

Second, an explanation of the branch that completes the composition, the actual summary of the treatise. This has three topics: A. How long the teachings will remain, B. The summary of the treatise itself, and C. The manner of completing the explanation.

A. How long the teachings will remain. This has two points.

1. The teachings

39ab The Teacher's True Dharma is twofold:
In essence, scripture and realization.

How long will this true abhidharma that explains the aspects of dharmas—defiled, undefiled, level, focus, aspects, and so forth—remain? you ask. **The Teacher's True Dharma is twofold: in essence**, it is the Three Baskets of **scripture** and **realization**, the factors of enlightenment.

2. How long they will remain

39cd These are upheld only by those
Who teach them and accomplish them.

What is it to uphold the Dharma of scripture? you ask. According to the scriptures, **these,** the scriptures, **are upheld only by those who,** after coming to know them, **teach them** to others with an unafflicted intention. This is also called upholding the baskets, upholding the scriptural Dharma, and upholding the teachings. **And** those who uphold realization **accomplish them,** the dharmas of the factors of enlightenment, within their being and practice them. As there are no upholders of the teachings or True Dharma other than these two, the word *only* is said.

The upholders of the scriptures are the supports for those who speak and accomplish. The unerring supports for the scriptures are those with accomplishment. Only those who have accomplishment are the upholders of realization because without accomplishing it, one cannot teach the meaning one has realized.

Therefore the True Dharma will remain as long as there are beings who speak and accomplish the Dharma. In particular, as far as the teachings of the Teacher Shakyamuni, the autocommentary explains, "They will remain for a thousand years." Some say that this is in terms of realization, but that the scriptures will remain a thousand years longer than that. This latter is also the explanation of the authors of the *ṭīkas.* The Prince explains:

> "The scriptures will remain for a long time" means that they will remain another thousand years. I view this position only as logical.

From *The Good Aeon:*[347]

> The True Dharma of the Thus-Gone Shakyamuni will remain for a thousand years. For another five hundred years, a pseudo True Dharma.

The *Minor Topics* also say Dharma will remain for a thousand years. The *Sutra Requested by Candragarbha*[348] explains that it will remain for two thousand years and be destroyed by the strife of Kaushambir. Master Kamalaśīla says in his commentary on the *Vajra Cutter Sutra,* "It is renowned among the learned that the teachings will last five times five hundred years."

In the *Commentary on the Hundred Thousand,*[349] it is said that by dividing five thousand into sections, there are ten periods of five hundred years. In the first, many arhats will appear; in the second, many nonreturners, and in the third, many stream-enterers, so these are the three chapters of the period of results. In the fourth period, there will be many who abide by the trainings of full knowing. In the fifth, by the trainings of mind, and in the sixth, by the trainings of discipline, so these are the three chapters of the period of accomplishment. In the seventh, there will be many who uphold the abhidharma; in the eighth, who uphold the basket of sutras, and in the ninth, who uphold the vinaya, so these are the three chapters of the period of scripture. The tenth is called the chapter of those who hold merely the signs, and it is also labeled the last five hundred. After that the True Dharma will disappear. At that time, the lifespan of humans in the Rose-Apple Land will be fifty years. Now the lifespan is sixty years and it is the period of the abhidharma, it says.

According to the calculations in the Glorious Rangjung Dorje's *A Clarification of the Four Times of the Omniscient Lord,*[350] the duration the teachings will remain is set at strictly five thousand years. Calculating from this Fire Rat year (1576), in the completed year of the Female Wood Pig (1575), 952 years had passed since the completion of the three five-hundred-year periods of results. Another 2548 years are thought to remain.

B. The actual summary of the treatise itself. This has three topics: 1. How the treatise was composed, 2. Confessing mistakes, and 3. Advice to be careful.

1. How the treatise was composed

40ab I mostly have explained this abhidharma
According to the Kashmiri Exposition.

Is the abhidharma explained in this treatise the abhidharma that the Teacher explained? you ask. **I,** Vasubandhu, have explained this Dharma of the *Treasury of Abhidharma* partially according to the tradition of the Sutra school and the Aparāntaka Great Exposition. However, I **mostly have explained this abhidharma according to** the school of **the Kashmiri** Great **Exposition,** because I explained it in Kashmir strictly according to the Exposition.

2. Confessing mistakes

40cd Any mistakes herein are solely ours;
The Sages are the authority in Dharma.

Any mistakes in words or meaning **herein,** in this treatise, **are solely my,**[351] the author's, own errors and mistakes. However, it is not a great wonder that someone like me would confuse the words and meaning in explaining the meaning of the scriptures: **the** Bhagavan **Sages** and their children, arhats who have the eye of the Dharma, **are the authority in** the words and meaning of the True **Dharma.**

> This completes the eighth area called "Teachings on the Absorptions" from the *Verses of the Treasury of Abhidharma.*

This completes the explanation of **the eighth area called "Teachings on the Absorptions" from** *The Explanation of* **the** ***"Verses of the Treasury of Abhidharma"*** called *The Essence of the Ocean of Abhidharma, The Words of Those who Know and Love, Explaining the Youthful Play, Opening the Eyes of Dharma, the Chariot of Easy Practice.*

3. Advice to be careful. This has two points.

a. Teaching the dangers of carelessness

41. The Teacher, the eye of the world, has been closed;
    The beings who were witness have mostly perished.
    Those who haven't seen thatness, those who are bad logicians
    And headstrong have confounded the teachings.

42. The one self-born, those who cherish his teachings,
    Have passed into the supreme peace. There's no refuge
    Or counsel for beings, and the stains that slay qualities
    Run rampant in this at their pleasure.

43a–c And so, as we know that for the Sage's teachings,
    It's as if the last breaths now rasp in the throat,
    That this is a time when the stains have great strength:

As he taught his disciples the distinction between what is the path that leads to liberation and what is not, **the Teacher,** the Bhagavan, is like **the eye of the world.** That eye **has been closed**—he has passed into nirvana—and it is as if worldly folk have been left sightless. **The beings** other than the Buddha **who were witness** to the dharma, the noble beings such as Kaśyapa, **have mostly** passed into nirvana and **perished.** Blinded by ignorance, **those** ordinary individuals **who have not seen** the **thatness** of Dharma and **who are bad logicians and headstrong,** following pseudo reasoning without relying on the Teacher's scriptures, **have confounded the teachings** of the Teacher through exaggeration and denigration.

The one Bhagavan, who is **self-born,** having found wisdom in his last existence without anyone to explain the scriptures, and **those who cherish his,**

the self-born's, **teachings have passed** without any remainder of the aggregates **into the supreme peace** that is superior to samsara. Without the Buddha or his children, **there is no refuge or counsel** who can give correct instruction **for beings, and the stains** of bad views and so forth **that** are the cause that **slays** the previously explained **qualities** and makes the teachings disappear **run rampant in this** world **at their pleasure,** or indiscriminately.

And so, as we who are intelligent **know that for the Sage's teachings,** the teachings of the Buddha, **it is as if,** for example, **the last breaths** at the approach of the time of death **now rasp in the throat** and will not remain long, and as we know **that this is a time when the stains** of bad views **have great strength,** follow the forthcoming advice.

b. Advice to rely on carefulness.

43d All those who want freedom, be careful!

In this manner, **all those who** fervently **want** the **freedom** of nirvana, **be careful** in everything! is the heartfelt advice. That is the root of all virtuous dharmas. In the words of the Bhagavan:

> Carefulness is a place of deathlessness;
> Carelessness is a place of death.
> Those who are careful will not die;
> The careless always die.[352]

The meaning of these is explained in *Letter to a Friend:*[353]

> A place of nectar, carefulness; but a place
> Of death is carelessness, the Sage declared.
> Thus to develop virtuous qualities,
> You always should act with respect and care.

Also from *Individual Liberation:*[354]

> Venerable ones, aging and death will truly come, and the teachings of the Teacher will be destroyed, so the venerable should practice the yogas of carefulness. The enlightenment of the Bhagavan Arhat Complete Perfect Buddha and the virtuous dharmas that are compatible with it, the factors of enlightenment, all attained through carefulness.

Thus it is said.

C. The manner of completing the explanation. This has two points.

1. Teaching the completing words

> This completes the *Verses on the Treasury of Abhidharma* composed by Master Vasubandhu.

2. The translator's colophon

> Translated into Tibetan by the Indian Abbot Jinamitra and the Tibetan translator Bande Kawa Paltsek and then corrected and finalized.

And now to say a few words about the reason for completing this work:

On Vindhya's lofty slopes of two accumulations,
The *kushu* stalks of powers and other qualities
Flourish with utter brilliance of youthfulness—
Great sage and master of the spring, please grant me refuge.

Sagara's sons, the beings of degenerate times,
Are stained and sullied by their various views.
At once you cleanse them with the natural Ganges:
Master Bhagīratha, grant me protection.[355]

Upon the Snow Land's eastern mountain face of merit,
The fully waxing light of good and virtue
From Konchok Lama, Shakyamuni's true disciple,
Conquers at once all darkness on three levels.

What need have we of tales of how in Magadha
The Shakyan prince bestowed three Dharma Wheels
On the three families? The perfect Buddha is here
And truly present as the wish-fulfilling jewel!

Additionally, my master, the great scholar
Renowned as the victorious over all,[356]
Is the most venerable in the Snow Land,
As rich in peace and tameness as Upāli.

If with his acumen in proofs and rebuttals
He destroys the logic of the six extremist teachers,
What need is there to talk of lesser opponents?
Thus in debate he is truly Dharmakirti!

From both my masters' kindness, I have not
Been stricken by the poison of the objects
Nor distracted by desire's illusory dance.
I take the burden on to free my mothers
And have faith in the ways of the Buddha's teachings.

The friend of day,[357] the master of the Shakyas,
Knowing the basket of the Abhidharma
To be discernment that will stop afflictions,
Thus taught it to his gatherings of students.
These teachings were in bits and pieces which
Shariputra and the rest compiled in *Seven Treatises.*

Afterwards seven hundred arhats at
Mount Vindhya wrote great treatises explaining
The meaning of the *Seven Treatises.*
Vasubandhu collected all the precious
Jewels of their meaning in this *Treasury.*

Then he himself wrote his own commentary,
And the son of a lord, Prince Yaśomitra,
The scholar Purṇavardhana, and other
Great Indian scholars wrote their explanations.

There is the chariot of the Practice Lineage,
The treatise that is called *The Springtime Cow.*
Upon the repeated requests of my true master
Great Namgyal Drakpa and from students Dogyü Gyatso

And others, for the benefit of future followers,
I have combined all aspects of these explications
And then explained this *Youthful Play* without
Any vagrant hearsay or my own fabrications.

When I was eighteen I received the full
And complete explanation and transmission
For Mikyö's commentary as well as

The *Treasury of Abhidharma* from
The omniscient glorious lama, Konchok Yenlak.
Then the great master trained me thoroughly in
The difficult points and dispelled my doubts
About the root, the commentary, and
The explanation, so that I have attained
Full mastery of the meaning of the words.
But if there may be any contradictions,
Mistakes, or faults herein, I ask all those
Who have the eyes of Dharma for their patience.

If any of my followers should wish
To gain the wish-fulfilling jewel of freedom
From the vast oceans of the abhidharma,
Embark upon this ship of *Youthful Play.*

May the rich nectar from the stamens of
The blossoming white lotus of this virtue
Nourish with deathless sustenance the bees
Who long for the teachings of the glorious Dakpo.

From now until I reach enlightenment's essence,
I ask the great master, the perfect buddha,
To dwell inseparably in my heart's drop.
May the nectar of my speech spread to all beings!

May they master unmistakenly and entirely
The meaning of the Baskets and the Tantras,
Have the intelligence to teach, write, and debate,
And strive to listen, contemplate, and meditate all day
and night.

May this essence of the ocean of abhidharma
That opens our eyes to the Dharma,
The place for clear-minded youths to play,
Spread over all the world and blaze!

When during his second uncountable aeon on the path of learning our Teacher, the unequalled king of the Shakyas himself, was the merchant Prajñābhadra, he formed his resolve in front of the tathagata Konchok Yenlak himself, who had arisen as the essence of all aspects of the body, speech, and mind of all the victors and was the sole refuge, support, land, and friend for all wanderers who fill space. I received this from the full moon of the face of the guru, omniscient glorious Konchok Shakya Choggi Tsowoy Bang, as well as from him, whose moon of wisdom that knows all there is to know is full and shines the light renowned as victorious in all directions that fills all the realms of the world. The crown jewel of vows, diligence, and scholarship in this Land of Snow, the one who is without peer in teaching, writing, and debating is Vijayakīrti's. I place the stainless dust from these two masters' feet on the crown of my head.

The monk of the Shakyas, Palden Mipham Chökyi Wangchuk Dorje Garwang Chokle Nampar Gyalway Nyingpo Khyabdak Tenpay Nyima, or by another name bestowed by the Khenpo of Uḍḍiyāna Padmasambhava, Vajreśvara, began this at the age of twenty in the great place of practice Sha Uk Tiger Gate. I completed it when called a twenty-one-year-old in the second half of the month of the Pleiades on the sixth day of the waning phase, of the Male Fire Rat year (1576) in the solitary place of White Mountain Cave near the great Dharma Wheel of Thupten Karma Sungrab Gyatso Ling. The scribe was Bhikshu Ānandarāja.

Virtue! Virtue! Virtue!

APPENDIX A

English Equivalents of Tibetan Terms

Terms are alphabetized according to Tibetan alphabetical order.

kun 'gro. universals.
kun tu 'gro ba'i rgyu. universal cause.
kun nas dkris pa. entangler.
kun nas nyon mongs pa. all-afflicted.
kun 'byung gyi bden pa. truth of origin.
kun sbyor. fetter.
kun rdzob. relative.
kun shes ldan pa'i dbang po. faculty of having all-knowing.
kun shes pa'i dbang po. faculty of all-knowing.
kun shes byed pa'i dbang po. faculty of producing all-knowing.
rkyen. condition.
skad cig ma. instant.
skal mnyam gyi rgyu. cause of same status.
skyabs. refuge.
skye mched. sense bases.
skye ba'i srid pa. birth state.
skyes nas thob pa. attained upon birth.
skyes nas mya ngan las 'da' ba. nirvana upon birth.
skyes nas myong 'gyur gyi las. karma experienced on birth.
skyes bu dam pa'i 'gro ba. holy wanderers.
skyes bu byed 'bras bu. personal result.
bskal pa grangs med. uncountable aeons.
bskal pa chen po. great aeon.

kha na ma tho ba. unwholesome.
khams. element.
khong khro. anger.
khyad par gyi lam. distinctive path.
khyab pa 'du byed kyi sdug bsngal. pervasive suffering of formation.
khro ba. aggression.
khrel med. immodesty.
khrel yod. modesty.
'khon 'dzin. grudge.
'khor lo'i dbyen. schism of the Wheel.

gong du 'pho ba. bound for higher.
gong ma cha mthun. those that lead to the higher.
gya nom snang ba. Excellent Appearance.
grang dmyal. cold hells.
dga' ldan. Joyous Land.
dge rgyas. Full Virtue.
dge chung. Lesser Virtue.
dge bsnyen. pursuer of virtue.
dge 'dun. sangha.
dge ba. virtue.
dge ba'i rtsa ba chad pa. severing the roots of virtue.

dge sbyong gi 'tshul. spiritual way.
dge sbyong gi 'tshul 'bras. results of the spiritual way.
dge tshul. novice.
dgra bcom pa. arhat.
'gog pa'i snyoms 'jug. absorption of cessation.
'gog pa'i bden pa. truth of cessation.
'gog pa'i rnam thar. emancipation of cessation.
'gyod pa. regret.
'gyur ba'i sdug bsngal. suffering of change.
'gro ba. wanderer.
rgod pa. agitation.
rgyas byung. produced by development.
rgyags pa. arrogance.
rgyu. cause.
rgyu mthun gyi 'bras bu. causally compatible result.
rgyu mthun pa. causally compatible.
rgyun zhugs pa. stream-enterer.
rgyu'i rkyen. causal condition.
sgom. meditation.
sgom spang. discards of meditation.
sgom lam. path of meditation.
sgyu. pretense.
sgra mi snyan. Unpleasant Sound.
bsgribs la lung ma bstan. obscured neutral.

nga rgyal. pride.
ngo bo nyid kyi rtog pa. essential thought.
ngo tsha. shame.
ngo tsha med pa. shamelessness.
nges pa'i las. definite karma.
nges par rtog pa'i rtog pa. thought that recognizes.
nges 'byed cha mthun. precursor to clear realization.
dngos po. thing.
dngos su log par zhugs pa. direct mistaken engagement.
mngon rtogs. clear realization.
mngon par 'du byed pa med pa mya ngan las 'da ba. nirvana without effort.
mngon par 'du byed pa mya ngan las 'da ba. nirvana with effort.
mngon shes. clairvoyance.
mngon sum. direct perception.
sngun dus. previous state.

ci yang med. Nothingness.
bcas pa'i kha na ma tho ba. prohibited unwholesome.

chags bcas. desirous.
chags pa. greed.
chags pa med pa. nongreed.
chags bral. detached.
cho 'phrul. miracle.
chos. Dharma, phenomena
chos kyi 'khor lo. Wheel of Dharma.
chos kyi rjes 'brang. follower of dharma.
chos kyi phung po. aggregates of Dharma.
chos mngon pa. abhidharma.
chos can. dharma base.
chos mchog. supreme dharma.
chos bzang. Good Dharma.
chos bzod. dharma forbearance.
chos shes. dharma knowing.
chu bo. floods.
'chab pa. concealment.
'chab pa. hypocrisy.
'chi ba'i srid pa. death state.
'chi bar sems pa'i chos can. one with volition for death.
'ching ba. bonds.

'jig rten. world.
'jig rten pa'i yang dag pa'i lta ba. correct worldly view.
'jig lta. personality view.
'jig tshogs la lta ba. view of personality.
'jig sred. craving destruction.
rjes shes. subsequent knowing.
rjes su dran pa'i rtog pa. thought that remembers.
rjes su srung ba'i chos can. protected one.

nyon mongs. affliction.
nyon mongs dri ma. afflicted filths.
nyon mongs pa'i sgrib pa. afflictive obscurations.

nyon mongs med pa. unprovocative.
nyi 'og pa. Aparāntaka.
nying mtshams sbyor ba. rebirth-linking.
nye 'khor dmyal ba. neighboring hell.
nye ba'i nyon mongs. near afflictions.
nye bar len pa. grasping.
nye bar len pa'i phung po lnga. aggregates of grasping, five.
nyer len gyi rgyu. grasping cause.
gnyid. sleep.
mnyam bzhag. equipoise.
snyoms 'jug. absorption.
snyoms 'jug gi sgrib pa. obscurations to absorption.
snyoms 'jug dag pa pa. pure absorption.
snyoms 'jug ro myang ldan. absorption concurrent with enjoyment.
bsnyen gnas. fasting vows.

ting nge 'dzin. samadhi.
gti mug. delusion.
gti mug med pa. nondelusion.
btang snyoms. equanimity, neutral feeling.
btags yod. nominally existent.
rtog pa. considering.
rtogs pa'i skal pa can. capable to realize.
lta na sdug pa. Lovely to Behold.
lta ba. view.
lta ba mchog 'dzin. overesteeming views.
stong pa. empty.
stong spyi phud. general prime thousand.
stobs. power.
brten bcas. active.
bstan bcos. treatise.

tha ma cha mthun. those that lead to the lowest.
thang cig. minute.
thams cad yod par smra ba. Sarvastivada.
thar pa cha mthun. precursor to freedom.
thod rgal gyi snyoms 'jug. skipping absorption.
thod rgal gyi ting nge 'dzin. skipping samadhi.
thogs bcas. obstructive.
thogs med. unobstructive.
the tshom. doubt.
theg pa dman pa. Foundation Vehicle.
thub pa. sage.
mthar lta. extreme view.
mthar 'dzin lta ba. view of holding extremes.
mthong chos myong 'gyur gyi las. visibly experienced karma.
mthong spang. discards of seeing.
mthong bas thob pa. attained through seeing.
mthong lam. path of seeing.
'thab bral. Conflict Free.

dad pa'i rjes 'brang. follower of faith.
dad pas mos. convinced through faith.
don dam. ultimate.
de ma thag rkyen. immediate condition.
de mtshungs. inactive.
de yi skad cig. instant of that.
dud 'gro. animal.
dus dang sbyor. occasional.
dus dang mi sbyor. nonoccasional.
drang srong. sage.
dran pa. mindfulness.
dran pa nye bar bzhag pa bzhi. foundations of mindfulness, four.
drod. warmth.
bdag rkyen. dominant condition.
bdag po'i 'bras bu. dominant result.
mdo. sutra.
'dod khams. Desire realm.
'dod chags. desire.
'dod pa la 'dun pa. pleasure-seeking.
'dod pa'i sred pa. craving for desire.
'du byed. formation.
'du byed kyi phung po. aggregate of formation.
'du shes. conception.
'du shes kyi phung po. aggregate of conception.
'du shes med 'du shes med min. Neither Conception nor Non-Conception.
'dun pa. intention.
'dus byas. composite, compound.

'dus ma byas. noncomposite, noncompound.
rdo rje lta bu ting nge 'dzin. vajra-like samadhi.
rdul phra rab. atoms.
rdul phran. molecules.
ldan min 'du byed. nonconcurrent formation.
sdom pa. vow.
sdom min. wrong vow.
sdig pa. misdeed.
sdug bsngal. suffering.
sdug bsngal gyi bden pa. truth of suffering.
sdug bsngal gyi sdug bsngal. suffering of suffering.
sdug pa'i rnam thar. emancipation of loveliness.

nam mkha'. space.
nam mkha' mtha' yas. Infinite Space.
gnas thams cad du 'chi 'pho ba. one who dies in all realms.
gnas pa las mi bskyod pa. unshaken from abiding.
gnod sems. malice.
mnar med pa. Incessant Hell.
rnam grol lam. path of liberation.
rnam thar pa. emancipation.
rnam par rgyal byed. Fully Conquering.
rnam par nyams pa. forfeit.
rnam par mi 'tshe ba. nonhostility.
rnam par 'tshe ba. hostility.
rnam par rig byed ma yin pa'i gzugs. imperceptible form.
rnam par shes pa'i phung po. aggregate of consciousness.
rnam byang. utterly pure.
rnam smin gyi rgyu. cause of full ripening.
rnam smin gyi sgrib pa. ripened obscurations.
rnam smin gyi 'bras bu. fully ripened result.
rnam g.yeng. distraction.
rnam shes. consciousness.
rnam shes mtha' yas. Infinite Consciousness.

brnab sems. covetousness.

dpyod pa. examining.
spang bya. discard.
spong ba'i lam. paths that abandon, paths that discard.
spel sgom. alternating meditation.
spyod lam. path of activities.

phal chen sde pa. Majority school.
phung po. aggregate.
phyin ci logs pa bzhi. errors, four.
phyir mi 'ong ba. nonreturner.
phyed du 'phar ba. half leapers.
phra rgyas. kernel.
phrag dog. envy.
'phar ba. leapers.
'phags lam yan lag brgyad. noble eightfold path.
'phen byed kyi las. propelling karma.
'phrul dga'. Joy of Emanations.

ba lang spyod. Bountiful Cow.
bag chags. imprint.
bag med. carelessness.
bag yod. carefulness.
bar gyi bskal pa. intermediate aeon.
bar chad med lam. path of no obstacles.
bar do'i srid pa. between state.
bar dor mya ngan las 'da ba. nirvana in the intermediate.
bar sdom. mid-vow.
byang chub. enlightenment.
byang chub phyogs kyi chos. factors of enlightenment.
byang chub yan lag bdun. branches of enlightenment, seven.
byang chub sems dpa'. bodhisattva.
bying ba. torpor.
bye brag smra ba. Great Exposition school.
byed rgyu. enabling cause.
blo. mind.
dbang po. faculty.
dbang po lnga. faculties, five.
dbang po 'pho ba. refine faculties.
'byung gyur. source-derived.

'byung ba. sources.
'byung ba chen po bzhi. great sources, four.
bral ba. removal.
bral 'bras. result of removal.
'bras gnas. abider in result.
'bras bu. result.
'bras bu che ba. Great Result.
'bras bu thos rgal ba. skipping results.
'bras bu mthar gyis pa. successive results.
sbyor ba. yoke.
sbyor 'byung. attained by training.
sbyor lam. path of joining.
sbyin pa. generosity.

ma bsgribs lung ma bstan. unobscured neutral.
ma nges pa'i las. not definite karma.
ma dad pa. nonfaith.
ma dros pa'i mtsho. Unheated Lake.
ma 'dres pa'i chos. unshared qualities.
ma byin par len pa. stealing, taking what has not been given.
ma mo. matrix.
ma yin dgag. not-negation.
ma rig pa. ignorance.
mar me mdzad. Dipamkara.
mos pa. interest.
mos pa las byung ba'i yid la byed pa. attention produced by interest.
mi. human.
mi skye ba shes pa. knowing nonarising.
mi skye ba'i chos can. nonarising dharma base.
mi dge ba. nonvirtue, unvirtuous.
mi lcogs med pa. Not Unable.
mi che ba. Not Great.
mi mjed 'jig rten gyi khams. Unbearable World Realm.
mi rtag pa. impermanent.
mi gdung ba. Without Pain.
mi g.yo ba'i chos can. unshakable one.
me mar mur pa. Burning Ground.
med dgag. no-negation.
me'i khams. fire element.
dmigs rkyen. objective condition.
dmyal ba. hell.

rmongs pa. delusion.
smon nas shes pa. knowing from aspiration.

rtsa ba'i nyon mongs. root afflictions.
rtse gcig pa. one-pointedness.
rtse mo. peak.
brtson 'grus. diligence.
tshad med dge. Immeasurable Virtue.
tshad med 'od. Immeasurable Light.
tshangs chen. Great Brahma.
tshangs pa mdun na 'don. Brahma's Ministers.
tshangs par spyod pa. Brahmic conduct.
tshangs ris. Brahma's Abode.
tshor ba. feeling.
tshor ba'i phung po. aggregate of feeling.
tshogs na spyod pa'i rang sang rgyas. congregating self-buddha.
tshogs lam. path of accumulation.
tshe cig bar chad cig pa. one lifetime, one obstacle.
tshul khrims. discipline.
tshul khrims brtul zhugs mchog 'dzin. overesteeming discipline and austerity.
mtshan nyid. characteristic.
mtshan gzhi. character base.
mtshams med kyi las. heinous karma, heinous deeds.
mtshungs ldan. concurrent.
mtshungs ldan rgyu. concurrent cause.
mtshungs pa de ma thag rkyen. concurrent immediate condition.
'tshig pa. contentiousness.

'dzam bu gling. Rose-Apple Land.
rdzas yod. substantially existent.
rdzogs byed kyi las. completing karma.
rdzu 'phrul gyi rkang pa bzhi. feet of miracles, four.

zhag mi thub. impossible day.
zhe sdang. hatred.
zhe sdang med pa. nonhatred.
gzhan 'phrul dbang byed. Mastery over Others' Emanations.

zag bcas. defiled.
zag pa. defilement.
zag med. undefiled.
zad pa shes pa. knowing extinction.
zad par gyi skye mched. all-encompassing sense bases.
zad par gyi skye mched bcu. ten all-encompassing sense bases.
zad mi skye shes pa. knowing extinction and nonarising.
zil gyis gnon pa'i skye mched. overpowering sense bases.
gzugs. form.
gzugs kyi phung po. aggregate of form.
gzugs khams. Form realm.
gzugs can gzugs la lta ba'i rnam thar. emancipation of viewing external form while conceiving of internal form.
gzugs med kyi rnam thar. formless emancipations.
gzugs med khams. Formless realm.
gzugs med nyer 'gro. bound for Formless.
gzugs su nyer 'gro. bound for Form.
bzod pa. forbearance.

'og min. Below None.
'od chen. Great Light.
'od chung. Lesser Light.
'od gsal. Radiant Light.

yang dag pa'i ngag. right speech.
yang dag pa'i ting nge 'dzin. right samadhi.
yang dag pa'i rtog pa. right consideration.
yang dag pa'i lta ba. right view.
yang dag pa'i dran pa. right mindfulness.
yang dag pa'i rtsol ba. right effort.
yang dag pa'i 'tsho ba. right livelihood.
yang dag pa'i las kyi mtha'. right action.
yang dag par spong ba bzhi. complete abandonments, four.
yong su nyams pa'i chos can. regressed one.
yongs su nyams pa. regress.
yi dwags. hungry ghost.
yid. mind.
yid la byed pa. attention.
yud tsam. hour.

yul can. subject.
g.yo. deceit.

rang bzhin kha na ma tho ba. inherently unwholesome.
rang sang rgyas. self-buddha.
ris mthun pa. likeness.
rigs. family.
rigs nas rigs. from family to family.
reg pa. contact.
reg pa. touch.
rlung gi khams. air element.
srog gi dbang po. faculty of life force.
srog bcod pa. taking life.
srid pa lan bdun pa. seven timer.
srid pa'i rtse mo. Peak of Existence.
srid pa'i sred pa. craving for existence.
sred pa. craving.

lan grangs gzhan myong 'gyur gyi las. karma experienced in other lifetimes.
lan cig phyir 'ong ba. once-returner.
lam. path.
lam gyi bden pa. truth of path.
las. karma.
las kyi sgrib pa. karmic obscurations.
las kyi dbyen. ritual schism.
las kyi lam. karmic path, path of karma.
log par g.yem pa. sexual misconduct.
logs zhugs. mistaken engagement.
le lo. laziness.
legs spyad. fine conduct.
lung ma bstan. neutral.
lus kyis mngon sum byed. made manifest by body.
lus 'phags po. Superior Body.

shin tu mthong ba. Great Vision.
shin tu sbyangs. pliancy.
shes nas dad pa. faith from knowing.
shes pa. cognition.
shes bya'i sgrib pa. cognitive obscuration.
shes bya'i gzhi lnga. bases of the knowable, five.
shes bzhin min pa. nonawareness.
shes rab. full knowing.

shes rab kyang grol. freed just by full knowing.
shes rab kyi cha las rnam grol. liberated through the aspect of full knowing.

sa 'pho ba. shift level.
sangs rgyas. buddha.
sa'i khams. earth element.
so so skye bo. ordinary individual.
so sor yang dag par rig pa. unhindered knowledge.
so sor brtags pa'i 'gog pa. analytic cessation.
so sor brtags min 'gog pa. nonanalytic cessation.
so sor thar pa. individual liberation
sems. cognition or mind.
sems pa. volition.
sems pa'i las. volitional karma.
sems 'byung. mental factor.
ser sna. stinginess.
sum cu rtsa gsum. Heaven of the Thirty-Three.
slob lam. path of learning.
bsam gtan khyad par can. special dhyana.
bsam gtan gyi nyer bsdogs. preparations for dhyana.
bsam gtan rab kyi mtha'. highest end of concentration.
bsam pa'i las. intended karma.
bsod nams skyes. Merit Born.
bsod nams cha mthun. precursor to merit.
bsod nams bya ba'i gzhi. bases of meritorious action.
bse ru lta bu rang sang rgyas. rhinolike self-buddha.

lha. god.
lha ma yin. demigod.
lhag pa tshul khrims kyi bslab pa. superior training in discipline.
lhag pa shes rab kyi bslab pa. superior training in full knowing.
lhag pa sems kyi bslab pa. superior training in mind.
lhag med myan ngan las 'das pa. nirvana without remainder.
lhan skyes. coemergent.
lhan cig 'byung rgyu. coemergent cause.

APPENDIX B

English Equivalents of Sanskrit Terms

The Sanskrit terms listed below come primarily from the edition of the root text prepared by V.V. Gokhale and the Tibetan-Sanskrit concordances compiled by Hirakawa. Terms are alphabetized according to the Devanagari alphabet.

akaniṣṭha. Below None.
akiṃcanya. Nothingness.
akuśala. nonvirtue, unvirtuous.
akopyadharman. unshakable one.
agradharma. supreme dharma.
aṇu. molecules.
atapas. Without Pain.
adattādāna. stealing, taking what has not been given.
adveṣa. nonhatred.
adhicittaṃśikṣā. superior training in mind.
adhipatipratyaya. dominant condition.
adhipatiphala. dominant result.
adhiprajñaṃśikṣā. superior training in full knowing.
adhimuktimanaskāra. attention produced by interest.
adhimokṣa. interest.
adhiśīlaṃśikṣā. superior training in discipline.
anapatrāpya. immodesty.
anabhisaṃskāraparinirvāyin. nirvana without effort.
anavatapta. Unheated Lake.
anāgāmi. nonreturner.
anāgāmya. Not Unable.
anāsrava. undefiled.
anitya. impermanent.
anivṛtāvyākṛta. unobscured neutral.
anutpattidharmin. nonarising dharma base.
anutpādajñāna. knowing nonarising.
anurakṣaṇādharman. protected one.
anuśaya. kernel.
anusmaraṇavikalpa. thought that remembers.
anekāsaṃkhyeyaṃ kalpam. uncountable aeons.
antaḥkalpa. intermediate aeon.
antagrahaṇa. view of holding extremes.
antagrāhadṛṣṭi. extreme view.
antarāparinirvāyin. nirvana in the intermediate.
antarābhava. between state.
anvayajñāna. subsequent knowing.
apatrāpya. modesty.
aparaparyāyavedanīya. karma experienced in other lifetimes.

aparāntaka. Aparāntaka.
apratigha. unobstructive.
apratisaṃkhyānirodha. nonanalytic cessation.
apramāṇaśubha. Immeasurable Virtue.
apramāṇābhā. Immeasurable Light.
apramāda. carefulness.
abhijña. clairvoyance.
abhidharma. abhidharma.
abhidhyā. covetousness.
abhibhvāyatana. overpowering sense bases.
abhisamaya. clear realization.
araṇā. unprovocative.
ardhapluta. half leapers.
arhat. arhat.
alobha. nongreed.
avadya. unwholesome.
avamagna, nimagna. torpor.
avara bhāgīya. those that lead to the lowest.
avijñapti. imperceptible form.
avidyā. ignorance.
avihiṃsā. nonhostility.
avīci. Incessant Hell.
avṛhā. Not Great.
aveṇikadharma. unshared qualities.
avetyaprasāda. faith from knowing.
avyākṛta. neutral.
aśraddhya. nonfaith.
asaṃvara. wrong vow.
asaṃskāra. noncomposite, noncompound.
asamayika. nonoccasional.
asura. demigod.

ākāśa. space.
ākāśānantya. Infinite Space.
ākṣepikakarma. propelling karma.
ājñatāvindriya. faculty of having all-knowing.
ājñasyāmindriya. faculty of producing all-knowing.
ājñātendriya. faculty of all-knowing.
ānantaryamārga. path of no obstacles.
ānantaryāṇikarmāṇi. heinous karma, heinous deeds.
āyatana. sense bases.
ārūpyaga. bound for Formless.
ārūpyadhātu. Formless realm.
āryaaṣṭānggikamarga. noble eightfold path.
ālambanapratyaya. objective condition.
āsrava. defilement.
āsvādanāsaṃprayukta. absorption concurrent with enjoyment.
āhrīkya. shamelessness.

indriya. faculty.
indriyasaṃcāra. refine faculties.

īryāpatha. path of activities.
īrṣyā. envy.

uttarakuru. Unpleasant Sound.
utpattilābhin. attained upon birth.
utsada. neighboring hell.
uddhata. agitation.
upakleśa. near afflictions.
upanāha. grudge.
upapattibhava. birth state.
upapadyaparinirvāyin. nirvana upon birth.
upavāsastha. fasting vows.
upādāna. grasping.
upādānakāraṇa. grasping cause.
upāsaka. pursuer of virtue.
upekṣā. equanimity.
upekṣā. neutral feeling.

ūnarātra. impossible day.
ūrdhvabhāgīya. those that lead to the higher.
ūrdhvasrotas. bound for higher.
ūṣman. warmth.

ṛṣi. sage.

ekavīcika. one lifetime, one obstacle.
ekāgra. one-pointedness.

ogha. floods.
aupacayika. produced by development.

karma. karma.
karmapatha. karmic path, path of karma.

karmabheda. ritual schism.
karmāvaraṇa. karmic obscurations.
kāmacchanda. pleasure-seeking.
kāmatṛṣṇā. craving for desire.
kāmadhātu. Desire realm.
kāyasākṣin. made manifest by body.
kāraṇahetu. enabling cause.
kukūla. Burning Ground.
kulaṃkula. from family to family.
kuśala. virtue.
kuśalamūlasamuccheda. severing the roots of virtue.
kṛtsnāyatana. all-encompassing sense bases.
kaukṛtya. regret.
kauṣīdya. laziness.
krodha. aggression.
kleśa. affliction.
kleśamala. afflicted filths.
kleśāvaraṇa. afflictive obscurations.
kṣaṇa. instant.
kṣanti. forbearance.
kṣayajñāna. knowing extinction.
kṣayānutpādijñāna. knowing extinction and nonarising.

khaḍgamviṣāṇakalpa. rhinolike self-buddha.

gati. wanderer.
gotra. family.
godānīya. Bountiful Cow.

cakrabheda. schism of the Wheel.
caturṛddhipāda. feet of miracles, four.
catvāri samyakprahāṇāni. complete abandonments, four.
catvāro viparītāsāḥ. errors, four.
citta. cognition or mind.
cetana. volition.
cetanākarma. volitional karma.
cetayitvākarma. intended karma.
caitasika. mental factor.

chanda. intention.

jambudvīpa. Rose-Apple Land.
jīvitendriya. faculty of life force.
jñeyāvaraṇa. cognitive obscuration.

tatkṣaṇa. instant of that.
tatsabhāga. inactive.
tiryaka. animal.
tuśita. Joyous Land.
tṛṣṇa. craving.
tejodhātu. fire element.
trayastrimsa. Heaven of the Thirty-Three.

darṣanaheya. discards of seeing.
darśanamārga. path of seeing.
daśakṛtsnāyatana. ten all-encompassing sense bases.
dāna. generosity.
dīpaṃkara. Dipamkara.
duḥkha. suffering.
duḥkhaduḥkhatā. suffering of suffering.
duḥkhasatya. truth of suffering.
duścarita. harmful conduct.
dṛṣṭadharmaphalakarma. visibly experienced karma.
dṛṣṭi. view.
dṛṣṭiparāmarśa. overesteeming views.
dṛṣṭiprāpta. attained through seeing.
deva. god.
dravyatamanta, dravyasat. substantially existent.
dveṣa. hatred.

dharma. dharma, phenomenon.
dharmakṣānti. dharma forbearance.
dharmacakra. Wheel of Dharma.
dharmajñāna. dharma knowing.
dharmaskandha. aggregates of Dharma.
dharmānusārin. follower of dharma.
dharmin. dharma base.
dhātu. element.
dhī. mind.
dhyānāntara. special dhyana.

nāraka. hell.
nikāyasabhāga. likeness.

nirupadhiśeṣanirvāṇa. nirvana without remainder.
nirūpaāṇvikalpa. thought that recognizes.
nirodha satya. truth of cessation.
nirodhasamāpatti. absorption of cessation.
nirmāṇarati. Joy of Emanations.
nirvedhabhāgīya. precursor to clear realization.
nivṛtāvyākṛta. obscured neutral.
niṣyanda. causally compatible.
niṣyandaphala. causally compatible result.
naivasaṃjñānāsaṃjñā. Neither Conception nor Non-Conception.

pañcānām ānantaryāṇām. heinous deeds, five.
pañcendriyatva. faculties, five.
pañcopādānaskandha. aggregates of grasping, five.
Paranirmitavaśavartin. Mastery over Others' Emanations.
paramāṇu. atoms.
paramārtha. ultimate.
pariṇamaduḥkhatā. suffering of change.
parihāṇadharman. regressed one.
parihīṇa. regress.
Parīttaśubha. Lesser Virtue.
Parīttābhā. Lesser Light.
paryavasthāna. entangler.
paryudāsapratiṣedha. not-negation.
pāpa. misdeed.
puṇyakriyāvastu. bases of meritorious action.
Puṇyaprasava. Merit Born.
puṇyabhagīya. precursor to merit.
puruṣakāraphala. personal result.
pūrvakālabhava. previous state.
pūrvavideha. Superior Body.
pṛthagjanatva. ordinary individual.
pṛthivī. earth element.
prakṛtisāvadya. inherently unwholesome.
prajñaptita, prajñaptisat. nominally existent.
prajñā. full knowing.
prajñāvimukti. liberated through the aspect of full knowing.
praṇidhijñāna. knowing from aspiration.
pratikṣepaṇasāvadya. prohibited unwholesome.
pratigha. anger.
pratimokṣa. individual liberation.
prativedhanādharman. capable to realize.
pratisaṃkhyānirodha. analytic cessation.
pratisaṃvid. unhindered knowledge.
pratisandhi. rebirth-linking.
pratyakṣa. direct perception.
pratyaya. condition.
pratyekabuddha. self-buddha.
pradāsa. contentiousness.
Prabhāsvara. Radiant Light.
pramādita. carelessness.
prayoga. yoke.
prayogaja. attained by training.
prayogamārga. path of joining.
praṣabdhi. pliancy.
prasajyapratiṣedha. no-negation.
prahāṇamārga. paths that abandon, paths that discard.
prāṇātipāta. taking life.
prātihārya. miracle.
prāntakoṭika. highest end of concentration.
preta. hungry ghost.
pluta. leapers.

phala. result.
phalasthita. abider in result.

bandhana. bonds.
bala. power.
buddha. buddha.
bṛhatphala. Great Result.
bodhi. enlightenment.
bodhipakṣya. factors of enlightenment.
bodhisattva. bodhisattva.
brahmakāyika. Brahma's Abode.
brahmacarya. Brahmic conduct.
brahmapurohita. Brahma's Ministers.

bhavarāga. craving for existence.
bhavāgra. Peak of Existence.
bhāva. thing.
bhāvanā. meditation.

bhāvanāmārga. path of meditation.
bhāvanāheya. discards of meditation.
bhūta. sources.
bhūmisaṃcāra. shift level.
bhautika. source-derived.

mada. arrogance.
madhyastha. mid-vow.
manas. mind.
manaskāra. attention.
manuṣya. human.
maraṇabhava. death state.
mahākalpa. great aeon.
mahābrahmāṇa. Great Brahma.
mahābhūta. great sources, four.
mahāsaṃghika. Majority school.
mātṛkā. matrix.
mātsarya. stinginess.
māna. pride.
māyā. pretense.
mārga. path.
mārgasatya. truth of path.
mithyācāra. sexual misconduct.
middha. sleep.
muni. sage.
muhūrta. hour.
mūrdhatva. peak.
mūlakleśa. root afflictions.
mokṣabhāgīya. precursor to freedom.
moha. delusion.
mrakṣa. concealment.
mrakṣa. hypocrisy.

yāma. Conflict Free.

rāga. desire.
rūpa. form.
rūpadhātu. Form realm.
rūpaskandha. aggregate of form.
rūpopaga. bound for Form.

lakṣaṇa. characteristic.
lakṣya. character base.
lava. minute.
loka. world.
lobha. greed.
laukikī samyagdṛṣṭi. correct worldly view.

vajropamasamādhi. vajra-like samadhi.
vāsana. imprint.
vāyudhātu. air element.
vicara. examining.
vicikitsā. doubt.
vijñāna. consciousness.
vijñānaskandha. aggregate of consciousness.
vijñānānta. Infinite Consciousness.
vitarka. considering.
vipākaphala. fully ripened result.
vipākahetu. cause of full ripening.
vipākāvaraṇa. ripened obscurations.
vipratipanna. mistaken engagement.
viprayuktasaṃskāra. nonconcurrent formation.
vibhavecchā. craving destruction.
vimuktimārga. path of liberation.
vimokṣa. emancipation.
viṣayin. subject.
viśeṣamārga. distinctive path.
visaṃyoga. removal.
visaṃyogaphala. result of removal.
vihiṃsā. hostility.
vihīna. forfeit.
vīrya. diligence.
vedanā. feeling.
vedanāskandha. aggregate of feeling.
vaijayanta. Fully Conquering.
vaibhāṣika. Great Exposition school.
vyavakīrṇabhāvita. alternating meditation.
vyavadāna. utterly pure.
vyāpannacitta. malice.
vyutkrāntakasamāpatti. skipping absorption.
vyutkrāntakasamāpatti. skipping samadhi.

śaraṇa. refuge.
śāṭhya. deceit.
śāstra. treatise.
śītanāraka. cold hells.
śīla. discipline.
śīlavrataparāmarśa. overesteeming discipline and austerity.

śuddhaka. pure absorption.
śubhakṛtsna. Full Virtue.
śūnya. empty.
śaikṣa mārga. path of learning.
śraddhādhimukta. convinced through faith.
śraddhānusārin. follower of faith.
śrāmaṇera. novice.
śrāmaṇya. spiritual way.
śrāmaṇyaphala. results of the spiritual way.

saṃkleśa. all-afflicted.
saṃgha. sangha.
saṃjñā. conception.
saṃjṇāskandha. aggregate of conception.
saṃpradhṛ. fine conduct.
saṃprayukta. concurrent.
saṃprayuktakahetu. concurrent cause.
saṃbhāramārga. path of accumulation.
saṃyojana. fetter.
saṃvara. vow.
saṃskaraduḥkhatā. pervasive suffering of formation.
saṃskāra. composite, compound, formation.
saṃskāraskandha. aggregate of formation.
sakṛdāgāmin. once-returner.
satkāyadṛṣṭi. personality view.
satpuruṣagati. holy wanderers.
saptakṛtvaḥparamaḥ. seven timer.
saptabodhyanggāni. branches of enlightenment, seven.
sapratigha. obstructive.
sabhāga. active.
sabhāgahetu. cause of same status.
samanantarapratyaya. concurrent immediate condition.
samādhi. samadhi.
samāpatti. absorption.
samāhita. equipoise.
samudayasatya. truth of origin.
samyakkarmānta. right action.
samyaksaṃkalpa. right consideration.
samyaksamādhi. right samadhi.
samyaksmṛti. right mindfulness.
samyagājīva. right livelihood.
samyagdṛṣṭi. right view.
samyagvāka. right speech.
samyagvyāyāma. right effort.
samvṛti. relative.
sarāga. desirous.
sarvacyuta. one who dies in all realms.
sarvatraga. universals.
sarvatragahetu. universal cause.
Sarvāstivāda. Sarvastivada.
sahaja. coemergent.
sahabhūhetu. coemergent cause.
sahalokadhātu. Unbearable World Realm.
sābhisaṃskāraparinirvāyin. nirvana with effort.
sāmayika. occasional.
sāsrava. defiled.
sāhasraścūḍikaḥ. general prime thousand.
sudṛśa. Excellent Appearance.
sudharma. Good Dharma.
sūtra. sutra.
skandha. aggregate.
sthitākampyas. unshaken from abiding.
sparśa. contact, touch.
smṛti. mindfulness.
smṛtyupasthāna. foundations of mindfulness, four.
srotaāpattiphalapratipannaka. entering stream-enterer.
srotaāpanna. stream-enterer.
svabhāvavikalpa. essential thought.

hīnayāna. Foundation Vehicle.
hetu. cause.
hetupratyaya. causal condition.
hrī. shame.

Notes

Notes on Area I

1. The autocommentary also has a ninth area, "Teachings on the Individual," which refutes the existence of an individual self. Tibetan sources generally explain that Vasubandhu wrote the ninth chapter later than the root verses, at the time that he was writing the autocommentary. The fact that this area comes after Vasubandhu's concluding advice—"All those who want freedom, be careful!"—tends to support this position. The verses for this area do not appear in the Derge Tengyur root verses, and *Youthful Play,* like most Tibetan commentaries, does not comment on this area.

2. Mi bskyod rdo rje, 2003, vol. 1, 98.

3. Skt. *matṛika,* Tib. *ma mo.* Another term for abhidharma because it classifies phenomena into groups or matrices of two or three.

4. The Fifth Shamar Konchok Yenlag.

5. Skt. *pratyekabuddha,* Tib. *rang sang rgyas.* Although commonly translated as *solitary realizer,* that translation is awkward and not entirely accurate, as not all self-buddhas attain realization in solitude. In the Tibetan, the syllable *rang* indicates that they attain enlightenment on their own, without a teacher in their last lifetime. Hence they are self-awakened or a *self-buddha.*

6. For example, such as the Prince Siddharta before he attained enlightenment.

7. The internal sense bases are the eye, ear, nose, tongue, body, and mind, and the external sense bases are form, sound, scent, taste, touch, and dharmas.

8. Some non-Buddhists believe that the gods such as Brahma or Śakra can liberate beings through their miraculous powers or by bestowing holiness or blessings upon them.

9. The eighteen original schools of Buddhism.

10. Skt. *anuśaya*, Tib. *phra rgyas*. The six are the subtle afflictions of desire, anger, pride, ignorance, view, and doubt. The kernels are discussed at length in area V.

Many translations from the Tibetan translate this term as "subtle-expander" or a similar term, matching the literal meaning of the Tibetan compound and reflecting Vasubandhu's explanation of the meaning of the Sanskrit term in V.39. However, this sounds clumsy and awkward in English. Translations from the Sanskrit often either leave the Sanskrit *anuśaya* untranslated or translate it as "predilection." The word *predilection* has some merits but is frequently used in a positive sense in English. As the kernels are always afflicted, that seems inappropriate. The word *kernel* matches the meaning of *phra rgyas* in that a kernel is something small that can develop into something larger.

Additionally, different schools of Buddhism have differing opinions as to the nature of the kernels. Theravadins and the Kashmiri Vaibhashikas posit that they are latencies, like seeds, whereas the Great Vehicle abhidharma presents them as manifest, though subtle. The English word *kernel* can mean seed, but it also is used in other contexts to describe a manifest but subtle quality, as in the phrase "a kernel of truth." Thus *kernel* can be used to describe both the Theravada and the Great Vehicle positions without prejudice.

11. Tib. *med dgag*. A no-negation generally negates the existence of something. In other words, the Sutra school proposes that liberation is merely the absence of obscurations, but is not in itself a thing. The same term is sometimes translated as *nonaffirming negation,* but here a simpler translation is preferred, although one must note that just as not every Tibetan negation that uses the word *med* is a *med dgag,* not every negation that uses *no* is a no-negation.

12. That is, Vasubandhu's autocommentary.

13. *See* III.96d.

14. An actual antidote is unable to coexist with what it discards, so therefore other wisdoms, which unlike the wisdom of the ten powers can coexist with the causes of unknowing, are not their actual antidote.

15. The Kashmiri Great Exposition asserts that the attainment or possession of something is itself a substantial thing separate from that which is possessed. *See* II.36 ff.

16. Variously translated in other translations as wisdom, discernment, supreme knowledge, or left untranslated but anglicized as *prajna,* this term refers to both an ordinary mental factor present with every cognition as well as, especially in Great Vehicle scriptures and treatises, the sixth transcendence, transcendent full knowing. Although at first glance, these might seem to be entirely different, the Buddha characterizes both in the sutras as *fully distinguishing dharma from nondharma.* In other words, it is fully knowing what is true and what is not, or intelligence.

The English word *wisdom* seems a good translation for the term *ye shes (jñāna)*, so it seems best not to use it for *shes rab* to avoid confusion between the two. *Discernment* seems quite appropriate for the mental factor that accompanies ordinary cognitions but somehow "transcendent discernment" does not sound particularly inspiring. *Supreme knowledge* is a very literal translation of the Tibetan explanations of the etymology of the word, but it is rather opaque. No one could argue that *prajna* has the wrong meaning, but English speakers do not naturally understand it and might think of it as being something exalted and foreign—not something that is associated with everything that happens in our minds. For these reasons, *full knowing* seems the best translation.

17. Prince Yaśomitra's *Sphuṭārthābhidharmakośavyākhyā,* an explication of the autocommentary.

18. That is, phenomena can be either defiled or undefiled. They cannot be both, nor can they be neither.

19. That is, in all times and all situations.

20. That is, there are some future composite phenomena that exist but will not happen.

21. The defilements are types of afflictions. *See* V.35.

22. They develop or expand either when they observe or focus upon an object or when they are concurrent or associated with a cognition that focuses on an object. *See* V.17–18.

23. Phenomena or bases that have the characteristic of being defiled.

24. The non-Buddhist Vaiśeṣika school.

25. Prince Yaśomitra's commentary is a textual explication of the autocommentary. The phrases in quotation marks are phrases from the autocommentary itself.

26. It is unobscured neutral because it is neither virtue nor nonvirtue, and it is not concurrent with any affliction. *See* II.30bc.

27. For example, when one attains the state of arhat, all of the afflictions and other discards of seeing and meditation have been discarded, so they cease. That cessation is attained by the power of full knowing, so it is *analytic cessation.*

28. The four classes discarded by seeing the truths of suffering, origin, cessation, and path plus the one class discarded by meditation.

29. This passage is quoted in its entirety in Mikyö Dorje's *Springtime Cow.*

30. *See* VIII.43d.

31. This refers to the Eighth Karmapa Mikyö Dorje's commentary *grub bde'i spyi 'jo (The Springtime Cow of Easy Accomplishment),* which is called the *Karmakaṭīka* (*Karmapa's Commentary*) in Sanskrit, or *Karṭik* or *Ṭīka* for short.

32. *'du shes, saṃjñā.* This is commonly translated as *perception,* but that has several meanings in English and this aggregate refers to only one of them. The aggregate of feeling, part of the aggregate of formations, and the aggregate of consciousness are also perception, and so calling this aggregate *perception* is potentially confusing and misleading. What this aggregate refers to is the mental process of forming an idea about the object: it is like when one sees a vase and thinks "That is big" or "That is small." Additionally, in other contexts the word *'du shes* matches the usage of the English words *conception* or *idea.*

33. The Sanskrit *loka* and Tibetan word *'jig rten* translated as *world* literally mean "disintegrating support."

34. *See* I.11.

35. The *Abhidharmasamuccaya* by Asanga.

36. Non-Buddhist schools are called *extremist* because they hold views of the extremes of either permanence or nihilism.

37. I.e., Master Vasubandhu.

38. The eight substances are earth, water, fire, air, form, scent, taste, and touch. Material objects in the Desire realm, such as vases, are made out of at least these eight substances. *See* II.22ff

39. *See* II.22ab.

40. That is, sounds produced by matter that is considered part of a being's body and is pervaded by the faculties. *See* I.34bc. *Sources* refers to earth, water, fire, and air; *see* I.12–13.

41. The Great Exposition school posits that vows and some other actions have actual, substantial forms that cannot be perceived. These forms stay with the being who took the vow until the vow is forfeited. The Sutra and Mind Only schools do not accept such forms as real or substantial. These are discussed further in area IV.

42. *See* II.36c ff.

43. Tib. *'byung ba,* Skt. *bhūta.* Although earth, water, fire, and air are commonly called *elements* in English, the literal translation of *sources* is used to avoid ambiguity because of other uses of the word element, as in the eighteen elements. In Tibetan, *'byung ba* and *khams* (element) can both refer to earth and so forth, so *source* is used when the Tibetan uses the word *'byung ba* and *element* when the Tibetan word is *khams.*

44. The Sanskrit word *dhātu* derives from the verb that means "to hold."

45. *Jñānaprasthāna* by Kātyāniputra.

46. Formations that are not concurrent or associated with mind, such as attainment, etc. *See* II.35b ff.

47 Tib.: *gnas bcu bstan pa.*

48. Form, nonconcurrence, and noncomposites. The Kashmiri Great Exposition posits *five bases of the knowable*—form, mind, mental factors, nonconcurrent formations, and noncomposites—which have substantial existence.

49. That is to say, a future mind consciousness is supported by the cognition that immediately precedes it, which is also in the future (in most instances).

50. The eye consciousness has the dominant condition of the eye, the ear consciousness the dominant condition of the ear, etc.

51. The four ways bodhisattvas magnetize or attract beings: generosity, pleasant speech, meaningful conduct, and agreement in purpose.

52. Bhikshus, bhikshunis, and male and female householders who hold the five lay precepts.

53. In other words, the ten sense bases that have form are by their nature the aggregate of form and possess the characteristics of form. They do not possess the characteristics of feeling, etc. It is not a nominal inclusion where what is included and what includes have different characteristics.

54. The Sanskrit and Tibetan words actually mean "caste," which has a sense of potential or cause, hence the explanation of the term as "origin." Because the word *caste* has negative connotations in English, it is commonly translated as "family."

55. The four erroneous conceptions are of the permanent, self, clean, and blissful. *See* V.9.

56. I.22cd.

57. As opposed to substantial existence. In other words, they would merely be labels applied by the mind to a collection of other things.

58. The fourth Formless level of Neither Conception nor Non-Conception.

59. *See* I.35.

60. *dkon mchog ta la'i gzungs.*

61. The aggregates of discipline, samadhi, full knowing, liberation, and the wisdom that sees liberation.

62. *See* VIII.36–7.

63. *See* VIII.35.

64. A synonym for the four Formless absorptions.

65. The Eighth Karmapa's commentary.

66. Mind and mental factors.

67. *See* I.4cd.

68. Tib. *ngo bo nyid kyi rtog pa*, *nges par rtog pa*, and *rjes su dran pa'i rtog pa.*

69. *mdo sde gdags pa*

70. A reference to the Buddha's voice as he is sometimes called *Brahma*. *See* VI.54.

71. *Cause of same status*, *universal cause*, and *cause of full ripening* are discussed in II.49ff.

72. The first moment of the path of seeing. *See* VI.28.

73. In this context, *active* means that the element of dharma always supports the consciousness that perceives it.

74. A school of Buddhism noted for its unorthodox positions, notably that there is an inexpressible self of the individual.

75. Severing the three roots of virtue—nongreed, nonhatred, and nondelusion—is ceasing to have them. *See* IV.79–80.

76. *See* V.7.

77. This is because there is no consideration or examination on those levels. *See* VIII.13.

78. Lion's milk is said to be so potent that it will shatter a vessel made of anything other than gold.

Notes on Area II

79. *See* I.48d.

80. *See* I.7a.

81. Faculties that are not performing their function. *See* I.40.

82. A *likeness* is the continuum of similarity throughout a being's lifetime. The Tibetan word *ris mthun pa* refers both to the continuum of a being in a similar body during the course of one lifetime and to discards that are of similar types. In this translation, when it refers to the continuum of a being, the term *likeness* is used, as the Tibetan *ris* can also mean an image or likeness of something.

83. That is, if the mind is virtuous, then the actions and so forth that arise from its power will also be virtuous.

84. Beings in the between state, so called because they cannot eat solid food but subsist on scent instead.

85. Fully ripened results are always unobscured neutral. *See* 57d.

86. The nine causes of mental unhappiness are: thinking they have hurt me, they are hurting me, or they will hurt me; thinking they have hurt, are hurting, or will hurt my friend or relative; and thinking they have helped, are helping, or will help my enemy.

87. *See* III.38a.

88. A fully ripened result must be unafflicted neutral, so the afflicted mind consciousness at birth cannot be a fully ripened result.

89. *See* III.98.

90. Beings born in a single instant by miraculous birth likewise die in a single instant without a gradual process of death.

91. The Great Exposition asserts that some arhats temporarily regress or fall from the state of arhatship when subtle afflictions arise in their beings. *See* VI.22.

92. Childish beings are ordinary beings who have not yet matured into nobles by directly seeing the four noble truths.

93. *Attached* means still attached to the Desire realm—that is, not having abandoned the afflictions that lead to rebirth in Desire.

94. That is, they are made out of the four sources and four source-derived.

95. *See* verse 32b.

96. *See* III.33–34.

97. Nonawareness is a weak aspect of full knowing, distraction is weak samadhi, and forgetfulness is weak mindfulness.

98. The last three views are wrong view, over-esteeming views, and over-esteeming discipline and austerity. *See* V.7.

99. Personality view is viewing the aggregates as me or mine, and extreme view is holding the self to be permanent or to have a definite end. *See* V.7.

Many translations from the Tibetan translate *personality view* rather literally as "view of the transitory collection". Here the example of translators from the Theravada tradition who say *personality view* is followed for ease of comprehension.

100. *See* V.53ab.

101. In other texts, the distinction between shamelessness and immodesty is said to be whether one disregards oneself or another when committing misdeeds.

102. Since afflictions are only abandoned starting from the second moment of the path of seeing, nobles on the first moment of the path of seeing who have not previously attained the dhyanas have not yet abandoned any afflictions and thus have not

been freed from any of their bonds. Once they attain the second moment, they possess the analytic cessation of the afflictions that focus on suffering in Desire. *See* IV. 61 *and* VI.28.

103. Wrong vows are commitments to perform misdeeds. *See* IV.13.

104. *Jñānaprasthāna.*

105. That is, experienced in one's next rebirth. *See* IV.50bd.

106. The Sanskrit root text assembled by V.V. Gokhale here reads *saṃjñā* or *conception,* not *name.* This translation follows the Tibetan.

107. Note that in Sanskrit and Tibetan, the letter is considered the phoneme or sound, not the sign on the page.

108. *See* II.52a.

109. *See* II.46c.

110. The isolate is what we perceive when we think of an object. Here the mere isolate refers to the thing itself.

111. The last aggregates of an arhat passing into nirvana without remainder do not produce any subsequent aggregates, so they are not same status causes.

112. These six types of individuals will be explained in VI.29, 31 & 56.

113. Universal kernels are kernels that focus on all levels and classes of discards. *See* V.12–13.

114. This last sentence does not appear in Wangchuk Dorje's commentary but was filled in from Mikyö Dorje's *Springtime Cow* so that all the words of the root text would be explained.

115. That is, when present same-status and universal causes issue results, the result arises in the immediately following moment. When past same status and universal causes issue result, the result arises after an interruption in time. (Mchims 1989, 201)

116. That is to say, someone who sees a vase, for example, has only one eye consciousness that perceives the vase but may have another consciousness, such as an ear consciousness, simultaneously. Each of the consciousnesses has its own set of concurrent mental factors.

117. In other words, when a cognition arises, the mental factors that are concurrent with it and dharmas that are coemergent with it are not its objective conditions—they are not its object in that specific instance. In general terms, however, they are suitable to be the objective condition for another cognition.

118. The virtuous pure mind of a higher level is the worldly virtuous absorption of a higher level of dhyana or Formless. *See* VIII.6.

119. Minds of emanation are the cognitions that arise when a being emanates something. *See* VII.49ff.

120. A type of affliction. *See* V.47ff.

121. A metaphor for the sun, which is said to be pulled through the sky by seven chariots.

Notes on Area III

122. These explanations of the different wanderers reflect the Sanskrit names for the five different types of wanderers: *naraka, preta, tiryañc, manuṣya,* and *deva.*

123. The three levels of the first dhyana are Brahma's Abode, Brahma's Ministers, and Great Brahma. The three levels of the second dhyana are Lesser Light, Immeasurable Light, and Radiant Light. The three levels of the third dhyana are Lesser Virtue, Immeasurable Virtue, and Full Virtue.

124. The three impure levels of the fourth dhyana are Cloudless, Merit Born, and Great Result.

125. The alternation of dhyanas is where nobles switch rapidly back and forth between the defiled and undefiled dhyanas. There are five different levels of alternation. *See* VI.42–43.

126. The five pure abodes are Not Great, Without Pain, Excellent Appearance, Great Vision, and Below None.

127. The aggregates of feeling, conception, formations, and consciousness. *See* III.30a.

128. *ma yin dgag.* This is a negation that primarily blocks the attributes of something, such as thinking in this context, "It is not a thing." A not-negation is characterized as a negation in which after the object of negation is negated another dharma is implied. This is sometimes translated as an "affirming negation."

129. Wandering sentient beings, who wander from realm to realm in samsara.

130. The state prior to death, or in other words, this life. Note that although it is called the previous state, it comes after birth. *See* III.13cd.

131. *Yogacāryābhūmi* by Asanga.

132. A reason that proves the prior existence of its cause. For example, the presence of smoke proves the prior existence of smoke-producing fire.

133. It is traditionally explained that a new being is born in a womb when the father's semen, the mother's blood, and the consciousness of the between state come together.

134. Chim Jamyang, whose commentary on the *Treasury* is the basis for most later Tibetan commentaries.

135. The *Saptabhavasūtra* (*srid pa bdun pa'i mdo*).

136. *mgnal 'jug gi mdo*. In Minor Topics (Dergye Tengyur, 'dul ba, vol. tha, pp. 136ff).

137. *skye bu dam pa'i 'gro ba bdun ston pa'i mdo*.

138. That is, the Great Vehicle abhidharma.

139. I.e., from the *Ṭīka* he wrote during his previous incarnation as Mikyö Dorje.

140. There are three types of self-buddha: the rhinolike who achieve realization in solitude, and the greater and lesser congregators who achieve realization in groups of five hundred.

141. In birth from the womb, egg, or warmth and moisture, the being develops in stages, so all twelve links arise in order. In miraculous birth, the being arises all at once, there are not the separate stages of development of each of the links.

142. The four divisions are the infantry, cavalry, elephants, and chariots.

143. One page of the original Tibetan manuscript is missing, so the commentary on the next three points is excerpted from Mikyö Dorje's *Springtime Cow.*

144. The Tibetan word literally means "not-action."

145. Because ignorance is a condition, it must be a thing and cannot be mere absence, which is noncomposite and not suitable to act as a condition.

146. This concludes the section excerpted from Mikyö Dorje's *Springtime Cow.*

147. These five are autonomous because they are concurrent only with ignorance, not other afflictions. *See* V.52ab.

148. The world is destroyed by fire, water, and wind. *See* III.100ff.

149. One billion worlds. *See* III.75.

150. This world is called *Unbearable* because beings here have strong afflictions that make it difficult to tolerate and because the bodhisattvas who take birth here have exceptional fortitude.

151. One league is 20,000 cubits. *See* verse 88.

152. A clear and transparent blue crystal, the color of the sky. Frequently mistranslated as lapis lazuli, it is more likely blue beryl.

153. Another name for Mount Meru.

154. The eight qualities are that the water is sweet, cool, soft, light, pure, clean, does not harm the throat, and benefits the stomach. The seas are called *playful* because the kings of the nagas disport in and enjoy their waters. (Bod rgya tshig mdzod chen mo, p. 2730.)

155. Carts whose sides slope down between the two wheels, making a nearly triangular shape when viewed from behind, can still be seen hauling improbable loads of hay and sugarcane in rural parts of northern India.

156. An earshot is 500 fathoms. *See* III.88.

157. This usually falls in early October in the Gregorian calendar.

158. In the ancient India tradition, the day was divided into 30 hours, not 24. *See* III.89.

159. Śakra is another name for Indra.

160. These realms are in order, Conflict Free, Joyous, Joy of Emanations, and Mastery over Others' Emanations.

161. For example, when gods of the realm of Brahma's Ministers descend to Brahma's Realm, the gods of that realm can see them because they are similarly on the level of the first dhyana, but if they should descend to the Desire realm, beings who have not attained the level of first dhyana could not perceive them.

162. There are eighty intermediate aeons per great aeon. *See* III.94a.

163. The Tibetan original gives a figure of 1,900,000 years, which appears to be a misprint. According to the calculation, it should be 15,000 years.

164. That is, single particles of the individual sources and the source-derived.

165. *See* Cf. I.9ab.

166. To compare with modern units of time, an "instant" would be 13.333 milliseconds. An "instant of that" is 1.6 seconds. A "minute" is 96 seconds. An "hour" is 48 modern minutes.

167. *See* I.7c.

168. "Age of Threefold Qualities" refers to the second age during an aeon. The first age is the Age of Perfection, during which humans have six qualities: 1) bodies as radiant as the gods of Form, 2) the ability to mentally create things with magic, 3) enjoyable food to eat, 4) all their limbs complete, 5) all faculties complete, and 6) equality and long life for all sentient beings, et cetera. This is the age referred to in verse III.97c. During the Age of Threefold Qualities, humans have the three qualities of primarily giving up the three misdeeds of mind, as during the time of the Buddha Kanakamuni. Alternatively, it is an age when humans have three of the six qualities of the Age of Perfection. (Mi bskyod rdo rje 2004, vol. 2, 728–729).

169. During the Age of Twofold Qualities, humans have two qualities of primarily giving up malice and covetousness, as during the time of the Buddha Kashyapa. Alternatively, it is an age when humans have two of the six qualities of the Age of Perfection. The Age of Strife is an age of great turmoil, as during the time of the Buddha Shakyamuni. (Mi bskyod rdo rje 2004, vol. 2, 729).

170. *See* VIII.11.

Notes on Area IV

171. As taught in the Vinaya, the seven material and immaterial merits are merit that "increases always and continuously, whether one is going, staying, lying down, or not lying down" (Dge 'dun grub, 647). The autocommentary clarifies that if there were no imperceptible form, it would not be logical for merit to increase in such a way (folio 169).

172. The Buddha or a listener disciple of the Buddha (Dge 'dun grub, 647).

173. Author's note: As undefiled sources are impossible, these are the sources of the level where the individual's bodily support was born.

174. That is to say, the sources that produce the imperceptible form of abandoning taking life are not separate from the sources that produce the imperceptible form of abandoning stealing, sexual misconduct, and so on.

175. Here, the three types of karma are volitional karma, perceptible karma of body and speech, and imperceptible karma of body and speech. *See* IV.1 & 2.

176. That is, a neutral mind that is thinking about sitting, going, standing, and so forth.

177. The Sanskrit *saṃvara* and Tibetan *sdom pa* normally translated here and in many other works as "vow" actually mean restraint of one's actions, not necessarily an oath or oral commitment. The dhyana and undefiled vows are thus the restraints on one's behavior that naturally arise out of abandoning the discards and attaining the dhyanas or undefiled paths.

178. That is, if a male bhikshu should lose his male sexual organs and gain female organs, he becomes a bhikshuni. There are stories of such spontaneous sex changes in the sutras and vinaya.

179. Two things that cannot exist without harm on the same basis at the same time are said to be simultaneously exclusive. Traditional examples include owls and crows, or discards and antidotes.

180. The Sanskrit word *śīla* translated as "discipline" literally means "cool."

181. Karmas have three aspects: preparation, the actual basis or action, and the aftermath. *See* IV.68, *below*.

182. The preparations for dhyana are levels of meditation that discard the obscurations that prevent one from attaining dhyana. *See* VIII.22.

183. *See* II.51cd

184. The preparations for the first dhyana, so called because it can act as the antidote for the discards of all levels. *See* VI.47cd.

185. That is, someone who becomes a Noble in one lifetime loses the perceptible at death. When they are reborn, even as a baby they still have the imperceptible form, but they do not possess the perceptible until they actually do something virtuous.

186. *Five supports* refers to the first five disciples, All-Knowing Kauṇḍinya, Aśvajit, Vaṣpa, Mahānāman, and Bhadrika, who became bhikshus when they developed certainty in the Buddha's first teaching of the Sutra of the Wheel of Dharma.

187. Mahāprajapatī and other five hundred first bhikshunis received their vows when they accepted the eight additional strictures for bhikshunis, called here *dharmas of respect* but also sometimes called *heavy dharmas*. (Dge 'dun grub, 72).

188. Dharmadinnā had been betrothed since before birth but wished to go forth and become a bhikshuni. Her parents would not let her, but the Buddha sent a nun as a messenger to give her dharma instructions, through which she achieved the result of stream-enterer. On the day she was to be sent off to be married, the Buddha once again sent the nun to give her vows and instructions, and through these instrutions she achieved the state of arhat. She was then released from her betrothal and went to join the bhikshunis. (Dge 'dun grub, 73ff).

189. A righteous pursuer of virtue is one who takes the eight precepts of the fasting vow for the rest of their life, not just one day.

190. *Ming chen gyi mdo*

191. This is a text recited during the ceremony for taking the vow in which one promises to turn away from killing, stealing, and so forth, just as the Noble arhats did.

192. There are two types of unwholesome actions: inherently unwholesome acts and prohibited unwholesome acts. Inherently unwholesome acts include killing, stealing, and so on, which are unwholesome by their very nature. Prohibited unwholesome acts are actions such as consuming intoxicants or eating after noon that the Buddha prohibited lay practitioners or bhikshus from doing. According to the Prince, although they are not necessarily unwholesome, someone who has vows commits a misdeed by doing them because they have disrespected the word of the Buddha. *See* IV.122c.

193. Here basis refers to the aggregates, elements, and sense bases.

194. That is to say, the bhikshu vows give up all seven misdeeds of body and speech; the lesser vows only give up four: killing, stealing, sexual misconduct, and lying.

195. The five qualifications are setting qualifications with regards to sentient beings, branches, places, time, and occasion—that is, saying one will only abandon killing certain sentient beings, or only abide by certain branches in certain places or for a certain time, etc.

196. *Fields* are the categories of recipients of the action. *See* IV.117. For the material merits *See* IV.4a.

197. The service conducted by bhikshus on the full and new moons to purify any transgressions and restore their vows.

198. That is, when the force that propelled the potter's wheel or arrow is used up, the wheel stops and the arrow falls to the ground.

199. For example, if one makes a commitment to circumambulate a stupa every day for a year but that stupa is destroyed before the end of the year, the mid-vow of the commitment is canceled.

200. The obscurations of full ripening are rebirth in the lower realms, Conception Free, and Unpleasant Sound. *See* IV.96.

201. *See* IV.95ab.

202. Cf. II.7c–8a.

203. According to Mikyö Dorje, when the feeling of pleasure is being experienced, it does not depend upon another feeling to be experienced: the other two feelings are blocked and an additional feeling of its own class is also blocked, so there can be no additional feeling on which it depends. Thus it is directly experienced.

204. That is, they propel a new being that will maintain a continuum of similarity or likeness.

205. *See* VI.60ab.

206. The five periods in the womb are mushiness, oval, oblong, round, and hands and feet moving. *See* III.19. The five periods of this life are childhood, youth, prime of life, middle age, and old age.

207. That is, the eleven results are all visibly experienced within the continuum of the being in the between state, before that being dies again.

208. A reference to an ancient Persian custom of euthanasia.

209. *See* VII.36.

210. *See* II.10c.

211. This passage refers to the different moments and paths that one progresses through as one discards the defilements. The *forbearances of knowing dharma* (or *dharma forbearances*) are the moments of the path of seeing where one can withstand seeing each of the four truths of the desire realm. The *knowing of dharma* (or *dharma knowings*) are the knowings that arise out of seeing the truths of Desire. There are also the *subsequent forbearances* that can withstand seeing the nature of the truths of the two higher realms and the *subsequent knowings* that arise from those. There is a dharma forbearance, dharma knowing, subsequent forbearance, and subsequent knowing for each of the four truths. *See* VI.28. The undefiled paths of meditation of no obstacles refers to the nine paths of no obstacles that abandon the discards of meditation for the Desire realm. *See* VI.33.

212. Afflictions and karma are exclusive of one another because they are the two separate classifications of the truth of origin and because the afflictions cause karma.

213. Skt: *Saṃcetanīyasūtra*, Tib.: *ched du bsam par bya ba'i mdo*.

214. *See* verse IV.16bc.

215. A hallucinogenic plant, *datura alba*.

216. A type of affliction. *See* V.47–53.

217. When someone takes full ordination as bhikshu, the vow is attained on the third repetition of the motion to grant them ordination, which is why the imperceptible and perceptible actions at that moment are the actual basis.

218. *See* III.44cd.

219. The *Śīlaskandhikā* (*sh'i la'i mdo*).

220. *See* V.12.

221. Tib. *nges 'byed cha mthun*, Skt. *nirvedha-bhāgīya*. The four stages of the path of joining that lead to the path of seeing. Most translators from the Tibetan translate this term as either "partial concordance with definite discernment" or "aids to penetration," neither of which seem particularly informative. The Sanskrit *bhāgīya* means "leading to," so here *precursor* is used to indicate that these four stages of the path of joining are the precursors to the clear realization of the path of seeing. *Clear realization* is used rather than "penetration" or the literal "definite discernment" for comprehensibility.

222. *See* IV.101a.

223. Devadatta created the schism during the Buddha's time by convincing his followers that the Buddha's behavior was not sufficiently ascetic and that bhikshus should not drink milk, eat meat, and so forth.

224. The last of the precursors to clear realization. *See* VI.19bc.

225. That is, offerings are made to the Three Jewels and those superior to oneself out of respect, and gifts are given to those below oneself out of a wish to help.

226. See the commentary to IV.4a.

227. Attaining the mind's ornament means miraculous powers. The mind's necessities are the eightfold noble path. The collection of yogas are tranquility and insight meditation. The supreme purpose is attaining arhatship and nirvana. (Mi bskyod rdo rje 2005, Vol. 3, 331)

228. That is, before he attained the Noble paths while sitting under the Bodhi tree in Bodhgaya.

229. That is, the associated mental factors.

230. Both individuals who have entered the path and those who have not entered the path have the precursors to merit. The precursor to freedom is equivalent to the path of accumulation. (Mi bskyod rdo rje 2003, vol. 2. 127)

231. *See* VI.17ff.

Notes on Area V

232. *Nirnayasaṃgraha* (*rnam par gtan la dbab pa bsdu ba*) by Asanga.

233. *Abhidharmasamucchaya* (*mngon pa kun las bstus pa*) by Asanga.

234. Subsequent knowing of the path is the sixteenth moment of clear realization. *See* VI.25–27.

235. Entering fire refers to the non-Buddhist practice of sitting in the middle of five fires: fires in each of the four directions and the sun above. Entering water refers to ritual bathing in the Ganges and so forth.

236. *Universal* means a kernel that can focus on any of the classes of discards. Nonuniversals can only focus on their own class. For example, a universal kernel of seeing suffering can focus on the discards of seeing any of the truths or meditation, but a nonuniversal kernel of suffering can only focus on the truth of suffering.

237. Discards of seeing are sometimes called "mistaken engagements," and they are classified in two types: direct mistaken engagements and mistaken engagements of mistaken engagements. Direct mistaken engagements focus on one of the four truths in an erroneous manner. For example, doubt that is discarded by seeing cessation actually focuses on the truth of cessation but sees it mistakenly, doubting its truth. Mistaken engagements of mistaken engagements focus not on the actual truth, but on one of the direct mistaken engagements. For example, desire discarded by seeing the path does not focus on the path, but might take the form of attachment to the view of holding austerity and discipline supreme, etc. (Mi bskyod rdo rje 2003, vol. 1, 357–8)

238. Shariputra has past kernels from when he was an ordinary individual, but because he has become an arhat, they do not develop.

239. For example, craving that is concurrent with enjoyment. Cf. VIII.5.

240. Specific afflictions are afflictions that arise because of a specific object. For example, when focusing on a pleasant object, desire arises. When focusing on an unpleasant object, anger arises. When one focuses on a pleasant object and gets conceited, pride arises.

241. Yaśomitra explains that just as flax is directed toward the production of its flowers and seeds, future phenomena must be directed toward an object of any of the three times. (Tengyur, ngu pa, 113A).

242. General afflictions can arise with regard to any object.

243. In this and following points, *time* refers to composite dharmas of the past, present, and future. *See* I.7c. In other words, the Great Exposition school posits that past and future objects have substantial existence in the same way that present objects do.

244. This is one point where Wangchuk Dorje's position differs from the autocommentary. The autocommentary says these stains have been abandoned but not removed, answering the question posed in 28ab.

245. I.e., the discards of seeing suffering, of seeing origin, and of meditation.

246. *See* V.47ff.

247. There are four graspings presented in the sutras: grasping at Desire, grasping at views, grasping at overesteeming discipline and austerity, and grasping at belief in a self (Mchims 2009, p. 471). Since unlike the floods, ignorance is combined into the other graspings, some people might wonder how there could be four graspings, and Wangchuk Dorje is addressing such a concern with this statement.

248. This is an explanation of the Sanskrit *anuśaya* (kernel) as a compound of words meaning "subtle" and "expand." The Tibetan term *phra rgyas* literally means "subtle expander."

249. The words for *defilement* in Sanskrit and Tibetan, *āsrava* and *zag pa,* literally mean the pus and nastiness that oozes out of wounds.

250. *Put* and *ooze* are the explanations of defilement, *carry away* is the explanation of flood, *attach* is the explanation of yoke, and *grasp* is the explanation of grasping.

251. *Kṣudravastaka* or *gzhi phran tshegs.*

252. *See* II.27.

253. *See* I.30–31 and II.12.

254. Stream-enterer, once-returner, nonreturner, and arhat. *See* VI.51–53.

255. As will be explained below in areas VI and VII, the forbearances are solely on the path of seeing; the path of meditation is made up of the knowings which follow that.

256. *See* VI.47cd.

257. *Moment* here refers to the fifteen moments of the path of seeing. *See* VI.27–28.

258. A nonreturner who progresses through the results in succession.

259. That is, the elephant.

Notes on Area VI

260. I.5a.

261. I.6a.

262. I.8c.

263. When a vase is destroyed by a hammer, someone who looks at its remains will think of them as shards, not as a vase. When one examines water with full knowing, one sees that it is merely a collection of particles of the eight substances and no longer conceives of it as water. Thus vases and water are said to exist only in relative or conventional terms.

264. When examining form, for example, whether one tries to destroy it or exclude it with mind, the perception of form is not discarded.

265. The sixteen aspects of the four truths are described in VII.13.

266. In other words, if the attainments were part of the four precursors to clear realization, then noble beings, who have the manifest attainments of the four precursors, would still have the four precursors in a manifest way. However, the precursors are no longer manifest in nobles, who have progressed on to higher levels.

267. Someone who first attains supreme dharma as a woman and then subsequently changes sex and attains a male body (either in the same life or the next), reattains supreme dharma on that male support as well.

268. Precursor to freedom or liberation is a synonym for the path of accumulation.

269. *See* VI.20b–d.

270. *khams mang po'i mdo.*

271. *See* VI.38ab.

272. The highest development of the fourth dhyana. *See* VIII.41.

273. *See* VI.56a.

274. That is, freedom from the nine meditation discards of their level.

275. *See* VI.37cd.

276. That is, they dwell in bliss in this lifetime, which is visible because we can see it in this life.

277. Samadhi that is afflicted with craving. *See* VIII.6.

278. *See* VI.1c.

279. That is to say, since the first three dhyanas are all characterized by different feelings, someone with sharp faculties is able to switch from the feeling of a lower to the higher and attain the higher level on the basis of the actual practice. Someone of dull faculties is unable to do so and must go through the preparations. The "final path of liberation" is the path of liberation that arises from abandoning the last of the discards to the higher level.

280. That is, stream-enterer, once-returner, nonreturner, and arhat.

281. *bcu tshan bcu ston pa'i lung.*

282. VI.50ab.

283. *sol ba'i phung po lta bu'i mdo.*

284. VI.41cd.

285. Liberated through both full knowing and samadhi, as explained in VI.64.

286. In this passage, "clearly knowing" is a translation of the Sanskrit *abhijña* and Tibetan *mngon shes,* which in many instances refer to clairvoyance. However, from the descriptions in various commentaries, it appears in this context to refer to merely knowing something clearly, not clairvoyance.

287. The *four foundations of mindfulness* are mindfulness of body, feeling, mind, and dharmas, discussed above in VI.14ff. The *four complete abandonments* (also called *right endeavors*) are abandoning nonvirtuous dharmas that have arisen, preventing those that have not arisen from arising, producing virtuous dharmas that have not yet arisen, and developing virtuous dharmas that have arisen. The *four feet of miracles* are developing faith, being diligent, taking control of the mind, and fully engaging oneself to manifest wisdom. The *five faculties* are faith, diligence, mindfulness, samadhi, and full knowing, described above in II.1. The *five powers* are the same as the faculties, but more highly developed. The *seven branches of enlightenment* are mindfulness, full discernment of dharmas, diligence, joy, pliancy, samadhi, and equanimity. The *noble eightfold path* is right view, right thought, right speech, right action, right livelihood, right effort, right mindfulness, and right samadhi.

288. Cf. VI.15ab.

289. That is, the foundations of mindfulness arise on the path of accumulation. The complete abandonments arise on warmth, the feet of miracles on the peak, the faculties on forbearance, the powers on supreme dharma, the branches of enlightenment on the path of meditation, and the noble eightfold path on the path of seeing.

290. That is, Wangchuk Dorje's teacher Shamar Konchok Yenlag.

Notes on Area VII

291. A divine robe clear on both the outside and inside.

292. Knowing, view, and forbearance.

293. It appears that *rhinolike* is used here as a general term, inclusive of the congregating self-buddhas as well as the rhinolike self-buddha: the autocommentary states that self-buddhas in general have three knowings.

294. This line appears slightly differently in the autocommentary and Chim Jamyang's commentary: "because it first arises in the continuum of a being whose action has

been completed." This might be the result of a typographical error: the Tibetan only differs by two letters. However, the meaning in both instances is similar.

295. *See* VII.13.

296. According to Yaśomitra, "the mind which does not possess" means undefiled, "place" here means characteristics, and "basis" means cause. (Tengyur ngu pa, 251A–B).

297. The three fires of greed, hatred, and delusion.

298. In other words, the Sutra school posits that when we perceive something, we do not directly perceive it. Instead, we perceive its aspect, a mental image or impression of the object. For example, when we see a vase, there is an image of the vase that arises in our mind, and that image is the aspect. The Great Exposition, on the other hand, posits that when we perceive an object, our consciousness engages it directly. The aspect is thus more like what we think about it. For example, when contemplating the five aggregates of grasping, nobles consider them as impermanent, suffering, and so forth, so those are the aspects. Since this is in essence full knowing—distinguishing the true nature of the object—the Great Exposition posits that the aspects are full knowing.

299. Not Unable, four actual practices, and special dhyana.

300. The previous six plus the first three levels of Formless.

301. That is, mind and mental factors.

302. Prince Yaśomitra provides an example: someone who on the support of Not Unable becomes detached from Desire and achieves the first dhyana attains two future relative knowings: one of Not Unable (the level of the path) and one of the first dhyana (the level attained for the first time). (Tengyur ngu pa, 262).

303. In Yaśomitra's example, when someone on the support of the second dhyana becomes detached and attains the third dhyana, the path (the path of liberation over the ninth discard of the second dhyana) is on the level of the second dhyana. The level that is attained by removal of attachment is the third dhyana. Upon achieving that level, the yogi attains undefiled knowings of the level of the path (the second dhyana), the attained level (the third dhyana), and also the lower levels such as the first dhyana, special dhyana, and Not Unable. (Tengyur ngu pa, 262–263).

304. Mikyö Dorje explains this example further: when you cut the cords that bind a basket, it springs back to shape as if it were a living thing. (Mi bskyod rdo rje 2005, vol. 3, 290)

305. The Great Exposition holds that the Bodhisattva can only attain complete awakening to Buddhahood on the support of a male body. Women attain a male body (in a future life) in order to completely awaken. *See* IV.109. This position is not necessarily accepted by all schools of Buddhism.

306. The way all dharmas are divided into ten categories is described above in VII.18ab: there are concurrent and nonconcurrent dharmas for each of the three realms and the undefiled, virtuous noncompound, and neutral noncompound.

307. In Sanskrit, the powers are called *prākṛtahastin, gandhahastin, mahānagna, praskandin, varāṅga, cāṇūra,* and *nārāyaṇa.*

308. That is, other than the resultant touches of soft, rough, and so forth described in I.10d.

309. Here *ṭīkas* refers to Indian commentaries in general, not specifically to Mikyö Dorje's commentary.

310. That is, compassion is in essence nonhatred and great compassion is nondelusion. Compassion focuses on one realm and great compassion on three. Compassion has the one suffering of suffering as its aspect, and great compassion all three types of suffering. Compassion is on all four dhyanas; great compassion on the fourth. Compassion is found among the listeners and great compassion among the Victors. Compassion is attained by detaching from Desire; great compassion by detaching from the Peak of Existence. The compassion of the listeners and self-buddhas does not have the power to fully protect beings from samsara, but great compassion does. Compassion sees suffering beings partially; great compassion sees all beings impartially. (Mi bskyod rdo rje 2005, vol. 3, 308)

311. Such as discards of seeing. *See* VI.58ab.

312. The unprovocative samadhi and knowledge from aspiration.

313. That is, one starts in Desire, enters the first dhyana, second dhyana, and so forth up to the Peak of Existence. Then one returns down through Nothingness and so forth to the first dhyana and Desire. Then one ascends to the fourth dhyana.

314. As in the four alternatives of two dharmas: something can be the first, or the second, or both, or neither. There is no possibility beyond the fourth alternative.

315. *See* VII.5cd & 6.

316. The divine eye is the clairvoyance of knowing death and rebirth.

317. The miracle of addressing is telling someone, "Your mind is like this." The miracle of teaching is teaching correctly just as things are. (Yaśomitra, Tengyur ngu pa, 281).

318. For instance, transforming oneself into a lion is connected to one's own being. Emanating a lion separate from oneself is connected to another being. (Tengyur ngu pa, 281).

319. An unafflicted, defiled dhyana. *See* VIII.5–6.

320. Skt.: *Dīrghāma;* Tib.: *lung ring po.*

321. A type of ghost.

322. *See* I.39cd.

323. That is, they see the general prime thousand, the middle world realm, and the three thousands described in III.73 and 74.

324. Tib. *rin chen phreng ba*, Skt. *Ratnāvāli.*

Notes on Area VIII

325. III.2cd.

326. *See* III.3.

327. *gang yang bsus po che mdo.*

328. *rnam par bsgyur ba'i mdo.*

329. *bsam tan gyi yan lag bstan pa'i mdo.*

330. The sense consciousnesses excluding scent and taste, which are not present in the dhyanas. *See* I.30b–d.

331. One of the classifications of the pure absorption. *See* VIII.17–18.

332. The Tibetan and Sanskrit verses literally read "up to three levels," but this is counting the level that one is on inclusively as the first of the three levels. In common English parlance, this would generally not be counted, and so here it is translated as *two levels.* The meaning is the same: from an undefiled third dhyana, for example, one can skip up two levels to Infinite Space, but not higher to Infinite Consciousness, etc.

333. Skt.: *Abhisamayālaṅkāra.* Tib.: *mngon rtogs rgyan.*

334. *See* VI.47cd.

335. In the first of these, attention on thorough knowledge of the characteristics, one considers the lower realm coarse and the upper realm peaceful. In the second, attention produced by interest, one discards the hindrances to generating the third. In the third, attention on complete withdrawal, one discards the three greater sets of meditative discards. In the fourth, attention on taking delight, one feels joy and pleasure at having abandoned the greater discards and discards the three medium sets of discards. In the fifth, attention on examination, one examines oneself to see which discards remain. In the sixth, attention on the end of training, one abandons the three lesser meditative discards. (Mi bskyod rdo rje 2003, vol. 1, 286–7)

336. The preparations for the second dhyana and higher.

337. The first emancipation, viewing external form while conceiving of internal form, is viewing external forms and meditating on them as repulsive while conceiving of one's own form as existing. The second is the same, except the conception of one's own form has been demolished. (Yaśomitra, Tengyur ngu pa, 306B). For more on the repulsiveness meditation see VI.9d ff.

338. *See* II.43.

339. Asanga, according to Mikyö Dorje. (Mi bskyod rdo rje 2005, vol. 4, 438)

340. *Cassia fistula.*

341. Yaśomitra quotes the passage from the sutras as follows: "While conceiving that there is no internal form, view a blue external form, blue-colored, that is seen as blue, that radiates blue, for example, a flax flower or an excellent fabric from the land of Varanasi that is blue, blue-colored, that is seen as blue, that radiates blue, and know that those forms have been overpowered, see that they have been overpowered. That sort of conception is the fifth overpowering sense base..." It continues similarly for yellow, red, and white. (Tengyur ngu pa, 308).

342. *See* I.13cd.

343. *See* I.13cd.

344. *Yogacāryābhūmi* by Asanga.

345. *Bsdu ba chen mo.*

346. II.43ff.

347. *bskal bzang las.*

348. *zla ba snying pos zhus pa'i mdo.*

349. *'bum ṭīk.*

350. *dus bzhi gsal byed.*

351. The Tibetan root text is ambiguous about whether this is singular or plural, and Wangchuk Dorje comments on it as if it were singular. The Sanskrit, however, is specifically in the plural, and so in the root text, it is translated in the plural.

352. *Udānavarga,* chapt. 4, verse 1.

353. Nagarjuna's *Suhṛllekha* (Tib. bshes pa'i spring yig).

354. *so so thar pa.*

355. This compares Namgyal Drakpa to King Bhagīratha, who is said to have brought the Ganges down to earth to purify the ashes of his ancestors, the sixty thousand sons of Sagara.

356. This is a play on the name of Wangchuk Dorje's master Namgyal Drakpa, whose name means "Renowned as victorious."

357. A synonym for the sun common in Sanskrit and Tibetan poetry; here it is a metaphor for the Buddha.

Works Cited

The works listed here are the editions consulted during the translation or referred to by the translator in the notes. This list does not include the many works cited by Vasubandhu or Wangchuk Dorje, many of which would be difficult to find, and some of which may have been lost.

Sources in the Tengyur

Vasubandhu. *Abhidharmakoṣakārikā (chos mngon pa'i mdzod kyi tshig le'ur byas pa)*, Derge Tengyur (Vol. *mgnon pa ku pa*)

_______. *Abhidharmakoṣaṃbhāṣyaṃ (chos mngon pa'i mdzod kyi bshad pa).* Dergye Tengyur (Vols. *mgnon pa ku pa* and *khu pa*)

Yaśomitra. *Sphuṭārthābhidharmakośavyākhyā (chos mngon pa'i mdzod kyi 'grel bshad don gsal).* Dergye Tengyur (*mngon pa gu pa* and *ngu pa*).

Other Tibetan sources referred to in the text

Dge 'dun grub (2001). *Legs par gsungs pa'i dam pa'i chos 'dul ba'i gleng gzhi dang rtogs brjod pa lung sde bzhi kun las btus pa rin po che'i mdzod ces bya ba bzhugs so.* Varanasi: Geluk Students Welfare Committee of the Central Institute for Higher Tibetan Studies.

Mchims 'jam pa'i dbyangs (1989). *Chos mngon pa mdzod kyi tshig le'ur byas pa'i 'grel pa mngon pa'i rgyan.* Krung go'i bod kyi shes rig dpe skrun khang. (Reprinted by Yasodhara Publications, Delhi, 2003)

_____ (2009). *Chos mngon pa mdzod kyi tshig le'ur byas pa'i 'grel pa mngon pa'i rgyan.* Institute of Tibetan Classics.

Dbang phyug rdor je (2002). *Chos mngon pa mdzod kyi rnam par bshad pa chos mngon rgya mtsho'i snying po mkhyen rtse'i zhal lung gzhon nu rnam rol legs bshad chos mig rnam 'byed grub bde'i shing rta zhes bya ba bzhugs so.* Baijnath: Dpal spungs gsung rab nyams gso khang.

_____ (2003). *Chos mngon pa mdzod kyi rnam par bshad pa chos mngon rgya mtsho'i snying po mkhyen rtse'i zhal lung gzhon nu rnam rol legs bshad chos mig rnam 'byed grub bde'i shing rta zhes bya ba bzhugs so.* Varanasi: Vajra Vidya Library.

Mi skyod rdor je (2003). *Shes rab kyi pha rol tu phyin pa'i lung chos mtha' dag gi bdud rtsi'i snying por gyur pa gang la ldan pa'i gzhi rje btsun mchog to dgyes par ngal gso ba'i yongs 'du sa brtol gyi ljon pa rgyas pa* (Vols. 1–2). Seattle: Nitartha international Publications.

_____(2005). *Chos mngon pa mdzod kyi 'grel pa rgyas par spros pa grub bde'i spyid 'jo* (Vols. 1–4). *(The Springtime Cow of Easy Accomplishment: An Extensive Commentary on the Treasury of Abhidharma).* Varanasi: Kagyu Refugee Protection Committee of the Central Institute for Higher Tibetan Studies.

Zhwa dmar chos kyi dbang phyug (2007). *Mngon pa mdzod kyi spyi don dbyig gnyen bzhad pa.* Varanasi: Vajra Vidya Institute Library.

Sanskrit source

Gokhale, V.V. *The Text of the Abhidharmakośakārikā of Vasubandhu, Journal of the Bombay Branch, Royal Asiatic Society,* n.s., vol. 22, 1946, pp. 73-102.

Index

Tibetan and Sanskrit equivalents for English terms are given in parentheses.

May All Beings Be Happy